Iran and the Surrounding World

INTERACTIONS IN CULTURE

AND CULTURAL POLITICS

IRAN

and the SURROUNDING WORLD

Interactions in Culture and Cultural Politics

NIKKI R. KEDDIE

RUDI MATTHEE

Editors

UNIVERSITY OF WASHINGTON PRESS

Seattle and London

Copyright © 2002 by the University of Washington Press
Printed in the United States of America

Library of Congress Cataloging-in-Publication Data

Iran and the surrounding world : interactions in culture and cultural
    politics / Nikki R. Keddie, Rudi Matthee, editors.
        p.   cm.
    Includes bibliographical references and index.
    ISBN 0-295-98206-3 (pbk.)
        1. Iran—Civilization.   2. Iran—Intellectual life.   3. Iran—Relations.
    I. Keddie, Nikki R.   II. Matthee, Rudolph P.
    DS266.I636   2002
    955—dc21
                                                                    2002002791

The paper used in this publication is acid-free and recycled from 10 percent post-
consumer and at least 50 percent pre-consumer waste. It meets the minimum
requirements of American National Standard for Information Sciences—
Permanence of Paper for Printed Library Materials, ANSI Z39.48–1984.

Contents

Acknowledgments   *vii*

Note on Transliteration   *ix*

Introduction   *3*

NIKKI R. KEDDIE

Part I. Overviews

1 / Iranian Culture and South Asia, 1500–1900   *15*

JUAN R. I. COLE

2 / Beyond Translation:
Interactions between English and Persian Poetry   *36*

AHMAD KARIMI-HAKKAK

3 / Turk, Persian, and Arab: Changing Relationships
between Tribes and State in Iran and along Its Frontiers   *61*

THOMAS J. BARFIELD

Part II. The Safavid, Qajar, and Pahlavi Periods

4 / The Early Safavids and Their Cultural Interactions
with Surrounding States   *89*

ABOLALA SOUDAVAR

5 / Suspicion, Fear, and Admiration: Pre-Nineteenth-Century
Iranian Views of the English and the Russians   *121*

RUDI MATTHEE

6 / The Quest for the Secret of Strength in Iranian
Nineteenth-Century Travel Literature: Rethinking
Tradition in the *Safarnameh*   *146*

MONICA M. RINGER

7 / Cultures of Iranianness:
The Evolving Polemic of Iranian Nationalism　*162*
FIROOZEH KASHANI-SABET

8 / Foreign Education, the Women's Press, and the Discourse
of Scientific Domesticity in Early-Twentieth-Century Iran　*182*
JASAMIN ROSTAM-KOLAYI

Part III. Culture in the Islamic Republic in Relation to the World

9 / International Connections of the Iranian Women's Movement　*205*
NAYEREH TOHIDI

10 / The Presentation of the "Self" and the "Other"
in Postrevolutionary Iranian School Textbooks　*232*
GOLNAR MEHRAN

11 / Cinematic Exchange Relations: Iran and the West　*254*
HAMID NAFICY

Part IV. Political-Cultural Relations with the Muslim World

12 / The Failed Pan-Islamic Program of the Islamic Republic:
Views of the Liberal Reformers of the Religious "Semi-Opposition"　*281*
WILFRIED BUCHTA

13 / Revolutionary Iran and Egypt:
Exporting Inspirations and Anxieties　*305*
ASEF BAYAT AND BAHMAN BAKTIARI

14 / The Iranian Revolution and Changes in Islamism
in Pakistan, India, and Afghanistan　*327*
VALI NASR

Part V. The Politics of Iran's International Relations

15 / Iran's Foreign Policy: A Revolution in Transition　*355*
GARY SICK

The Contributors　*375*
Index　*379*

Acknowledgments

This book originated in an international conference held at UCLA in 2000, "Iran and the Surrounding World since 1500: Cultural Influences and Interactions," sponsored by UCLA's G. E. von Grunebaum Center for Near Eastern Studies (Irene Bierman, director) and the university's Center for 17th & 18th Century Studies and William Andrews Clark Memorial Library (Peter Reill, director). The highly successful conference was accompanied by a film program; a concert combining Iranian, South Asian, and Arab music, led by Ali Jihad Racy; and a reception to greet the festschrift *Iran and Beyond: Essays in Middle Eastern History in Honor of Nikki R. Keddie,* edited by Rudi Matthee and Beth Baron and published by Mazda in the same year as the conference.

Generous cosponsors of the conference and the reception were UCLA's Division of Social Sciences, Division of Humanities, International Studies and Overseas Programs, Department of History, Department of Near Eastern Languages and Cultures, Center for Modern and Contemporary Studies, Center for the Study of Women, Center for Social Theory and Comparative History, Center for Medieval and Renaissance Studies, Center for European and Russian Studies, Center for International Relations, Center for Jewish Studies, Center for the Study of Religion, the Franklin D. Murphy Chair, the "1939 Club" Chair, the James S. Coleman Chair, and the Henry J. Bruman Chair. All sponsors and cosponsors helped ensure the high level of the conference and ultimately made this book possible. For their excellent organization of the conference, special thanks are also due to the staff of the UCLA Near Eastern Studies Center, especially Associate Director Jonathan Friedlander, and to the staff of the Center for 17th & 18th Century Studies.

In addition to the authors of this book, the following people participated in the conference in various capacities, and their comments on the papers were very helpful to the editors: Janet Afary (who commented on the entire manuscript), Barbara Metcalf, Leslie Peirce, Hossein Ziai, Hamid Algar, and Thierry Zarcone. Thanks are due as well to Houchang Chehabi (who also commented on the entire manuscript) and to our excellent University of

Washington Press editors, Michael Duckworth and Xavier Callahan. We also give special thanks to our authors for their additional work in updating their papers, and to the few authors whose papers were added after the conference, when we found that they were working on important subjects relevant to the book.

NIKKI R. KEDDIE
Los Angeles, California

RUDI MATTHEE
Metuchen, New Jersey

Note on Transliteration

Transliteration in a work that involves several Middle Eastern languages inevitably involves some solutions that may not satisfy everyone. We have tried to recognize differences in local pronunciations without overloading the text with variations. The system of transliteration used for Arabic, Persian, and Turkish is that of the *International Journal of Middle East Studies,* and for Urdu and Russian that of the Library of Congress, with some modifications. Vowels are *i* and *u* in Arabic, Turkish, and Urdu, and *e* and *o* in Persian (with Qizilbash and Isma`il as exceptions). Diphthongs are *ai* and *au* (*ei* in Turkish, as in the name Suleiman). Certain proper nouns, when they refer to persons or items important in Islamic history, are given a standard spelling: (Prophet) Muhammad, (Imam) Husain, Fatima, Quran. The definite article in Arabic is not normally assimilated to the noun, though it is assimilated in the terms Ayatollah and Hojjatoleslam and in a modern Persian name such as Abol Hasan. The letter `ain is not rendered when it occurs at the beginning of a word. The silent *h* is given as *eh* in Persian but as *a* in Arabic and Urdu. No diacritical marks are used with transliterated forms. Names with an established English spelling appear in their anglicized forms: Uzbek, Khomeini, Khamenei, Mawdudi, Soroush, Dariush Mehrjui. Dates are given according to the Common Era calendar.

Iran and the Surrounding World

INTERACTIONS IN CULTURE

AND CULTURAL POLITICS

Introduction

NIKKI R. KEDDIE

This book deals with Iran's relations with the surrounding world since 1500, concentrating on the cultural and cultural-political spheres, with emphasis on the period since the rise of the Islamic Republic in 1979. By many in the West, Iran's interaction with the rest of the world is often associated with two salient but contradictory images. On the one hand, there is some recognition of Iran's important cultural contributions, usually prefaced by the adjective *Persian,* including Persian carpets, Persian miniatures, and Persian poets, especially those popular in the West, such as Omar Khayyam and Jalal al-Din Rumi. Iranian cinema, music, and exile literature have recently been added to the cultural achievements recognized outside Iran's borders. On the other hand, there are images of Iranians as fanatical nationalist or political-religious opponents of the United States, which appeared both in the period of oil nationalization under prime minister Mohammad Mosaddeq (1951–53) and again during and since the "Islamic" revolution of 1979. The images of fanaticism are frequently exaggerated, and the concerns of a people who feel heir to a proud nation and culture under threat from a dominant West are seldom appreciated in that West. Yet these contrasting, culturally positive but politically negative images, however simplified, in some ways reflect real features of Iran's history. This history is contradictory in many ways. Iran has a long and distinguished history of major contributions to the world's cultures, while at the same time Iran's political record, both domestically and in relation to the outside world, has often been problematic.

Iran's history has been characterized by many autocratic and repressive rulers and regimes, and by frequent popular revolts and major protest movements, often, though not always, having a religious form. These movements have usually been brutally suppressed and, even if successful, lost much of their original populist program and adopted less spiritual and more autocratic practices. This is true of the Abbasid caliphs after their victorious revolt c. 750 C.E., of the Safavid dynasty (1501–1722), which began by supporting a radical Shi`i movement, and of the Islamic Republic, which came to power representing a multifaceted revolt against the Pahlavi regime.

3

Naturally, there were variations within this very broad pattern, affected by such major events as the Islamic conquest of Iran, later Turko-Mongol nomadic conquests, and the coming of the West and the modern world. But even with these changes, the phenomenon of cultural strength combined with problematic politics, particularly on the part of ruling groups, generally holds. And, as the examples of the great medieval poets Sa'di and Hafez demonstrate, the best art was often created under the worst political circumstances. Even autocratic rulers often patronized excellent art, while in more recent periods the arts developed in part under patronage and in part in opposition to dominant regimes.

This book contains essays discussing both culture and politics, often in interaction, that serve to deepen our understanding of the links between these two spheres, and stresses Iranian cultural and political interactions with the surrounding world. A number of the chapters point up the close relationship between culture and politics, including cultural-political interactions with outside areas, a relationship these chapters show to exist whether or not the politics were (or are) expressed in Islamic terms, and whether the culture involved is in support of the ruling system or is oppositional.

Iran's interaction with the outside world has hitherto largely been studied for the period before 1500, with a concentration on the transmission of ideas, religious beliefs, and art forms. Those who discuss more recent periods tend to focus on political and economic relations with the West, with little discussion of culture and scant attention to Iran's relations with the Arab, South Asian, and Turkic worlds closest to it. While political and political-economy approaches are extremely important, this volume tries to create the basis for a more comprehensive view of Iran's cultural and political relations with the world since 1500. Political relations with the West make up parts of several chapters, but the emphasis is on other relationships—both geographically, in dealing also with South Asia, the Middle East, and Central Asia, and in subject matter, including literature, film, art, religion, education, the role of women, and ideology, where interactions were often more fruitful and longer lasting than they were in politics. With such a vast framework there is no attempt to cover the entire subject—rather, we commissioned fine papers from people in various disciplines working on this range of topics, in order to suggest the parameters and importance of Iran's cultural-political interactions with the surrounding world since 1500.

The book includes both overviews and papers that fall within defined periods. Although Iran's history may be periodized in different ways, here, in order to orient readers, we would suggest the following outline—which includes some very broad divisions for periods before 1500, periods mentioned here because their images and realities continue to influence Iran in the modern world. (1) The period c. 1500–500 B.C.E. includes the formation of the Zoroastrian religion and the creation of Iran's first states and empires, ruled by those who spoke old Persian, an Indo-European language. (2) From c. 500 B.C.E. to 740 C.E., Iran saw the rise and fall of several agrarian-based empires and the spread in them of Zoroastrianism, and also major interactions with Near Eastern, Greek, Hellenistic, and Byzantine cultures. (3) 740 C.E. marked the Arab-Islamic conquest, which over time brought the conversion of most Iranians to Islam and its culture, while over the centuries Iranian modes of government and ideas were of major importance in the development of a cultural synthesis that spread through the Islamic world. (4) The invasions of Iran and Anatolia by the Seljuq Turks from the mid-eleventh century brought in new nomadic tribes, and began a period of Turko-Mongol nomadic invasion and rule in Iran that lasted until the rise of the Safavids in 1501. (5) The Safavids, 1501–1722, initially relied on Turkic tribes, but they were able to create countervailing forces and set up a centralized state roughly corresponding to today's Iran. They were also important for converting Iran to the Shi`i branch of Islam. The Safavids were conquered by Afghans, and the eighteenth century was one of division and internal warfare. (6) The Qajar period, 1796–1925, saw Western military and economic encroachments but only weak attempts to respond to them on the governmental level, although Western and modern ideas began to influence many individuals. (7) The Pahlavi dynasty, 1925–79, was characterized by top-down modernization, centralization, autocracy, and ties to Western powers, along with neglect of traditionally oriented, usually less prosperous, classes and their culture, all of which helped bring revolution. (8) The Islamic Republic, 1979–today, has seen a re-creation in twentieth-century terms of Islamic norms, but has been mostly authoritarian and top-down in its approach, despite some beginnings of greater democracy.

Regarding the subject of this book, relations with the surrounding world since 1501, under the Safavids the most important cultural contacts were with South Asia and the Turkic and Arab worlds, while since the Qajar period the main interactions have been with the West. Many aspects of Iran's interactions with the surrounding world before 1501 remained important after that date, including those in the spheres of religion, ideas, art, and governmental organization. After the Arab-Islamic conquest of Iran, interactions between the Muslim Arabs and Iran in the above and other spheres resulted in syntheses of ideas and cultural practices, with many novel developments appearing in such fields as art, literature, philosophy, and theology. Such cultural elements and syntheses, expressed both in Persian and in Arabic and dating both to pre-Safavid and post-Safavid periods, were very influential both in

South Asia and among Turkic peoples as they had earlier been among the
Arabs. Persian influence in some cultural spheres also spread to the west. There
were also important influences going the other way, from South Asia and from
Turks, Arabs, and, later, the West, into Iran.

A major area of Iranian influence abroad from pre-Islamic times onward
was in the realm of religion. Scholars are increasingly stressing that Iranian
Zoroastrianism influenced early Judaism and, mainly via Judaism, Christianity and Islam. This influence occurred in key points of belief and escha-
tology, including belief in an afterlife and day of judgment, angels, and a
supernatural, evil Satan. At least one scholar believes Zoroastrianism began
the whole Western or Judaeo-Christian-Muslim concept of progressive time.[1]
The Zoroastrian-influenced religion Manicheanism, with its transformation
of Zoroastrian dualism into a belief that matter was evil and spirit good,
influenced a whole series of religious movements in East and West, which
were characterized as heresies by both Christians and Muslims.

The most influential later religious interactions came after the Arab-Islamic
conquest of Iran and the rest of the Middle East, when Islam was gradually
adopted by local populations who also greatly influenced the development
of this religion. The minority, Shi`i, branch of Islam, though begun by Arabs,
was adopted by some Iranians, but only after 1501 did it become the state religion of Iran and acquire a particularly Iranian identity. Iranian forms of
Shi`ism have spread in the Muslim world since then and they continue to do
so today. Under the Safavids and later, Iranian-influenced Shi`ism became
important, especially in South Asia and in Arab areas near Iran. Under the
Islamic Republic, its brand of Shi`ism has spread, mainly by influencing the
beliefs and practices of those who already adhere to the Shi`a.

Iranian religious interactions with the outside world in the period since
1500 are discussed in several chapters within. The chapters by Juan Cole and
Vali Nasr highlight the changing influence of Iranian Shi`ism in South Asia
since 1500, while Wilfried Buchta, Asef Bayat, and Bahman Baktiari show the
difficulties of spreading the influence of a highly politicized form of Shi`ism
in non-Shi`i areas of the Middle East. The political aspects of the religio-
political movement identified with the leader of the Iranian Revolution and
Islamic Republic, Ruhollah Khomeini, have in recent years been more
influential than have been its religious aspects. Only in Shi`i communities in
the Muslim world has there been a widespread acceptance of Khomeini's
vision. As the Buchta and Bayat/Baktiari chapters show, there have been several obstacles in the way of early hopes within the Islamic Republic that Iran's
model of an Islamic revolution and an Islamic state might be followed in countries following the majority, Sunni, view of Islam.

In the visual arts, what has mainly come down to us from pre-Islamic times are buildings and bas reliefs that evince Iranians' mastery of design and often depict human and animal figures frequently in symbolic interrelationship. These elements continued in Islamic times, when Iran became a center for the revival of figurative art, with miniatures in books being the best-known form. This figurative art was influenced, after invasions by Central and East Asian nomads, by the arts of Eastern peoples, and it in turn influenced painting and other arts in India and the Ottoman Empire in the period covered by this book. Abolala Soudavar's chapter shows how the Safavids followed an artistic-cultural policy that helped spread Iranian influence in these areas.

Regarding literature, the greatest Iranian poets lived before 1500, but their influence abroad grew after that date. Western writers and literary audiences have been interested in Persian poetry at least since the eighteenth-century translations by William Jones, and the popularity of this poetry has most recently been expressed in Jalal al-Din Rumi's being the bestselling poet in the U.S. for several years. Ahmad Karimi-Hakkak analyzes the masterful, non-literal translations done by Jones of Hafez and by Coleman Barks of Rumi. A contemporary aspect of Iranian world influence in the visual arts is Iranian cinema, analyzed by Hamid Naficy, which provides a current example of great, humanistic, and often implicitly oppositional art created under a repressive regime.

If Iran had major cultural influence abroad before and after 1500, it was also strongly influenced by people coming from other cultures. This often took place via conquests, the most important of which was the Arab-Islamic conquest, but a less emphasized and understood series of conquests by Turko-Mongol nomadic states that began in the eleventh century were also of great importance. Thomas Barfield's chapter summarizes the nature of the Turko-Mongol conquests and the states they produced in Iran and elsewhere, noting that these people had the basis for far longer-lived and more stable states than did the Arab Bedouins or other pre-Turkic nomads (on whom Ibn Khaldun's model for a short, three-generation state was based). The interaction between Persians and Turks, while not involving as important a religious and cultural change as did the Arab conquest, reinforced the role of nomadic tribal federations in Iran and was crucial to the creation of the Safavid state. The Safavids made Shi'ism the religion of the overwhelming majority of Iranians, giving Iran a cultural adhesive that helped it hold together through turbulent times and despite major ethnic differences.

After the Safavids took power, they had important political, economic, and cultural relations and interactions with a wider number of areas than any previous Iranian state, owing largely to the rise in importance of Europe and its traders. Abolala Soudavar's chapter shows how Safavid rulers effectively utilized Iranian brilliance in the arts to launch a cultural policy, largely via gift-giving to foreign rulers, which helped Iranian influence abroad. Juan Cole shows the spread of Iranian influence in South Asia in the Safavid and subsequent periods, while Rudi Matthee deals with Iranian attitudes toward the British and the Russians, whose trade and expansion were beginning to encroach on Iran in the Safavid period. Matthee suggests that even before the nineteenth century Iranians showed an eagerness to learn from foreigners, coupled with a profound suspicion of those foreigners' motives, prefiguring later attitudes toward the West.

In the nineteenth century, a number of educated Iranians began to be concerned with Iran's "deficiency," later seen as "backwardness" as compared to Europe, and this was reflected in the literature of those who went abroad and wrote about it in ways detailed in Monica Ringer's chapter. In the same period began expressions of Iranian nationalism, discussed in Firoozeh Kashani-Sabet's paper. This was doubly influenced by contact with the West: first, because such contacts both showed up Iran's weaknesses and provided a model for self-strengthening, and second, because Western nationalist and racist theories provided a model for Iranian nationalists, especially since, because Persian is a language in the Indo-European or "Aryan" family, nationalists could adopt widespread Western racial theories saying that "Aryans" were superior to others. Kashani-Sabet also discusses the vicissitudes of nationalism under the Pahlavis and the Islamic Republic.

Western cultural influence grew in a number of domains in the late nineteenth and twentieth centuries, among them the spheres of education and of refashioning the position of women, covered in Jasamin Rostam-Kolayi's paper. The Qajar government did little in the sphere of education, and almost nothing in girls' education, so the role of foreign schools, mostly of religious background, was especially important. These schools pioneered in modern education for girls, and, along with a general modern curriculum, stressed what is here called "scientific domesticity," including household management and hygiene. This approach greatly influenced middle and upper-class women (while the practices of other classes were often denigrated) and was taken over by Reza Shah in his policies, which also supported some new roles for women.

The importance of interactions with foreign, especially Western, countries to the position of women is again stressed in Nayereh Tohidi's paper on the period since 1979. While the leaders and ideologues of the Islamic Republic originally reacted strongly against what were seen as un-Islamic and Western-based Pahlavi reforms in the position of women, over the years both internal forces and foreign contacts led to a reinstatement of many of these reforms. Tohidi shows the importance in promoting such changes of Iranian women's international contacts and conferences. Less optimistic is Golnar Mehran's chapter on images of the "other" in Iranian textbooks: she shows that textbooks inculcate the superiority of male Muslim Iranians and do not give adequate representations of other groups, although this may change in time.

The international impact of the ideology and related practices of the Islamic Republic is discussed in several papers. Wilfried Buchta shows how the theoretical desire of some early leaders of the Republic to work toward an ecumenical Islam that would unite Shi`i and Sunni Islam has been effectively undermined by the overwhelming power of religious conservatives who insist on the very features that divide Shi`is from Sunnis. Only those he calls "semi-oppositional," notably Abdol Karim Soroush, point to what would be needed for genuine ecumenism within Islam. Asef Bayat and Bahman Baktiari discuss the influence over time of the Islamic Republic on the Egyptian public, and note that this influence has been greatest when there have been signs of liberalism and democratization, as under Mohammad Khatami's presidency since 1997, and smallest when the country has been more repressive of free thought and action. Vali Nasr's discussion of influence is perhaps the most pessimistic one, as he deals with the role of the Islamic Republic as both model and instigator of an increasingly organized, exclusive, communal view of Shi`ism by many Pakistani and South Asian Shi`is, which has contributed to a rise of communal animosities within South Asian Islam. More optimistic is Gary Sick's paper on the relations of the Islamic Republic with the outside world, which sees cause for hope, especially in some recent developments.

This book emphasizes the period since 1979, which has been subject to less scholarly scrutiny than have earlier periods, and within the decades of the Islamic Republic it stresses cultural and cultural-political aspects of Iran's attitudes to and relations with the outside world. The roots of recent attitudes may, however, be seen in earlier periods, and often in cultural divisions that appeared especially since the onset of Western influences. Regarding women, for example, although many middle- and upper-class women and men were happy to rearrange gender relations on a more Western model, as shown in Rostam-Kolayi's chapter, this left out many men and women of the popular and bazaar classes, who retained many elements of an older view of gender relations and of women that resurfaced in the revolution and the Islamic Republic. But early strictness has given way, due to internal necessity, women's pressures, and foreign contacts. Somewhat similarly, regarding Shi`ism, while there were liberal clerics and secular laypersons, there remained large groups of clerics and non-clerics convinced that Iranian Islam was threatened by the West and by deviations from strict Islamic law and practice, and these people gained power after 1979. They, too, have had to adjust considerably to the realities of the modern world. Some important clerics now accept or even promote more liberal views than previous clerics, while others try to preserve as much strictness and clerical power as possible.

In the larger cultural sphere, the arts went from being primarily tied to courts and patronage to being largely, at least implicitly, oppositional, a position they retain under the Islamic Republic. It is often not realized outside Iran that, even with recent crackdowns on the periodical press, book publication remains remarkably free and sometimes even openly oppositional in the Islamic Republic, while other aspects of the arts are constantly pushing the boundaries that have been set up for them. In this, foreign influences in cinema, writing, music, and art reach Iran and are important, while Iranians both at home and in the diaspora are having increasing influence in world culture.

Iran's resistance to the world race toward globalization and free trade has some positive aspects. Free trade in film, for example, could swamp Iran's film industry as it has those of many countries. On the other hand, no country today can be an island, and Iran's continuing economic crisis seems to guarantee continued efforts to improve relations with the outside world. Khatami's "dialogue of civilizations," a phrase he first voiced in 1997 that has since been widely adopted even outside Iran, may seem an indirect route to solving economic and political problems in relations with the West, especially the U.S., but it may be more feasible today than the U.S. government's desire for direct governmental negotiations. For one thing, increased Western respect for the culture of Iran and for Islam, topics covered in this volume, would provide a new and more even playing field for eventual negotiations than does the attitude of U.S. superiority that has characterized past relations. Khatami's speech on U.S. television praising many aspects of American culture and politics in essence invited a similar response (not yet heard, aside from President Clinton's few remarks on Iran's great cultural traditions) from U.S. leaders regarding positive aspects of Iranian culture. We may hope that Western leaders will gain a greater acquaintance with this culture, as well as with the reasons for Iran's past reactions against the West and especially the U.S., as a prelude to improving relations with Iran, which in turn could improve Iran's internal situation. To such an outcome this book might make a modest contribution. Its contributions to a better understanding of many aspects of Iran's recent history are more certain. While none of its authors tries to predict the future, all provide material and insights that contribute to our understanding of the forces at work in today's Iran and in countries interacting with Iran, giving a more complete picture than one which concentrates only on political and crisis aspects of Iran's relations with the surrounding world.

NOTE

1. Norman Cohn, *Cosmos, Chaos and the World to Come: The Ancient Roots of Apocalyptic Faith* (New Haven: Yale University Press, 1993).

Part I

Overviews

1 / Iranian Culture and South Asia, 1500–1900

JUAN R. I. COLE

This chapter treats the Persian cultural influences on India and interactions between India and Iran in the centuries from 1500 to 1900. It surveys the place of the Persian language in Indian government, chancery practice, and imperial decrees, and the manner in which state adoption of it created a very large class of Persian-speaking bureaucrats, scribes, translators, and other intellectuals in the subcontinent. It is argued that in the Mughal period perhaps seven times as many readers of Persian lived in India as in Iran. The chapter looks at Indo-Persian travel writing, works on comparative religion, and the impact of religious groups with strong ties to Persian-speaking Iran, whether Twelver Shi`is or the much smaller Isma`ili and Zoroastrian communities. It pays special attention to the Shi`i-ruled kingdoms that were common in India in the early modern period.

Iran had, in the period 1500–1900, an enormous amount of interaction with South Asia (comprising the present-day countries of Pakistan, India, Bangladesh, and southern Afghanistan). Qazvin, Isfahan, and then Tehran served in important ways as cultural and political trendsetters for Muslim (and some Hindu) courts and scholars in the subcontinent. The centrality of the Persian language to chancery and bureaucratic practice in South Asia contributed to the creation of a large Persophone population who could transmit Iranian cultural achievements in poetry, philosophy, theology, mysticism, art, travel accounts, technology, ethics, statecraft, and many other fields from one area to the other. Indian writing on these subjects also circulated in manuscript in Iran in the early modern period, to an extent that is difficult to appreciate now that national boundaries have solidified and national languages (Urdu, Hindi, and Bengali) have been adopted and standardized. The cadre of Persophone bureaucrats and scholars in the subcontinent, which included large numbers of Hindus as well as Muslims, acted as a vast audience for Iranian ideas, but more than that they participated in a far-flung *ecumene* of Persian culture, with both local and cosmopolitan traditions and impact.

In addition, the establishment of the Safavid dynasty in Iran from 1501 and the conversion of a majority of those who lived on the Iranian plateau to Shi`ism over the succeeding two centuries constituted among the more important religious developments in early modern Islam. It is comparable in significance to the conversion to Islam of the inhabitants of western Punjab, of eastern Bengal, and of the islands that became Indonesia, which occurred in the same period. Iran was, geographically speaking, a large country, more than three times the size of modern France, but it had a tiny population, at four to five million, compared to most of its powerful neighbors. (The Indian subcontinent in 1600 had an estimated population of 120 million.) Iran was nevertheless a relatively wealthy and influential state, able to fend off the Ottomans, the Uzbeks, and the Mughals and even sometimes to grow at their expense. Its Qizilbash tribal army, later supplemented by Georgian slave soldiers, and its lucrative silk trade lent it importance in world affairs. Along with tribal armies and silk, however, it was a font of the Persian language, Sufi mysticism, philosophy, minority religions such as Isma`ilism and Zoroastrianism, and, with the Safavid conquest, Shi`i Islam. Iran, like most of the Muslim world, had been a majority Sunni society until the Safavids made Shi`ism the state religion and promoted it for most of the succeeding two centuries.

Nearly simultaneously with the rise of the Safavids in Iran, the Mughal dynasty was established in North India.[1] Its founder, Babur, was a descendent of Timur Lang from the Ferghana Valley in Central Asia, Chaghatay-speaking (a Turkic language), and a strict Sunni Muslim. Ironically, his empire became Persian-speaking and came to have an ecumenical mixture of Sunnis, Shi`is, and Hindus in its elite. Let us begin, then, with language, and ask how Persian attained its position in Mughal India. Muzaffar Alam has written a fine and thorough consideration of the subject, to which the following four paragraphs are primarily indebted.[2] He argues that the predominance of Persian at the Mughal court was not a foregone conclusion, saying that other Turkic conquerors, such as the Ottomans and the Uzbeks, gave it a less prominent place than did the Mughals in India. Although Persian had a long history among Indian Muslims as a language of government, religion, and the chronicling of history by the time of the Mughal conquest, its position was not unassailable. An occasional bureaucratic use of Hindavi, the local North Indian dialect infused with Persian vocabulary, was seen in the Afghan Lodi state just prior to the Mughal advent. While Alam's caution against our taking this development as "natural" is useful, I do not entirely agree that the adoption of Persian by the Mughal state was as contingent and dependent on a few elite decision-makers as he suggests. There had been a long tradition of Turko-Mongol rulers in Central Asia who had retained the Persian scribal class (*dabirs*) to perform bureaucratic work and adopted Persian as the court language. Iran itself under Mongol, Timurid, and Safavid rule fit this description. Whatever the attitude of the Uzbeks to Persian, it remained strong as the spoken language in cities like Bukhara and Samarqand and played a role in polite letters and as a chancery language. As late as the nineteenth century, the archives of the Emirate of Bukhara were kept in Persian despite the Turkic origins of the ruling family. There is a sense, then, in which the Mughals in supporting Persian were doing nothing unusual for post-Timurid states in the region; it is the Ottomans in the far west who innovated, by doing record-keeping in Ottoman Turkish.

Moreover, the Sanskrit-derived dialects of North India were not standardized and so lacked utility for imperial purposes. Alam quotes Amir Khusrau as saying in the fourteenth century that "Persian parlance enjoyed uniformity of idiom throughout the length of four thousand parasangs, unlike the Hindavi tongue, which had no settled idiom and varied after every hundred miles and with every group of people."[3] Without governmental support to homogenize such a set of local dialects, they remained diverse, lacking the advantage of a scribal Persian that had been honed to its purpose over centuries. Two other factors seem to me important, though they are not emphasized by Alam. A large preexisting Persophone scribal establishment existed in India, on whose talents the Mughals could draw immediately without having to train thousands of Indians in Chaghatay Turkish (anyway not a language of bureaucracy even in Central Asia). Second, Persian, as an Indo-European language, was close in grammar and vocabulary to the North Indian dialects and so could be learned more easily by the scribes of Lahore, Delhi, and Agra than could an Altaic language like Turkish.

The Mughal emperor Akbar made Persian the official language of court and bureaucracy by decree, as Alam explains. Imperial edicts were issued in that language, as were local and provincial documents regarding land tenure and government appointments. Akbar strove to attract intellectuals and administrators from Iran. He also ordered Persian taught in Quran schools, and urged that much less time be spent teaching the Arabic alphabet as opposed to the substance of the Persian language. He contracted with Iranian educational administrators in Shiraz, in particular, to come to head up a string of *madrasas* or secondary schools, not all of them exclusively Muslim. At some points, Mughal rulers and lexicographers launched "purification campaigns" to purge Persian of Indian words or local usages and spellings, and occasional attempts were made to update usage to mirror that in contemporary Iran, rather than that in the medieval classics. Large numbers of Hindus from the Kayasth and Khatri castes (which specialized in scribal and bureaucratic work) flocked to Persian tutors or, where possible, to schools so as to receive training in Persian for subsequent bureaucratic work as accountants, clerks, and corresponding secretaries.[4] These Hindu castes soon produced fine Persian prose stylists and poets, and their epistolary handbooks became models for all government letter writers. As outsiders to the language, they also were prolific in producing grammars and lexicons, as were local Indian Muslims. Alam insists that Persian became the language of choice not only for the Mughal nobility but for a sizeable middle stratum throughout the empire that included Muslims, Hindus, bureaucrats, educationists, and merchants. The Persian language and sensibility of a travel account like that of Anand Ram Mukhlis in the mid-eighteenth century point to the emergence of a Persophone world-civilization in the early modern world that did not exclude by virtue of religion or regional origin.[5] It is impossible to know exactly how many Persophone intellectuals existed in the subcontinent at any particular time in the premodern period. But the subcontinent's population in 1700 was around 170 million, and at that time probably about ten percent of these were Muslims. Indian Muslims were highly urban, in contrast to Hindus, and therefore far more likely to be literate, and the language of Muslim literacy was Persian. If only five percent were literate (a proportion that statistics for early-nineteenth-century small towns in the British Gazetteers make plausible), this assumption would yield nearly a million in 1700. That number would certainly be reached if we added in the tens of thousands of Hindu scribes and accountants who knew Persian as well. Given that Iran's population in 1700 was probably around five million and that the overall literacy rate there was likely only about two or three percent, we arrive at an upper figure of 150,000 literate Iranians. (Remember that about half of Iranians were pastoralists, and almost all pastoralists are illiterate.) We may conclude from this heuristic exercise, in any case, that there were certainly far more readers of Persian in the subcontinent at the apex of the Mughal empire than in late-Safavid Iran. Indeed, a likely proportion seems seven to one in India's favor.

A market existed in Central Asia and Iran, as well as among Persophone strata throughout the subcontinent, for travel accounts of India, which could convey political intelligence, cultural information, and reports of natural and supernatural wonders. Such descriptions of India are more numerous than previous generations of historians estimated and constitute a distinct genre of Persian literature. The corpus includes straightforward travelogues as well as travel narratives embedded in chronicles, letters, and other genres. Contributors to it often came from Iran or Central Asia, but others were Indian Muslims or Hindus who journeyed to unfamiliar parts of the vast subcontinent. Such works include the travelogue of the Central Asian traveler Mahmud Balkhi, which is remarkable for its humanist naturalism and its frank admission that the author went native in India.[6] Other important travel authors who wrote accounts in Persian of India in our period included Abd al-Razzaq Samarqandi, Faizi Fayyazi, Asad Beg Qazvini, Abd al-Latif Gujarati, Mirza Nathan Esfahani, Shehab al-Din Talesh, Nek Rai, Khwaja Abd al-Karim Kashmiri, Anand Ram Mukhlis, and Aqa Ahmad Behbahani.[7]

In addition to travelers, large numbers of Iranian poets, courtiers, scribes, clergymen, and merchants migrated to India.[8] The chronicles sometimes speak as though tens of thousands of Iranians came into a particular area at a particular time. Western travelers at times blame large-scale Iranian migration to Mughal India for a decline in Iran's population.[9] Emigration to India was unlikely to have been demographically so significant for Iran, but one could imagine that in southern and eastern Iran whole clans might during times of drought or political instability pick up and go to India, creating some ghost towns upon which travelers might remark. Because of the ways in which they could rise high in Indian Muslim courts, these Iranian migrants played a significant role in Indian political and economic life. The reasons for the emigration to the subcontinent were diverse. In the sixteenth century, as the Shi`i Safavids were establishing themselves, many Sunni notable families fled to escape expropriation and death if they refused to convert. The prominence of Khorasan as a point of origin for Iranians in India is related to its having been a continued site of Sunni resistance against Shi`ism, in Herat, Khaf, and Torbat-e Haidariyeh. Other groups now defined as heretical, such as the esoteric Noqtavis and many Sufis, also took refuge in India. Minorities such as the Zoroastrians or Parsis found asylum there in times of political turmoil, and their position in Yazd and Gujarat allowed them to engage in trade between the two. Many Shi`i Iranians also came to settle in the Sunni Mughal empire, and opportunities for trade or advancement in the bureaucracy were significant pull factors. India in the early modern period, with its rainfall agriculture and system of irrigation canals that often allowed two growing seasons, as well as its spice and textile trades, was simply far richer than Iran. Enough Iranians had already settled there and corresponded with relatives and friends back home for this fact to have become widely known and to contribute to chain migration (albeit on a relatively small scale compared to modern instances of such phenomena).

Subrahmanyam has argued that the Iranian immigrants in India cannot be seen as a diaspora community, defined as an immigrant group that occupies a single niche in a wider society. Rather, Iranian immigrants to Bijapur, Golconda, and the Mughal Empire performed a wide variety of occupations, and sometimes a single person was a courtier, merchant, and poet. Bijapur and Golconda were both Shi`i-ruled for much of their history, which encouraged Iranian immigration, and ministers there actively sought Iranian warriors, scribes, and clergymen through agents in Iran. The help the Safavid state gave to Humayun in reestablishing his control of India in the sixteenth century included sending with him a large number of Iranian courtiers, whose numbers grew under Akbar and Jahangir. Indeed, Jahangir's queen, Nur Jahan, was from a Tehrani notable family.[10] He had substance abuse problems, leaving the field open for Nur Jahan to become extremely influential in the governance of the country, and significant numbers of her clan were appointed to high office, including some provincial posts. Iranians were seen by European travelers and other observers of the Mughal Empire in the first quarter of the seventeenth century as the most powerful and privileged ethnicity in the realm. In the late seventeenth century they constituted nearly a third of the five hundred highest officeholders, and nearly half of the wealthiest of these.[11] These Iranian officials at the Mughal court were in turn among the richest and most powerful persons in the early modern world. Even after the decentralization of the Mughal state in the eighteenth century, Iranian immigration to India continued to be significant. It was impelled in part by the frequent political turbulence in Iran beginning in the teens of the eighteenth century, which led to the fall of the Safavid dynasty in 1722, the wars of Nader Shah in the 1730s and 1740s, and the subsequent interregnum when no chieftain controlled much of the country, until the rise of the Zands in the 1760s. A pull factor was the rise of regional courts, some of them, like Awadh and Bengal, Shi`i-ruled, which continued to offer patronage on a substantial scale to Iranian immigrants, such as the extended family of the Behbahani clan.[12] In the important eighteenth-century Bengal port of Hughli, which hosted trading establishments from a number of nations, the Iranian merchants in the early part of that century had more capital than any of the others.[13]

The Safavid rulers, who over time gave more influence and power to the strict Shi`i clerics, tended to deny patronage to panegyric poets, whom they saw as pursuing a worldly and trivial occupation, as well as to Sufi authors, provoking the emigration of substantial numbers of Iranian poets to India in the sixteenth and seventeenth centuries.[14] In the syncretic and unconventional atmosphere of India they were free to experiment with what they called a "new discourse" (*tazeh-gu`i*).[15] They frequently took tropes from classical Persian poetry and built on them, producing complex metaphors that are, probably, also often influenced by Indian literary norms. This style can be compared, for its cerebral tone, extended metaphors, humanism, and "violent yoking of unlike ideas," with that of the "Metaphysical" poets of seventeenth-century Britain, such as John Donne, though it was far more baroque and difficult. A reaction against the new style began in the eighteenth century among some Iranian litterateurs, and in the early twentieth century it began being condemned by Iranian nationalists as foreign. Yet the "Indian style" was the predominant form of Persian poetry in the early modern period, since little great poetry was produced under Safavid patronage.

An exemplar of the new style in Persian was Bidel (1644–1721), born in Patna into an old Turkic family.[16] Bidel began by patterning his verse on that of the classical Persian poets, but after he settled in Delhi in 1664 he gradually turned to the complex and abstract Indian style. In his extensive travels through India, during which he met adherents of many religions, he became increasingly religiously tolerant and gained a deep understanding of Hindu thought. He died and was buried in Delhi. Siddiqi writes that "Bīdel's mystical and passionate *gāzals* are among the best in the Indo-Persian literary tradition; only Amīr Ḵosrow equals him in quality and quantity." He admits, however, that the baroque abstractions of the Indian style make Bidel's verses difficult to interpret in some instances. He adds that "the actual extent of Bīdel's influence on Indo-Persian, Urdu, Afghan and Tajik literature, however, is beyond measure, and it seems to have increased with each succeeding generation of poets and writers in Central Asia." Despite his popularity in some quarters, Bidel and the Indian style provoked great controversy. In the eighteenth century he was attacked by Ali Hazin, a prominent emigrant from Nader Shah's Iran to Banaras, for departing from the simplicity of classical Persian verse. The Indian style was defended, however, by local Indian Persian poets such as Arzu (who was also the first to publish on the similarities between Persian and Sanskrit).[17]

Persian became the primary language of the chronicle of political events in early modern India.[18] Writers of Iranian heritage contributed significantly to this corpus of works, with names such as Astarabadi and Khafi being prominent. They brought with them Iranian historiographical models.[19] They also played a role in the development of other sorts of prose writing.[20] The Iranian contribution to Mughal miniature painting and architecture is legendary, and it derives not only from the work of immigrant artists and architects (such as Mir Sayyed Ali, with his laconic court scenes, or Ghiyas al-Din, who designed the lovely mausoleum of Humayun) but also from their influence on subsequent Muslim Indian and Hindu practitioners of these arts.[21]

Religion was another huge area where Iranians and Persian culture were extremely important. The position of Persian as a lingua franca allowed unusual amounts of cultural interchange among adherents of various religions and cultures in this period. A substantial literature on Hinduism existed in Arabic and Persian. The great medieval Iranian savant Abu Raihan Biruni (973–1048) authored, around 1030, a wide-ranging description of Hinduism that became a classic.[22] Medieval and early modern Muslim political ascendancy in North India led to a vast amount of translation from Sanskrit sources into Persian, the language of the bureaucracy and of most Indo-Muslim learning. A large number of authors combined elements of Hindu and Islamic learning in this period. The Persophone Hindu stratum even participated in the translation of the Hindu scriptures into Persian for its own use, and it has been argued that more Hindus read the Bhagavad Gita in Persian than in Sanskrit in late Mughal times.[23] It should not be lost sight of, however, that throughout this period cultural production, especially by Hindus, continued vigorously in local Indian languages, in everything from Braj Bhasha to Telegu, and these were more important for Hinduism than was Persian, a minority taste.[24] Many works by Brahmins on Hindu subjects in these languages do not so much as acknowledge that Islam or the Mughal Empire existed.

The number of Muslim scholars who collaborated with Hindu pandits in making Sanskrit works available was considerable. Nizam al-Din Panipati rendered the widely influential *Yoga Vasistha* into Persian late in the sixteenth century at the behest of the Mughal ruler Jahangir while he was still a crown prince. The Mughal prince Dara Shikuh (1615–1659) himself did much to expound Hindu tenets in Persian, as well as translating important works such as the Upanishads.[25] Since many Hindus also wrote in or translated into Persian, very large numbers of such manuscripts circulated among the literate classes, and many of these books demonstrably reached Iran. Among them was the Persian translation of the *Yoga Vasistha* (*Jug-Basisht*), a work on Hindu mysticism probably written in the thirteenth century c.e. Cast in the form of a dialogue purportedly between the Vedic sage Vasistha and his pupil Rama, this work shows influences of Vedanta, Yoga, and even Mahayana Buddhism. As noted above, Nizam al-Din Panipati carried out a translation of this book in the late 1500s. The Safavid-era Iranian mystic Mir Fendereski (d. 1641) selected and commented on portions of Panipati's rendering of the *Yoga Vasistha*. Mir Fendereski gained a reputation at the court of Shah Abbas at early-seventeenth-century Isfahan for asceticism, and he is said to have become, after his journeys in India, a vegetarian and an adorer of the sun who refused to go on pilgrimage to Mecca lest he be forced to sacrifice sheep. The *Yoga Vasistha* appears to have been a popular work among those with Indo-Persian interests from about 1600 onward.[26] Many of the same intellectuals involved in the study of Hinduism were also prominent in the study of philosophy, and a lively tradition of Iran-influenced philosophy, with commentaries on great Safavid thinkers such as Mulla Sadra, continued in Indian seminaries and study groups into the twentieth century.

Persian descriptions of Hinduism, though varying in quality, were also quite numerous. An example of this literature is the anonymous *School of Religions* (*Dabestan-i mazaheb*), which examines Zoroastrianism, Hinduism, and both branches of Islam at some length, and includes a brief description of Christianity. The author was probably a Zoroastrian of Iranian extraction, brought up in Patna, North India. The *School of Religions* was lithographed at least three times in the nineteenth century.[27] As this book attests, the small Zoroastrian community, known in the subcontinent as Parsis, also played a disproportionate cultural and economic role in India. Parsis continued to be in contact with Iranian Zoroastrians and thus with Iranian culture, and Zoroastrian immigrants from Iran came to the subcontinent, especially to Bombay during the nineteenth century.[28]

Despite the importance of Sufi mysticism in India, contemporary Iranians made fewer and fewer contributions to Sufism in India as Iran's conversion to Shi`ism progressed and monarchs such as Shah Abbas turned against the orders. The Ne`mat-Allahi order was among the very few that survived vigorously, by adopting a Shi`i coloration; it had a major outpost in South India, from which missionaries came to Iran in the later eighteenth century to revive the order there.[29] Despite the relative lack of Sufi affiliations between Iran and India, Persian spirituality remained at the center of the Sufi experience in the subcontinent.[30] Innumerable commentaries were written in Persian upon Persophone Sufi greats such as Rumi, Jami, and other classical mystics into the nineteenth century (after 1850 or so, such commentaries were increasingly in Urdu).

Given Iran's turn to Shi`ism, it is unsurprising that Iranians should have contributed mightily to the development of this branch of Islam in the subcontinent. The split in Islam between Shi`is and others goes back to the crisis of succession that followed the Prophet Muhammad's death. The partisans (Shi`a) of the Prophet's son-in-law and cousin, Ali ibn Abi Talib, supported his accession to power. A permanent constituency grew up for Ali and his descendants, the House of the Prophet, which sought to transform heredi-tary charisma into political power. Several branches of Shi`ism emerged, depending on which branch of Ali's descendants adherents followed. From a Twelver point of view, the Isma`ili line diverged when they followed Isma`il rather than Kazim ibn Ja`far as seventh imam. The esoteric Druze developed out of Fatimid Isma`ilism in medieval Egypt. The Twelver line ended in exo-teric history with Hasan al-Askari, alleged to have a young son (Muhammad al-Mahdi) who disappeared into a supernatural realm and would return even-tually to fill the world with justice. The Twelver branch afterwards developed as a scripturalist religion with ulama who often studied with Sunni scholars and used similar techniques to elucidate texts. Those who followed an eso-teric folk religion based on belief in the Twelve Imams but emphasizing Ali's divinity became known as Nusairis. The rest of the Muslims, rejecting the hereditary claims of the Alid lines, recognized the prior rights of four early elected caliphs (only the last being Ali) and then acknowledged the subse-quent sultan-caliphs. Twelvers remained a minority in most places, though various sects of Shi`ism gathered great numerical strength in medieval Syria, southern Iraq, and eastern Arabia, as well as some towns in Iran. In the eleventh century, Isma`ilis ruled Fatimid Egypt and Twelver Buyids ruled Iran and Iraq. But this interlude of Shi`i power ended with the Turkish Seljuq invasions and the victory of the Sunni Ayyubids over the Crusaders and Fatimids.

The rise of the Shi`i Safavid dynasty in Iran coincided with the establish-ment of several new Muslim dynasties in India, the rulers of which looked to Iran as the model for imperial style.[31] Iran's preeminence in this regard had several roots. Iran was often called *velayat*, literally "authority," but here apparently in the sense of "the metropole," among South Asian Muslims. The Safavids thus assumed not only the throne of Iran but also the position of role models for other dynasties. Of course, the Uzbeks, the Mughals, and the Ottomans committed themselves to Sunni Islam, but most were generally rooted in claims to legitimacy having to do with descent from Turko-Mongol conquerors, and they based their power on a Sunni Turkic tribal cavalry. Other rulers, lacking this strong source of legitimacy, were more open to establishing it by modeling themselves loosely on the Safavid court, even to the extent of adopting Shi`ism. Further, Shi`i Iranian émigrés at regional courts often played a key role, both in founding new dynasties in South Asia and in encouraging the conversion of newly established regional rulers. In this regard, the trade routes between Iran and India became an important conduit of religious ideas, bringing them along with silk, grain, horses, raisins, and wine from Shiraz and Bandar Abbas to Surat, Bijapur, Golconda, and Hughli.

Yusuf Adil Shah (r. 1489–1510) was an Ottoman adventurer and exile who had formed ties to Shah Isma'il of Iran. He was even rumored to have been a son of Ottoman Sultan Murad II. He established himself as ruler of an area in South India that had formerly been under the control of the Muslim Bahmani dynasty, with his capital at Bijapur. On hearing of Shah Isma'il's victory and announcement of his Shi'ism, Yusuf Adil Shah issued a 1502 proclamation that Shi'ism was the state religion of his realm. Shi'ism remained influential at this court, with one two-decade interlude, until late in the sixteenth century. Ultimately, this state was absorbed by the Sunni Mughal Empire in the course of the seventeenth century. Yusuf Adil Shah and his Shi'i successors went so far as to declare themselves vassals of the Safavids, though the latter could hardly exercise much real power given the distances involved. Many Shi'i Iranians emigrated to the hospitable Bijapur court, and horse merchants, bureaucrats, and military men made careers there. The Adil Shahis maintained a corps of three hundred pious Iranians to pronounce ritual curses on the first three caliphs, honored by Sunnis but excoriated by Shi'is as usurpers of Ali's rights. Ritual cursing of Sunni holy figures, which was also promoted in Iran by the Safavids, provoked riots among Bijapur's Muslim population, which remained largely Sunni and was often oriented to Sufism or mystical Islam.

A similar story could be told about Ahmadnagar, to Bijapur's northwest, ruled from 1490 by the Nizam Shahi dynasty. Under the influence of an Iranian exile who had adopted Twelver Shi'ism, the second monarch in this dynasty, Burhan Nizam Shah (1508–53), converted to Shi'ism. Shi'ism remained influential in Ahmadnagar's elite political culture for generations, though it, too, ultimately fell to the Sunni Mughals. Likewise, for a brief time (1561–89) a Shi'i ruling house, the Chak dynasty, came to power in Kashmir. Initially, this Kashmiri clan had adopted the Nurbakhshi Sufi order, but with the rise of the Safavids many Nurbakhshis, who had had a strong Shi'i tendency, formally became Twelvers, and this was the case with the Chaks. The conversion of the ruling house created tensions with local Sunnis, leading to religious riots similar to those in Bijapur. The Mughal Akbar made these disturbances a basis for his invasion of the region and its annexation to his empire. A Shi'i minority remained, however, which included influential military men and notables.

The most long-lived and important of the early modern Shi'i dynasties in India was that of Golconda, ruled by the Qutb-Shahi dynasty (1512–1687). It was actually founded by an Iranian from Hamadan, Sultan-Quli Qutbu'd-Din, a Turkmen. Like the sixteenth-century Shi'i Bijapuri rulers, this dynasty had Friday prayers said in the name of the Twelve Imams and the Safavid monarch. Shi`i ulama flocked to the city of Golconda (now Hyderabad, Andhra Pradesh), where they were given stipends, endowment monies, and other perquisites by the ruling family, which also built Shi`i seminaries, buildings for the commemoration of the martyrdom of Imam Husayn, and burial grounds. Many Iranians emigrated to join the Golconda upper classes, including military men, bureaucrats, poets, ulama, and great merchants. (Golconda was a premier source of diamonds in the early modern period.) The Mughal emperor Shah Jahan reduced Golconda to nominal vassalage in 1636, insisting that the Qutb-Shahis cease holding Shi`i Friday prayers and desist from having the sermons said in the name of the Safavids. In 1687, the arch-Sunni Mughal emperor, Aurangzib, had the satisfaction of conquering Golconda and unseating its Shi`i dynasty.

Not only Shi`i mourning culture and clerical institutions grew up in Golconda, but also the mystical Shi`i Sufi order, the Ne`mat-Allahiyeh. Initially, this had been a Sunni order, but most members became Shi`is in the course of the sixteenth century. The order established an outpost in Golconda in the early modern period, which became extremely useful when the later Safavids began persecuting Sufi orders. It was possible for the leaders to escape to Golconda and make it their headquarters. From there, in the mid to late eighteenth century, they launched a revival of the Ne`mat-Allahi order in Zand and early Qajar Iran. Iran's religious influences abroad frequently came back to roost in the home country.

We may conclude that the religious revolution wrought by the Safavids had an immediate effect on the Muslim courts of the Indian subcontinent, helping turn the tide toward Shi`i rule throughout the old Bahmanid realms of South India during the sixteenth century, as well as, briefly, in Kashmir. Where these Shi`i dynasties survived into the seventeenth century, however, they faced increasing pressure from the Sunni-ruled Mughal empire, which ultimately dethroned them all and absorbed their kingdoms. If the sixteenth was the Shi`i century in the Muslim east, the seventeenth was a period of Sunni revivalism everywhere but Iran itself. The demographic implication of the turn to Shi`ism in the 1500s was, however, limited in India. In part, this slight impact simply tracked with the relatively low rates of conversion to Islam more generally in heavily Hindu South India. The three areas where any substantial proportion of the population accepted Islam in early modern South Asia were western Punjab, Kashmir, and eastern Bengal, and all were under Sunni Mughal rule for most of this period. In addition, there is little reason to believe that most monarchs in this era had any particular desire to see very large numbers of their subjects adopt their religion. Many rulers appeared to see the court religion as a sign of regal distinctiveness, rather than as a message for the masses, and few showed any interest in projects of mass conversion.

In the course of the eighteenth century, the Mughal empire disintegrated, relinquishing power to its major provinces, which emerged as royal courts in their own right. The western Deccan and central India fell to the Hindu Marathas, the eastern Deccan was devolved on the Sunni Nizam of Hyderabad, Punjab fell to the Sikhs, Kabul and Peshawar to the Sunni Dorrani dynasty. Bengal, Sind, and Awadh each developed local Shi`i dynasties that began as regional Mughal governorships. Especially after about 1725, these increasingly became post-Mughal successor states. Shi`ism in Bengal throve in the eighteenth century, with ample government patronage for Shi`i practices and institutions such as seminaries. Many Iranians immigrated to the nawabate, as merchants and Muslim learned men. Shi`ism lost this privileged position, however, when the British conquered the province from 1757.

The Talpur nawabs of Sind in the northwest of the subcontinent were Baluchi in ethnicity but, unlike the majority of the Baluch, were Shi`is rather than Sunnis. Under their influence the practice of Islam in Sind took on a strongly Shi`i coloration, though one could not call the unlettered Sindi peasants who commemorated Imam Husain and other members of the Prophet's family Shi`is, exactly. Among the more important effects of this ruling house was their influence on the Jalali Sohravardi order. This Sufi brotherhood was one of four (along with the Qadiris, Naqshbandis, and Chishtis) that provided some of the framework for the conversion of what is now Pakistan to Islam, having come to Punjab and Sind from Bukhara in the thirteenth century. The ancestral seat of the paramount leader of the order was Ucch, which was on the border of Sind and the Sunni nawabate of Bahawalpur. Around 1805, the old leader of the order died and a fight broke out among two claimants to succeed him. One claimant was backed by the nawab of Bahawalpur, and the other sought the help of the Talpurs in Sind. The latter agreed, but conditioned this aid on the Sohravardi leader adopting Shi`ism. The Talpur armies defeated Bahawalpur and put their man at the head of the Sohravardi order in Ucch. He honored his pledge and converted to Shi`ism. The Sohravardi leaders, or *Bukhari pirs*, saw themselves as generally related to one another and were centered in shrines of their pious ancestors dotting Punjab. Gradually, many of the other shrine-based leaders followed their prestigious cousin in Ucch by declaring for Shi`ism, as in Jhang Siyal and several other sites. Typically, these Sufi leaders were great landholders, having had great estates bestowed on their lineages by the Mughals, and their Sufi followers or *murids* were often also the peasants who worked their estates. Their enormous prestige helped ensure that when they adopted Shi`ism over the course of the nineteenth century, many of their peasants did as well. Some significant percentage of Punjabi Shi`is appear to have come into the religion through their *pirs* who had converted. This distinctive form of Shi`i Sufism in what became Pakistan helped influence the lyrics of mystical music or *qavvali*. Despite its cultural reach, the specifically political power of Shi`ism in Sind declined, and in the 1840s both Sind and Punjab fell to the British.[32]

AWADH (OUDH)

The most important and long-lived Shi`i successor state to the Mughals was Awadh, ruled by the Nishapuri dynasty 1722–1856.[33] Situated between Bengal and Delhi at the foot of the Nepalese Himalayas, it was founded by Mir Muhammad Amin Nishapuri (d. 1739), known as Burhan al-Mulk, the first nawab of Awadh. He came to the Mughal empire from eastern Iran in 1708 and rose rapidly in government service. He became governor of Awadh (the British "Oudh") in 1722 and quickly formed an alliance with Sunni townsmen and rural Hindu rajas, the local intermediate elites. He resisted the Mughal emperor's one attempt to transfer him to another province, a sign of Awadh's increasing autonomy, and he later collaborated with the Iranian invader Nader Shah, who rewarded him by conferring Awadh on him and his descendants as a hereditary nawabate. Nader Shah also left behind a substantial contingent of Shi`i Qizilbash cavalrymen, who joined the Awadh military. The nawabs gradually consolidated their hold on Awadh and began in a minor way to build up local Shi`i constituencies and institutions. Shi`is never became more than a very small minority in the province. Some 90 percent of the population was Hindu, and only three percent of the Muslims were Shi`is. Shi`ism as the royal religion, however, had a vastly disproportionate impact on politics and culture throughout the nineteenth century.

Awadh, which was among the powers defeated at Baksar by the British East India Company army in 1764, was thereafter gradually surrounded by the British. The indemnities and other payments levied by the East India Company forced Awadh into debt. The British demanded the concession of some Awadh territory in the north later in the century, and then annexed over half the province in 1801 to pay for the claimed arrears in Awadh tribute. The rulers of the province were thus deprived of the opportunity for expansion, and instead lost substantial territory, after which they were surrounded by the British on three sides. It is not surprising that they should have invested their wealth in culture rather than in the military, and that culture had strong Shi`i components.

Thousands of immigrants came into Awadh from Iran over the decades, serving as physicians, bureaucrats, military men, poets, chroniclers, and clerics or ulama. They remained a small minority overall, but they were a noticeable component of the urban population. Persian could be heard spoken by some common people in the streets of the capital, Lucknow, in the late eighteenth century, as well as at court and among literary figures. Enormous numbers of Persian words entered local speech, contributing to the further development of Urdu, which began enjoying an important place in Awadh culture. Urdu was a mixture of what we would now call Hindi grammar with Persian vocabulary, written in the Arabic script, and was increasingly championed by North Indian intellectuals as a vehicle for local culture in the late eighteenth and early nineteenth centuries. Ironically, the nawabs of Awadh, despite their Persian ancestry, became the foremost patrons of Urdu poets in the late eighteenth and early nineteenth centuries, leading to a flourishing of the language there. This prominence of Urdu helped differentiate the Awadh court from the old Mughal court at Delhi, which had favored Persian. The foundational texts of modern Urdu literature often have a strongly Shi`i tinge because they were written in Lucknow, and *marthiyah* or traditional elegies in commemoration of the martyred Shi`i Imams constituted a major genre. Still, all the great early Urdu writers also wrote extensively in Persian, so that language hardly fell into disuse in the late eighteenth and early nineteenth centuries.

The Awadh nawabs supported the creation and growth of a Shi`i clerical corps, made up both of local Shi`i ulama and of immigrant Iranians. A rather lively set of debates was conducted about whether the local clerics or the Iranians were better Shi`is. Because of their knowledge of local court protocol and customs, the Indian Shi`i ulama tended to become ensconced in positions of influence, such as Friday prayer leader and seminary teacher, and to receive the patronage of the Shi`i nawabs (later kings) of Awadh. Iranian clerics sometimes preferred to settle among Shi`i communities ruled by the British, where they were free from the demands made on them by the Awadh state. The Awadh nawabs respected the great Shi`i jurisprudents of the Iraqi shrine cities, most of whom were Iranians, and bestowed on them enormous amounts in patronage and put them in charge of large-scale philanthropic works such as canal building.[34] As in the Shi`i-ruled South Asian kingdoms, in Awadh the Shi`is remained a tiny minority of the population, and the religion functioned more as a symbol of royal distinctiveness and prerogatives than as a missionary faith aimed at converting the masses. The chroniclers do maintain, however, that in the 1840s hundreds of Hindus and thousands of Sunnis became Shi`is.

The Shi`i establishment in Awadh was much reduced in power and influence in 1856 when the British annexed the province, after which the decline of Shi`i patronage led to a great slackening if not a total halting of Iranian immigration into the area (unlike the situation in Bombay). Shi`is in British India often went to Iran for seminary study or to master Persian poetry, and a small number of them could afford the pilgrimage to the shrines of the Imams in Iraq, so that contacts between Iran and South Asian Shi`is continued.

The emigration of the Isma`ili Agha Khan leaders of Mahallat in Iran to British Bombay in the aftermath of a failed 1840s revolt against the Qajars established another Iran-India relationship among adherents to that branch of Shi`ism. It has remained strong ever since (Isma`ilism had an old history in India but was not necessarily connected to Iran, whereas the Agha Khanis were).[35] In our period, Shi`i influence was carried from Iran by the prestige of the court, the prestige of the Persian language, the networks of Iranian merchants in the Indian Ocean, and the emigration of thousands of Iranians to South Asia (many of them from the upper strata and so able to rise high in Indian governments). The influence of Shi`i Sufi orders, and the resonances of Safavid Shi`ism with South Asian Muslim folk traditions of devotion to the family of the Prophet, were also important in this development.

PERSIAN CULTURE IN THE EIGHTEENTH
AND NINETEENTH CENTURIES

The story of Iranian and Persian influences in the subcontinent does not end in Bengal with the rise of the British. Not only did regional courts such as Awadh and Hyderabad continue to patronize Persian works, but so, too, did the British themselves. Knowledge of Persian was common among nineteenth-century British administrators in India, and they promoted the beginnings of the print and lithograph revolution in that language.[36] Mastery of Persian and the commissioning of Persian works by local scribes and chroniclers were key to the early process by which the British gained access to networks of local intelligence about the subcontinent, which were crucial to their establishment of empire. Persophone historians in turn did much to shape British and subsequent views of Mughal "decline" and its causes.[37] Nor did the Hindu castes that had cultivated it forsake Persian in the early nineteenth century. The great Hindu reformer Ram Mohan Roy edited a Persian-language newspaper in Calcutta in the 1820s and wrote some of his reformist treatises in Persian. Interest in India and things Indo-Persian remained strong in nineteenth-century Iran, as well. Mansoureh Ettehadieh Nizam-Mafi has demonstrated that of the 48,439 manuscripts calligraphed in the Qajar period according to the bibliographer Monzavi, 1,538 (comprising 309 distinct titles) consisted of histories of India. Of these, 751 were written prior to the late eighteenth century and subsequently recopied, and 787 were authored during the Qajar era. Only 1,986 manuscripts were produced on Iranian history in this period. Thus, about 44 percent of all history manuscripts produced in Iran during the Qajar era were about India! Moreover, in the nineteenth century at least 912 Persian books were printed in India, many of them dealing with Indian themes, compared with 2,569 books printed in all of Iran.[38] All of this is to say that India bulked large in the educated Iranian imagination in the nineteenth century, and knowledge of it was quite common among readers.

Nevertheless, the gradual decline in knowledge of Persian among most Indians after about 1850 began to limit Iran's influence. The rise, first of Urdu and Hindi, and then of Hindi-English medium schools after independence, along with the new projects of Indian and Pakistani nationalism, helped foster among those South Asian groups that had been Persophone a certain amount of independence and a turn inward to local traditions. For the Shi`is among them, this tendency was not interrupted in a major way until the Islamic Revolution of 1978–79.

CONCLUSION

The cultural and political exchanges between Iran and the Indian subcontinent in 1500–1900 depended strongly upon a linguistic network within India of Persophone intellectuals. As Subrahmanyam has demonstrated, however, Persian did not function as an enclave language for a narrow diasporic community of Indo-Iranians. Rather, ethnic Iranians filled a wide range of social roles, including bureaucrat, merchant, warrior, clergyman, mystic guide, and artisan. Persian was used by millions of non-Iranians over the centuries. There were perhaps seven times more readers of Persian in the subcontinent than in Iran at the height of the Mughal empire, creating a far-flung network of consumers for travel accounts, chronicles, translations from the Sanskrit, how-to manuals, and poetry. As the language of the Mughal court, Persian carried the prestige of symbolic power. It became the favored language for the writing of political history and attracted the talents of thousands of panegyric and other poets. Even much later in history, both the nineteenth-century poet Ghalib and the twentieth-century Muhammad Iqbal believed that they had done by far their best work in Persian. The "new discourse" of the early modern poets, with its subtle takeoffs from the classics and difficult extended metaphors, produced a new concept of individualism. Persian was also a cosmopolitan language for the production of travelogues recounting the wonders of the subcontinent that incidentally allowed the display of the individual's own adventures and personal quirks. The sense of curiosity and naturalism that characterize so much of Mughal Persian writing extends to investigations into Hindu philosophy, with translations of key works such as the Upanishads and the Bhagavad Gita. This "translation movement" and engagement with the philosophy of another civilization can be compared in its scope and seriousness to only two other moments in Islamic history. These are the Baghdad translation movement that brought Greek learning into Arabic under Harun al-Rashid, and the nineteenth-century translation movement centered in Cairo and Istanbul that introduced readers for the first time to Voltaire, Montesquieu, and other French authors. The contribution of the Mughal Persianists to the field of comparative religion, however, has not received the same recognition in scholarship as have the other two moments of civilizational encounter. The place of Persian works in India continued to be highly significant into the nineteenth century, when many British merchants and bureaucrats joined the multiethnic Indo-Persian *ecumene.*

Persian culture informed early modern India in areas other than language, as well. The tradition of Persian miniature painting was taken up avidly in the subcontinent and developed with reference to Indian themes; through European influence, sometimes even perspective was introduced. Indo-Persian architecture produced some of the loveliest buildings still extant in that architecturally rich region, from Nur Jahan's mausoleum in Lahore to that of Humayun in Delhi.

Iran's influence on Islamic thought was also enormous. The great medieval Sufis, such as Rumi, al-Ghazali, Sohravardi, Jami, and many others were widely read, commented upon, and imitated. The School of Isfahan in Safavid philosophy, with its emphasis on Neoplatonic Illuminationism in the tradition of Sohravardi, found many followers in India, and its works were taught in seminaries. Commentaries on great Iranian philosophers such as Mulla Sadra were produced in the hundreds. Among the more important religious influences exerted by Iran on India from the Safavid period forward has been in the area of Twelver Shi'ism. This branch of Islam remained a small minority among Indian Muslims, but because it was adopted by some ruling houses and great landed nobles, it had an influence far beyond what its mere numbers might suggest. The biggest impact of Iranian culture in India, however, was not so narrowly sectarian. Indo-Persian writing was largely characterized by a broad humanism to which nothing human was foreign. In this sense it was a truly early modern phenomenon and a worthy contemporary of the European Renaissance.

NOTES

1. Good basic overviews of Mughal history can be found in Muzaffar Alam and Sanjay Subrahmanyam, eds., *The Mughal State, 1526–1750* (Delhi: Oxford University Press, 1998); and John F. Richards, *The Mughals* (Cambridge: Cambridge University Press, 1993).

2. Muzaffar Alam, "The Pursuit of Persian: Language in Mughal Politics," *Modern Asian Studies* 32 (1998): 317–49.

3. Ibid., 331–32.

4. Cf. Stephen P. Blake, *Shahjahanabad: The Sovereign City in Mughal India, 1639–1739* (Cambridge: Cambridge University Press, 1991), 108–12, 130–34, cited in Muzaffar Alam and Sanjay Subrahmanyam, "Discovering the Familiar: Notes on the Travel-Account of Anandram Mukhlis, 1745," *South Asia Research* 16 (1996): 131–54, which deals in an extended way with a Khatri writer of a Persian travel account.

5. Alam and Subrahmanyam, "Discovering the Familiar."

6. Muzaffar Alam and Sanjay Subrahmanyam, "From an Ocean of Wonders: Maḥmûd bin Amîr Walî Balkhî' and his Indian Travels (1625–1631)," in *Récits de voyages asiatiques. Genres, mentalités et conceptions de l'espace*, ed. Claudine Salmon (Paris: Ecole française d'Extrême-Orient, 1996), 161–90.

7. Alam and Subrahmanyam, "Discovering the Familiar"; Simon Digby, "Some Asian Wanderers in Seventeenth-Century India: An Examination of Sources in Persian," *Studies in History*, new ser., 9 (1993): 247–64; Juan R. I. Cole, "Mirror of the World: Iranian 'Orientalism' and Early 19th-Century India," *Critique: Journal of Critical Studies of Iran and the Middle East* 8 (Spring 1996): 41–60.

8. Sanjay Subrahmanyam, "Iranians Abroad: Intra-Asian Elite Migration and Early Modern State Formation," *Journal of Asian Studies* 51 (1992): 340–63.

9. Sir John Chardin, *Travels in Persia* (London: Argonaut Press, 1927), 130, 139.

10. Ellison Banks Findly, *Nur Jahan, Empress of Mughal India* (New York: Oxford University Press, 1993).

11. M. Athar Ali, *The Mughal Nobility under Aurangzeb* (Bombay: Asian Publishing House, 1966), 19–20, 175–271.

12. Juan Cole, "Shi`i Clerics in Iraq and Iran, 1722–1780: The Akhbari-Usuli Conflict Reconsidered," *Iranian Studies* 18 (1985): 1–33.

13. Sushil Chaudhry, "The Rise and Decline of Hughli—a Port in Medieval Bengal," *Bengal Past and Present* 86, no. 1 (1967): 33–67; Holden Furber, "Glimpses of Life and Trade on the Hugli 1720–1770," *Bengal Past and Present* 86, no. 2 (1967): 13–23; Ashin Das Gupta, "Trade and Politics in 18th-Century India," in *Islam and the Trade of Asia*, ed. D. S. Richards (Oxford: Bruno Cassirer, 1970), 199.

14. Yar Muhammad Khan, *Iranian Influence in Mughul India* (Lahore: Punjab University Press, 1978), 10–35.

15. Paul E. Losensky, *Welcoming Fighani: Imitation and Poetic Individuality in the Safavid-Mughal Ghazal* (Costa Mesa, CA: Mazda, 1998).

16. Moazzam Siddiqi, "Bīdel," in *Encyclopaedia Iranica* (London and New York: Routledge and Kegan Paul, 1989), 4:244–46.

17. Alam, "Pursuit of Persian," 341–42.

18. Aftab Asghar, *Tarikh-nevisi-ye farsi dar Hend va Pakistan: Timuriyan-e bozorg az Babor ta Aurangzib, 932–1118 H.Q.* (Lahore: Khaneh-ye farhang-e Jomhuri-ye Eslami-

ye Iran, 1985); see also Peter Hardy, *Historians of Medieval India: Studies in Indo-Muslim Historical Writing* (London: Luzac, 1960).

19. See Sholeh Quinn, *Historical Writing during the Reign of Shah Abbas: Ideology, Imitation and Legitimacy in Safavid Iran* (Salt Lake City: University of Utah Press, 2000); idem, "The Historiography of Safavid Prefaces," *Pembroke Papers* 4 (1996): 1–25; and idem, "Notes on Timurid Legitimacy in Three Safavid Chronicles," *Iranian Studies* 31 (1998): 149–58.

20. Yar Muhammad Khan, *Iranian Influence*, 35–39.

21. Ibid., 39–46. Fine surveys of these fields in the new Cambridge History of India monograph series that attend to Iranian influences are Catherine Asher, *Architecture of Mughal India* (Cambridge and New York: Cambridge University Press, 1992); and Milo Cleveland Beach, *Mughal and Rajput Painting* (Cambridge and New York: Cambridge University Press, 1992).

22. Muhammad Abu Rayhan al-Biruni, *Kitab fi tahqiq ma li al-Hind*, ed. Edward Sachau (Leipzig: Otto Harrassowitz, 1925); trans. Edward Sachau, *Alberuni's India* (London: K. Paul, Trench, Trübner & Co., Ltd., 1910).

23. Fathullah Mujtabai, *Aspects of Hindu Muslim Cultural Relations* (New Delhi: National Book Bureau, 1978).

24. Cf. Sanjay Subrahmanyam, "Hearing Voices: Vignettes of Early Modernity in South Asia, 1400–1750," *Daedalus* 127, no. 3 (Summer 1998): 75–104.

25. See Dara Shikuh, trans., *Serr-e Akbar (Upanishad)*, ed. Tara Chand and S. M. Reza Jalali Na'ini (Tehran: Ketabkhaneh-ye tahuri, 1357/1978); Dara Shikuh, *Montakhab-e asar*, ed. S. M. Reza Jalali Na'ini (Tehran: Taban, 1337/1958); Bikram Jit Hasrat, *Dara Shikuh, Life and Works* (New Delhi: Munshiram Manoharlal, 1943; 2d ed., 1982).

26. The *Yoga Vasistha* exists in many versions, and the one that was translated was an abridged edition properly known as the *Laghu Yoga Vasistha*. See Fathullah Mujtabai, "Muntakhab-i Jug-basasht or, Selections from the Yoga-vasistha attributed to Mir Abu'l-Qasim Fendereski" (Ph.D. dissertation, Harvard University, 1976), esp. xxii–xxiii; for a modern English rendering of this work see Swami Venkatesananda, trans., *The Concise Yoga Vasistha* (Albany: State University of New York Press, 1984); for some analysis of its tales see Wendy Doniger O'Flaherty, *Dreams, Illusions and Other Realities* (Chicago: University of Chicago Press, 1984), 127–296. For Mir Fendereski, see Seyyed Hossein Nasr, "Findiriski, Mir," in *Encyclopedia of Islam-2*, Suppl. (1982), 308–9, and Akbar Hadi Hosainabadi, *Sharh-i hal-e Mir Damad va Mir Fendereski bi enzemam-e divan-e Mir Damad va qasideh-ye Mir Fendereski* (Esfahan: Entesharat-e maisam timar, 1363/1984), 57–163.

27. David Shea and Anthony Troyer, trans., *The Dabistan or School of Manners* (Washington and London: M. Walter Dunne, 1901), 183–84 (quote), 196; [Kai-Khosrau Esfandiyar], *Dabestan-e mazaheb*, ed. Rahim Rizazadeh Malek, 2 vols. (Tehran: Ketabkhaneh-ye tahuri, 1362/1983), vol. 1, 127–28, 134; cf. Klaus K. Klostermaier, *A Survey of Hinduism* (Albany: State University of New York Press, 1989), 228–33.

28. Nancy Singh and Ram Singh, eds., *The Sugar in the Milk: The Parsis in India* (Delhi: Institute for Development Education/ISPCK, 1983); Susan Stiles Maneck, *The Death of Ahriman: Culture, Identity, and Theological Change among the Parsis of India* (Bombay: K. R. Cama Oriental Institute, 1997); Christine E. Dobbin, *Asian Entrepreneurial Minorities: Conjoint Communities in the Making of the World-Economy, 1570–1940* (Richmond, Surrey: Curzon Press, 1996).

29. Nasro'llah Pourjavady and Peter Lamborn Wilson, *Kings of Love: The Poetry and History of the Nimatu'llahi Sufi Order* (Tehran: Imperial Iranian Academy of Philosophy, 1978); and William Royce, "Mir Ma`sum Ali Shah and the Ni`mat Allahi Revival, 1776–77 to 1796–97" (Ph.D. dissertation, Princeton University, 1979).

30. Saiyid Athar Abbas Rizvi, *A History of Sufism in India,* 2 vols. (New Delhi: Munshiram Manoharlal, 1975–1983).

31. For Shi`ism in India from Safavid times to 1856, see Sadiq Naqavi, *Iran-Deccan Relations* (Hyderabad: Bab-ul-Ilm Society, 1994); S. A. A. Rizvi, *A Socio-Intellectual History of the Isna `Ashari Shi`is in India,* 2 vols. (Canberra: Ma`rifat Publishers, 1986); and Juan R. I. Cole, *Roots of North Indian Shi`ism in Iran and Iraq* (Berkeley and Los Angeles: University of California Press, 1989).

32. J. Cole, "Conversion to Imami Shi`ism in India," in *Encyclopaedia Iranica* (Costa Mesa, CA: Mazda, 1994), 6:232–34 and the sources cited therein.

33. See especially Muzaffar Alam, *The Crisis of Empire in Mughal North India: Awadh and the Punjab, 1707–48* (Delhi and New York: Oxford University Press, 1986); Richard B. Barnett, *North India between Empires* (Berkeley: University of California Press, 1980); Michael H. Fisher, *A Clash of Cultures: Avadh, the British and the Mughals* (London: Sangam, 1988); and Cole, *Roots of North Indian Shi`ism.*

34. Juan Cole, "'Indian Money' and the Shi`i Shrine Cities of Iraq," *Middle Eastern Studies* 22 (1986): 461–80; Yitzhak Nakash, *The Shi`is of Iraq* (Princeton: Princeton University Press, 1994), 249, 252–53; Meir Litvak, *Shi`i Scholars of Nineteenth-Century Iraq* (Cambridge: Cambridge University Press, 1998), s.v. "Oudh bequest" in index; Meir Litvak, "A Failed Manipulation: The British, the Oudh Bequest and the Shi`i `Ulama of Najaf and Karbala," *British Journal of Middle Eastern Studies* 27 (2000): 69–89; and M. Litvak, "Money, Religion and Politics: The Oudh Bequest in Najaf and Karbala', 1850–1903," *The International Journal of Middle East Studies* 33 (2001): 1–21.

35. Farhad Daftari, *The Isma`ilis* (Cambridge: Cambridge University Press, 1990).

36. P. Thankappan Nair, "Origin of the Persian, Urdu and Hindi Printing and Press in Calcutta," *Indo-Iranica: The Quarterly Organ of the Iran Society* 43, nos. 3–4 (Sept.–Dec. 1990): 8–69.

37. Kumkum Chatterjee, "History as Self-Representation: The Recasting of a Political Tradition in Late Eighteenth-Century Eastern India," *Modern Asian Studies* 32 (1998): 913–48; Christopher A. Bayly, *Empire and Information: Intelligence Gathering and Social Communication in India, 1780–1870* (Cambridge: Cambridge University Press, 1996); Mohamad Tavakoli-Targhi, "Orientalism's Genesis Amnesia," *Comparative Studies of South Asia, Africa, and the Middle East* 16, no. 1 (1996): 1–14; and idem, "Modernity, Heterotopia, and Homeless Texts," *Comparative Studies of South Asia, Africa, and the Middle East* 18, no. 2 (1998): 2–13.

38. Mansoureh Ettehadieh Nizam-Mafi, "The Emergence of Tehran as the Cultural Center of Iran," in *Téhéran. Capitale bicentenaire,* eds. C. Adle and B. Hourcade (Paris and Tehran: Institut français de recherche en Iran, 1992), 133–38.

2 / Beyond Translation: Interactions between English and Persian Poetry

AHMAD KARIMI-HAKKAK

Over the past two centuries, hundreds of translators have brought Persian poetry to speakers of English; only a handful have attracted attention beyond the confines of literary scholarship. This essay examines interactions with Persian poetry that go beyond translation to create versions that relate to their originals in ways that need to be studied further. Comparing Sir William Jones's eighteenth-century rendition of one famous ghazal with Coleman Barks's recent version of Rumi's "Song of the Reed Flute," it argues that, contrary to the widespread impression that literal translation means close translation, translators who go beyond lexical equivalence at times achieve greater proximity with their original texts; they also stand a better chance of attracting attention among general readers of poetry. Historically, such attempts have helped foster greater interactions between Persian and English poetic traditions.

In the last decade or so, the immense popularity of Coleman Barks's versions of Rumi's poems has impressed on us, once more, issues surrounding the translation of Persian poetry into English. In this essay I hope to demonstrate that Barks's approach has an illustrious pedigree stretching over two centuries, and that this approach has played an important part in popularizing Persian poetry in the English-speaking world and beyond. That examining approaches of this type can deepen our understanding of the intertextual relations between original poems and their rendition into other languages, and of the poetic translator's craft in general, ought to be obvious. Beyond that, creative encounters with Persian poetry show the possibility of transcending the binary opposition between the scholarly objective of approximating foreign poetry through more or less literal translations augmented by scholarly apparatuses such as notes, commentaries, and analyses, on the one hand, and efforts rooted in more creative impulses such as Coleman Barks has brought to his work on

Rumi. Ultimately, increasingly complex and multifaceted manifestations of cultural interactions point to the need to explore what lies beyond our present dichotomies in translation studies as we enter a new century and millennium.

In *The Essential Rumi,* Barks enters the debate between scholars and creative "translators" in as playful a manner as I have seen anywhere. "The design of this book," he says wistfully, yet pointedly, in his prefatory note, "is meant to confuse scholars who would divide Rumi's poetry into the accepted categories."[1] In framing the issue in this way, Barks goes beyond anticipating scholarly objections to state something relevant to the poems he is making accessible to new audiences: Rumi's poetry cannot and should not be divided into "accepted categories" because it aspires to transcend all such divisions and categories. He returns to the scholarly-versus-creative binary at the end of his book, where he recalls his own initiation into the world of the Persian poet. "I had never even heard of Rumi until 1976, when Robert Bly handed me a copy of A. J. Arberry's translations, saying, 'These poems need to be released from their cage.'"[2]

We may question whether Barks's translations of Rumi achieve that end, or whether the metaphor of the poem caged in scholarly translations is, in general, accurate or appropriate. Yet there is no denying that Barks's versions— to which he also refers as translations, renditions, interpretations, etc.—have gained the kind of popular acclaim denied to all the previous translations of Rumi, scholarly or otherwise. In search of the reasons for this popularity, I propose to go back in the history of poetic translation from Persian into English to as close a moment as we may term originary. The excursion will, I believe, reveal important salutary features of translation activity unfettered by scholarly or elitist concerns. A better understanding of those features may allow us to view the larger issues of esthetic interaction between old and established cultures from a fresh perspective.

WILLIAM JONES'S TRANSLATION OF HAFEZ'S "TURK OF SHIRAZ"

Tensions between the desire of the literary scholar for accuracy and that of the general reader for art have led to important strides in the history of translation. In the seventeenth century, the conflict among Biblical translators and scholars—some stressing literal accuracy, others stylish prose—was partly responsible for the King James Bible.[3] By the beginning of the eighteenth century, critical comments on translation began to break free from the tendency to discuss the problems faced in translating individual texts to give way in time to general discussions on the limitations and possibilities of translation in general. As late as 1791, Alexander Tytler complained that despite its importance the art of translation had not received proper theoretical treatment. "There is perhaps," he wrote in the introduction to his *Essay on the Principles of Translation,* "no department of literature which has been less the object of cultivation than the Art of Translating."[4]

Of all the neoclassical statements on translation theory in England, the most carefully reasoned, and by far the most influential, came from John Dryden. In his "Preface to the Translation of Ovid's Epistles," Dryden distinguished three types of translation according to the degree of their closeness to the original: *metaphrase,* or "turning an author word by word and line by line, from one language into another"; *paraphrase,* or "translation with latitude, where the author is kept in view by the translator, so as never to be lost, but his words are not so strictly followed as his sense; and that too is admitted to be amplified, but not altered"; and, finally, *imitation,* where "the translator (if now he has not lost that name) assumes the liberty, not only to vary the words and sense, but to forsake them both as he sees occasion; and, taking only some general hints from the original, to run divisions on the ground work, as he pleases."[5]

Dryden mentions the first option, metaphrase, only to reject it as a futile pursuit. "It is almost impossible," he concludes, "to translate verbally, and well, at the same time."[6] The basic reason for this impossibility rests on the assumption that the words and sense of a literary work are irreconcilable in translation. Striving to keep both, metaphrase—or literal translation, as we call it—would place itself in an impossible bind. On the other end, Dryden all but excludes possibilities for translation, properly so called, that might go beyond what he terms paraphrase. He does so because he envisions that any attempt to vary the sense of a work causes the translator to feel himself free from all constraints except "some general hints from the original," as he states above. In the true fashion of neoclassical thought on cultural processes great and small, his view of translation is one-dimensional and linear. Consequently, the translator is left with one option only, paraphrase—"translation with latitude," in his words—where he strives to maintain the sense of the original work, while at times amplifying, but not altering, its words. In doing this, the translator must exercise his judgment as to the essence, harmony, and metrical effects of the original, and then try to reproduce these effects in the target language. Speaking of Virgil in his preface to *Sylvae,* Dryden says, "The turns of his phrase, his breakings, his numbers, and his gravity, I have as far imitated as the poverty of our language . . . would allow."[7] Here and elsewhere Dryden limits the creative role of the translator to determining the various effects of the original and finding ways to transport these into the new language.

When Sir William Jones, pioneer Orientalist and leading scholar and translator of Persian poetry in eighteenth-century Europe, began translating Persian poetry into Latin, French, and English, neoclassical translation theory held sway in England. As the most prominent literary figure of his time, Jones was totally immersed in all aspects of neoclassical literature and esthetic thinking.[8] He was also keenly aware that he was in fact charting the course of Oriental studies for generations to come. Esthetically, Jones stood between the neoclassical literary culture and an emerging revolt against its most cherished principles, which later came to coherence in Romanticism. Naturally, Dryden and Pope constituted some of the most formative influences on his thinking. Yet he had already questioned the notion of poetry as an "imitative" art, making one of the most original contributions to the emergence of an "expressive" theory of poetry.[9] Certainly, he was not going to be "imitative" in his translations.

Fortunately, Jones has left a fairly detailed record of his various attempts in translating Persian poetry. Although for obvious reasons I will have to illustrate his approach to poetic translation by examining a single work, the conclusions can be extended to almost all his attempts at what he called "Englishing" Persian poetry. In translating Hafez's famous "Turk of Shiraz," Jones made two versions, one, simply titled "a literal translation," appended to the other, an English ode titled "A Persian Song of Hafez." Therefore, from the perspective assumed in this essay, a detailed examination of this work may afford us a glimpse into the process by which he has arrived at a more or less final version of his work, and, ultimately, of his approach to translating Persian poetry. Although I do not have space here to examine other, similar works, the approach must be seen as generalizable to other efforts, most famously Edward Fitzgerald's versions of Omar Khayyam's *Rubaiyyat*. First, let us read Jones's final product in its complete form:

> Sweet maid, if thou would'st charm my sight,
> And bid these arms thy neck infold;
> That rosy cheek, that lily hand,
> Would give the poet more delight
> Than all Bocara's vaunted gold
> Than all the gems of Samarcand.
>
> Boy, let yon liquid ruby flow,
> And bid thy pensive heart be glad,
> Whate'er the frowning zealots say:

Tell them, their Eden cannot show
A stream so clear as Rocnabad,
A bower so sweet as Mosellay. .

O! when these fair perfidious maids
Whose eyes our secret haunts infest,
Their dear destructive charms display;
Each glance my tender breast invades,
And robs my wounded soul of rest,
As Tartars seize their destin'd prey.

In vain with love our bosoms glow:
Can all our tears, can all our sighs,
New luster to those charms impart?
Can cheeks, where living roses blow,
Where nature spreads her richest dyes,
Require the borrow'd gloss of art?

Speak not of fate:—ah! Change the theme,
And talk of odours, talk of wine,
Talk of the flowers that round us bloom:
'Tis all a cloud, 'tis all a dream;
To love and joy thy thoughts confine,
Nor hope to pierce the sacred gloom.

Beauty has such resistless power,
That even the chaste Egyptian dame
Sigh'd for the blooming Hebrew boy;
For her how fatal was the hour,
When to the banks of Nilus came
A youth so lovely and so coy!

But ah, sweet maid, my counsel hear
(Youth should attend when those advise
Whom long experience renders sage):
While musick charms the ravish'd ear;
While sparkling cups delight our eyes,
Be gay; and scorn the frowns of age.

What cruel answer have I heard!
And yet, by heaven, I love thee still:
Can aught be cruel from thy lip?
Yet say, how fell that bitter word

From lips which streams of sweetness fill
Which nought but drops of honey sip?

Go boldly forth, my simple lay,
Whose accents flow with artless ease,
Like orient pearls at random strung:
Thy notes so sweet, the damsels say;
But O! far sweeter, if they please
The nymph for whom these notes are sung.[10]

Here is the opening line of Hafez's *ghazal,* followed by Jones's literal translation:

Agar an Tork-e shirazi beh dast arad del-e ma ra
Beh khal-e hendu-yash bakhsham Samarqand o Bokhara ra[11]

If that lovely maid of Shiraz would accept my heart,
I would give for the mole on her cheek the cities of Samarqand
    and Bukhara.

Jones's literal translation is not a literal translation of the type that Dryden had dismissed as impossible. To begin with the most obvious of the liberties he has taken, Jones renders the word *Tork* into "lovely maid." Clearly, the selection has been made in light of Jones's understanding of the word's connotation in the Persian *ghazal* tradition, where the legendary beauty of Turkish women provides the basis for a conventional trope. Turkish women were considered as ravishingly beautiful as Turkish warriors were thought ruthless in their plunder, a convention that Hafez utilizes by depicting an irresistibly beautiful yet utterly ruthless beloved. Through the phrase "lovely maid," Jones strives for a similar effect, at least in terms of the trope's conventional root. In a counter move, he omits the modifier *hendu* for the *khal* (mole), which specifies its black color and anchors the contrast between the association of Turks with the color white and of Indians with the color black. No translation could have captured the double binary embedded in the two terms of ethnic designation. The content of the speaker's wish, articulated through the compound verbal phrase "del beh dast avardan" (literally, bringing someone's heart into hand, meaning being kind to someone, looking favorably on someone's request, or granting someone's wish), remains unspecified, allowing us only to surmise that the poetic persona is longing for union with a hopelessly unyielding beloved.[12]

Relying on the construct "accepting one's heart" to carry the sense of the Persian compound verb, Jones foregoes the poet's adherence to a convention generic to the Persian *ghazal*, namely that of pairing body parts, here "heart" and "hand." The choice eliminates the possibility of grasping the relation between the beloved's "heart" and "hand" and a third body part, namely the mole.

The contrast between the persona's native city of Shiraz and the faraway riches hidden in fabled twin cities of Central Asia fares similarly in the translation. The black circles that mark Samarqand and Bukhara on some map the poet may have in mind revive the memory of the beloved's mole, and that memory provides the basis for the poem's main theme: the opposition between that which is near and accessible and that which is far away, between the pleasures of this world and the promise of heavenly delights in the afterlife. This train of thought ultimately leads to the idea that life can be enjoyed without too profound an urge to question its beginning or end, its purpose or meaning. The line that stretches between the persona's humble city and the riches of the ancient city of Bukhara or the famed capital of Tamerlane may be lost to the English reader unaware of the operations of the original poem. Like so much else, the loss has occurred in spite of the translator's attempt to produce as literal a translation as possible.

As we move from an examination of Jones's literal translation to that of his poetic version, we must expect greater losses, at least if we keep in mind Dryden's articulation of the translator's choices. In fact, a closer examination of "A Persian Song of Hafez" reveals a series of strategies aimed at recapturing as much of the original poem's lyric thrust, stylistic features, and semiotic density as possible. For example, in the opening line, which Jones has expanded into a six-line stanza, several motifs absent from the literal translation have been worked back into the poem:

> Sweet maid, if thou would'st charm my sight,
> And bid these arms thy neck infold;
> That rosy cheek, that lily hand,
> Would give the poet more delight
> Than all Bocara's vaunted gold
> Than all the gems of Samarcand.

The first remarkable difference between the Persian original and Jones's literal translation, on the one hand, and the "Song," on the other, has to do with the latter's rhetorical situation. In Hafez's *ghazal*, as in Jones's literal translation, the line comprises a lover's statement about what he is willing to forgo, should the beloved—absent from the scene of the utterance—grant his wish. In "Song," this gives way to the lover's address to the beloved: "Sweet maid, if thou. . . ." It shifts back in the second stanza to the pattern set by the original Persian poem as the speaker addresses the cupbearer (*saqi*), "Boy, let yon liquid ruby flow," and follows the original's moves toward greater abstractions through the penultimate line. It shifts back once again to the song itself in the closing line where the persona bids his song to "go forth boldly" into the world. In other words, the shifting perspectives of Jones's "Song" correspond to those of the Persian original except in the opening and closing. Through these shifts, Jones comes marvelously close to what Hafez has done in his composition, except in those crucial junctures where he feels bound to adhere to generic conventions in English lyric poetry. Both the first and last lines, addressed respectively to the beloved and the poem, follow conventions of the Renaissance and Tudor love lyric prevalent in a great many genres, including Shakespearean and Spenserian sonnets as well as the English odes from Marvell and Milton to Pope and beyond.[13] Without slavishly following his original in each line, Jones has sought a way to graft Hafez's poem to the English poetic tradition.

Let us ponder the issue of the rhetorical situation in the two poems a moment longer. In Jones's second stanza, the speaker's address to the cupbearer, "Bedeh saqi mai-ye baqi," is replicated as "Boy, let yon liquid ruby flow." Through the middle stanzas, 3–6, where the discourse of the Persian *ghazal* is elevated to philosophic musings, Jones's "Song" approximates the ascent in the greater abstraction implied in the absence of a specific addressee, only to return once again, as does the Persian poem, to address the beloved in stanzas 7–8. Finally, in the concluding line, Hafez falls back on a well-known convention in the Persian *ghazal* tradition, distancing himself from the persona he has created through the use of his pen name as a separate poetic entity. It is as if the speaker occupies the position of an external voice hailing someone else called "Hafez," bidding him to sing his *ghazal* in melodious song: "beya vo khosh bekhan, Hafez!" The convention has no parallel in English poetry, and may have been judged strange or potentially misleading if adopted literally.

Rather than attempt to reproduce the original's words and risk unforeseeable effects, Jones falls back on a well-known convention in English poetry, where the speaker closes by addressing the poem itself: he bids his song go forth and proclaim his beloved's matchless beauty to the world. In doing so, Jones seems to refashion the terms according to which his "Song" captures the spirit of the original by departing from its apparent surface. Instead of trafficking back and forth between the two texts in search of rhetorical parity, Jones traverses through one poetic tradition, that of the original, to his own. Rhetorically, then, Jones's "Song" approximates Hafez's *ghazal* in the impression it evokes rather than by reproducing the postures or situations inherent in the original. The multiplicity of perspectives intimated in the Persian poem through shifting rhetorical situations is approximated in the English "Song" through the convention of the poem as evidence of the poet's love.

Jones's departures from the diction of the original are even more illustrative than his lexical and rhetorical maneuvers. The appellation "sweet maid," which he uses twice, exemplifies one such departure, revealing his strategy of concretizing those abstractions in the original poem that he must have judged too removed from the English readers' sensibilities. The move, while severing his version from a significant feature of the original poem, namely its verbal correspondences with mysticism, makes his "Song" more palpable as a love lyric. In fact, Jones must have sensed the impossibility of trying to translate Hafez's mystical allusions, and decided instead to make his poem as much a love song as possible. He does so in the face of necessity: he must assign a gender to Hafez's genderless beloved. As Persian pronouns and nouns are gender-free, the translator of Persian *ghazals* into English is forced sooner or later to assign a gender to such entities as "that Turk of Shiraz" (*an Tork-e shirazi*) or "these sweet, tricky, riotous gypsies" (*in luliyan-e shukh-e shirin-kar-e shahr-ashub*).[14]

In doing this in the way he does, Jones gains significant advantages for his "Song." The phrases he uses not only refer to female human beings as familiar as possible to his immediate readers—respectively "sweet maid" and "these fair perfidious maids"—they also buttress his "Song" as an English love poem. Consequently, while Hafez's poem, in addition to its central character as a love poem, has the potential to function as a brief against the hollow promises of religion—and/or as a mystical or pseudo-mystical position statement—Jones focuses his reader's attention on an aspect that is not only present in the original, but has through the centuries been privileged by those commentators who have seen in this poem an instance where the poet elevates the worldly over the divine. While Jones's strategy abandons or de-emphasizes a latent aspect of the poem's meaning, it strengthens and amplifies the sense in the poem that has been most prevalent in its reception history. The lyricism of Hafez is not only transported to its new readers in the English-speaking world; it has been actualized and accentuated.

In the original poem, the image of "Tork-e shirazi" is first generalized into the mass of "luliyan-e shukh-e shirin-kar-e shahr-ashub," and later associated with the persona's beloved in the way he chides her: "bad-am gofti o khorsand-am" and "nasihat gush kon jana." The move registers the moral superiority of the speaker over the addressee, while allowing a gradual elevation of the discourse from the specific to the general and then to the universal. The beloved, who is addressed in a succession of imperatives—"hadis az motreb o mai guy" (speak of the musician and the wine), "raz-e dahr kam-tar ju" (stop seeking the secrets of the world), and "nasihat gush-kon" (hearken to [my] advice)—is depicted as young and impressionable, in need of guidance by the old and knowing speaker. Only in this context can the abstract-in-concrete image of Potiphar's wife—Zolaikha in Islamic cultures—be related to the overall theme of the poem. Embedded as it is in a Biblical and Koranic myth, and recalling the irresistible power of love, the allusion is poignantly relevant to the poem's general argument if it is spoken by a man of superior knowledge. It links the situation at hand with the mythical arche-type of the loss of control that marks love and that is to account for the per-sona's plea.

In all their linguistic and cultural specificity, the moral or mystical allu-sions of the Persian *ghazal* ought by definition to remain inaccessible to the English reader, making it impossible to reconstruct a non-lyrical reading of them. To the extent that such features function as sources of polysemy, and give rise to the possibility of readings that transcend the love situation, they create areas of ambiguity which scholar-translators often attempt to make comprehensible to their readers through notes, glosses, and commentaries of various kinds. Yet, in the poem under examination here, Jones seems to have recovered part of that transcendent thrust in the way he has rendered the line in question:

> Man az an hosn-e ruz-afzun keh Yusof dasht danestam
> keh `eshq az pardeh-ye `esmat borun arad Zolaikha ra
> (I knew from the daily-enhancing beauty that was Joseph's
> that love would drag Zolaikha out of her veil of chastity)

> Beauty has such resistless power,
> That even the chaste Egyptian dame
> Sigh'd for the blooming Hebrew boy;
> For her how fatal was the hour,
> When to the banks of Nilus came
> A youth so lovely and so coy!

Here, the names of the two Biblical figures, Yusof (Joseph) and Zolaikha (Potiphar's wife), have been recoded in the phrases "the chaste Egyptian dame" and "the blooming Hebrew boy." Working through allusion rather than through naming, Jones's "Song" attempts to bring its references to more or less same level of familiarity for the English reader as the original's have for the native Persian speaker, all their polar antitheses in place.[15] Once again, in transcending literalism, Jones has aimed for a text that is likely to be perceived by its readers in ways not too different from that in which he thought the original must have been perceived by its immediate audience.

As we have seen, Jones expands the Persian *ghazal*'s nine distichs into nine six-line stanzas, each displaying the rhyme pattern of *abc, abc.* He also opts for a rather rare form of four accented iambic feet. In these formal features, which determine the shape of the poem on the page and its sound to the ear, he clearly departs from specific features of the original, yet puts the regularity and predictability of the original poem on display. More importantly, his diction combines the familiar with the quaint in a way that seems to suspend the poem's diction between that of a Shakespearean sonnet and an as yet unidentifiable yearning that we see in poets like Keats and Shelley. In all this, Jones communicates not only the most palpable general commonalities between Persian and English poetry—i.e., the presence of rhyme, meter, and a lofty diction, features that mark a text as a poem—but, more significantly, its basic thematic thrust and as much of its individual motifs as possible, given his readers' rudimentary familiarity with the poem's esthetic underpinnings.

Yet the exotic is not far to seek in Jones's rendition, even if it is transformed into the kind of effect that any connoisseur of English poetry may recognize. For instance, Hafez's mention of Bukhara and Samarqand has been concretized and made tangible in the twin images that bespeak the wealth hidden in those legendary cities of the Silk Road: "Bocara's vaulted gold" and "the gems of Samarcand." The effect thus produced is enhanced in the next stanza, where the persona bids the cupbearer to tell "the frowning zealots" that their heaven is no match for his favorite retreat, thus reiterating the advantages of the here-and-now. As we move further on, the mystery of human fate is recalled in the advice to the youthful beloved to give up all thoughts of penetrating "the sacred gloom." In sum, the English poem parades a series of topoi that challenge the reader to integrate the exoticism of the original into an understanding of the greater universal condition that is the human lot.

Through this process of expansion, Jones further opens up the possibility of moving beyond literal translation to search for those expressive devices that he perceives to be present in the original, if only by implication, and which may be in need of explicit expression to produce comparable effects on the English reader. Because he has allowed himself more lexical liberties than a literal translation might sanction, he can afford to render the single word *luliyan* as "fair perfidious maids," and to elaborate each of the adjectives describing them in a separate line. Hafez's three words *shukh, shirin-kar,* and *shahr-ashub* thus turn into fully developed adjectival clauses helping to bring about an understanding of the *luliyan* through descriptions of their eyes, the effect of their charm, and the aggressive nature of the glances they cast toward the lover:

> O! When these fair perfidious maids
> Whose eyes our secret haunts infest,
> Their dear destructive charms display;
> Each glance my tender breast invades,
> And robs my wounded soul of rest,
> As Tartars seize their destin'd prey.

Using a more accommodating form, Jones conveys both the familiarity of the metered line and the novelty of the imagery that communicates the effect of the beloved's behavior. His diction brings together a combination of the carefully culled phrases that characterize neoclassical poetry and the fecundity of the original in its implications beyond the lyrical. We know from Jones's critical writings that the possibility of using the trope of love to speak to and of the transcendental and the divine impressed him as a hallmark of Persian lyric poetry. In the case at hand, it is worth noting that the mention of the mole on the beloved's cheek has been discarded. Meanwhile, the relationship between the lover's desire and his supposed sacrifice, which in the original connotes unreasonable profligacy, has been changed to one where the lover seeks "delight."

At the same time, in the last stanza, the notion of a poem "whose accents flow with artless ease" solidifies an image in the fourth stanza where the beloved's beauty is described as needless of "the borrow'd gloss of art." The allusion at the poem's end thus caps the speaker's argument about the difference between the beauty that nature has bestowed on the beloved's cheeks—"where nature spreads her richest dyes"—and "the borrow'd gloss of art," and weaves into the poem the nature-versus-art dichotomy so prevalent in eighteenth-century English poetry. Moreover, it enforces the notion of the Orient through the sensuous depiction of a rich and colorful nature. Jones seizes on both potentialities to fill the space made available by his strategy of amplifying the discourse of the original with his own inventions, mostly words of the same semantic field as he has found in the original. As the poem's persona reiterates his beloved's superior beauty, the hierarchy Jones has constructed begins to come into full view: whereas love poems in general are artifacts and therefore artificial, his poem displays an artless ease that makes it superior. Yet even such a poem pales before the beauty of the beloved, made of nature's "richest dyes." Such devices help the fourteenth-century Persian poet articulate an esthetic commensurate with neoclassical English preoccupation with decorum and balance, giving rise to feelings about Persian poetry that transcend both local cultures.

Finally, as a pioneer Orientalist, Sir William Jones knew well that in Persian poetry the genre of *ghazal* had for centuries been the site of intense energy and attention in understanding and communicating human emotions—love, grief, and joy—rather than pondered and polished sentiments of a public nature. The poem here makes explicit what is often implied in so many other examples of the genre, namely that Persian *ghazals* are often sung to musical accompaniment. Hafez's explicit mention of the verb *khandan* (to sing) in the closing line leaves no doubt that the poem's persona conceives of the singing as the culminating act that follows the poem's composition; that, in an important sense, it completes the act of composition by presenting it to the audience. Perhaps finding it impossible to communicate that fact to his readers, Jones transforms the original poem's oblique, yet significant, allusion both to singing and to the ritual whereby the royal patron scatters pearls at the poet's feet as he or a professional minstrel is singing the "song." He may have concluded that any attempt to transmit this aspect of the poem would exoticize it to the extent that it may not be able to convey its most universal message of love and beauty. In view of that impression, Jones takes one final step to bring "A Persian Song of Hafez" closer to an English love song: his persona ends his professions of love by bidding his "simple lay" to go forth into the world and proclaim his beloved's superior beauty through its "notes so sweet."

In sum, Jones charts a course between the Persian *ghazal* and an English "Song" that passes through translation but does not stop there; rather it appropriates as much of the target language's poetic and cultural resources as it needs to acclimate itself to its new environment.[16] Through their diction, meter, and rhyme scheme, texts thus produced evoke the memory of familiar texts in the mind of the reader, in this case primarily Shakespearean sonnets or the most familiar odes of a Milton or Marvell. The combination of apostrophic lyricism, on the one hand, and the formal features of the Augustan ode, on the other, give the late-eighteenth-century English reader the feeling that "A Persian Song of Hafez" is at once near and far, English and Persian, a poem and a translation.[17] As such, the poem's internal dynamics begin to modify concepts of near and far, old and contemporary, exotic and familiar. Rather than giving an impression of unbridgeable chasms separating Hafez from his eighteenth-century English reader, Jones's creative and transformative strategies have resulted in a text that links new readers to the Persian poet.

COLEMAN BARKS'S TRANSLATION
OF RUMI'S "NAI-NAMEH"

Twentieth-century conceptualizations of translation and interpretation provide important new insights into the ways in which translation-based activities mediate between original texts and the new contexts in which they are made to operate. Rooted in abstract, at times metaphysical, inquiries of continental philosophers like Wittgenstein, Heidegger, and Gadamer into the nature of the human mind, on the one hand, and the emergence of transformational and generative theories of language and grammar, on the other, twentieth-century translation theories have had important consequences for the art and craft of poetic translation.[18] Cognizant of the advances in information and communication theories and their application to poetic translation, all late-twentieth-century discussions of poetic translation tend to view the activity of translators and interpreters as a process consisting of, and happening in, stages that begin before the first word is replaced by a foreign word, and continue long after the last word has been decided. Literal translation, then, is seen not as the end of the interpretive endeavor but as its midpoint, · the beginning of a stage that looks back and, if at all possible, moves back toward the original text. Lying beyond translation, this looking back and moving back is seen primarily as an attempt at restituting some of the aggression and violence that the act of translation may have necessitated against an original text. This conceptualization has given rise to a novel understanding of what fidelity in translation is ontologically and what it entails in practice. The implications that have thus emerged for the practice of poetic translation are developing as we enter a new century and millennium.

Let us consider briefly some of the questions that operate at the interface of the new literary theories and the practice of poetic translation. In general, semioticians and other poststructuralists often distinguish between the primary and secondary functions of language, where the former conveys semantic or content-oriented information and the latter expresses emotive or rhetorical information. Poststructuralist literary theory also places renewed emphasis on the representational aspect of the translated text, namely the impression that a translation-based text in some way "stands for" its original, and that the locus of this representation-function lies not only beyond the lexicon but outside all verbal or content-based equivalence. Needless to say, the role of this representation-function is more pronounced in poetry than in other types of texts. At times, for example, translators may consider the symbolism, or even the sound structure of an original poem, more "meaningful" than its semantic content; they may therefore decide to forgo a piece of semantic information in favor of a particular poetic or stylistic effect.

Based on their initial assessment of the priorities in the poems they work with, creative translators may depart from certain apparent features in order to approximate an emotive impact which they wish to communicate to their readers. In doing so, they transform their original, either by moving beyond its lexical content and thematic thrust, or by discarding certain of its generic codes or conventions. Instead, they infuse their texts with qualities that bring them nearer to the original in its representation-function. Let us remember that the basic criteria by which translated texts are judged as different from original poems are essentially introduced by readers. Whereas the quality of an original poem is ultimately determined on an axiological plane, that of all types of translations is first and foremost referential. In the case of an "original" poem, readers ask simply whether it is a good poem, while in evaluating a translated poem, they ask, in addition—and perhaps primarily—whether the work in question is really a translation of a particular "original."

Predictably, such considerations take us beyond the tradition of translation-based scholarship, and give rise to tensions between scholarly and creative approaches not unlike those mentioned above, between Biblical scholars and translators of seventeenth-century England. In the history of poetic translation from Persian into English, scholars have held sway, with the result that, by and large, Persian poetry is known far more to scholarly and academic communities than to general readers of poetry. Coleman Barks's recent translations of Rumi must be seen within the context of other recent efforts to make Persian poetry available to a larger readership than the academic study of Persian literature has achieved thus far. At such a juncture, greater attention to the representation-function mentioned above may be helpful in developing the terms for clarifying the distinction between creative efforts like Barks's and the tradition of scholarly translation in the last two centuries. I certainly hope it will help break the cycle of attack and counterattack that has characterized the debate between scholars and creative translators.

Of all the Persian poets, perhaps Rumi has the largest mind. His thought unit is neither the human moment nor the national memory, and he pens his thoughts in strokes larger than words and lines. To him, language is a medium inherently inadequate to express what he wishes to communicate, the stories he tells insufficient to the sense he seeks to covey. He often ends up demonstrating this inadequacy and insufficiency by placing distant meanings in everyday images or anecdotes. For these reasons, the poetry his experience suggests to his mind often demands a hermeneutic of reading that goes beyond the dichotomies between surface and depth, between meaning and sense, between translation and interpretation. It would be as wrongheaded for the Rumi translator to clutch at every word as it would be to forgo the meaning of each word or phrase in search of the sense behind it, and futile to abandon any particular turn of phrase that places the translation at the edge of comprehensibility in search of its more common equivalent. Rumi's is a shared sense of the universal poetry that lies beyond this or that language; it demands an integrative approach unfettered by binaries.

Nor is his experience a stable entity easily transportable to a new language; one would have to work out a dynamic narrative of experiential empathy that readers can feel emotionally and intuitively. In a sense, to translate any mystical poetry is to transform it into something else, forever beyond the circumstances of the poem's creation, much as the meanings residing in mystical narratives catapult the reader to new planes of understanding. The reed flute that ushers in Rumi's *Spiritual Couplets,* and governs it throughout, aims to go back to where it was and what it was before it became what it is in the poem. What happens to it makes it both different from and more than what it was in the reed-bed: the flute is not the reed, however much it may crave that former state. This requires an approach to translation that would have as its goal a textual existence capable of producing a comparable reading experience.

Regardless of the approach, to translate Rumi is to transform him, and that, I think, is what Barks aims for. In evaluating Barks's versions of Rumi's poems, we need to look at those Rumi motifs, those trains of thought that, recurring and permeating the text, epitomize the potential to rise above the limitations of all texts, all language. I propose to illustrate this potential by analyzing the twenty-three lines that make up "The Reed Flute's Song" and serve to introduce the monumental *Spiritual Couplets.* I give the Persian first, followed by Barks's version:

> Beshnau az nai chun hekayat mikonad
> az joda'iha shekayat mikonad
> k-az naiyestan ta ma-ra bobrideh-and
> az nafir-am mard o zan nalideh-and
> sineh khaham sharheh sharheh az feraq
> ta beguyam sharh-e dard-e eshtiyaq
> harkasi k-u dur mand az asl-e khish
> baz juyad ruzegar-e vasl-e khish
> man beh har jam`iyyati nalan shodam
> joft-e bad-halan o khosh-halan shodam
> harkasi az zann-e khod shod yar-e man
> az darun-e man najost asrar-e man
> serr-e man az naleh-ye man dur nist
> lik chashm o gush ra an nur nist
> tan ze jan o jan ze tan mastur nist
> lik kas ra did-e jan dastur nist
> atash ast in bang-e nai o nist bad
> harkeh in atash nadarad nist bad

atash-e eshq ast k-andar nai fetad
jushesh-e eshq ast k-andar mai fetad
nai harif-e harkeh az yar-i borid
pardehha-yash paradehha-ye ma darid
hamcho nai zahri o taryaqi keh did
hamcho nai damsaz o moshtaqi keh did
nai hadis-e rah-e por-khun mikonad
qessehha-ye eshq-e majnun mikonad
mahram-e in hush joz bi-hush nist
mar zaban ra moshtari joz gush nist
dar gham-e ma ruzha bigah shod
ruzha ba suzha hamrah shod
ruzha gar raft gu rou bak nist
to beman ai an keh chun to pak nist
harkeh joz mahi ze ab-ash sir shod
harkeh bi ruzi-st ruz-ash dir shod
dar-na-yabad hal-e pokhteh hich kham
pas sokhan kutah bayad vas-sallam[19]

Listen to the story told by the reed,
of being separated.
"Since I was cut from the reedbed,
I have made this crying sound.
Anyone apart from someone he loves
understands what I say.
Anyone pulled from a source
longs to go back.
At any gathering I am there,
mingling in the laughing and grieving,
a friend to each, but few
will hear the secrets hidden
within the notes. No ears for that.
Body flowing out of spirit,
spirit up from body: no concealing
that mixing. But it's not given us
to see the soul. The reed flute
is fire, not wind. Be that empty."

Hear the love fire tangled
in the reed notes, as bewilderment

melts into wine. The reed is a friend
to all who want the fabric torn
and drawn away. The reed is hurt
and salve combining. Intimacy
and longing for intimacy, one
song. A disastrous surrender
and a fine love, together. The one
who secretly hears this is senseless.
A tongue has one customer, the ear.
A sugarcane flute has such effect
because it was able to make sugar
in the reedbed. The sound it makes
is for everyone. Days full of wanting,
let them go by without worrying
that they do. Stay where you are
inside such a pure, hollow note.
Every thirst gets satisfied except
that of these fish, the mystics,
who swim a vast ocean of grace
still somehow longing for it!
No one lives in that without
being nourished every day.
But if someone doesn't want to hear
the song of the reed flute,
it's best to cut conversation
short, say good-bye, and leave.[20]

A comparison between the translation and the Persian original shows a surprising sense of fidelity that runs well below the surface of the words and relates more to the poem's mystical thrust than to any specific image, conceit, or motif. As in the original, Barks keeps the frame fiction of the speaker's invitation to the reader to listen to the story of the reed flute, followed by the reed flute's own words as it expresses the pain of separation from the reedbed and describes its new, imperfect companions. Here, too, I will begin the discussion with an examination of the poem's rhetorical situation. The voice that utters all the Persian lines except the opening one can be said to be the reed flute's. In that sense, the plaintive reed flute occupies more or less the position of the fulfillment-seeking lover in Hafez's "Turk of Shiraz" *ghazal.* Yet the absence of punctuation in premodern Persian poetry makes it plausible to imagine an end to the flute's speech at some point, envisioning the rest of the poem to be uttered by the speaker of the first line and intended as human observations on the flute's condition.

The resulting indeterminacy opens a space wherein the two figures of the speaker and the persona of the reed flute converge, and the poem attains its universality. In his version, Barks closes the quotation he had opened in the second line halfway into the poem, after the words "be that empty." The rest privileges only one of the two readings possible in the original. The second half of Barks's version consists of the speaker's reflections on the reed flute's foregoing utterances. Thus, the English poem eliminates the possibility of envisioning the whole as spoken by the persona. Instead, Barks reiterates the speaker's opening invitation: "Hear the love fire tangled/ in the reed's notes." In choosing the word "notes," he raises the possibility that the speaker's words provide a "gloss" on the reed flute's speech.

Structurally, then, Barks's version begins with an invitation and ends by bidding the reader (or a certain type of reader) good-bye. It thus features the reed flute inviting the reader to its song and proceeds to tell that story in the rest of the poem, first by the reed flute itself, then by a human speaker. Once inside the reed flute's narrative, Barks harnesses the same disparate sets of images, and works through more or less the same antitheses. Barks's reed flute, like Rumi's, is a seeker of intimacy who makes his way through "the laughing and grieving" (*khosh-halan o bad-halan*) and depicts "[b]ody flowing out of spirit,/ spirit up from body." It concludes the presentation by stating that "it's not given us/ to see the soul." This is strikingly close to the original Persian assertion that "none is allowed to see the soul" (*kas ra did-e jan dastur nist*).

The last statement that Barks places in the mouth of the reed flute merits special consideration: "The reed flute/ is fire, not wind. Be that empty." Rumi's statement here goes thus: "atash ast in bang-e nai o nist bad/ harkeh in atash nadarad nist bad" (This the reed flute song is fire, not wind/ May he who does not have this fire not be). Clearly, no translation, literal or otherwise, could recreate the homonymous phrase *nist bad* ("not wind"/ "may he . . . not be"), which the Persian uses twice, each time privileging a different sense. Yet the enigmatic command "be that empty" in Barks's version harbors within it an ambiguity that points in the same direction. The flute reed that is hollow inside and the sounds which it produces, and which fill the air, are as empty as empathic readers who may seek to assign to those sounds meanings and senses of their own making. Functioning as a demonstrative pronoun, the word "that" can give the sentence the meaning "be that thing which is empty"—i.e., the reed flute ("me," as the words are spoken by the reed flute itself). Functioning in the sense of "as empty as," the same word may convey the sense that the emptiness of the audience should come to equal that of the reed flute. Though not the lexical equivalent of the Persian, the new double entendre serves the poem as productively, because it allows possibilities that take the mind from the command to the mysterious sense behind it.

Stylistically, Barks's "The Reed Flute's Song" is not just an attempt to communicate the general impression that Rumi's poetry is composed in a simple language, but to remind readers that Rumi does not create an artificial style and that he in fact considers all stylization antithetical to the spirit of poetry. Phrases like "be that empty," while having no parallel in the original and therefore appearing as departures from it, enhance the mystical aura of the poem. In comparing such constructs with Rumi's own masterful use of phrases that look and sound the same but convey different senses, readers familiar with the original may miss the poem's surface meaning as it begins to weave the problematic of appearance versus reality in all human constructs into the tapestry of mystical ideas. Such losses are indeed inevitable, a common feature of all attempts at translation. Yet the general style of Barks's poems has a strikingly similar impact on the reading process. Finally, given the absence of punctuation in the original Persian, why does Barks close the reed flute's speech where he does? Attentive readers can't fail to note that in the four lines that follow the *nist bad* pun, the word *nai* (reed flute) is repeated five times, whereas the previous passage is dominated by the words "I" (*man*) and "me" (*ma-ra*), indicating the presence of a first-person speaker. Whether Barks has noted the more personal tone of part one or not, the effect his version produces is not unlike that of the original: general remarks following specific descriptions.

In the second part, too, the English poem works with the same theses and antitheses as the original. The uniquely dense hemistich "pardehha-yash pardehha-ye ma darid" (Its [the reed flute's] notes/drapes/covers/veils have torn asunder our veils/covers/drapes/notes) may serve as an example. Barks's rendition is structured in this way: "The reed is a friend/ to all who want the fabric torn/ and drawn away." The aggressive sense of the original is absent from the translation, of course. Yet the verb "want" implies certain select spirits in whom the desire to have their "fabric torn and drawn away" has brought about the will to submit to the reed flute's transgressive design. Most often, Barks juxtaposes phrases containing pairs of antithetical concepts to words or phrases that mediate between them or bridge the gulf that separates them, a strategy that constitutes a basic building block in Rumi's poetry. Thus, as an equivalent to the Persian *zahr/taryaq* (poison/antidote) dichotomy, the phrase "hurt and salve combining" evokes feelings in line with conventional articulations of mystical experience in Persian poetry. Similarly, his "intimacy/ and longing for intimacy" is as effective a rendition as the one communicated by the *damsaz/moshtaq* (close as breath/eager seeker) binary. Yet, once he has established the linguistic and rhetorical frames of references to Rumi's poem, Barks turns quite literal. The deceptive simplicity hidden in the literal translation of the lines in Rumi that follow the antithetical pairs above is a case in point:

> mahram-e in hush joz bi-hush nist
> mar zaban ra moshtari joz gush nist

> The one who secretly hears this is senseless.
> A tongue has one customer, the ear.

By contrast, where he finds it necessary, Barks expands an image in the original, as if to provide keys to interpretation. The image of the mystics as fish thirsting for water as they swim in the ocean provides a clear illustration. Whereas Rumi implicitly identifies the mystic with the image of "thirsty fish," Barks makes the identification explicit:

> harkeh joz mahi zeh ab-ash sir shod
> harkeh bi ruzi-st ruz-ash dir shod

> All creatures but the fish tire of drinking water
> The day drags on for anyone who's hungry
> Every thirst gets satisfied except
> that of these fish, the mystics,
> who swim a vast ocean of grace
> still somehow longing for it!

Barks, it seems, feels he needs to remind his readers—as Rumi never did—that the fish in the poem does not refer to an animal and that therefore the ocean is not to be taken literally either. Such passages serve to alert English-speaking readers to the basic premises of Persian mystical poetry. Through them, a translator who has proved himself quite adept at offering literal translations does not shy away from a free-floating turn of phrase where he sees the need. The cohabitation of the two strategies, often conceived as mutually exclusive, exudes an echoic integrity that moves his version beyond the dualism of literal versus free translation, of lexical archaisms versus slangy colloquiality, of false choices between stylish and simple diction, or of diametrically different tendencies toward exoticism or domestication. It is as if the translator aspires to replicate the mystical experience that lies at the heart of the original poem by creating the impression that he approaches his original without a master plan. Having decided to move beyond all rationalistic divisions, Barks welcomes the transformative power of his original and seems prepared to be transported into any mental state which would enable him to produce his version of Rumi's poems.

CONCLUSION

Perhaps our modern tendency to submit everything to a regime of reason, of a plan, of conscious control, has moved us away from the world as imagined by poets like Rumi and Hafez. The massive influx of reason, specifically in the form of heightened control over the nature of the poetic experience and of access to it, may have hardened us into positions of rigid religiosity or outright rejection of all things spiritual or mystical, for example. Our very thought processes may militate against imaginative conceptualizations of the other-as-mystery. Just as we wonder if it is even possible to imagine surrendering to transformative experiences, we may also wonder if it makes sense to begin to translate without prior commitment to this or that theory or approach. The spontaneity of the poetic expression seems to be the very thing that our scientific or rational culture tends to suppress. The capacity for the sudden surprise that awaits the poet at every turn along his path escapes us all too easily. Is that why the only approach to translation that appeals to our age is one predicated on the existence of stable forms of experience—or at least a single stable form of each experience?

Yet we cannot forget that the representation-function of translated texts means that translations are always already approached and received "in light of" the original texts that lie behind them. A poem in translation is always already viewed as somehow a substitute in the new language for the original. This necessitates a renewed search in every generation for fresh ways of comparing original texts with their translations. Because poststructuralist theory views poetic texts as multilayered, our age must modify existing notions of equivalence in such a way as to move beyond the lexicon, the syntax, or the style of the translation in relation to the original on which it depends. Individual variety, historical or geographical fluidity, or constantly shifting interpretive horizons are essential to understanding the other.

It is true that in every age what distinguishes a "close" translation from its opposite involves some general "perception" of the "distance" between it and the original. At the same time, it is also true that both "perception" and "distance" are dynamic concepts that change with every passing generation. When distance is understood in a linear way, as it was in the eighteenth century, the closer the words of the translated text were to those of the original, almost in a dictionary sense, the closer the translated text was thought to be. For over two centuries, the linear view of distance, anchored in the notion that language is more or less the sum total of its lexicon, has bound translation activities to a binary opposition between the literal and the free. Twentieth-century understandings of the dynamics of language and literature seem to have given rise to the general impression that a linear notion of the distance between an original text and its "translation" is inadequate and in need of rethinking. Although they differ in their specific strategies for looking and moving back to the original texts they tackle, the two "interpreters" of Persian poetry whose work I have examined in this article seem to share the willingness to recognize that need. By scouring the semantic field of words and images in the original and eyeing the original poets' universes of discourse with the intention of reconstructing it in accordance with their own traditions, both Barks and Jones have performed acts more akin to those involved in the process of original creativity than to those common to the scholar-translator. At the heart of their strategy lies the desire to move beyond the dichotomy between literal and free and the will to challenge the impression, dominant in so many scholarly translations from Persian, that moving away from the former and closer to the latter inevitably results in texts that are farther removed from the original.

In recalling Robert Bly's words about the necessity of "releasing" Rumi's poems from their "cage," Barks makes a point that can be generalized to his overall design—and to that of Jones's approach to Hafez, as well as to other similar attempts, most notably Edward Fitzgerald's celebrated translations of Omar Khayyam's *Rubaiyyat*. Such works empower readers of various generations to make connections between cultures of vastly different times. Whether we refer to them as translations, adaptations, or versions, there can be little doubt that they have given expression to the sumptuous lyricism of Hafez, the rebellious spirit of Khayyam, and the mystical transcendentalism of Rumi. Most importantly, they have helped turn the works of a few Persian poets from recommended reading for graduate students of humanities to texts cherished by a far wider circle of readers. We are all the richer for having them.

NOTES

1. *The Essential Rumi,* trans. Coleman Barks, with John Moyne, A. J. Arberry, Reynold Nicholson (San Francisco: Harper, 1995), 290.
2. Ibid.
3. For a perceptive and pioneering study of the evolution of translation theories

in English, see Flora Ross Amos, *Early Theories of Translation* (New York: Octagon Books, 1973).

4. Alexander Tytler, *Essay on the Principles of Translation* (London: Cadell and Davies, 1813), 1.

5. John Dryden, *The Works of John Dryden,* 18 vols. (Edinburgh: Archibald Constable and Co., 1821), 12:11–12. For a detailed discussion of Dryden's theory and practice of translation see William Frost, *Dryden and the Art of Translation* (New Haven: Yale University Press, 1955).

6. Dryden, *Works,* 12:12.

7. John Dryden, *The Essays of John Dryden,* ed. W. P. Ker, 2 vols. (Oxford: The University Press, 1926), 2:255; cited in Amos, *Early Theories,* 162.

8. For the most authoritative account of Jones's literary career and his involvement with "Oriental Literature," see Garland H. Cannon, *Oriental Jones* (New York: Asia Publishing House, 1964). See also the essay on Jones in Arthur J. Arberry, *Oriental Essays: Portraits of Seven Scholars* (New York: Macmillan & Co., 1960).

9. The most extensive discussion of Jones's ideas in this regard occurs in an exceedingly influential essay titled "On the Arts, Commonly Called Imitative," published in 1772. In his work *The Mirror and the Lamp* (London: Oxford University Press, 1953), M. H. Abrams assesses this essay as "an explicit and orderly reformulation of the nature and criteria of poetry and of poetic genres," an "extension of the expressive concept to music and painting," and an "inversion of aesthetic values" (pp. 87–88). He calls Jones "the first writer in England to weave these threads into an explicit and orderly formulation." Yet, surprisingly, Abrams does not make the connection between Jones's esthetic outlook and his exposure to Oriental literatures.

10. William Jones, *The Works of Sir William Jones,* ed. Lord Teignmouth, 12 vols. (London: J. Hatchard, 1807), 10:251–3. Jones's "A Persian Song of Hafez" enjoyed immense and lasting popularity on its composition in 1771 and was published in numerous periodicals in England and elsewhere in Europe as well as in India, before the appearance of his *Works.* The most notable among these include *Annual Register* 15 (1772): 198, and 29 (1787): 178; *Gentleman's Magazine* 56 (Jan. 1786): 58; *Monthly Review,* 77 (July–Dec. 1787): 184; and *Town and Country* 18 (July 1786): 381.

11. Shams al-Din Mohammad Hafez, *Divan-e Hafez,* ed. Parviz Natel Khanlari (Tehran: Kharazmi, 1359/1980), 22. All subsequent citations refer to this work. The version available to Jones may not have been the same as the one cited here. However, Jones's "literal translation" provides a fairly reliable guide to its exact wording and line order.

12. For a more detailed discussion of the role of persona in this *ghazal,* see Julie Scott Meisami, "Persona and Generic Conventions in Medieval Persian Lyric," *Comparative Criticism* 12 (1990): 125–51.

13. On these conventions, see Jane Hedley, *Power in Verse: Metaphor and Metonymy in the Renaissance Lyric* (University Park, PA: The Pennsylvania State University Press, 1988). See, particularly, Hedley's discussion in ch. 5, "'Your monument shall be my gentle verse': Sonneteering and the Metaphoric Way," 77–111.

14. In discussing Hafez's poem and Jones's translation, John D. Yohannan, while crediting the English translator for the fact that he has managed to make a poem, considers the assignment of feminine gender to the beloved an unjustified departure. "Credit must be given Jones for making an English poem out of Hafiz's ghazal, for

not every translation of a poem is itself a poem. But he has done it at some cost. Apart from the obvious liberties taken, it should be noted that the ascription of a feminine gender to the Shiraz Turk is unjustified in the original, as the Persian pronoun is the same for all three genders." John D. Yohannan, *Persian Poetry in England and America: A 200-Year History* (Delmar, NY: Caravan Books, 1977). This type of assessment ignores the fact that, in all translations from Persian into English, translators are forced to opt for specific gender designations wherever they find gender-related indeterminacies in their originals, and that each such choice presents problems of one kind or another.

15. In addition to the above, Jones relates his strategy in deciding to convey the sense of his original in English translation through allusion, rather than naming, to metrical differences between Persian and English. "The reader," he says in one of his essays, "will excuse the singularity of the measure which I have used, if he considers the difficulty of bringing so many Eastern proper names into our stanzas." See Jones, *Works*, 5:316.

16. Interestingly, Jones's strategy here closely resembles the strategy many early-twentieth-century Iranian poets adopted as they began to appropriate European poetry for their culture. See Ahmad Karimi-Hakkak, *Recasting Persian Poetry: Scenarios of Poetic Modernity in Iran* (Salt Lake City: University of Utah Press, 1995), 137–85.

17. See Patricia Berrahou Phillippy, *Love's Remedies: Recantation and Renaissance Lyric Poetry* (London: Associated University Presses, 1995).

18. Throughout the discussion that follows, I am indebted to George Steiner's groundbreaking overview of the relationship between linguistic theory and the practice of literary translation in the twentieth century. See George Steiner, *After Babel: Aspects of Language and Translation* (Oxford: Oxford University Press, 1975), particularly ch. 4, "The Claims of Theory," 236–95.

19. Reynold A. Nicholson, ed., *The Mathnawi of Jelal ad-Din Rumi*, edited and translated with commentary, 8 vols. (London: Luzac & Co., 1925–40), 1:3. All subsequent citations refer to this edition.

20. *The Essential Rumi*, 17–19.

3 / Turk, Persian, and Arab:

Changing Relationships between Tribes

and State in Iran and along Its Frontiers

THOMAS J. BARFIELD

Tribal peoples of many origins have played a large role in Iranian politics: as founders of ruling dynasties, as powerful regional confederations, and as disruptive transborder populations. This paper examines the long-term interactions between successive Iranian governments and tribal peoples of different historical and cultural traditions, both within its territory and along its frontiers. Far from being static, this relationship changed over time and has had a profound cultural and political impact on the development of Iran as a nation.

A cursory examination of Iran's history over the last thousand years reveals an almost unbroken sequence of important empires and dynasties of tribal (mostly Turkish) origin: Seljuqs, Ghaznavids, Khwarazm Shahs, Mongol Il-Khans, Timurids, Aq-qoyunlu, Qizilbash, and Qajars, to name just some of the more prominent. Even the most notable exception, the non-tribal Safavid dynasty (1501–1722), was founded on the mobilization of nomadic Turkish tribes who then dominated the court for the next eighty years and would play a critical role in the states that emerged after its fall. Of equal importance were large numbers of tribal groups that maintained continual social and political cohesion through perennial opposition to state rule in frontier areas. These included Arab tribes in the southwest, the Kurds in the northwest, the Turkmen in the northeast, and the Baluch in the southeast. Uneasily encapsulated within Iran itself, there were large tribal confederacies that periodically came to prominence, such as the Bakhtiari, Lurs, Shahsevan, Qashqa'i, and Khamseh, whose relationships with the central government were always subject to negotiation.

The Safavid dynasty, in particular, marked a watershed between two distinct periods. The first (1000–1500) saw Iran conquered and ruled by a series of invading Turko-Mongolian tribes originating in Central Asia. The second period (1501–1925) also saw the continued domination of Iran by leaders of tribal groups, but these were no longer invaders—rather, they were tribes of more diverse ethnic origin, long resident in Iran, who had distinct regional roots in the country. One problem in examining these evolving relationships is that, while the organization and history of major dynasties in Iran are relatively well documented, the organization and history of the tribes are not. It is too often assumed that they were all alike, all nomads, and that they were "primordial" groups impervious to change, with political organizations that were just simple extensions of their kinship relations. Seemingly, it was just one group replacing another with no rhyme or reason for their rise or fall. But this was not the case, as a closer examination will reveal.

UNDERSTANDING TRIBAL ORGANIZATIONS

Tribal political structures are those that (at least in theory) employ a model of kinship to build groups that act together to organize economic production, preserve internal political order, and defend the group against outsiders. In these structures people therefore identify themselves as members of a defined social group, not as residents of a particular place. While most nomadic pastoralists have a tribal organization, it is also found widely among seminomadic or even sedentary peoples. These sedentary groups occupy marginal regions where state control is weak, and include groups like the Kurds who inhabit the mountainous borderlands of Iran, Turkey, and Iraq, and the Pushtuns of Pakistan.

Although tribes define themselves on the basis of genealogy, "actual" kinship relations (based on principles of descent, marriage, or adoption) are evident only within smaller units: nuclear families, extended households, and local lineages. At higher levels, clans and tribes often find it necessary to establish relationships that are more politically based, because kinship is problematic as the organizing model for very large groups, where the pretense that they are genealogically related cannot be maintained. For this reason, it is important to distinguish between a tribe, which is the largest unit of incorporation based on a genealogical model, and a tribal confederation, which combines openly unrelated tribes to create a supratribal political entity.

Tribe-state relations in Iran generally involved tribal confederations, not genealogically based tribes. Such confederations swallowed up whole tribes and made local leaders subordinate to the central rule of a khan. This was usually achieved by a leader who either conquered neighboring tribes or brought them under his control more voluntarily by means of alliances. Although over time the specific tribes and clans that made up the confederation might change, confederations often had life spans of centuries. The creation on the Iranian plateau of such long-lived confederacies with powerful khans was in striking contrast to the fragmented political system of the Bedouin tribes of Arabia and North Africa, where supratribal confederations were rare and very unstable. After the early Islamic conquest, Bedouin tribes of Arabian origin played a diminishingly small role in Iran, while Turkish nomads from Central Asia came to dominate the political landscape both among the tribes and as rulers of sedentary states. The differences between Turkish and Arab-Bedouin nomads had both cultural and political roots.

EGALITARIAN VERSUS
HIERARCHICAL TRIBAL STRUCTURES

There were two very different types of tribal cultural traditions, with different styles of tribal political organization, present in the Near East.[1] The first was the segmentary egalitarian–lineage type most closely associated with the Bedouins of Arabia and North Africa, although it was also characteristic of the more sedentary Pushtuns and Kurds. The second was the hierarchical tribal model characteristic of the Turko-Mongolian peoples who came into the Iranian and Anatolian plateaus from Central Eurasia. The former had leaders (*shaikhs*) who generally ruled, as "first among equals," over populations that rarely reached into the tens of thousands. The latter had permanent leaders (*khans*) who commonly ruled over as many as a hundred thousand people or more in Iran, and, along the Mongolian borders with China, periodically formed empires that organized millions.

These two types of organizations displayed very different political dynamics. Tribes composed of egalitarian lineages had leaders who ruled by means of consensus or mediation. Their tribal dynamics are often called "segmentary," which means that cooperation or hostility between particular groups was determined by the scope of the problem at hand. The numerous petty disputes that ordinarily divided egalitarian lineages would be set aside when they were faced with a common outside threat. They would then return to their old rivalries and disputes once the common enemy was gone. The egalitarian nature of these societies also made them resistant to accepting the permanent authority of any paramount leader who came from a rival kin group. For this reason, as Ibn Khaldun first noted, only a leader who stood outside the tribal system, generally in the guise of a religious prophet, could expect to gain the cooperation of enough quarrelling tribes to create a supratribal organization.

Bedouins can acquire royal authority only by making use of religious coloring, such as prophethood or sainthood, or some great religious event in general. The reason is because of their savagery, the Bedouins are the least willing of all nations to subordinate themselves to each other, as they are rude, proud, ambitious and eager to be leaders. Their individual aspirations rarely coincide. But when there is religion (among them) through prophethood or sainthood, then they have some restraining influence upon themselves. The qualities of haughtiness and jealousy leave them. It is easy then to unite (as a social organization). . . . This is illustrated by the Arab dynasty of Islam. Religion cemented their leadership with religious law and its ordinances, which, explicitly and implicitly, are concerned with what is good for civilization.[2]

The Arab tribes therefore had their greatest impact in Iran during the early days of Islam when religion united them. In general, however, egalitarian tribes saw little need for supratribal organization, because they were normally confronted only by small regional states rather than centralized empires, and because such tribes had a symbiotic relationship with neighboring cities and often shared a common culture with their region's agricultural and urban populations.

By contrast, the Turkish nomads who entered the highland plateaus of Iran and Anatolia after 1000 C.E. had a very different concept of political organization. Largely of Central Eurasian origin, they drew on the cultural traditions of the horse-riding peoples from the steppes of Mongolia. These Turko-Mongolian tribal systems accepted the legitimacy of hierarchical differences in kinship organization that made social distinctions between senior and junior generations, noble and common clans, and the rulers and the ruled.[3] The acceptance of hierarchy as a normal feature of tribal life made it much easier for their leaders to create supratribal confederations by variously incorporating individuals, local lineages, clans, and whole tribes as the building blocks of a political/military organization that could present a united front to the outside world. These tribal confederacies incorporated hundreds of thousands of people from a variety of tribes, whose political unity was often all they had in common. The authority of a ruling dynasty, once established, became strictly hereditary and was rarely challenged from below. Their khans met Ibn Khaldun's criteria for having true royal authority: they possessed the right to command obedience (by using force if necessary), collect taxes, administer justice, and handle all external political relations.[4] Such dynasties often lasted for centuries, but they needed a substantial flow of revenue to sustain them.

If Turko-Mongolian tribal culture was more accepting of hierarchy and royal charisma than the egalitarian Bedouin tribes, it was in part because historically they were confronted by larger states and empires than the tribes of Arabia and North Africa. As William Irons put it, "Among pastoral nomadic societies hierarchical political institutions are generated only by external relations with state societies and never develop purely as a result of the internal dynamics of such societies."[5] (The same statement applies to most non-nomadic tribes.) The size and complexity of nomads' political organization appears to be directly related to the organization of the sedentary states they opposed and to their ability to maintain independence from them. Looking very broadly cross-culturally at historic and ethnographic cases, we find that Iran falls in the middle of an arc of growing political centralization, running from tribes without any rulers in East Africa to the powerful centralized steppe empires in Mongolia.[6]

TRIBES AND IRANIAN STATES

Historically, the dynamic of state and tribe relations in Iran has varied depending on what type of state confronted what type of tribe. At times, Iran was the center of large centralized empires that had broad frontiers running from Mesopotamia and Anatolia to the borders of India, and from the Caucasus and Central Asia to the Persian Gulf. At other times, it was divided into regional states centered on regions such as Khorasan and Azerbaijan, or cities such as Isfahan or Shiraz. The more powerful the state, the more influence it had on the tribes. But, more important, for most of the last thousand years it was the tribes that provided the rulers of Iran, creating a state that had two arms: a tribal, predominantly Turkish, military, and a civil administration composed of urban-based officials, predominantly Persian. This tribal origin of Iranian rulers was, however, a mixed blessing for the tribes that produced them. Although a new ruler might be "one of their own," in general it was state policy to reduce the role of tribes to that of subjects like any other. Rulers showed little hesitation in executing any close relatives who treated the state as a common tribal patrimony, and they often ended up suppressing rebellions among the very tribes who had earlier brought them to power.

The impetus for forming large confederations within Iran came from outside the tribes. Nomads and other tribal groups throughout the region were either surrounded by powerful states and empires or lived on their borders.

The creation of a tribal confederacy was a means by which tribes confronted the threats posed by sedentary states. In general, the degree of centralization of tribal confederations was correlated with the power of the states they faced. For example, those inside the borders of Iran formed large confederations with powerful khans, while those on the borders maintained a much looser political organization. In examining the history of the tribes within Iran over the past thousand years, we find the following general patterns, often used by different tribes simultaneously.

1. Tribal confederations that used their organization to conquer sedentary states
2. Tribal confederations that used their organization to maintain autonomy from state control
3. Tribal confederations that were manipulated by sedentary governments to rule mobile populations
4. Fragmented tribal groups in frontier areas that avoided state control by staying beyond the range of Iranian power

EXTERNAL NOMADIC CONQUERORS

The majority of the dynasties that conquered Iran came from Central Asia and invaded the Iranian plateau via Khorasan. This is a pattern that has a long history, dating back at least to the Bronze Age when, during the middle of the second millennium B.C.E., cattle-keeping peoples speaking Indo-European languages overran Iran, Anatolia, and India. Later, the most important dynasties of the western Iranian world—Achaemenid (558–330 B.C.E.), Parthian (250 B.C.E.–224 C.E.), and Sassanian (224–637 C.E.)—all had their origins in Central Asia. The pattern was disrupted by the Muslim Arab invasion, which not only conquered Iran but also went on into Central Asia. Later, there was a sequence of local Iranian dynasties (Saffarids, Samanids, Buyids) under whom there was a flourishing of culture and economic development. This lasted until around 1000 C.E., when a new wave of Turko-Mongolian tribes rolled over southwestern Asia and initiated a period of Turkish and Mongol political domination of the region in which tribes played a very powerful role in governing Iran.

The period of Turko-Mongolian invaders began with the Seljuqs in 1038 and ended with the collapse of the Mongol Il-Khanate in 1353. These dynasties had a reputation for destructiveness (well deserved by the Mongols) and apparently had greater difficulty in governing than earlier dynasties. However, the interaction of a Turko-Mongolian military elite with representatives of an older Persian tradition of civil administration, culture, and religion eventually created a synthesis that was the foundation of most of the dynasties that followed them.[7] Invading conquest dynasties faced a series of problems after they came to power. These included:

1. moving away from a grand form of raiding and extortion to create a proper civil administration that preserved peace and brought in revenue;
2. separating the state's interests from those of the conquering tribal confederation; and
3. coping with growing class differences between ordinary tribesmen, who remained nomadic pastoralists, and the tribal elite, who became urbanized.

Unlike the Arabs, who were very familiar with the sedentary world around them before they began their conquests, the steppe nomadic tribes were unfamiliar (or at least unconcerned) with the basics of agriculture and urban life. They devalued farmers and farming, had little concept of regular taxation or other aspects of state administration, and were prone to seek what they wanted through raiding, extortion, or long-distance trade. Their leaders were adept at appropriating wealth rather than facilitating its production. Familiar with the intricacies of trade and the profits of raiding, they were surprisingly unsophisticated about the way in which this wealth ultimately depended on a base of ordinary peasants who produced the agricultural surplus that supported the state. The mismatch between military power and administrative ignorance of Turko-Mongolian dynasties was most apparent in their initial neglect of agriculture and urban life, the result of their skewed development in Mongolia, where extortion was the key to political success.[8] While such a strategy was effective against China, with its vast population and large productive capacity, it was less successful in Central Asia and Iran, where irrigated agriculture was much more susceptible to disruption and where state structures were more fragile.

The need to educate new tribal rulers in basic administration is well documented. For example, when the Seljuqs first entered Khorasan and conquered Nishapur in 1038, their leader Toghril had difficulty in restraining his brothers from looting the city. He had to point out to them that, as the conquerors and new rulers of the land, they were in fact destroying their own property.[9] Such examples could be cited for almost all newly arrived tribes. The worst case was that of the Mongols. Only after forty years, during the reign of Ghazan Khan (1295–1304), did they begin to come to grips seriously with creating a civil administration that protected the agricultural population from tribal predation. Ghazan's rebuke to his fellow tribesmen underscores their severe deficiencies in appreciating the simplest principles of governing a sedentary state.

> I am not on the side of the Tazik ra`iyyat [Persian peasants]. If there is any purpose in pillaging them all, there is no one with more power to do this than I. Let us rob them together. But if you wish to be certain of collecting grain and food for your tables in the future, I must be harsh with you. You must be taught to reason. If you insult the ra`iyyat, take their oxen and seed, and trample their crops into the ground, what will you do in the future? . . . The obedient ra`iyyat must be distinguished from the ra`iyyat who are our enemies. How should we not protect the obedient, allowing them to suffer distress and torment at our hands?[10]

In creating a state administration, tribal leaders needed the help of skilled administrators. These they found among the urbanized Persian population. Such men became ministers who ran the state and attempted to influence their masters into carrying out more productive policies. It is during this period that the figure of the somewhat slow-witted Turkish shah at odds with his wily Persian vizier becomes a literary fixture in works such as Sa`di's *Golestan* (1258). For example, in one story Sa`di focuses on the strategy of a vizier who counters the plans of a ruler to gain renown by giving away the entire treasury as gifts to his subjects by arguing that

> If thou distributest a treasure to the multitude
> Each householder will receive but a grain of rice.
> Why takest thou not from each a barley-corn of silver
> That thou mayest accumulate everyday a treasure?[11]

Underlying this story is a cultural conflict. The tribal nomadic khans maintained power by constantly emptying their treasuries whenever revenue came in, in order to keep their followers happy. By contrast, a sedentary ruler relied on a full treasury with which he could buy (or buy off) the troops he needed when necessary. A Persian minister, Nezam al-Molk (1018–1092), famous advisor to the Seljuqs, wrote his *Book of Government* (*Siyasat-nameh*) to explain to his prince how such administration should be carried out.[12] One aspect of Persian political ideology that appealed to all the new Turkish and Mongolian rulers was its emphasis on the shah or sultan as the absolute leader and key figure in the administration of the state.

Establishing a proper administration put limits on the ability of ordinary tribesmen to loot and kept state and royal property from being divided among the tribal elite. This was only the first of many cleavages that developed between Turko-Mongol rulers in Iran and their own tribespeople. The relationship between tribes and states was always problematic under dynasties of tribal origin. To the extent that the tribes claimed kinship with the ruling dynasty, they often posed a threat to its stability by assuming a too active role in politics. In a tribal system, the spoils of war, including conquered land, were supposed to be distributed among the participants. Yet no dynasty could allow itself to be dismembered in such a manner and expect to survive. Hence arose the difficult game of providing benefits to the tribal supporters while at the same time building a separate standing army and administration outside of the tribal system. This included the use of various sorts of military fiefs (*iqta`*) granted to supporters of the dynasty, and the movement of tribal troops to the empire's frontier, where they could be kept employed fighting outsiders. The danger was that some of these groups could (and periodically did) turn on their erstwhile masters and displace them. One way to prevent this was for the ruler to take advantage of the state's dual organization to play off the two key factions of the state against each other: his tribal military against his urban civil officials, and vice versa. Each provided the ruler with different tools that, if used skillfully, could keep him master of the state without serious rivals outside of his own family.

The adoption of a new way of life also set up cultural differences between the nomadic elite and ordinary tribesmen. As the elite became part of a sophisticated and urbanized ruling class, it developed a polish and interests alien to its more rural kinsmen. One recently researched aspect of this cultural shift was the change from a high public role of women in the Turko-Mongol tribes, even in fighting and ruling circles, to increased seclusion of women among those who became settled and urbanized.[13] In addition, revenue that had gone to maintain the loyalty of a broad tribal base was diverted into other endeavors such as building projects, luxury goods production, and the distribution of ever larger rewards to the members of the court. Although invading dynasties were established with the mobilization of tribal troops under their own indigenous leadership, as time went by there was a tendency to rely more on a fixed body of troops financed by the government. The large-scale mobilization of tribal troops was reserved for auxiliary use in times of crisis, because rulers could no longer count upon the automatic loyalty of tribal armies.

The Mongol solution to this problem was to detribalize their armed forces by turning tribes into military units run by centrally appointed commanders. The Mongols were so successful with this policy that the autonomous tribes that were incorporated into their empire ceased to exist. Only when Mongol power declined did a new set of tribes arise in Iran. For this reason, when the Mongol Il-Khanate ended in Iran during the mid-fourteenth century there were no large supratribal organizations left in the country that might seize power on their own. Instead, we find a large set of tribes under the label "Turkmen," who had formerly existed on the edge of Mongol-controlled areas, competing with one another, none too successfully, to reestablish some sort of central order. In the end they did not succeed, but a new dynasty of Iranian origin did: the Safavids (1501–1722).

THE SAFAVID ADMINISTRATIVE REVOLUTION

The collapse of Mongol authority in Iran in 1353 led to a period of fragmentation and unstable regional states. Timur (Tamerlane) invaded from Central Asia in 1380 and within twenty years had conquered as far west as Baghdad, Damascus, and Ankara, and as far south as India. Under his son, Shah Rokh (r. 1405–47), Iran was part of a single state ruled from Herat, but Azerbaijan was only loosely controlled and then lost to the rising power of Turkmen tribes. These Turkmen tribes eventually took control of all of Iran and displaced the Timurids in the late fifteenth century.

The organization of Turkmen tribal groups in western Iran was decentralized. They appear to have lost any supratribal organization they may have had under the Mongol Il-Khans. Indeed, it was always Mongol policy to prevent the rise of any supratribal group by keeping tribes under strong state control. Hence, when the Mongol Il-Khanid state ended, it left in its wake relatively weak and disorganized tribal groups within Iran. Those tribes with the most cohesion at that time had preserved their autonomy in the borderlands between the more powerful states established by the Seljuqs, Ottomans, and Il-Khans. There in the borderlands straddling Anatolia, Azerbaijan, and northern Syria, they became frontier freebooters, rapidly rising and falling in power. The term "Turkmen" itself appears to have been applied to them as a sort of a residual category for a type of Turko-Mongolian frontier tribe that lived independently just beyond the control of state power. It was as much a political category as an ethnic label, and their larger units had mostly geographically based names (Rumlu [Anatolian], Shamlu [Syrian], etc.). Whenever they became powerful enough to establish state rule, they took on a more specific tribal name drawn from the ruling tribe or clan.

The Turkmen competed for control of Azerbaijan and eastern Anatolia, the former base of Mongol power, with far more powerful states such as the Timurids in the east and the Ottomans to the west. They were never unified but instead fought one another, most notably in the long-running conflict between the Qara-qoyunlu (1375–1468) and Aq-qoyunlu (1378–1508) (Black

Sheep and White Sheep clans, respectively). The Aq-qoyunlu eventually succeeded in displacing their rivals to establish their hegemony over Iran. However, within a generation their power was undermined by civil wars after the death of their leader Ya`qub in 1490. It was then that the new Safavid dynasty picked up the pieces and began a period in which the tribes came firmly under the control of the central government.

In its rise and in its tribal policies the Safavid dynasty represented a sharp break from the past, but one that demonstrated just how closely bound the Turkish tribal and Iranian nontribal elites had become since the time of the Seljuqs. The Safavid Shah Isma`il, who founded the dynasty, was an Iranian of nontribal background and the hereditary leader of an important Sufi order based in Ardabil. But he also had strong ties to the Turkish tribal world because his father and grandfather had traveled throughout Eastern Anatolia seeking alliances and military backing from the Turkmen tribes there. Isma`il's own maternal grandfather was the famous Aq-qoyunlu khan Uzun Hasan. Because these Turkmen tribes followed a popular brand of Shi`ism, the Safavid order abandoned its Sunni roots and espoused this popular Shi`ism itself. This enabled Isma`il to recruit an army composed of a variety of Turkmen clans who followed him in the name of religion against the tribal Aq-qoyunlu dynasty. While the organization of disparate tribes by a religious leader had been common among the Arabs, as Ibn Khaldun noted, it was rare among the Turks. But Shi`i Islam had long attracted great numbers of tribal peoples throughout Anatolia who declared themselves *murid*s, or personal disciples, of a religious leader. Given the weakness of the Turkmen dynasties ruling various regions of Anatolia and Iran, such religious structures had great political potential for any leader capable of making this religious attachment also a political one. Isma`il succeeded in this and built an army composed of a wide variety of Turkmen tribes who pledged politico-religious loyalty to him personally. Although they retained their clan identities (which would later play a great role in court politics), the Turkmen members of his army became known collectively as Qizilbash (redheads) for the distinctive headgear that marked their allegiance to Isma`il and to the twelve Shi`a imams. However, the Safavid failure to break down the Turkmen tribal organization during the formation of the dynasty was to have repercussions for its entire existence.

In its internal organization, the Safavid dynasty was a less radical break with the past than it might appear. As with the Turkish dynasties that had preceded it, the government was divided between "men of the sword," mostly Turks, and "men of the pen," mostly Persian. Thus, while the leader of the dynasty promoted Persians to more high offices than previously (they had always been the bulwark of civil administration for earlier Turko-

Mongolian governments), the Turks still maintained a large degree of control over the state because there was no substitute for their military expertise. Shah Isma'il was particularly effective in giving Persians important positions at court, until his disastrous defeat at Chaldiran by the Ottomans in 1514, when his influence over the Turkmen tribes declined and they moved to seize greater influence. Although the gunpowder revolution had reached the region, military power still lay in the use of horse cavalry, and it was the Turkish tribes that could supply the bulk of these.

During the early part of the reign of his successor, Shah Tahmasb (r. 1524–76), the Turkmen continued to dominate court politics and military affairs. At that time there were four main Turkmen clans (Ustajlu, Takkalu, Rumlu, and Zu'lqadir) that held most of the military positions in the Safavid government, as well as a number of border tribes in the northeast, including the Afshars and Qajars. These clans were bitter rivals for power, and each clan staunchly supported its own leaders. When Tahmasb appointed a member of one clan to the highest office, that of Great Amir, the new amir would use the opportunity to pack as many of his fellow clansmen as possible into subordinate positions. This quickly led to the disaffection of the other clans, the eventual overthrow of the amir (they averaged only about three years in office), and his replacement by a new amir from another clan. The tribe of the clan that lost would then revolt, and the problems of the court would quickly move to the provinces where each of these clans had its base. By the time almost all the clans had cycled through the top jobs during the course of a decade, creating havoc in their wake, Tahmasb realized he could use their rivalries against them. Beginning in 1533, he successfully played one clan off against another and placed Persians in high positions as counterweights to tribal leaders. While this was resented by the tribes, they were too jealous of each other to be able to unite. Indeed, when Tahmasb died in 1576, factional fighting among the Turkmen reemerged with greater intensity.

The death of Tahmasb opened a period of bloody warfare in which the Turkish tribes regained much of their power at court under Isma'il II and Khodabandeh. However, when Shah Abbas (r. 1588–1629) succeeded to the throne, he effectively restored central power and established the policies that would be used by later rulers to undermine tribal influence. The Safavid dynasty reached its height under Abbas in no small part because he was able to end the turmoil created by the tribes and focus on economic development, reform the army, and restore Iran's power vis-à-vis the Ottomans, Mughals, and Uzbeks. Although he had been put in power by a cabal of Turkmen amirs, Abbas refused to play their puppet. He executed those amirs who conspired against him and stripped others of their offices. Then, rather than play one clan against another, he chose to rebuild the Safavid army by creating a core of troops and officials loyal to him, with no tribal affiliation. This he did by expanding on a policy started by his predecessors of recruiting Christian captives from the Caucasus, converting them to Islam, and making them slaves (*gholams*) of the shah who then served at his pleasure. This was a policy similar to that of the Ottomans, who also countered the influence of the tribes by creating the janissaries, military units of similar origin. The advantage of such recruitment was that their members had no tribal groups to support them, no landholdings of their own, and no relatives. Abbas's reorganization of the royal army included the creation of nontribal units of *tofangchis* (musketeers) numbering 12,000 men and artillery units of 12,000 men with 500 cannons. He also created a unit of 10,000 royal *gholams* and a bodyguard of 3,000.[14] These units served as a counterweight to the tribal cavalry that had hitherto dominated the military. At the same time, he reduced the economic independence of his Turkmen amirs by confiscating the estates of those he found disloyal and declaring them to be crown or state land, a policy that greatly expanded during his reign and was continued by his successors. The control of this additional source of local revenue both weakened the former fief holders and strengthened the central government. It also sent a message to other provincial leaders that the price of opposition was now very steep. To prevent tribes from revolting against their loss of power, Abbas implemented a widespread policy of exile in which parts of practically every strong tribe found themselves uprooted from their homelands and moved to a frontier, usually Khorasan, to defend the dynasty against invaders. What is interesting about this transfer was that it included not just Turkmen clans, but groups such as the Kurds and Bakhtiari who had not been prominent at court.[15] For the first time one could say that the Iranian government had a tribal policy.

Abbas succeeded better than any shah before him in getting the tribes out of the court and gaining control of the countryside, but in foreign affairs he was faced with the reality that Iran had lost as much as half the territory it had ruled under Tahmasb. The series of civil conflicts inside Iran had made it difficult for the dynasty to fend off invasions by the Uzbeks in Khorasan in the northeast and by the Ottomans in Azerbaijan in the northwest. Both these regions became contested frontiers, so contested, in fact, that over time the dynasty's capital was moved from Tabriz to Qazvin and eventually under Abbas to Isfahan to remove the court from danger.

At the time of Abbas, the Ottoman Turks were at the height of their power. While the Safavids regained control of Tabriz in Azerbaijan and much territory in the Caucasus, they were unable to restore their former power in eastern Anatolia. Similarly, while Abbas did retake Baghdad and throw the Portuguese out of Hormuz, after his death most of Mesopotamia, with the exception of Khuzestan at the head of the Persian Gulf, returned to Ottoman control, and the border between Ottomans and Safavids stabilized. The Treaty of Qasr-e Shirin (Treaty of Zohab) in 1639 confirmed this boundary and brought an end to nearly 150 years of frontier warfare. From that time, neither side encroached much upon the other. In terms of tribal policy this had two repercussions. The first was to reduce the importance of Iran's relations with the Arab tribes, most of which now fell under Ottoman administration. The second was that the creation of a firm border between the Ottomans and Safavids left no room for autonomous Turkmen tribes. What had been lawless frontier areas became garrisoned border provinces, and tribes there found themselves under the thumb of one or the other of these two powerful empires.

Safavid battles against the Uzbeks were somewhat more successful because the Safavids, though less technologically advanced than the Ottomans, had better cannons than the Uzbeks, and went on to recover western Khorasan from them. However, it was during this period that eastern Khorasan (Afghan Turkestan) began to drift out of Iran's orbit. The old Timurid capital of Herat became a contested city that would fall in and out of Iranian hands over the next three centuries. The deserts to the north between Marv and Khwarazm became home to a set of Turkmen tribes that, while they could not conquer Iranian territory, created no end of trouble through slave raiding and banditry. It was in order to confront these Turkmen tribes along the northeastern border (particularly the Yomut Turkmen) that Abbas resettled so many tribes from other parts of Iran there. Trouble with the Mughals in India was relatively less than along Iran's other frontiers, except around Qandahar in Afghanistan, where the Safavids seized territory that the Mughals thought should be in their sphere of influence. This brought Iran in contact with the eastern tribes of Afghanistan, including the Dorrani Pushtuns around Herat, their rival Ghelza'i Pushtuns in Qandahar, and the Baluch to the east, whose khans dominated the arid territories south of Sistan to the Makran coast. Ironically, it would be these Afghan tribes, and not tribes in Iran, that would bring the dynasty down, but this would not occur for almost one hundred years, so strong was the legacy that Abbas left.

Abbas's rule was so successful that it set the parameters of tribal policy for future dynasties. It clearly established Iran as a state with a distinct geographical identity and a Persian cultural heart. From Abbas's time, tribes were much more clearly either inside or outside the state's purview. This had not been the case at the beginning of the dynasty, when, following the Turkmen tradition, the Safavid state could just as easily have been a secondary Turkish state vying with the Ottomans for Anatolia and the Timurids for Central Asia. For better or worse, Iran was now clearly a state between the two, with no serious designs on its neighbors. Abbas weakened the old dual organization of Turkish military and Persian administration to create a more unified government that used outsiders loyal to the throne and a standing army to give the state preeminence. By deporting tribes to distant frontiers, abolishing the presumption that some tribes had the right to rule particular provinces, and giving both the state and the ruler direct control of provincial revenue, he set a mark that all succeeding dynasties attempted to meet, some more successfully than others. His foreign relations, though failing to restore all the territory that Iran had once occupied, created the stable boundaries that have essentially lasted until today.

THE QAJARS AND THE REGIONAL TRIBAL CONFEDERATIONS IN THE NINETEENTH CENTURY

Abbas's successors were weaker rulers. Still, Abbas had so thoroughly eliminated the threat of invasions by outsiders and so undermined the tribes inside Iran that the dynasty lasted another century. It was not until 1722 that the Ghelza'i Afghans based in Qandahar revolted against the Safavids and marched on central Iran. With amazing luck and facilitated by what can only be described as gross incompetence, they defeated the Safavid army and seized both the capital and the reigning Shah Soltan Hosain, who was forced to cede power to them. This was the downside of the Safavid policy of cutting the tribes out of the military and depending on a small standing army. Failure could and did lead to the collapse of the whole structure. The short-lived Afghan coup opened a period of tribal resurgence, first under Nader Shah Afshar (r. 1736–47), who mobilized a wide variety of tribal forces to create a powerful but ephemeral empire most notable for its defeat of the Mughals and the sack of Delhi. To hold his troops together, he had to reward them lavishly with loot from campaigns and with payments derived from heavy taxes on all the territories under his rule. His state collapsed with his death. The east broke away under one of his lieutenants, Ahmad Shah Dorrani, who created a new empire that encompassed today's Afghanistan and the Mughal borderland of Sind, Punjab, and Kashmir. Iran itself devolved into a set of regional power centers that vied to reestablish central control.

One consequence of the Safavid collapse and Nader Shah's failure to create a durable state was that the tribes first deported by Abbas returned to their homelands. In the absence of central authority, each attempted to create a regional power base and then to expand its control to the rest of Iran, or, failing that, to come to terms with other similar groups trying to accomplish the same end. It was at this time that we see another structural change in the organization of Iran's tribes: the rise of confederations in central Iran along the Zagros Mountain chain, each with close ties to important cities in their regions. Previously, areas of tribal strength had been primarily Azerbaijan (Tabriz) and Khorasan (Mashhad), and while these areas remained the homes of powerful tribal groups, the dominant tribal political players now came from the areas surrounding Shiraz, Isfahan, and Tehran; that is, from the more Persianized or encapsulated tribes. This began with the Zand dynasty (1751–95), which was led by a small tribe under the leadership of Karim Khan Zand. He established a base in Shiraz and by the 1760s had gained control of Iran with the exception of Khorasan, but the dynasty's hold on its outer territories was weak. With the death of Karim Khan in 1779, the Qajars were able to mobilize a more powerful army in north-central Iran and defeat both the Zands and Nader's descendants, who still ruled Khorasan. By the beginning of the nineteenth century the Qajars ruled all of Iran, but found themselves confronting strongly rooted tribal confederacies in central and northwestern Iran. These included the Qashqa'i and Khamseh confederations around Shiraz, the Bakhtiari around Isfahan, the Kurds in Kermanshah, and the Shahsevan in Azerbaijan. Throughout the Qajar period, these tribal confederations and their leaders played an important role in government and often dominated their local areas in opposition to central control.

The range of strategies they employed was quite diverse. Leaders of some strong tribal confederations served as allies of a ruling dynasty, acting as its governors for their own regions. Since control of marginal places and peoples could be had only at great financial cost, such alliances were seen as beneficial by both sides, particularly when the state was weak. When the state was powerful, the tables were often reversed, with the state administration attempting to destroy the tribal leadership of confederations or co-opt it as a tool in a policy of indirect rule by means of official appointments and subsidies. Between these extremes, ruling dynasties established a modus vivendi with the leaders of tribal confederations in which the latter simply acted as intermediaries between the state and the nomads. (Just who was manipulating whom in such relationships was often difficult to tell.)[16] Tribal confederations in Iran regularly moved from one relationship to another as state power waxed and waned over the centuries.

What distinguished a confederation leader from other political actors was his role as the accepted legal authority for the tribes he controlled. Inside the confederation the khan was equivalent to the government, regardless of whether he was perceived as an oppressor acting as an agent for a powerful dynasty, or, more favorably, as the protector of local tribal territorial and political integrity against outside demands. The leadership of these confederations straddled the borders of two worlds. They were the leaders of tribes, but were usually based in cities and had strong relationships with the nontribal elite of Iran. In most cases they were members of the tribe themselves, but this was not always the case. In one notable example, the Qajars actually created a whole new confederacy, the Khamseh, from a variety of Arab, Turkish, and Iranian tribes as a counterweight to the more powerful Qashqa'i, and then appointed its leader from the Qavvam family, who were originally influential merchants from Shiraz. Even the Qashqa'i khans, who celebrated their tribal heritage, only visited their tribal followers in the summer, when they set up chiefly camps to receive their nomad followers. Tribal nomads themselves saw no contradiction in this because the confederation was designed to serve a political end. The job of the khan was to represent the tribal confederation's interests at the highest levels of government and to mediate disputes between tribal peoples and local officials.

The Qashqa'i of southern Iran, whose leaders have been key figures in regional, national, and international politics for the past two centuries, offer one of the classic examples of a powerful confederation. Beginning with their appointment as governors of the tribes of Fars province in the late eighteenth century, an unbroken line of rulers, or *il-khans*, created a powerful confederacy out of a diverse set of tribes. They owed their success to the strategic location of their territory along key trade routes to the Persian Gulf, to their territory's possessing substantial resources for agriculture as well as pastoralism, and to both nomads and the Iranian state's seeking a political intermediary to meet their needs. During the First World War, even foreign powers (British and German) competed for the support of the Qashqa'i khans. Their paramount leadership "defined the state and the tribe for each other while simultaneously drawing its vital sources of power from both."[17]

The Qashqa'i and other Iranian confederations proved remarkably long lasting. While their histories are often filled with bloody disputes within ruling lineages, the confederacy leadership remained within these lineages for centuries. This was due in part to a disposition in Turko-Mongolian political culture to limit supreme leadership to the descendants of the confederacy's founder. In this tradition, completely new leadership could come about only with the creation of a new confederacy. Internal revolts against ruling khans or their destruction by external forces brought about new confederations with new names, not the reorganization of existing ones. Therefore, few twentieth-century confederations had a history more than two hundred years

Qashqa'i shepherds, 1978.
Photos by Nikki Keddie.

Qashqa'i rug weaving, 1978. Photo by Nikki Keddie.

Qashqa'i girl, 1978.
Photo by Nikki Keddie.

Qashqa'i migration, 1978. Photo by Nikki Keddie.

Shahsevan women, 1978. Photo by Nikki Keddie

old, before which time we find a whole host of other confederations occupying the same territory.

If the centralization of tribes into large confederations was primarily a product of the relationship between nomads and the state, then, as we would expect,
in border areas where state power was weak the tribal nomads were organized into much smaller groups. Here they maintained their autonomy either
by inhabiting the frontier zones between states (allowing them to play one
power off against another) or by fleeing from the territory of one state to
another. The strategy of border tribes depended on the existence of a political no-man's-land between two states beyond the control of either. Because
these frontiers were political rather than geographic, their boundaries could
shift over time as state power expanded or contracted. The classic example
of this type of frontier was, for a long period, the borderland between Turkey
and Iran, which was the home of powerful Turkmen tribes described earlier.
This frontier zone had disappeared by the time of the Qajars because both
sides were under state control. However, the northeastern frontier with Central Asia in the late nineteenth century provided another long-lasting example of the ability of tribal nomads to exploit the rivalries between weak
sedentary states to their own advantage with very little formal organization.

Of all the Central Asian tribes, the Turkmen, who straddled the borderland between northeastern Iran and the Uzbek khanates of Bukhara and Khiva
in Central Asia, were in the best position to manipulate the inability of Qajar
shahs and Uzbek amirs to dominate the frontier regions that divided them.
When either the Iranians or Uzbeks attempted to coerce them, the Turkmen
employed movement as a strategy to resist state authority, transferring their
camps from one side of the frontier to the other to avoid taxes or escape military retaliation. In general, it was observed that those Turkmen who lived
closest to towns and cities were the most law abiding, while those who inhab-
ited the more distant deserts were prone to violence as a political and economic strategy. Many of these took up slave raiding as a profession, selling
captive Iranians in the bazaars of Central Asia or holding them for ransom.
The Sunni Turkmen justified this trade on the grounds that Iranians, as Shi`i
heretics, were legitimate targets of slave raiding. Despised as savage robbers
in Iran, they were welcomed as valued customers in Khiva and Bukhara, which
benefited from a slave trade they refused to close down. Such an infamous
commerce could only thrive as long as the states of Iran and Central Asia
were simultaneously too weak to police their frontiers and too hostile to cooperate with one another. The Turkmen strategy ultimately failed, however, when
the expansion of Tsarist Russia into Central Asia first cut off their slave markets and then led to their conquest in 1884 with the capture of the oasis of

Marv. With no place to run, the Turkmen lost both their political independence and their military power.[18] A similar but less pervasive problem of
raiding tribes also occurred in the southeast, where Baluch tribes straddled
the old frontier between Safavid Iran and Mughal India.

THE DECLINE AND DEMISE OF TRIBAL
INFLUENCE IN TWENTIETH-CENTURY IRAN

If tribes were so important to the historic development of politics and government in Iran, why do they play such a small role now? Tribes remained
politically significant in Iran long after they had been marginalized in neighboring Ottoman Turkey, Russian Central Asia, or British India. Thus, when
the modernization of Iran became the policy of the new Pahlavi dynasty
(1925–79) founded by Reza Shah, dealing with the tribes took on prime importance. It was not that the tribes were so much stronger at the end of the Qajar
period, but that the central government was so weak. All over Iran, tribal confederations and their elites dominated many provincial governments (particularly in the south), in some places as appointed governors and in others
as local notables who could influence policy. But this power was vulnerable,
largely for structural reasons, to military, economic, and political changes that
would move the tribes to the margins, although their leaders would maintain an important role as traditional members of the landowning upper class.

The basis of tribal military power had always been its ability to mobilize
horse cavalry, historically the most important arm of any Iranian army. Most
of the tribal peoples in Iran were nomads who maintained a horse-raising
tradition as part of their pastoral economy. Although, with the introduction
of cannons, but more especially rifles, the predominance of the horse cavalry declined, it still remained important. And while cannons gave the state
army an advantage, rifles gave strength to tribal people because they were so
compatible with the strengths of existing tribal organization.

A tribal military had a low maintenance cost. Tribal warriors could be
expected to provide their own horses, supplies, and guns and to maintain them
at their own expense when not in use. They were not paid except when they
were on campaign. By contrast, even when they were not in use, government
troops had to be paid regularly by the state, garrisoned or transported to where
they were needed, and supplied with training and weapons. The tendency of
the weak Qajar government was to economize by letting the military slide,
and to turn a blind eye to the peculation of officers and government officials
who found it advantageous to pocket the money for themselves. This was particularly true in provincial areas where troops and police were at the end of

the central government's pipeline and were often no match for local tribal confederations.

The troops of a nomadic tribal confederation, however, were ordinarily no match for well-organized state armies. It was not that the tribes were so much outgunned (although this would be the case in the twentieth century) as out-organized. A properly led modern army might be defeated, occasionally, but could repeatedly return to pacify a region if the central government had the political will. Under Reza Shah the state's military power was increased, and he destroyed the foundation of tribal power. This was made easier because so many of the powerful tribal confederations in Iran were nomadic. Simply by placing troops at strategic points, the Iranian government could block their migrations and destroy their economic base, which Reza Shah did in his policy of forced settlement of nomads. By contrast, non-nomadic tribes in the region retained more ability to resist state control because they were less vulnerable to such indirect strategies.

New nonmilitary factors also altered the balance of power between tribes and state. Tribal people had historically been able to preserve their local autonomy because they lived in mountain, desert, or steppe regions that were difficult to control and expensive to occupy. However, the development of new transportation technologies, including railroads and then paved motor roads, reduced the effective distance between the tribes and state power. This allowed direct state power to be more easily projected into regions that it had not previously penetrated, particularly in regions where there was oil-related development. The government no longer needed to use tribal leaders as intermediaries between the tribes and themselves, which was the main function served by tribal confederations. Reza Shah was therefore effective in removing tribal leaders from power and taking direct control of the provinces. Later, his son, Mohammad Reza, continued his policies of more directly controlling the tribes by giving military officers the authority to supervise nomadic migrations and declaring that all pastureland was state property and not a tribal patrimony.[19] When the revolution of 1978 broke out, urban Iran dominated it. The tribal groups found themselves unable to take advantage of the fall of the Pahlavis to regain their former autonomy and influence.

The military pacification of tribal groups had been temporarily successful under the later Safavids, but what made this change permanent in the twentieth century was the integration of tribal peoples more closely into the national political and economic structure. With the rise of the oil economy, even the formerly important role they played in the economy became more marginal. For example, as late as the 1950s animal products constituted one-third of Iran's non-oil domestic production and a similar fraction of its exports, and at least half of this was produced by migratory peoples.[20] Tribal peoples also became more insignificant demographically as Iran's overall population grew. In the early nineteenth century they made up more than a third of Iran's population, but their significance declined as the sedentary population greatly expanded while tribal population remained static (about two million).[21] With a population greater than 60 million at the end of the twentieth century (almost 60 percent of whom are urban), tribal peoples today now constitute just one of many interest groups in Iran, and a small one at that. As in earlier periods of centralized rule, the tribes that have retained the most autonomy entering the twenty-first century are those groups residing on the margins of Iran rather than those encapsulated within it. These include the Baluch in the southeast, who still have a transborder strategic reserve area and a great supply of modern weapons diverted from Afghanistan. Similarly, the Kurds, who have armed co-ethnics in Iraq and Turkey, have been able to manipulate their frontier position, although to a much lesser extent.

However, as we have seen, it would be a mistake to project the relative weakness of today's tribal populations into Iran's past. In terms of a political legacy and cultural patrimony derived over the course of the whole millennium, it could be said that the modern nation of Iran itself was the by-product of the struggles between successive dynasties and tribal confederations within and outside of Iran. In particular, the symbiotic relationship between Turkish and Persian elites throughout this period was striking in all Iranian central governments through the beginning of the twentieth century. Though Iran may now have transcended these roots as it enters a new millennium, the roots are still clearly there.

NOTES

1. Thomas J. Barfield, "Tribe and State Relations: The Inner Asian Perspective," in *Tribes and State Formation in the Middle East*, ed. Philip Khoury and Joseph Kostiner (Berkeley: University of California Press, 1991), 153–85.

2. Ibn Khaldun, *The Muqaddimah: An Introduction to History* [abridged edition], trans. Franz Rosenthal (Princeton: Princeton University Press, 1967), 120–21.

3. Charles Lindholm, "Kinship Structure and Political Authority: The Middle East and Central Asia," *Comparative Studies in Society and History* 28 (1986): 334–55.

4. Ibn Khaldun, *Muqaddimah*, 120–121.

5. William Irons, "Political Stratification among Pastoral Nomads," in *Pastoral Production and Society*, ed. L'Equipe écologie et anthropologie des sociétés pastorales (Cambridge: Cambridge University Press, 1971), 362.

6. Thomas J. Barfield, *The Nomadic Alternative* (Englewood Cliffs, NJ: Prentice-Hall, 1993), 17.

7. Robert Canfield, ed., *Turko-Persia in Historical Perspective* (Cambridge: Cambridge University Press, 1991).

8. Thomas J. Barfield, *The Perilous Frontier* (Oxford: Blackwell, 1989).

9. C. E. Bosworth, "The Political and Dynastic History of the Iranian World (AD 1000–1217)," in *The Cambridge History of Iran: The Seljuq and Mongol Period*, ed. J. A. Boyle (Cambridge: Cambridge University Press, 1968), 5:20–21.

10. I. P. Petrushevsky, "The Socio-economic Condition of Iran under the Il-Khans," in *The Cambridge History of Iran: The Seljuq and Mongol Period*, ed. J. A. Boyle (Cambridge: Cambridge University Press, 1968), 5:494.

11. Sa`di, *The Gulistan*, trans. Edward Rehatsek (London: Allen & Unwin, 1964), 95.

12. Nizam al-Mulk, *The Book of Government; or, Rules for Kings: The Siyasat-nama or Siyar al-muluk*, trans. Hubert Darke (New Haven: Yale University Press, 1960).

13. Important articles about women in Iranian societies ruled by dynasties of Turko-Mongol origin are in *Women in the Medieval Islamic World*, ed. Gavin R. G. Hambly (New York: St. Martin's Press, 1998), especially Priscilla P. Soucek, "Timurid Women: A Cultural Perspective," Maria Szuppe, "The 'Jewels of Wonder': Learned Ladies and Princess Politicians in the Provinces of Early Safavid Iran," and Kathryn Babayan, "The 'Aqa'id al-Nisa': A Glimpse at Safavid Women in Local Isfahani Culture."

14. Laurence Lockhart, "The Persian army in the Safavid period," *Der Islam* 39 (1959): 89–98.

15. John Perry, "Forced Migration in Iran during the 17th and 18th Centuries," *Iranian Studies* 8 (1975): 199–215.

16. There are now a number of specific studies on nomadic confederations in Iran: Gene Garthwaite, *Khans and Shahs: A Documentary Analysis of the Bakhtiari in Iran* (Cambridge: Cambridge University Press, 1983); Lois Beck, *The Qashqa'i of Iran* (New Haven: Yale University Press, 1986); Richard Tapper, *Frontier Nomads of Iran: A History of the Shahsevan* (Cambridge: Cambridge University Press, 1997).

17. Beck, *The Qashqa'i of Iran*, 163.

18. William Irons, "Nomadism as Political Adaptation: The Case of the Yomut Turkmen," *American Ethnologist* 1 (1974): 635–58.

19. Fredrik Barth, *Nomads of South Persia* (Boston: Little, Brown, 1961).

20. Thomas R. Stauffer, "The Economics of Nomadism in Iran," *Middle East Journal* 19 (1965): 284–302.

21. Charles Issawi, *The Economic History of Iran: 1800–1914* (Chicago: University of Chicago Press, 1971), 20.

Part II

The Safavid, Qajar, and Pahlavi Periods

4 / The Early Safavids and Their Cultural Interactions with Surrounding States

ABOLALA SOUDAVAR

This study briefly surveys the interaction of the nascent Safavid state with its three immediate neighbors, the Ottomans of Anatolia, the Uzbeks of Transoxiana, and the Mughals of India. Through a discussion of diplomatic correspondence and exchanges of gifts and paintings, the cultural savvy of the Safavids is juxtaposed with that of their neighbors in order to show that, in a world strongly affected by a common Persian cultural heritage, the Safavids enjoyed a psychological advantage beyond military might and political clout.

In the year 1500, Isma`il the Safavid (r. 1501–24)—barely twelve years old—set out to conquer the world. Conquer he did, not the whole world but a sizeable empire that stretched from the shores of the Oxus River to the Persian Gulf, Mesopotamia, and Anatolia. Scion of the Sufi sheikhs of Ardabil and venerated by his followers as a demigod, he drove his troops from one victory to another, preaching a militant brand of Shi`ism that lauded the Imam Ali and his eleven descendants to a degree that almost eclipsed the Prophet himself.

As a symbol of their veneration for the Twelve Imams, the Safavid militants adopted a twelve-sided baton cut of red scarlet and planted it into their turbaned headgear. They thus became known as Qizilbash ("redhead" in Turkish).[1] Since Ali, the Prophet Muhammad's cousin and son-in-law, was only the fourth successor to the Prophet, the first three, Abu Bakr, Umar, and Uthman, were branded as usurpers. Cursing their names (*sabb* and *la`nat*) became the rallying cry of the Qizilbash. Daily processions through the cities' most populated areas, such as the bazaars, were conducted by Qizilbash provocateurs, called the *tabarra`iyan*, who vilified the name of the three "usurpers" and chanted defamatory slogans.[2] Slogans, rather than theological arguments, were meant to establish the righteousness of Shi`ism over Sunnism. Lauding the House of Ali was meant to bring added legitimacy to the Safavids, who, through a forged genealogy, presented themselves as progeny of the seventh imam, Musa al-Kazem, and the standard-bearers of legitimate Islam.

These claims and slogans obviously did not sit well with Isma`il's Sunni neighbors, who, in turn posing as champions of "true [i.e., Sunni] Islam," denounced Isma`il's religious policies as "heretical." Even though the underlying reason for their actions was mostly political, they sought confrontation by invoking a duty to reestablish true Islam. As we shall see, depending on the relative strength of Isma`il's neighbors and how threatening his expansionist endeavors were viewed to be, the reaction to Safavid religious activities ranged from sympathetic to belligerent.

Of the three major neighbors, the Ottomans (r. 1281–1924) were the most powerful and launched a coordinated assault on all fronts: religious, commercial, and military. The Uzbeks, on the other hand, paid lip service to religious differences but emphasized their hereditary claim on Khorasan. Despite repeated inroads into Khorasan, they were unsuccessful at gaining a permanent foothold there and did not present a serious military threat. Finally, the Mughals of India, whose founder Babur (r. 1526–30) had sought military help from Isma`il and for a while even donned the Qizilbash headgear,[3] never challenged the Safavids on religious grounds.

Interestingly, Isma`il's successor Tahmasb (r. 1524–76) confronted the exact same relationship problems that his father had experienced, with each new protagonist continuing the policies of his predecessor. The relative military strength of the government remained the same, but what constituted a marked change with prior times was Tahmasb's exploitation of Persian culture within a world influenced by a strong Persian heritage. This forced his neighbors to admire with envy the new Safavid cultural ethos and gave Tahmasb a psychological advantage beyond military might and political clout. In what follows, we shall examine the relationship of the early Safavids with each of the three above-mentioned neighbors and the role of cultural diplomacy in that context.

ISMA`IL AND THE OTTOMANS

Isma`il's meteoric rise to power coincided with the reign of the aging Ottoman sultan Bayezid II (r. 1481–1512), son of Muhammad II, the conqueror of Constantinople. Their early relationship was conditioned by their respective ruling positions within the Islamic community: Bayezid was the paramount emperor of the Islamic lands engaged in holy war against "Christian infidels," and Isma`il was a ruler of unruly Turkmen tribesmen who was aspiring to forge a kingdom in Persian lands. The tone of their early correspondence clearly reflected this: Isma'il addressed Bayezid as the one who "through the authority conferred by God"[4] had become the "sultan of the Islamic sultans,"[5] and the elder monarch returned the compliment by calling his young rival "Shah Isma'il" and the one who "through the authority conferred by God" was now the "ruler of Persian lands and the Lord (*noyan*) of the lands of the Turks and Dailamites."[6]

But from Trebizond (Trabzon), where he was stationed, Bayezid's son Selim (the future Selim I, r. 1512–20) had a different perspective. He had experienced at first hand the popularity that Isma'il enjoyed amongst the Turkmen of Anatolia and understood their immense devotion to him. Finding his father too complacent towards Isma'il, and fearing a devastating blow from yet another eastern conqueror—as his ancestor Bayezid I had suffered at the hands of Timur a century ago[7]—he forced his father to abdicate and seized the throne by eliminating rival contenders with the help of the janissaries, the Ottoman elite troops. The change of power resulted in an immediate tone shift in political correspondence. Instead of "Shah Isma'il," the Safavid ruler was now addressed as "Amir (commander) Isma'il," the "Lord of the Land of Injustice" and the "joy of rascals and leader of rogues."[8]

Selim was obsessed with Isma'il, and as he prepared for war against him, the European campaigns were temporarily suspended. Since the eastern Anatolian provinces had been the most important source of Qizilbash manpower, Selim quickly moved to close the border in eastern Anatolia and block Isma'il's recruiting efforts in the region. By so doing, he also deprived the Safavids of an important source of revenue, namely, the taxation of commercial caravans that now avoided passage through Iran. Before marching eastward, he ordered the massacre of forty thousand Turkmen who might have been sympathetic toward their Qizilbash kinsmen. To arouse the religious zeal of his own troops, he obtained a religious edict (fatwa) which proclaimed that in God's eyes "the killing of each Iranian Shi'i was equivalent to seventy Christian infidels."[9]

Selim finally confronted Shah Isma'il in 1514 on the plain of Chaldiran, where the outnumbered Qizilbash troops were defeated by the devastating Ottoman artillery. Despite their victory, the Ottomans sustained heavy casualties. So weakened were their forces that, eight days after occupying the Safavid capital, Selim had to evacuate Tabriz and head back towards Anatolia.

Determined to eliminate Isma'il, Selim began preparations for a second campaign immediately after his return. Meanwhile, Isma'il tried to enlist the support of the Mamluk ruler of Egypt, Qansu al-Ghuri (r. 1501–16). Selim responded by attacking the Mamluks and annexing their possessions, including Mecca and Medina, to his empire. In one quick swoop, Selim had not only put an end to the 267-year-long reign of the Mamluks, but also added the prestigious title of Khadim al-Haramain al-Sharifain (Servitor of the two Holy Cities [of Mecca and Medina]) to his own long string of epithets.

While a certain sarcasm was previously embedded in Isma'il's correspondence with Selim,[10] his tone now turned conciliatory. The more conciliatory he became, the more adamant was Selim in his demand that his adversary should forgo "heretical" affiliations and adopt "true religion." To publicize his contempt for Isma'il's conciliatory proposals, Selim arrested his ambassadors. To put further pressure on him, he betrothed the Safavid monarch's captured wife, Tajlu Khanom, to one of his officers, claiming that previous marriages to Shi'is were null and void.[11]

Despite his setbacks, Isma'il behaved not as a vanquished man but as a cunning tactician who, through direct and indirect means, by alternating offers of concessions to Selim with parades exaggerating Qizilbash troop and artillery strength, attempted to dissuade the Ottomans from mounting a second attack. In the end, Isma'il's psychological warfare bore fruit and undermined the janissaries' willingness to undertake another eastern campaign. Selim's second campaign was aborted, and Isma'il obtained a much needed respite to consolidate his position.[12]

SAFAVID PRINCELY EDUCATION

In the person of Selim, Isma'il had found a formidable adversary who overpowered him not only militarily but also intellectually. Indeed, Isma'il's early wanderings, from incarceration in Fars to the hiding period in Gilan before his "emergence" in 1500, did not allow him to receive a proper princely education. One can detect in his diplomatic correspondence, despite the Persian scribes' tendency to the contrary, a liking for simplified and shortened prose replete with *luti* (street brotherhood) slogans.[13] He could compose poems in Turkish but lacked Persian literary sophistication. Selim, on the other hand, had a solid command of Persian that allowed him to be named among the Persian poets of his era.[14] In order to overcome his own educational shortcomings, Isma'il decided to activate the royal library-atelier of Tabriz and provide his sons with the best possible education.

Since the Mongol period, the curriculum (*farhang-e shahaneh*) of Turko-Mongol rulers of Iran required royalty both to be educated in Persian literature and to patronize the sumptuous reproduction of its major works.[15] The following dynasties, especially the Aq-qoyunlu (r. 1378–1508) and the Timurids of Iran (r. 1370–1506), had pushed the standards of princely education to new heights. Isma'il, being the grandson of Uzun Hasan Aq-qoyunlu (r. 1453–78), was fully aware of the *farhang-e shahaneh* requirements, and in the aftermath of the Chaldiran debacle, as consolidation of dynastic rule took precedence over conquest, princely appearance and activities had to be emphasized more than ever before. In this context, the production of a royal illustrated *Shah-nameh* manuscript was de rigueur.

As the conqueror of the Aq-qoyunlu capital of Tabriz and the Timurid capital of Herat, Isma`il had inherited an unparalleled crop of talented intellectuals, administrators, literary figures, and artists. Calligraphers and painters from Herat, under the leadership of the aging Behzad, joined the Tabriz atelier headed by the celebrated painter Soltan Mohammad to participate in an unprecedented project that reflected the grandiose visions of Isma`il: the most sumptuous and grandly illustrated manuscript perhaps ever made, the *Shah-nameh-ye shahi*.[16] The project was also meant to get Tahmasb interested in the fine arts. Tahmasb came to Tabriz in 1521, and, under the tutelage of Behzad and Soltan Mohammad, acquired painting skills that reputedly allowed him to teach and even rectify painters and their works later on. After the death of Isma`il in 1524, the *Shahnameh-ye shahi* project continued until its completion some ten or fifteen years later. The bulk of the manuscript thus reflects Tahmasb's taste, and its dedicatory *rosace* bears his name rather than Isma`il's.

Though Isma`il was a descendant of the Aq-qoyunlu, it was the Timurid standards of *farhang-e shahaneh* that he sought to establish for his sons. Hence, the Timurid epithet of *mirza* was adopted for Safavid princes, in lieu of *beg*, used for Turkmen princes. As a diminutive of *amir-zadeh* (son of commander), an epithet adopted by the Timurids in deference to the title *amir* used by their progenitor Timur, *mirza* sounded less noble than the traditional Persian word for prince, *shah-zadeh* (son of shah). But such was the erudition of Timurid princes that, by the end of the fifteenth century, the word *mirza* had become synonymous with "learned prince," and their capital city of Herat had become the uncontested cultural center of the Persian lands. Thus, Tahmasb and, after him, Sam Mirza were sent to Herat to act as governors of Khorasan and, at the same time, get acquainted with the sophisticated ways of that city. A particularly fashionable Herati exercise was the *mo`amma*, or the art of poetical riddles, the solving of which required the undoing of several layers of entangled meanings.[17] Following the Timurid model, the *farhang-e shahaneh* of Safavid princes included Persian literature, fine arts, and *mo`amma*. Thus, in a praising biographical note on his brother Bahram Mirza, Sam Mirza wrote that, "in the realm of calligraphy, especially *nasta`liq*, he was most famous and in the practice of drawing, poetry, and *mo`amma* he was unparalleled."[18] True to their *mirza* epithet, the Safavid princes who had acquired Herati sophistication maintained their own library-ateliers and used them to convey complex messages to each other through poetical manuscripts designed with multiple levels of meaning embedded in each illustration.[19]

The one exception among first-generation Safavid princes was Isma'il's second son, Alqas, who for unknown reasons was treated as an outcast in his father's time. When Tahmasb was summoned to Tabriz, Alqas was bypassed in favor of his younger brother, Sam Mirza, who replaced Tahmasb as nominal governor of Herat. According to the chronicler Qazi Ahmad Qommi, Alqas was deprived of education and remained semiliterate.[20] Yet it is this least educated of the Safavid princes who had the greatest cultural impact on the Ottoman court. When Alqas rebelled against his brother Tahmasb and defected to the Ottomans in 1547, he brought along a small retinue of administrators that included his scribe, Fathollah Arefi Shirazi. Arefi composed for the Ottoman Sultan Suleiman the Magnificent (r. 1520–66)—who, like his father Selim I, was well versed in Persian poetry—a multiple-volume versified history of the Ottoman dynasty, volume five of which was entitled *Solaiman-nameh*, or the *History of Suleiman*. It was composed in the same meter as Ferdausi's *Shahnameh* and established a genre emulated by subsequent poet laureates. He was succeeded in this task by another member of Alqas's retinue, his librarian, Aflatun Shirvani. The latter was in turn succeeded by Loqman Ormavi, who composed the *Selim-nameh* (also called *Shahnameh-ye Selim Khan*), an ode to Suleiman's successor, Selim II (r. 1566–74).[21]

The original royal manuscript of the *Solaiman-nameh* was copied in 1558 by Ali b. Amir Beg Shirvani, also a member of Alqas's retinue; this manuscript and the 1581 *Selim-nameh* (see fig. 1) both display a standard of calligraphy and illustration techniques much inferior to those of contemporary Safavid works.[22] It is a testimony to Safavid cultural achievements and Ottoman paucity in literary figures and arts-of-the-book artists that the small entourage of the fleeing, semiliterate Alqas became the instruments of his endearment to Suleiman, with much impact on Ottoman courtly art and literature.

ISMA'IL AND THE UZBEKS

In 1506, as Isma'il was conquering the Aq-qoyunlu empire, the Timurids of Herat were threatened by the Uzbek warlord Mohammad Khan Shibani, who had already captured Samarqand. As a descendant of Shiban, grandson of Changiz Khan, he had a hereditary claim on Khorasan and considered the Timurids as usurpers.[23] The last of the Timurid sultans, Soltan Hosain Baiqara, died en route to meet the Shibani khan, and the task of defending

Herat fell to his two sons, Badi' al-Zaman Mirza and Mozaffar Hosain Mirza, who were no match for the invading Uzbeks. They were swept away and Shibani Khan triumphantly entered Herat as a rightful ruler reclaiming lost territory. There were no reprisals against the Heratis and there was no deportation of artisans and artists.

With the conquest of Timurid territories, the Shibani khan was inevitably headed for confrontation with Isma'il. As with the Ottomans, the first skirmishes were diplomatic rather than military. The khan derogatorily addressed Isma'il as *darugheh* (the title of local commanders appointed by the Mongols in conquered territories) or *shaikh-oghlu* (son of *shaikh*), and chided him for his kingly pretensions "even though none of his forefathers was a king."[24] Isma'il responded that by this logic the first of the Iranian dynasties, the Pishdadians, should have never been supplanted, and that Changiz Khan was a usurper as well.[25] Isma'il then admonished him for not keeping his word by invading Iran en route to Mecca on pilgrimage. Isma'il prided himself on having accomplished his own pilgrimage to Mashhad, as vowed, even though the khan had vacated the city and was not there to greet him with full honors![26]

In 1509, Isma'il encircled the citadel of Marv, where Shibani Khan was awaiting Uzbek reinforcements. He lured him out of the citadel before the arrival of fresh troops and, after cornering him in a ruined caravanserai, massacred the entire garrison that accompanied him. The khan's body was retrieved from under a mound of corpses and beheaded. His scalp was sent to the Ottoman sultan Bayezid, his hand to another supporter, and his skull was made into a wine cup.

The death of Shibani Khan shattered all hopes for a unified command of the Uzbeks. They remained a loose federation of clans more content to join in plundering expeditions than to pursue hereditary territorial claims. Despite inflicting severe casualties upon Qizilbash troops in Ghojdovan in 1512, the Uzbeks avoided direct confrontation with Safavid troops and retreated to Transoxiana each time the Safavid monarch approached Khorasan. The Oxus became once again the de facto borderline between Iran and its northeastern Turkic neighbors.

ISMA'IL AND BABUR

As the Uzbeks pushed south and conquered Timurid domains in the early sixteenth century, a number of wandering Timurid princes, including Soltan Hosain's successor and eldest son, Badi' al-Zaman Mirza,[27] flocked into Safavid territory. Isma'il received them with full honor. Had the Timurids been the

Fig. 1. (above and opposite). Selim II receiving Tahmasb's envoys, c. 1581. Topkapi Saray Museum, no. A3595.

masters of Khorasan when Isma`il embarked on his eastern conquests, his attitude towards the Timurids would have been perhaps different. As it turned out, they had a common enemy in the person of the Shibani Khan. Thus, when the latter was killed, Isma`il and Badi` al-Zaman Mirza celebrated the demise of their common enemy by drinking wine out of a cup made from his skull.[28]

Another Timurid prince who had suffered defeat at the hands of Shibani Khan was Babur. He was a prince in search of a kingdom. In 1501 he had briefly occupied Samarqand but had been ousted by Shibani Khan, and now, with the demise of his enemy, he sought Isma`il's help to recover Samarqand.[29] Isma`il provided troops and Babur conquered Samarqand, but his victory was short-lived, as Isma`il's help came with strings attached: Babur had to wear the Qizilbash headgear and have the Friday sermon recited in the name of Isma`il according to Shi`i rites. Within three months, the Sunni population of Samarqand rebelled against him and he was evicted from the city. Babur again joined forces with the Safavids. Against a major Uzbek contingent trapped in Ghojdovan, the combined Qizilbash and Timurid forces were placed under the command of the Persian vizier Najm-e Sani, who could control neither of them. As the Uzbeks counterattacked and the Qizilbash fell into disarray, Babur decided to abandon the battle scene and head south with his forces. He conquered India shortly after the death of Isma`il. Isma`il I's initial relationship with the Mughal emperor Babur set the tone for the Safavid-Mughal relationship, which remained courteous and friendly despite the Mughals' adherence to Sunni Islam.

TAHMASB AND THE UZBEKS

Like most of his illustrious Turko-Mongol predecessors, Isma`il died at an early age of excessive alcohol consumption. He was succeeded by his ten-year-old son, Tahmasb. Tahmasb had barely reached adolescence when the traditional Uzbek inroads into Khorasan resumed. Led by Shibani Khan's nephew, Obaidollah Khan, the Uzbeks hoped for a quick victory against the young and inexperienced Tahmasb. They confronted the Qizilbash army near Jam, and Tahmasb emerged victorious. Wounded and narrowly escaping death, Obaidollah retreated to Transoxiana.

Tahmasb's victory in Jam had important consequences for the future of the Safavid state. Domestically, he gained the respect of Qizilbash commanders who had witnessed his patience, courage, decisiveness, and choice of strategy. Vis-à-vis the Uzbeks, he gained a confidence he never lost. But, most importantly, he understood the effectiveness of firepower against the Uzbeks, who lacked firearms. From then on he carefully husbanded his artillery for the eastern front and refused to waste it against the superior Ottoman forces on the western front.

As for the Uzbeks, the debacle in Jam revived the memory of the earlier defeat of Shibani Khan and reminded them that, far from their supply bases, they could not be effective against the better-equipped Safavid imperial troops. No matter how much Obaidollah emphasized their hereditary Changizid claim over Khorasan, his Uzbek peers did not welcome the prospect of a costly conquest.

At fourteen, Tahmasb had defeated the most respected leader of the Uzbeks, a prestigious descendant of Changiz Khan. His victory was not accidental, and subsequent events only confirmed Tahmasb's military abilities. In 1534, Tahmasb launched his first—and last—self-initiated campaign against the Uzbeks. The vanguard of the Qizilbash army was already marching towards Bukhara when news of an imminent Ottoman attack prompted Tahmasb to abort his campaign and head west.[30] For the next few years Tahmasb rushed from one frontier to the other, as Ottomans and Uzbeks alternated attacks. The Uzbeks never dared to confront Tahmasb himself, and, after each raid, evacuated Khorasan before his arrival.

Since Obaidollah refused military confrontation with Tahmasb, the latter launched a rhetorical campaign against him. Intellectually, the Uzbek khan was a man to be reckoned with. He was an accomplished poet, skilled calligrapher, talented musician, and renowned composer who had turned his capital, Bukhara, into a second Herat.[31] Nevertheless, Tahmasb's *farhang-e-shahaneh* provided him with enough ammunition to challenge Obaidollah on cultural grounds as well. In the ensuing war of words, mixing prose with poems of his own, he first derided Obaidollah for evading confrontation.

> When I left, you raised an army,
> and when I came back, you rapidly fled;
> If you wish to be a king, come to the battlefield,
> God shall determine whom among the two of us merits the throne[32]

Next, with a couplet borrowed from a poem written by Pir Budaq to his father, Jahanshah Qara-qoyunlu (r. 1438–67), he reminded Obaidollah of his own youthful good fortune and threatened to eradicate him from the world.

> Both my fortune and I are young:
> do not attempt to fight with two young ones[33]
> I shall so throw you up and down,
> That no sign shall remain from you or your name[34]

He also viciously attacked Obaidollah's physical features and weaknesses.

O impatient lowly *deaf* man
Beware of me and my good fortune
You are *deaf* and your fortune is blind
How can a *deaf* and blind one wield power
It is time to fight like a man
Let your sword be tainted red by blood, O *yellow-skinned* man
  [*i.e.*, Mongol] [my emphasis].[35]

But it was in fending off attacks against Safavid Shi`ism that Tahmasb proved to be most imaginative. As Obaidollah criticized Qizilbash "heretical" behavior, in particular their act of prostration before their spiritual leader, which he equated with idolatry, Tahmasb replied that even though prostration to worship a human being was a sin, prostration to honor a man was permitted, since the parents of the Prophet Joseph had similarly honored him (Quran XII:100).[36] And God had ordered all angels to prostrate themselves before Adam, but Satan, who refused to do so, was forever damned (Quran II:32).[37] He knew the Quran well, and time and again made effective use of it.

A NEW ROLE FOR THE LIBRARY-ATELIERS

The library-atelier of Tahmasb had surpassed in prestige those of the Aqqoyunlu and Timurids, but the library-atelier of the erudite Obaidollah, whose *farhang-e shahaneh* was no slighter than Tahmasb's, lacked competent artists. Shibani Khan had allowed the former Timurid artists to remain in Herat, and, as a result, most were inherited by the Safavids. It was only through laying siege on Herat and pressuring artisans and artists to leave for Bukhara that Obaidollah finally mustered a nucleus of respectable artists for his library-atelier. The two most important ones were Mir Ali, the uncontested *nasta`liq* master-calligrapher of his age, and Shaikhzadeh, a prolific painter and illuminator who single-handedly illustrated most of the Herati manuscripts of this period. The two had worked for the library-atelier of Sam Mirza and left Herat prior to its fall to the Uzbeks in 1529.[38] Their combined efforts lifted the Bukhara library-atelier of Obaidollah and his son, Abd al-Aziz, to unprecedented levels.

As the level of their respective library-ateliers rose, painting and manuscript illustration offered another sparring arena for the two opponents. When Tahmasb repented of past sins in 1534 and banned music and the consumption of alcohol from his realm, the continued drinking habits and musical activities of Obaidollah became a source of ridicule at the Safavid court. Tahmasb's close companion and chief painter, Aqa Mirak, drew an ink caricature of Obaidollah seated on a golden throne with a wine gourd resting on his arm, playing a musical instrument (fig. 2).[39] Its message was clear: how could Obaidollah pretend to be the champion of true Islam if he drank wine and played music?

TAHMASB AND THE OTTOMANS

Tahmasb's attitude toward the Uzbeks was in sharp contrast to his handling of the Ottomans. Towards the former he felt a psychological superiority that allowed him to remain scornful of their leaders. But in dealing with the Ottomans, Tahmasb gradually abandoned mockery in favor of cautious respect.

After the janissaries refused to follow Selim I in a second campaign against Isma`il, the Ottomans resumed their European campaigns. Selim's successor, Suleiman, was a relentless campaigner who in rapid succession conquered Belgrade, Rhodes, and Hungary and even laid siege to Vienna and Corfu. In between the European campaigns he undertook three major campaigns against Tahmasb. Nonetheless, unlike his father, Suleiman did not harbor a grudge against the Qizilbash. Even though he constantly demanded they abandon their insulting *sabb* and *la`nat* practice, annihilating them was not a priority. In fact, none of his eastern campaigns were launched on his own initiative; each time, he was lured into it by a Safavid renegade.[40]

Opting for a scorched-earth strategy, Tahmasb refused confrontation and harassed the enemy through guerilla warfare.[41] Ironically, Tahmasb's evasive tactics attracted the same rebuke from Suleiman as the one Tahmasb had formerly thrown at Obaidollah. As he recounts in his own diaries, Suleiman told him, "your father Shah Isma`il fought me. If you have any claim on bravery let us fight and, if you don't want to fight, stop pretending to be brave."[42] Tahmasb's justification for evading the Ottomans is testimony to his coolheaded response to provocation and subtle use of Quran-based rhetoric: "God has said: 'don't throw thyself unnecessarily into death when fighting the infidels' [quoting Quran II:195], and, if such an action is forbidden against infidels, how then can I justify fighting against a Muslim army ten times larger than mine?"[43] But Tahmasb was not content with justifications alone: every Ottoman attack had to be reciprocated with stinging rhetoric. He thus chided Suleiman for acting like a "veiled woman" when hiding behind a curtain of artillery, and challenged him to come out and fight like a man.[44]

Like his father, Tahmasb could also use *luti* rhetoric, especially in the phase

Fig. 2. Caricature of Obaidollah Khan, c. 1535. Art and History Trust, Arthur M. Sackler Gallery, Washington, D.C.

of correspondence when mutual belligerence was at its height. Whereas Bayezid I had qualified Isma`il as *siyadat entesab* (descendant of the Prophet), Suleiman blatantly attacked Tahmasb's forged genealogy by calling him *siyadat ektesab* (one who pretended to be a descendant of the Prophet). Tahmasb responded by asking how Suleiman dared question his lineage, "you whose forefathers are renowned to be idiots and of rotten seed through marriage with Anatolian [*rumi*] and Frankish [*i.e.,* Christian] slaves."[45] It is perhaps at this stage that Aqa Mirak painted another mocking caricature of a disheveled Suleiman in short pants, holding a dog, the very symbol of an "unclean" Christian foreigner in the eyes of the Muslims (see fig. 3).[46]

Worn down by an unwinnable war, the two enemies finally concluded the peace treaty of Amasia in 1555. The Safavid loss of territory was minimal, restricted to Baghdad and certain areas of eastern Anatolia. In return, Suleiman recognized Safavid sovereignty. With the initiation of the peace process, the correspondence between the two became courteous and even flowery, as on the occasion of the arrival of Suleiman's son, Prince Bayezid. Bayezid was chased by the combined forces of his father and his brother, Selim, and took refuge with Tahmasb after extracting a religiously binding oath that was supposed to block all paths to treachery.

It was a wonderful opportunity for Tahmasb to put pressure on Suleiman by refusing compliance with his extradition request. But, eager to preserve his peace with Suleiman, Tahmasb—by his own admission—found a way to renege on his promise: he had vowed not to deliver the prince to Suleiman and his men, but made no vow regarding Selim (the future Selim II)![47] The unfortunate prince and his sons were delivered to Selim's men, who beheaded them on the spot.[48]

Obaidollah died in 1540, and the 1555 treaty lifted the threat of Ottoman attacks. Possibly hampered by a hereditary ophthalmic disease that weakened his eyesight,[49] and free from the threat of belligerent neighbors, Tahmasb eased into semiretirement. In the post-1555 period he did not ride a horse and saw no need for a standing army; for the last fourteen years of his reign, he simply stopped paying his army.[50] As he lost confidence in his brothers and most valiant son, Isma`il (the future Isma`il II, r. 1576–78),[51] he increasingly hid behind female relatives, first his sister, Soltanom (d. 1562), and then his daughter, Pari Khan Khanom (d. 1578), neither of whom was allowed to marry.

Handicapped as he was, Tahmasb cherished the Ottoman truce and spared no effort to maintain it. Thus, when Selim II succeeded his father Suleiman, Tahmasb personally supervised the production of a congratulation letter to Selim 70 ells (*zar*) long. We have a first-hand account of Tahmasb's direct involvement in this project through one of the scribes, the young

Fig. 3. Caricature of Sultan Suleiman by Aqa Mirak, c. 1550. Courtesy J. Soustiel.

Qazi Ahmad Qommi: over a period of eight months, Persian administrators and members of the cultural elite recited prose and poetry to the monarch, who personally chose passages for inclusion in the letter.[52] Never in the history of Persian diplomatic correspondence had so much time and attention been devoted to a single letter.

In 1567, a Safavid delegation was sent to carry this letter. It was accompanied by 320 officials and 400 merchants, with gifts laden on thirty-four camels. An Ottoman list of the gifts, ranked in descending value, enumerated objects that included a jewel box holding a pear-sized ruby, two pearls weighing forty drams, a tent topped with gold, and twenty silk carpets. At the very top were listed two precious manuscripts: a Quran reputedly copied by the Imam Ali and the *Shahnameh-ye shahi,* the pride of Tahmasb's library.

The arrival of the Safavid delegation is described and illustrated in the royal manuscript of the *Selim-nameh,* copied in 1581 (fig. 1, see also the Appendix to this chapter). A row of attendants at the bottom carry the gifts sent by Tahmasb. First and foremost are the manuscripts. The one domain in which the Safavids had achieved absolute superiority was the art of the book. As Persian was still the dominant literary language of the Ottoman court, illustrated and illuminated Persian manuscripts were in high demand. Hence, a superior position was accorded to the Safavid manuscripts brought by the Persian delegation.

GIFT OF ILLUSTRATED MANUSCRIPTS

The gift of Tahmasb's own illustrated manuscripts set a precedent that successor Safavid rulers felt obliged to follow, especially after the accession of the Ottoman Sultan Murad III (r. 1574–95), who was a renowned bibliophile and avid collector.[53]

Tahmasb was succeeded by his son Isma'il II, whose long incarceration at the dungeon of Qahqaheh had allowed him to delve into poetry but deprived him of a library-atelier.[54] Upon ascending to the throne, he revived the royal Safavid library-atelier and commissioned the production of a new illustrated copy of the *Shahnameh.*[55] According to the contemporary chronicler Budaq Qazvini, he sent Murad III "fifty illustrated manuscripts copied by unrivaled master-calligraphers, not one of which could be found in the Ottoman sultan's library. Even though [his cousin] Ebrahim Mirza impertinently repeated that such manuscripts were irreplaceable and [the Ottomans] could not appreciate their value or their beauty, and that other items should be sent instead, [the shah] replied, 'I need peace and security, not books and manuscripts that I never read or see.'"[56]

The sudden death of Isma`il II, followed by the reign of his almost blind elder brother, Shah Mohammad Khodabandeh (r. 1578–88), tipped the balance of power in favor of the Ottomans. They invaded Tabriz and, despite several attempts by Shah Mohammad's valiant son Hamzeh Mirza to liberate it, remained in full control, and threatened to annex the Safavid sacred city of Ardabil. Hamzeh Mirza sued for peace and accepted the Ottoman condition of sending his infant son, Haidar Mirza, as hostage to the Porte, with the proviso that the Ottoman sultan would in turn—nominally—appoint him governor of Tabriz.[57]

The Safavid delegation accompanying the young prince was to present lavish gifts. Given Hamzeh Mirza's dire military position, no gift could be more effective than precious illuminated manuscripts that projected Safavid refinement in the highest sphere of kingly activities, namely, the patronage of the art of the book. Since previous gifts to the Ottomans had depleted the illustrated manuscripts of the Safavid royal library,[58] Hamzeh Mirza undertook the refurbishing of existing text manuscripts by adding illumination, illustration, and sumptuous lacquer bindings to them.[59] He was killed in 1586 before his infant son could leave for Istanbul.

The death of Hamzeh Mirza left the blind Shah Mohammad in a precarious position and prompted him to write the most apologetic letter that a Safavid ever addressed to the Porte. Blaming Isma`il II for the renewed Safavid-Ottoman hostilities,[60] he recognized Ottoman suzerainty over his domain and asked Murad III to bestow back on him the nonoccupied areas of Iran as a hereditary fiefdom (olka).[61] But he was soon deposed and replaced by his younger son, Abbas. Dealings with the Ottomans resumed the course agreed upon by Hamzeh Mirza: Haidar Mirza was to go to the Porte as promised. When the Safavid delegation finally set out for the Porte, magnificent manuscripts from Hamzeh Mirza's personal library-atelier were added to the gifts, to express regret for the delayed arrival of the young hostage prince.[62]

TAHMASB AND HUMAYUN

History repeated itself when, in 1544, Babur's son Humayun (r. 1530–56) came to the Safavid court seeking Tahmasb's help in recapturing his kingdom. It was a wonderful opportunity for Tahmasb to take advantage of this royal visit to score a diplomatic coup and pressure Humayun to act as a Shi`i, in the same way that his father had pushed Babur to don the Qizilbash headgear.

Humayun was received with great fanfare and Tahmasb issued specific orders to various princes and governors, spelling out in great detail the welcoming preparations that they each had to undertake.[63] Once Humayun was at his mercy, Tahmasb asked him to put on the Qizilbash headgear—also called *taj-e haidari* (Haidar's crown)—and to accept Shi`i affiliation. Humayun donned the *taj,* saying he was accepting it as a crown of honor, but refused to become a Shi`i. His refusal so angered Tahmasb that he threatened to execute him along with his retinue.[64]

Tahmasb's favorite sister, the princess Soltanom, interceded on behalf of the Mughals. The shah agreed to spare their lives and to provide troops against Humayun's treacherous brother, Kamran Mirza, who held Qandahar. Kamran Mirza was defeated and Qandahar was captured. It was to belong to the Safavids, but, under duress and fearing the approaching winter, Humayun ousted the Qizilbash contingent from Qandahar and proceeded to recapture his lost kingdom on his own.[65]

In the following decades, Qandahar repeatedly changed hands.[66] With each change of hand, the victor, whether Safavid or Mughal, presented a disarming excuse for his conquest and emphasized that such a "minor event" should not affect the solid foundation of their mutual friendship.[67] This façade of courteous relations between the two neighbors remained unscathed, except for a brief period during the reign of Shah Abbas II (r. 1642–66).

After the military successes of the Sunni conservative Aurangzib (r. 1658–1707) over his brother Murad Bakhsh, whom Abbas II had supported, the mood at the Safavid court turned against the Mughals. Belittling the Mughals became the order of the day, and, by royal command, the court painter Ali Qoli Baig Jebadar prepared a painting that depicted Babur kissing the hand of Isma`il I (fig. 4). Even though Babur had never met Isma`il in person, the painting referred to Babur's initial oath of allegiance towards the Safavids. By its shape, the painting seems to be the prototype of a mural painting such as the one in the audience hall of the Chehel Sotun palace in Isfahan, which depicts a previous royal encounter, Tahmasb receiving Humayun.[68] Perhaps it was intended to adorn another wall of the same hall.

THE MUGHALS AND PERSIAN CULTURE

The encounters of the first two Mughal emperors with the Safavids became symbols of a cordial relationship between the two neighboring empires that was emphasized over and over again in subsequent diplomatic correspondence. Yet, more than friendship, it is the cultural ties between the two that prevented the flaring of religious and political animosity as they each grew richer and stronger.

As a scion of the Timurids, Humayun's appreciation for works of art was immense. Fortuitously, his arrival coincided with Tahmasb's loss of vision and loss of interest in his own library-atelier. At Tahmasb's court, Humayun was dazzled by the masterpiece of the Safavid royal library-atelier, and offered a huge sum for the release of the aging painter Mir Mosavver, whom the shah had previously dismissed. Tahmasb responded by giving Humayun an illustrated manuscript prepared for his great grandfather, the Timurid Abu-Sa'id, with magnificent illuminated borders added by his chief painter, Aqa Mirak, that were supposed to emphasize Safavid artistic superiority over Timurid traditional painting.[69]

Humayun's largesse, on the one hand, and Tahmasb's disinterest in illustrated manuscripts, on the other, prompted the exodus of Safavid artists, including Mir Mosavver, to the Mughal court. Mir Mosavver's son, Mir Sayyed Ali, along with another migrating painter, Abd al-Samad, are credited with launching the Mughal school of painting.

CULTURAL EXCHANGES AND THEIR RAMIFICATIONS

The initial exodus to the Mughal court was followed by several waves of migrating artists, literary figures, administrators, and judges.[70] The constant flow of these men between the two courts maintained a climate of mutual respect and friendship that did not exist between the Safavids and their other neighbors. Rapid Turkicization on the part of the Ottomans probably diminished the appeal for Persian administrators of migration to the Porte. But, as the Mughals remained entrenched in their Persian cultural heritage, men of experience were increasingly imported to administer their expanding empire.

With or without migrating Persian administrators, the Safavids wielded enormous influence on their neighbors through the high standards their library-ateliers had achieved in calligraphy, illumination, and painting. Under the Timurids and the Aq-qoyunlu, a new style of script, *nasta'liq*, had been developed for Persian literature. Safavid calligraphers improved on it and *nasta'liq* conquered the administrative domain as well. Literary manuscripts, royal decrees, and governmental correspondence were all gradually penned in the new script. The sudden popularity and dominance of *nasta'liq* further consolidated Safavid supremacy in the arts of the book, but the flight of Mir Ali to the Uzbek court briefly positioned Bukhara as a new center for *nasta'liq* propagation that eventually much influenced the Mughal style of calligraphy.[71]

The loss of a master here and there, however, neither challenged the supremacy of the royal Safavid library-atelier nor created lasting competition for it. None of its neighbors disposed of the vast resources that production centers such as Shiraz offered.[72] Even when royal patronage was at its low-

Fig. 4. Babur kissing the hand of Esma(il I, c. 1665. Art and History Trust, Arthur M. Sackler Gallery, Washington, D.C.

est, Shiraz ateliers continued to produce impressive quantities of illustrated manuscripts that fed not only the Persian commercial markets, but also Indian and Ottoman export markets, where the possession of such items had become a symbol of prestige and social standing. In the process, talented artists were discovered and trained, many of whom subsequently joined the princely Safavid library-ateliers.

Without such a pool of talent to tap into, neighbors of the Safavids could not sustain a high-quality output in their library-ateliers. After each down-turn they had to await the arrival of a new Safavid defector to raise the level once again. The one exception was perhaps Mughal painting. When the Mughal ateliers shifted into a high-gear production mode to satisfy the aspirations of the energetic emperor Akbar (r. 1556–1605) for the illustration of a grand-scale *Hamzeh-nameh* with more than 1,400 full-page paintings, a vast number of local Indian painters were recruited to work under the supervision of the two aforementioned Persian masters, Mir Sayyed Ali and Abd al-Samad. The Timurid tradition of princely patronage, coupled with an abundant Indian workforce, assured continued excellence for Mughal royal painting.

Inevitably, the local painters exercised their influence and, despite the constant arrival of new waves of Persian artists, steered the Mughal style away from Persian miniature painting. The early Mughal style had followed the Persian canons of painting, especially in stylized portraiture (see, for instance, a portrait of Akbar's brother Muhammad Hakim Mirza in fig. 5). But, in time, Mughal painting adopted a naturalistic style of portraiture that valued exact likeness (fig. 6).[73] On the other hand, due to a lack of local tradition, Persian influence remained strong in Mughal calligraphy and illumination.

Unlike the Uzbeks and the Mughals, the Ottomans substituted Turkish for Persian in the administrative domain. It was not a drastic change. As Turkish lacked a long-standing administrative tradition, the initial switch of language was mainly achieved through a change of verbs; sentence structure and most other words read very much like Persian and/or Persianized Arabic. The switch of language limited further Persian influence. For the writing of decrees, for instance, the Ottomans rejected *nasta`liq* and transformed the traditional *ta`liq* script into their famous *divani* script. But when it came to creating ornate decrees, they had no choice but to apply Safavid illumination techniques and use Persian-trained illuminators.[74]

CONCLUSION

Shah Isma`il I's emphasis on the revival of the royal library-atelier and on the education of his sons in literature and fine arts not only brought prestige to the Safavids but provided a very effective means of diplomacy. Within a world dominated by a common Persian cultural heritage and in which Persian administrators, literary figures, and artists were in demand, neighboring royalties were eager to claim that they shared the same *farhang-e shahaneh* that the Safavids had inherited. Educated in the best of Herati traditions, Shah Tahmasb skillfully used cultural diplomacy to supplement his military initiatives by mixing vilifying rhetoric with bombastic praise and by sending lavish works of art to dazzle his adversaries. For lack of military strength, Tahmasb's successors had no choice but to continue his style of cultural diplomacy in order to project a hazy image of imperial dignity.

APPENDIX

The celebrated 1567 gift of Tahmasb to Selim II, the *Shahnameh-ye shahi* manuscript, remained in the Ottoman library until the early nineteenth century. Indeed, later flyleaves inserted opposite each illustration bear a synopsis of the related *Shahnameh* story, written in Turkish c. 1801 by the "Keeper of the Guns" of Selim III (r. 1789–1807), Muhammad Aref.[75] Unlike their illustrious sixteenth-century predecessors, the later Ottoman sultans could not read Persian; therefore, a Turkish translation was necessary to understand the relationship between text and illustration.

By the end of the nineteenth century, the manuscript was in the possession of Baron Edmond de Rothschild in Paris.[76] The intriguing question is, how did this manuscript come out of the Topkapi Palace Library in Istanbul?

Compounding the mystery is the fact that the *Shahnameh-ye shahi* was initially accompanied by a sumptuous copy of the Quran, reputedly copied by the Imam Ali (d. 661), that has also disappeared from Topkapi. That one important manuscript was stolen is perhaps conceivable, even though unlikely, given the hefty size of the *Shahnameh-ye shahi* (approx. 48 × 18 cm); but to think that two historically important manuscripts, so different in size and subject (and at different shelf locations), were both stolen from the usually impenetrable Topkapi Palace Library is unimaginable. The only plausible alternative is that the two were given back to Iran on the occasion of a peace treaty between the Ottomans and Qajar Iran in the nineteenth century.

Such a theory finds added support from a Quran manuscript recently sold on the London art market. It first appeared at Christies in London, where, after a private viewing, I suggested that the manuscript was undoubtedly the companion Quran to the *Shahnameh-ye shahi*.[77] It had a sixteenth-century Safavid binding, and at the same time had the crushed-mother-of-pearl-sprinkled *toghra* sign of the Topkapi Palace Library (fig. 7). Moreover, it was an extremely fine ninth-century Quran, with an added colophon-like *kufic* inscription inserted into the last two illuminated pages (fig. 8), reading "*katabahu Ali*" (copied by Ali). It was common practice throughout the ages in the Muslim world to attribute the provenance and/or penmanship of preciously old Quran manuscripts to the Imam Ali, his son Hasan, or the caliph Uthman. It is not clear whether Tahmasb or his librarians knew about the apocryphal nature of the colophon. But, if they knew about it, chances are that they relied on their less experienced Ottoman counterparts to accept the spurious attribution, for, in those days, the Ottoman market was constantly fed with fakes and semi-fakes of Iranian origin.[78]

More importantly, notations on the first page of the Quran (fig. 7) indicate that it was in Iran in 1863. We might then presume that, in a twist of fate, the two manuscripts were given back to Iran, most probably on the occasion of the treaty of Erzerum in 1824. This treaty came in the wake of successful military campaigns conducted by the valiant Qajar prince Mohammad Ali Mirza Daulatshah (1788–1821). He had started negotiations with the Ottomans,

Fig. 5. Portrait of Muhammad Hakim Mirza and a courtier (detail), 1584. Signed by Farrokh Beg. Kabul. Golestan Palace Library, Tehran, no. 1663, fol. 47.

Fig. 6. Seated nobleman, Mughal, 17th century. Art and History Trust, Arthur M. Sackler Gallery, Washington, D.C.

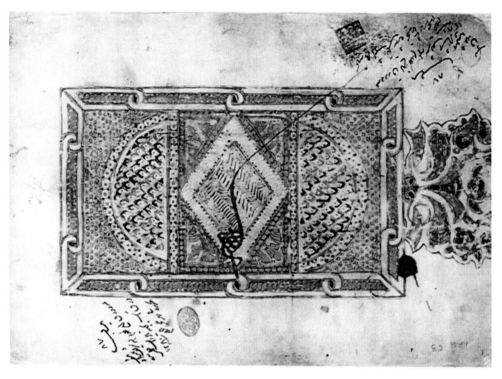

Fig. 7. *Illuminated page of the Koran offered by Tahmasb to Selim II, with Topkapi Saray Library toghra sign.*

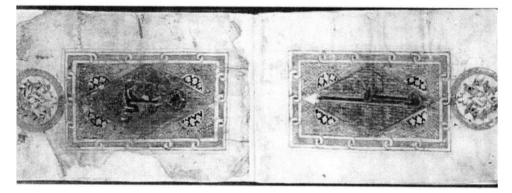

Fig. 8. *Colophon double page of the Koran offered by Tahmasb to Selim II, with added signature in the name of Ali.*

and, in correspondence with his brother and crown prince Abbas Mirza, he had highly praised the intellectual capacity of the military commander who was negotiating on behalf of the Ottoman sultan.[79] The basis for negotiations was the original 1555 treaty of Amasia, amended by subsequent treaties concluded with successive Safavid and Afsharid rulers. Facing military pressure in the field, the Ottomans found it an opportune time to buy goodwill. The learned and bibliophile Qajars were certainly able to appreciate the historical significance of the return of these two exceptional manuscripts, a return that was perhaps conceived and suggested by the knowledgeable Ottoman military commander so highly praised by Daulatshah. Reciprocating the magnanimous gesture of Tahmasb would also be a reminder of the long history of war and peace between the two nations. To this day, research into Qajar-Ottoman treaties has not revealed any direct reference to such a gift, except for the fact that the Erzerum treaty constantly refers to the Imam Ali and Shahnameh characters. One may hope that researchers with access to Iranian archives will one day find concrete evidence to this effect.

NOTES

1. Turkish was the common language of Safavid militants, who were mostly of Turkic stock.

2. For further information on the *tabarra`iyan* and their practices see Jean Calmard, "Les rituels shiites et le pouvoir. L'Imposition du shiisme safavide: eulogies et malédictions canoniques," in *Etudes safavides,* ed. Jean Calmard (Paris: Institut français de recherche en Iran, 1993), 115–17, 127–31.

3. Mirza-Haydar Dughlat, *Tarikh-i rashidi,* ed. Wheeler M. Thackston (Cambridge, MA: Harvard University Press, 1996), Persian vol., 208.

4. "Al-mu`ayyad min `ind-Allah."

5. Abdol Hosain Nava'i, *Shah Isma`il Safavi, majmu`eh-ye asnad va mokatebat-e tarikhi va yaddashtha-ye tafsili* (Tehran: Arghavan, 1368/1989), 55.

6. Nava'i, *Shah Isma`il,* 63.

7. Timur had defeated Bayezid I in 1403 and held him captive in a cage until he died. This ignominious defeat provided ammunition for a stinging rhetoric that Isma`il and, later on, his son Tahmasb used against the Ottomans. See Nava'i; *Shah Isma`il,* 168; and Abdol Hosain Nava'i, *Shah Tahmasb Safavi. Asnad va mokatebat-e tarikhi hamrah ba yaddashtha-ye tafsili* (Tehran: Arghavan, 1368/1989), 236.

8. "Malek-e khetteh-ye zolm o setam," "sorur-e shorur va sardar-e ashrar"; Nava'i, *Shah Isma`il,* 55.

9. Nava'i, *Shah Isma`il,* 145.

10. For instance, in one of his replies to Selim, Isma`il attributed the rough tone of Ottoman letters to the fact that they were written by addicted scribes in want of opium, and mockingly said that he was sending them back a boxful; Nava'i, *Shah Isma`il,* 168.

11. Jean-Louis Bacqué-Grammont, *Les Ottomans, les Safavides et leurs voisins. Contributions à l'histoire des relations internationales dans l'orient islamique de 1514 à 1524* (Istanbul: Nederlands historisch-archaeologisch instituut te Istanbul, 1987), 51–52 and 80.

12. Bacqué-Grammont, *Les Ottomans,* 233.

13. His letters constantly reiterate slogans such as "ya Ali madad" (Help me O Ali) and "har keh ba al-e Ali dar-oftad var-oftad" (whoever fought Ali's progeny passed away); Nava'i, *Shah Isma`il,* 71–72.

14. Sam Mirza, *Tohfeh-ye sami,* ed. V. Dastgerdi (Tehran: Forughi, 1352/1973), 19; Khorshah b. Qobad al-Hosaini, "Tarikh-e ilchi-ye nezam-shah-e dakkani" (London: British Library, ms. OR153), vol. 6, fol. 102b.

15. Abolala Soudavar, "The Saga of Abu-Sa`id Bahador Khan, The Abu-sa`id-namé," in *The Court of the Il-Khans, 1290–1340,* ed. Julian Raby and Teresa Fitzherbert (Oxford: Oxford University Press, 1996), 95 and 160; Abolala Soudavar, "The Grand Sedition and Abol-mozaffar Shah Tahmasb Safavi," *Iranshenasi* 9, no. 1 (Washington, DC, 1997): 68–69.

16. Also known in Western literature as the *Rothschild* or *Houghton Shahnameh.* See, for instance, Martin B. Dickson and Stuart C. Welch, *The Houghton Shahnameh* (Cambridge, MA: Harvard University Press, 1981).

17. Soudavar, "Grand Sedition," 68–70.

18. Sam Mirza, *Tohfeh-ye sami,* 9.

19. Soudavar, "Grand Sedition," 62–74.

20. Qazi Ahmad Qommi, *Kholasat al-tavarikh,* ed. Ehsan Eshraqi (Tehran: Tehran University Publications, 1359/1980), 556–57; Soudavar, "Grand Sedition," 72.

21. Cornell Fleischer, "Alqas Mirza," *Encyclopaedia Iranica* (London: Routledge & Kegan Paul, 1985), 1:908; J. M. Rogers, Filiz Çağman, and Zeren Tanindi, *The Topkapi Saray Museum, The Albums and Illustrated Manuscripts* (London: Thames and Hudson, 1986), 206–7.

22. Topkapi Saray Museum, H1517 and A3595. See, for instance, Rogers *et al., Topkapi Saray Museum,* 152–57.

23. The descendants of Changiz's first son, Jochi, had a hereditary claim on the territories west of the Oxus; Mohammad b. Ali Shabankareh'i, *Majma` al-ansab,* ed. M. H. Mohaddes (Tehran: Amir Kabir, 1363/1984), 290; Peter Jackson, "From Ulus to Khanate," in *The Mongol Empire and Its Legacy,* ed. Reuven Amitai-Preiss and David O. Morgan (Leiden: E. J. Brill, 1999), 28–29.

24. Nava'i, *Shah Isma`il,* 81.

25. Qazi Ahmad Tatavi, *Tarikh-e alfi* (Tehran: Fekr-e ruz, 1378/1999), 342–43.

26. Nava'i, *Shah Isma`il,* 87

27. Badi` al-Zaman Mirza became a resident of Tabriz but was forced to follow Selim I back to Istanbul after the latter's brief occupation of Tabriz in 1514.

28. Mirza Baig Hasan b. Hosaini Jonabadi, *Rauzat al-safaviyeh,* ed. Gholamreza Tabataba'i Majd (Tehran: Bonyad-e mauqufat-e doktor Mahmud Afshar, 1378/1999), 241.

29. Babur had first occupied Samarqand for a very short time in 1497.

30. According to Budaq Monshi Qazvini, "Javaher al-akhbar" (St. Petersburg Library, ms. Dorn 288, dated 1576), fol. 306a, Alqas Mirza had already marched for two days towards Transoxiana, accompanied by Hosain Khan Shamlu.

31. Dughlat, *Tarikh-i rashidi*, 234–35.

32. Qommi, *Kholasat al-tavarikh*, 226; Nava'i, *Shah Tahmasb*, 38.

33. Wheeler M. Thackston, *A Century of Princes: Sources on Timurid History and Art* (Cambridge, MA: Harvard and MIT, 1989), 46.

34. Qommi, *Kholasat al-tavarikh*, 227; Nava'i, *Shah Tahmasb*, 37.

35. Qommi, *Kholasat al-tavarikh*, 227.

36. Nava'i, *Shah Tahmasb*, 41. The verse in question is clearly talking about Joseph's "parents," yet the edited Persian text mentions the brothers of Joseph as the ones prostrating themselves before him. As Tahmasb cites the original Arabic verse in his letter, we can only presume that the inclusion of "brothers" instead of "parents" was due to scribal error, and therefore I took the liberty of correcting it. Interestingly, God and not Joseph is recognized as the subject of the parents' prostration in the Persian translation of this verse; Quran-e Karim, trans. M. Elahi Qomsheh'i (Tehran: Sazman-e chap va entesharat-e javidan, n.d.), 188. Such altered translation must be an attempt to solve a theological problem perceived by the translator: that human beings should not prostrate themselves before one another.

37. Nava'i, *Shah Tahmasb*, 41.

38. Soudavar, "Grand Sedition," 78.

39. For a color reproduction, see Abolala Soudavar, *Art of the Persian Courts* (New York: Rizzoli, 1992), 180–81.

40. The first campaign was instigated by the renegade governor of Tabriz, Olameh Takkalu, and the next two by Alqas.

41. In his memoirs, Tahmasb provided a simple reason for this approach: he estimated the Ottoman troops at 300,000, and "if each had one servant that number should be doubled, each has a mount, and as mount and man consume two *man* [approx. 3 kgs] of food per day it would amount to 15,000 hundred *man kharvar* [i.e., 1,500,000 *man*]. Even if they have brought along 500,000 or 600,000 camel-loads of food, it would only last for a month, and since we have burnt everything how can they survive?" While the Ottoman figures may be exaggerated and the calculation slightly inaccurate, the basic reasoning is sound; Shah Tahmasb, "Tazkereh" (British Library, ms. OR5880), fol. 52a.

42. Ibid., fol. 27a.

43. Ibid., fol. 27a and b. A rhetorical stance that backfired with the Ottomans was Tahmasb's viziers' reminding their Istanbul counterparts that their king had repented from past sins and abandoned wine drinking and other forbidden activities, as a true Muslim ruler should. The Ottoman viziers amusingly replied that monarchs were by definition sinless and above the law, and claimed to be outraged at the thought that Tahmasb could ever commit a sin that required repentance. These were deeds that the Persian viziers must have imagined; the Ottomans could not conceive of making such allegations against him. Navai'i, *Shah Tahmasb*, 242.

44. Ibid., 209. Throughout his letter, Tahmasb engaged in a tit-for-tat reply that countered every Ottoman attack with new rhetoric or insult, such as calling the Ottomans *Rumiyeh-ye shumiyeh* (forsaken Anatolians) in response to the mocking term *Qizilbash-e aubash* (lowly redheads) used in Suleiman's correspondence. In one passage alone, the string of insults thrown at Suleiman covered eight lines of text; ibid., 207.

45. Nava'i, *Shah Tahmasb*, 213. Tahmasb evidently had forgotten that his own

grandmother and great-grandmothers were Christians from the ruling Comnenos House of Trebizond (Trabzon). The word "slave" was perhaps used to create a distinction between his own ancestry and Suleiman's.

46. The portrait is problematic. As in the "Caricature of Obaidollah Khan," Aqa Mirak depicts the special ribbons knotted around the headgear, and the three feathers, designating royalty. The headgear, though, is neither Uzbek nor fully Ottoman. It may represent a version of the janissary headgear as imagined by Aqa Mirak. The mace is more Uzbek than Ottoman, but the shorts seem to designate a ruler at seaside.

47. Tahmasb, "Tazkereh," fol. 85b.

48. Suleiman offered 400,000 florins and his son Selim added another 100,000 florins to induce Tahmasb to deliver Bayezid, but the money was held in Erzerum and only sent after the execution of the unfortunate prince. In addition, Suleiman and Selim reportedly wrote a joint letter stating that, together with their progeny, they were obligated to uphold the right of the Safavids over their dominions and respect the tenets of the peace treaty that they had recently concluded; Sharaf Khan Bedlisi, *Sharafnameh,* ed. V. Véliaminof-Zernof, 2 vols. (St. Petersburg, 1860–62; repr. Tehran: Asatir, 1377/1998), 2:218–19.

49. Abolala Soudavar, "Between the Safavids and the Mughals: Art and Artists in Transition," *Iran* 37 (London: British Institute of Persian Studies, 1999): 51–52.

50. Hasan Baig Rumlu, *Ahsan al-tavarikh,* ed. Abdol Hosain Nava'i (Tehran: Haidari, 1357/1978), 635.

51. Bahram Mirza died of excessive alcohol consumption in 1549. Sam Mirza, Alqas Mirza, and Isma'il II were all incarcerated in the fortress of Qahqaheh.

52. Qommi, *Kholasat al-tavarikh,* 1:477–78. The final version of this letter was penned by Qazi Kuchak Moshref.

53. Filiz Çağman and Zeren Tanindi, "Remarks on some Manuscripts from the Topkapi Palace Treasury in the Context of Ottoman-Safavid Relations," *Muqarnas* 13 (1996): 132. For an overview of gift-giving in the Safavid period, see Rudi Matthee, "Gifts and Gift-giving in the Safavid Period," in *Encyclopaedia Iranica* (New York: Bibliotheca Persica Press, 2001), 10: 609–14.

54. He used the pen name Adel; see Jonabadi, *Rauzat,* 579.

55. Basil Robinson, "Isma'il II's Copy of the Shahnama," in *Iran* 14 (London: British Institute of Persian Studies, 1976): 1–8; Soudavar, *Art of the Persian Courts,* 250–54.

56. Budaq, "Javaher al-akhbar," fol. 134a.

57. Eskandar Baig, *Tarikh-e alam-ara-ye abbasi,* ed. Iraj Afshar, 2 vols. pag. as one, 2nd ed. (Tehran: Amir Kabir, 1350/1971), 1:344–46.

58. At least two other embassies, one sent by Tahmasb to Murad III in 1576, and the other sent by Shah Mohammad on the occasion of the much publicized circumcision festivities organized for Murad's son in 1582, are recorded as carrying manuscripts; see Çağman and Tanindi, "Remarks," 144–45; and Ivan Stchoukine, *La Peinture turque d'après les manuscrits illustrés, 1ère partie, de Sulayman 1er à Osman II, 1520–1622* (Paris: Librairie orientaliste Paul Geuthner, 1966), 30.

59. Abolala Soudavar, "The Age of Muhammadi," *Muqarnas* 17 (2000): 17–68.

60. Blaming Isma'il II for Ottoman animosity was unjustified, since he had officially banned the *sabb* and *la`nat* practice of the Qizilbash to alleviate tensions

between his own Shi`i and Sunni subjects, and to remove a major bone of contention in the Safavid-Ottoman relationship.

61. See Nava'i, *Shah Abbas*, 1:92. The letter that Nava'i produces is titled "letter of Shah Abbas to Sultan Murad." However, since the author of the letter refers to Hamzeh Mirza as "my son" and refers to his death as a recent event, it must have been written at a time that Shah Abbas had not claimed the throne and Shah Mohammad was still the nominal and acting ruler of Iran.

62. Soudavar, "Age of Muhammadi," 60.

63. Nava'i, *Shah Tahmasb*, 53–61.

64. Riazul Islam, *Indo-Persian Relations* (Tehran: Iranian Culture Foundation, 1970), 29.

65. Kamran's treasure was, however, left to the Qizilbash as agreed upon.

66. After the death of Humayun, Tahmasb wrested Qandahar out of Mughal hands in 1558. Akbar took it back in 1594 when the Safavid prince Rostam Mirza took refuge with the Mughals. Shah Abbas recaptured it in 1622. Shah Jahan got it back in 1638 when its Safavid governor, Ali Mardan Khan, switched sides, but lost it to Shah Abbas II in 1649. See Islam, *Indo-Persian Relations*, 49, 57, 82, 104, 113.

67. Ibid., 83 and 105.

68. Ronald W. Ferrier, ed., *The Arts of Persia* (New Haven: Yale University Press, 1989), 215.

69. Soudavar, "Between the Safavids and the Mughals," 49–50.

70. Some were political refugees fleeing harassment and persecution, and some were intellectuals attracted by the enlightened court of the Mughal emperor Akbar.

71. For Mughal royal albums built around Mir Ali's calligraphy, see M. C. Beach, *The Imperial Image: Paintings for the Mughal Court* (Washington, D.C.: Freer Gallery of Art, 1981), 156–91.

72. Sometime prior to 1576, Budaq Qazvini wrote, "There are in Shiraz many writers of *nasta`liq*, all copying one another, making it impossible to distinguish among their work. The women of Shiraz are scribes, and if illiterate, they copy as if they were drawing. The author [of these lines] visited Shiraz and ascertained for himself that in every house in this city, the wife is a copyist *(kateb)*, the husband a miniaturist (mosavver), the daughter an illuminator *(mozahheb)* and the son a binder *(mojalled)*. Thus, any kind of book can be produced within one family. Should anyone be desirous of procuring a thousand illuminated books, they could be produced in Shiraz within a year"; Budaq, "Javaher al-akhbar," fols. 109a–09b.

73. This new style eventually came back to Iran to influence Persian painting towards the end of Safavid rule; Soudavar, *Art of the Persian Courts*, 365–68.

74. See for instance A. Nadir, ed., *Imperial Ottoman Fermans* (London: Exhibition Catalogue, 1986), 46–67.

75. Dickson and Welch, *Houghton Shahnama*, 1:270.

76. Like so many other precious manuscripts given—or sold—to foreigners by the Qajar court, the *Shahnameh-ye shahi* found its way to the European market. Arthur Houghton Jr. bought it in the 1950s from the Rothschild estate and partially dispersed it during the 1970s and 1980s. In 1994, the remainder of the manuscript came into the possession of the government of Iran in exchange for a modern painting, "Woman III" by De Kooning.

77. Sale Catalog, *Islamic Art, Indian Miniatures, Rugs and Carpets* (London: Christies, 20 Oct. 1992), lot 232.

78. See, for instance, Abolala Soudavar, "The Concepts of 'Al-aqdamo asahh' and 'Yaqin-e sabeq,' and the Problem of Semi-fakes," *Studia Iranica* 28 (1999): 264–66; idem, "Forgeries; Introduction," in *Encyclopaedia Iranica* (New York: Bibliotheca Persica Press, 1999), 10:92.

79. Mirza Abol Qasem Qa'em Maqam Farahani, "A letter," in *Hezar sal nasr-e Parsi*, ed. K. Keshavarz (Tehran: Entesharat va amuzesh-e enqelab-e eslami, 1371/1992), 3:1217–18.

5 / Suspicion, Fear, and Admiration: Pre-Nineteenth-Century Iranian Views of the English and the Russians

RUDI MATTHEE

It is generally assumed that there is a linear, causal relationship between nineteenth-century British and Russian interference in Iran's affairs and the suspicions and resentment this bred among Iranians. An examination of both the nature of the operations of these two countries in Iran prior to the 1800s, and the ways in which these were interpreted by Iranians, yields a more complex picture. Before the rise of the Qajars, the Iranian treatment of the English was mostly courteous, combining customary hospitality and pragmatism. Until the mid-eighteenth century, when neighboring India came under British control, the Iranians exhibited less suspicion of English activities than admiration for their naval skills and political system. The Russians, by contrast, were already feared for their expansionism and held in contempt for their boorishness in Safavid times. Though this perception remained constant, the remarkable changes in eighteenth-century Russia did not go unnoticed in Iran, and by the late 1700s even Russian rule was seen by some as preferable to the tyranny of their own rulers.

"The English and the Russians are the only two nationalities at all generally known in Persia. . . ." C. E. Yate, *Khurasan and Sistan* (Edinburgh and London, 1900), 396–97.

I ran has long felt the impact of the outside world. Often overrun and conquered, the country has been ruled by foreigners for most of its recorded history. No period is as sensitive in this regard as the nineteenth century. Russia and Britain never formally colonized Iran, which made their political and economic meddling in the country's domestic affairs throughout the Qajar period as overpowering as it was elusive. Over time, their role, and especially that of Britain, became the stuff of myth, assuming proportions far beyond the historical record. A few conspiracy-oriented Iranian historians have projected outside interference much further back in time, exposing supposed machinations of the English East India Company in Safavid court affairs or portraying European missionaries, who lived and worked in Safavid Iran in great numbers, as a force furthering imperialist projects of their home countries.[1] Abdol Hadi Ha'eri wrote an entire book documenting the dark intentions and designs of the Western powers in Iran—which he contrasts to the benefits and marvels of Western civilization—and throughout his narrative wonders why Iranians in the premodern age rarely recognized the activities of the many foreign merchants, missionaries, and diplomats who visited and lived among them as brazen intrigues in the service of imperialism.[2]

Lacking a less reductionist exploration of the issue, one is left with the impression that Russia's aggression against Iran and Iran's fear of Russian expansionism date from the wars the two countries fought in the early nineteenth century, and that Iranians merely reacted to the British diplomatic and commercial overtures toward their country during the Napoleonic period. Cause and effect, moreover, are likely to remain linear as long as it is believed that outside meddling preceded and caused the widespread suspicion and resentment of foreign activities in Iran. Finally, the approach of Ha'eri and others like him, obsessed with the evil intentions of foreigners, leaves no room for the awe and admiration that were as much aspects of the tangled story of Iran's interaction with the West as suspicion and resentment. The reality, it will be argued, is more complex, involving a multifaceted relationship between action and perception that long precedes the Qajar period. Concentrating on the main players in the nineteenth and early twentieth century, England and Russia, both countries with which the Iranians have had relatively close contact since the late 1500s, this essay will test the idea that the image of *Rus-e manhus*, "ominous Russia," and *Englis-e por tadlis*, "perfidious England," appeared ex nihilo as a reaction to their machinations in the early nineteenth century. Some observations on the position of foreigners in pre–nineteenth-century Iran and the ways in which Iranians viewed and treated Westerners will precede the discussion.

WESTERNERS IN SAFAVID IRAN

In discussing the historical reception of foreigners in Iran, it is useful to begin by making a distinction between the ways they were treated as individuals and the views Iranians held of these same individuals and their motives, as well as those of the corporations or nations that they represented. Ha'eri and others are struck by and seem frustrated at how welcoming Iranians from the Safavid period on often were to the very same foreigners who, as they see it, were out to plunder their country and bring it under political and military control. What they overlook is that, for all the tolerance and hospitality shown to individual visitors from abroad, Iranian misgivings about their motives are nevertheless discernible, even if the Persian sources are little explicit about this. The Safavids, it seems, had no illusions about the ulterior motives of the Western merchants who took the time and trouble to visit their country. They suspected that these outsiders were driven by a desire for profit and fame, and, convinced as they were of Iran's wealth and the majesty of its ruler, believed that both were to be found in abundance in their country. European missionaries encountered opposition of a different kind. They aroused resentment from the Shi'i clergy as well as from members of Iran's local Armenian population, who resisted the missionaries' efforts to convert them to Roman Catholicism. Under Shah Abbas, this latter endeavor is said to have led royal advisors to insinuate that the missionaries were out to incite a revolt among the Armenians in case a European nation were to invade Iran.[3] Non-clerical foreigners also encountered resistance. Though little is known about its composition and activities, a xenophobic faction seems to have existed at the court.[4] Concrete fears, moreover, underlay the suspicions the Iranian elite harbored about the motives of West European nations that tried to enlist Iran's assistance against the Ottoman Empire. The Safavids were nervous about the Western powers because they believed that they might eventually turn on Iran. As they saw it, only the Ottoman Empire provided a defensive barrier against such aggression; hence, religious differences and the long-standing Safavid-Ottoman military conflict notwithstanding, the Iranians had no interest in a definitive victory of the Western powers over the Ottoman Empire.[5] Yet Iranians in this period were not just hospitable to foreigners, making them feel welcome and treating them with much courtesy, but allowed them to move about in relative freedom. The narratives of Western visitors to Safavid Iran reflect this. They are generally positive in their evaluation of the country and at times effusive about the treatment offered them. Some, speaking in comparative terms, commented on the striking freedom and tolerance enjoyed by Westerners (Franks) in Iran as opposed to other lands. Olearius, comparing Russia and Iran, noted how hemmed in he had felt in Russia and how in Iran he had more freedom of movement than the Iranians themselves.[6] Typically, they compared Iran favorably to the Ottoman Empire, hailing the safety of the country's roads and the refinement of its inhabitants and pointing out how these features contrasted with the situation in Ottoman territory.[7] The tolerance shown them by Iranians brought praise as well. One missionary who visited Iran during the reign of Shah Abbas I was astounded at the freedom enjoyed by Westerners in Iran, even those who, he said, misbehaved by getting drunk and by galloping their horses across city squares while hitting people. He insisted that the "Persians will allow Franks to do everything except forcing the harams of the elite, because the Shah so wills it."[8] Nor was this confined to Shah Abbas I. Another missionary at the end of the seventeenth century expressed a similar sentiment when he noted the remarkable privileges and powers enjoyed by foreign ambassadors, claiming that the boldness of some would not be accepted anywhere but in Iran.[9]

The question this raises is, what motivated Iranians in welcoming Westerners in such numbers? Part of the answer surely lies in the nature of the Safavid state and society. Safavid Iran was not a nation-state with firm social boundaries and an exclusionary approach to belonging and identity, but a society that, despite a clear majority religion and a sociopolitical hierarchy, knew and allowed a great deal of ethnic and religious heterogeneity. Its very diversity lent it a plasticity that permitted it to accommodate and subordinate those who did not "belong." Part of the answer also has to do with the perceived usefulness of outsiders. Shah Abbas received Western European envoys warmly, to the point of courting them, and permitted Christian missionaries to operate in his realm, because he saw them as representatives of nations that might join forces with him in his struggle against the Ottomans. A need for cash revenue and hopes of naval assistance prompted him and his successors to accord foreign merchants special status. Safavid rulers granted the East India Companies privileges in the expectation that their trade would fill the shah's coffers and with the understanding that their ships would be at his disposal to keep the waters of the Gulf safe from pirates. Pleas for naval support ultimately took the form of requests to assist the Iranians in building their own navy. The Safavid elite also took advantage of other facilities offered by the maritime companies, such as passage on their ships. Several Safavid envoys traveled abroad on the ships of the Dutch East India Company (VOC). In 1670, Shah Solaiman decreed that for reasons of safety no Iranian freight should be carried from the Persian Gulf ports on other than European vessels.[10] Five years later, the authorities in Bandar Abbas, dismayed at the high fees Iranian hajj pilgrims were forced to pay in Basra, asked the Dutch to transport at least 1,000 pilgrims on their ships to Mocha.[11]

At bottom, a fascinating paradox existed with regard to Westerners. As non-Muslims, they were officially considered unclean, *najes,* and many people reportedly shunned their company, refusing to eat with or touch them. Yet this did not prevent the Safavid elite from being intensely curious about European visitors, from engaging them in philosophical and religious debate, from admiring their skills and ingenuity. Iranians in the Safavid period seem to have regarded those who traveled with no discernible concrete purpose with suspicion. Yet the Safavid elite also adopted and emulated numerous things Western, artifacts and styles, selectively and generally in a superficial manner, but with great gusto.[12] Some Iranians admired European skills in the manufacture of arms, building fortresses, and the art of navigation.[13] The well-known scholar-cum-traveler Mohammad Ali Hazin Lahejani expresses this when, having arrived in Bandar Abbas with the intent of setting sail for Arabia, he says, "A company of Europeans residing in that port were on terms of the kindest and most friendly intimacy with me. As their ships and pack- ets are very spacious and are fitted up with convenient apartments, and their navigators are more expert on the sea and more skillful in their art than any other nation, I chose to go by a vessel of theirs."[14] Hazin, who lived and trav- eled in the waning days of the Safavid regime, and whose observations doc- ument a period when Iran suffered terrible misrule and became engulfed in political and economic chaos, offers us a glimpse of another sentiment as well, and one that was to be become loudly proclaimed in the nineteenth century. Lamenting the country's miserable state, he said

> in these times there is not to be found on the whole surface of the earth a chief who possesses the proper qualities for governing: on the con- trary at the present moment each of the soltans and chiefs and com- manders throughout the universe is . . . of meaner worth and more without rule than any or most of their subjects; except some of the rulers of the Frank kingdoms, who in the institutes and ways of life, and in the government and regulation of their states, are strong and constant. From them, however, by reason of their immense distance, little or no advantage is derived towards the condition of the people who inhabit the coasts and regions of other climes.[15]

THE ENGLISH

All the above observations apply to the English and their operations in Iran from the Safavid period onward. Agents of the British East India Company (EIC) arrived in the Persian Gulf in 1617, keen to establish a trading post in Iran and to set up trade in Iranian silk, and harboring hopes that they might compete in the overland trade through the Ottoman Empire. The Iranians from the outset were friendly and forthcoming, but the English never achieved the conditions of trade they hoped for, namely, the export of silk against imported merchandise such as broadcloth. The Safavid court, starved for cash, wanted ready money for its precious silk, and cash is what the EIC sorely lacked. Having lent assistance to Shah Abbas's project of ousting the Portuguese from Hormuz, the English after 1622 enjoyed a brief moment of favored status, manifested in an agreement whereby they were to receive half of the toll income from Bandar Abbas (Gombroon) in perpetuity. They failed to capitalize on this opportunity, mostly because of a lack of financial means but also because their imports did not include any commodity that the Iranians coveted (they offered nothing remotely similar to the Dutch with their valuable spices). The Iranians always found excuses to pay them less than the agreed-on sum in toll money.[16] As the memory of the naval assistance wore off, their prestige diminished accordingly. As important, the English soon lost their connection at court. Initially, they had a powerful friend in the person of Imam Qoli Khan, the vizier of Fars, but with his death in 1633 their access to those in power waned. From that time on, they were rebuffed in all attempts to get special commercial status, and continued to be tolerated in large measure because they provided a counterweight to the VOC and because their armed ships might be used as a deterrent against Omani Arab marauders in the Persian Gulf.

This, in addition to cultural norms and patterns reflected in the Persian court chronicle, makes it scarcely surprising that little of the English presence is reflected in Persian-language sources. The well-known Safavid historian Eskandar Monshi is rare in giving the English their due in his lengthy description of the combined English-Iranian assault on Portuguese-held Hormuz in 1622.[17] A Persian poem celebrating the same event barely acknowledges their presence and assistance in Shah Abbas's expulsion of the Portuguese.[18] The Safavids, it seems, saw the English as yet another group of outsiders who had come to Iran with the evident aim of becoming rich—at the expense of the country's gold and silver stock, which was siphoned off to India. As they did with other foreign nations in possession of shipping facilities, the Safavids frequently requested the use of their vessels to transport envoys or even soldiers, to convey merchandise, or to assist them in naval operations. In 1650, an Iranian envoy traveled to Golconda in southern India on board the English ship *Friendship*. A year later, Khalifeh Soltan, the Safavid grand vizier, requested that EIC agents carry Iranian silk and merchants to England via Surat.[19] In 1672, the governor of Bandar Abbas asked the EIC agent to lend him a ship in order to transport two guns and some sixty soldiers to Gwadar on the Makran coast, to serve as reinforcements to the land army that had previously been sent to the area.[20] In 1685, Hosain Beg, the Safavid envoy to Siam, traveled from Bandar Abbas to Bombay on an English ship, accompanied by the returning Siamese ambassador.[21] And in 1702, the governor of

Bandar Abbas informed the English agent that Shah Soltan Hosain had ordered that any available EIC ship should be used to assist the Iranians in fighting the Arabs from Oman. As usual, the English refused to oblige, citing a lack of authority.[22]

The reality of the English position in the Persian Gulf and in Iran proper should suffice to dispel the anachronistic myth of English (British) interference in Iran's domestic affairs going back to Safavid times. It is impossible to trace meddling that far back, if meddling means trying to have appreciable influence on policy decisions, or (the usual implication) that a concerted and sinister policy directed and controlled from outside was behind such efforts. Time and again the East India Company directors admonished their agents in Iran to concentrate on business and not to get entangled in Safavid politics. The reality was not that simple, for doing business inevitably entailed having to conduct negotiations with political authorities. That did not, however, translate into control and domination. Like everyone else, the English tried to influence the Safavid court to their own advantage, yet none of these outsiders at the time was remotely powerful enough to achieve lasting results. At bottom, no long-term objective other than commercial profit informed the operation of the English in Iran. Territorial claims remained limited to port cities and entrepôts, and aimed at securing trade rather than at a military presence in the interior. Iran's interior would in any case have been difficult to control. In India, cultural fragmentation and geographical proximity eventually gave the East India Companies access to areas of production, enabling the EIC to attract producers to its settlements and in the eighteenth century to establish a cloth monopoly in the south.[23] Iran, by contrast, was ruled by supremely self-confident regimes that would have prevented outsiders like the maritime companies from establishing territorial control, while in the 1700s it descended into the kind of chaos that made such control equally unfeasible. Many of the country's productive areas, moreover, lay outside the reach of the Europeans. This was especially true of the silk-producing regions, which were located far north, more than a thousand kilometers from the Persian Gulf ports. Frustrated at their annual failure to obtain their entire share of the toll revenue of Bandar Abbas, the company officials at Surat or Gombroon occasionally argued in their internal correspondence that force might be the only way to get the Iranians to comply.[24] Yet, realizing their limitations in terms of personnel and military strength, the board of directors in London never authorized the use of violence, fearing that "the charge and hazards of such an undertaking may be greater then can be foreseene at present."[25]

This picture outlived the Safavid dynasty, and the expectation of naval assistance continued to be a strong incentive for Iranian rulers to be cordial to the English. Like the Safavids before him, Nader Shah (r. 1732–47) realized that he would not be able to rule effectively in the Persian Gulf area without a navy. In 1734, he turned to the EIC and the VOC for assistance. Both companies perforce and reluctantly complied, facilitating the purchase of ships in Surat. The first operation of the Iranian navy–an attack on Basra in 1735–briefly created a hostile climate between the Iranians and the English, as the Ottomans forced the English to defend the port with their ships. Since Nader Shah continued to depend on the EIC for naval assistance, however, this incident did little to mar long-term relations, and in 1735 he granted the EIC customs privileges.[26] It was also an Englishman, John Elton, who, following a career in the service of the Russian state, in the 1740s entered the service of Nader Shah and helped him organize a Caspian fleet.

Under Karim Khan Zand, relations were generally cordial as well. Impressed by their rising power in India and in need of naval assistance, Karim Khan, too, was keen to solicit British good will. He went further than any previous Iranian ruler by granting them the sole right to establish a factory at Bushehr in 1763, though it is an exaggeration to say, as Ha'eri does, that by so doing Karim Khan gave up Iranian sovereignty.[27] The concessions were mitigated by clauses designed to protect Iranian interests, such as a prohibition of assistance to enemies of Iran, and obligations to pay fair prices for Iranian merchandise and not to export all their proceeds in specie but rather to take commodities as part of payment for their goods. The British also negotiated with Karim Khan to give him needed military assistance in exchange for his cooperation in their project of routing the Ka'b Arabs, and in that context they tried to secure the island of Kharq in the Gulf. They failed in all their objectives.[28]

Rather independent of the British crown until 1773, the EIC for the better part of the eighteenth century tended to its business interests in the Persian Gulf, but deemed these less important than its operations in India. In India, the English in the late 1600s turned to violence, albeit reluctantly and initially against the wishes of the directors at home. Yet, here, too, the excuse for mobilizing military power was the defense of business interests. The riches of the subcontinent and the huge anticipated profits these would yield made it worthwhile to do so, and a crumbling central authority made the task relatively easy. In Iran, the commercial stakes were never high enough to risk the hostility of whichever power held sway over all or part of the country. Territorial conquest, never before seriously part of English thinking in Iran, was contemplated in 1750 in the form of a suggestion to relocate the agency to either Bahrain or Qeshm, in order to evade possible Iranian retaliation. The

Bombay directors soon gave up on the idea, however, for fear that it would anger the Iranians and thus endanger business.[29] Whereas the English assumed increasing political control in India, they chose not to advance any territorial claims on Iran. Confronted with the presence of various petty Arab states on Iran's southern littoral and a chaotic political situation on the mainland, they failed to establish a hegemonic position even in the Persian Gulf, let alone in Iran. To argue otherwise is to conflate seventeenth-century English commercial activities in the Persian Gulf basin with the eighteenth-century British territorial penetration and administrative takeover of India, a takeover accompanied by an invasion of what Bernard Cohn calls an epistemological space.[30] By amassing a body of knowledge of India, its languages, its judicial system, its religious traditions, the British "tamed" the country, making it ready for inclusion in their vision of history and imperial domination. Nothing like this happened in Iran before the nineteenth century, and even then Iran's continuing formal independence prevented the British from replicating the Indian example. To portray the EIC as imperialist, implying domination and hegemony,[31] therefore is to apply a false label.

Only in 1773, with the Regulating Act, did the English Parliament and government establish a certain control over the EIC, which included the appointment of a governor-general. Paradoxically, however, this measure, rather than bringing the Persian Gulf and Iran within the purview of a state desirous to extend its territory, caused the British to focus on India, deemed far more important. Trade in the Persian Gulf diminished in volume and profitability, to the point where in 1777 the British would have given up on it altogether were it not for fear that Karim Khan might not let them leave.[32] It was only the rise of Napoleon and his Asian ambitions centering on India, combined with Russia's aggression against Iran from 1805, which revived British interest in the Persian Gulf. Changing geopolitical conditions now added a political and territorial dimension to existing commercial interests.

THE RUSSIANS

Given the little information on early relations between Iran and Russia available in the Western scholarly literature, one could be forgiven for thinking that a keen Iranian awareness of Russia only began with the reign of Tsar Peter the Great (1689–1725).[33] Similarly, it is often assumed that Iran's fears of Russia, its military might, and the threat it posed to Iran's territorial integrity date from the turn of the nineteenth century, when the two countries fought a series of wars that led to Russia's annexation of large pieces of Iranian land. Yet a close look at the sources preceding the rise of the Qajar dynasty reveals that Iranians had a long-standing and mostly adversarial relationship with Russia that, on the Iranian side, combined contempt for the perceived barbarism of Russians with intense suspicion of their motives and objectives. This goes back to the first encounter between the two in the Caucasus during the reign of Shah Tahmasb I in Iran and Tsar Ivan IV in Russia, and to their fierce struggle over influence and control in the Caucasus that broke out shortly thereafter. Russia's association with Gog and Magog, the two tribes against whose attacks Alexander the Great is said to have built a barrier and who figure in the collective Muslim mind as part of the story of the end of time, did not help the Iranian image of Russia as an aggressive power. A constant fear of the Iranians—one that would persist over the next two centuries— was the building of fortifications as part of Russia's expansionism. Russia had built its first fortress in the northern Caucasus in the 1560s.[34] Iranian fear of a creeping Russian influence among the peoples of the Caucasus, facilitated by the Christianity of some of them, and of a military union between Russia and Georgia directed against Iran, began with Shah Abbas, who expended diplomatic and military effort trying to halt Russia's encroachment on his northwestern flank. It continued under his successors, whose fear that the principalities would side with Russia and seek its protection proved justified more than once.

Despite these tensions, the attention paid to Russia and its inhabitants in the premodern Persian-language sources barely exceeds that reserved for the English. Shah Abbas alone sent some fifteen missions to Moscow between 1589 and 1617, and the Russians reciprocated with at least ten embassies between 1590 and 1626. Only a few of these contacts are mentioned in the main Safavid histories, such as the *Tarikh-e alam-ara-ye abbasi.* More puzzling are the sparse references in the Persian sources to Peter the Great's aggression against Iranian territory in 1720, when Russian troops invaded and occupied the northern provinces of Talesh, Gilan, and Mazandaran. Defeat and occupation did not fit the mold of the court chronicle, a genre designed to extol the glorious exploits of the ruler and especially his conquests. The embarrassment of having been invaded by a non-Muslim neighbor may account for some of the reticence of the official chroniclers. Another factor may have been the existence of an anti-Afghan alliance between the Russians and Shah Tahmasb II, a son of Shah Soltan Husain who had escaped Isfahan during the Afghan siege to take refuge in the north in an attempt to salvage Safavid rule. Finally, the Russian invasion of the Caspian littoral was only a sideshow to the tumultuous events that were shaking the central parts of the country at the time. Hazin, who hailed from Gilan, is typical in being not just sparing but rather neutral in his reference to Russian aggression. In describing the invasion he limits himself to stating, "At the same time the generals who were sent with a swarm of troops by the Emperor of the Russians, landing from the sea, made themselves masters of most of the considerable towns of Gilan." Of the ensuing occupation he only says, "A large body of the Russian army was stationed in the town of Astara, and had built there a fort."[35] The authors of the *Zobdat al-tavarikh* and the *Majma` al-tavarikh,* respectively, are scarcely more informative. The former narrates the Afghan invasion and its culmination, the siege and sack of Isfahan, in considerable detail, but omits any reference to the Russian invasion and the plight of the Caspian provinces in the same period.[36] The latter offers a brief and factual description of the Russian invasion and then refers the reader to the account of the same events in the *Tarikh-e naderi,* before returning to his narrative of the Afghan onslaught on Iran.[37] The *Tarikh-e jahangosha-ye naderi* does provide a fuller description of Peter the Great's attack on Iran. Yet here, too, the narrative stands out for its factual and almost impartial tone. Astarabadi, the author, relates the events that led to the cession of the areas between Niazabad and Astarabad in exchange for Russian protection against Iran's enemies. He notes how the Iranian envoy Isma`il Beg had gone to Moscow to ask for Russian assistance on behalf of Tahmasb Mirza, the son of Shah Soltan Hosain, who had proclaimed himself shah in Qazvin, and how the Russians justified their march on Iran by referring to the fact that they had been invited by the Iranians.[38] Astarabadi also recounts the battle between Iranian and Russian forces that took place in 1723 near Rasht, and frankly tells his readers that the outcome was a defeat for the Qizilbash troops.[39]

The rather factual tone of the indigenous sources cannot conceal the negative feelings that Iranians harbored for the Russians. Russia shared this fate with Portugal, the other Western country with a history of aggression and violation of Iranian territorial integrity (excluding the short-lived Dutch occupation of the fortress of Qeshm in 1684).[40] As for the Russians, they were not just seen as dangerous, but also as uncouth and primitive, and their embassies were regularly treated with contempt. Examples occur throughout the seventeenth century. All must be put in context and in every case a specific cause can be adduced for anger and resentment: existing disagreements, a previous affront, a perceived breach of protocol by the Russians, or a sense that the gifts carried by an envoy were an insult to a Safavid monarch. Yet none of these justify or fully explain the poor treatment meted out to envoys and ambassadors, representatives who were supposed to be immune to prevailing sentiments. There is the mission originally led by Vasilei Vasil'evich Tiufiakin, sent to Iran in 1597, whose surviving members were treated in a rather uncivil manner by Shah Abbas.[41] In 1614, Russia, impoverished after more than a decade of civil strife and turmoil, sent Tikhanov to Iran. He also received an undiplomatic reception in Isfahan.[42] And Ivan Ivanovich Chicherin, the head of a delegation that visited Iran in 1618–20, was made to dismount and enter the *maidan* of Qazvin on foot, even while an Indian ambassador who was to be received in audience simultaneously was allowed to keep riding.[43]

The issue is not confined to diplomatic envoys. If Shah Abbas and his successors did not generally allow foreign merchants to be molested and made sure that they traveled throughout his realm in freedom and security,[44] this was not always true for those coming from Russia. The issue of Russian merchants' being obstructed, harassed, and taken captive is a running one in Russo-Iranian relations in Safavid times, and it is not always clear whether the shah, good intentions notwithstanding, was unable to prevent their oppression, or whether the central state applied less pressure on local officials to improve their behavior toward Russian traders than it did in the case of Western European merchants. Yusof Khan, the governor of Shamakhi in the 1610s, not only refused to grant legal protection to Russian merchants but actively oppressed them, taking a number of them captive.[45] Russian merchants returning to Astrakhan in 1619–20 complained about mistreatment and abuse in Ardabil and Gilan.[46] And one of the demands of the Lobanov-Rostovskii mission that in 1653 came to Isfahan to seek an improvement in the tense Russo-Iranian relations was the release of all Russian merchants detained in Iran.[47] Ambassador Artemii Volynskii, too, sought the release of Russian captives in Iran during his mission to Isfahan in 1716–17.[48] Cornelis de Bruyn, passing through Shamakhi in 1707, noted how the Iranians were ill-treating the Russian merchants in town.[49] One of Peter I's excuses for invading Iran, finally, was the harassment of Russian merchants in the Safavid realm.

All this shows that tensions between Russia and Iran were not confined to the reign of Shah Abbas I. Abbas's policy vis-à-vis the Russians was marked by ambivalence. He alternated attempts at deterrence and containment with pledges to lend financial support to the impoverished Russian state and an oft-repeated promise to join Moscow in a wider European anti-Ottoman league. This ambivalence gave way to intermittent, low-key relations under Shah Safi (r. 1629–42), and to outright hostility under Shah Abbas II (r. 1642–66). From 1648 to 1653, Iran and Russia came to blows over Georgia. In a replay of the events of a century earlier, this conflict was triggered by the building of a Russian garrison on the south bank of the river Terek—considered the Iranian side by Iran.[50] By this time the foreign sources suggest that, in the Iranian perception of Russians, loathing prevailed over fear and that the Russians' reputation for boorishness and filthiness earned them the nickname

"Uzbeks of Europe" in Iran. Several observers recount the affair of the Russian delegation that visited Isfahan in 1664, whose members were pulled from their horses and treated with contempt at the Safavid court. A few years later, relations between Iran and Russia became strained over the Sten'ka Razin rebellion in the lower Volga region. By taking the port of Astrakhan, Sten'ka Razin severely disrupted commercial traffic in the Caspian Sea region and along the Volga route, and his Cossacks staged several sea-borne irruptions into Gilan and Mazandaran. The Safavid court, it is said, harbored deep suspicions about the role of the Russian state in this unrest, believing that it had stirred up the revolt to suit its own expansionist aims. For its part, Russia resented the Safavid state for receiving a mission sent by Sten'ka Razin.[51] It is likely that the humiliating reception that awaited the next Russian envoy to Iran, ambassador Feodor Voznictsyn, who visited Isfahan in 1672, was directly related to this mutual animus. Voznictsyn was forced to approach Shah Solaiman on his knees, and the Safavid monarch neglected to ask the obligatory question about the tsar's health at the outset of the audience.[52] Voznictsyn's successor, K. Khristoforov, who was in Iran in 1673, was similarly rebuffed by the Iranian authorities, who evidently did not want to accommodate the Russians in their desire to have Iran join an anti-Ottoman league and thereby jeopardize its own relations with the Ottomans. The next Russian envoy to fare poorly at the Safavid court was Vasilei Kuchukov, who in early 1698 arrived in Iran with the intent of becoming the Russian resident in the country. His violation of Safavid custom by insisting on handing his credentials personally to Shah Soltan Hosain, rather than to the grand vizier, was seen by Iranians as deliberate rudeness designed to cause a break in Russo-Iranian relations. He was thrown into prison, and upon release expelled from Iran.[53]

The reign of Tsar Peter furthered Iranian suspicions of Russian motives. In 1699, Peter sent a reconnaissance mission to the Caspian Sea area. Two years later the rumor spread that the Russian monarch had demanded the cession of Gilan, whose harbors would be suitable for the Russian navy and whose forests he wished to use for shipbuilding.[54] The most illuminating example of the mutual perceptions of Iranians and Russians in this period is the embassy of the aforementioned Artemii Petrovich Volynskii. The ostensible aim of his mission was to conclude a commercial treaty with Iran and to establish a transit trade between Russia and India via Iran, involving free trade for Russian merchants. He was also to raise the question of the violence and injustice done to Russian merchants in Iran. Behind this formal mandate lurked ulterior and secret motives. Volynskii was to gather intelligence on Iran's geographical, political, and economic conditions, its military strength, and especially the state of its fortresses. Throughout his stay in Iran Volynskii encountered obstacles, some of which had to do with the loss of central control during the continuing disintegration of the Safavid state, and some with Iranian attitudes and perceptions. How deep-rooted the Russian reputation of boorishness went is suggested by the fact that Volynskii was told to approach the khan of Shamakhi without shoes.[55] When he reached Isfahan, he was received with intense suspicion about the hidden motives of his mission. Suspicion turned to hostility when it transpired that the Russian mission of Alexander Bekovich-Cherkasskii, which in 1717 had been sent to Central Asia as an exploratory expedition, had constructed fortresses on the eastern shores of the Caspian Sea. Volynskii was also asked about the strength of the Russian Caspian Sea fleet, as rumors circulated that Russian ships had been spotted near the coast of Gilan.[56]

The post-Safavid period exhibits the same patterns. Little direct reporting of the opinion of Iranians regarding Russia and Russians has come to us from the period between the fall of the Safavids and the rise of the Qajars, and it cannot be proven that the antipathy carried over across the tumultuous eighteenth century. There is anecdotal evidence to suggest that fear, suspicion, and superciliousness remained alive, however, and that the issue of fortresses remained sensitive. Jonas Hanway, who traveled in Iran under Nader Shah, reported that the inhabitants of the southern Caspian shore "having been often plundered by the Ogurtjoy and Russian pirates" were "under great apprehension" when the ship on which he traveled dropped its anchor in the bay of Astarabad. Elsewhere, Hanway said of the Iranians, "Being ignorant of the vast improvements that are being made by their neighbours the Russians, they consider themselves in general as greatly superior to them," adding, in mitigation, "the truth is that they see very few but their unpolished merchants or ruder seamen."[57] In 1780, following the death of Karim Khan Zand, the Russians sent a flotilla to Astarabad with the aim of putting pressure on the local ruler, Agha Mohammad Khan Qajar, to cede the town of Ashraf to them as a trading post. Agha Mohammad Khan initially gave in, granting the Russians a different site, but changed his mind as he became suspicious of the military preparations the Russians were making. As George Forster, who in 1783 visited the area, tells it, a year earlier a Russian squadron had arrived in Ashraf in Mazandaran and had erected a large building near the Caspian shore "for the purpose of accommodating his crew, and probably lay the basis of some future plan." Agha Mohammad invited the commander and his men for the celebration of a religious holiday and proceeded to arrest them, expressing "much resentment at the conduct of the Russians, in having erected without permission, so large and solid a building in his country." He only released them after the Russians had demolished the building.[58] In a reminder of the aforementioned plight of Russian merchants in Iran,

Forster also asserts that "Russian traders, chiefly a low class of people, are exposed in all parts of the government of Aga Mahomed to severe oppression and insult."[59]

CHANGES IN PERCEPTION

The Iranian image of the British evolved in the late eighteenth century following more direct and intensified contact. India rather than Iran is where Iranians first became acquainted with British nationals other than merchants and the occasional envoy, and with aspects of British society in a quasi-English setting. In Shi`i Lucknow, especially, resident Iranians served the British, mingled with them, befriended them, and generally spoke highly of them. A good example is Abol Fath Mirza. A descendant of the Safavids who after many peregrinations wound up in Lucknow, where he received a stipend from the East India Company until his death in 1232/1816–17, he was effusive in his Anglophilia to the point of embarrassing his benefactors. An anonymous Iranian in his entourage offered Governor-General John Shore a copy of a book he had written, titled "The Victories of the Company" (*Fotuhat-e kompani*).[60] Much of the more realistic image Iranians began to form of the English at this time is to be found in the travelogues that were written at the turn of the nineteenth century. It is of interest that many of the early works on Britain and its people appearing in India were written by Iranians or by Indians of Iranian origin. Authors such as Mirza Abu Taleb Esfahani, Abd al-Latif Shushtari, Aqa Ahmad Behbahani, Gholam Hosain Khan Tabataba'i, and Mir Mohammad Hosain are generally positive in their description of the British as a people and, later, of England as a country, focusing on the efficiency, cleanliness, and orderliness of the society and its people.[61]

In Iran itself, things were slower to evolve. The governor of Shiraz, Sadeq Khan, a brother of Karim Khan Zand, questioned the Danish traveler Carsten Niebuhr about the intentions of the British in India, demonstrating both an awareness of their growing presence in the subcontinent and fear of what that presence might spell for Iran.[62] A similar incipient distrust of English motives and methods is conveyed in a conversation that supposedly took place between Karim Khan Zand himself and an English envoy, during which the ruler is presented as unmasking the true intentions of the English in wanting to trade with Iran. The envoy is most likely George Skipp, who visited Shiraz in 1767 as representative of the EIC and who was indeed badly treated by Karim Khan.[63] The narrator is Rostam al-Hokama, an early-nineteenth-century man of letters whose memoirs are an often amusing jumble of fact and fiction covering the period between the last Safavids and the early Qajars. "I know their real aim," Rostam al-Hokama has Karim Khan Zand say about the English: "with flattery and diplomatic niceties do they intend to become the masters of Iran, just as they have brought India under their control with ruse and lies and deceit."[64] Going back no further than 1779–80, Rostam al-Hokama's memoirs are not contemporary testimony for this encounter, and the lack of straightforwardness in much of his work puts the account's verisimilitude into doubt. Yet the spirit of the story is the same as that conveyed by Niebuhr about his conversation with Sadeq Khan. Also, Karim Khan reportedly rejected Skipp's presents, saying that he "had no need of European trade, because such trade had caused money to leave the country." The theme of Iran's self-sufficiency in this response has the ring of authenticity, being reminiscent of Safavid self-perceptions.[65] Hence, Rostam al-Hokama's anecdote should not be dismissed as an example of spite retroactively imputed to a ruler who, some of his acts suggest, may have been favorably inclined toward the English. It is plausible that Karim Khan Zand had ambivalent feelings about the English. Like the Safavids, he realized their usefulness, indeed their indispensability for his strategic designs, and he may have admired heir technical prowess, but that does not mean he had illusions about their motives. Ambivalence is detectable in Rostam al-Hokama's own portrayal of Westerners, including the English. Ha'eri cites Rostam al-Hokama as a rare example of an early-nineteenth-century Iranian who was aware of the duplicitous practices of the English in Asia. That may be true, but Rostam al-Hokama also expressed admiration for the English, crediting them with the virtues of order and justice, at least at home.[66] In an assessment that recalls Hazin's, Rostam al-Hokama declared that the rule and regency of the well-behaved European monarchies "is so strong and stable because their principles are linked to reason, wisdom and discernment. . . ."[67] He also ranks the English among the Western nations which thrived by virtue of laws, regulations, norms, and intelligent order. In these countries, he goes on, chaos, corruption, turmoil, and disorder never arise and their people live quietly.[68] This assessment is all the more poignant when juxtaposed to the same author's jeremiads about the decline of the Iran he knew, a country in which "there is no proper accounting practice and accountability, where good customs and desirable laws are not found, and which is always disturbed by tyranny and oppression on the part of the contumacious and always in a state of ruin because of the conflict of tyrants."[69] In a distich directed at the Qajar monarch, he brings the two together.

Ai padeshah   qanun-e rumi-ra bekhan
rasm-e farangi-ra bedan   Khademan va zanan va mollayan-e
                               molk-ra pishgar mibinam

Kaferan-ra zeh qist-e qavi   ghaleb va kamkar mibinam[70]

Oh ruler, read the law of the Westerners
and learn about the customs of the Franks
I see how the slaves and the women and the mullahs of the realm
    are servants
I see how the infidels are victorious and accomplished
By virtue of their strong justice

In the meantime, the image of Russia had also been somewhat modified. The most important catalyst for a change in perception was the reign of Tsar Peter I, followed by that of Catherine II (1762–96). Both were known as modernizers and as such were held up by some Iranian commentators as symbols of all that their country lacked. Mirza Mohammad, the *kalantar* of Fars under Karim Khan Zand, provides a good early example of the altered image Russia conjured up for Iranians in the mid to late eighteenth century. Lamenting that, at the time of his writing, Iran had become bereft of (real) men, he proclaimed that it would be good if, as in Russia, a woman of the stature of Catherine came to power in his country.[71] This is but one step removed from a sentiment already detected by Cornelis de Bruyn, who in 1707 had noted how not only the Russian merchants in Shamakhi but a number of the shah's own subjects in town as well would welcome a Russian occupation as a liberation from Safavid oppression.[72] Such feelings may have been widespread, and not just among the Christian population, though the source of oppression seems to have varied. Hanway claimed that, during Peter I's invasion of Iran, the "inhabitants of Baku earnestly desired the protection of the tsar against the insults of the Lezgees, who had vexed them with inroads for two years."[73] P. Chekalevskii, the Russian consul in Tabriz, alluded in 1754 to a similar desire on the part of the local Azerbaijani population to be relieved of the extortionate taxes imposed by Nader Shah and to be ruled by Russia rather than Iran.[74] James Fraser conveys a similar sentiment for the early Qajar period. Traveling in Iran's north in the 1830s— *after* the Russians had humiliated the Iranians by defeating their armies and annexing their land—Fraser noted how the inhabitants of those regions detested the Russians and feared their advance, but that they hated the Qajars and their tyranny so much that they would rather become Russian serfs than be ruled by the Qajars.[75]

It seems that, in its perception of Russia, Iran at the turn of the nineteenth century was like Japan, where fears about Russian expansion were "joined (though not replaced) by an intense admiration for Catherine the Great and her rule."[76] Iranians had come to see Russia as a country busy catching up with the West. Whatever its success in doing so, the associations it now evoked went far beyond those of the boorish and primitive land Iranians had previously assumed it to be. As a Qajar chronicler of the Russo-Iranian wars put it, Peter the Great had "brought the Russian people up from the level of animals to that of humans."[77] Mirza Shafiʿ, the vizier of Tehran, spoke in similar terms to Jaubert, the French envoy who in 1806 visited Iran on behalf of Napoleon. Lamenting the current state of Iran, he observed how far it had fallen behind Western nations. The Russians, he noted, "whom we used to despise because of the profound ignorance to which they had sunk, have now surpassed us in many respects."[78] The underlying apprehension remained, though, and for good reason. Many Iranians in the northern parts of the country may have wished they were subjects of the tsar rather than the shah, and Peter and Catherine may have appeared as modernizing rulers more than as aggressors, but what Iran received from Russia in the nineteenth century had little to do with Enlightenment and modernization and everything with violence and imperialism.[79] When war broke out and the Russians set out to occupy Georgia—in response to Agha Mohammad Khan's bloody sack of Tiflis in 1795—Qajar religious and political leaders were quick to condemn them in the fiercest of terms. The negative terminology employed in the various anti-Russian jihad tracts that appeared following the peace treaty of Golestan (1813) was in part ready-made, for, as non-Muslims, the Russians could be branded as infidels. But in reaction to Russia's aggression and the barbarous tactics its generals used in the Caucasus, they could also draw upon a reservoir of unflattering images and negative stereotypes that had built up over the centuries.[80]

CONCLUSION

It is generally assumed that British and Russian interference in Iran's domestic policies goes back to the early nineteenth century, and that a linear causal relationship exists between the involvement of these nations in the country's affairs and the suspicion and resentment this bred among Iranians. An inquiry into the nature of these two countries' operations in Iran prior to 1800, and the ways Iranians interpreted them, yields a more complex picture.

An amalgam of pragmatism, curiosity, admiration, and suspicion seems to have characterized the Safavid outlook on Westerners, their motives, and those of the nations they represented. Iranians had no illusions about the self-interest that motivated Europeans who visited their country, suspecting that even those who professed to be motivated solely by a love for travel pursued ulterior motives. Yet Europeans were generally well received in premodern Iran, appreciated for their usefulness as potential allies, and admired for the quality of their weaponry and the justice thought to characterize their political system.

The English are a case in point. They entered Iran in the early 1600s intent on the pursuit of trade, preferably trade with minimal political involvement. Joining the myriad outside groups operating in Safavid territory, they were treated courteously and allowed to operate on Iranian soil under conditions set by the court. As their ships were equipped with cannon, they proved useful in helping the Iranians oust the Portuguese from Hormuz in 1622, but their reluctance to engage in similar ventures later cost them much goodwill, and since they offered too little in the way of preferred commodities or hard cash, they could never claim privileged status. Despite the large amount of specie they (illegally) siphoned off to India, they continued to be tolerated because the gain the shah derived from their commercial activities and military strength was seen to exceed the value of these shipments. Still, their role in politics rarely went beyond that of petitioners, and the Iranians never saw them as more than one outside party among many competing for attention and favor.

The EIC operation had tremendous power behind it, though it did not directly operate under this power, at least not until the later eighteenth century, when it was mobilized, and then only in India. Around the mid-eighteenth century, as Iran was engulfed in chaos, the English more and more concentrated on India, which they deemed more profitable and easier to access. Karim Khan Zand's suspicions of British intentions show the concern the territorial penetration of India was beginning to raise in Iran. Such suspicions never turned into a realistic assessment of the momentous changes that were afoot, however. Iranians, convinced of their own uniqueness and superiority, seemed hardly aware of the changing world, represented by the foreigners operating among them, in which countries like Iran were about to be marginalized and ultimately absorbed into a Western-dominated hegemonic system. To suggest, as Ha'eri does, that they should have been aware of the sword of Damocles that was hanging over their heads reflects a modern nationalist agenda rather than a scholarly conclusion. What some Iranians did seem aware of was that England was governed differently from Iran, that English orderliness and accountability and the attendant justice and stability stood in stark contrast to the tyranny and oppression then experienced by Iranians. Iranian admiration for the ways of the Europeans in their own countries is detectable as early as the Safavid period, and makes up the bulk of early Indo-Iranian writing about the English. In the Qajar era, this theme would become a topos, albeit one that increasingly had to compete with a growing mistrust and suspicion of British behavior abroad.

The story of Russia's interaction with Iran before the Qajars is an altogether different one. It is difficult to generalize on the basis of isolated examples, especially if these span long periods of time. Yet one is struck by a pattern combining the contempt and fear in Iranian views of the Russians. As early as the Safavid period, Iranians looked down on Russians as uncouth and primitive. Their fear of Russian (in reality, often Cossack) raiding of the Caspian littoral, and the building of fortresses as frontier outposts designed to facilitate expansionism, dates from the same period. As Hanway explained, the contact Iranians tended to have with certain groups, mostly merchants and marines, neither of them known for their sophistication, must also have nurtured their sense of superiority over the Russians.

Yet here, too, sentiments were complex and rich in paradox. Hanway epitomizes this in his story of how his traveling companion, Hajji Mohammad Khan, faced with the presence of a Russian servant in the room where he stayed, made "some remarks on the unpolished manner of the Russians; adding, however, that under their government Gilan was rich, and that he believed the inhabitants would not think it bad if the Russians were again masters of that province."[81] The preference of some or many Iranians for living under Russian rule may go back to Peter's invasion, which brought relief from the extortionate governance of late-Safavid provincial authorities. Armenian inhabitants of Gilan, weary of forced conversion and curtailed in their business activities, in the dying days of Safavid rule fled to Russia in large numbers.[82] Probably many Muslims would also have preferred to be governed by infidels if they behaved better than their own rulers. Such sentiments may explain the absence of anti-Russian invective in the accounts of Hazin and others. It says something about both the extent of misrule suffered by Iranians during much of the period discussed, and the ambivalence they felt toward foreigners, that even Russia, the epitome of cultural barrenness and expansionist aggressiveness, could be admired. As early as the eighteenth century, Iranians would begin to put the real blame for their misfortune at the doorstep of their own rulers, and gamble that foreign intervention might provide relief, even if they probably had little faith in the ultimate benefits of such intervention.

NOTES

1. See, for example, Khan Malik Sasani, *Dast-e penhan-e siyasat-e Englis dar Iran* (Tehran, n.d. [1952]), 1, who opens his book by stating that "Since the Iran of Nader

Shah, with a population of 100 million [sic], frightened the East India Company, the English government came up with a specific and detailed plan to divide the country." See also Abol Qasem Serri, preface to Willem Floor, ed., *Ashraf Afghan bar tahtgah-e Esfahan* (Tehran: Entesharat-e tus, 1367/1988), iv–xi; and Abdul-Hadi Hairi, "Reflections on the Shi`i Responses to Missionary Thought and Activities in the Safavid Period," in *Etudes safavides,* ed. Jean Calmard (Tehran-Paris: Institut français de recherche en Iran, 1993), 151–64.

2. Abdol Hadi Ha'eri, *Nakhostin ruyaru'iha-ye andishehgaran-e Iran ba do ruya-ye tamaddon-e burzvhazi-ye gharb* (Tehran: Amir Kabir, 1367/1988). For the Iranian penchant to engage in conspiracy thinking with regard to outside interaction with their country, see Ahmad Ashraf, "Conspiracy Theories," in *Encyclopaedia Iranica* (Costa Mesa, CA: Mazda, 1993), 6:138–47; and idem, "The Appeal of Conspiracy Theories to Persians," *Princeton Papers, Interdisciplinary Journal of Middle Eastern Studies* 5 (1996): 57–88.

3. See Arnulf Hartmann, O. S. A., "William of St. Augustine and His Time," *Augustiniana* 20 (1970): 222. This is probably related to a belief reported among Iran's Armenian population that their present state of misery would end through the appearance of a European monarch who would revive the ancient Armenian kingdom. See Aschot Johannissjan, *Israel Ory und die Armenische Befreiungsidee* (Munich: Müller & Sohn, 1913), 78.

4. H. Dunlop, ed., *Bronnen tot de geschiedenis der Oostindische Compagnie in Perzië 1611–1638* (The Hague: Martinus Nijhoff, 1930), 746–47, diary Jan Smidt.

5. N. Sanson, *Estat présent du royaume de Perse* (Paris: La veuve de Jacques Langlois, 1694), 140–04. See also Rudi Matthee, "Iran's Ottoman Diplomacy During the Reign of Shāh Sulaymān I (1077–1105/1666–1694)," in *Iran and Iranian Studies: Essays in Honor of Iraj Afshar,* ed. Kambiz Eslami (Princeton: Zagros Press, 1998), 148–77.

6. Adam Olearius, *Vermehrte newe Beschreibung der Muscowitischen und Persischen Reyse,* ed. Dieter Lohmeier (Schleswig, 1656; facs. reprint, Tübingen: Max Niemeyer Verlag, 1971), 136.

7. See, for example, John Cartwright, "Observations of Master John Cartwright in his voyage from Aleppo to Hispaan, and back again," in Samuel Purchas, *Hakluytus Posthumus or Purchas his Pilgrimes* (Glasgow: James MacLehose and Sons, 1905–07), 8:504–05; Pietro della Valle, *Viaggi di Pietro della Valle il pellegrino,* 2 vols. (Brighton: G. Gancia, 1843), 1:440, 612; Père M. Gaudereau, "Relation du voyage de M. Gaudereau," in Archives des Missions Etrangères, Paris, vol. 348, fol. 492. Even in 1734, following the destruction of the Afghan invasion, one Italian missionary compared Iran favorably to the Ottoman Empire. See Paola Orsatti, "Il Carmelitano Leandro di S. Cecilia viaggiatore in Oriente (1731–1751)," in *La conoscenza dell'Asia e dell'Africa in Italia nei secoli XVIII e XIX,* 2 vols. (Naples: Istituto universitario orientale, 1985), 2:516.

8. [H. Chick, ed.], *A Chronicle of the Carmelites in Persia and the Papal Mission of the XVIIth and XVIIIth Centuries,* 2 vols. (London: Spottiswood, 1939), 1:104.

9. [Bénigne Vachet], "Journal du voyage de Perse commencé au mois de décembre de l'année 1689," Bibliothèque Nationale, Paris, Mss. Fr. 24516, fols. 497–98. The privileges enjoyed by foreign envoys in premodern Iran indeed far exceeded those of emissaries in Europe. In Iran an envoy was lodged and fed and received a per diem state allowance known as *mehmandari,* from the moment he arrived in the country until he left Iranian soil.

10. Algemeen Rijksarchief (ARA), The Hague, VOC 1278, v/d Dusse, Gamron to Batavia, 16 May 1670, fol. 1809r.

11. ARA, VOC 1307, Bent, Gamron to Batavia, 12 Dec. 1675, fol. 638.

12. For this, see Rudi Matthee, "Between Aloofness and Fascination: Safavid Views of the West," *Iranian Studies* 31 (1998): 219–46.

13. See, for instance, Eskandar Beg Monshi, *Tarikh-e alam-ara-ye abbasi,* ed. Iraj Afshar, 2 vols. pag. as one, 2nd ed. (Tehran: Amir Kabir, 1350/1971), 982, who called the fort of Hormuz a rare example of Western skill (*karnameh-ye nadereh-ye Farangiyan*).

14. Mohammad Ali Hazin, *Tadhkirat al-ahwal,* trans. F. C. Belfour as *The Life of Shaikh Mohammed Ali Hazin* (London: J. Murray, 1830), 215 (p. 196 of the Persian text).

15. Ibid., 214 (195).

16. In 1657, for instance, the Iranians refused to pay the full amount, with the argument that the agreement had been made with the English king and that the English did not have a king at that point. See R. Ferrier, "British-Persian Relations in the 17th Century" (Ph.D. dissertation, Cambridge University, 1970), 99.

17. Monshi, *Tarikh-e alam-ara-ye abbasi,* 981–82.

18. The poem appears in Luigi Bonelli, "Il poemetto persiano jang nameh-ye Keshm," *Atti della Reale Accademia dei Lincei* 287, Rendiconti 6 (1890): 291–303; and in Maria Cristina Pudioli, "Qadri di Širāz e la 'guerra di Kešm,'" *Studi Orientali e Linguistici* 4 (1987–88): 66–95.

19. William Foster, ed., *The English Factories in India 1651–1654* (Oxford: At the Clarendon Press, 1915), 73, 55, 66.

20. India Office Records (IOR), London, G/40/2, Surat to Company, London, 12 Jan. 1672, fol. 78.

21. IOR G/36/109, Bombay to Surat, 28 July 1685, fol. 215.

22. IOR G/36/117, first section, Bruce, Gombroon to Bombay, 12 Dec. 1702, fol. 3.

23. For the various reasons why India was susceptible to colonial influence (in contrast to China), see Rhoads Murphey, *The Outsiders: The Western Experience in India and China* (Ann Arbor: University of Michigan Press, 1977), especially chs. 3–5.

24. See, for instance, IOR, G/36/85, Surat to Gombroon, 15 Feb. 1660, fol. 75; IOR, E/3/36, #4163, Swally to London, 17 Jan. 1676, unfol., where a strong case is made for war against Iran in order to force the Safavids to honor the toll agreement; and IOR E/3/42, #4820, Gombroon to Surat, 16 May 1682, where it is argued that only two ships would be needed to inspect all goods entering and leaving Bandar Abbas, and that it should be just as easy to lay a blockade around Bandar Abbas.

25. IOR, E/3/88, London to Persia, 11 March 1675, fol. 143.

26. Abdul Amir Amin, *British Interests in the Persian Gulf* (Leiden: E. J. Brill, 1967), 17–19.

27. Ha'eri, *Nakhostin ruyaru'iha,* 209.

28. Amin, *British Interests,* 74–75, 92ff.; and J. G. Lorrimer, *Gazetteer of the Persian Gulf, Oman, and Central Arabia* (Calcutta, 1915; repr. 1986), 4:1780–1801.

29. Amin, *British Interests,* 30–32.

30. Bernard S. Cohn, *Colonialism and Its Forms of Knowledge: The British in India* (Princeton: Princeton University Press, 1996), 53.

31. Ha'eri, *Nakhostin ruyaru'iha,* 193.

32. Amin, *British Interests,* 108–09, 115.

33. For this awareness, see Maryam Ekhtiar, "An Encounter with the Russian Czar: The Image of Peter the Great in Early Qajar Historical Writing," *Iranian Studies* 29 (1996): 57–70.

34. B. B. Piotrovskii, ed., *Istoriia narodov severnogo Kavkaza s drevneishikh vremen do kontsa XVIII v.* (Moscow: Nauka, 1988), 317.

35. Hazin, *Tadhkirat al-ahwal,* 135 (123–24) and 169–70 (157). For a similar tone, see Mohammad Ali b. Abi Taleb Hazin Laheji, *Rasa'el-e Hazin Laheji,* ed. Ali Aujabi *et al.* (Tehran: A'eneh-ye miras, 1367/1998), 196.

36. Mohammad Mohsen Mostaufi, *Zobdat al-tavarikh* (Tehran: Entesharat-e daneshgah-e Tehran, 1375/1996), 128–38.

37. Mirza Mohammad Khalil Mar`ashi Safavi, *Majma` al-tavarikh dar tarikh-e enqeraz-e safaviyeh va vaqa`eh-ye ba`d ta sal-e 1207 hejri qamari,* ed. Abbas Eqbal Ashtiyani (Tehran: Sana`i-Tahuri, 1362/1983), 74.

38. The inhabitants of cities such as Darband, Baku, and Rasht, as well as Tahmasb Mirza, had indeed invited the Russians to come assist them, but not so much against the Afghans, who were not much of a threat to northern Iran, as against the Lezgis, who had ravaged Shirvan in previous years. See Laurence Lockhart, *The Fall of the Safavi Dynasty and the Afghan Occupation of Persia* (Cambridge: Cambridge University Press, 1958), 186, 245.

39. Mirza Mahdi Khan Astarabadi, *Tarikh-e jahangosha-ye naderi* (Tehran: Donya-ye ketab, 1368/1989), 22–23.

40. See [Chick, ed.], *Chronicle,* 101–4.

41. See Molla Jalal al-Din Monajjem, *Tarikh-e abbasi ya ruznameh-ye Molla Jalal* (Tehran: Entesharat-e vahid, 1366/1987), 212; and P. P. Bushev, *Istoriia posol'stv i diplomaticheskikh otnoshenii russkogo i iranskogo gosudarst v 1586–1612 gg.* (Moscow: Nauka, 1976), 294–320.

42. P. P. Bushev, *Istoriia posol'stv i diplomaticheskikh otnoshenii russkogo i iranskogo gosudarstv v 1613–1621 gg.* (Moscow: Nauka, 1987), 49ff.

43. Della Valle, *Viaggi,* 1:832; 2:41.

44. [Chick, ed.], *Chronicle,* 104

45. P. P. Bushev, "Posol'stvo V. G. Korobina i A. Kuvshinova v Iran v 1621–1624 gg.," in *Iran. Ekonomika, istoriia, istoriografiia, literatura. Sbornik statei* (Moscow: Nauka, 1976), 149.

46. Bushev, *Istoriia posol'stv i diplomaticheskikh otnoshenii, 1613–1621,* 203–4.

47. E. S. Zevakin, "Konflikt Rossii s Persiei v serednie XVII stoletiia," *Azerbaidzhan v nachale XVIII veka* 8:4 (1929): 27.

48. P. P. Bushev, *Posol'stvo Artemiia Volynskogo v Iran v 1715–1718 gg.* (Moscow: Nauka, 1978), 58–59. In the chaotic period following the assassination of Nader Shah, we again hear of Russian merchants being molested and plundered in various parts of northern Iran. See Johann Jacob Lerch, "Nachricht von der zweiten Reise nach Persien welche der kaiserl. russische Collegienrath Herr D. Johann Jacob Lerch von 1745 bis 1747 gethan hat," *Magazin für die neue Historie und Geographie* 10 (Halle, 1776): 459.

This does not mean that Iranian merchants were never oppressed in Russia. For Russian harassment of Iranian merchants, see Bushev, *Istoriia posol'stv, 1613–21,* 139; and K. A. Antonova *et al.,* eds., *Russkie-Indiiskie otnosheniia v XVII veka. Sbornik dokumentov* (Moscow: Nauka, 1958), 178–79.

49. As cited in Lockhart, *Fall of the Safavi Dynasty,* 62.

50. Zevakin, "Konflikt Rossii s Persiei," 24–31.

51. A. G. Vorob'eva, "K voprosu o prebyvanii Stepana Razina v Azerbaidzhana i Persii," *Izvestia Akademia Nauk Azerbaidzhanskoi SSR. Seriia istorii filosofii i prava* 3 (1983), 35.

52. Vahan Baiburdian, *Naqsh-e Aramaneh-ye irani dar tejarat-e bain al-melali ta payan-e sadeh-ye 17 miladi*, trans. Idik Baghdasariyan (Girimanik) (Tehran, 1375/1996), 140–42.

53. [Chick, ed.], *Chronicle*, 1:489. See also Bushev, *Posol'stvo Artemiia Volynskogo*, 8; and Lockhart, *Fall of the Safavi Dynasty*, 61–62.

54. Johannissjan, *Israel Ory*, 118.

55. Bushev, *Posol'stvo Artemiia Volynskogo*, 23–24, 48, 59, 94–96. Much of this was no doubt related to cultural misunderstandings. Just as Kuchukov's insistence on handing his credentials personally to the shah violated Safavid but not Romanov protocol, so Volynskii followed a Russian custom but broke Safavid rules by wishing to be received in audience by the shah himself before having talks with any other court officials.

56. Bushev, *Posol'stvo Artemiia Volynskogo*, 58, 107–08.

57. Jonas Hanway, *An Historical Account of the British Trade over the Caspian Sea*, 4 vols. (London: Mr. Dodsley, 1753), 1:166, 122.

58. P. G. Butkov, *Materialy dlia novoi istorii Kavkaza, 1722–1803*, 3 vols. (St. Petersburg: Tip. Imp. Akademii Nauk, 1869), 2:84–99; and George Forster, *A Voyage from Bengal to England through the Northern Part of India, Kashmire, Afghanistan, and Persia, and into Russia, by the Caspian Sea*, 2 vols. (London, 1798; repr. New Delhi: Munshiram, 1997), 2:201.

59. Forster, *Voyage from Bengal*, 2:210.

60. Giorgo Rota, "Un sofi tra i nababbi. L'ultimo safavide a Lucknow," in *Ex libris Franco Coslovi*, ed. Daniela Bredi and Gianroberto Scarcia (Venice: Poligrafo, 1996), 353, citing Abol Hasan Qazvini, *Fava'ed al-safaviyeh*, ed. Maryam Ahmadi (Tehran, 1367/1988), 111. See also C. A. Bayly, *Empire and Information: Intelligence Gathering and Social Communication in India, 1780–1870.* (Cambridge: Cambridge University Press, 1996), 80.

61. For the first three, see Juan R. Cole, "Invisible Occidentalism: Eighteenth-Century Indo-Persian Constructions of the West," *Iranian Studies* 25 (1992): 3–16. The latter two are discussed in Gulfishan Khan, *Indian Muslim Perceptions of the West during the Eighteenth Century* (Karachi: Oxford University Press, 1998), 84–95.

62. Carsten Niebuhr, *Reisebeschreibungen nach Arabien und anderen umliegenden Ländern*, 2 vols. (Copenhagen: N. Möller, 1774–78), 2:104.

63. For the likelihood that Rostam al-Hokama's model was George Skipp's mission, see Ann Lambton, "Some New Trends in Islamic Political Thought in Late 18th and Early 19th-Century Persia," *Studia Islamica* 39 (1977): 95–128; and John Perry, *Karim Khan Zand. A History of Iran, 1747–1779* (Chicago: The University of Chicago Press, 1979), 261–62, 267.

64. Rostam Hashem Asef (Rostam al-Hokama), *Rostam al-tavarikh*, ed. Mohammad Moshiri, 2nd ed. (Tehran: Amir Kabir, 1352/1973), 383.

65. [Chick, ed.], *Chronicle*, 1:667–68. For the Safavid analogy, see Matthee, "Between Aloofness and Fascination."

66. Birgitt Hoffmann draws attention to this point in the preface to her transla-

tion of Rostam al-Hokama's work. See Birgitt Hoffman, *Persische Geschichte 1694–1835 erlebt, erinnert und erfunden. Das Rustam at-tawārīh in deutscher Bearbeitung,* 2 vols. (Berlin: Klaus Schwarz, 1986), 1:82.

67. Rostam Hashem Asef, *Rostam al-tavarikh,* 395.

68. Feraidun Adamiyat and Homa Nateq, *Afkar-e ejtemaʿi va siyasi va eqtesadi dar asar-e montasher nashodeh-ye dauran-e Qajar* (Tehran: Entesharat-e agah, 2536/1977), 55.

69. Rostam Hashem Asef, *Rostam al-tavarikh,* 395; trans. in Lambton, "Some New Trends," 107.

70. Adamiyat and Nateq, *Afkar-e ejtemaʿi,* 31.

71. Mirza Mohammad Kalantar-e Fars, *Ruznameh-ye Mirza Mohammad Kalantar-e Fars,* ed. Abbas Eqbal (Tehran: Tahuri, 1362/1983), 89.

72. As cited in Lockhart, *Fall of the Safavi Dynasty,* 62. Among those were certainly many Armenians who saw Tsar Peter as the European monarch who would liberate them. See Aldo Ferrari, "Gli Armeni e la spedizione persiana di Pietro il Grande (1722–23)," *Annali di Ca' Foscari* 35, no. 3 (1996): 181–98.

73. Hanway, *Account,* 3: 156.

74. T. Mamedova, *Russkie konsuly ob Azerbaidzhane 20-60-e gody XVIII veka* (Baku: Elm, 1989), 87.

75. James Baillie Fraser, *A Winter's Journey from Constantinople to Tehran with Travels through Various Parts of Persia,* 2 vols. (London: Hard Bentley, 1838), 1:404–05. Of course, remarks like this fitted neatly into the world view of Soviet historians keen to justify Russian expansionism as liberation and eager to demonstrate that the inhabitants of northern Iran (and northeastern Turkey) had long been oriented toward Russia, and that their country had always been a haven for oppressed peoples, especially those suffering under Muslim rule.

76. Donald Keene, *The Japanese Discovery of Europe, 1720–1830* (Stanford: Stanford University Press, 1969), 57.

77. Mirza Mohammad Sadiq Vaqaʿeh-negar, *Ahang-e sorush. Tarikh-e jangha-ye Iran va Rus,* ed. Hosain Azar (Tehran, 1369/1990), 64.

78. P. Amédée Jaubert, *Voyage en Arménie et en Perse fait dans les années 1805 et 1806* (Paris: Pélicier/Nepveu, 1821), 224.

79. Ha'eri, *Nakhostin ruyaru'iha,* 375.

80. The mutual antipathy is unmistakable. Like Volynskii a century earlier, Russian commanders in the Caucasus were very outspoken in their opinion of Iranians as treacherous, savage, and inferior in civilization. See Muriel Atkin, *Russia and Iran 1780–1828* (Minneapolis: University of Minnesota Press, 1980), 73, 153–54.

81. Hanway, *Account,* 1:222.

82. Vazken S. Ghougassian, *The Emergence of the Armenian Diocese of New Julfa in the Seventeenth Century* (Atlanta: Scholars Press, 1998), 46.

6 / The Quest for the Secret of Strength in Iranian Nineteenth-Century Travel Literature: Rethinking Tradition in the *Safarnameh*

MONICA M. RINGER

Throughout the nineteenth century, Iranian travelers abroad sought the secret of European strength and the reasons for the growing power disparity between Iran and Europe. In the process of identifying elements of European civilization which were deemed "relevant" and worthy of adoption, travelers reevaluated their own traditions (political, religious, cultural) and grappled with the issue of achieving "progress" through reform. Could Iran modernize without at the same time Westernizing? Was there an alternate route to modernization? What about thorny issues of cultural authenticity? The resolution of these problems differed throughout the century and mirrored the changing nature of the discourse of modernization in Iran.

Mirza Saleh Shirazi, a student dispatched to London from 1815 to 1819, congratulated himself on his earnestness:

From five hours before midday when I woke up until ten in the morning I studied French. . . . After lunch I again studied and after that until two in the afternoon I read other French books. Afterwards I changed into English-style clothes and went to the home of my printing master, where I remained . . . until four-thirty in the afternoon. After this I ate dinner . . . returned home, read some Roman, Greek, Russian, Ottoman and Iranian history and some stories in English, and then translated a page from French to English.[1]

While Mirza Saleh Shirazi's industriousness was certainly exemplary, his experiences as a student in Europe, charged with learning "useful sciences and languages," were followed by those of some sixty-five students who, like him, were sent abroad at government expense throughout the nineteenth century. Indeed, it is the dispatch of students abroad, as part of Crown Prince Abbas Mirza's program of defensive military modernization—the *Nezam-e jadid*—that is often cited as the beginning of the process of modernization in Iran. More fundamentally, Mirza Saleh Shirazi's travel account marks an essential shift in the rationale behind travel abroad. For the first time, Iranians were consciously embarking on a quest for the secret of European strength—a quest that underlay the emergence of a discourse of modernization. Mirza Saleh Shirazi's account thus is evidence of the onset of tremors that would shake Iran in the nineteenth century to its foundation.

The nineteenth century was a period of deep change for Iran. The country witnessed processes of modernization, Westernization, and the rapid internationalization of Iran's domestic affairs. The effects of reforms (and no less so the increasingly apparent *lack* of substantive and lasting reforms) occupied center stage throughout the entire century. Above all, the discourse of modernization that resulted involved a fundamental rethinking of tradition, history, and the role of religion. This discourse involved a reformulation of identity, culture, and even language, and entailed an intimate and immediate challenge to existing intellectual foundations, social elites, and the basis of legitimacy of the monarchy.[2]

It is no coincidence that the travel account (*safarnameh*) enjoyed its heyday in nineteenth-century Iran. It was in part a result of increased contact between Iran and Europe, following a hiatus as a result of the overthrow of the Safavids in 1722 and the political turmoil that persisted intermittently until the late eighteenth century. Yet the nineteenth century is certainly not the *only* period of Europe-Iran relations, trade, or reciprocal travel. It would be instructive to ask *why* it was in this period that so many *safarnameh*s were written. Unlike the Ottoman Empire, where officials dispatched abroad were required to keep an account of their official dealings which would then be submitted to the Porte in the form of a diplomatic report, Iranian diplomats were not in the habit of writing about their experiences abroad. For example, the Iranian envoy to the court of Louis XIV in 1714–15 kept no written account. Indeed, his lack of interest in things European (whether social, political, or cultural) both astonished and insulted his European hosts, who themselves frequently complained of his complacency and obvious sense of superiority.[3] Those Iranian travelers who journeyed to Europe in nonofficial capacities were few, and their written testimonies fewer still. Prior to the nineteenth century, Iranians viewed Europe with an "unquestioned assumption of cultural superiority."[4]

The relative frequency of the nineteenth-century *safarnameh* was due to the changing nature of the contact between Iran and Europe. The notion of a resumption, and rapid intensification, of international relations between Iran and Europe was prevalent in early-nineteenth-century travel literature. More significantly, travelers, particularly in the early part of the century, clearly attempted to compile a wide variety of information about Europe. This was a direct result of the increasingly apparent disparity in power between Iran and European nations. Iranians voyaging abroad wrote *safarnamehs*, either consciously or unconsciously, as a means of exploring the reasons behind this disparity, and as a means of evaluating possible ways of correcting it. *Safarnameh* literature thus resulted from the notion of Europe as somehow *relevant* to Iran—relevant in the sense of applicable. Europe emerged in the beginning of the century as a model of development, modernization, and reform. It is important to note, however, that Iranians were very selective in their use of Europe as a model of change. The process of selection differed throughout the century, with different aspects of European technological and sociopolitical advancements held up for emulation by many travelers abroad. The changing nature of Iranian understanding of Europe and its relevance to the Iranian context is particularly evident in the *safarnameh* literature, which serves as a window into the rationale and process of evaluation, selection, and rejection.

Mirza Saleh Shirazi's *safarnameh* is unthinkable prior to the nineteenth century and marks a shift in genre of the *safarnameh* itself, as demonstrated by the difference in both the purpose of travel and the audience for whom the account is written. Mirza Saleh Shirazi belongs to a different period and a self-consciously new era, an era in which Iran began to feel the inequality of its relationship with Europe. The first inkling of this "deficiency"—as it was not initially conceived of as backwardness *per se*—resulted from a series of military defeats of Iranian forces by the Russians early in the century.[5] As a result of the disruption of the Iranian sense of security, Mirza Saleh Shirazi and others set out on a quest for the secret of European strength. The *safarnameh* as a tool of historical inquiry is just this: an account of the quest and an implicit comparison and exploration of Iran's deficiency. The accounts can be analyzed on three levels. First, for the information they contain and what this indicates about the level of Iranian awareness and understanding of life and events abroad. Second, the *safarnameh* was the vehicle for analysis, presentation, and the construction of the European "Other." Third, in construing the primary Other as Europe, the *safarnamehs* also served the related process of the reformulation of the Iranian "Self." This construction of the Self-Other dichotomy is nowhere more apparent than in travel literature of this period and served as a primary channel of the crystallization of conceptions of identity, culture, and tradition.

Travel literature as a genre is by nature particularly suited to uncovering layers of Self—and to the associated process of creating the Other. Through travel, an individual undergoes a transformative experience. At the most basic level, the traveler is exposed to new places, new peoples, and new customs. The traveler thus undergoes experiences impossible in the absence of such travel, experiences that highlight both the differences and similarities of these new places to the travelers' own. Insofar as self and place are integrated realities, molded by environment, the traveler in some sense divests himself of his identity through the physical act of departure and the abandonment of his indigenous environment. The individual, as he leaves home, family, and his daily occupations, is also in some sense stripped down to his essential character—a character which is tested by this very process and thereby emerges as though from an ordeal, fortified and wiser. He is therefore also freed up for the creation of new realities and new selves. Separation from home presents an opportunity, whether recognized and embraced as such or not, to recreate the self.[6] These processes are intensified in travel across cultures. Cross-cultural travel generates a new kind of self-consciousness, a new collective self-awareness, as the travelers themselves realize what they share with other cultures, and, equally as important, what they do not. As described by Freya Stark, a woman who fully embraced travel as a process of divesting the "Self," "one great interest in [Middle Eastern] civilization is that it gives you a sudden fresh view of your own; the nearest in fact to getting out of the world and examining it as an object."[7]

The transformative experiences of individual travelers were recorded in their *safarnameh*s and in some sense imparted to and vicariously shared by their readers. The *safarnameh* thus served to represent the examination of collective culture and the formulation of a conscious identity. To the extent that the travel accounts also sought the secret of European strength and served to locate the source of the current power disparity with Europe, they also (whether consciously or unconsciously) served to formulate a collective Self-Other dichotomy and new self-consciousness.[8] In the process of identifying the elements of European civilization which were deemed "relevant" and worthy of adoption, the *safarnameh* literature reveals a rethinking of tradition as travelers questioned what was essential and must be maintained, what could be dispensed with, what simply eliminated, and what modified. This new genre of *safarnameh* literature was not an exclusively Iranian phenomenon. Travelers departed from North Africa and Egypt, the Ottoman Empire, Afghanistan, Central Asia, and India on similar voyages of discovery. The earliest examples of these travel accounts hail from the eighteenth-century Ottoman Empire and (British) India—both of which experienced earlier and more intensive contacts with Europeans and European power than had Iran.[9] In particular, the accounts of the travels of Mirza E`tesham al-Din and Abu Taleb Khan Esfahani to Europe in 1766–69 and 1799–1802, respectively, were composed by Iranian Indians in the Persian language. These accounts were read by Iranians living in both India and Iran, and are examples of the Perso-Indian culture that spanned current political boundaries. Although their reference point is clearly Indian society, their evaluations of the power disparity with Europe resonated in Iran as well.[10]

It is difficult to calculate with any precision the popularity of books in an era before mass printing. It is certain that many nineteenth-century *safarnameh*s, particularly those written by diplomats on official missions and by the reigning monarchs themselves, were widely read in court circles. Later travelers often mention their predecessors' journeys and experiences. With the spread of printing throughout the century, some of the most popular Iranian travel accounts—as well as other Persian-language accounts written by Indian Iranians and published in India—were printed and available in Iran. But *safarnameh* literature enjoyed an impact quite out of proportion to its circulation statistics for several reasons. First, the majority of accounts of travel to Europe were composed by members of the social and political elites— landowners usually associated (either themselves or through a close male relative) with the court. Second, the travelers—already an influential elite—were by and large reform-oriented and thus in a position to shape ideas concerning Europe, and, specifically, Europe as a model of change. Moreover, the travelers were the movers and shakers in much of court life and particularly in diplomatic circles. They served (whether prior to or after their return from abroad) as ministers, diplomats, editors, and translators in the government. They thus served as the prism through which much information and, more importantly, the *interpretation* of information into patterns of meaning understandable and relevant to Iranians was refracted.

THE NEW ERA (ASR-E JADID)

The growth of *safarnameh* literature in Iran as a vehicle for the exploration of the secret of European strength roughly coincides with the rule of Fath Ali Shah (1797–1834), and, more importantly, with the duration of Crown Prince Abbas Mirza's modernization program, the *Nezam-e jadid* (c. 1803– 1833). This stage is best represented by the travel accounts of Mirza Saleh Shirazi and Mirza Mostafa Afshar, who journeyed to Great Britain in 1815 and Russia in 1829, respectively. Shirazi participated in a five-member student mission to England from 1815 to 1819. Afshar was the assistant of Abbas Mirza's personal secretary, whom he had sent as part of an official delegation headed by his son, Prince Khosrau Mirza, to St. Petersburg to apologize for the killing of the Russian diplomat and well-known author Griboyedov in Iran.[11] In the introduction to his travel account, Afshar explained that he had been charged with recording what he saw and heard on the trip. Both Shirazi and Afshar thus were closely associated with Abbas Mirza's court and his reform program. Both were dispatched personally by Abbas Mirza to uncover the secret of European strength. They were conscious explorers—enjoined to report back on what should be done to strengthen and protect Iran.

The defining characteristics of this period of travel literature include, first, a clear recognition of the dawn of a new era: *asr-e jadid.* The components of the new era are new knowledge, new rules, new government, and, thus, the necessity of a new paradigm—a new solution to Iran's deficiency. Thus, a reestablishment of the traditional system, or the reestablishment of a just order, is not sufficient or even relevant. There is a deep feeling of the qualitatively new secret that must be appropriated in order for Iran to get on the bandwagon of "progress," or, alternately, to be left behind and inevitably dominated if not conquered.[12]

Second, Shirazi and Afshar articulate the secret of European strength as the source of "progress" (*taraqqi*). The urgency of survival thus meant that Iran must modernize. Modernization in turn was conceived of as the adoption of Western technology and the establishment of an ordered government with the potential of promoting prosperity. Third, both emphasize the role of education in modernizing, and present the example of Russia as having implemented a successful program of modernization and Westernization which enabled her to start down the path of "progress" and prosperity. They urge Iran to follow Russia's lead down the same path. According to Shirazi, Peter the Great believed that "the reason for the prosperity of Western countries is the spread of sciences, industries, and knowledge."[13] Education was identified as a principal means of modernizing by both Shirazi and Afshar. Afshar identifies Peter the Great's policy of training and then enlisting the nobility in government service as a key source of Russia's enormous progress. He forcefully insisted that Iran could do the same.

> The establishment of [European-style schools] in the kingdom of Iran would be extremely simple and easy. A few masters of Western sciences could be brought to Iran, and one of the schools for the children of the nobility of the land could be selected and they could be gathered together there, and several people of high moral conduct could be selected to supervise them [the students], who would learn both Iran-

ian sciences from Iranian teachers as well as Western sciences from Western teachers.[14]

Not only did Afshar not take into account the domestic opposition that such educational reforms might (and eventually would) engender, but, more fundamentally, he did not comprehend the depth and breadth of the ramifications of such educational reforms. Like Shirazi and others, Afshar was unaware of the context of European institutions, whether in terms of education, technology, or even governmental systems. He therefore did not recognize the problems of the transferability of foreign institutions to the Iranian context. This attitude was widespread and persisted throughout much of the nineteenth century. One corollary of this superficial view of adoption, particularly as concerned technology, was that the path to modernization was conceived of as a unique one. There was thus little recognition of the importance of alternate routes to modernization.

ROYAL POLITICS

Safarnameh literature of the subsequent period—from the death in 1834 of Fath Ali Shah (who outlived his son Abbas Mirza by only a year) until the reign of his great-grandson Mozaffar al-Din Shah in 1896—is singularly lacking in analysis of Iranian domestic conditions, or, inversely, of European power. There are several reasons for the relative intellectual paucity of accounts in this sixty-year period (1834–96), which spanned the reigns of both Mohammad Shah and Naser al-Din Shah. First, the strain on relations with Britain, and growing alarm concerning European political and economic inroads and the accompanying "meddling" of European powers in Iranian affairs, resulted in a degree of insecurity and retrenchment on the part of the monarchs which was not conducive to either serious introspection or concerted attempts at exploring the European "Other."

Second, the centrality of diplomacy meant that the few diplomats sent abroad were almost exclusively occupied in negotiations. They were not given a mandate to seek the secret of European strength, but rather to conclude alliances and economic treatises. Third, much of the tone of reform in the Naser al-Din Shah period (1848–96) was set by the Pivot of the Universe himself. While His Majesty enjoyed the distinction of being the first Iranian monarch to ever travel to Europe, his three journeys (in 1873, 1878, and 1889) and the travel accounts that resulted reveal his underlying conservatism and lack of commitment to the reform process. Naser al-Din Shah's *safarnamehs* are replete with description of train travel, dinner parties, ballets, theater, operas, and the variety of animal species found in the zoo. However, only occasional and vague reference is given to the serious diplomatic negotiations, and introspection and analysis are singularly absent. Even one of the most interesting accounts of the period, the *safarnameh* of Momtahen al-Dauleh, relating his experiences as a student in France, contains much anecdotal information but no conscious analysis or exploration.[15]

The shah's marked ambivalence towards Europe, however, is in and of itself revealing. It marks a new stage in the relationship between Iran and Europe, a stage fraught with insecurity and disappointment. Politically, Naser al-Din Shah adroitly carried on a balancing act between the two regional superpowers, Great Britain and Russia. At the same time, reformers' hopes that Great Britain would champion their cause remained illusory. The shah's travel accounts demonstrate the deepening crisis in Iran, as the notion of Iran's "deficiency" takes on increasing connotations of social inferiority vis-à-vis Europe. Throughout his accounts, the shah is acutely sensitive of his treatment by his European hosts and takes care to record the respect shown him by monarchs and the European population at large, as though he were promoting the image of Iran in European eyes. He also is careful to avoid any overt awe or unseemly admiration for European institutions that might suggest critical comparison to Iran. Naser al-Din Shah was also not averse to attempting to minimize Iranians' knowledge of Europe. Through a policy of censorship and the imposition of a ban on travel to Europe in 1867, he hoped to prevent any unfavorable comparisons between Europe and Iran. He admitted as much to his secretary Amin al-Dauleh when he declared, "My servant and the people of this country should not be informed of any other places except Iran and their own world. . . . if they hear the word 'Paris' or 'Brussels' they should not know whether these two [things] are edible or wearable."[16]

Hajji Pirzadeh, writing in the late 1880s, was less ambivalent than Naser al-Din Shah concerning the benefits and dangers of Europe. He unequivocally warned of the dangers of Westernization in Iran. Pirzadeh's *safarnameh* of a trip to Europe in 1886–89 is one of the few nineteenth-century travel accounts written by one of the ulama. Pirzadeh, a dervish, enjoyed the uncommon position of being popular in both ulama and court circles. He was close to Mozaffar al-Din Shah's court and was also a close friend of reformist prime minister Mirza Hosain Khan, the two having lived together in Istanbul. In 1886, during Naser al-Din Shah's reign, Pirzadeh was chosen to accompany courtier Mo`ayyad al-Molk to Europe for medical treatment. His *safarnameh* reflects many contemporary Iranian attitudes towards Europe, and is more representative of travel accounts written by individuals who are critical of Europe and Europeans than are many of the *safarnameh*s we have discussed that were written by reform-minded individuals. Pirzadeh's *safarnameh* is dominated by two characteristics. First, he was unabashedly impressed with European technological advances, inventions, and innovations affecting productivity. He noted Europe's obvious wealth, standard of living, ordered government, and the cleanliness of cities, towns, and even villages he passed through. His account is also highly descriptive and seeks to compile as much detailed information possible about Europe—but Europe perceived as a land of curiosities and wonders, a distinctly alien "Other."

Second, Pirzadeh's wonder and amazement at European technology and inventions in no way mitigates his open criticism of European society. Pirzadeh clearly warns of the dangers inherent in political reform that takes the form of Westernization. In painting a negative portrait of European society, Pirzadeh displays a typically late-nineteenth-century conception of the connection between morality, culture, and religion. The status of women is an integral part of this equation. Pirzadeh sees Europe (especially Paris) as lacking in morality. Women are deliberately presented as sexually licentious and Europeans as endlessly frivolous and self-indulgent. Pointing to the apparent liberty of European society as exemplified in its women, Pirzadeh insists that European conceptions of liberty and freedom are destructive and lacking in religious content. In fact, he goes so far as to caution against dispatching Iranians to study abroad, since he believes the temptations of Europe could lead them to abandon their religion entirely. Europe is thus declared a clear and present danger.

CRISIS AND TRANSLATION

The sudden death of Naser al-Din Shah and the accession to the throne of his son, Mozaffar al-Din Shah, in 1896 inaugurated a dynamic period of intensive exploration and introspection in *safarnameh* literature that lasted until the early twentieth century. Mozaffar al-Din Shah, if not radically more committed to reform than his father, at least was less willing to impose restrictions. In the caustic words of a contemporary commentator, "Mozaffar al-Din Shah, contrary to [his] father, was not opposed to the spread of education. Or, I should say, during the reign of Mozaffar al-Din Shah everybody did whatever they pleased."[17]

The *safarnamehs* in this period are markedly more sophisticated than those earlier in the century, and the authors evidence an understanding of issues of contextuality, transferability of foreign institutions, and the associated issues of cultural authenticity in their analyses of Iran, Europe, and prospects of modernization. No longer do the authors embark on quests for the secret of

European strength. Rather, they are seeking a solution, a synthesis, an adaptation. In other words, they are conscious of the need to map an alternative route to modernization, a route not traveled by Europe, a route appropriate for Iranian pilgrims seeking progress and strength.

Two of the most important *safarnameh*s in the 1896–1906 period include those of Prime Minister Amin al-Soltan's voyage around the world, written by his traveling companion Mehdi Qoli Khan Hedayat, and that of Prince Zell al-Soltan. In contrast to earlier nineteenth-century travelers, authors of *safarnameh*s in this period were, by and large, not on official functions (excepting Mozaffar al-Din Shah himself). Rather, they were reform-minded individuals on private trips abroad, actively engaged in cultural exploration of the societies they encountered. For the first time, travelers ventured beyond Europe into Asia (China, Japan) and even to the United States. Their sensitivity and commitment to understanding different societies and cultures is also revealed in the informal, personal nature of the accounts, which are noticeably replete with the authors' own emotions, considered reflections, and more intimate descriptions of nature and scenery.

After his dismissal from the position of Prime Minister in September 1903, Amin al-Soltan Atabak decided to embark on a trip abroad. He requested that his friend and fellow courtier, Mirza Qoli Khan Hedayat Mokhber al-Saltaneh, join him on the voyage. Hedayat, himself a powerful and respected reform-minded courtier, educator, school principal, and Minister of Sciences, accepted the invitation. In the *safarnameh* that he kept of their travels, he wrote that in agreeing to accompany the Atabak, he hoped that the Atabak would be more favorably inclined to support the reform agenda once he had seen Europe firsthand.[18]

In order to secure permission to travel abroad from Mozaffar al-Din Shah, Amin al-Soltan presented the trip as a pilgrimage to Mecca. The Shah gave Amin al-Soltan permission to travel, but stipulated that he should not be gone from Iran for more than seven months. Keeping his intended itinerary secret even from Hedayat, Amin al-Soltan announced upon leaving Iran that they would be traveling through Russia to China and Japan. Accompanied by their two sons and a few servants, the Atabak and Hedayat thus traveled around the world via Asia, then across America, through Europe to Istanbul and Damascus en route to their officially declared destination of Mecca—a trip which would take them an entire year.

Hedayat's *safarnameh* is a fascinating report on local customs, traditions, religion, and society, including lengthy sections on women. The most detailed sections are on China and Japan. Japan, in fact, appears to be the principal, although undeclared, destination of the Atabak. In late-nineteenth-century reform literature, Japan was frequently upheld as an example of successful modernization, effectively replacing Russia as a model of emulation for Iran. This was partly due to the worsening of Iranian-Russian relations and the increasing alarm about possible Russian designs on Iranian territory and/or sovereignty. Iranians were concerned not to become another Russian Central Asian Khanate. The emergence and popularity of Japan as a model of reform had other reasons, however—reasons intrinsic to the nature of the reform movement itself. First, reformers were forced to take seriously the continual increase in opposition on religious and cultural grounds to Westernization and Western influence in Iran. Some countered opponents' claims that reforms were essentially designed to initiate, or at the very least could not avoid, a process of Westernization by denial—asserting that the importation of European institutions would not lead to a concomitant Europeanization. However, this tactic was largely bankrupt in the later part of the century. The principal reform figures in the Mozaffar al-Din Shah period were more sophisticated than their predecessors and recognized the validity of much of the concern over the loss of cultural traditions and issues of authenticity. In seeking to promote the necessity of continued reform, they argued that Iran could selectively borrow and critically adapt foreign institutions to Iranian needs and to the Iranian context. Japan in particular was upheld as having successfully appropriated the ultimate secret of European strength: a constitution. Reformers furthermore asserted that Japan had done so without having compromised her cultural or religious traditions. Despite frequent allusions to Japan as an example of the discovery of an alternate path to modernization in the nineteenth century, however, very little was actually *known* about the details of the Japanese experience.[19] It is not surprising then that Amin al-Soltan set out for Japan in search of more concrete information.[20] The interest in Japan as an example of successful reform illustrates the recognition of the importance of composing a blueprint for reform that would maintain Iran's religious and cultural traditions and identity—in essence, an indigenous solution.[21] It also explains Hedayat's long forays into Japanese society, customs, religion, and cultural traditions.

The *safarnameh* indicates a strong sense of the urgency of reform and modernization and the belief in a causal connection between education, reform, and constitutionalism. Hedayat's *safarnameh* contains descriptions of educational institutions and their role in modernization, as well as lengthy accounts of discussions with Japanese ministers. Hedayat records one conversation between the Atabak and a close advisor to the Japanese emperor. When asked by the Atabak how the government proceeded to implement European-style governmental organization and education, the minister replied that their first priority was to train qualified personnel to support a new state organization. Students were sent to Europe and the United States in all branches of science and industry. The next stage in solidifying reform was to establish a comprehensive system of universal, European-style education nationwide.[22] Hedayat took care in his presentation of Japanese educational reform to stress that it included a strong moral foundation in line with traditional Japanese mores. In conclusion, Hedayat stated simply that "the Japanese, who [initially] had only a few ships, today are the victors against the Russians" (in the Russo-Japanese war of 1905).[23]

In 1905, the royal prince and governor of Isfahan, Zell al-Soltan, found himself compelled to travel to Europe to be treated for malaria.[24] In the company of a number of his sons, Zell al-Soltan voyaged to Austria and France. Unlike his father, Naser al-Din Shah, or reigning brother, Mozaffar al-Din Shah, Zell al-Soltan was not on an official state visit and did not compose his account for public consumption. Indeed, he only intended to make it available posthumously.[25] For this reason, Zell al-Soltan was remarkably candid in his *safarnameh*—even going so far as to admit his desire for the throne.

Despite his stated reluctance to journey to Europe, he enjoyed himself immensely and interacted easily with his many European hosts, describing his pleasure in their company. He also traveled with a special book that he requested the foreign heads of state he encountered to sign—a courtesy which Zell al-Soltan reciprocated by sending them thank-you cards.[26] He was particularly smitten by Paris and even wrote of missing it while briefly in the south of France. He was also impressed with the various visual and plastic arts that he encountered, such as painting and porcelain works.

Zell al-Soltan presented Iran as a country lost between its glorious past and an uncertain future. Whereas Iran has lost much of the arts of her past, Europe revels not only in its *own* past, but appreciates and in a sense appropriates that of Iran as well–by putting it on display in museums in Europe.[27] On a trip to Versailles, Zell al-Soltan remarked that the French preserved their own past in museums and in paintings, even going so far as to have their pets memorialized.

In tune with contemporary reform currents, Zell al-Soltan placed his hopes for progress and prosperity for Iran in the establishment of the rule of law. "I want constitutional government," he stated firmly in his *safarnameh,* and went on to elaborate that he believed a constitutional monarchy like that in Great Britain to be superior to the French Republican system, since "a government without a Sultan is like a body without a head."[28]

Zell al-Soltan also echoed many reformers of the period by emphasizing the key role of educational reform in any substantive political change. He suggested that the government take a greater role in promoting European-style education. In order to create an educated leadership cadre qualified to spearhead reform, he proposed that the government compel officials to send their sons to Europe for education at their own expense. This policy would result in the formation of an elite leadership, yet at the same time allay any opposition to spending government funds on such a project. In fact, Zell al-Soltan described the European state as a "people-making workshop." Citizens are educated not just in sciences, but also in civic duties and responsibilities, the result of which is order, justice, power, and social stability.[29]

While in France, Zell al-Soltan visited Mirza Malkom Khan, a long-time correspondent and fellow reform advocate. The *safarnameh* includes a note of lavish praise for Malkom Khan, describing him as a great and patriotic reformer. Like Malkom Khan, Zell al-Soltan insisted that the role of the ulama in state affairs must be curtailed. Religious affairs should be limited to the otherworldly, since the power of the ulama is always a hindrance to the necessary strength of the state. In keeping with many other like-minded reformers, Zell al-Soltan insisted that the establishment of a constitution had no bearing on religion, whether Islam, Christianity, or Judaism. "The issue of religion is a problem of the hereafter . . . and the issue of order and education (*nazm va tarbiyat*) [of the government] an issue of this world." In an impassioned plea for reform in Iran, Zell al-Soltan addressed his fellow Iranians and urged them to action, yet cautioned them that becoming like Europe, although desirable and certainly possible, would not be easy or quick.[30]

CONCLUSION

Safarnameh literature offers unique insight into the development of the Self-Other construction. It also illustrates some of the concerns about the benefits and dangers of reform, Westernization, and the related problems of indigenous traditions. The majority of *safarnamehs* written in the nineteenth century were somewhat self-selective with regard to reform in that they were written by elite individuals with close ties to the court and with vested personal interests in the system. Moreover, by virtue of having observed European (and/or Asian and American) society firsthand, the *safarnamehs* do not idealize the European model. Europe is described with both positive and negative attributes. For these reasons, the travelers do not represent the more radical ends of the discourse of reform. It is also clear that the *safarnameh* literature echoes the ups and downs in the reform current, with the most introspective and analytical accounts written in the Abbas Mirza and Mozaffar al-Din Shah periods. Nor is it surprising that some of the most important accounts were composed by travelers associated with Abbas Mirza's *Nezam-e jadid* program, and by individuals committed to the reform process later in the century.

Of particular interest is the fact that the *safarnameh*s display a close connection between ideas concerning the benefits of Europe as a model of reform and the presentation of European women. There is a direct correlation between views of Europe and the depiction of women. Those travelers early in the century who were actively seeking the secret of European strength and who recommended that Iran jump on the bandwagon of "progress" (Mirza Saleh Shirazi and Mirza Mostafa Afshar) make little mention of European women. What they do note are types of girls' education, and the benefits attributed to it by Europeans themselves. Hedayat, writing later in the century, discussed marriage practices, girls' education, and traditional female dress in various societies. These matter-of-fact and even sociological discussions of women differ greatly from the manner in which women are depicted by Pirzadeh and others such as Sahhafbashi in the latter part of the century.[31] Pirzadeh, as a result of his convictions about the immorality and spiritual corruption of European society, not surprisingly takes great pains to depict European women in a negative light. Women are described as out of control, sex-starved, and lacking honor. The discrepancy in the portrayal of women epitomizes the travelers' attitudes towards European freedom and society. Those travelers who are more inclined to adopt European institutions and political ideas of constitutionalism present European society in a positive light. Those who are uncomfortable with the Europeanization of Iran and who fear a loss of cultural and religious traditions believe that freedom—and its embodiment in male-female relations as conceived of in Europe—is a threat. Naser al-Din Shah's marked ambivalence concerning the benefits and dangers of reform and European influence is manifest in his portrayal of the beauty of European women; yet also of their "freedom," which takes the form of his ability to take the hands of other men's wives in social settings—an act which would be entirely inappropriate in Iran. In nineteenth-century *safarnameh* literature, women's bodies are a terrain upon which debates concerning social change, identity, and national honor are contested.[32]

Whereas those travelers like Pirzadeh who are concerned with Islam and religious identity in a changing Iran are clear in their defense of Iran's cultural and religious traditions, travelers more inclined to accept the European model are noticeably ambivalent. Many reformers criticized the ulama as an impediment to change and an obstacle to progress. At the same time, Islam itself was not openly disparaged, and many travelers were themselves pious and equally concerned about issues of cultural identity. The *safarnameh*s thus do not evince an idealization of Europe, nor a concomitant rejection of Iranian culture or society. Although pro-reform travelers are conscious of a need to break with the past, they are less sure of what exactly such a break entails. Clearly, the late-century *safarnameh*s such as Hedayat's recognize the importance of charting an alternate path to modernization, yet do not actually map out such a path. The recognition of issues regarding the contextuality and transferability of foreign institutions, cultural authenticity, and political change clearly marks the latter travel accounts with a sophistication not found earlier in the century. However, the elusive indigenous solution had not yet been found.

NOTES

1. Mirza Saleh Shirazi, *Majmu`eh-ye safarnameh-ye Mirza Saleh Shirazi* (Tehran: Nashr-e Iran, 1364/1985), 345.

2. On the discourse of reform and the critical reevaluation of tradition in nineteenth-century Iran, see Monica Ringer, *Education, Religion, and the Discourse of Cultural Reform in Qajar Iran* (Costa Mesa, CA: Mazda, 2001).

3. See Maurice Herbette, *Une ambassade persane sous Louis XIV* (Paris: Perrin et companie, 1907), 201–2.

4. On the Safavid weltanschauung, see Rudi Matthee, "Between Aloofness and Fascination: Safavid Views of the West," *Iranian Studies* 31 (1998): 219–46, particularly p. 227.

5. The first Russo-Persian War of 1803–15 culminated in the Treaty of Golestan, and the second Russo-Persian War of 1826–28 resulted in the Treaty of Torkmanchai.

6. Eric J. Leed, *The Mind of the Traveler: From Gilgamesh to Global Tourism* (New York: Basic Books, 1991), 6, 10, 34.

7. As quoted in Leed, *Mind,* 45. Freya Stark traveled to the Middle East in the 1920s and 1930s.

8. Leed, *Mind,* 20–21.

9. On this shift in genre in the Ottoman Empire, see Fatma Müge Göçek, *East Encounters West: France and the Ottoman Empire in the Eighteenth Century* (New York: Oxford University Press, 1987). On the eighteenth-century Indian travel accounts, see Juan R. I. Cole, "Invisible Occidentalism: Eighteenth-Century Indo-Persian Constructions of the West," *Iranian Studies* 25, nos. 3–4 (1992): 3–16.

10. While I concur in rejecting the strict compartmentalization of culture and intellectual traditions according to contemporary political borders, the Perso-Indian accounts are not included in this discussion of "Iranian" *safarnameh* literature due to their point of reference. Despite their readership in Iran, they are not making observations on the Iran-Europe relationship, power disparity, or possible solutions.

11. Russian minister plenipotentiary Griboyedov was killed by a mob in Tehran over an incident involving the alleged confinement of two Georgian women in the Russian embassy after they had been forcibly removed from an Iranian harem. On the significance of this episode, see Nikki R. Keddie, *Qajar Iran and the Rise of Reza Khan, 1796–1925* (Costa Mesa, CA: Mazda, 1999), 25.

12. Anxiety over the loss of territory was a major and constant theme in nineteenth-century reform literature. See Firoozeh Kashani-Sabet, *Frontier Fictions: Shaping the Iranian Nation, 1804–1946* (Princeton: Princeton University Press, 1999).

13. Shirazi, *Safarnameh*, 129.

14. Mirza Mostafa Afshar, *Safarnameh-ye Khosrau Mirza beh Peterzburg*, ed. Mohammad Golbun (Tehran: Ketabkhaneh-ye mostaufi, 1349/1970), 236–37.

15. See Mirza Mehdi Khan Momtahen al-Dauleh, *Khatarat-e Momtahen al-Dauleh* (Tehran: Amir Kabir, 1362/1983). On Naser al-Din Shah's life and reign, see Abbas Amanat, *Nasir al-Din Shah Qajar and the Iranian Monarchy, 1831–1896* (Berkeley: University of California Press, 1997).

16. Mirza Ali Khan Amin al-Dauleh, *Khaterat-e siyasi-ye Mirza Ali Khan Amin al-Dauleh* (Tehran: Ketabha-ye Iran, 1341/1962), 131. See also p. 48.

17. Abol Hasan Bozorg Omid, *Az mast keh bar mast* (Tehran: Donya-ye ketab, 1363/1984), 95.

18. Mohammad Qoli Hedayat Mokhber al-Saltaneh, *Safarnameh-ye Makkeh* (Tehran: Entesharat-e tiraj, 1304 A. H./1886–87), 3

19. See, for example, Abd al-Rahim Talebof, *Ketab-e Ahmad* (Tehran: Sazman-e ketabha-ye jibi, 1346/1967), and Zain al-Abedin Maragheh'i, *Siyahatnameh-ye Ebrahim Beg* (Tehran: Asfar, 1364/1985).

20. Indeed, according to British diplomat Sir N. O'Conor, Amin al-Soltan profited much from his travel to Japan, the United States, and Europe, and would make use of the lessons learned should he return to power in Iran. See PRO, London, 248/898. Nikki Keddie informed me in a conversation that Amin al-Soltan was impressed with Japan's constitutional monarchy and may have looked upon constitutionalism in Iran more favorably after his firsthand experience in Japan.

21. For an in-depth discussion of the "indigenous solution," see Ringer, *Education.*

22. Hedayat, *Safarnameh*, 164.

23. Ibid., 191.

24. Mas'ud Mirza Zell al-Soltan, *Safarnameh-ye Farangestan* (Tehran: Entesharat-e asatir, 1368/1989), 3.

25. Zell al Soltan, *Safarnameh*, 106.

26. Ibid., 138.

27. Ibid., 143–48.

28. Ibid., 107, 114.

29. Ibid., 169–70.

30. Ibid., 160–61, 170, 176, 190.

31. Ebrahim Sahhafbashi, *Safarnameh-ye Ebrahim Sahhafbashi Tehrani* (Tehran: Sherkat-e mo'alefan va tarjoman-e irani, n.d.).

32. See the pioneering work on women and the "Self-Other" construction by Mohammad Tavakoli-Targhi in "Imagining Western Women: Occidentalism and Euro-eroticism," *Radical America* 24, no. 3 (1993): 73–87.

7 / Cultures of Iranianness:

The Evolving Polemic of Iranian Nationalism

FIROOZEH KASHANI-SABET

The theme of nationalism has emerged as a prominent polemic in the study of modern Iran, despite the lack of consensus on the meanings of Iranianness. Some early-nineteenth-century Iranian nationalists invoked patriotism to link their troubled nation to a glorious ancestral past, while modernists from the Reza Shah era drew on this constructed past and other—often European—sources to "renew" the Iranian citizen and his nation through attire, language, and body. Instead of exemplifying any single theme in the changing agenda of the Iranian nationalists, the Iranian citizen came to encompass myriad cultures of Iranianness, as the nation took on new challenges to its sovereignty and independence.

W hat is a nation?" asked Ernest Renan in 1882. Although this was a deceptively simple question, the meaning of nationhood would baffle and inspire Iranian intellectuals, as it did French thinkers, for over a century.[1]

The historiography on Iranian nationalism is varied and multifaceted, much like the changing icons of the nationalists themselves. As Nikki Keddie has pointed out, there are many different emphases in Iranian nationalism, including linguistic, territorial, ethnic, and religious.[2] What is perhaps unique to the nationalist discourse in Iran is the way in which the varying emphasis on these complementary but often competing articulations of nationalism has transformed Iranian politics in radical ways. If at one time language was the primary defining characteristic of the modern Iranian, at another juncture religion would supplant language as the principal marker of Iranianness. Given the country's recent history, it is perhaps fair to conclude that the most contentious and least enduring aspects of Iranian nationalism have occurred in the sociocultural sphere, whereas the most persistent themes have concerned the nation's territorial integrity. Whatever the controversies, Iranian nationalism continues to shape policy and stimulate debate. What have been the distinctive features of modern Iranian nationalism, and how have different constructions of nationalism related to different stages of Iran's modern history and changing relations with the outside world?

Compared to many modern nations, Iran had several premodern features favorable to the development of nationalism. The concept of a territorial Iran (or *Iranshahr*) went back to ancient times. A single state or empire had ruled a territory roughly comparable to modern Iran in some pre-Islamic centuries and again under the Safavids (1501–1722), with a revival of unity beginning under the Qajars (1796–1925). There was also a widespread identification with Persian language and literature, even though this was not coterminous with Iran's borders. On the one hand, Persian was the court language through much of South Asia and an important cultural language in Caucasia, Central Asia, and other primarily Turkish-speaking areas. On the other hand, half or more of Iran's population spoke other native languages, although many of them also knew Persian. Persian was, however, both a major cultural language and the most important language within Iran's borders. About 90 percent of Iranians were united in their adherence to Shi`i Islam, which differentiated them from their neighbors and was a more potent unifying "national" factor than is often recognized. Finally, increasing numbers of Iranians from the nineteenth century on took advantage of the historical accident that their language was in the Indo-European language family, and that by many Europeans the predominance of an Indo-European language was interpreted as a racial advantage, an idea used by nationalists of countries where such languages were dominant. On the downside, as far as the emergence of modern nationalism in Iran was concerned, was Iran's late development of modern socioeconomic factors, including a national infrastructure, industry, major urbanization, and large-scale trade, which in countries all over the world accompanied the development of a national market and other ties among different parts of bordered nations. This meant that modern nationalism appeared later in Iran than in many other countries, but once it developed it soon spread to be passionately believed in by many in all strata of the population, however much its forms differed in different periods.

In 1828, after Iran signed the Treaty of Torkmanchai accepting defeat at the hands of the Russians, some in the ruling elite pondered the reasons for this loss, which had caused Iran to renounce portions of its frontier territory. Thus began the process of self-questioning that led several Iranian thinkers later in the century, such as Mirza Malkom Khan and Mostashar al-Dauleh, to express in prose and poetry their patriotic yearnings for effective government, cultural dominance, or territorial irredentism. Since then, as Iran has faced other challenges to its frontiers and its natural resources, nationalist ideology has inspired both populist activism and, especially after 1921, state policy, making nationalism a prevailing philosophy in the culture and politics of Iran. Although nationalism stands out as a dominant discourse, it has changed significantly over time. The markers of authentic Iranianness have vacillated with political and socioeconomic circumstances and with the regimes themselves. Who, then, is the Iranian?

NATIONALIST DISCOURSE UNDER THE QAJARS

In the 1850s, when Joseph Arthur de Gobineau visited Iran, he observed the manners and culture of his hosts, commenting on the history and contemporary society of this "ancient nation." Writing with a distinctly French sensibility attuned to nationalist rhetoric, he discussed the meanings of the phrase "Iranian nation," which he understood to denote an amalgam of races that had come together within a particular territory.[3] To Gobineau, one of the most striking features of Iran was that it possessed a sort of "immortal" patriotism. Despite being subjected to foreign invasion, "Iranian individuality" could not be suppressed. In true patriotic spirit, Gobineau concluded, "One mutilates Persia in vain, one divides it, one can take away its name, she will remain Persia."[4] Gobineau's fascination with Iran, it appeared, stemmed in part from the fact that the country possessed an antiquity that lent itself well to nationalist mythmaking.

An existing widespread belief in one version of Iranian history was partly responsible for making nationalism a subject of polemic in the study of modern Iran. In discussing Iran's past, Gobineau was struck by the interest that Iranians showed in their history. Despite his recognition that "the history of the Persians is certainly hardly exact," he observed people's interest in their country's past, concluding that "a nation that attaches such value to its antecedents evidently possesses . . . great energy."[5] The willingness to imagine a shared history and to partake of a collective future lent this community national solidarity. As Ernest Renan summed it up, therein lay the definition of nationhood. "A nation is therefore a large-scale solidarity, constituted by the feeling of the sacrifices that one has made in the past and of those that one is prepared to make in the future. It presupposes a past; it is summarized, however, in the present by a tangible fact, namely, consent, the clearly expressed desire to continue a common life."[6]

Contributing to the rise of Iranian nationalism were a preexisting identification with Iran, reaction to nineteenth-century territorial losses and threats from abroad, early contacts with European nationalist and racial thought, growing centralization of the Qajar state, and the need felt by many for an ideology with which to oppose Qajar failures both to stand up to encroaching foreign nations and to adopt more modernizing policies that could strengthen Iran. Many early Iranian patriots would agree with Renan's definition, as they voiced similar statements affirming national honor, historical grandeur, and territorial existence in their writings.

The first late-nineteenth-century figures in Iranian nationalism were nearly all oppositional, and highly critical of the Qajars and of existing social, economic, and political realities. One of the early figures of Iranian nationalism was Mirza Fath Ali Akhundzadeh, who came into contact with ideas of the French Enlightenment by reading Russian and English translations.[7] Ironically, despite his identification with Iran, Akhundzadeh had spent most of his life outside of Iran in Russian-conquered Transcaucasia. In his work, *Maktubat-e Kamal al-Dauleh,* he spoke longingly of the prosperity of the Iranian nation (*mellat-e Iran*) under the ancient Persian kings, a prosperity that disappeared with the coming of the Arabs.[8] This work is also revealing as it demonstrates a limited knowledge of French political philosophy and literature. He defines for his readers terms such as *civilisation, changement, parlement,* and *poésie,* which he uses throughout the text. He also refers to Voltaire and Renan in his effort to promote the freedom of expression.[9] Although it is difficult to gauge with accuracy Renan's direct influence on Akhundzadeh, there are certainly echoes of Renan's ideas concerning Aryan and Semitic culture in the *Maktubat.* As A. H. Shissler has argued, "Renan basically attributes every positive aspect of society and civilization to his 'Indo-European' peoples, except monotheism."[10] That Akhundzadeh considered pre-Islamic Iran, which was in his view free of Arab/Semitic influence, a paradise in which justice prevailed, and the subsequent period of Iranian history, following the Arab invasions, a period of decay, suggests that Akhundzadeh shared Renan's basic belief that progressive contributions to civilization could be traced to the Indo-Europeans, with whom Iranians shared a linguistic root. As Nikki Keddie has pointed out, "some of the nineteenth and early twentieth century orientalists and other writers who wrote about the Orient were pioneers in the widespread racist theories that most western scholars of that period believed. This was especially the case of the Comte de Gobineau . . . and also Ernest Renan, who saw himself as the originator of the popular 'racial' distinction between 'Aryans' and 'Semites.'"[11]

The belief found in many Iranian nationalists from Akhundzadeh on that Iran was great until it was ruined by the (Muslim) Arabs conforms to a typical model found among ethno-racial nationalists in many countries, who find it useful to blame other ethnic groups for their perceived decline from an early period of greatness. Many Arabs similarly blamed Ottoman rule for their decline, while Turkish nationalists often blamed both Arabs and Persians. Similar ideas are found outside the Middle East. The Iranian "Aryan" view was reinforced by its conformity to a view widespread among Europeans, who were often admired and envied in Iran as in other Asian countries, but parallel nationalist views and myths were constructed about the superiority of the ancient Turks, the Arabs in the early Islamic period, and so forth.

Other intellectuals and historians of pre-Islamic Iran would follow in Akhundzadeh's footsteps. In 1891, Mirza Aqa Khan Kermani sought to write the history of the "Aryan" nation (*mellat-e aryan*) in his work, *A'eneh-ye sekandari*. Although *A'eneh-ye sekandari* was not the earliest "nationalist" text on ancient Iranian history, his use of the term "Aryan nation" revealed the influence of Orientalist scholarship on his thoughts. Like European Orientalists, Kermani offered his unique speculations on the Persian language, though his theories were to be discredited by Iranian linguists such as the poet laureate Mohammad Taqi Bahar, Malek al-Sho`ara.[12] In one passage, for instance, he claimed that the French term *histoire* derived from the Persian word *ostovar*, meaning solid, since "for the firmness of the nation we do not possess anything better than history."[13] *A'eneh-ye sekandari* contains numerous other French terms, indicating Kermani's familiarity with European historiography of Iran. In another work, *Seh maktub*, an imitation of Akhundzadeh's *Maktubat*, Kermani again idealized the ancient history of Iran before the invasion of the "barbarous" Arabs, whom he believed had launched the country's precipitous decline. Like Akhundzadeh, Kermani seemed to subscribe indirectly to the European bifurcation of Semitic and Aryan languages and cultures—a position that privileged Iran's Indo-European roots over its subsequent arabized culture.

Akhundzadeh and Kermani were not unique in expressing patriotic sentiment, though their oppositional, implicitly or explicitly anti-Islamic, views represented but one angle of Iranian nationalism. Along with scripting the myths of old Iran, nineteenth-century patriots also expressed a nationalism focused on land. In the aftermath of the Russo-Persian Wars, and, later, Iran's loss of Herat, glorifications of the country often centered on land. History writing, in particular, defined as Iranian an expansive territory that had once belonged to the ancient Persian monarchs. Increasingly, intellectuals voiced their attachment to the Iranian homeland (*vatan*)—a territory that embodied the history, culture, ethnicity, and myths of the emerging nation. As one writer explained in 1900, "*Vatan* is a piece of land on which a person is born and is his place of growth and life. . . . Then it expands from the soil and stone . . . to include the home, the neighborhood, the city, the country and the whole of existence."[14] The Iranian *vatan* was thus deified to inspire individual fealty to the homeland.

During the constitutional revolution (1905–1911), the ideas of citizenship and national sovereignty took hold of a broad public, as women and men called for the creation of a parliament, the most conspicuous symbol of Iran's progress and renewal. With the creation of the Majles in 1906, the nation's delegates strove to outline the parameters of political participation in the nation as they prepared Iran's first constitution. Nationalist ideology clearly influenced the evolving political process. The electoral laws, for instance, stipulated that Majles representatives had to be Persian-speaking and male.[15] Oppositional nationalist thought, strong already among intellectual and merchant participants in the revolution, was now manifested also among the lower urban *bazaaris*, who were also prominent in the revolution, and was even expressed by clerics and their students who spoke out against the increasing sale of Iran's resources and productive capacities to Europeans. There was a temporary alliance of secular nationalists, who now tended to hide their criticisms of Islam and the clergy, and clerical and religious ones, who stressed the dangers to Islam coming from non-Islamic foreigners.

Iranian nationalism, like other nationalisms, became at once a statement of inclusion and a policy of exclusion. By privileging one language or religion over another, the nation ran the risk of alienating its excluded members. Iranian intellectuals grappled with the myriad markers of Iranianness—ethnicity, race, territory, and religion—acutely aware of the divisive forces that threatened to segregate the country. Recognizing the hazards of divisiveness, newspaper editors, many of whom were ardent constitutionalists and self-avowed patriots, stridently called for unity. In one issue, the journal *Rahnema,* edited by Abd Allah Qajar, noted, "It is for unity that inhabitants of the land of Iran should join hands. . . . It is unity that causes the Muslim and the Armenian and the imprisoned one to be equal."[16] The striking feature about Iranian nationalism is the overt recognition by its proponents that religious, ethnic, and linguistic diversity actually existed within the nation. At least during the constitutional years, unity was not meant to come about through the complete erasure of individual differences, but rather through the acceptance of an Iranian identity that acknowledged difference but privileged certain characteristics over others.

Iranian constitutionalists also drummed the theme of love of homeland (*hobb-e vatan*) as territorial threats continued to beleaguer the nation. As one writer desperately proclaimed, "Iran is our homeland! Iran is our life!"[17] At this time, there was a danger of territorial obliteration, particularly in the aftermath of the signing of the Anglo-Russian Treaty of 1907 that divided Iran into spheres of influence. The signing of the Anglo-Russian Treaty became a subject of debate in the popular newspaper *Habl al-Matin,* as well as in other constitutionalist journals.[18] Similarly, Iran's western boundary with the Ottoman Empire remained under siege. As territorial concerns intensified, Iranian patriots recalled the country's past. Like Akhundzadeh and Kermani, who had longingly described the vast territorial empire of the ancient Persian suzerains, journalists also described the boundaries of that other Iran, regretting the loss of land and lamenting the nation's comparatively reduced domain.[19] Even during the constitutional years, the popular historiographical narrative imagined the nation's ancestry through the possession of land.

As the nation crossed the threshold of modernity, one writer, focusing on the southern provinces of Iran, acknowledged the distinctly tribal nature of Iranian society. Recognizing the commanding role they maintained in the southern regions even after the establishment of constitutional rule, he proposed measures for reining in tribal power to the nation's advantage. After all, tribes were among the "natural forces of this water and soil [*i.e.,* homeland]," so it seemed politic to enlist their support in revamping Iran's military.[20] For, without a competent military force, the territorial integrity of the nation could not be safeguarded. This patriot, unlike many of his fellow activists, appreciated the diversity and markedly tribal features of the Iranian nation. In this instance, national unity was to come not from suppressing the tribes but from inviting them to participate in the defense of *their* nation. This accepting point of view did not typify the attitude of other patriots, who considered tribal power a threat to central power and, therefore, a danger to Iranian sovereignty—an opinion that would prevail and lead to the eventual disarmament of the tribes under the Pahlavi regime.

However quixotic such appeals to unity may have been, they reflected the desire of certain nationalists to treat diversity as an asset rather than a liability. To them, unity made sense because the whole was undoubtedly greater than the sum of its parts, not just for Persians or Muslims but for all groups involved. Still, with the victory of the constitutionalist faction in the Civil War of 1908–1909, certain strands of Iranian nationalism gained prominence, in particular the promotion of the Persian language and Shi`i identity, and, for some leaders, a stress on secular modernity. Each of these emphases, while useful to nationalism in some ways, could also exclude and devalue sections of the population, and hence might later undermine national unity. Linguistic nationalism was reinforced in various ways during the period of the Second Majles. For instance, one of the many social-political associations formed during this period, the Society for the Progress of Iran (*Jam`iyat-e taraqqi khahan-e Iran*), declared Persian "the official and scholarly language of Iran." It also listed among its goals the promotion of women's education, making for two themes that Reza Shah's regime would take up over a decade later.[21] Unsurprisingly, during the second constitutional period, many patriots became even more vociferous that "Iran must be cultivated with the hands of Iranians"— a slogan that a subsequent generation of citizens would repeat in an effort to nationalize the Iranian oil industry.[22]

The Great War proved a difficult time for Iran. In 1915, one newspaper article summed up the situation as follows: "The poor Iranian nation. . . . In spite of its neutrality . . . its northern and southern regions have been subjected to the attacks of the troops of the countries at war . . . and each day a new attack is being made on its independence."[23] The nation's territorial integrity seemed more at stake now than it did after the loss to Russia in 1828. Still, Iranian nationalists managed to endorse the themes of Persianization and to reinvoke the memory of the valiant Achaemenid kings in advancing the nation's cause. In particular, the newspaper *Kaveh*, published in Berlin under the editorship of the prominent constitutionalist and nationalist Sayyed Hasan Taqizadeh, used pre-Islamic symbols to support nationalist activity against the passivity of Iran's central government.[24] It would not be until the conclusion of the war, however, that the nationalist agenda, which called for guarantees of the nation's territorial independence and promotion of the Persian language and antiquities, could be implemented. Effective opposition to a proposed Anglo-Persian treaty of 1919, which would have created a de facto protectorate, and support for governmental suppression of several postwar regional autonomy movements demonstrated and contributed to a great spread of mass support for a strong government that could deal with internal and external threats. This sentiment made many Iranians welcome the February 1921 coup d'état led by Reza Khan, and his work to strengthen the army and the state. The new government's nationalism was also manifested through the introduction of relevant cultural institutions. One of the first steps taken in this regard after the war was the conversion to the Persian solar calendar that is still commonly used in Iran. Approved by parliament, the law was to take effect with the Persian New Year (*Nauruz*) of 1304/1925 C.E.[25]

Toward the end of the Qajar reign, then, territory, language, and history remained the symbols of Iranian identity. Perhaps the most marked difference between the nationalism of the Qajar and Pahlavi years, however, would be the self-conscious, orchestrated, and public way in which Reza Shah and his son, Mohammad Reza Pahlavi, strove to ingrain their select ideas of Iranian nationalism among the Iranian public. Their policies raised broad questions about the meanings of Iranian identity and the shifts in its usage since the days of the Qajars.[26]

"RENEWAL" OF NATIONAL IDENTITY
UNDER THE PAHLAVIS

In the years following the war and his coronation in 1926, Reza Shah, the quin-
tessential and often heroic military man,[27] endorsed the creation of many cultural institutions to disseminate the nationalizing agenda of the state and to
conceive the modern Iranian. Qajar thinkers had broached the theme of
modernity as well, but they had lacked the power to make it a state policy
that concerned the private and public facets of the citizen's life. Modernity,
moreover, acquired different connotations as the process of nation-building
took shape under the Pahlavi regime. The question was no longer "who is
the Iranian," but rather "who is the *modern* Iranian?" This was not a question left to the ordinary citizen to answer. Rather than invent this persona
from naught, the architects of Reza Shah's nationalist policies forged the modern Iranian through "renewal" (*tajaddod*)—that is, the remaking of every Iranian, man or woman. It is no surprise then that such a process required
cosmetic changes as well as intellectual indoctrination. In other words, the
modern Iranian literally had to embody this message of renewal in mind, body,
and attire—a distinction that set the modernist debates of the Pahlavi era apart
from those of the Qajar period.

In 1928, the government took a portentous step toward launching its
renewal project by passing a law outlining the proper dress code for its male
citizens. Iranian men were enjoined to wear Pahlavi hats (although the style
of the hat would later be revised), jackets, shirts, and pants. Moreover, the
Pahlavi hats were not to contain any "distinguishing marks" or to be in "off-
putting colors."[28] Religious scholars and students, however, were exempted
from this law if they could provide necessary documentation verifying their
vocation. Those who did not abide by this directive faced punishment in the
form of either fines or incarceration.[29] The state, rather than the individual,
decided what was modern and appropriate, even in something as personal
as someone's daily attire. While socially enforced dress codes expressing ethnic, social, professional, and gender status previously existed, only now did
dress come to be nationally legislated. As in other arenas, European mores
influenced modern Iranian sartorial choices. Such legislation, while defining
the modern Iranian male citizen, at the same time suppressed his individual
choice. The individual became a medium for the implementation of social
and cultural policy and thus could not assert himself or diverge from the norm
through the use of conspicuous and suggestive signs, colors, or fashions, for
such differentiation might breed subversion. Perhaps most important to the
official nationalist project, other individual distinctions such as ethnicity or

religion would also be effaced through uniform clothing, since at least in their outward appearance most Iranian men, regardless of geographic or linguistic predilection, appeared to have something in common. As Houchang Chehabi has argued, "In sum, Iranians would be more willing . . . to imagine each other as a community if they all looked alike."[30]

As part of the Pahlavi nationalist efforts toward unification of Iranians and lessening the power of organized and exclusive Shi`ism, Reza Shah also worked to lessen discrimination against religious minorities. This had already been part of the program of liberal nationalists, and Zoroastrians, as followers of an ancient Iranian religion, had already seen their low status reversed by many nationalists. Under Reza Shah, the Baha'is, though still seen as seceders from Islam by the orthodox, were freer than before and did not experience the persecutions felt earlier in the century; attitudes toward Jews, Iranian Sunnis, and Armenian and Nestorian Christians also improved. On the other hand, Reza Shah's nationalist policies and in particular his vigorous efforts to homogenize Iran's educational system led him to put restrictions on the operation and curricula of schools run by and for minorities.

Women, too, had to be made modern, and in May 1935 the Society for Women (*Kanun-e banovan*) was founded to "renew" the Iranian woman. It is noteworthy that one of Reza Shah's daughters, Shams Pahlavi, presided over the Society for Women in an honorary capacity, for, as exemplars of the state, the members of the royal family were to embody its message of renewal as well.[31] The modernized Iranian woman, who was charged with becoming both patriotic mother and skilled professional, would not project an image of progress if dressed in the traditionalist garb of the veil. One year later, in 1936, to complete the women's renewal project, Reza Shah decreed the mandatory unveiling of women. Although there was widespread resistance to the unveiling law, poets such as Mohammad Taqi Bahar and Parvin E`tesami welcomed the change.[32] Yet clothing was at best an elusive national adhesive. The dress code regulations for women during the Reza Shah regime would not only alienate the religious classes and many women accustomed to veiling, but they were also short-lived.[33] In fact, they ceased to be enforced after Reza Shah's abdication in 1941. Furthermore, despite their limited success as national policy, they provided a blueprint for the Islamic Republic of Iran to enforce its unique dress codes for women and men decades later.

Attire was only one facet of the regime's "renewal" project. The citizen's body itself became a feature of nationalist topography, stirring debate and spurring the rise of supporting institutions. Citizens healthy in mind and spirit could best serve the nation. Educational indoctrination, inculcated through the study of manners or ethics (*akhlaq*) as well as the pursuit of physical fitness, would promote dynamism and vigor in the modern Iranian. Even before the establishment of the Pahlavi dynasty, the culture of exercise and physical fitness was being promoted through the armed services. In 1923, a journal appropriately titled *Pahlavi* that covered issues related to the military discussed the ethos of sports—a discussion that, although intended primarily for the military man, also extended to the ordinary citizen. Among the first conditions of hygiene, it claimed, were physical strength and the maintenance of a healthy body. However, in order for exercise to become more than just a passing fad, it had to be made a part of every Iranian's daily life; in other words, a culture of health, fitness, and athleticism had to be forged. In saying so, this article created an antecedent for Iranians' purported penchant for sports by pointing out that sports had historically been a prominent feature of the great civilizations of the Greeks and the Romans, as well as of the glorified society of pre-Islamic Iran. In those cultures, too, physical exercise was considered a "regular activity" in people's lives.[34]

In 1927, a law was passed making physical fitness programs a requirement in schools and introducing sports in the daily life of Iranian youth. The law stipulated that physical exercise would become mandatory in schools and that, except for holidays, exercise would form a regular part of the school regimen.[35] Athletic instructors had to pass a medical exam and be well versed in different exercise techniques. A charter for the Pish-ahangi (Boy Scouts) of Iran was also established as a way of promoting "virtuous behavior" and to ingrain the culture of fitness and health throughout the country. It was followed by a Girl Scouts organization. Not surprisingly, scouting instructors had to be Iranian, to uphold the nationalist ideals of the state.[36] Through this charter, the state hoped to open scouting offices in the provinces and thus help to make fitness and sports a commonplace in the daily culture of the modern Iranian. In Isfahan, for instance, an office was created under the leadership of Ahmad Aram between the years 1926 and 1927. Although the office functioned for over a year, it ceased to operate between 1928 and 1929 because of lack of interest. By 1935, a new office was set up to promote scouting activities around the country.[37] Sports gained more visibility in society in part because the crown prince, later king, Mohammad Reza Pahlavi, engaged in soccer during his youth and thus set an example for the rest of the nation.[38] In 1936, a special office for physical training and scouting was founded to facilitate the instruction and promotion of sports in Iran.[39] As Sa'id Nafisi, a well-known scholar and university professor, remarked in reflecting on the creation of the Boy and Girl Scouts and the establishment of athletic facilities in Iran, "The stronger, the more powerful, and the healthier the human body is, the more a person will advance in his work, and [thus] his mind will be healthier . . .

and his aptitude greater for the acquisition of knowledge."[40] Nafisi regarded scouting as an effective way to promote physical and spiritual fitness in the interest of forging a more industrious and powerful citizenry.

For women, physical vigor became equally important. Like her male counterpart, the modern Iranian woman was exhorted to engage in physical exercise to become a more productive member of the national polity. As Hajar Tarbiyat, the head of the Society for Women, explained, "Women more than men require bodily and spiritual health. . . . Therefore, it is necessary to pay attention to the bodily health of girls and their engagement in physical exercise from childhood."[41] Presumably, women's bodies needed specialized and constant training to assist them with the difficult ordeal of pregnancy and the necessary task of nurturing "strong-minded men" for the nation.

Bodily "renewal" of the modern Iranian, however, would be incomplete without a concomitant transformation of the citizen's mind. Intellectual indoctrination occurred in schools through the publication of carefully crafted texts, and an institution was formed expressly for this purpose toward the end of Reza Shah's reign. In 1939, an establishment called the Organization for the Cultivation of Thought (*Sazman-e parvaresh-e afkar*) was created to spread the nationalist ideals of the state through various media, including the press, the theatre, and public lectures. Its primary members consisted of university professors who in certain instances had helped to define the nationalist mores of the modern Iranian.[42] The public lectures, in particular, became an expedient way to reach out to the populace, and the Organization for the Cultivation of Thought approved several topics for these talks. As expected, many of these lectures focused on ethics, or themes with specific nationalist import such as the importance of exercise and cleanliness. Records concerning the number of people attending these lectures were kept by the officials of the organization.

Intellectual indoctrination would also occur in the writing of history textbooks. As an academic topic, history lent itself especially well to nationalist purposes, for two strategic reasons. First, it repeated a narrative derived in part from, and thus endorsed by, European Orientalist scholarship, thus providing a false yet welcome veneer of authenticity.[43] Second, it aggrandized Persian culture and antiquity, assisting Iranian nationalists in their expected mechanical task of linking the celebrated past to the present. Two academic textbooks written during Reza Shah's reign illustrate this point. In 1933, a history textbook composed by a writer holding a diploma in political affairs discussed the definition and terminology of "Iran." Unsurprisingly, it began with the alleged European understanding of the term. "By Iran, Europeans refer to a plateau . . . that lies between the three plains of Mesopotamia, Turan, and Sind and the Caspian Sea and the Gulf of Oman, whose vastness comprises three million square kilometers. Thus, today's country of Iran forms a large part of the aforementioned plateau, not all of it."[44] But "Iran" was not just a locale, it was also the progenitor of a race (*nezhad*), and it was in this plateau that the "center of life and formation of the civilization of the Iranian race" had emerged.[45] Geography played a visible role in assigning racial characteristics to peoples and civilizations. This same textbook, moreover, pointed out that the word "Iran" was derived from the term "Arya." Clearly, Iranian scholars with some knowledge of Orientalist scholarship popularized select European usages of the term "Iran," but, curiously, they made little effort to discuss uses of the term in non-European literature. Schoolbooks became an easy and accessible way for Pahlavi policy makers to promote the state's agenda of nationalism, as they had a captive and impressionable audience in students, and facilities for ideological dissemination through established institutions such as schools.

Abbas Eqbal Ashtiyani, a prolific historian of the Pahlavi years, composed several such history texts. In one work, used in the first year of Iranian high schools, he talked about the history of "old Iran." Predictably, the section on the history of Iran began with reference to the Aryans in the territory that formed the Iranian nation—a chronology that echoed Orientalist scholarship on the subject—who were "of the white race."[46] In a brief section, he offered a telling explanation of race. Noting that human beings from different geographic regions also had different physical characteristics, he, following many Western scholars, divided them into four races: the white race, the yellow race, the black race, and the red race. According to Eqbal Ashtiyani, members of the white race possessed a high level of intellectual aptitude, as did some individuals of the yellow race. However, those belonging to the black race, whose members predominantly lived in Africa, "are considered the least talented people and still live in barbarity."[47] The matter-of-fact manner in which Eqbal Ashtiyani dispersed his opinions made his racialist comments all the more alarming, as they indicated the acceptance of such notions among certain cadres of the modernist literati. That discussions of history and race became self-congratulatory was a given. In fabricating a lineage that the modern nation could be proud of, nationalist historians readily adopted and adapted the racial-linguistic views characteristic not only of Orientalists such as Ernest Renan and Gobineau, who had been familiar with Persian antiquity as well as its contemporary culture and society, but also of many Western scholars and laypersons in the century from 1850 to 1950.[48]

In the tradition of Qajar monarchs, Reza Shah also had to forge an ancient and distinguished lineage for himself. A document found in the archives of the Iranian Ministry of Foreign Affairs clearly makes this point. Written in English, this short biographical sketch of Reza Shah was presumably meant to be distributed to foreign governments in contact with Iran. It most likely served as the "official" chronicle of the monarch's life. According to this source, Reza Shah not only had "descended from a very ancient and noble family of Iran," but his birthplace, Savad Kuh in Mazandaran, was home to "the purest stock of the Iranian race, whose blood has not been contaminated by any heterogenious [sic] strains." Moreover, the king belonged to a people "who have made themselves famous for their heroism and their patriotism."[49] It is significant that as the ultimate embodiment of the nation, Iran's latest monarch had to portray himself as having "pure" Persian ancestry. By becoming a true, unadulterated Persian, he legitimated his power and stood out against the Safavid and Qajar kings who had descended from Turkic tribes. Unlike Ahmad Shah Qajar, whom Reza Shah had replaced, it was suggested that Reza Shah's commitment to the country was unequivocal because of both his heritage and his military deeds. The monarch's official biography contrasted with the version presented by British sources, which did not speak of his pedigree, instead noting simply that he had come "of a small family from Sawad Kuh in Mazanderan."[50]

Increasingly, the modern Iranian citizen had to embrace ethnic homogeneity. Such uniformity could be forced through the imposition of a language that represented the chosen ethnic identity of the state. The contradictions in and impractical application of such racial claims and policies were not probed in nationalist circles. Rather, Persianization proceeded apace with the creation of the language academy, Farhangestan, in 1935. Aside from striving to cleanse the Persian language of certain foreign words, the Farhangestan also sought to promote literary activities, and it included in its membership scholarly figures such as Mohammad Taqi Bahar, Isa Sadeq, Ali Akbar Dehkhoda, Sa`id Nafisi, and education minister Ali Asghar Hekmat.[51]

Domestically, the period from 1926 to 1941 was a busy time for Iranian modernists. In this interval the government also tried to subdue tribal rebellions and to maintain peace along its volatile borders. Although internally the mantra for reform was "renewal," externally the country struggled against old ghosts. In 1933, Iran revised the terms of its oil agreement with Britain. The shah also took a much celebrated trip to Turkey, whose ruler Mustafa Kemal Ataturk he admired. In a letter thanking the Turkish president for his hospitality, Reza Shah remarked, "It was with complete pleasure that I witnessed the enormous progress of the nation of my friendly neighbor, which was accomplished with complete speed in a short period of time under the patriotic guidance of its august leader."[52] Reza Shah, too, strove to move Iran toward the path of progress, a concept that increasingly became synonymous with Europeanization and with top-down legislation that often emulated Ataturk's policies. Moreover, the country strove to maintain a semblance of stability along its frontiers through the eventual recognition of its new neighbor, Iraq, and the signing of the Sa`d Abad Pact (1937).

Perhaps the shah's main miscalculation was his gravitation toward Germany in the later years of his reign. Here, it should be emphasized that although historically Iran had turned to Great Britain and France for ideas of enlightenment and reform, Germany was an object of interest and curiosity for Iranian statesmen and intellectuals as early as the nineteenth century. After France's loss in the Franco-Prussian War (1871), many Iranian intellectuals became interested in Bismarck and looked for the secrets of Germany's military success against a power that the Iranians had long admired. There are many extant nineteenth-century manuscripts on the Franco-Prussian War, and historians of modern Iran have often overlooked this interest.[53] The growing ties with Germany until 1941 were political, economic, and ideological. Notable after 1933 was Germany's promotion in Iran of Nazi "Aryan" ideology, which went far beyond what had been put forth by scholars, and related increased political and economic ties between Germany and Iran to the common "Aryan" superiority of both countries. Reza Shah's affinity for Germany as an alternative power to Great Britain and the Soviet Union had contemporary reasons, but it must be placed in the proper historical context.[54] Whatever the purported benefits from this alliance, it cost Reza Shah his crown when he was forced out of the country by Great Britain and the Soviet Union in 1941.

In 1930, more than a decade before Reza Shah's downfall and several years before some of the regime's controversial cultural policies would be implemented, Abol Hasan Forughi, the younger son of the nineteenth-century journalist Mirza Hosain Khan Zoka al-Molk, reflected on the meaning of the terms "renewal" and "nationality." According to him, "renewal," as interpreted by the state, referred to reforms undertaken in an attempt to acquire the accoutrements of European civilization. The modern Iranian renewed himself not by reincarnating or refurbishing an old identity, but by making himself an extension of the European persona. In other words, renewal was nothing more than imitation. Forughi saw this blind imitation as contradicting the nationalist mission of the state. For Forughi, true nationalism consisted of a nation fulfilling its humanitarian historical mission. He challenged the racist claims of his peers, who glorified the supposed "pure" Iranian race of the Sassanians and saw the reason for Iran's decline in the mixing of the Iranian race with other races.[55]

Criticisms such as this would rekindle debate on the meaning of Iranianness and pose challenges to the definitions provided by the modernists of the Reza Shah era. Commenting on his reign more than ten years after the fact, one writer remarked, "Many things are said about Reza Shah the Great. . . . No sooner had he been sent . . . [away] than there was not a single insult that had not been directed against him." Despite such criticism, this writer, Taqi Binesh, regarded Reza Shah as a "patriotic man" who had made important contributions to the nation.[56]

Although there was little consensus on the legacy of Reza Shah's national-ist policies, the theme of nationalism remained salient in the political culture of Iran. In 1941, when Mohammad Reza Pahlavi succeeded to the throne, the country faced the hardships of the Second World War. Among the most imme-diate challenges that the young monarch had to cope with was the Azerbai-jan Crisis of 1945—a crisis that once again placed land and frontiers at the forefront of patriotic debate and invited foreign interference in Iran's polit-ical affairs. To the Iranian nationalist, Azerbaijan formed an irrevocable part of Iran; the Iranian nation was inconceivable without this contested province. The Azerbaijan crisis, occurring at a moment of transition in Iranian poli-tics, showed an ambivalent international public the powerful nationalist ide-ology that was driving the Iranian state. It also demonstrated Iranian frustration with foreign presence on its soil and with outside influence in its political affairs.[57]

It is perhaps ironic that, despite the substantial capital and creativity Reza Shah invested in spreading his nationalist vision of renewal, the most cele-brated nationalist moment in modern Iranian history would occur *after* his reign, when Mohammad Mosaddeq launched his campaign to nationalize Iranian oil. Although an analysis of the particulars of this movement is beyond the purview of this essay, it is a commonplace of modern Iranian historiog-raphy that "Mosaddeq's defense of Iranian independence . . . his charisma, and his overthrow with American and British support helped make him an enduring national hero."[58] Unlike Reza Shah, Mosaddeq came to represent a nationalism that was deemed distinctly antiforeign, as it was directed against foreign control of Iran's most profitable resource, and therefore authentically Iranian. Moreover, nationalist discourse during the oil crisis was not cosmetic in nature. Rather, it related to one of the most abiding symbols of Iranian-ness: the nation's land and its resources.

After Mosaddeq's fall, Mohammad Reza Pahlavi pursued a nationalist agenda akin to his father's. He took on the grand title "Arya Mehr," mean-ing light of the Aryans, and revived Persian mythology by hosting a lavish and much reviled 2,500th-year celebration of the monarchy in 1971. He was, however, more closely allied with foreign powers, especially the United

States, than his father had been. Increasingly, the religious establishment, led by Ayatollah Khomeini, became emboldened and attacked the policies of the Pahlavis, particularly the regime's dependent relationship on the United States.[59] As during the Mosaddeq period and, to a large degree, in the constitutional revolution, Iranian nationalism was largely expressed through juxtaposition of the Iranians to threatening foreigners, notwithstanding the cultural claims to uniqueness and antiquity made by the state.

In 1980, one of the first national challenges the Islamic Republic faced was the defense of the country's frontiers. Although the nation would be preoccupied with the war against Iraq, it would still find the time to recast the Iranian citizen. Like the Pahlavi state, the Islamic Republic of Iran transformed the modern Iranian through attire, historiography, and religion, forging yet another culture of Iranianness in the process. Religious fundamentalism, in other words, had become one more expression of nationalism.

CONCLUSION

When Ernest Renan delivered his speech at the Sorbonne in 1882, he observed, "More valuable by far than common customs posts and frontiers conforming to strategic ideas is the fact of sharing, in the past, a glorious heritage and regrets, and of having, in the future, [a shared] programme to put into effect, or the fact of having suffered, enjoyed, and hoped together. These are the kinds of things that can be understood in spite of differences of race and language."[60] For Iranian nationalists, however, conveying a shared past and outlook proved elusive, for they did not always have the same historical memories or future aspirations. If anything, by tracing the articulations of Iranianness for over a century, one is struck by the difference in emphasis placed by various nationalists on the bases of nationhood. Still, there was something holding this nation together. For Iranian nationalists of whatever breed, the world beyond Iran was often either a land to reclaim as part of the national heritage, or a society simultaneously to emulate and to mistrust. Perhaps the one thread of commonality in this discourse was the desire to define and defend a land and culture as uniquely Iranian. Rather than embodying any single vision, the modern Iranian became an amalgam of these trends, seen as contributing to the good of the nation.

NOTES

    I would like to thank Rudi Matthee for his useful comments on this paper. I am especially grateful to Nikki Keddie for her many important additions and contributions to this essay.

1. My analysis of nationalism in this essay has been informed by the following theoretical works: Benedict Anderson, *Imagined Communities: Reflections on the Origin and Spread of Nationalism* (London and New York: Verso, 1983, repr. 1991); P. Chatterjee, *The Nation and Its Fragments: Colonial and Postcolonial Histories* (Princeton: Princeton University Press, 1993); idem, *Nationalist Thought and the Colonial World: A Derivative Discourse?* (London: Zed Books, 1986); Homi Bhabha, ed., *Nation and Narration* (London and New York: Routledge, 1990); Ernest Gellner, *Nations and Nationalism* (Oxford: Blackwell, 1983); Eric Hobsbawm, *Nations and Nationalism since 1780: Programme, Myth, Reality* (Cambridge and New York: Cambridge University Press, 1990).

2. Nikki Keddie, "Viewing Nationalism in Iran: History and Theory," unpublished paper.

3. Joseph Arthur de Gobineau, *Trois ans en Asie* (Paris: Editions A. M. Métailié, 1980), 212.

4. Ibid., 217.

5. Ibid., 206.

6. Ernest Renan, "What is a Nation?" in *Becoming National: A Reader,* ed. Geoff Eley and Ronald Grigor Suny (New York and Oxford: Oxford University Press, 1996), 52–54.

7. Maryam Sanjabi, "Rereading the Enlightenment: Akhundzada and His Voltaire," *Iranian Studies* 28 (1995): 39. Also, Juan R. I. Cole, "Marking Boundaries, Marking Time: The Iranian Past and the Construction of the Self by Qajar Thinkers," *Iranian Studies* 29 (1996): 35–56.

8. Mirza Fath Ali Akhundzadeh, *Maktubat-e Jalal va Kamal al-Dauleh ya seh maktub,* 1285 A.H./1868 (manuscript at the Ketabkhaneh-e Melli-ye Iran, no. 1123), 21 and 200–01.

9. Sanjabi, "Rereading the Enlightenment," 52.

10. A. H. Shissler, "A Student Abroad in Late Ottoman Times: Ahmet Ağaoğlu and French Paradigms in Turkist Thought," in *Iran and Beyond: Essays in Middle Eastern History in Honor of Nikki R. Keddie,* ed. Rudi Matthee and Beth Baron (Costa Mesa, CA: Mazda, 2000), 43.

11. Nikki Keddie, "Viewing Nationalism in Iran: History and Theory," unpublished paper.

12. For a study of Kermani, see Iraj Parsinejad, "Mirza Aqa Khan Kermani and Literature," *Iran Nameh* 8 (1990): 541–66. Parsinejad notes that Malek al-Sho`ara Bahar criticized Kermani's linguistic theories.

13. Mirza Aqa Khan Kermani, *A'eneh-ye sekandari* (Tehran, 1906), 14. Also, see Mohamad Tavakoli-Targhi, "Refashioning Iran: Language and Culture during the Constitutional Revolution," *Iranian Studies* 23 (1990): 77–101; and idem, "Tarikh-pardazi va Iran ara'i," *Iran Nameh* 12 (1373/1994): 583–628.

14. *Habl al-Matin* 41, no. 3, Sept. 1900, 15–16. For further analysis of the Iranian homeland, see Firoozeh Kashani-Sabet, *Frontier Fictions: Shaping the Iranian Nation, 1804–1946* (Princeton: Princeton University Press, 1999).

15. Janet Afary, *The Iranian Constitutional Revolution, 1906–1911: Grassroots Democracy, Social Democracy, and the Origins of Feminism* (New York: Columbia University Press, 1996), 64.

16. *Rahnema,* 17 Rajab 1325/27 August 1907, 3.

17. *Tamaddon,* 14 Safar 1326/16 March 1908, 2.

18. *Habl al-Matin,* nos. 112, 113, 114, 115, 116, 9–15 Sept. 1907, as examples. Also, Mangol Bayat, *Iran's First Revolution* (Oxford: Oxford University Press, 1991), and Cyrus Amir-Mokri, "Redefining Iran's Constitutional Revolution" (Ph.D. dissertation, University of Chicago, 1992).

19. *Tamaddon,* no. 14, 20 Rabi` al-avval 1325/1907, 3.

20. *Jonub,* no. 12, 10 Rabi` al-avval 1329/1911, 2.

21. *Jonub,* no. 16, 11 Rabi` al-thani 1329/1911, 4.

22. *Jonub,* no. 11, 3 Safar 1329/1911, 8.

23. *Ettehad,* 30 Rabi` al-avval 1333/15 Feb. 1915, 1.

24. For discussions of *Kaveh,* see Amir-Mokri, "Redefining Iran's Constitutional Revolution," 182–83.

25. Iran, National Archives, Ma`aref "B," Folder 18, Document 373.

26. Here, I am not suggesting that the "state" was monolithic and unchanging during the Pahlavi years. Yet, in the area of cultural nationalism, there were certain continuities and it is important to highlight such long-term trends.

27. For instance, the journal *Pahlavi* often referred heroically to Reza Khan. For more on the army, see Stephanie Cronin, *The Army and the Creation of the Pahlavi State in Iran, 1910–1926* (London: Tauris Academic Studies, 1997).

28. Iran, National Archives, Ma`aref "B," File 51006, Document 324, "Nezam-nameh-e mottahed al-shekl nemudan-e albaseh," 3 Bahman 1307/1928.

29. Iran, National Archives, Ma`aref "B," File 51006, Document 324, "Qanun-e mottahed al-shekl nemudan-e albaseh-ye atba`-e Iran dar dakheleh-ye mamlakat," 10 Dai 1307/1928.

30. Houchang Chehabi, "Staging the Emperor's New Clothes: Dress Codes and Nation-Building under Reza Shah," *Iranian Studies* 26 (1993): 225. This article includes an English translation of the dress code law.

31. Iran, National Archives, Ma`aref "A," File 51006, Document 568, "Nezam-nameh-e kanun-e banovan."

32. Badr al-Moluk Bamdad, *From Darkness into Light: Women's Emancipation in Iran,* ed. and trans. F. R. C. Bagley (New York: Exposition Press, 1977). For more on the idea of patriotic womanhood, see Firoozeh Kashani-Sabet, "Patriotic Womanhood: The Culture of Feminism in Modern Iran," paper presented at the Biennial Conference of the Society for Iranian Studies, Bethesda, May 2000.

33. Sina Vahid, *Qiyam-e Gauharshad* (Tehran, 1987).

34. *Pahlavi,* no. 19, 19 Jumada al-ukhra 1342/1923, 3–4.

35. *Vezarat-e ma`aref va auqaf va sana`i-ye mostazrafeh: Ehsa'iyeh-ye ma`aref va madares (1307–1308)* (Tehran: Matba`eh-ye raushana'i, n.d.), 27.

36. Iran, National Archives, Ma`aref "A," File 51006, Document 441, "Asasnameh-ye tashkilat-e pish-ahangi-ye Iran." Also, A. Reza Arasteh, *Education and Social Awakening in Iran, 1850–1968* (Leiden: E. J. Brill, 1969).

37. *Salnameh-e ma`aref-e Esfahan, sal-e tahsili-ye 1313/1314* (n.p., n.d.), 37–39.

38. For more on other aspects of the history of sports in Iran, see Houchang Chehabi, "A Short History of Iranian Soccer," *Iran Nameh* 27 (1999): 89–113; and idem, "Sport and Politics in Iran: The Legend of Gholamreza Takhti," *International Journal of the History of Sport* 12, no. 3 (Dec. 1995): 48–60.

39. Iran, National Archives, Ma`aref "B," File 51006, Document 402, "Asasnameh-ye edareh-ye pish-ahangi va tarbiyat-e badani."

40. Sa`id Nafisi, *Sokhanraniha-ye sazman-e parvaresh-e afkar* (Tehran: Chap-khaneh-ye Ferdausi, 1318/1939), 154–55.

41. *Khatabehha-ye kanun-e banovan* (Tehran, 1314/1935), 13.

42. Iran, National Archives, Prime Ministry Files, 108011/3268. "Tashkilat va che-gunegi-ye karha-ye sazman" and "Asasnameh-ye sazman-e parvaresh-e afkar."

43. M. Tavakoli-Targhi has prepared a manuscript on Orientalism and national-ism in Iran, although I have not seen his work. For his discussions of historiography and language in early Iranian nationalism, see Tavakoli-Targhi, "Refashioning Iran" and "Tarikh pardazi."

44. Hosain Farhodi, *Daureh-ye omumi-ye tarikh* (Tehran, 1312/1933), 89.

45. Ibid., 89.

46. Abbas Eqbal Ashtiyani, *Daureh-ye tarikh-e omumi* (Tehran, 1315/1936), 133. For the importance of history and historiography in Iranian nationalism during the Qajar period, see Tavakoli-Targhi, "Refashioning Iran"; and idem, "Tarikh pardazi."

47. Ashtiyani, *Tarikh-e omumi*, 17–18.

48. For a critique of Orientalist scholarship, see Edward Said, *Orientalism* (New York: Pantheon, 1978).

49. Iran, Archives of the Ministry of Foreign Affairs, Year 1313/Carton 20, "The Pahlavi Dynasty," 1.

50. *Iran Political Diaries,* ed. R. M. Burrell (Buckinghamshire: Archive Editions, 1997), 8:73.

51. Iran, National Archives, Ma`aref "B," 51006/523.

52. Note to Ataturk, Archives of the Ministry of Foreign Affairs, Tehran, 1313/1934, Carton 20.

53. In 1302 A.H./1884 the newspaper *Sharaf,* for instance, wrote a brief and favor-able biography of Bismarck. A few years later, the newspaper *Sharafat,* which suc-ceeded *Sharaf,* also published a biographical sketch of Bismarck. See *Sharaf,* no. 24, Moharram 1302/1884; *Sharafat,* No. 27, Rabi` al-thani 1316 A.H./1898. For more on Iran-ian interest in the Franco-Prussian War, see Kashani-Sabet, *Frontier Fictions,* ch. 3.

54. On German-Iranian relations, see Ahmad Mahrad, *Dokumentation über die persisch-deutschen Beziehungen von 1918–1933* (Bern: Herbert Lang, 1975). Also, idem, *Iran unter der Herrschaft Reza Schahs* (Frankfurt/Main: Campus-Verlag, 1977).

55. Abol Hasan Fo”ughi, *Tahqiq dar haqiqat-e tajaddod va melliyat* (Tehran: Chap-khaneh-ye ettehadiyeh, 1309/1930), 34.

56. *Azadi,* 8 Esfand 1331/1952, 1.

57. Ervand Abrahamian, *Iran between Two Revolutions* (Princeton: Princeton Uni-versity Press, 1982), 388–415.

58. Nikki R. Keddie, *Roots of Revolution: An Interpretive History of Modern Iran* (New Haven: Yale University Press, 1981), 141. For more on the oil nationalization issue, see Mostafa Elm, *Oil, Power, and Principle: Iran's Oil Nationalization and its After-math* (Syracuse: Syracuse University Press, 1992).

59. Keddie, *Roots of Revolution,* 158–60.

60. G. Eley and R. Suny, *Becoming National,* 52–53.

8 / Foreign Education, the Women's Press, and the Discourse of Scientific Domesticity in Early-Twentieth-Century Iran

This article notes how the ideology of scientific domesticity—the modernist discourses on hygiene, disease prevention, and household management—was introduced by foreign and missionary girls' schools in Iran and taken up first by the Iranian women's press, specifically the journal Alam-e Nesvan (Women's World, 1920–1934), and eventually by the state. Education for women came to center on scientific domesticity as the Iranian women's press and Reza Shah's new Pahlavi state (1925–41) embraced this modern notion.

The role of foreigners in Iranian education has been a controversial one. Some have seen it as an aspect of semicolonial dominance,[1] while others have regarded it more positively and sympathetically.[2] In a reevaluation of foreign and missionary institutions, their agendas, and influence on modern education, it is important to understand the complexities of the cultural encounters as experienced by both foreigners and Iranians. The rise of modern female education in Iran and its guiding discourses were intimately tied to foreign educational projects. But, rather than a domination of the powerful West over the weak East, this was a complex interaction between foreign-initiated efforts and Iranian private and state initiatives in the context of changing socioeconomic processes. Adopting this perspective allows us to evaluate the active contribution of Iranians themselves and how they fashioned foreign influences and models to fit their own needs.

Changing socioeconomic and political conditions provided possibilities for new ways of imagining the role of women in the household and society. In this context, foreigners and missionaries had an agenda for Iranian women to follow Western models of education and domestic management. Central to this agenda was the discourse on scientific domesticity that received grow-ing indigenous support, exemplified in the women's journal *Alam-e Nesvan*.

The advocacy of ideals of household management and domesticity (albeit modern and scientific) might appear paradoxical in light of today's feminism, where career and domestic roles are at opposite poles. But in the early twen-tieth century, it was a project of expanding opportunities for upper- and middle-class Iranian women. This project was realized under Reza Shah Pahlavi (1925–41), when the previous government's neglect of female educa-tion was to a large extent overcome.

THE EARLIEST FOREIGN AND MISSIONARY GIRLS' SCHOOLS IN IRAN

Foreign missionaries and organizations from Britain, France, and the United States opened schools in Iran in the nineteenth century. The creation of schools for girls and the spread of foreign and missionary education in Iran radically changed the nature of female education, traditionally limited to religious instruction and primarily an avocation of the wealthy. One of the oldest and most widespread forms of education available to girls and women was the *maktab* system that taught religious subjects, the Quran, and basic reading, writing, and arithmetic. For the great majority of *maktab* students, educa-tion did not continue after the elementary level, and girls usually attended until the age of eight or nine years. Private tutoring for girls of the highest social classes has been documented for the Safavid and Qajar periods, but was most likely present among the ruling classes before. Royal women of the court received private training in Quranic studies, reading, writing, calligraphy, and Persian.[3]

Although the British had a major political and economic presence through-out the country, their missionary educational activity in Iran was not as exten-sive as that of the French and the Americans. As early as 1869, however, the English Church Missionary Society set up a mission and school in Iran. British Anglican missionary schools were focused in the cities of Isfahan, Kerman, Yazd, and Shiraz.[4] French and American missionary educational projects con-centrated in the north and northwest, in the cities of Tehran, Hamadan, Tabriz, and Orumiyeh.

By the turn of the last century, increasing numbers of Iranian Muslims were becoming attracted to French and American missionary education, which had begun by catering primarily to Iranian Christians and Jews. French edu-cational missions varied in their intended audience, one focusing on Iranian Jews and the others on Iranian Christians and Muslims. But they aimed less at conversion and more at promoting French language and secular values. Muslim conversion to Christianity was considered apostasy according to Islamic law and was punishable by death or loss of property. The Qajar state eventually forbade missionaries from converting Iranians of any religion, due to complaints launched by leaders of the Armenian community. As a result, missionaries looked increasingly toward educational projects as avenues for "improving" Iranian lives through modernization and Westernization. Such efforts were particularly important in relation to female education, where state activity and sponsorship was lacking.

French foreign and missionary schools made the strongest cultural and educational impact on Iran until the mid-twentieth century, when U.S. influence stepped in to replace it. French missionary and foreign schools included the Lazarist Catholic Mission, the Alliance Française, and the Alliance Israélite Universelle. The Lazarists opened a school in Tabriz in 1839, while the Alliance Française and Alliance Israélite established their schools in the late nineteenth century. Lazarist schools were organized in opposition to American Mission schools, which emphasized religious instruction.[5]

In the 1860s, the French Catholic order of the Sisters of Saint Vincent de Paul opened girls' schools in Tehran, Orumiyeh, Tabriz, and Isfahan.[6] The Tehran branch (later renamed Jeanne d'Arc) was established in 1875 and offered instruction in reading, writing, French, and some history and geography. Sewing, ironing, and housekeeping were also included,[7] constituting the beginnings of a new educational curriculum for girls.

The Alliance Française, a French cultural organization founded in Paris, focused primarily on teaching French language and literature. By the late nineteenth and early twentieth century, it had set up schools in Tehran, Rasht, Borujerd, Shiraz, and Tabriz and provided financial and educational assistance to missionary and Iranian schools that taught French.[8]

The Alliance Israélite Universelle, founded in Paris in 1860, was primarily concerned with improving the educational, moral, legal, and social status of Jews internationally.[9] Its first school, Ettehad, opened in Tehran in 1898,[10] and, due to popular demand from the Tehran Jewish community, the Alliance set up a girls' school in the same year.[11] Soon after, schools for Jewish girls and boys were established in Hamadan (1900), Isfahan (1901), Shiraz (1903), and Kermanshah (1904).[12] The Alliance Israélite's specific educational and moral goals were "improving" Jewish Iranian women's lives, teaching girls to become worthy companions for male graduates, and helping eradicate child marriage.[13]

The legacy of French cultural and educational programs in Iran in the nineteenth and early twentieth centuries was considerable. Most educated Iranians of the early twentieth century knew some French, and many of those who held high political office had studied in France or at French schools. In addition, many foreign instructors employed by the state were recruited from France. By the Reza Shah period, a solid foundation of French influence in the organization of Iranian education was in place. The administration, laws, regulations, schools, pedagogical techniques, textbooks, curriculum, examinations, and standards of the Iranian educational system were borrowed heavily from the French model. By 1930, the Ministry of Education employed twenty-three French instructors, and almost all state secondary schools of the period taught French as a second language.[14]

THE AMERICAN PROTESTANT MISSION AND THE CURRICULUM OF MODERN HOUSEHOLD MANAGEMENT

Despite the tremendous impact of French schools on modern education, the most significant activity on behalf of female education in Iran was led by the American Protestant Mission, the largest U.S. missionary institution in Iran. In the 1830s, the Mission established elementary schools in northwestern Iran, where a large Christian minority population resided. The first school for boys opened in Orumiyeh in 1836 and for girls in 1838.[15] These earliest schools initially worked among the Assyrian Christian population and later included Armenians, Jews, Zoroastrians, and Muslims as they branched out to other cities in Iran. Because of the religious character of the schools, children of Iranian Christians had more opportunity and incentive to attend them. However, shortly thereafter, the American Mission opened separate schools for Muslims at the request of Mohammad Shah (r. 1834–48).[16]

The American Mission's most famous schools in Iran were located in Tehran. In 1872, it opened a boys' primary school in Tehran, which in 1925 branched out to include a high school called the American College of Tehran, renamed Alborz College in 1935. The Mission opened a girls' primary school called Iran Bethel in 1874, which later expanded to include a middle school and high school (called Nurbakhsh).[17] Iran Bethel enrolled initially only European and Iranian Christians, until 1888, when small numbers of Jewish and Zoroastrian girls entered. As the number of girls enrolled in Iran Bethel increased, Muslim girls joined as well. By 1913, out of a total of 345 students, 154 were Muslims.[18] The first female instructors of the school were American and Iranian Armenian, and eventually Iranian Muslim women joined the faculty.[19]

The American and other foreign and missionary schools were not encroaching on state or religious territory, but instead moved into a noncompetitive arena. In the nineteenth century, the Qajar state had not yet taken an active role in sponsoring schools for boys and girls, while the ulama-run *maktabs* were for Muslim children only and taught primarily the Quran and religious subjects. Acting cautiously, American missionaries initially served the Iranian Christian communities with the aim of "reviving" their Christianity, rather than converting Muslims. However, their work among Iranian Christian minorities was not uncomplicated. Iranian-Armenian opposition to French and American missionary activity forced Mohammad Shah to issue a decree in 1840 prohibiting missionary proselytizing among both Christians and Muslims in Iran.[20]

During Naser al-Din Shah's reign (1848–96), American missionary schools increased in number, opening in Tehran and other large cities. The Tabriz mission established the Boarding and Day School for Armenian and Muslim Girls in 1873.[21] By 1895, in northwestern Iran alone, the American Mission had 117 schools, enrolling 2,410 students. By the late 1890s it operated 147 schools throughout Iran with a total of approximately 1,000 girls enrolled.[22] Muslims gradually became interested in the educational opportunities these schools offered their children and asked for admission. The Tehran, Tabriz, and Hamadan schools, especially, had a growing Muslim contingent.[23] A few Muslim women reportedly even lied about their age to gain admission to Iran Bethel.[24] Some Muslim parents had strong misgivings about sending their daughters to a foreign school and would make surprise visits to check up on their activities.[25]

In spite of the increasing popularity of American schools and perhaps because of it, Naser al-Din Shah and Mozaffar al-Din Shah (r. 1896–1907) wavered between acknowledging their contributions to Iran, limiting their activities, and ordering their closure.[26] In 1903 Mozaffar al-Din Shah ordered parents to remove their daughters from Iran Bethel, "where they were being taught to wear high shoes with long shirts," referring perhaps to the American-style women's attire worn by missionary teachers in the school. Such threats did not do long-term damage to the American school, for it was up and running after ten days and within a month all of the girls had returned.[27]

The American Mission saw its work among Iranian women as a means of instituting larger social change. By the 1850s, Presbyterian groups in the United States came to regard women as important resources of missionary work and as targets of such work.[28] As Mary Park Jordan, teacher at the Tehran American Boys' School and wife of Samuel Jordan, the school's illustrious founder and principal, often had her students memorize, "No country rises higher than the level of the women of that country."[29] Women trained in Mission schools were expected to be role models and leaders in their homes and communities.

The curriculum of the American schools differed in significant ways from that of the French schools, but shared some features with them as well. The earliest American Mission schools had a largely religious curriculum. Separate schools for Muslim students offered comparable subjects, with the exception that the Bible was used as a textbook and not an instrument of conversion and/or profession of faith.[30] Later, and certainly by the time of the establishment in 1925 of the American College for Boys in Tehran, the American Mission curriculum expanded to include physics, geometry, physiology, botany, literature, Persian, Arabic, and French.[31] While "Christian instruction was accepted in the curriculum as a matter of necessity rather than of choice,"[32] a growing number of students and their families were attracted to the science instruction. Like the Lazarist schools, American Protestant mission schools introduced a new scientific course of study for girls. Domestic science instruction, or what the Americans called "household arts," was considered an important and essential course of study for girls and young women.

Instruction in modern household management began as early as the mid-nineteenth century. In 1852 the American Mission girls' school in Orumiyeh, headed by Fidelia Fiske, offered "household arts" to the fifty students enrolled. As the record stated, "The conviction had grown on this practical educator that it was [as] important for the girls to learn household arts [as] to learn the sciences and this conviction she put into vigorous execution." Once assigned to the Orumiyeh school, Fiske was told to "begin Mount Holyoke in Persia," referring to Fiske's all-women's alma mater in the United States.[33] The orthodox Protestantism of the American Mission insisted on gender differences as the foundation of social and religious order and socialized its female students to adhere to a middle-class-American model of domesticity that did not always sit well with the school's Iranian upper-class clientele.

By the early twentieth century, American Mission teachers elaborated further upon the domestic science curriculum in their girls' schools. Iran Bethel shared the same basic curriculum with its male counterpart in Tehran, with the exception of training in domestic management and household sciences that would prepare girls for modern womanhood. Boyce taught a self-designed course called "Household Arts" (which she later called "Home Economics," *khaneh-dari* in Persian) at Iran Bethel, while teaching English, Bible, and ethics at the Boys' School. The Household Arts course, which Boyce adjusted to suit Iranian needs as she saw them, taught girls the proper design, layout, and furnishing of a home; plumbing, water gathering, and water purification; heating; lighting; washing clothes; cooking; and designing and sewing clothes. According to Boyce, this new course counted as the most important instruction the girls would receive, for "it ensures so permanent a hold of the missionary on their lives after school days are over," and it did succeed in reaching into the Iranian households of girls who attended the school. Boyce's main goal "was to make the girls feel that household management was an art—not merely servant's work as many believed, and was worthy of the best efforts of educated girls." She upheld the importance of home economics, elevating it to an art, a dignified calling, and a "*science* [my emphasis] demanding as high a quality of mental activity as . . . other studies."[34] Thus, in American Mission schools, young men were expected to master courses in the physical and natural sciences, while girls were encouraged to be experts in "the science of household management."

The alliance of science and "household arts" situated Iran Bethel's curriculum in a global body of knowledge that, in the nineteenth and twentieth centuries, assumed that a hygienic, rationally controlled, scientifically ordered household fostered those same qualities in the larger nation and society. At Iran Bethel, this discourse was coupled with the "gospel of science," a component of American Protestant missionary schools in the Middle East. Missionaries incorporated into both male and female education the study of botany, zoology, astronomy, chemistry,[35] and, for girls only, the science of the household.

Important research of the past several decades has highlighted how movements of feminism, modernity, and nationalism in the late-nineteenth- and early-twentieth-century Middle East were tied to the dynamics of gender and class.[36] The literature on scientific domesticity in the European and North American context[37] has informed studies on similar movements in Asia, the Middle East, and Africa, with a major modification that takes into consideration colonialism and empire-building.[38] In the Middle Eastern context, the influence of scientific domesticity was greatest in the arena of female education and the foundation of girls' schools.[39] The discourse of scientific domesticity was tied to the general movement for female education in Iran, but it was first and foremost the concern of a particular social group—the new, modern, urban middle class. As such, it was shaped by modern socioeconomic changes that linked Iran to the world economy, in increasing contact with Europe and later the United States.

The international movement of scientific domesticity, coupled with Protestant missionary zeal, functioned also as part of broader colonial discourses that deemed women in the Middle East, especially Muslim women, to be "backward" and "uncivilized." These assumptions were later picked up by Iranian reformers of the early twentieth century and especially by some of those who were active in the women's press. Iranian women who received an education from American schools were expected to be modern, scientifically astute wives and mothers, as opposed to traditional, illiterate, ignorant, and superstitious women. Since missionaries were forbidden to engage in direct conversion of Iranians, they perceived their educational goals as at least "improving" Iranian women's lives and delivering them from the "darkness" of child marriage, temporary marriage, and polygamy.

Boyce's course on household management was influenced both by the international movement of scientific domesticity and by the American missionary ethos of the "dignity of labor." The new curriculum and its hands-on approach to domestic work were not embraced initially by Boyce's students, who reportedly approached Household Arts "not unmingled with scorn," for they did not think it as worthy a subject as their other courses in astronomy, pedagogy, and literature.[40] Girls from elite and upper-middle-class families, who were the bulk of students at Iran Bethel at the time, were not accustomed to doing housework and viewed it as demeaning and below their station. Well-to-do families had a retinue of servants hired to do such work, and, consequently, housework was servant's work.

The American Boys' School, too, challenged Iranian notions of manual work as limited to servants and instituted training in the "dignity of labor" by requiring students to perform chores on campus. Students took turns waiting on tables, so that "a prince or a son of the prime minister serve[d] food to a student who was so poor that he was on full scholarship."[41] Students were also responsible for making their beds and straightening their rooms. As Arthur Boyce, vice-president of the American Boys' School, wrote, "It was not uncommon for parents to ask if they could hire a servant for their son and free him from these requirements."[42] Thus, American missionary education helped redefine traditional social-class roles and shaped a new model of Iranian womanhood. But it did not challenge class differences, since American Mission efforts mainly catered to upper- and upper-middle-class Iranians.

By and large, children of the Muslim elite, as well as those from wealthy Iranian religio-ethnic minority families, attended missionary schools. Protestant missionaries prided themselves on serving the Iranian power-holding classes, whose outlook was believed to be more Western and modern, as defined by American Protestant values.[43] Samuel Jordan, president of the American College for Boys (later renamed Alborz College), made a direct connection between the American Mission's goal of modernizing and Westernizing Iran and working with the upper classes. In 1935 he wrote:

[In] Iran since the beginning of the century, American schools have been patronized by the leading men of the country. Among the students have been enrolled sons of the princes of the royal family, first and second cousins of former Shahs, the only grandson of the present Shah, sons of Prime Ministers and other Cabinet ministers, of members of the *Majlis* (Congress), of tribal chieftains, of provincial governors, of other influential men. . . . Probably no other school in the world has ever enrolled so many of the children of the leading men of any country. . . . Our students imbibed liberal ideas, they agitated for reforms, they cooperated with other forward-looking patriots in transforming the medieval despotism of thirty years ago into the modern, progressive democracy of today.[44]

Jordan said this at the peak of Reza Shah Pahlavi's modern dictatorship, illustrating the American Mission's approval of the authoritarian modernization of Iran.

American Mission schools and hospitals originally offered services free of charge. In 1882, Iran Bethel did not charge fees and furnished free board and clothing to students.[45] However, by the early twentieth century, Mission schools did away with the free tuition and board policy, believing instead that charging tuition would "bring a higher grade of students."[46] Boyce noted that the boys who came from all corners of Iran to attend the Boys' School were mostly from "better class families as all pay board except the few who are on scholarship." Less well-to-do families were encouraged to pay what they could, even as "little as five cents a month."[47]

However, by the 1930s, Iran Bethel served a varied religious-ethnic population, encompassing the modern, urban, Iranian middle classes. As a former Iran Bethel student, who was a member of the Qajar royal family, recalled:

I now found myself sitting side by side not only with Moslems . . . but with Iranians who were also Armenian Christians or Zoroastrians or Jews, with Kurds and Azeris and Bakhtiari chieftains' daughters. Many were girls I would have never met otherwise because they were the daughters of middle-class factory owners or pharmacists or grocers, and, as they were not related to us, weren't part of our social set.[48]

Even though we do not have a complete record of its graduates, we know from existing sources and biographies that women from influential political and intellectual families attended Iran Bethel. Iran Taimurtash, daughter of Reza Shah's powerful Court Minister; Moluk Khanom Jalali, daughter of an Isfahan governor; Mehrtaj Rakhshan, educationalist and daughter of Agha Emam al-Hokama; Sattareh Farman Farmaian, founder of the professional field of social welfare in Iran and daughter of Qajar prince Abdol Hosain

Mirza Farman Farma; and Parvin E`tesami, a celebrated poet and daughter of journalist and publisher Yusof E`tesami, are among some of Iran Bethel's graduates.

The autobiography of Sattareh Farman Farmaian stands as testimony to the extent to which the learning and knowledge transmitted at Iran Bethel reached directly into the households of Iranian families.[49] Farman Farmaian's science studies in biology, health, and hygiene gave her license to advise her mother on health matters. Commenting on her mother's bleeding gums, she warned her not to rinse her mouth out with dirty water from the courtyard pool. "I am rinsing my teeth the way God says, praise be to Him . . . and I don't need your Americans to tell me what is right," her mother responded. Referring to the dangers of repeated pregnancies, the daughter counseled her mother, "Khanom, . . . perhaps you should not have so many babies. Mrs. Payne, our hygiene teacher, says you lose something from yourself every time you do."[50] Girls at the American Mission school were socialized to become a different type of woman than women of their mother's generation. Knowledge of the domestic science, hygiene, and health instruction that was part of Iran Bethel's curriculum for girls was perceived as a cure for the social ills of the twentieth-century Iranian household.

In sum, the Iranians who attended foreign and missionary schools were not interested in religious training or conversion, but in educational opportunities that would enable young men to move into political or bureaucratic service and young women to become "modern" wives and mothers. Like girls' schools and women's colleges in the U.S. of this period, American Mission education in Iran was devoted to promoting and spreading female education in order to make better household managers. But many students at Iran Bethel initially resisted the domestic science curriculum in favor of a more "academic" education. Training in the domestic sciences did not lead Iran Bethel graduates to secluded lives at home. On the contrary, many became immersed in Iranian public life as teachers, new professionals, and participants in the burgeoning Iranian women's press.

FOREIGN WOMEN, THE "NEW" IRANIAN WOMAN, AND *ALAM-E NESVAN* (*WOMEN'S WORLD*)

Alam-e Nesvan (1920–34), the longest-running Iranian women's journal of the early twentieth century, played the role of an educational manual for Iranian mothers and wives, coaching them in the modern methods of hygiene, childcare, household management, and cooking. It was published by the Alumnae Association of Iran Bethel and edited by a group of its graduates.

An average issue of the journal was forty pages in length and had sections on
hygiene, childcare, household management, women's modern dress, world
news on the progress of women, and literary topics. In addition to its
longevity, which was unique during a period of increasing state censorship,
Alam-e Nesvan was an exceptional periodical for Iran due to its collabora-
tive structure and heterogeneous makeup. Most independent periodicals of
the period, *i.e.,* those not sponsored by the state, were written and edited
by one person and financed by a wealthy patron and subscriptions. *Alam-e
Nesvan's* editorial board and contributors were a diverse community of Muslim, Armenian, Jewish, and Zoroastrian Iranians and American and European missionary educators and medical doctors. All members of the editorial
board were women, even though men sometimes held important positions
in production and management.

Given *Alam-e Nesvan's* background, it is no surprise that it carried
discussions of foreign, especially American and European, women. Such discussions were a common feature of the late-nineteenth- and early-twentieth-
century Middle Eastern women's press in general.[51] Biographical sketches of
foreign women in the section entitled "News on the Progress of Women"
appeared frequently in early issues of *Alam-e Nesvan.* Unlike Egyptian and
Ottoman women's journals, *Alam-e Nesvan* communicated a discernible U.S.
influence, due to its sponsorship by the American Mission and its production by the graduates of Iran Bethel. While coverage of European and American women predominated by a slight margin, news of women in Ottoman
Turkey, Egypt, Japan, China, and India enjoyed a prominent showing in the
journal. Such articles highlighted internationally famous personalities like the
British Queen Victoria, French scientist Marie Curie, Japanese social activists
Madames Yoshima and Hayeshi, and Turkish Minister of Education Halide
Hanom.

The United States and Europe were held up as setting the standards of modern women's "progress" in the area of motherhood and household management. In particular, they excelled in personal and familial hygiene, health
matters, and child rearing. Most of the articles in *Alam-e Nesvan's* "Disease
and Hygiene" and "Child Rearing" sections were written by American, European, and Western-trained Iranian medical doctors and made reference to
the scientific and medical progress of the United States and Europe. An article on hygiene by M. Jalali complained that Iranians did not yet know "the
meaning of the truth of cleanliness."[52] A translated article by Dr. Stamp
lamented the sad state of dental health and the field of dentistry in Iran.[53]

Articles on child rearing followed Western, bourgeois models of motherhood that necessitated a rational division of time and a scientific, orderly

method of care. For instance, detailed instructions on how to properly nurse, feed, clean, and dress children of various ages frequently appeared. The journal endorsed keeping children on strict sleeping and eating schedules[54] and taking them regularly to the doctor.[55] It even offered instructions on appropriate behavior in the doctor's office.[56]

Inculcating good morals and behavior in children was pursued in articles on how to prevent children from cursing, lying, and being disobedient.[57] An article entitled "The Happy Mother" best summed up *Alam-e Nesvan*'s discourse on modern motherhood: a perfect mother had to cook, clean, take care of and teach children, and be in the best possible moral and physical health.[58] The journal's discourse on motherhood appeared to go largely unchallenged by the readership, with rare exceptions. One reader sent in a letter asking why most of the articles in the journal were about "feeding children." The editors' blunt response evoked the nationalist preoccupation with modern motherhood: "Children are going to form the future society, and Iranian mothers are still as before ignorant of how to feed their children. As a result, they would raise weak and incapacitated individuals for the future generation."[59]

As Marilyn Booth has written for Egypt, brief biographies of foreign women appearing in the early-twentieth-century women's press "elucidate agendas as much as they point up conflicts."[60] They highlighted changes in gender roles during the 1920s and 1930s and suggested programs for change, using foreign women as guides for "Eastern" women. Iranian contributors to *Alam-e Nesvan* addressed the contradictions and conflicts in subscribing to European and American models of women's emancipation. The treatment of foreign, especially American and European, women in *Alam-e Nesvan* was fraught with ambivalence and tension. While contributors generally did not take issue with the journal's model of Western, bourgeois motherhood, some treaded carefully around the issues of European-style dress and leisure activity. In the later years of the journal, veiling and unveiling became openly discussed topics and a variety of opinions were aired. In the context of these heated debates on unveiling, partisans of both sides denounced blind imitation of European and American women.[61] "The Issue of Intermarriage Between Iranians and Foreigners," an article referring specifically to marriage between Iranian men and European women,[62] hinted at broader concerns of national identity, morality, and relations between the sexes, as it suggested Iranian ambivalence toward the European "other."

Dr. Reza-Zadeh Shafaq, a regular contributor, raised the topic of intermarriage in *Alam-e Nesvan* in 1930 and 1931.[63] Subsequent issues did not continue the discussion, perhaps because it was too delicate, given the American

missionary support for *Alam-e Nesvan*. Reza-Zadeh Shafaq presented the
terms of the debate: Would the "civilized" European woman be a proper
mother for an Iranian child? Would the "backward" Iranian mother be any
better or worse a nurturer? How could a nation progress if its women had to
compete with foreign women? Would national strength and vitality suffer as
a result? Feelings of inferiority dominated many of the discussions of current Iranian social conditions. In the global hierarchy, Iran was always
deemed at the bottom, not only in relation to Europe and the United States,
but also to parts of the Middle East and East Asia.

While European and American women were held up as models of scientific
motherhood, Egyptian, Turkish, Indian, Japanese, and Chinese women were
constructed as progressive women of "the East" in *Alam-e Nesvan*. Muslim
Egyptian women were social reformers, raising money for schools, founding
women's organizations, working in government offices, and getting a higher
education.[64] Turkish women fought in World War I and were "making rapid
progress toward Western civilization"[65] by holding public office, voting, and
getting a higher education. They were also adopting more "stylish" clothes,
showing their faces like European women and mixing in public with men.[66]
Japanese women had access to primary, secondary, and university education
and were social reformers, organizing the temperance movement.[67] Chinese
women protested foot binding and Japanese occupation, while they worked
in factories and set up teacher-training schools for women.[68] Indian women
were also going to school and forming associations made up of women of
various religious backgrounds (Hindu, Muslim, Zoroastrian, Jewish, and Bud-
dhist). Like Ottoman and Chinese women, they too were involved in anticolonial struggle, against the British.[69] What were Iranian women doing all
the while? An editorial in *Alam-e Nesvan* used the metaphor of clothing and
appearance to explain the plight of Iranian women.

> We invite women who are so observant to look with us at the East. They
> will see a gathering with Lady Japan, Lady India, Lady Ethiopia, Lady
> Ottoman, and Lady Egypt. Lady Japan is wearing a dress called Edu-
> cation and her shoes are named Industry. Lady India is wearing a dress
> called the Movement. Lady China just awoke, washed her face, and
> dressed hastily. . . . Lady Ottoman, in addition to her exalted dress
> named Literature, has adorned herself with a tiara of Ministership, a
> bracelet of Parliamentarianism, and a necklace of Patriotism. Lady Egypt
> is wearing a dress called Social Reform. Lady Ethiopia is wearing a dress
> called Humanity and is present at the gathering, proud with a dark and
> luminous face. Each lady is wearing a headscarf named Awakening. . . .

But Lady Iran is wearing a worn-out dress and has fallen asleep in the corner and is totally oblivious to the world. . . . She is snoring.[70]

Such extreme depictions of Iranian backwardness filled the pages of *Alam-e Nesvan,* coupling the sad state of Iranian women with the disunity of the nation, for Iran had not yet joined in on "renewing her nationhood through the women's awakening."[71]

SCIENTIFIC DOMESTICITY AND REZA SHAH'S REFORMS

As the previous discussion illustrated, the editors of *Alam-e Nesvan* looked primarily to Europe and the United States when seeking to change their own society, and, to a lesser degree, to Japan, Turkey, Egypt, China, and India. The West had already experienced extensive socioeconomic change that created the conditions for rescripting women's roles and identities. The dichotomy of the public and private, in which women were associated increasingly with unpaid housework and child rearing in the "private home," first took root in Europe as far back as the seventeenth century. The effects of capitalist production, manufacturing, urbanization, and their attendant ideological trends, such as individualism and feminine moral virtue, had shaped the new definitions of scientific domesticity. By the 1840s, this notion had gained such cultural currency among English middle-class writers, for example, that it was simply assumed to be the most natural arrangement.[72] It was this modernist model of domestic discourse that affected the rest of the world, along with other features of European domination.

A seemingly paradoxical impact of a modernist discourse that associated women with the domestic arena was that women's public roles were expanded. Women's increasing access to education and the professions was in part facilitated by the movement for scientific domesticity, which, some have argued, rationalized and justified modern training and education for girls and women. As mothers, women were expected to bring up the citizens of the emerging new nation-states. Therefore, they needed to be properly educated themselves in order to fulfill such a lofty role. Women's general education, built around the knowledge of child rearing and domestic management, was then cited as a form of intellectual empowerment and professional expertise that qualified them for wider participation in public life, if not for full citizenship.[73] Middle-class European and North American women had already adopted this discourse of scientific domesticity, as it enhanced and elevated their status and tied their work in the home to social and economic progress.

The entrance of European and American women into educational institutions and the professions was noted and celebrated by articles in *Alam-e Nesvan*. As was the norm with Iran's modernizing elite, *Alam-e Nesvan* looked toward the West as a model of emulation, because adopting the discourse of scientific domesticity had proven a successful strategy to expand women's political and social authority gradually. Western women had in fact achieved, through much struggle and conflict, some features of "modernity," such as university education, municipal suffrage, family law reform, and expanded access to public life and certain professions.

Antoinette Burton writes of the ways in which imperialism and colonialism informed European feminist ideologies, especially in Britain, and articulated many of the assumptions of the European women's movement.[74] Even though Iran was not formally colonized, but, rather, subjected indirectly to British and Russian political and economic influence, the power of "imperial feminism" left its mark on the discourse of *Alam-e Nesvan*. As products of American Mission schools and representatives of the newly emerging Iranian middle class, graduates of Iran Bethel shared certain assumptions with their American educators. They, too, viewed their Iranian sisters—with the exception of rural peasant women, whom they romanticized—as backward, victimized, and in need of moral uplift and progress. Like European and American feminists, they, too, used the periodical press and the language of nationalism to make their claims for expanding women's access to education.

The middle-class composition of the Iranian and American women's movements and their common reliance on the discourse of scientific domesticity as grounds for expanding women's social roles is clear. However, to note such important historical parallels between Western and Iranian feminism is not to argue that the Iranian women's movement copied its American or European counterparts. The relationship here is more complex and multifaceted. Iranian women had been using the periodical press and scientific domesticity discourses as a strategy for reform before American Mission graduates opened *Alam-e Nesvan* in 1920. Women's political participation during the constitutional period (1906–11), which has been widely documented,[75] and women's efforts to establish girls' schools[76] were early-twentieth-century movements formed in part against European encroachment and incursion into Iranian affairs.

The new domestic science curriculum of the early girls' schools and its accompanying discourse of scientific domesticity was formulated as a rejection of existing domestic arrangements in Iran, such as gender segregation, seclusion, and veiling, that were deemed "backward" and "uncivilized." The new education, its practitioners and proponents believed, would bring scientific methods and techniques to the home, rationalizing the household, reordering its members, and transforming the women who now managed it. Household management and child rearing would no longer be the sole labor and concern of servants. Mothers and wives themselves would be the center of home management and would employ their scientific knowledge about cleanliness, hygiene, nutrition, and disease prevention to care for others. Women managers of the household would be the beneficiaries of a new kind of professional training.

In the late 1920s and 1930s, scientific domesticity as an ideology tied to the movement for female education became hegemonic and was adopted by the state in the curriculum of the earliest public girls' schools and in the "Women's Awakening" propaganda of the Reza Shah era. The curriculum of state-sponsored girls' schools resembled closely the domestic science curriculum advocated by *Alam-e Nesvan* and put into effect earlier in the foreign and missionary girls' schools of the late nineteenth and early twentieth centuries. Girls shared the same curriculum as boys, studying the Quran and religion, Arabic, Persian, history, mathematics, geography, drawing, physical education, and social studies. In addition, childcare, hygiene, household arts, and "household practices" (cooking, sewing, and laundry) were included.[77] Instead of reading favored *maktab* texts, such as *Mush va gorbeh* (*Mouse and Cat*), *Hosain-e Kord* (*Hosain, the Kurd*), and *Chehel tuti* (*Forty Parrots*), female students studied domestic education textbooks. These included *Tarbiyat al-banat* (*Education of Women,* translated from French by Mirza Aziz-Allah Khan, 1906), *Hefz al-sehheh-ye zanan va dokhtaran* (*Hygiene of Women and Girls,* by Morteza Golsorkhi, 1925), and *Akhlaq* (*Morals,* by Badr al-Moluk Bamdad, 1931).[78]

During the Reza Shah era, the state promoted the hygiene and health of its citizens, an agenda advocated by reformers of the late nineteenth and early twentieth centuries, including *Alam-e Nesvan.* The state sponsored public health projects, such as nationwide inoculations, maternal and child health care, a women's hospital with a training school for medical assistants, and training centers for nurses and midwives.[79] Hygiene gained national significance on a par with industry and commerce in the pages of one government publication of the period, which placed a lengthy article on child care and children's hygiene between articles on agriculture and commercial law.[80]

State propaganda in the post-1935 period, when Reza Shah launched the official "Women's Awakening" campaign, could have come straight from the pages of *Alam-e Nesvan,* with the rhetoric portraying women as educated mothers, scientific household managers, and modern wives. This discourse of modern Iranian womanhood, actively propagated and shaped in the press, had become dominant by the 1930s. The Iranian state of the 1920s and 1930s built on agendas and discourses that had already been in circulation in the women's and general-interest periodical press. It is not surprising then that the editors and contributors of *Alam-e Nesvan* supported reforms of the Reza Shah period that included state support for female education and scientific domesticity and privileged Western clothing, dress styles, and social interaction between women and men. The journal enthusiastically endorsed Reza Shah's agenda, which addressed issues such as reforms in female education, hygiene, and public health, and, later, in family law, women's employment, and dress. They, like other reformers of the period, had every confidence that a strong, centralized state with a broad range of powers could at last carry out reform ignored by previous rulers and long overdue. The state had finally come to administer over its national household, just as women were managing their familial household.

CONCLUSION

The discourse of female education and scientific domesticity, first introduced in foreign and missionary girls' schools in the late nineteenth century, became an Iranian concern by the early twentieth century and reached its culmination during the Reza Shah period. In the nineteenth and twentieth centuries, foreign and missionary schools made the first inroads in providing education for girls, and in setting a curriculum of scientific domesticity from which Iranian-initiated private and state educational projects would borrow heavily in the early twentieth century. The teaching of household management to Iranian girls was novel for Iran. In addition to teaching literacy and new subject matter such as history, science, and foreign languages, schools like Iran Bethel promoted training in hygiene, disease prevention, and child-care. Traditional *maktab*s and private tutors did not broach such a curriculum. The Iranian women's press stands as testimony to the novelty of such ideas, as its pages were full of this modern science of the home and body.

As female education and training in scientific domesticity in Iran became associated increasingly with national progress in early-twentieth-century Iran, they created new roles for women, with an emphasis on household management, scientific motherhood, and modern wifehood. Modern education became a means of restructuring society in line with the emergence of new political and economic needs and social groups. This education, including scientific domesticity, soon opened the door for women to go outside the domestic sphere and enter new professions. Modern education for a minority also led to disdain for the uneducated and for much of Iranian culture, thus contributing to the "two cultures" phenomenon that has been so important in twentieth-century Iran. While education served to expand individual and social opportunities for the upper and new middle classes, it also created new professional roles for women both inside and outside the home and reso-cialized them to serve the nation through their expanded duties in families and households.

NOTES

1. See, for example, Jalal Al-e Ahmad, *Gharb-zadegi* (Tehran: Azad, 1341/1962).

2. See, for example, Michael Zirinsky, "A Panacea for the Ills of the Country: American Presbyterian Education in Inter-War Iran," *Iranian Studies* 26 (1993): 119–37; and idem, "Render Therefore unto Caesar the Things Which Are Caesar's: American Presbyterian Educators and Reza Shah," *Iranian Studies* 26 (1993): 337–56.

3. Maria Szuppe, "The Jewels of Wonder: Learned Ladies and Princess Politi-cians in the Provinces of Early Safavid Iran," in *Women in the Medieval Islamic World*, ed. Gavin R. G. Hambly (New York: St. Martin's Press, 1998); and Shohreh Gholsorki, "Pari Khan Khanum: A Masterful Safavid Princess," *Iranian Studies* 28 (1995): 143–56.

4. Denis Wright, *The English among the Persians* (London: Heinemann, 1977), 117–18.

5. See Monica M. Ringer, *Education, Religion, and the Discourse of Cultural Reform in Qajar Iran* (Costa Mesa, CA: Mazda, 2001), 138.

6. Homa Nateq, *Karnameh-ye farhangi-ye farangi dar Iran* (Paris: Khavaran, 1375/1996), 180–82.

7. Ringer, *Education, Religion,* 126.

8. Ringer, *Education, Religion,* 131–33, and Nateq, *Karnameh-ye farhangi,* 106.

9. See, for example, *Bulletin de l'Alliance Israélite Universelle*, deuxième série, no. 29 (1904): 59–68.

10. Albert Confino, "L'Action de l'Alliance Israélite Universelle en Iran" (Algiers, 1942), cited in *Hommage aux fondateurs de l'Alliance Israélite Universelle/Dorud beh mo'assesan-e aliyans-e ezra'elit-e universel* (New York: The Committee to Honor the Alliance Israélite Universelle, 1996), 5–6.

11. Joseph Cazès, letter dated August 8, 1898, Archive AIU, Iran, XIIIE, 132, cited in *Hommage aux fondateurs de l'Alliance Israélite Universelle,* 8.

12. See *Bulletin* nos. 28–36 (1903–11).

13. Cazès, in *Hommage aux fondateurs de l'Alliance Israélite Universelle,* 8; and *Bul-letin,* deuxième série, no. 29 (1904): 67.

14. Issa Sadiq, *Modern Persia and Her Educational System* (New York: Bureau of Publications, Teacher's College, Columbia University, 1931), 37–39.

15. Justin Perkins, *A Residence of Eight Years in Persia among the Nestorian Chris-tians* (Andover, MA: Allen, Morrill, and Wardwell, 1843), 249, 337, 497.

16. Ibid., 404–05.

17. Annie Stocking Boyce, report, June 30, 1938, Presbyterian Historical Archive (PHS), RG 91-7-4.

18. Board of Foreign Missions of the Presbyterian Church in the U.S.A., *A Cen-tury of Mission Work in Iran, 1834–1934* (Beirut: American Press, 1936), 87–88.

19. C. Colliver Rice, *Persian Women and Their Ways* (London: Seely, Service, and Co., 1923), 153.

20. On the Qajar shahs' reactions to foreign educational activities and missionaries in Iran, see Ringer, *Education, Religion*. On Armenian-Iranian opposition to missionary education, see Houri Berberian, "Armenian Women in Turn-of-the-Century Iran: Education and Activism," in *Iran and Beyond: Essays in Middle Eastern History in Honor of Nikki R. Keddie*, ed. Rudi Matthee and Beth Baron (Costa Mesa, CA: Mazda, 2000), 70–98.

21. Board, *Century*, 84.

22. Ibid., 88; and Reza Arasteh, *Education and Social Awakening in Iran, 1858–1968* (Leiden: E. J. Brill, 1969), 164.

23. John G. Wishard, *Twenty Years in Persia: A Narrative of Life under the Last Three Shahs* (New York: Fleming H. Revell Co., 1908), 239–40; and Rice, *Persian Women*, 152.

24. Boyce, report, June 30, 1915–June 30, 1916, PHS.

25. Rice, *Persian Women*, 152.

26. Ringer, *Education, Religion*.

27. Board, *Century*, 87–88.

28. K. Pelin Basci, "Shadows in the Missionary Garden of Roses: Women of Turkey in American Missionary Texts," in *Deconstructing Images of "the Turkish Woman,"* ed. Zehra Arat (New York: St. Martin's Press, 1998), 104.

29. Yahya Armajani, "Samuel Jordan and the Evangelical Ethic in Iran," in *Religious Ferment in Asia*, ed. Robert J. Miller (Lawrence: University of Kansas Press, 1974), 33.

30. Perkins, *Residence*, 13, 250–51, 316, 404–05.

31. Boyce, chapter 3, unpublished memoirs, PHS, RG 91-18-11, 1–2.

32. Board, *Century*, 98.

33. Ibid., 77–78.

34. Boyce, "Household Arts for Tehran Girls," c. 1916, PHS, RG 91-18-11.

35. See, for example, Helen Barrett Montgomery, *Western Women in Eastern Lands* (New York: The MacMillan Company, 1910). See also Basci, "Shadows in the Missionary Garden," in Arat, ed., *Deconstructing Images*, 106.

36. See, *e.g.*, Beth Baron, *The Women's Awakening in Egypt: Culture, Society, and the Press* (New Haven: Yale University Press, 1994); Margot Badran, *Feminists, Islam, and Nation: Gender and the Making of Modern Egypt* (Princeton: Princeton University Press, 1995); Leila Ahmed, *Women and Gender in Islam* (New Haven: Yale University Press, 1992); Juan R. I. Cole, "Feminism, Class, and Islam in Turn-of-the-Century Egypt," *International Journal of Middle East Studies* 13 (1981): 397–407; Afsaneh Najmabadi, "Zanha-yi millat: Women or Wives of the Nation?" *Iranian Studies* 26 (1993): 51–71.

37. Leonore Davidoff, *Worlds Between: Historical Perspectives on Gender and Class* (New York: Routledge, 1995); Leonore Davidoff and Catherine Hall, *Family Fortunes: Men and Women of the English Middle Class 1780–1850* (Chicago: University of Chicago Press, 1987); Mary Poovey, *Uneven Developments: The Ideological Work of Gender in Mid-Victorian England* (Chicago: University of Chicago Press, 1988); Mary Ryan, *The Empire of the Mother: American Writing about Domesticity* (New York: The Hayworth Press, 1985).

38. See, *e.g.*, Shakry, "Schooled Mothers and Structured Play: Child Rearing in Turn-of-the-Century Egypt," in Lila Abu-Lughod, ed., *Remaking Women: Feminism and*

Modernity in the Middle East (Princeton: Princeton University Press, 1998), 126–70; Booth, "'May Her Likes Be Multiplied': 'Famous Women' Biography and Gendered Prescription in Egypt, 1892–1935," *Signs* 22 (1997): 827–90; and Karen Transberg Hansen, ed., *African Encounters with Domesticity* (New Brunswick: Rutgers University Press, 1992).

39. See, *e.g.*, Mona L. Russell, "Creating the New Woman: Consumerism, Education, and National Identity in Egypt, 1863–1922" (Ph.D. dissertation, Georgetown University, 1997); Elizabeth Frierson, "Unimagined Communities: State, Press, and Gender in the Hamidian Era" (Ph.D. dissertation, Princeton University, 1996); and Najmabadi, "Crafting an Educated Housewife in Iran," in Abu-Lughod, ed., *Remaking Women*, 91–125.

40. Boyce, "Household Arts for Tehran Girls," 1–3.

41. Armajani, "Samuel Jordan," 33.

42. Arthur C. Boyce, "Alborz College of Tehran and Dr. Samuel Martin Jordan, Founder and President," in *Cultural Ties Between Iran and the United States,* ed. Ali Pasha Saleh (Tehran: Sherkat-e chapkhaneh-ye bistopanj-e Shahrivar, 1976), 196.

43. For more discussion of this, see Zirinsky, "Render Therefore unto Caesar."

44. Samuel Jordan, "Constructive Revolutions in Iran," *The Moslem World* 26 (1935): 348.

45. Board, *Century,* 87.

46. Wishard, *Twenty Years in Persia,* 239–40.

47. Boyce, January 11, 1936, PHS, RG 91-18-11, and ch. 3, 3–4.

48. Sattareh Farman Farmaian, *Daughter of Persia: A Woman's Journey from Her Father's Harem Through the Iranian Revolution* (New York: Doubleday, 1992), 59.

49. For a comparable example, see Julia Clancy-Smith, "Envisioning Knowledge: Educating the Muslim Woman in Colonial North Africa, c. 1850–1918," in Matthee and Baron, ed., *Iran and Beyond,* 112.

50. Farman Farmaian, *Daughter of Persia,* 104–5.

51. See Baron, *Women's Awakening;* Frierson, "Unimagined Communities"; Marilyn Booth, "Biography and Feminist Rhetoric in Early Twentieth-Century Egypt: Mayy Ziyada's Studies of Three Women's Lives," *Journal of Women's History* 3 (1991): 38–64; idem, "May Her Likes Be Multiplied," and idem, "The Egyptian Lives of Jeanne d'Arc," in Abu-Lughod, ed., *Remaking Women,* 171–211.

52. M. Jalali, "Cleanliness," *Alam-e Nesvan* 4, no. 1 (Sept. 1923): 4–5.

53. Dr. Stamp, "What Do Teeth Do?" trans. Mirza Jalal Khan Shafa, *Alam-e Nesvan* 3, no. 2 (Nov. 1922): 6–10.

54. Grace Taillie, "Child Rearing," trans. S. Afshar, *Alam-e Nesvan* 2, no. 3 (Jan. 1922): 9–13; Grace Taillie, "The Right Hour to Put Children to Bed," trans. S. Afshar, *Alam-e Nesvan* 2, no. 4 (March 1922): 14; Mrs. (Doctor) McDowell, "Announcement," trans. S. Afshar, *Alam-e Nesvan* 3, no. 1 (Sept. 1922): 7–10.

55. Mrs. Paine, "Rules of Taking Care of Children," trans. Mehranu [*sic*] Sami'i, *Alam-e Nesvan* 4, no. 1 (Nov. 1923): 13–14.

56. Ibid.

57. See, for instance, Mrs. (Doctor) McDowell, "Child Rearing," *Alam-e Nesvan* 2, no. 1 (Sept. 1921): 17–20; idem, "Modesty," *Alam-e Nesvan* 3, no. 2 (Nov. 1922): 25–9; idem, "Cultivation of Children," trans. F. Dayhim, *Alam-e Nesvan* 12, no. 1 (Jan. 1932): 14–19; idem, "Obedience in Child Rearing," *Alam-e Nesvan* 12, no. 5 (Sept. 1932): 229–34.

58. Mrs. Paine, "The Happy Mother," trans. S. Afshar, *Alam-e Nesvan* 4, no. 4 (April 1924): 9–14.

59. "Criticism," *Alam-e Nesvan* 11, no. 3 (May 1931): 140.

60. See Booth, "Biography and Feminist Rhetoric," 38.

61. For a more detailed discussion, see Jasamin Rostam-Kolayi, "The Women's Press, Modern Education, and the State in Early Twentieth-Century Iran" (Ph.D. dissertation, University of California, Los Angeles, 2000).

62. Articles in the general-interest Iranian press demonstrate that some reformers were concerned that Iranian men studying and traveling abroad might meet and marry European women, due to a shortage of modern Iranian women. For discussion of this, see Camron Michael Amin, "Attentions of the Great Father: Reza Shah, 'The Woman Question,' and the Iranian Press, 1890–1946" (Ph.D. dissertation, University of Chicago, 1996), 238–40.

63. Dr. Reza-Zadeh Shafaq, "The Issue of Intermarriage of Iranians with Foreigners," *Alam-e Nesvan* 11, no. 1 (Jan. 1931): 10–16.

64. "The New Women of Egypt," *Alam-e Nesvan* 2, no. 3 (Jan. 1922): 18–20.

65. "News of Women's Progress—The Progress of Muslim Women," *Alam-e Nesvan* 3, no. 1 (Sept. 1922): 18–19.

66. "Sending Off the Troops," *Alam-e Nesvan* 2, no. 1 (Sept. 1921): 34; "News of Women's Progress—The Progress of Muslim Women," "News of Women," *Alam-e Nesvan* 11, no. 3 (May 1931): 131.

67. "The Education of Japanese Women," *Alam-e Nesvan* 2, no. 1 (Sept. 1921): 28–34; and "Extraordinary Japanese Women," *Alam-e Nesvan* 2, no. 4 (March 1922): 25–27.

68. "Daughter of China," *Alam-e Nesvan* 2, no. 5 (May 1922): 20–21; and "The Establishment of a School for Women," *Alam-e Nesvan* 12, no. 3 (May 1932): 137–39.

69. "Indian Women," *Alam-e Nesvan* 2, no. 6 (July 1922): 20–22; and "News on Women's Progress," *Alam-e Nesvan* 11, no. 6 (Nov. 1931): 275–79.

70. "Among Peers," *Alam-e Nesvan* 2, no. 5 (May 1922): 1–2.

71. "The New Women of Egypt," 18–20.

72. Davidoff, *Worlds Between,* 74; Davidoff and Hall, *Family Fortunes,* 175, 181; and Poovey, *Uneven Developments,* 10.

73. Davidoff and Hall, *Family Fortunes,* 171, 183, 186; and Judith Newton, "'Ministers of the Interior': The Political Economy of Women's Manuals," in *Starting Over: Feminism and the Politics of Cultural Critique,* ed. Judith Newton (Ann Arbor: University of Michigan Press, 1994), 144–46.

74. Antoinette Burton, *Burdens of History: British Feminists, Indian Women, and Imperial Culture, 1865–1915* (Chapel Hill: The University of North Carolina Press, 1994).

75. See Janet Afary, *The Iranian Constitutional Revolution, 1906–11* (New York: Columbia University Press, 1996); and Abdol-Hosain Nahid, *Zanan-e Iran dar jonbesh-e mashruteh* (Saarbrücken: Navid, 1979).

76. See Rostam-Kolayi, "The Women's Press, Modern Education, and the State."

77. Sadiq, *Modern Persian,* 56.

78. "Education—Women's Education in the Pahlavi Period and After," in *Encyclopaedia Iranica* (Costa Mesa, CA: Mazda, 1998), 8:235.

79. Ruth Frances Woodsmall, *Women and the New East* (Washington, D.C.: The Middle East Institute, 1960), 57–58.

80. Amir Jahed, *Salnameh-ye Pars* (Tehran, 1933–34), 80–96.

Part III

Culture in the Islamic Republic
in Relation to the World

9 / International Connections
of the Iranian Women's Movement

NAYEREH TOHIDI

This chapter shows the impact of transnational contacts, especially connections with global feminist discourse and women's movements, on the women's rights movement in Iran. Since the revolution, Iranian women's international connections have been of three kinds. First, the missionary approach of those who wanted to export Islamic revolution and a single model of "Islamic womanhood." Second, a pragmatic approach that gradually replaced the first one through interaction with women in countries in the Middle East and in Europe. Third, the international connections sought by dissident secular feminists, religious minorities, and gender-egalitarian Islamic women reformers disillusioned with theocracy. Attention is drawn to the new women's press that promotes reform and to the positive role of the UN-sponsored international conferences in facilitating gender sensitization and in the development of women's NGOS.

Iranian women activists have had international connections since the early twentieth century, but here I will be concerned with the connections established since 1979. The chronology of international contacts among Islamist women and of international pressures exerted on the ruling Islamists make the significance of international factors clear. Despite the Islamists' feigned disregard of the international community's opinions, they have been quite sensitive, though wary, about how they are perceived and received by the world community. The history and internal dynamism of Iranian society, particularly the social praxis of Iranian women, have played the main roles in shaping the course of women's movements. The main concern of this paper, however, is the role of external or international factors—the impact of global feminism on the women's movement in Iran.

"FREEDOM IS NEITHER EASTERN NOR WESTERN; IT IS UNIVERSAL"

In the past two decades, there has been an urgent attempt by Iranian feminists to prove that contemporary demands for women's rights in Iran are not simply a foreign or Western import. Rather, the Iranian women's movement and feminism have indigenous roots going back 150 years, when Iran began to modernize. This quest for "authenticity" by the women's movement has developed as a result of the anti-West discourses of secular nationalists and also of the Islamists who took power in 1979. Branding freedom and democracy as Western, and hence alien to Iranian Islamic culture, conservative Islamists began imposing new restrictions on women's rights and freedom.

Women, therefore, were the first group to display signs of opposition to the Islamic Republic of Iran (IRI). Initially, this opposition took the form of militant demonstrations. Later, in the face of harsh repression, women pursued a course of subtle and slow yet persistent resistance and subversion. The first display of overt defiance coincided with an unprecedented, massive celebration of International Women's Day (March 8, 1979) that turned into a week-long protest against Khomeini's declaration of mandatory veiling, regressive measures in regard to women's personal status and family laws, and other areas of women's rights. One of the main banners raised by thousands of women protesters read, "Freedom is neither Eastern nor Western; it is Universal!" Such acts of resistance or any manifestations of feminism in the 1970s and 1980s were, for the most part, ignored or branded as divisive and as "bourgeois deviations" by many secular leftists, or as Western and "Westoxicated" by nationalists and Islamists.[1]

During the first decade of the Islamist regime, which coincided with the Iran-Iraq war, secular women activists and feminists experienced a period of brutal repression and demoralization, resulting in exodus and passive resistance. After the war and Khomeini's death in 1989, secular activism, especially that of women, began gradually in artistic films and literary creativity, journalistic critical writings, and scholarly revisiting of Iranian women's history and identities. An important factor contributing to the effectiveness of women's resistance and their surprising achievements in many realms has been the gradual convergence and collaboration of secular feminists and reform-oriented Islamic women activists. The latter group has been identified in the West as "Islamic feminists," since their views and demands have gradually come closer to gender-egalitarianism.

Through a vigorous campaign, the ruling clerics prescribed and dictated a uniform and exclusively Islamic identity for women in Iran, modeled after key non-Iranian Islamic women, chiefly Fatima (daughter of the Prophet and wife of the First Imam of Shi`i Muslims). In practice, however, this "model of Muslim woman" has remained ambiguous, contradictory, and irrelevant to contemporary realities. Furthermore, there has been no agreement among Islamist ideologues over the characteristics of this model, other than that of the *hejab* (cover). The extent and form of *hejab* have also been matters of contest, ranging from a full black chador to a short, colorful head scarf along with a loose overcoat.

In opposition to conservative clerical prescriptions of a restrictive and homogeneous gender identity, some women tried to discover and configure a more inclusive, multiple, and fluid identity for Iranian women based on Iran's pre-Islamic and Islamic history. Like the secular reformers of the late nineteenth and early twentieth centuries, some current reformers refer to the pre-Islamic history of Iran in order to construct a model of womanhood supposedly rooted in Iran's indigenous culture. A good example of this trend is an impressive volume by two prominent secular feminists, Shahla Lahiji and Mehrangiz Kar, *The Quest for Identity: Images of Iranian Women in Prehistory and History.*[2]

Disillusioned with the failed promises of clerics to bring about justice for all and resentful of intensified sexual discrimination, a growing number of female Islamic intellectuals and activists joined secular feminists in their search for more modern, practical, and egalitarian gender identities. They have become more willing to adopt identities that are not based solely on Islamic tradition, but are rooted in the diverse realities of past and present Iran and are also informed by international women's movements and feminist discourses. In this context, a sense of urgent need has arisen to prove that women's quest for equality and emancipation is universal rather than Western; thus, attempts are made to provide evidence for the history of women's movements in the East, including the Muslim world. Many women activists in Iran are trying to show that their current support for feminism and search for equality is not simply a Western import but has an indigenous national background, the roots of which were planted during the Constitutional Revolution of 1906–11.

A good example of this trend is the publication of a Women's Calendar (*Salnameh-ye Zanan*) for the first time in Iran. This calendar was initiated in 1998 by a young feminist writer and publisher, Nushin Ahmadi Khorasani, and has been published for three years now. It attempts to place current feminist activities and discourse in historical perspective and also to show hidden links between the Iranian women's movement and global feminist movements. The efforts to discover the national roots of Iranian feminism and argue for the "authenticity" of the women's movement in Iran have not led to ignoring the important influence of international factors, including feminist discourses and women's movements in the West and in other parts of the world.

In postrevolutionary Iran, various groups or categories of women have been interested in establishing three types of international connections for three different purposes: missionary and ideological, diplomatic and prag-matist, and integrative and networking. The first category consists of those Islamist women whose main purpose in establishing international contacts has been ideological propagation of an Islamic revolution and an Islamic model of womanhood. The second category, which has gradually replaced the first, draws from the new elite of professional and highly educated Islamic women, well connected to the state organs and the new bureaucracy. Their active presence at international conferences and work to establish inter-national connections are supposed to be in the service of public relations and diplomatic strengthening of the Islamic state, especially regarding its gender image. Yet, in the process of their own experience with sexist barriers and their contacts with the international community, especially with women's organizations and feminist discourse, they have come to be less ideological, more open-minded and pragmatist, and more conscious of women's rights.

The third category includes independent and/or dissident women activists and feminists inside and outside Iran who have sought international con-nections with women's organizations in various parts of the world. Their pur-poses have included earning publicity for their cause, exchanging ideas and experiences, gaining a support network and solidarity in their fight against sexism and repression in Iran, and becoming a united part of the interna-tional women's movement. The size and diversity of this group have been increasing as more women, religious as well as secular, members of religious minorities and Muslims, inside as well as outside Iran, join the forces of reform movements or radical opposition because of their disillusionment with the Islamist state. Several examples of the views, activities, and accomplishments of each group will follow.

The Missionary Connections

The first category is Islamist women associated with ruling hard-liners. These women waged a missionary campaign, making visits to and inviting women's delegations from as many Muslim countries as possible, in order to propagate or export the Islamic Revolution and their constructed "model of Muslim woman" (*olgu-ye zan-e mosalman*) to the rest of the world.[3] This model refers to a traditional, patriarchal gender regime, emphasizing sex differences and a sex-based division of labor rather than equality of male-female rights and roles. Initially most active in this category was the Women's Society of Islamic Revolution, founded by radical Islamist women like Zahra Rahnavard and Fereshteh Hashemi. This group was soon marginalized through factional conflicts, though, while another group called the Women's Society of the Islamic Republic (wsIR), founded by female relatives of Khomeini, became more prominent. Each issue of their quarterly publication, *Neda* (directed by Zahra Mostafavi, Khomeini's daughter, and edited by Fereshteh A`rabi, Khomeini's granddaughter), includes reports about women in other parts of the (usually) Muslim world or interviews with women converts to Islam in western countries.

One reason for recent moderation in the orientation of *Neda* and in the approach of such radical Islamist women is the failure of their extremist goals both inside and outside Iran. An example is their failure to establish Fatima's birthday as Woman's Day in all Muslim countries, and to set up Fatima as an Islamic counterpart to the Catholic Church's Mary. The impact of radical Islamist women in foreign countries has usually been limited to aspects of dress code and the revival of some traditions and rituals, rather than conversion of other Muslims to Khomeinism or Islamic revolution. Islamist ideology "exported" by these missionary women is usually reconstructed and transformed in the context and practice of each foreign community. For instance, their impact in one community can result in a rise in violence against women not wearing the proper *hejab;* in another community, they may trigger an interest in wearing head scarves. Another reason for the inconsistency of impact is the inconsistency of the message and the messenger. For instance, many Iranian Islamists said in the 1980s "contraception is anti-Islamic," and then endorsed it as Islamic when the Iranian government waged a campaign for population control in the 1990s.

Certain recent developments in various Muslim countries, however, have been considered manifestations of the Iranian Islamist impact. Among them are the attempt by the Bashir regime in Sudan to impose the Iranian Islamist version of the veil (chador) on Sudanese women in the early 1990s, as well as the increase in *mut`a* (temporary marriage or *sigheh*), even in some Sunni communities, in countries like Algeria and Sudan.[4] Mut`a marriage was previously permitted only in Shi`i shari`a, and was unknown or condemned among Sunnis.[5]

In terms of political influence, the Shi`a-Sunni divide has outweighed Islamic unity in neighboring countries and regions like Iraq, Turkey, Pakistan, Saudi Arabia and all Gulf states, Central Asia, and the Caucasus. Home-grown Islamist movements in countries like Pakistan and Afghanistan have more conflict than unity with Iranian Islamists. According to Shahla Haeri, women members of the Jama`at-i Islami of Pakistan show no interest in the Iranian version of Islamism. "What turns them off the most is the black chador."[6] Ordinary Muslim women in Pakistan talk about Iranian "excesses" and "contradictions." For instance, they were shocked to see the wife of the Iranian Ambassador to Pakistan wear very Western dress underneath her chador. Pakistani women, who maintain a colorful native dress code, often asked Haeri, "Do not the Iranian Islamists see the contradiction in wearing Western clothing under their chador?"

In the Caucasian and Central Asian Muslim communities, too, radical Islamist women from Iran have not been well received. For most women in these Muslim communities, the black veil, glorified by Iranian radicals, is the most noticeable reason for dismay. Even in the Shi`a-majority Azerbaijan Republic, where the wsir and many Iranian male Islamists have campaigned to win broad support, the Islamist trend is diverse, influenced by not only Iran, but also Turkey, the United Arab Emirates, Saudi Arabia, and Pakistan.

In June 1992, when a delegation of twenty-two Islamist women headed by Zahra Mostafavi visited Baku, Azerbaijan, their heavily-covered figures in chadors in Baku's hot summer brought stares and disdainful reactions every-where they went. They met with the same reaction from women in Tajikistan and the rest of Central Asia during visits in the early 1990s. On one occasion, a middle-aged Azeri woman asked me to translate a question to two com-pletely covered younger visitors. "Don't you feel hot under this heavy black garment in this hot summer?" she asked. "But the fire in hell is much hotter if one fails to follow Allah's orders," one of the Iranians replied. Baffled by her response, the Azeri woman mumbled, "What a cruel God you have! The Allah of Islam that I know of is much kinder to women."

International negative reaction to the chador was so broad and obvious that it engendered a heated debate back home, even in the print media, among Islamist women activists, male Islamist diplomats, and associates of the For-eign Ministry. Some male politicians, like Abbas Maleki, the former deputy foreign minister for education and research who was also the editor of the *Iranian Journal of International Affairs,* argued against women delegates wear-ing the chador while attending international events in foreign countries because of its "counterproductive impact." Instead of the chador, he rec-ommended wearing the modest *hejab* known as *manto-rusari* (head scarf with a long, loose overcoat) worn by less conservative Muslim women. But some extremist women Islamists like Soraya Maknun (a Ph.D. from an American university and a professor at Al-Zahra University in Tehran) insisted that they should not compromise on such a critical "Islamic symbol" and should not succumb to international pressures.[7]

For the pragmatist ruling male elite in Iran, the geopolitical stake is high in the Caspian region. For both internal interethnic and external geopolitical reasons, Azerbaijan holds a special and sensitive place in Iran's foreign policy. In Iran's rivalry with Turkey, Russia, and Western powers over political and economic influence in the Caspian region and Central Asia, an ideological compromise by the IRI in regard to the form of *hejab* might seem a small concession. Yet it took over seven years, a change of president, and then a change in the orientation of the Majles (parliament) after the recent elections to revive the debate around the question of chador versus *manto-rusari*. This debate has resurfaced with more vigor than before through the recently more open and reform-oriented print media. It was initiated by three newly elected (February 2000) female Majles representatives who are determined to wear a moderate *hejab* (*manto-rusari,* rather than chador) in the Majles. Supported by a few other women representatives, they note that the majority of Muslim women worldwide and in Iran wear other modes of dress.[8] Some prominent, newly elected male deputies, including Hojjatoleslam Hadi Khamenei (the reformist brother of the conservative supreme leader) and Dr. Mohammad-Reza Khatami (the president's liberal brother), made public statements in support of the new female deputies' arguments.

Until very recently, any criticism of the chador, especially by a woman, was taboo. In May 1999, for instance, secularist Turkish deputies barred an elected female deputy, Marveh Kavakchi, from taking her seat in parliament because she was wearing a head scarf. As a reaction to this in Iran, about two hundred chador-clad women, led by a conservative female deputy, took to the streets of Tehran to protest against the Turkish deputies "for violating the basic rights of a Muslim woman." Kavakchi, however, voiced her anger against this demonstration, saying, "I do not need the support of those who do not believe in democracy and the right to choose one's style of life and dress code, be it the Iranian Islamists or Turkish secularists."[9] She was proved right when less than a year later the same Islamist women in Iran threatened to bar elected deputies from parliament because they chose not to wear a chador.

Hence, one of the first impacts of international contacts with Muslim women outside Iran, especially with post-Soviet Azerbaijan, has been a challenge to the chador, a challenge that helped open debate, negotiation, and criticism about the *hejab*. Some influences of Iranian Islamists on Azerbaijan are also noteworthy. One is a trend in support of Islamic *hejab*—not the chador, but the *manto-rusari*—among some Azeri women. This trend is in line with a similar style worn in neighboring Turkey, but those Azeri women activists who are pushing for adoption of the head scarf are closely connected to the pro-Iran Islamic Party of Azerbaijan.[10]

In late 1999, following an intense campaign and petitions, Azerbaijani Islamic women activists won a court case in support of their demand for the right to choose a hair-covered picture for a woman's passport. Previously, the authorities in Azerbaijan refused to issue a passport with a picture of a woman wearing a head scarf. There were, however, reasons in addition to political Islam behind this pro–head scarf trend. Many of the Azeri Shi`i women who have begun to wear the head scarf are those who have been financially able to travel to Iran for a pilgrimage to Mashhad or have made a pilgrimage to Mecca. One resolution they make during such pilgrimages is to wear modest dress for the rest of their lives. These pilgrimages earn women the honorific titles of *Mashhadi khanim* or *Hajjiyeh khanim,* and wearing a head scarf would signify the right to such titles, which are also indicative of class status.

Another impact of Iran on gender issues in Shi`i-majority Azerbaijan relates to the so far failed attempts to formally restore the shari`a in family law. Some religious authorities and even some women have suggested legalization of "conditional polygyny" and an informal revival of the practice of temporary marriage as a solution for the current imbalance in sex ratios.[11] In the Azerbaijan Republic, due to increasing economic hardships, war, the growing exodus of young males, and the tradition of endogamy, a large number of young women are finding no chance to marry and raise a family. In the strongly family-centered society of Azerbaijan, this is viewed as a "catastrophe" for women. In the mid-1990s, due to the growing rate of marriage between Azeri women and Iranian male visitors to Baku (some already married), the Iranian authorities, worried about unwanted political implications, introduced rules and legal restrictions against such transnational marriages.

The Pragmatist Connections

A turning point in international connections and dialogue for both Islamist women activists and secular women was the 1995 UN-sponsored Fourth World Conference on Women in Beijing. During this conference it was clear how the earlier, strict ideological or missionary approach of the IRI's delegations was giving way to a relatively moderate and pragmatist one informed by the UN language and contemporary debates around gender issues. This was striking when compared with the missionary discourse, sectarianism, intolerance, hostility towards diversity, and ignorance about feminism and women's issues both nationally and internationally displayed by the IRI delegations at the Third World Conference on Women in Nairobi in 1985. I was present at both conferences as a participant observer, and I noticed both changes and continuities in the quantity and quality and the class composition and appearance of the delegations from one conference to the other.[12] At the Beijing conference, the diversity and difference in discourse and behavior of the Iranian participants were obvious. Their relatively tolerant attitude toward women of different persuasions, nationalities, cultures, and sexual orientations was reflective of the changes under way within Iran.[13]

Despite some movement toward moderation, a disturbing continuity was reflected in the IRI's opposition to certain egalitarian aspects of the Beijing Platform for Action, placing Iran among the leading conservative Muslim states in alliance with conservative Catholic states led by the Holy See. According to Amnesty International, even during the June 2000 Beijing-Plus-Five World Conference on Women in New York, "the unholy alliance formed by the Holy See, Iran, Algeria, Nicaragua, Syria, Libya, Morocco and Pakistan has attempted to hold to ransom women's human rights."[14]

Nevertheless, the Islamist women's international interactions, especially at UN-sponsored conferences, have contributed to the transformation from a sectarian and missionary approach to pragmatic tolerance. This shift, however, has been due not only to the international factor but also, and perhaps more so, to changing domestic realities, including the economic imperatives of growing urbanization and educational attainment among women. As reported by Poya, "throughout the 1980s and 1990s, more and more families have been relying on auxiliary or solely female earnings. . . . Factors such as inflation, male unemployment, and the war economy increased women's active participation in the workforce."[15] In their real life and practice, then, Islamic women would need more compatible role models than Fatima. Moreover, the moderation in the gender ideology of many Islamists has coincided with a moderation in the IRI's foreign policy—a shift from an isolationist and anti-West position to seeking to integrate into the world market.

The following examples are offered to illustrate the dynamism, contradictions, and process of change within Islamist women's organizations, facilitated by their international contacts. One useful illustration is in the contrasting content and results of the first and second international conferences held by a leading Islamist women's organization in Iran. Coordinated by the Women's Society of the Islamic Republic (WSIR) the first one, the International Congress on Woman and Islamic World Revolution, was held in February 1987 in Tehran, coinciding with the birthday of Fatima. President Khamenei inaugurated the Congress with a speech stating, "We should admit that, contrary to the Islamic order, women's status in many Muslim societies, including our own, is inappropriate and women are under various forms of oppression." At the end of the three-day congress, a twelve-item resolution was issued, including several items related to international relations. This resolution reemphasized "Islam as the only liberator of oppressed peoples and the Quran as the most complete guide for the lives of human beings." It reiterated "women's loyalty to Imam Khomeini and his prophetic leadership, the determination to export Islamic revolution to the whole world, to support all liberation movements, to reject any Western or Eastern [Soviet] models of womanhood constructed by blasphemous and imperial systems, and to believe in Fatima as the sole Islamic model for personal and social development of all women in the world." It condemned "the Western criminals headed by the U.S. and the Eastern deceivers." While condemning the "repressive and oppressive regimes that prevent Muslim women's entry into scientific, cultural, and social centers because of the Islamic *hejab* of those women—the very *hejab* that is the symbol of resistance against blasphemy and arrogance," they demanded that "all their freedom and Islamic and human rights be observed by those regimes."[16]

As this resolution and previous examples suggest, the IRI authorities, including those in its women's organs, resort to universal concepts and standards of "human rights" and "freedom of choice" only in defense of Muslims in minority positions within a non-Muslim or secular Muslim (*e.g.,* Turkish) context. When it comes to the violations of human rights under Islamist rule, they question the relevance of the notion of "universal human rights" to a Muslim context.

One year later (1988), coordinated by the Women's Society of the Islamic Republic of Iran (WSIRI), the second International Congress on Woman and Islamic World Revolution was held, again in February. This time, as reported in *Zan-e Ruz,* over seventy guests from inside and outside Iran were present, including the Philippines, France, the Soviet Union, Lebanon, Sierra Leone, Kenya, and Pakistan. During the third and last day of the Congress, led by three members of the WSIRI, three workshops were formed to discuss the "Role of Woman in Self and Societal Improvement."

In one workshop, attended by most of the foreign invitees and wives of ambassadors to Iran, some unexpected statements and ideas were brought up that resulted in a hurried interruption by the organizers. For instance, Dr. Stepanian (a woman from the Soviet Union) made some provocative suggestions. She encouraged Iranian women to play "a more active role in the legislative organs in order to legalize their natural rights and improve their literacy levels and educational and employment opportunities." Among several issues to be raised in both the Soviet Union and Iran, said Stepanian, is that "Women should be free to choose to work inside or outside the home.

What needs to be changed is people's attitude towards the husband's role and duties in the family. We should pass laws requiring salaries for women's house-work and we should liberate women from this enslavement to housework."[17]

The next speaker to make provocative points was the wife of the French Ambassador, who said:

> Women all over the world have certain problems and series of barri-ers before their advancement that have to be dealt with. . . . I think in your country the belief system of men and women about gender roles needs to be changed. This is a cultural and ideological issue that needs long-term work to change. Unfortunately, in your society it seems just natural that women should stay at home and men should work out-side the home, and equality between women and men is not seen as an important issue.[18]

Following these remarks, one of the organizers of the meeting, Ms. Avani, tried to end the session in a hurry, despite the objection of the foreign par-ticipants, who wanted to continue the discussion. When one of the foreign participants asked about the Congress resolution, the WSIRI members responded, "No decision about whether a resolution will be issued or not and about what its content should be has been made yet. The results of the Con-gress will be sent to the Majles for ratification and subsequently a resolution will be issued next month." The foreign participants objected, arguing that every international congress should end with a resolution, the content of which should be discussed and approved by the participants. Nevertheless, the state-ment announced later as the Congress resolution included the following:

> Let it be known that, given the WSIRI's support for Imam Khomeini, members of this organization and all the liberated women participants in this Congress have declared their opposition to and condemnation of any program, under any name or guise, that tries to suggest appli-cation or imposition of the decadent Western or Eastern [Soviet] cul-tures or any other corrupt cultures to or on our society. We are proud that the model for Muslim women in terms of any family or social affairs is Her Excellency Fatima Zahra.[19]

Compared with the resolution of the previous conference, this one seems to be more defensive than aggressive or missionary.

THE IMPACT OF THE UNITED NATIONS CONFERENCES

My studies and observations of the Iranian and post-Soviet Muslim republics testify to the largely positive impact of the UN efforts on women and chil-

dren. One of the factors that helped moderate the strictly ideological, male-
and state-controlled international agendas of Islamist women in Iran was their
increasing contact with transnational women's NGOs (nongovernmental
organizations) in UN-sponsored regional and world conferences. Such contacts provided many women with unique opportunities for cross-cultural,
cross-national, and cross-ideological exposure, learning, and dialogue. The
potential for the emergence of some internationally well-connected Iranian
NGOs has been stimulated or helped by UN projects. Actualization of this
potential can speed up and facilitate the development of the women's movement, which is a crucial part of any civil society.

To appreciate the positive role of women's international contacts, I quote
from an article in a right-wing paper known for its anti-women and anti-
democracy position. This lashing out against women's international contacts
came in the wake of the impact of the Beijing conference. The article is also
meant as a criticism of a relatively moderate position that the supreme leader
(Khamenei) took during his speech on the occasion of the Iranian Woman's
Day, a few months after the Beijing conference.

> In order to deceive public opinion, particularly among the inexperi-
> enced women of Muslim countries, world conferences and international
> congresses on women are held nowadays one after another by the Mafia
> forces of Zionism. They use all sorts of tricks to impose their satanic
> goals on Muslim societies step by step. . . . What is the use of this
> "Woman's Day" and "Woman's Week" during which our pious girls
> are made to perform public shows and ceremonies that remind us of
> the propagandist demos of the Soviet bloc and *Taghuti* ["idolatrous,"
> *i.e.,* Western] states? . . . What have we gained from wasting the state
> budget to send women delegates to various countries in the world and
> what are the criteria for selection of the delegates? . . . How are we pro-
> tecting our young and naive women who take part in these conferences
> from the bad influence of the West? . . . Has not the rise of the divorce
> rate to 17 percent terrified our authorities involved in women's issues? . . .
> Those influenced by the "Western model of woman". . . cannot appre-
> ciate our family values and our women's primary identities as mothers
> and wives.[20]

Since 1990, Iran has been elected (for three consecutive periods) to serve
among the forty-five voting members of the UN Commission on the Status
of Women. Reports about the participation of Iranian NGOs and governmental
organizations have usually appeared in women's journals like *Zanan, Farzaneh,*
and *Payam-e Hajar* (*PH*). The latter is published by the Islamic Institute of

Women (iiw), led by Azam Ala'i Taleqani (daughter of the late, popular Aya-tollah Sayyed Mahmud Taleqani), a group that has been keen on women's movements internationally and has kept taking part in UN-sponsored regional and world conferences concerning women. In each issue of *PH*, there is a short (about five pages) section in English.

According to statements in *PH*, the iiw has maintained its independence as an NGO and has financed its international travels through charity and loans. Participation in international gatherings on women is viewed as part of the "mission" of the iiw. Taleqani's group has pursued a cautious and mild yet consistently critical stance against male domination and extremist Islamists inside Iran, and a rather conciliatory tone toward the international women's movement.

An example is a report by a representative of the iiw about her partici-pation in the Symposium on Women and Development, with attendees from twenty-eight Asian countries, held in November 1993 in Jakarta. She notes without objection or comment the discussion supporting separation of state and religion, quoting a Malaysian delegate who insists that no single religion should be used as the basis for family law, as in her country and many oth-ers, where there are Christians, Hindus, and Buddhists as well as Muslims. She also quotes a delegate from Pakistan as saying that if people were asked in Pakistan to vote on whether they want an Islamic government or not, the majority would vote no.[21] In the same issue of *PH*, there is another report without comment about the final document of the World Conference on Human Rights (Vienna, 1993), with its emphasis on universal human rights.[22]

Taleqani has gradually become bolder in her critiques and more outspo-ken, especially since the growth of the reform movement and the presidency of Khatami. She was among the nine women whose presidential candidacies were rejected by the Council of Guardians. In a recent issue of *PH*, she reveals an interesting pattern of monopolization of UN resources in 1992–93 by state-controlled women's organs under the presidency of Rafsanjani, depriving NGOS of financial resources from such international agencies. According to *PH*, Shahla Habibi, head of the Office of Women's Affairs (OWA) under President Rafsanjani, along with a number of other women, submitted a proposal to the UN according to which any UN aid to women's NGOS should be stopped, and all UN projects aimed at helping female-headed families or supporting educational programs for women previously conducted by NGOS were to be incorporated into a single "national" project. They told the UN office it had no right to assist NGOS without OWA's confirmation, and that OWA should receive all UN support. "This is exactly the type of monopolization that has existed in the government," Taleqani writes, "resulting in much corruption and nepotism. The OWA has spent lots of money on national and international conferences, but no data bank or information center on women has been created yet to help us with planning on the basis of women's needs and realities."[23]

Another illuminating case of an Islamist woman going through different ideological and practical phases is Zahra Rahnavard, a multitalented radical Islamist intellectual. She was active in the early stage of Islamist women's international contacts, promoting the export of Islamism "as an alternative system to both capitalism and socialism for the oppressed toiling masses of the third world." She wrote a book on her visit and experiences in India, discussing her contacts with and impressions of Indian women.[24] She was critical of Iranian diplomats based in foreign countries for keeping their women out of politics, instead of engaging women in active political missions around the Iranian consulate and embassies.[25] One of her (failed) missionary goals was to establish the birthday of Fatima as a Woman's Day throughout the Muslim world.[26] Some of Rahnavard's writings have been translated into Arabic, English, Turkish, and Urdu.[27] In 1989, as a member of the Women's Social-Cultural Council, she chaired the international committee of this council and tried to "expand the international connections among women scholars" by organizing and holding international conferences in Iran. She criticized the regime's policies toward women, arguing, "Just as we do not have any clear strategy in regard to the economy, foreign policy, or culture, likewise we have no specified strategy about women's place in the Islamic Republic."[28]

Rahnavard was not in the Iranian delegation to Beijing, yet she became engaged in the theoretical challenges posed by such international involvement of Iranian women. One of the requirements for delegations' participation in the Beijing Conference was the preparation of a reliable, jargon-free "National Report" on women's conditions. During the preparatory meetings for Beijing, many elite Islamist women felt compelled to come up with an accurate report. The prepared report, which noted the lack of accurate statistics about women, was sent to the ruling male elite organs for confirmation. Apparently, it revealed an embarrassing situation regarding women, and so was held up and went through several changes.

This example of the eye-opening, educational, and challenging effect of preparation for a world conference on women brought home the relevance of feminist studies. The challenge of feminism had to be taken more seriously by the Islamist male elite and their women allies. In this context, Rahnavard tried to take up the challenge and deal with feminism, not in the women's press, but in the official organ of the Foreign Ministry, the *Journal of Foreign Policy*. Her article "Women, Islam and Feminism" shows that she is among those Islamist elite women who have grown closer to advocating women's rights and reform of the legal status of women in Iran. She tries to find convergent as well as divergent points between Western feminists and Islamists like herself. But her Islamist ideology confines her analysis to political polemics and propaganda in her continued attempt to "save" Western feminists rather than to build a mutual dialogue and exchange of ideas.[29] Since Khatami's presidency, Rahnavard has come back to the political scene with a moderate image and was appointed as the chancellor of the all-female Al Zahra University, replacing a male chancellor.

In short, while the WSIRI, under the leadership of Khomeini's daughter, Zahra Mostafavi, began to form a missionary international Islamist women's movement, what has been achieved so far is more a pragmatic international exchange with Muslim women's groups. In 1995, under the initiative of the Association of Women's Solidarity, led by Fatemeh Hashemi (daughter of former president Hashemi Rafsanjani), and with the cooperation of the OWA[30] and the WSIRI, the League of Muslim Women NGOs was established. It is claimed that women's NGOs from sixty-one countries have already joined the league. A similar attempt to establish a World Organization of Muslim Women, in conjunction with the World Conference of Islamic Countries held in Tehran in 1997, was blocked by the resistance of the male Muslim delegates to that meeting.[31]

Women's sports and transnational games have been another active arena for international contacts and connection building. Fa'ezeh Hashemi (Fatemeh Hashemi's sister), an active sportswoman herself, has played an important role in this area.

THE IMPACT OF THE AFGHAN TALIBAN

The gender dimension of the interaction between Iran and Afghanistan is particularly interesting. Despite the Taliban's extremist version of Islamism, especially in regard to women, Iranians perceive it as a product of the U.S. and its ally, Pakistan, the IRI's political rival in the region. Many Iranian Muslim reformers have identified conservative Islamists of Iran with the Afghan Taliban. For the Iranian conservatives, this has been a very damaging association in the electoral campaigns. For instance, in her *Zanan* editorial against conservative women deputies in the fifth Majles who proposed a law for sex segregation of hospitals, Shahla Sherkat began with this polemic: "The path you have taken ends in Afghanistan!"[32] Another piece of evidence of the ironic impact in Iran of the Taliban's version of Islamism is related to the debates led by Mohsen Sa'idzadeh. A prominent cleric known for his support for women's rights and feminist theology, Hojjatoleslam Sa`idzadeh was imprisoned and defrocked for writing a newspaper article critical of the conservative clerics in Iran who teach and preach a Taliban-like version of Islam in the Qom seminaries. His more subtle and damning point was that Islam is open to all sorts of interpretations, including a Taliban version, hence a choice of how to interpret Islam is just that, a choice.[33]

Reform-oriented Islamic women have emphatically opposed the Taliban. For instance, Ma`sumeh Ebtekar, Vice President on Environment, a leading member of the official delegation to the Beijing conference, visited the Afghan city Mazar-e-Sharif (which had not yet fallen to the Taliban) in 1998 and raised a loud voice against the Taliban and in support of Afghani sisters.[34] Residence in Iran by millions of Afghan refugees may also have made them more resistant to Taliban rule and practices.

The Integrative Connections

Long before Khatami's call for a "dialogue of civilizations," women's rights advocates had been trying to establish international dialogue, especially to "normalize" public attitudes toward Western women and to shatter the prevalent negative stereotypes of Western feminism. Most women intellectuals, political activists, and feminists in Iran have been interested in global trends and international events, particularly the international women's movement. Women activists in Iran, including religious ones, have not limited themselves to allying only with women of the Muslim world. They have shown as much, if not more, curiosity about the discourses, struggles, and achievements of their non-Muslim and nonreligious sisters in the West and in the developing world.

The ruling clerics pursued a vigorous campaign to construct a uniform model of Muslim womanhood, emphasizing Fatima. For instance, Fatima's birthday has been declared as Woman's Day in Iran, replacing the International Women's Day.[35] Despite such efforts, most women have rejected such premodern models. Women, including religious ones, have constructed diverse identities, mostly through a pragmatic and selective synthesis of the traditional and modern, the Islamic and the Western.

DE-ESSENTIALIZING THE "WEST" AND "WESTERN WOMAN"

De-essentialization of notions like "the West" and "Western" has been a significant and sensitive aspect of the new counter-discourse, especially among the Muslim "new thinkers," as well as secular feminists in Iran. This has occurred in parallel to efforts in the West by many scholars, writers, and feminists against essentialized Islam and negative stereotypes of Muslims, especially Muslim women.

The term *feminism* was initially viewed as a Western, hence a suspect and irrelevant, notion for Muslim women. It was only in the early 1990s that, for the first time, feminism and classic feminist literature from Britain, France, and the United States began to be translated and published as books and book chapters and in the pages of the emergent women's press. The journal *Zanan* (*Women*), edited by Shahla Sherkat, the former editor of *Zan-e Ruz,* played a pioneering role in this regard.[36] What some call "Islamic feminism"[37] gradually grew into a challenging voice within the legal opposition. The supreme leader, Khamenei, has now raised his voice against "feminism," marking the first time the term has been used in public by the leading Ayatollah.

To realize the extent of change, one should remember how, in October 1988, Khomeini issued a written order harshly scorning and even threatening with death a woman who had expressed in a radio talk show her preference for a Japanese role model, Oshin (based on a TV serial), over the "Fatima model" for Iranian women.[38] A decade later, Khamenei, Khomeini's successor, is faced with a much more serious challenge from women—not from an isolated voice on a radio show, and not just by secular feminists, but also by thousands of Islamic women who initially supported the Islamic government. Such women are moving increasingly away from support of totalitarian Islamist rule, by either rejecting a religious government altogether or reinterpreting Islam in a gender-egalitarian fashion while expressing a desire for secularization of Islam, the state, and law.

During the early years of the IRI, supportive words about Western women and feminist movements were taboo. In recent years, Muslim women reformers such as Jamileh Kadivar have spoken of "the significance of the international women's movement and its positive impact on the improvement of women's status in Iran." Kadivar is the wife of Mohajerani, the liberal Minister of Culture, and sister of Hojjatoleslam Mohsen Kadivar, a popular cleric who has been imprisoned because of his writings against theocracy. The large support she received in the Majles elections was not simply because of her ties to such popular male authorities. Her own reform-oriented writings and supportive stance on women's rights are positive credentials.[39] During the fifth parliamentary election, a very negative campaign was run against her from Shiraz. The city's Imam Jom'eh (head of the Friday prayer) called her a woman who stood for divorce and birth control. Ultimately, she was prevented from participating in a run-off election through what seemed to be vote fraud. In the February 2000 elections for the sixth Majles, however, Kadivar won the second highest number of votes in Tehran.[40]

Deconstruction of the negative and stereotypical image of the "Western woman" in general and of feminism in particular has remained a delicate and precarious task. The women's press has used every possible occasion to pursue this goal, slowly but consistently. *Zanan* has not been alone. In addition to *Payam-e Hajar* (*Hagar's Message*) and *Farzaneh* (*Learned*), which slowly and more cautiously followed suit, a number of more recent women's publications such as *Hoquq-e Zanan* (*Women's Rights*), edited by Ashraf Geramizadegan (former editor of *Zan-e Ruz*), *Zan* (*Woman*), run by Fa`ezeh Hashemi, and especially *Jens-e Dovvom?* (*The Second Sex?*) have joined the process of re-presentation of the West, feminism, and the global women's rights movement. The most internationally oriented and independent new publication on women is *Jens-e Dovvom?*, which has been coming out as a periodical anthology since 1998 under the editorship of a young secular-feminist publisher, Nushin Ahmadi-Khorasani, who also began publishing the previously mentioned women's calendar in 1998. Both in the calendar and the anthology, she has pursued an inclusive and internationalist approach. She has tried to bridge the gap between feminisms of various orientations, secular and Islamic, liberal and radical, Iranian and Western, by including pictures and short biographies of Iranian and non-Iranian women pioneers. The first issue of the calendar was harshly criticized in certain conservative publications and in threatening communiqués by vigilantes trying to "alert revolutionary people and government authorities, especially the ministry of culture, against the danger of feminist and deviant historiography . . . that promotes the pre-Islamic era, unworthy women, and symbols of promiscuity . . . and worships foreigners."[41]

Sophisticated analytical criticism of the distorted stereotypes about Western women and feminism appears in *Jens-e Dovvom?*, including an article by Khorasani herself, who writes about "the anxiety in the eyes of Iranian men when looking at the West and Western women."[42] *Zanan* and, more recently, *Jens-e Dovvom?* and *Hoquq-e Zanan* have included reports and pictures of non-veiled Western and non-Western women—movie stars, artists, writers, and scholars—as well as translations of feminist literature, including introductions to various feminist theories, feminist organizations, and women's NGOS.[43]

Among numerous examples in the women's press promoting a "dialogue of civilizations" is a report back from a visit to the United States by a prominent reformist cleric, Hojjatoleslam Hasan Yusofi Ashkevari, printed in PH. He expresses appreciation for cultural and political diversity in the U.S. and emphasizes the positive aspects of America. Most daring is his observation of religious freedom in the U.S. as resulting in "more genuine religious beliefs and sincere respect for religion" as compared to the prevalence of "pretentious religiosity" and "covert corruption under a despotic theocracy" in Iran.[44]

Another example is the newspaper *Zan,* which, before being shut down by conservatives in late 1999, included a number of writings supportive of the international women's movement and feminism, including Western women's achievements.[45] One daring piece is an interview with Professor Sa'ud al-Maula, General Secretary of the National Committee for Dialogue Between Muslims and Christians in Lebanon, during his visit by invitation to Iran in 1998. He makes several critical points about the lack of freedom and choice for women in Iran, especially regarding compulsory veiling. In line with Iranian Muslim modernist intellectuals and modern Lebanese theologians, he argues against the imposition of religion as a state ideology and forcing a single "Islamic model" on youth and women. He also criticizes the Saudi government for its "closed views on women while having open relations with the West." He even states, "you have lost your women, as I have found most of them to be pro-America. It is obvious that most of them wear this *hejab* out of fear, not by choice."[46] Expression of such views from Lebanon, the very country in which the Iranian Islamists have invested so much, politically, ideologically, and financially, may be an indication of the ideological failure of Islamism in regard to women not only in Iran but also in the countries with which Iran has maintained active foreign relations. Along with the women's press, women writers and artists, especially filmmakers like Rakhshan Banie'temad and Tahmineh Milani, are playing a significant role in cultural reconstruction of gender attitudes, women's roles, and images of Iranian women at both national and international levels.

THE IMPACT OF DIASPORA: EXILES AND MIGRANT WOMEN

A number of Iranian women scholars and activists living abroad have taken the initiative by playing the role of a bridge between Iranian feminists, inside and outside the country, and facilitating the connections of the Iranian women's movement with NGOs and women's movements in other countries. According to Shahin Nava'i, in 1999 there were ninety-seven Iranian women's groups outside Iran, on four continents, in sixteen countries and twenty-six cities, with the largest concentration in Europe, North America, Asia, and Australia.[47] Diaspora women activists have contributed to the women's movement inside Iran at different levels, including political, informational, theoretical, technical, and organizational. This is evident, for instance, in a written message from Nushin Ahmadi Khorasani to the tenth annual meeting of the Iranian Women's Studies Foundation (Canada, July 1999). She expressed her appreciation (along with some criticisms) of the significant help and support that Iranian women have received from their expatriate sisters.[48]

The activities of diaspora Iranian women include raising international awareness and mobilizing international pressures against violations of women's rights in Iran, sending in literature and supplying women activists inside Iran with materials and scholarly works published abroad, doing research on women in Iran (some of which gets translated and published in Iran as well as abroad), helping the women's press financially through distribution and sales among immigrant communities abroad, and providing Iranian women's rights pioneers with international forums, transnational connections, and visibility by inviting them to international academic conferences or political meetings.[49]

CONCLUSION

Because of language and geopolitical barriers, the women's movement in Iran had difficulty in establishing international connections. Compared to women in colonized countries, few Iranian women were armed with the languages of colonizers, which are also the languages of transnational feminist discourse. This, however, is changing, thanks not only to the growing numbers of highly educated women inside Iran, but also to a rise in the presence of Iranian women abroad. In the past, mostly men could go abroad for various purposes. Iranian women who live abroad have begun to help bridge the gap between Western and Iranian feminists. This they do by teaching, research, women's activist groups, and, more recently, Internet sites on Iranian women, international conferences that include speakers from inside Iran as well as those living abroad, and media appearances and interviews with women from inside and outside Iran. Among the most internationally active and vocal feminists living inside Iran are two prominent lawyers, Mehrangiz Kar and Shirin Ebadi, and writer and publisher Shahla Lahiji. Following their participation in a recent international conference on the Iranian reform movement (Berlin, April 2000), Kar and Lahiji and a number of male dissident intellectuals were arrested. Ebadi, too, who is a recipient of a Human Rights Watch award, was recently detained and tried behind closed doors. Thanks in part to an intense international campaign in their support, the three women were released on bail after being detained for several weeks.[50]

Recent scholarship, improved media coverage, and movies by Iranian women filmmakers are beginning to change the one-sided and stereotypical representation of Iranian women as mere victims and passive products of religious backwardness. An example of such films is *Zinat,* based on the life story of a real woman, Zinat Darya'i. She is a non-elitist activist from a village on the island of Qeshm in southern Iran, one of the least developed and most traditional areas of Iran. She was a highlight of this year's celebration of March 8th in Tehran. She has only a fifth-grade formal education, yet, since age eleven, she has been working as a primary health provider and midwife. In the 1980s, with "two kids and a husband to run," she received professional training as a health worker, during which she was obliged to take off her facial mask (worn in the Persian Gulf area). Because of this and having a career, she became an outcast in her village, even among her family and friends, for several years. However, as she stated in her passionate speech, "they gradually noticed the good that I was doing and how devoted I was. They grew to accept me, and in the last elections, those very people who cursed me voted me into the local council—I came in ahead of all the male candidates." Zinat's story represents not only the remarkable agency of some rural women; it also shows the dynamism and process of change in the attitudes of people in her village and in Iranian society at large.[51]

A comparison of the celebration of International Women's Day (IWD) in 1979 with that in 2000 provides an interesting reflection of changes that have occurred in both the national and transnational contexts of the women's movement in Iran. On March 8, 2000, two decades after the last public celebration of IWD in Iran, a coalition of independent women's groups succeeded in holding an open celebration in Tehran at the City Books Center.[52] The first celebration of the IWD turned into an immense, five-day-long (March 8–12, 1979) outburst of anger on the streets of Tehran against a whole series of measures in violation of women's rights. The year 2000 event, however, was a small, well-organized gathering to mark the precarious yet hopeful beginning of an opening towards democracy and women's rights. Though it was not publicized in the media, the place was packed. Women of various ages and backgrounds gave short speeches on a wide variety of women's issues. Several performances by young women musicians marked another sign of a small yet hopeful opening in the scope and liveliness of women's activism.[53] Several other points distinguish these two celebrations from each other, including their international links. While the 1979 IWD protest attracted some Western radical feminists like Kate Millet,[54] the one in 2000 brought in women from Afghanistan and Bangladesh to share their plight and hopes with their Iranian women counterparts.

This small yet significant event did not receive much coverage in the press, which might imply a lack of interest or courage in the new reformist press in covering women's nonconformist and feminist activities. Though this sounds familiar in the recent history of Iranian intellectuals' attitudes towards feminism, a significant difference has emerged. The active and established women's press now persistently criticizes these reformers about their passivity toward or negligence of the "Woman Question." The monthly *Zanan,* for example, started a series of interviews with prominent Islamic reformist men, clerical and lay, putting them on the spot to address women's issues theologically, theoretically, and regarding policy.[55] Iranian feminist women scholars from inside and outside Iran have also contributed to these debates by criticizing the shortcomings of Islamic reformers in regard to gender issues. Such lively gender debates and intellectual confrontation between feminists and leading intellectuals did not exist in the early years of the Islamic Republic, nor during the previous regimes.

At the March 8, 2000, event, Nushin Ahmadi Khorasani referred to the connections between the women's movement in Iran and those both in the West and in the Muslim world. She began her talk with a reference to the notion of global sisterhood, by stating that:

> The hope for a humane and just life for women is the main concern that has deeply bonded women together throughout the world. This bond goes beyond traditional relations, family and ethnic ties, and ideological orientations. I am talking about black women in Nigeria, the Muslim woman in Egypt, the secluded woman in Saudi Arabia, the women in Bangladesh and Syria. Despite many concerns and pains common between us and American and European women, I am not talking here about them. Because whenever we talk about them, we are accused of being Westernized. When we cook delicious foods in U.S.-made microwaves, we are praised. But God forbid if we talk about the intellectual productions and experiences of Western women in their struggles for equal rights. Never mind, though, we non-Western women, too, have many proud experiences. Regardless of whether there has been any talk about the word feminism or not, we have over a century of experience in the women's movement. . . . Regardless of any "ism" or school of thought, the quest for justice is what we women have nourished in our children's minds.[56]

Khorasani represents a new perspective in the feminist discourse and women's movement that is a product of postrevolutionary, post-Islamist Iran and pertains mostly to urban middle-class women thirty to forty years old. For this group, as Mahsa Shekarlu puts it, "the West is neither seductive nor threatening."[57] They do not share the same resentment, suspicion, and hostility, nor the infatuation and mimicry, that various strata of the older generations displayed towards the West.

Khorasani, like many other reformers in today's Iran, supports a normal relationship between Iran and the U.S. on an equal basis. Rejecting any simplistic representation of either side, she criticizes, for example, a CNN report on Iran by Christiane Amanpour (February 28, 2000) as exaggerating a pro-American cultural fascination among Iranian youth. As Khorasani states, "If you watch Iranian TV [controlled by hard-line Islamists], you'd think that all Americans want to be Muslim, and in the U.S. they show that all Iranians want to be American." She is critical of emphasizing women in the West as an object of emulation.

> We have always looked vertically and not horizontally. I am speaking more to the establishment of stable and lasting relations with our female neighbors. Maybe they can help us more effectively, because our situations are a bit more similar. Why should we always place more value on the West? While I am not condemning a look to the West, I'm also pointing to what's nearby. Look at Egypt, for example, they have a very strong history of a women's movement. Why not learn from their experiences?[58]

In short, a more moderate and reasonable attitude toward the West and a more global rather than isolationist approach to feminism and the women's movement have become widespread among both secular and many Islamic women activists. They seek to identify commonalities without ignoring differences. They acknowledge that "male-dominated systems are not unique to Iran; we see them everywhere throughout the world. . . . [it] is important to learn from other experiences of resistance."[59] Yet, rather than a fascination with the West and emulation of Western women, as was predominant in the past, a tendency that is emerging among many Iranian feminists entails a stronger interest in establishing relationships and dialogues with women in countries surrounding Iran, or in ones that share more cultural and historic ties or similarities with Iran.

NOTES

I am grateful to Nikki Keddie, Farideh Farhi, Evan Siegel, Alana Powell, Mohammad H. Hafezian, Janet Afary, and Eliz Sanasarian, who made helpful comments on the first draft of this paper. I am especially grateful to Nushin Ahmadi Khorasani, who provided me with many of the primary sources from Iran.

1. For the views of the secular left, nationalist, and Islamist groups toward women's issues during these years, see Azar Tabari and Nahid Yeganeh, eds., *In the*

Shadow of Islam (London: Zed Books, 1982); Farah Azari, *Women of Iran: The Conflict with Fundamentalist Islam* (London: Ithaca Press, 1983); Nayereh Tohidi, "The Woman Question and Intellectuals in the Recent Decades," *Nimeh-ye Digar* 1, no. 10 (1990): 51–95; Haideh Moghissi, *Populism and Feminism in Iran* (London: Macmillan, 1994); and Parvin Paidar, *Women and the Political Process in Twentieth-Century Iran* (Cambridge: Cambridge University Press, 1995), 234–56.

2. *Shenakht-e hovviyat-e zan-e irani dar gostareh-ye pish-tarikh va tarikh* (Tehran: Roshangaran, 1372/1993).

3. See Golnar Mehran, "The Creation of the New Muslim Woman: Female Education in the Islamic Republic of Iran," *Convergence* 23, no. 4 (1991): 42–52.

4. See *Sudan Women and Law Project* (Paris: Women Living Under Muslim Law, 1996).

5. Though *mut'a* marriage is promoted by some Shi'i ulama of the IRI, some Islamic women's groups have remained critical of it. See Shahla Haeri, *The Law of Desire: Temporary Marriage in Shi`i Islam* (Syracuse: Syracuse University Press, 1989).

6. Author's interview (5 March 2000) with Shahla Haeri, who has been doing field research in Pakistan.

7. During the Beijing world conference on women (Forum '95), I confronted Maknun on this issue. Her views had not changed.

8. See, for instance, the statement made by Elaheh Kula'i in the Tehran daily *Aftab-e Emruz*, 18 Esfand 1378/8 March 2000, 1.

9. For sources of citations and further discussion, see Nayereh Tohidi, "Jensiyat, moderniyat va demokrasi," *Jens-e Dovvom?* 3 (Tehran, 1378/1999): 10–23.

10. For a gender-focused discussion on Islam in Azerbaijan, see my paper "Islam and National Identity in the Post-Soviet Republic of Azerbaijan," submitted to the National Council for Eurasian and East European Research, June 1998.

11. See N. Tohidi, "Gender and National Identity in Post-Soviet Azerbaijan: A Regional Perspective," in *Gender and Identity Construction: Women of Central Asia, the Caucasus, and Turkey*, ed. F. Acar and A. G. Ayata (Boston: E. J. Brill, 2000), 249–92.

12. While *Zanan* 6, no. 25 (Shahrivar 1374/Aug.–Sept. 1995), printed my critical report on both the governmental and opposition delegations ("Gozareshi az didar-e zanan-e jahan dar Pekin"), *Payam-e Zan* (a more conservative journal based in Qom and run by men) printed a report in twelve installments (nos. 44–56) by Fariba Shirazi that toed the official line. Other relatively critical reports included those by Mahbubeh Abbasqoli-zadeh and M. Ebtekar in *Farzaneh* 2, no. 7 (Fall and Winter 1995–96); Ziba Jalali Na'ini in *Goftogu* 10 (Winter 1374/1995); and Akuchekian in *Payam-e Zan* 44 and 47 (1374/1995).

13. See N. Tohidi, "Fundamentalist Backlash and Muslim Women in the Beijing Conference," *Canadian Women Studies* 16 (Summer 1996): 30–34. See also Halleh Ghoraishi's report on the Beijing conference, "Iranian Islamic and Secular Feminists— Allies or Enemies?" Middle East Research Associates (MERA Occasional Papers no. 27, Dec. 1996).

14. News release issued by Amnesty International, AI Index Act 77/008/2000 (5 June 2000).

15. Maryam Poya, *Women, Work, and Islamism: Ideology and Resistance in Iran* (London: Zed Books, 1999), 12.

16. Author's translation from *Nimeh-ye Digar* 11 (Spring 1990): 172–74.

17. Ibid., 182.

18. Ibid.

19. Ibid., 183.

20. Mohandes Mohammad-Ali Ramin, *Sobh* 65 (Dai 1375/Dec. 1995).

21. *Payam-e Hajar* 218 (Winter 1372/1993): 3.

22. Ibid., 4.

23. *Payam-e Hajar* 229 (Summer 1376/1997): 4–5.

24. Zahra Rahnavard, *Safar be diyar-e zanan-e bot* (Tehran: Sorush, 1366/1987).

25. Ibid., 111.

26. Ibid., 115.

27. For a feminist critique of Rahnavard, see Janet Afary, "Islamist Women Leaders: Escape from Freedom or Tradition?" *Critique* 19 (Fall 2001): 47–78.

28. *Zan-e Ruz* 21 (Bahman 1368/Jan.–Feb. 1989).

29. *The Journal of Foreign Policy* 9 (1374/1995): 523–47.

30. Created since Khatami's presidency, the Office of Women's Participation, headed by Zahra Shoja`i, has replaced the former Office of Women's Affairs.

31. See *Zanan* 7, no. 39 (Azar 1376/Nov. 1997): 10–13.

32. *Zanan* 7, no. 42 (Farvardin and Ordibehesht 1377/April 1998): 2.

33. On Sa`idzadeh and other ongoing gender-related debates among the Iranian clerics, see Ziba Mir-Hosseini, *Islam and Gender: The Religious Debate in Contemporary Iran* (Princeton: Princeton University Press, 1999); and Haleh Afshar, *Islam and Feminisms: An Iranian Case-Study* (London: Macmillan, 1998).

34. Mark Heinrich, "Women's Day Focus on Afghan, Algerian Abuses," Reuters dispatch, 8 March 1998, via Internet.

35. Recently, Fatima's birthday has been declared "Mother's Day" as well as "Woman's Day."

36. For the evolution of Shahla Sherkat from radical Islamist to Muslim feminist reformer, and the collaboration of her type with secular feminists like Mehrangiz Kar, see Jane Bayes and Nayereh Tohidi, eds., *Globalization, Religion, and Gender: The Politics of Implementing Women's Rights in Catholic and Muslim Contexts* (New York: St. Martin's Press, forthcoming).

37. See, *e.g.,* Margot Badran, "Toward Islamic Feminisms: A Look at the Middle East," in *Hermeneutics and Honor: Negotiating Female Public Space in Islamicate Societies,* ed. Asma Afsaruddin (Cambridge, MA: Harvard University Press, 1999), 159–88.

38. See *Keyhan Hava'i,* 19 Bahman 1367/7 Feb. 1989. For a feminist analysis on this incident, see Afsaneh Najmabadi, "Olgu-ye zan-e mosalman ve fatva-ye Imam," *Nimeh-ye Digar* 9 (1989): 94–97.

39. Jamileh Kadivar's book *Zan* (Tehran: Entesharat-e ettela`at, 1368/1996), includes a chapter on the Beijing conference.

40. On Kadivar, see *Zanan* 9, no. 63 (Ordibehesht 1379/April–May 2000): 7–13.

41. See, *e.g.,* "Khatar-e gerayeshha-ye erteja`i dar taqvim-negari . . . ," *Jomhuri-ye Eslami* 5756, 9 Ordibehesht 1378/April 1999, 7.

42. *Jens-e Dovvom?* 2 (1378/1999): 15–30.

43. See, *e.g.,* Nayereh Tohidi, "De-Stereotyping Western Women: A Portrait of Nikki Keddie" (Kelisheh zeda'i az zanan-e gharb: Mo`arefi-ye yek chehreh), *Jens-e Dovvom?* 6 and 7 (1379/2000): 4–21.

44. *Payam-e Hajar* 233 (Farvardin 1377/March–April, 1998): 12–13.

45. See, *e.g.*, the article on feminism and Islamic feminism by woman activist and scholar Jaleh Shaditalab in *Zan*, 8 Esfand 1378/27 Feb. 1998, 9.

46. *Zan*, 26 Azar 1377/17 Dec. 1998, 11.

47. See *Ava-ye Zan* 38/39 (Winter 1999): 18.

48. Khorasani could not attend that conference, but her message was read and published in the conference proceedings.

49. Several Iranian women activist academics outside Iran have contributed to the debate by publishing articles in Persian in the women's press inside Iran or having their research reports translated and published in Iran. Frequent contributors include Afsaneh Najmabadi, Nayereh Tohidi, Azadeh Kian, Ziba Mir-Hosseini, and Farideh Farhi. Translations of Janet Afary and Parvin Paidar's books have also been published in Iran.

50. In addition to these three women, several other intellectual reformers, including the aforementioned cleric Yusefi Eshkevari, are still either imprisoned or under persecution by the Revolutionary Court for speaking out against extremist Islamist ideas and policies, including ones relating to gender politics.

51. For a study on such health workers, see Homa Hoodfar, "Volunteer Health Workers in Iran as Social Activists: Can 'Governmental Non-Governmental Organizations' Be Agents of Democratization?" (Occasional Paper No. 10, Women Living Under Muslim Laws, Dec. 1998).

52. Among the main initiators of this courageous move were Shahla Lahiji, director of the Raushangaran and Women's Studies Press, and Nushin Ahmadi Khorasani, director of Tause'eh Press and editor of *Jens-e Dovvom?*.

53. See the report by N. Tohidi in *Ava-ye Zan* 40 (Spring 2000): 6–8.

54. On the history of the women's movement in Iran, see Mangol Bayat-Philipp, "Women and Revolution in Iran, 1905–1911," in *Women in the Muslim World*, ed. L. Beck and N. Keddie (Cambridge, MA: Harvard University Press, 1978); Eliz Sanasarian, *The Women's Rights Movement in Iran* (New York: Praeger, 1982); Guity Nashat, ed., *Women and Revolution in Iran* (Boulder, CO: Westview Press, 1983); Paidar, *Women and the Political Process in Twentieth-Century Iran;* and Janet Afary, *The Iranian Constitutional Revolution, 1906–1911* (New York: Columbia University Press, 1996).

On women in contemporary Iran, see Erika Friedl, "The Dynamics of Women's Sphere of Action in Rural Iran," and Mary Hegland, "Political Roles of Aliabad Women: The Public-Private Dichotomy Transcended," in *Women in Middle Eastern History*, ed. N. Keddie and B. Baron (New Haven, CT: Yale University Press, 1992); Valentine Moghadam, *Modernizing Women: Gender & Social Change in the Middle East* (Boulder, CO: Lynne Rienner, 1993); Nayereh Tohidi, "Modernity, Islamization, and Women in Iran," in *Gender and National Identity*, ed. V. Moghadam (London: Oxford University Press, 1994); Mahnaz Afkhami, "Women in Post-Revolutionary Iran: A Feminist Perspective," in *In the Eye of the Storm*, ed. M. Afkhami and E. Friedl (Syracuse: Syracuse University Press, 1994); Ziba Mir-Hosseini, "Stretching the Limits: A Feminist Reading of Shari'a in Iran Today," in *Feminism and Islam: Legal and Literary Perspectives*, ed. M. Yamani (London: Ithaca Press, 1996); Homa Hoodfar, "Bargaining with Fundamentalism: Women and the Politics of Population Control in Iran," *Reproductive Health Matters* 8 (Nov. 1996): 30–40; Haleh Esfandiari, *Reconstructed Lives: Women & Iran's Islamic Revolution* (Baltimore: Johns Hopkins University Press, 1997); Azadeh Kian, "Women and Politics in Post-Islamist Iran," *British Journal of Middle Eastern Studies* 24 (1997): 75–96; Afsaneh Najmabadi, "Feminism in an Islamic Republic: Years of Hardship, Years of Growth," in *Islam, Gender, and Social Change,* ed. Y. Y. Haddad and J. L. Esposito (London: Oxford University Press, 1998); Haleh Afshar, *Islam and Feminisms: An Iranian Case Study* (London: Macmillan, 1998); Hisai Nakanishi, "Power, Ideology, and Women's Consciousness in Postrevolutionary Iran," in *Women in Muslim Societies: Diversity within Unity,* eds. H. Bodman and N. Tohidi (Boulder, CO.: Lynne Rienner, 1998); Poya, *Women, Work, and Islamism;* and Nikki R. Keddie, "Women in Iran since 1979," *Social Research* 67 (2000): 407–38.

55. See, e.g., *Zanan* 57–64 (Dec. 1999–June 2000).

56. Author's translation from the Persian text of Khorasani's speech, which she kindly faxed.

57. See the Internet journal, *Bad Jens* 1 (13 March 2000).

58. Ibid.

59. Ibid.

10 / The Presentation of the "Self" and the "Other" in Postrevolutionary Iranian School Textbooks

GOLNAR MEHRAN

Postrevolutionary Iranian authorities have used textbooks as key instruments of political-ideological education and identity construction, an important element of which is the identification of the "self" and the "other." A content analysis of primary-school books points to clear demarcation lines based on Iranian/non-Iranian, Muslim/non-Muslim, good/evil, friend/enemy, and male/female dichotomies. The "self" has an Iranian-Islamic identity and the role models are predominantly male. The "other" is good or evil only in relation to the interests of "us." The image of the world includes an ever-present historical enemy whose destruction requires rage and hatred, despite more recent calls for dialogue, understanding, and tolerance in Iran.

The final decades of the twentieth century witnessed a variety of international declarations and conventions emphasizing peace, tolerance, respect for differences, human rights, democracy, and nonviolence. A common theme among all is the task assigned to education—namely, fostering "respect for human rights as well as the cultural and national values of the child's country and that of others."[1] While all aspects of the educational system are important in the promotion of tolerance and the shaping of attitudes of openness and respect among schoolchildren, none has been emphasized as much as the content of basic education, with special attention to textbooks. The result has been a special demand placed on primary schoolbooks to bring about "knowledge, understanding and respect for the culture of others at the national and global levels."[2]

The central role of the school as an important socialization agent has long been recognized by the Islamic Republic of Iran. The postrevolutionary Iranian authorities have used textbooks as key instruments of political and ideological education, charged with teaching the younger generation about the values and attitudes deemed appropriate in the construction of the "new society." Textbook content has, therefore, been used to transmit the social, political, and cultural values of the regime. Postrevolutionary textbook content has been the focus of various studies addressing such diverse topics as ideology, gender roles, socialization, and identity.[3]

Here I will study the content of primary-school textbooks used in the Islamic Republic of Iran in order to (a) identify the values transmitted to young children regarding the self and others, and (b) recognize the image of the world presented to Iranian schoolchildren. Since the self and the other can be defined only in relation to each other, I will focus on both, in national and international contexts. My aim is to assess how the content of schoolbooks prepares young Iranians for national as well as global citizenship.

A major question posed is whether schoolchildren are educated in the spirit of the time in which they live. President Khatami is calling for a new period of tolerance, respect, and dialogue within and outside Iran. Many citizens of the world are seeking a culture of peace, human dignity, and equal rights in response to the century's brutal manifestations of violence, racism, violation of human rights, and national, ethnic, and religious intolerance. Does the content of Iranian textbooks prepare the young for the national and international ideals of the twenty-first century? To answer the question, passages and illustrations in primary-school textbooks in Iran are analyzed. The methodology used is content analysis with special attention to detecting national, gender, racial, ethnic, and religious biases and stereotypes. Such a textual and pictorial analysis is referred to as "reading against the text," here undertaken with special sensitivity to possible distortion in the presentation of the other.

IDENTITY CONSTRUCTION
AND THE IDENTIFICATION OF THE "OTHER"

Juan Carlos Tedesco argues that the construction of identity that occurs in the socialization process "implies the identification of what is 'different,' or the identification of a borderline."[4] The major distinguishing feature of one who is "different" is that he/she is not perceived to be "like us." In other words, the other can be identified only in relation to us and never in isolation. In fact, the third pillar of education identified by the International Commission on Education for the Twenty-first Century—namely, "Learning to Live Together"—clearly indicates that if one is to understand others, one must first know oneself; discovery of others depends on the discovery of the self.[5]

This essay further contends that traditional ties of solidarity such as national origin, gender, and religion as well as political ideology and social class continue to play an influential role in shaping the identity of schoolchildren in Iran. The latter are important points of reference in defining "us" and identifying the other.

An attempt will be made here to identify both "us" and "them" as introduced in elementary school textbooks in Iran. The primary-school level has been chosen since political education, as an institutionalized form of political knowledge acquisition, first takes place at the primary level. Realizing that elementary schooling is the first and at times the only exposure of Iranians to formal education, the Islamic Republic has made every effort to charge primary school textbooks with teaching the younger generation about the self and others. The extreme centralization of the Iranian educational system, with standard textbooks throughout the country, highlights the importance of schoolbooks in identity construction among the young.

The total number of textbooks used during the five years of primary schooling (ages 6–10) during the 1999–2000 academic year was twenty-six. They are classified within the following categories: Persian, Mathematics, Experimental Sciences, Quran Instruction, Religious Studies, and Social Studies, which includes geography, history, and civic education.

A content and pictorial analysis of textbooks used at the primary-school level points to the major role assigned to Persian, Religious Studies, and Social Studies books in teaching the young about the self and others. Although the pictures used in Mathematics, Experimental Sciences, and Quran Instruction books convey important messages, as well, identity construction is undoubtedly a task of the aforementioned textbooks, which will be the focus of attention here.

An in-depth analysis of the content as well as pictures presented in Persian, Social Studies, and Religious Studies textbooks points to the existence of the following dichotomies, representing "us" and "them" to young pupils: Iranian/non-Iranian, Muslim/non-Muslim, and male/female. It should be noted that throughout the textbooks two types of the other are introduced, the internal other and the external other, both of which will be discussed.

DEFINITION OF THE "SELF"

To identify the non-Iranian, it is important to know who is the Iranian and what his/her distinguishing features are. In other words, knowledge about the other is possible only after having known the self. Here, both the actual characteristics of Iranians (*i.e.,* who they really are), as well as the desirable features of the ideal citizen of the Islamic Republic of Iran (who the ruling authorities want him/her to be) are discussed. In this context, "us" is Iranian and the "other" is non-Iranian.

Who Is an Iranian?

The first introduction of Iran takes place in the first grade. The Persian (Grade 1) textbook devotes four lessons to an introduction of the country, its map, its people, and its customs.[6] The emphasis on us, our people, and our homeland clearly identifies the borderline with the others who are not part of us. In the brief introduction of Iran, the young are taught two important things. First, Iranians are bound together in a common land with clear geographic boundaries, celebrating a common feast called *Aid-e Nauruz,* and sharing a common national identity. They are also Muslims, sharing a religious identity as well. The only diversity portrayed is in a picture of men wearing different headgear, representing various ethnic groups living in Iran. There is no mention of religious or linguistic diversity. The same is true in the second-grade Persian textbook, where the diversity of Iranians is illustrated in two colorful illustrations of boys and girls wearing local costumes.[7]

The inseparability of Iran and Islam is clearly presented in the third-grade Persian textbook, where the reader is reminded that Iran is an Islamic land, and that the Iranian New Year is the best time to visit the tombs of the martyrs of Islam.[8] Even in the lesson titled "Patriotism" in the fourth-grade Persian textbook, the reader is told that patriotism is intermingled with Islam and the search for martyrdom.[9]

The same theme is repeated in the fifth-grade Persian textbook, where Iran is described as a land of the brave, the latter being the martyrs who cried "Allahu Akbar" (God is great) while fighting to defend their land, the bastion of Islam.[10] The deliberate combination of patriotism and religion is clearly evident in the lesson title "Islamic Homeland" in the third-grade Religious Studies textbook.[11] The heavy emphasis on Iran's being an Islamic country and Iranians being Muslims is most evident in the fourth-grade Social Studies textbook. The title of Lesson 9 is "The Islamic Country of Iran," where the Muslim nation of Iran is shown as trying to lead an Islamic life.[12] It seems that love of the land is permissible only if accompanied by religious feelings and an Islamic sense of belonging.

Throughout the textbooks, being Muslim is what is deemed important, with relatively little emphasis on being Shi`i. The stress is on what is accepted by all Muslims—namely, the Prophet Muhammad, praying, fasting, mosque, recitation of the Quran, Friday prayers, pilgrimage, and the various Islamic celebrations. Religious symbols stressing the Islamic identity of Iranians abound, but few refer directly to Shi`ism. Exceptions are the selection of Imam Ali as his successor by the Prophet Muhammad, the martyrdom of Imam Husain in Karbala, visits to the shrines of Shi`i Imams by Iranians, and *ta`ziyeh,* or the religious theater, portraying the events of the day of Ashura when Imam Husain and his followers were killed.[13] This is not to say Shi`ism is not discussed in textbooks; what is notable is that Iran is portrayed as a Muslim nation, with little emphasis on its Shi`i character. Politicized Islam in Iran is stressed, combining religion with the affairs of the state.

In the twenty-six primary-school textbooks analyzed, there is only one mention of non-Muslim Iranians. In the section on history in the fourth-grade Social Studies textbook, there is a brief mention of Zoroastrianism, introduced as the official religion of the Sassanians.[14] Since this is the only exposure that the young pupil has to non-Muslim Iranians, with absolutely no mention of other religious groups living in the country, he/she may believe that all Iranians are Muslims, and Zoroastrians lived only in ancient times. Furthermore, unless otherwise exposed, the elementary-school pupil is also led to believe that Persian is the only language used by Iranians. There is no mention of other linguistic groups in the country.[15] Despite the extensive emigration of Iranians since the 1979 revolution, school textbooks define as Iranian only those who live within the geographic boundaries of the country. There is no mention of millions of Iranians scattered throughout the world.

The Ideal Iranian

The ideal Iranian, possessing desirable qualities and bringing dignity and respect for us, is defined on the basis of political ideology and religiosity. Exceptions include renowned Iranian scientists and ministers who lived long ago. Examples are Ibn Sina, Biruni, and Razi, introduced first and foremost as Iranians and "sources of pride" for the country as great scientists, mathematicians, philosophers, and physicians.[16] Other exceptions are the Iranian ministers who helped administer Iran during the rule of the Arabs, Turks, and Mongols.[17] Other nonreligious role models introduced are the prime minister Amir Kabir and the early-twentieth-century Constitutional Revolution freedom-fighters Sattar Khan, Baqer Khan, and Mirza Kuchek Khan-e Jangali.[18] Recently, Mohammad Mosaddeq has also been introduced as the only nonclerical politician having an influential role in popular antiforeign movements.[19] Despite the fame and popularity of poets and poetry in Iranian culture, young pupils are introduced to poets such as Ferdausi and Sa`di only through their poems, without any discussion about their role and influence in society.

Contemporary Iranians are rarely introduced as role models, the exceptions being the immensely popular wrestling champion Takhti,[20] whose mysterious early death is linked to his opposition to the shah's regime, and the teacher Baghchehban,[21] who used sign language for the first time in Iran and established the first school for deaf children. In the twenty-six textbooks analyzed, there is absolutely no presentation of a single female Iranian role model. The ideal women are non-Iranian and revered for their religious attributes. The only Iranian female character mentioned in the textbooks is the famous poet Parvin E'tesami, whose name appears at the end of her poems; her role is never treated individually.[22] The message conveyed is that we do not have any female role models and no Iranian woman is deemed good enough to earn our regard as a source of pride and dignity for us.

The young pupil is told that the ideal member of "us," who is always male and a member of the ulama, combines admirable political ideology and religious status. The ulama are presented as being conscious, conscientious, self-sacrificing, and brave, as struggling against dictatorship and demanding independence from foreign rule.[23] The culmination of all positive features in the private and public domains is identified as Ayatollah Khomeini. Accounts of his political life and career as well as his personal characteristics, along with a variety of pictures of his public and private life, abound in primary-school textbooks. Every book begins with his picture and an anecdote about something he has said. There is an attempt to keep Ayatollah Khomeini alive for members of the new generation, who are either too young to remember him or who were born after his death. Ayatollah Khomeini is introduced as the ultimate role model among us, whose path is followed by Ayatollah Khamenei.

Thus, the young Iranian boy is clearly told whom to emulate. The ultimate, most perfect member of "us" in school textbooks is male, a devout Muslim, and preferably one of the ulama. Although famous scientists, doctors, teachers, and athletes (all male) are also introduced as role models, none has the status and prestige of the perfect ones. The question that remains is, whom should the girls look up to?

Presentation of Men and Women

The Iranian society depicted in primary schoolbooks is a traditional one with a clear division of labor between men and women. Both the written word and the pictorial presentation in textbooks reinforce the image of a masculine world outside and a feminine world inside the home, with few exceptions. In Persian, Social Studies, Mathematics, and Religious Studies textbooks, women are often portrayed as wives and mothers engaged in traditional domestic chores, such as cooking, cleaning, sewing, knitting, and washing. The ideal female model in schoolbooks is the perfect housewife, one who is responsible for the daily tasks at home, enjoys performing them, and is adept at them.[24] In the fourth-grade Social Studies textbook, the pupil is directly told what is expected of him/her during adult life. In a lesson titled "Family Life," it is stated that the father usually works outside the home and is responsible for providing food and clothing for his wife and children. The mother, on the other hand, "usually" works at home, cooking, cleaning, child-rearing, and helping pupils perform their school duties. Readers are told that this clear-cut division of labor is altered in two situations, when women also work outside the home. The exceptions are rural and nomadic women, who help their husbands in agricultural tasks and animal husbandry, and "some" urban women who work in schools, hospitals, factories, and offices.[25] The message conveyed is that women work outside the home only to help their husbands; there is no mention of women who have chosen a career for their own personal and professional growth. Furthermore, even if urban women work, they are engaged in traditionally "feminine" jobs deemed acceptable and permissible for women, such as teaching and nursing. Performing domestic chores at home and working at traditional jobs outside the home is the ideal future portrayed for young girls, who are shown in textbooks as "liking" to learn cooking and sewing from their mothers and aspiring to become teachers in the future.[26]

The only exceptions in the Persian and Social Studies textbooks studied are brief mentions of a female school principal and a female doctor in the third-grade Social Studies book.[27] The other exception is found in the fifth-grade Religious Studies textbook, in the lesson on "Islamic Behavior": for the first and only time, Muslim women are asked to learn military skills, along with nursing and first aid, in order to defend the country when needed.[28] Young girls are told that the protection of Quran and the defense of the Islamic country is an obligation for both men and women. The lesson reminds school-children that women are active in the various Islamic and revolutionary institutions, aiming at building a free and prosperous Islamic nation. Female pupils are also reminded that Islam demands that women be simple and covered at all times. The young girl is thus conveyed two important messages. First, her activity is permitted and welcome only in a certain political framework and within ideologically approved institutions. Second, despite her social-political activity outside the home, a woman should remain first and foremost a good Muslim, in the proper clothing. The boundaries set for female activity outside the home directly point to what is deemed appropriate for women; the shoulds and should-nots are clear.

The emphasis on the appropriate Islamic covering (*hejab*) is evident throughout the textbook pictures. Girls are always shown with the scarf (*rusari*) at home, the larger and more formal scarf (*maqna`eh*) at school, and the black veil (chador) as the ultimate form of covering. The majority of adult women portrayed outside the home wear chador. Exceptions are rural and nomadic women, shown wearing scarves and colorful traditional costumes, sharing the difficult physical labor performed by the male members of the family. Sex segregation outside the home, performance of daily domestic chores, engagement in traditional feminine jobs, and Islamic covering are the predominant images reflected in the textbook pictures. Such is the image of female existence portrayed for young girls at an age when female role models can play a crucial role in acquainting readers with the possibilities available for women in society.

The female image depicted in textbooks through content and illustrations limits women to the domestic realm and does not reflect the variation in female occupations and professions in the real world. According to 1996 statistics, 9 percent of Iranian women above the age of 10 were employed by public and private organizations. Among them, 28 percent were specialists such as scientists, physicians, university professors, lawyers, and the like; 23 percent were employed in the production sector; 5 percent were workers in the service sector; 2 percent were high-ranking authorities and managers; and the rest worked as technicians, assistants, industrial laborers, operators, saleswomen, and office workers. The statistics show that 27 percent of the women not employed were students and 58 percent declared themselves as housewives.[29] The stereotypical view of women's activities in the schoolbooks deliberately distorts the reality of female existence in the Islamic Republic.

A welcome change in the portrayal of girls in recent years has been in pictures included in science textbooks. Pictures of girls performing scientific experiments abound in Experimental Sciences textbooks throughout primary school. Girls engaged in physical activities such as running, playing ball, and jumping rope, and boys participating in household chores such as setting the dishes and helping the mother in cooking are nontraditional pictures that have appeared elsewhere, challenging the stereotypical images of feminine or masculine behavior.[30]

Counter Role Models

Within the male world presented to primary schoolchildren, there is also a good-evil duality in which counter role models are presented. Whereas the ulama are introduced as the ideal members of "us," the villains are repre-

sented by kings. As early as the first grade, the young Iranian pupil is conveyed the message that before the 1979 revolution, Iran was divided into good
(Ayatollah Khomeini and his followers) and bad (the shah, whose rule was
marked by dictatorship and oppression).[31] This theme continues in the
higher grades, where the name of the shah is always accompanied by mentions of oppression, corruption, tyranny, torture, and treason.[32] Pictures illustrating the luxurious living conditions of the shah and his family compared
to the bleak situation of life among the poor before the revolution aim at contrasting the two.[33]

The same theme is reflected in Social Studies textbooks, in which the kings
are referred to as *taghut* (tyrants) marked by plunder, luxury, waste, and force,
and hatred is deemed the appropriate feeling toward them.[34] The number-
one villains among us throughout history are the kings, beginning with the
Medes and ending with the last shah. The most evil kings are the Sassanian
monarch Khosrau Parviz, whose "selfishness" prevented him from accepting the Prophet Muhammad's invitation to Islam,[35] and Mohammad Reza
Pahlavi, who is portrayed in the darkest light throughout all textbooks. (The
villains among us are all male, just like the role models.) There are three exceptions to the rule that kings are the enemies of the people: Dariush, during
whose reign many public works were provided for Iranians;[36] Shah Isma`il,
the first Safavid shah, who made Shi`ism the official religion of Iran; and
Karim Khan Zand, praised for his kindness towards his enemies, avoidance
of war and bloodshed, and calling himself the "representative of the people,"
as opposed to "shah."[37]

Twenty years after the revolution and the abolition of monarchy in Iran,
the ruling authorities still feel the need to present monarchs as the primary
villains, justifying such negative feelings as hatred and detestation towards
them even though none of them remain. Primary schoolchildren age six
through ten have no idea what a king is and carry no memory of the late shah,
but this does not deter the textbook compilers from including vivid images
of these ever-present evil forces. After two decades, there still seems an urgent
need to keep alive the memory of monarchy in order to justify the present
form of governance. The villains are always cast as against the ideal citizens
among us—mostly the ulama, culminating in Ayatollah Khomeini, and the
common people. Schoolchildren are told that our friends are those who earn
their income through manual labor, such as carpenters, metal workers,
painters, gardeners, peasants, and construction workers.[38] They come from
lower socioeconomic ranks, have simple lives, survive under conditions of
austerity, usually engage in hard physical labor, and are, first and foremost,
good Muslims.

Recognizing that the above-mentioned role models may not be tangible for young schoolchildren, textbook authors have included two other categories of "us" with whom pupils may identify. One is the teacher, who is part of the daily life of schoolchildren. Pupils are told that teaching is the profession in which one can render the highest service to society and the people.[39] Children are asked to respect their teachers throughout various lessons, and most textbooks end with a note of gratitude to the teacher. Even the Prophet Muhammad is quoted as saying, "I am the teacher of the people."[40] The highest praise for teachers takes place in the fifth-grade Persian reader, in which the teacher is described as being free, a fighter, forgiving, an enlightener, and self-sacrificing.[41] He/she is portrayed as one who teaches kindness, courage, freedom, independence, struggle against oppression, justice, faith, and fraternity to the students, keeping them away from cruelty and selfishness. While teaching such respect for the teacher is worthwhile, it seems that the textbook authors are attempting to introduce the teacher—the representative of the educational system and probably the first formal authority in the pupil's life—as the ultimate leader and role model, ignoring the influence of the family.

The other, more heroic, role model who represents the best among us is the *shahid* (martyr) killed during the 1978–79 revolution or the 1980–88 Iran-Iraq war. The primary schoolchild is told that martyrdom is the highest form of sacrifice and martyrs are given the highest rewards by God, including entry to paradise. To give one's life for God and for the betterment of one's society is presented as the most desirable value among Muslims.[42] To render martyrdom more tangible for the young, an entire lesson is devoted to the characteristics and struggle of Shahid Hosain Fahmideh, a thirteen-year-old Iranian killed in action during the Iran-Iraq war by attaching a grenade to himself and creeping under an enemy tank to destroy it. His courage, commitment to the Islamic revolution, and will to drive the enemy from his land are lauded as representing the highest values among Iranians.[43] He is a hero among us. Detailed description of battlegrounds, tanks, machine guns, shells, artillery, fire, and death in primary schoolbooks written for the very young may seem contrary to the worldwide effort to condemn violence and teach peaceful conflict resolution. Yet such concepts are intentionally discussed in Iranian textbooks in order to keep alive the memory of the war, which was a climax in the consolidation of the Islamic Republic and remains heavily imbued with political, religious, patriotic, and ideological sentiments.

The world presented to young Iranians is a black and white one; there are no shades of gray. People are either good or evil, with nothing in between. The school pupil is never asked to judge for him/herself. Political education is open and direct in postrevolutionary textbooks: identities are imposed from outside and not allowed to be built individually. This is in contrast to Tedesco's statement that "the outstanding feature of the present historic period is precisely the importance assumed by the individual's own activity in constructing his or her identity."[44] It is true that the Iranian family plays a crucial role in socializing the young, followed by the peer group. Many members of the ruling authority in Iran have in fact expressed concern about the conflicting values of family and school in postrevolutionary society, and many intellectuals and educators have pointed to the fact that the "children of revolution" have constructed their own identities, often in direct contrast to what they have been taught in school. The above arguments notwithstanding, primary schoolchildren represent the most impressionable age group. The fact that the school is their first contact with formal social-political-cultural institutions implies that a heavy dose of ideology is used to put them in the "right path" from the beginning. Although the image of the world presented to the young may be radically transformed in their minds over time, it is important to recognize its features and how it is portrayed.

IDENTIFICATION OF THE "OTHER"

Once the self is defined and the ideal and undesirable members of us are identified, it is easy to determine who is the other. "Strangers," "foreigners," and "outsiders" are the labels used for non-Iranians in primary-school textbooks. How are "outsiders" identified and labeled? Content analysis of these textbooks points to friend/enemy, Muslim/non-Muslim, and male/female dichotomies, among others.

Friend/Enemy Dichotomy

The concepts of friend and enemy are clearly defined for primary schoolchildren. They are told that, although the specific enemy can change through time, feelings such as rage and hatred are always appropriate ones toward an enemy.[45] The pupil is taught that the enemy should be destroyed, leaving no room for tolerance or peaceful conflict resolution.

Who are Iran's enemies? They are different people at different times, yet they share a few points in common: they do not want Iran to advance, they want to divide the nation, they intend to interfere in the internal affairs of the state, and, at the most extreme, they want to destroy Iran.[46] The enemy is usually presented in two forms, mostly in the history section of Social Studies textbooks: those who have waged direct, physical war against Iran, and those who have plotted against the independence and dignity of the country. The only exception is the Arab conquest of Iran in the seventh century, which is depicted as a most welcome event for the common people, who experienced "nothing but poverty, illness, and hunger under Sassanian rule."[47] Pupils are told that the Muslim faith brought freedom and equality for all, and was, therefore, willingly accepted by the people. In fact, Arabs are never presented as enemies unless they mistreat the Shi`i Imams or disobey the rules of Islam and become oppressors, like the Umayyads and Abbasids.[48]

The dominant theme repeated in the discussion of foreign invasion or attack is that Iranians have always disliked the rule of foreigners and have always been successful in saving their country and regaining independence.[49] The Mongol and Iraqi attacks are the ones most emphasized in primary schoolbooks. The Mongol invasion of Iran is described using the most negative terms, such as "destruction," "cruelty," and "brutal murder."[50] The portrayal of the 1980–88 Iran-Iraq war is the most vivid, using stories and pictures of the physical damage and introducing war heroes to make the young pupil feel the significance of the whole event. Schoolchildren are told that Iraq's rulers imposed the war on us in 1980, forcing eight years of bloody war on the Islamic Republic.[51] Textbook compilers have been careful, however, in introducing the enemy to young Iranians: the villains are shown to be the Iraqi government, the Iraqi army, the forces of Saddam, and the Ba`athist nonbelievers,[52] as opposed to the people of Iraq, shown as Muslims and our neighbors. While there is a conscious attempt to keep the memory of the war alive in the minds of those who are too young to remember it, there is also an effort to separate the Iraqi people from their government. The fact that Iraqis are Arabs is also ignored in textbooks.

The second group of enemies introduced to primary schoolchildren has seldom conquered Iran physically; its invasion has taken the form of political interference and socioeconomic penetration. These are Westerners, particularly the Russians, British, and Americans, against whom Iranians had to restore their national sovereignty and dignity. The recent infiltration of Westerners is portrayed as indirect yet dangerous, undermining the very independence and identity of Iranians. Young pupils are told that the West has implemented its influence through its military might and the use of Iranian "satellites," notably the Qajar and Pahlavi kings and nobility. The image of Westerners in school textbooks is one of constant interference, aggression, and plunder, aimed at bringing about dependence, a sense of need, and a lack of will among Iranians.[53] Black and white are very clear in the discussion of relations between Iran and the West before the 1979 revolution. The main heroes of the struggle against the West in Iranian textbooks are the ulama.

Westerners and ulama are the two extremes of the evil-good continuum, with others falling in between.

A pattern recurring in the treatment of the other as the enemy is the positive image portrayed of the self. In every discussion of war, there is mention of Iranian bravery, courage, sacrifice, search for independence and dignity, and hatred of foreign rule or interference, culminating in the most esteemed act of martyrdom. It seems that foreign attack brings out the best in us. Young Iranians are repeatedly warned against the danger of the enemy, and taught the importance of being self-reliant and never needing the help of foreigners.[54] Partnership, negotiation, communication, dialogue, and cooperation in foreign relations are basically absent in the textbook discussion of ancient or modern Iranian history. The dominant messages are distrust, fear, and resentment. Pupils are informed that the Friday prayer leader always carries a gun in his hand, in order to show the enemies of Islam that Muslims are prepared to defend their lands at all times.[55] The message is that the enemy is always present and Iranians should be alert at all times.

Who are our friends? They are mostly the weak and the oppressed of the world.[56] The boundaries of religion, race, color, and national origin break down when it comes to the call to free the oppressed. This is the first exposure of the Iranian pupil to any concept of global citizenship. The young Iranian is asked to move across the borderlines defined by national citizenship to enter the global community and render service to it.

Another and more strictly defined category of friends are Muslims, collectively referred to as the Islamic community or *umma,* of which Iran is a member. Although this concept is narrower than that of global citizenship, it goes beyond race, color, language, and national origin, including all the Muslims of the world. While a clear line of demarcation still exists between Muslim and non-Muslim, here the pupil is taught to look beyond the borderlines of his/her own country. Here the borderline between us and them becomes blurred and the schoolchild is simultaneously exposed to both national unity and Muslim solidarity. He/she is asked to honor not only national sovereignty but also unity among Muslims, to prevent the rule of the enemy over Islamic nations.[57] Although the "enemy of Islam" is never clearly defined, the pupil is constantly reminded of its presence and ill intentions.

Male and Female Role Models

The evil foreigner, who is portrayed as an ever-present enemy always plotting against Iran, is not the only image offered of non-Iranians. The "other" is also presented in a positive light, mostly in the framework of role models.

Ideal non-Iranians are portrayed in the context of religious/nonreligious, male/female categories. The ultimate role models are religious figures, Muslim and non-Muslim, beginning with Noah and including all prophets and Shi`i Imams. They represent the ideal characteristics aspired to by all human beings, including faith, kindness, compassion, knowledge, strength, simplicity, justice, respect, sacrifice, and courage.[58] In addition to the detailed information about the life of the Prophet Muhammad in primary-school textbooks, the readers also cover the lives of other prophets, including Noah, Abraham, Moses, and Jesus Christ.[59] Only the religions deemed appropriate by the Islamic Republic are covered in any detail, including Islam, Judaism, Christianity, and Zoroastrianism, although there are brief mentions of the Buddhist and Brahmanic traditions in Asia, and a picture of a Brahmanic temple in India.[60]

Religious role models are not limited to male figures in Iranian textbooks. Both Muslim and non-Muslim women who played an important role in their own religion are portrayed. Yet all female figures are introduced in the context of their relation to the male prophets or imams, and the service they have rendered to their faith; none is presented as a role model by herself, independent of others. Examples are Khadija, the wife of the Prophet Muhammad; Fatima, daughter of the Prophet Muhammad, wife of Imam Ali, and mother of Imams Hasan and Husain; Zainab, the sister of Imam Husain; and Ma`sumeh, the sister of Imam Riza.[61] The ultimate female role models are Fatima and Zainab, who represent the two sides of female existence. Fatima, introduced as the "exemplary lady of Islam," is an ideal housewife, engaged in domestic chores and child rearing in the shelter of the home. Here is a description of Fatima in the fourth-grade Religious Studies textbook: "She was the best wife for her husband and the best mother for her children. She performed the domestic chores at home. She had a simple and clean life. . . . She tried to keep her covering. . . . Fatima loved her children very much, raising them as the best children according to the principles and traditions of Islam."[62] This is in contrast to Zainab, whose courage in recounting the events of Karbala and the martyrdom of Imam Husain and his followers, and open struggle against oppression, offers an image of female resistance in the outside world.[63] Both women are honored in schoolbooks for propagating Islam, and their roles inside and outside the home together represent the ideal woman of the Islamic Republic of Iran. No other female role models are introduced in primary-school textbooks outside the religious sphere. There is no mention of famous women in the realm of culture, literature, politics, or science outside Iran, either in historical or contemporary times.

Although male religious figures remain the ultimate non-Iranian role models—with special emphasis on the Prophet Muhammad, Imam Ali, and Imam Husain—Muslim and non-Muslim male scientists and inventors are presented as models to be emulated by young Iranians. Historical figures such as Jabir Ibn Hayyan, known as the "father of chemistry," are introduced both for their scientific achievements and for personal characteristics such as persistence and endurance.[64] Textbooks attempt to portray the "glory of the Islamic civilization" and convey the message that Muslim lands were once the center of science and culture. The emphasis on introducing Muslim scientists and reminding pupils that their works were once translated into European languages and taught in Western universities is part of an attempt to instill a sense of pride in young Iranians regarding their past and their identity. The discussion of more modern times includes Western figures, the most notable of whom are the Wright brothers, Alexander Graham Bell, and Thomas Edison.[65] Such men are highly praised for their service to humanity, industry, and science. There is no mention of foreign but non-Western role models in the schoolbooks, which ignore the achievements of Asians, Africans, and Latin Americans in various spheres of human life.

The detailed description of the scientific endeavors of Westerners presents a sharp contrast to the neglect of modern Iranian scientists, writers, and intellectuals. One can look at this issue from two points of view. On a positive note, textbook compilers aim at providing a global view of human achievement, regardless of national origin. From a more pessimistic viewpoint, however, it seems that despite the claims made by postrevolutionary authorities, we are still not able to see the best among us, due to a deep-rooted belief in our "inferiority," first imposed upon and then internalized by us. The contemporary world portrayed in schoolbooks is one filled with "superior" Western scientists and Iranian religiopolitical leaders. It seems that the only good Westerners are scientists, while no Iranians are deemed good enough to act as role models except religious authorities and political leaders. The rich culture and history of both the West and Iran are ignored in an attempt to introduce only ideologically approved figures. The situation is even worse when it comes to non-Western foreigners, of whom nothing is mentioned. Ironically, a Euro-American-centered worldview seems to permeate the minds of Iranian educational authorities, despite twenty years of anti-Western slogans.

IS HISTORY BEING REPEATED?

The self-other perspective presented in the textbooks of the Islamic Republic is not a new phenomenon. A review of textbooks compiled during the reign of Mohammad Reza Shah Pahlavi also points to a clear presentation of the "self" and the "other." The dichotomous view of the world has a long-standing history. What is important here are the changing definitions of self and other since the prerevolutionary period.

The self presented during the late Pahlavi period was mostly Aryan, taking pride in Iran's "superior" civilization, language, and culture, and filled with a sense of supremacy toward neighboring nations and cultures. What was important at the time was *Iraniyat,* or being an Iranian. Thus, government-sponsored schoolbooks, especially history and Persian-language textbooks, instilled a sense of Iranianness, Iranian spirit, and Iranian identity among the young. The message was that the full-blooded Iranian was "superior" compared to the "inferior" invaders who aimed at conquering Iran's insurmountable and invincible spirit—namely, the Arabs, Mongols, and Turks. The Iranian self was introduced as "culturally superior" to the others.

The self presented in the textbooks of the Islamic Republic is still Iranian. The concepts of nationhood and national solidarity continue to exist, and the love of *vatan* or homeland remains strong, although nationalism (*melli-gera'i*) and Iranianism are frowned upon. What is new is the shift to the Irano-Islamic identity, as opposed to the solely Iranian one. The national-religious identity has replaced the exclusive emphasis on national identity. The shift has been one from seeking pride in the Aryan-Iranian civilization and culture to searching for Islamic-Iranian roots. Iranianness, however, remains intact; the common denominator is, still, being an Iranian (*irani budan*). National identity's continued importance in the Islamic Republic may be surprising to those who believed the extreme attack on Iranianness during the early days of the revolution. An in-depth study of the national-religious symbols used during the Iran-Iraq war, however, and careful observation of how the children of the revolution are creating their own independent identities in spite of the guidelines provided by the ruling authorities, point to the failed attempt to delete the Iranian part of the Irano-Islamic identity. In the words of Haggay Ram, "the post-revolutionary state's endeavor to integrate the Islamic tradition more forcefully into the definition of Iranian self-identity . . . should not serve as an indication of a change of heart from pure 'Iranianism' to pure 'Islamism.'"[66]

Yet another and more significant shift in the postrevolutionary period has been the presentation of the other in textbooks. The shift in emphasis from proud membership in the Indo-European, Aryan-Iranian civilization to the equally proud sense of belonging to the Islamic civilization has altered the definition of the other. Prerevolutionary textbooks instilled a sense of pride and honor in sharing the same roots as Europeans, presenting them as "brothers" of the same blood and origin. Postrevolutionary Islamism, however, emphasizes common roots with other Muslims, especially Arabs, and glorifies

Islamic civilization. The message is that Muslims are morally superior. Thus, the Iranian sense of superiority is kept intact; the difference is the shift from "cultural superiority" to "moral superiority."

Within the political realm, the other is determined by the Islamic Republic's Third Worldism. The arrogant West is introduced as the number one enemy threatening Iranian national sovereignty and cultural identity. In the late-Pahlavi-era schoolbooks, the West was presented as the ideal towards which Iran was to strive. Western might and supremacy were justified for the young on the basis of its scientific, industrial, and technological advancement. The Western way was not shunned, and fascination and praise for Western civilization were in order, partly because "they" shared the same roots as "us." The West at the time comprised Europe and, later, the United States; Russia (later, the Soviet Union) was definitely excluded.

While the shah's regime emphasized the goodness of the West, accepting its path and attempting to emulate it, the Islamic Republic chose to focus on the dark side of the West, highlighting its historical aggression against Iran's national interests. Both the Pahlavi and the Islamic authorities suffer from what Siavoshi calls "a Manichean view of the global situation."[67] The black-and-white image of the world presented in the Pahlavi schoolbooks divided the globe into the evil forces of communism, led by the Soviet Union, and the good champions of freedom, represented by the West. A similar simplistic dichotomy exists in today's textbooks, in which the world is divided into "morally superior" Muslims and "corrupt" Westerners. It seems that the Iranian identity continuously needs a counter-hero in order to be able to define itself. This is certainly not limited to Iran; it is also true of the textbooks of other countries that feel obliged to highlight their differentness in order to instill a sense of independent identity in their young. Their attempts may include overt nationalism and a sense of moral/cultural superiority.

CONCLUSION

What is the message conveyed to primary schoolchildren in the Islamic Republic of Iran regarding the self and the other? An analysis of the content and pictorial presentation of textbooks used in grades one through five shows that patriotism and religion are combined to present an Iranian-Islamic identity. Thus, the "self" has a strong religious nature—decisively Muslim—that does not overshadow his/her national character. Despite heavy emphasis on Islamic unity and solidarity, schoolchildren are frequently reminded that they are Iranians who should keep their national interests in mind at all times. The national character presented in schoolbooks undermines ethnic and linguistic diversity, and the predominantly Muslim identity portrayed fails to take into account the different religious groups in the country. The role models presented are male, and they belong to an ideological order deemed superior to those of their compatriots due to their religious-political activities. Good and evil are clear, with manifest borderlines. Although the pupil is never conveyed the message that he/she is "better" because he/she is Iranian, being Muslim definitely puts him/her in a "superior" position. The schoolchild is told that Islam is "the best and most complete religion";[68] the Prophet Muhammad is superior to other prophets;[69] and whoever does not accept Islam and chooses another religion will "lose" and have a difficult time in the afterlife.[70] There is a clear line of demarcation between Muslim and non-Muslim in postrevolutionary textbooks, although "equality and brotherhood" are emphasized among Muslims, regardless of race, color, language, and nationality.[71]

The other is presented in relation to us; thus, evil is determined in relation to the national and political interests of Iran. Good, on the other hand, is defined in predominantly religious terms, emphasizing an Islamic sense of community. The West and Westerners continue to occupy a central place in the Iranian mentality despite revolutionary statements emphasizing Third-World unity and solidarity with the South. Western science is highly valued, while Western political domination and interference in national affairs are strongly condemned. Whether it is shown in a positive or negative light, the West is ever-present, pointing to the unresolved relation between us and the West. The other in Iranian schoolbooks is still predominantly the West, with whom "we" continue to have a love-hate relationship.

Do the content of postrevolutionary textbooks and the messages conveyed in them prepare young schoolchildren for the new millennium? Global citizenship, peace education, tolerance, acknowledgement of and respect for differences, nonviolence, conflict resolution, gender sensitivity, responsiveness to diversity, and nondiscrimination are key words used in international educational circles in preparation for the twenty-first century. It seems, however, that Iranian textbooks do not instill such values in schoolchildren. The few exceptions that do exist, emphasizing the need to help each other regardless of religious or national differences,[72] are brief and insufficient. The clear-cut demarcation lines between us and them in both national and international contexts, the existence of an ever-present "enemy" that threatens the country at all times, the deliberate avoidance of diversity, and the stereotypical presentation of women point to the fact that Iranian educational authorities do not take into consideration the above-mentioned key concepts in the compilation of textbooks.

Does the content of Iranian textbooks reflect the slogans of the Khatami period? The May 1997 elections and the presidency of Mohammad Khatami brought about a new political vocabulary in the country, in which respect for diversity, tolerance, and dialogue are also key words. President Khatami has introduced a new image of self and other to Iranians. In his viewpoint, "we" are not a homogeneous entity without diversity, yet the differences among "us" should not lead to separation or domination of one over the other. Iran belongs to all Iranians, and each Iranian "owns" Iran and "belongs" to Iran as much as any other Iranian.[73] Acknowledgement of and respect for diversity are important ingredients of Khatami's presentation of the self. The same theme appears vis-à-vis the other, who is neither all evil nor all good, only different from "us." Khatami calls for understanding and recognition of the other, which, according to him, is possible only after having known the self. Recognition, away from extreme love or hate, is the beginning of dialogue, which can lead to learning all the good that the other has to offer, while remaining independent and proud.[74] The words used for the "other" in Khatami's terminology—*digaran* and *ghair*—do not carry any negative connotation. In his call for understanding and dialogue, Khatami notes that kindness, freedom, justice, and human rights are the ideals that are to replace animosity, hatred, cruelty, ignorance, force, and violence in the new century, both in the national and international spheres—what he refers to as the "final victory of the word over the sword."[75]

Three years after the election of President Khatami and the beginning of a new phase in Iranian politics, textbooks continue, with only minor modifications, to instill the messages of the early days of the revolution. While altering textbooks is a slow and sensitive process, so far no attempt has been made to prepare the grounds for understanding and dialogue. The self portrayed does not represent the nuances of Iranian existence, and the other is a selective presentation of what is really out there. The existing schoolbooks do not help the young Iranian pupil explore the depth and complexity of his/her identity; they do not assist him/her in building a realistic and tangible sense of pride and dignity. Without a critical reflection upon the self, it is indeed difficult to expect a mature understanding of the other. More important is the lingering existence of a sense of fear and animosity that justifies hatred and violence. The absence of kindness, tolerance, and forgiveness in these textbooks shows that the word has not yet replaced the sword.

NOTES

1. "Convention on the Rights of the Child," adopted by the General Assembly of the United Nations on 20 November 1989.

2. Betty A. Reardon, *Tolerance—The Threshold of Peace: Teacher-Training Resource Unit* (Paris: UNESCO Publishing, 1997), 126.

3. To cite only works in English: Adele Ferdows, "Gender Roles in Iranian School Textbooks," in *Iran: Political Culture in the Islamic Republic*, ed. Samih K. Farsoun and Mehrdad Mashayekhi (London and New York: Routledge, 1994), 325–36; Patricia J. Higgins and Pirouz Shoar-Ghaffari, "Sex-Role Socialization in Iranian Textbooks," *NWSA Journal* 3 (1991): 213–32; Patricia J. Higgins, "Changing Perceptions of Iranian Identity in Elementary Textbooks," in *Women and the Family in the Middle East: New Voices of Change*, ed. Elizabeth Warnock Fernea (Austin: University of Texas Press, 1985), 337–63; Golnar Mehran, "Socialization of Schoolchildren in the Islamic Republic of Iran," *Iranian Studies* 22 (1989): 35–50; M. Mobin Shorish, "Textbooks in Revolutionary Iran," in *Textbooks in the Third World*, ed. Philip G. Altbach and Gail P. Kelly (New York: Garland, 1988), 247–68; Jacquiline Rudolph Touba, "Cultural Effects on Sex Role Images in Elementary Schoolbooks in Iran: A Content Analysis after the Revolution," *International Journal of Sociology of the Family* 17 (1987): 143–58.

4. Juan Carlos Tedesco, *The New Educational Pact: Education, Competitiveness, and Citizenship in Modern Society* (Paris: UNESCO, International Bureau of Education, 1997), 62.

5. *Learning: The Treasure Within*, Report to UNESCO of the International Commission on Education for the Twenty-first Century (Paris: UNESCO, 1996), 92–93.

6. *Farsi (Persian) (Grade 1)* (Tehran: Ministry of Education, 1999), 93–96.

7. *Persian (Grade 2)* (Tehran: Ministry of Education, 1999), 107–08.

8. *Persian (Grade 3)* (Tehran: Ministry of Education, 1999), 78–79 and 114–15.

9. *Persian (Grade 4)* (Tehran: Ministry of Education, 1999), 150–51.

10. *Persian (Grade 5)* (Tehran: Ministry of Education, 1999), 44–45.

11. *Ta`limat-e dini (Religious Studies) (Grade 3)* (Tehran: Ministry of Education, 1999), 2.

12. *Ta`limat-e ejtema`i (Social Studies) (Grade 4)* (Tehran: Ministry of Education, 1999), 142–43.

13. *Persian (Grade 5)*, 69.

14. *Social Studies (Grade 4)*, 109.

15. *Persian (Grade 5)*, 181.

16. *Persian (Grade 4)*, 54–55, 69–70.

17. *Social Studies (Grade 5)* (Tehran: Ministry of Education, 1999), 101–10.

18. *Social Studies (Grade 5)*, 123, 127, 130.

19. *Social Studies (Grade 5)*, 132.

20. *Social Studies (Grade 3)* (Tehran: Ministry of Education, 1999), 79–80.

21. *Persian (Grade 5)*, 32–38.

22. *Persian (Grade 5)*, 92, 188.

23. *Social Studies (Grade 5)*, 124–33.

24. *Religious Studies (Grade 5)* (Tehran: Ministry of Education, 1999), 47.

25. *Social Studies (Grade 4)*, 123–24.

26. *Social Studies (Grade 3)*, 3.

27. *Social Studies (Grade 3)*, 88, 95–96.

28. *Religious Studies (Grade 5)*, 37–38.

29. Women's Bureau, *Shakhesha-ye ejtema`i—eqtesadi-ye zanan dar Jomhuri-ye*

Eslami-ye Iran (Tehran: Presidential Office of the Islamic Republic of Iran, 1375/1996), 172–81.

30. *Persian* (Grade 1), 33, 47, 72, and 82.

31. *Persian* (Grade 1), 108–109.

32. *Persian* (Grade 3), 130.

33. *Social Studies* (Grade 3), 52–53.

34. *Social Studies* (Grade 3), 51, 55, 60.

35. *Social Studies* (Grade 5), 89–90.

36. *Social Studies* (Grade 4), 100–03.

37. *Social Studies* (Grade 5), 113, 117–18.

38. *Persian* (Grade 2), 80–81.

39. *Persian* (Grade 5), 33.

40. *Religious Studies* (Grade 2) (Tehran: Ministry of Education, 1999), 41.

41. *Persian* (Grade 5), 202.

42. *Social Studies* (Grade 5), 167–68.

43. *Persian* (Grade 4), 17–19.

44. Tedesco, *New Educational Pact,* 55.

45. *Persian* (Grade 3), 79.

46. *Social Studies* (Grade 5), 121–37.

47. *Social Studies* (Grade 4), 113–14.

48. *Social Studies* (Grade 5), 101–04.

49. *Social Studies* (Grade 4), 104–05.

50. *Social Studies* (Grade 5), 108–11.

51. *Social Studies* (Grade 5), 137.

52. *Social Studies* (Grade 3), 98.

53. *Social Sciences* (Grade 5), 143–44.

54. *Social Sciences* (Grade 3), 40–41.

55. *Religious Studies* (Grade 5), 68.

56. *Persian* (Grade 3), 131.

57. *Social Studies* (Grade 4), 144.

58. *Social Studies* (Grade 5), 90–100.

59. *Social Studies* (Grade 4), 84–93.

60. *Social Studies* (Grade 5), 50–51.

61. *Social Studies* (Grade 3), 24.

62. *Religious Studies* (Grade 4), 32.

63. *Social Studies* (Grade 5), 100.

64. *Persian* (Grade 5), 176–77.

65. *Persian* (Grade 5), 166–71.

66. Haggay Ram, "The Immemorial Iranian Nation? School Textbooks and Historical Memory in Post-Revolutionary Iran," *Nations and Nationalism* 6 (2000): 82.

67. Sussan Siavoshi, "Regime Legitimacy and High-School Textbooks," in *Iran After the Revolution: Crisis of an Islamic State,* ed. Saeed Rahnema and Sohrab Behdad (London: I. B. Tauris, 1995), 208.

68. *Religious Studies* (Grade 2), 31.

69. *Religious Studies* (Grade 2), 27.

70. *Religious Studies* (Grade 3), 22.

71. *Persian* (Grade 3), 63.
72. *Persian* (Grade 4), 95.
73. *Hezareh-ye goftegu va tafahom* (Tehran: Rasanesh, 1378/1999), 74.
74. Ibid., 70–72.
75. Ibid., 53.

11 / Cinematic Exchange Relations:
Iran and the West

HAMID NAFICY

Iran's relationship with the West has involved not only acts of violence but also acts of mutual imagination, including ones involving film. Iranian cinema began as early as 1900. During its first seventy years, it was highly dependent on the West for its techniques, ideas, and products and had little reciprocal influence on the West. This began to change with the "New Wave" cinema during the last decade of the late shah's rule, and more dramatically since the 1979 revolution, when Iranian cinema achieved artistic and financial success at home and abroad. This chapter relates and analyzes these developments, and attempts to explain the paradoxical successes, including major international recognition, of Iranian films under a clerical regime.

Throughout the twentieth century, the relationship of Iran and the West has involved not only acts of invasion, rebellion, coup d'état, political machination, and expropriation of natural resources, but also acts of mutual imagination, which were driven not only by individual and national self-interest but also by the attraction and repulsion of two cultures. The West, in particular the United States, tended to represent Iran in its movies and television programs in an Orientalist fashion as quaintly underdeveloped, ethnographically exotic, geopolitically premodern, or Islamically backward and violent.[1] Iranians, in turn, often sought to define and fashion themselves according, or in contradistinction, to these media representations. This kind of cinematic "self-othering," seeing the self through the eyes of the other, began with the introduction of film into Iran in 1900, where it has had a lasting psychological and ideological impact.[2] The interaction of Iran and the West, however, was not limited to the exchange of representations, for in the realm of cinema it involved a massive exchange of ideas, narrative forms, production procedures, and technical know-how, along with technological transfer and the marketing and distribution of films.

One of the oldest and most active cinemas in the Middle East and the Third World, Iranian cinema maintained from its beginning this multifaceted relation of exchange with the cinemas of the West. At first, it was only an importer of Western technology, ideas, production procedures, narrative modes, generic forms, and filming style. It would take it some seven decades to reverse the flow, to become in the 1970s an exporter of filmic ideas and products to the West, and another two decades to achieve the status of a vital international cinema. I will examine this cinematic exchange relation, which was part of the larger modernization process in the country and worldwide, by using a historical trajectory divided into the three major epochs of recent Iranian history.

THE QAJAR ERA

Thanks to the travel diary of Mozaffar al-Din Shah Qajar, we can pinpoint with rare accuracy the circumstances of the first Iranian film footage, which was shot in Europe—the first instance of exchange. The date was August 18, 1900; the location was the city of Ostend, Belgium; the occasion was Mozaffar al-Din Shah's review of a "flower parade" in which women riding some fifty floats threw flowers at the shah, which he joyously returned; the cinematographer was Mirza Ebrahim Khan Akkasbashi, the official court photographer; and his camera was a Gaumont that he had purchased on the shah's order a few weeks earlier in Paris.[3] That first real contact with Western cinema affected Akkasbashi, who upon his return to Iran continued to film what were called "actualities," documentary shots of daily events, such as the Moharram religious ceremonies and the lions in the royal zoo. These actualities, along with French and Russian newsreels, were shown in the royal palace and the houses of dignitaries during wedding, birth, and circumcision ceremonies, creating a model of a private, sponsored cinema.[4]

Iranian cinema also benefited from the demographic composition of its pioneers, which favored Westernization. Many of them were émigrés from the West who lived in Iran, or hyphenated Iranians, Armenians, and foreign-trained Muslims, among them Akkasbashi and Ohanian (below). Some of them, such as Ebrahim Khan Sahhafbashi, who set up the first commercial public cinema on Tehran's Cheraq Gaz Street in 1904, imported not only films and film equipment but also other Western scientific instruments and consumer products, including X-ray machines, steam-driven automobiles, and phonographs. Most of the pioneers were pro-West and liberal; some, such as Sahhafbashi, were constitutionalists, who favored replacing despotic monarchy with parliamentary monarchy. Cinema was, thus, integral to the Westernization of Iran and contributed to its consolidation.

During this era, Iranian cinema gradually evolved from the Qajar period's artisanal ways of making and exhibiting films to an industrial mode of production. This involved, among other things, both a rise in local productions and an increase in foreign film imports.

The Inward Flow

While in its first few decades of existence the traditional and religious strata condemned cinema as morally corrupting, Western-educated people welcomed it as a modernizing agent. *Mr. Hajji, the Movie Actor* (*Hajji Aqa, Aktor-e Sinema*, 1932), the first full-length feature film made by the Armenian-Russian-Iranian filmmaker Avanes Ohanian, inscribed at the level of theme and plot this social debate about cinema—constituting another form of exchange with the West. A technically sophisticated and delightful film, it dealt with the issue head on and in a humorous and self-reflexive manner.[5] In it, a traditional religious man (Hajji) is transformed from hating cinema to endorsing it as the most important means of educating Iranians. The conflict between religious traditionalism and Western modernity, which the film set up and resolved, would intensify in the Pahlavi period, both in society and on the screens.

Cinema also benefited from transnational interchanges between Iran and its more advanced neighboring countries. This occurred when sound entered the local cinema. The first Persian-language sound newsreel, shown in 1932, was apparently filmed by a Turkish photographer in Turkey and showed Iranian Prime Minister Mohammad Ali Foroughi conferring with the Turkish leader Kemal Ataturk and delivering a brief speech in Persian. The film apparently astonished audiences unaccustomed to hearing Persian spoken in the movies. The first Persian-language sound feature, *The Lor Girl* (*Dokhtar-e Lor*, 1933), was directed in India by Ardeshir Irani and written by the Iranian expatriate poet Abdol Hosain Sepenta, who also starred in it. The film, a melodramatic love story which also managed to extol Iranian nationalism and modernization under Reza Shah, was highly successful with Iranians, causing Sepenta to make for export a succession of talking pictures based on Persian folktales and epics.

The global ascendancy of the United States after World War II, which coincided with the rise of Iranian nationalism and the nationalization of the British-controlled oil industry under the popularly elected Prime Minister Mohammad Mosaddeq, had a profound impact on the institutionalization of the documentary cinema in Iran. As part of its program to win the hearts and minds of non-Communist nations, the United States Information Service (USIS's arm abroad) began in 1951 to show American-made newsreels and educational films to Iranians by means of its nationwide network of forty mobile film units. These films were dubbed into Persian, but soon a Syracuse University team of filmmakers and audiovisual specialists came to Iran, where it produced some twenty-two films on Iranian geography and on improving sanitation, nutrition, and agricultural methods. Perhaps "the first educational films to be made locally and tailored to Iranian needs," these films were distributed to schools by the mobile units, reaching a massive audience of some 350,000 people a month.[6]

More importantly, from 1951 until 1959, under the aegis of the Syracuse team and the Point IV Program, 402 issues of *Iran News* (*Akhbar-e Iran*) newsreel were made and shown in public cinemas. In addition, a large number of Iranians were trained in documentary film production, and up-to-date 35mm and 16mm production facilities, film processing plants, sound recording studios, and allied departments were set up at the Fine Arts Administration (FAA) in Tehran. With the help of newly trained locals, the American teams produced seventy-nine documentaries, which were screened in cinemas before feature films and were distributed to outlying areas by the mobile units. Finally, the American and Iranian collaboration led to the establishment of an "official" documentary style, which proved to be a very resilient model long after the demise of both USIS and FAA.[7]

In the 1960s–70s, the Pahlavi government's need for political control of the culture industry fit the interest of U.S. media companies in economic control of the world's markets. American companies began selling all kinds of products and services, from feature films to television programs, from TV receivers to TV studios, from communications expertise to personnel training. The impact on the nascent television industry was particularly strong. Although National Iranian Radio and Television (NIRT) became a vast institution, producing thousands of hours of sophisticated programming annually, 40 percent of its schedule in 1974 was taken up by Western imports, which were primarily American.[8] The Americans sold not only consumer products but also the consumer ideology.

The Outward Flow

The exchange relations, which had been limited to a generally one-way flow of Western ideas, people, and products into the Iranian cinema and media, changed in the early 1970s to the reverse flow, from Iran to the West. A principal impetus was the government's involvement in producing documentaries for foreign consumption and in supporting the New Wave film movement. Like the initial flow, the reverse flow was multifaceted and controversial. Seeking to improve its deteriorating political image abroad, the shah's government embarked on several coproduction projects with foreign companies to make films for foreign distribution, resulting in two prestigious multipart nonfiction projects. The eight-part series *Crossroads of Civilization* (1977) was coproduced by British journalist David Frost (Paradine Films) and the Iranian Ministry of Culture and Art. Its $2.5 million budget was underwritten by Bank Melli Iran; this did not count the money that the Iranian armed forces spent on equipment, manpower, material, and logistical services. Modeling itself on such acclaimed British television series as *Civilisation* and *Ascent of Man*, *Crossroads of Civilization* covered, in seven episodes, Iranian history from the early Medes to the present, using reenactments, paintings, photographs, interviews with experts, and fascinating historical film footage. The eighth program, a lengthy interview with Shah Mohammad Reza Pahlavi, was not released, apparently due to the brewing anti-shah social climate. The second project was a $250,000 contract between National Iranian Radio and Television and Michigan State University (MSU) for a number of films on Iranian history called *Ancient Iran* (1977). Produced by veteran USIS filmmaker and professor of film at MSU Mohammad Ali Issari, these films were designed for use in American high schools and colleges. The series caused controversy among the students and faculty of MSU because of its purported attempt to "legitimize the shah's regime," resulting in the cancellation of the contract after the completion of only three films.[9] While technically well made and historically valuable, these two series were compromised by their sponsorship by an increasingly discredited Iranian government.

On the fiction front, two films jolted the complacent local film industry, which had been producing generally low-quality, formulaic melodramas, comedies, and tough-guy action films—two films that set into motion new film genres and movements. If Masud Kimiai's *Qaisar* (1969) gave rise to a modernized tough-guy (*Jaheli* or *luti*) genre, Dariush Mehrjui's *The Cow* (*Gav*, 1970) led to what was later called the New Wave film movement. *The Cow* was about a farmer who, upon losing his cow, which is the sole source of his livelihood, begins to embody the animal in spirit and body. Its focus on villagers was regarded as a return to roots, echoing in a different genre the tough-guy films' return to the authentic bedrock of Iranian society and psychology. Its truthful portrayal of village life, using a sparse if somewhat primitive style, was regarded as a breath of fresh air, linking it to the Italian neorealist cinema. Finally, its adaptation of a story by a leading dissident writer, Gholamhosain Sa`edi, was a harbinger of a new alliance between educated filmmakers (Mehrjui had a B.A. in philosophy from UCLA) and oppositional contemporary writers.

Soon, powerful film production companies were set up with government aid, such as NIRT's Telfilm and the Film Industry Development Company of Iran, to invest in films directed by Iranians and to channel coproduction deals with international companies. Although coproduction arrangements consisted primarily of using Iranian petrodollar financing, and little use was made of local technical or on-camera talent, a certain amount of prestige and experience was gained from this arrangement.[10] These companies, along with an independent collective of dissident filmmakers called the Progressive Film-makers' Union (*Kanun-e Sinemagaran-e Pishro,* established in 1973), funded some of the best filmmakers of the 1970s. Many of them were foreign-trained and, like those in the Qajar period, had a significant collective impact on cinema (among them were Fereidun Rahnema, Farrokh Gaffary, Bahman Farmanara, Dariush Mehrjui, Kamran Shirdel, Parviz Kimiavi, Sohrab Shahid Saless, Khosrau Haritash, and Hajir Daryush). These, together with self-taught or locally trained directors, such as Bahram Baizai, Abbas Kiarostami, Masud Kimiai, Naser Taqvai, Parviz Sayyad, and Amir Naderi, formed a formidable, but all-male, cinematic force. The simultaneous emergence of a new generation of socially conscious leftist writers, such as Sa`edi, Sadeq Chubak, Hushang Golshiri, and Mahmud Daulatabadi, whose works these filmmakers adapted or with whom they collaborated on original screenplays, resulted in increasing realism and social criticism, deeper character psychology, and improved technical quality—hallmarks of the New Wave film movement.

Mehrjui's *The Cow* embodied the contradictions that were also the hallmark of this movement: its sponsorship by the state and its censorship and banning by the state. The film's release was withheld because the government feared that it might contradict "the official image of Iran as a modern nation of promise and plenty."[11] However, when the film was unofficially entered in the Venice International Film Festival in 1969 and garnered a top award, the ministry lifted the ban. From then on, international festivals became factors in the Iranian politics of cinema. Upon its release, the film was greeted with great critical and public enthusiasm, generating high box-office revenues.[12] The international and national success of *The Cow* opened the way for the government to support the New Wave, hoping to create a positive international profile at a time when it was under criticism by an increasingly vociferous population of Iranian students abroad (40,000 in the U.S. alone). However, the New Wave was essentially a "cinema of discontent," whose realistic and often critical assessment of contemporary social conditions, expressed

through allegory and symbolism, contradicted the aims of its sponsors, causing tensions in the relationship and censorship or confiscation of the works.
This, in turn, both compromised the films and heightened audience interest
in them, putting the filmmakers in a double bind. Their acclaim at international festivals raised the profile of filmmaking as an art, a form of intellectual labor, and a commercial enterprise. Foreign film festivals and filmgoers
became alternative audiences which these filmmakers began to address. This
bifurcated local and international audience proved to be a mixed blessing.
On the one hand, the New Wave filmmakers' success abroad generally guaranteed them more political or commercial freedom at home; on the other
hand, foreign audiences and their expectations impacted their works somewhat, earning them criticism at home on the ground of elitism and peddling
of Third World misery to outsiders. These were the sorts of criticism that
other successful Third World filmmakers were also receiving.

The New Wave filmmakers did not form a cohesive film movement, as they
were not driven by a monolithic ideology or by a programmatic project under-
girded by a singular financial infrastructure and film-industry practice. They
were a group of ambitious filmmakers with diverse class backgrounds and
ethnoreligious affiliations, and they maintained individualistic—sometimes
even antagonistic—tastes, aspirations, and styles. These factors along with
the divisive politics of the government and the commercial stranglehold of
major distributors discouraged these and other film industry members from
forming sustained independent organizations, such as professional unions
and pressure groups, through which they could represent themselves and exert
collective influence. Thus, the New Wave filmmakers remained largely atom-
ized and compromised at the same time that, like the great East European
directors of the same era, they bit the hand that fed them. Consequently, the
New Wave cinema was not so much a filmmaking movement as a filmmaking moment.

THE ISLAMIC REPUBLIC ERA

In this era, the exchange relations with the West by means of cinema became
even more complex and multifaceted than before. By 1978, the social turmoil
that would lead to a revolution was under way, a turmoil in which movie
houses were heavily implicated. Since cinema was condemned for what was
perceived to be its support of the shah's Westernization projects and the United
States' cultural hegemony, movie houses became a favorite target of revolutionary wrath. This was expressed most savagely in the August 1978 inferno
in Abadan's Rex Theater, apparently set by pro-revolution Islamist arsonists,

which killed nearly 400 spectators. After this event, burning or destroying cinemas became an integral part of the dismantling of the Pahlavi regime. By the time the Islamic government was installed less than a year later, 180 cinemas nationwide had been destroyed, leaving only 256 extant.[13] This created a shortage of exhibition sites from which the current cinema still suffers. However, unlike the Qajar-era clerical leaders, such as Shaikh Fazlollah Nuri, the clerical leaders of the 1979 revolution were not opposed to cinema per se. They were against what Ayatollah Ruhollah Khomeini called the "misuse" of cinema by the Pahlavi regime to morally corrupt and politically subjugate Iranians.[14] Consequently, instead of proscribing it, they advocated its adoption as an ideological apparatus to transform the Pahlavi culture into an Islamic culture.[15]

Many New Wave filmmakers stayed in Iran during the revolution and, after a period of forced hiatus, began to make films under the new regime; among them were Mehrjui, Kiarostami, Kimiai, Baizai, Kamran Shirdel, and Taqvai. They were instrumental in reviving the Iranian cinema and placing it on the map of world cinema. Others went into exile (some before the revolution), where they made films with mixed results; among these were Naderi, Shahid Saless, Sayyad, Manuchehr Tayyab, Reza Allamehzadeh, Mohammad Reza Aslani, and Marva Nabili. All of them, and many more newcomers who turned to filmmaking abroad, served to collectively create an Iranian exile and diaspora cinema—the most dramatic result of the cinematic exchange relations between Iran and the West.

Nearly twenty years after the fiery revolution, the Toronto International Film Festival and the New York Film Festival called the Iranian cinema of the 1990s one of the "preeminent" and "most exciting" national cinemas in the world, respectively.[16] This is a new, vital cinema with its own special industrial and financial structure and unique ideological, thematic, generic, and production values—and it is part of a more general transformation in the political culture of the country since the revolution. However, this is not an "Islamic" cinema that upholds the ruling ideology. Instead, at least three major types of cinemas evolved.

The first to emerge was the state-sponsored "Official Cinema" (my term), which explicitly supported the government's ideological projects and policies. The "Populist Cinema" is commercially supported; nonetheless, it affirms the postrevolutionary Islamic cultural values, not as manifestly as the Official Cinema, but embedded in the plot, theme, character, portrayal of women, and mise-en-scène.[17] The "Art Cinema," on the other hand, engages with those values and tends to critique, often implicitly, social conditions under the Islamic government. The Populist Cinema and the Art Cinema evolved almost simultaneously, gaining prominence as the Official Cinema waned. The struggle over the Art Cinema was intense as it once had been over the New Wave films. This is because Art Cinema filmmakers—at least in the first dozen years after the revolution—were, like their New Wave predecessors, largely dependent on state financing and support at the same time that they wished to remain ideologically and aesthetically independent, even critical, of their chief sponsor.

In terms of quantity, the Art Cinema is the smallest of the three forms, perhaps accounting for 10 to 15 percent of the national output, but in terms of quality, local and international prestige, and revenues, it is the most significant. Because of this disproportionate impact and the light that it sheds on the complexity of the exchange relations with the West, only the Art Cinema is dealt with here.

Many reasons account for the high quality of the Art Cinema films that have so impressed Western critics and audiences. Such reasons can be attributed to the peculiarity of the postrevolutionary political structure in Iran and the specificity of the emergent film culture and industry. Outstanding among them are government involvement in film financing, film production, and film censorship; government banning of foreign film imports; and the proactive and reactive actions of the filmmakers and moviegoers. The state's involvement in film financing, production, and censorship (features, also, of the Pahlavi-era cinema) intensified for a time after the revolution to the point of de facto takeover of all means of film production and distribution. However, after a period of uncertainty, excessive zeal, and draconian censorship, the government and the film industry gradually took some measures to rationalize the industry. In 1983, the Ministry of Culture and Islamic Guidance created the Farabi Cinema Foundation to centralize and control the import and export of films, raw stock, and film equipment and to encourage local productions, a task that it accomplished very successfully. The monopolization of many aspects of the industry meant that the government had to render some services in return, such as facilitating bank loans, streamlining cumbersome rules and regulations, and expediting the production and exhibition of films. By severely restricting foreign film imports, the government removed a key competitive obstacle to the rise of a viable local film industry. Because the industry was so weak, protectionism was at this point an enlightened and necessary policy. The result was that Iranian cinema found a captive audience, which gradually got to like what was made for it, and in turn influenced the filmmakers to make films to fulfill its desires. The doubling of the population since the revolution (to nearly 70 million) extended the industry's potential audience base, as did the increasing involvement of the private sector in filmmaking. Foreign films found their way in through pirated videos and satellite television channels that were widely, but clandestinely, available.

These and other, similar measures helped to protect the nascent film industry and to bolster both the quantity and the quality of the films—factors that facilitated the reverse flow of films from Iran to the West. According to Ataollah Mohajerani, Minister of Culture and Islamic Guidance, in 1998 Iranian cinema ranked tenth in the world in its output, surpassing Germany, Brazil, South Korea, Canada, and Australia and far exceeding the traditionally high-volume Middle Eastern film producers, Egypt and Turkey.[18] The output of the last five years ranged between forty-five and sixty feature films annually.

An important but controversial aspect of rationalization, with an impact on the quality of the films, was the institutionalization of a centralized censorship system which subjected all films to several stages of official review and approval, from the film's idea to the finished film. The imposition of strict rules of censorship, modesty, and gender segregation was highly stifling and led, among other things, to an unrealistic filmic representation of the private lives of Iranians and of male-female relations.[19] However, these rules, which were increasingly interpreted liberally, seem, ironically, to have also had a positive effect on the quality of the films. Like many authoritarian regimes, such as those of Communist Poland and Hungary and of Pahlavi-era Iran, the Islamist regime, by limiting the explicit expression of ideas through official censorship, forced Iranian filmmakers to develop creative and subversive alternatives for indirect expression, resulting in hermeneutically rich films and thus contributing to their auteurist style. Kiarostami has repeatedly pointed to this unexpectedly positive outcome of censorship without condoning it.[20] The tight grip of the censors also encouraged the filmmakers to develop alternative indigenous subjects, genres, narrative structures, and modes of storytelling.

One significant result was the emergence of a new wave of Art Cinema since the late 1980s which is characterized by a type of nontheistic humanism. Fatemeh Mo'tamed Aria, a prominent actress, described it as a "compassionate cinema," saying, "It is our plea for compassion that is capturing the world, not our advanced technique or our high technology. Our cinema is being presented to the world because of the kindness of a child towards his sister, or the compassion of a mother towards her child."[21] This concern for others is tied to a communitarian, optimistic, and spiritual worldview. Accordingly, in this cinema individual efforts for the collective good are rewarded, for people are not thought of as autonomous and self-centered individuals only, but also as interdependent beings whose well-being inextrica-

bly binds them to each other. Surprisingly for a theocratic state, the humanist cinema is generally less concerned with human beings' relations with a
religiously defined God than with their relations either with one another or
with an unidentifiable, universal, and transcendent force (Majid Majidi's *The
Color of Paradise* [*Rang-e Khoda*, 1999] is an example).

While the humanist Art Cinema films, such as those of Majidi, Makhmalbaf, Baizai, Panahi, Mehrjui, and Banie'temad, do not advocate the official
religious culture and ideology directly—and they often critique it—their
emphasis on humanism, optimism, ethics, and spirituality implicates them
to some extent in the dominant ideology, in so far as these values are similar to the so-called Islamic values which the regime has professed but rarely
practiced. As a result, the government has tolerated, even welcomed, whatever implicit or explicit criticism they offer, for they fundamentally oppose
neither the ruling doctrine nor the ruling power structure.

INTERNATIONAL MARKETING, DISTRIBUTION, EXHIBITION

Despite high inflation, the production cost of Iranian films is very low, hov-
ering between one hundred and two hundred thousand dollars. Such relatively low investments can be recovered and profits made, given the size and
captivity of the primary audience in Iran. But without foreign competition
at home and foreign exchange revenues from audiences abroad, the Iranian
film industry's capacity for sustained innovation and increased income is
rather limited. However desirable, the lifting of the import ban is likely to
cause a total reconfiguration of the film industry and an initial plunge in the
quality and quantity of locally produced films. With the formation of the
Farabi Cinema Foundation and the production of an increasing number of
quality films, the marketing of Iranian Art Cinema films abroad became a
serious and ultimately profitable business in which commercial and independent companies also increasingly participated. After the success and the
controversy surrounding a major festival of Iranian films at UCLA in 1990,
screening of Iranian films—individually or in touring film packages—by
nationwide art-house and commercial cinemas became a reality in the United
States (and in Europe). Some exiled opponents of the Islamist government,
particularly entertainers and filmmakers such as Parviz Sayyad, vehemently
objected to the UCLA and subsequent foreign film festivals, because, they
claimed, these events lent legitimacy to the government.[22] They called for the
boycott of Iranian film festivals abroad and campaigned against the films,
filmmakers, and festival organizers.[23] Despite their efforts, however, the
quality of the films was so high, they were so numerous, and audience response

was so enthusiastic that these specialized festivals grew in number and popularity, turning the Iranian Art Cinema into a transnational cinema.

The established international film festivals had a major hand in this process. In 1986, only two postrevolutionary films were shown in foreign festivals, while 230 films were screened in 1990 in some seventy-eight international festivals, winning eleven prizes.[24] According to press reports, which are not entirely reliable, by 1998 Iranian films had been shown on some five thousand screens abroad, winning nearly 330 international prizes.[25] A case in point is the history of Iranian cinema's presence at the Cannes International Film Festival, the most prestigious festival in the world. While Iranian films had been screened at Cannes starting in 1963 (with Ahmad Faruqi Qajar's *Dawn of the Capricorn* [*Tolu`-e Fajr*]), until 1992 the festival showed Iranian films only occasionally and only one or two at a time, and no film won a top award. This number increased exponentially, though, as thirteen films were shown at Cannes in 1992 alone.[26] Over the years, several Iranian films garnered the festival's top filmmaking awards,[27] with the year 2000, in which they won three major awards, being the most notable.[28]

No filmmaker has received more critical and popular acclaim in the West than Kiarostami, whose picture appeared on the cover of the July–August 1995 issue of the renowned periodical *Cahiers du Cinéma* (no. 493) above a caption which simply declared, "Kiarostami le magnifique." Inside, nearly fifty pages were devoted to discussing his work. In 1998, the French Ministry of Culture decorated Mohsen Makhmalbaf with the highly regarded title of "Officier de l'ordre des arts et des lettres." Other auteur filmmakers who received wide international recognition and honor were male directors Dariush Mehrjui, Bahram Baizai, Majid Majidi, Jafar Panahi, and Abolfazl Jalili, and female directors Tahmineh Milani, Rakhshan Banie`temad, and Samira Makhmalbaf.

These are auteur filmmakers because their vision and personality dominate the entire filmmaking process, from conception to completion, and because certain common thematic, narrative, and stylistic features recur in their films. In addition, many of them write their own screenplays (Kiarostami, Mehrjui, Baizai, Majidi, Banie`temad, Milani, and Mohsen Makhmalbaf) and several collaborate with others in their writing (Mehrjui, Banie`temad), thereby consolidating their authorship. A few directors edit their own films, further ensuring their control over their film's parentage.[29] A recent development is the collaboration of directors with their spouses or children on their films. For example, Mehrjui's wife supervises his film's production design and sets, Banie`temad's husband produces her films, and Samira Makhmalbaf's father Mohsen helped her with the screenplays and editing of her fea-

ture films *The Apple* (*Sib*, 1997) and *Blackboards* (*Takhteh Siyah*, 2000). A study
of the films' ending credits will reveal the important contribution of the web
of familial and familiar associations to authorship, in a film industry and in
a society that are fraught with uncertainty and anxiety.

The increasingly international outflow of Iranian films, which expanded
beyond Europe, North America, and Canada to encompass Latin American,
Far Eastern, and Central Asian countries, not only garnered prestige for the
filmmakers and the Iranian cinema, but also guaranteed a needed inflow of
cash. These revenues proved helpful in rescuing the Art Cinema filmmakers
from their dependence on state sponsorship (with its strings attached), on
commercial producers (with their preoccupation with the box office), and
on local audiences (with their fickle taste). This is a highly significant aspect
of the relations of exchange between the Iranian cinema and the West, for it
is reciprocal, dynamic, multifaceted, and financially significant. The many
awards that auteurist filmmakers have regularly garnered from international
film festivals opened not only these festivals as potential sources of audiences
for Iranian cinema, but also foreign television networks, art-house cinemas,
commercial theaters, mainstream video chain stores (such as Blockbuster),
and mail-order houses (such as Facets Multimedia).

For the first time, the income from these sources is significant enough to
change the hitherto dual basis of filmmaking in Iran (state and commercial
funding). This third source of financing (foreign currency earnings) is economically important for the film industry as a whole and for individual
filmmakers, who thereby gain a relative measure of independence—a new
phenomenon in Iranian cinema. The foreign earnings are not small, considering the relatively low production budgets of less than $200,000, and the
lopsided exchange rate, which in 1999 reached almost 10,000 Iranian rials to
one United States dollar. Considering these factors, some films did very well
in their commercial release abroad. For example, by the end of 1999,
Kiarostami's *Taste of Cherry* (distributed by Zeitgeist Films) had generated a
respectable $340,658 in its United States commercial distribution, playing in
147 art-house, university, and commercial cinemas across the country.[30] No
doubt this income far exceeded the film's production cost. Majid Majidi's
Oscar-nominated film *Children of Heaven* (*Bachehha-ye Aseman*, 1997, distributed in the U.S. by Miramax Films) did even better. It earned over one
million dollars in four months in ten Hong Kong cinemas alone, taking a position among the top ten box-office earners of the summer.[31] In the United
States, too, the film earned nearly one million dollars (exact figure: $933,933).
According to the Director of International Relations of the Farabi Cinema
Foundation, it became the top-grossing Iranian film of all time abroad.[32]

Majidi's next film, *The Color of Paradise* (*Rang-e Khoda,* 1999, distributed by Sony Classic Pictures), which received universally positive reviews in the West, became a veritable blockbuster for Iranian films. It grossed $130,000 in its first two weeks, far ahead of the $50,000 that Majidi's own widely touted *Children of Heaven* had earned in the same period.[33] According to Yahoo!'s "U.S. Top Box Office Actuals" (May 30, 2000), in its ninth week of exhibition in twenty-four theaters nationwide, *The Color of Paradise* had grossed $714,442.[34]

The capacity of Iranian filmmakers to generate box-office revenue abroad has led to a type of coproduction arrangement that is very different from those prevalent in the Pahlavi era. In the past, the Iranian government provided European and American directors with coproduction funds; the new arrangement, however, involves European and American film companies (such as MK2 Productions in France and Miramax Films in the U.S.) investing in the films of Iranian directors. The production financing and marketing muscle of these companies have been in part responsible for the globalization both of Iranian cinema and of certain directors, such as Mohsen Makhmalbaf, Kiarostami, and Majidi.

Multiple transnational audiences, new coproduction arrangements, and the financial independence of the Art Cinema directors have resulted in several curious situations. One is that independently produced Art Cinema films that are banned in Iran, such as Mohsen Makhmalbaf's *The Silence* (*Sokut,* 1998), made money abroad—money the director did not have to share with anyone, as he had financed the film himself. Another is the emergence of art-house films that have become box-office sensations both at home and abroad, such as Majidi's *The Color of Paradise,* which not only did well internationally but also drew more than 600,000 spectators in Iran, earning $166,394 in the Tehran theaters alone. It thus became the seventh-ranking film in Tehran in terms of its box-office earnings for 1999. Milani's *Two Women* (*Do zan,* 1999), which also had done well in the festival and commercial circuits in the U.S., became the second-ranking film in its earnings in Tehran, with $390,747.[35] Another is the unforeseen social consequences of such transnational exchanges. For example, Iranian president Mohammad Khatami was so moved by the story of the blind boy in *The Color of Paradise* that he gave the lead actor, Mohsen Ramazani, who is blind, a house in Tehran; an American charity, similarly affected, bought a minibus for the Shahid Mohebbi Institute for the Blind in the Aryashahr district of Tehran.[36] Finally, transnational traffic of the type described here helped the semi-independent filmmakers to come into their own, not only financially, but also stylistically.

However, not all the consequences are positive, as globalization has opened the Art Cinema directors to the charges of being elitist, unduly critical of Iranian social conditions, xenophilic, unpatriotic, and even un-Islamic. Some have argued that by their choice of films to show and award, foreign film festivals tend to distort indigenous cinema (as though an indigenous, "pure" cinema without exchange with the rest of the world were viable). For example, Iranian critics have argued that since political, pro–Islamic Republic films have little chance of entering the international film festivals, certain Art Cinema directors, such as Kiarostami, have become apolitical, tackling only safe topics in order to ensure the entry of their next film into the festival circuit.[37] Exiled filmmakers, on the other hand, have argued the opposite point: since political, anti–Islamic Republic films made in exile are unlikely to be accepted at the international festivals as Iranian entries, antigovernment filmmakers are deprived of this important venue for their films unless they are willing to represent their host country.[38] Once Art Cinema filmmakers are invited to attend, however, these festivals offer them fora in which they can state with relative impunity their opinions about Iranian society and cinema, publicly and candidly—opinions that are often critical of the Iranian government's policies regarding culture, cinema, and censorship. For example, Samira Makhmalbaf, upon winning the coveted Jury Prize at the 2000 Cannes International Film Festival for *Blackboards,* boldly stated, "This prize is to honor the heroic affairs of all the younger generation who are struggling for democracy and a better life in Iran."[39] Baizai, too, in his personal appearances at foreign film festivals, has been highly critical of the government's censorship policies. These festivals not only do not whitewash the intolerant politics, policies, and practices of the Islamist regime, they also provide venues in which these politics, policies, and practices can be discussed and criticized, even by nonpolitical, safe directors. No film at international festivals is divorced from the politics of home or host countries. Because of this, even festival films that on the surface may not appear to be political are often read politically by all sides, as was the case with Samira Makhmalbaf's *The Apple.* The film was highly praised in Europe and the West as a fresh and realistic look at her society by a precocious teenage woman. Its very success at commercial theaters and festival circuits abroad, however, made the film controversial at home. Some local critics ascribed the film's success in part to its criticism of Iranian society's failure to adequately take care of its citizens, particularly its women and children—a type of washing the national dirty laundry in public. Others credited the contributions of Samira's father Mohsen for its success.[40] The politicized reading of films at international festivals is part of the translational processes that typically occur in such venues, where a source film text is transformed into a new target text by new audiences and critics. This text then becomes a new source text, which is circulated back to the home country, causing its own politics of translation and interpretation.

A fascinating but under-studied aspect of the politics of crosscultural translation has to do with subtitling, titling, retitling, and rating of foreign films. The subtitling of Iranian films into Western languages, particularly English, has improved considerably, even though awkward phrasing and misspelling of words continue to surface from time to time. This is because most of the subtitling is carried out in Iran by persons whose first language is not English (this is true of the subtitling of other foreign films). Like subtitling, and sometimes dubbing, titling is usually done to increase the films' comprehensibility and marketability (although politics also play a part). The title of Majidi's film *Rang-e Khoda,* which translates as "the color of God" in English, was changed to *The Color of Paradise* for U.S. distribution. Likewise, the title of Kiarostami's *Zendegi va Digar Hich,* which translates as "life and nothing else," was changed to the more optimistic *And Life Goes On.* Mohsen Makhmalbaf's *Naser al-Din Shah, Aktor-e Sinema,* which translates as "Naser al-Din Shah, the movie actor," was changed to *Once Upon a Time Cinema* (1992), and his *Nun va Goldun,* which means "bread and vase," was retitled *A Moment of Innocence* (1996). Before major distributors picked up Iranian films for wide commercial distribution, the films were exhibited in the United States without rating. However, they are now being classified according to the Motion Picture Association of America's rating system. Curiously, Majidi's two popular films *Children of Heaven* (distributed by Miramax Films) and *Color of Paradise* (distributed by Sony Classic Pictures) are both rated PG (parental guidance required) instead of G (general admittance), even though both involve children and are bereft of violence, sex, and bad language. It is not known whether this classification has had a negative bearing on these films' box office, but given that film producers and directors usually fight tooth and nail to have their films classified G (or, at worst, PG), one can assume lower revenues as a result of the rating. The full explanation for these films' PG classification is also not known, although the reason for so classifying *Children of Heaven* was intriguingly listed as "mild profanity"![41]

The enhanced presence of Iranian films on art-house, university, and commercial theater screens and on television screens has led to an explosion in the West of publications about Iranian cinema, in both the mainstream and academic press. Several doctoral dissertations have been written or are in the process of being written, in Europe and North America, on this subject, and the annual Middle Eastern, Iranian, and film studies conferences regularly feature presentations by scholars on aspects of Iranian cinema. Likewise, several books in Italian, German, French, and English on the topic have been published or are in production. Finally, judging from the increasing number of inquiries that I have been receiving in recent years, Iranian cinema has become a subject for full film courses at several universities in Europe, North America, and Canada.

This surge of interest abroad has intensified efforts inside Iran to bolster the marketing of films to foreign film distributors and television channels. Two efforts are worth mentioning. One is the establishment in the early 1990s of *Film International* (edited by Mohammad Atebbai), a quarterly periodical edited in Iran in English (associated with the respected *Mahnameh-ye Sinema'i-ye Film*, edited by Houshang Golmakani) which contains news and information about the latest productions, biographies of directors and stars, film reviews, scholarly and critical essays, and information and statistics about all aspects of Iranian cinema. It provides distributors and broadcasters with necessary information on a regular basis and in a well-designed format. The other is the creation in 1988 of an annual "international film market" in Tehran to facilitate the exchange of information with foreign concerns and to market Iranian films more aggressively. Significantly, the market is designed to be all-inclusive, involving not only Iranian public-sector filmmakers but also the private-sector film companies. This is another way in which the exchange with the West is gradually changing the character of the local film industry, from one that was totally centralized and government financed and controlled to one that is moving towards a mixed economy and ideological pluralism.

ADAPTATION, COPYING, COPYRIGHTING

The globalized flow of Iranian films is forcing more urgently than ever a political decision at home. Iran has never been a signatory to the international copyright conventions. This stance was once perhaps justified, from an Iranian point of view, because Iran was not a producer of world-class knowledge, scientific or artistic, which needed protecting. As such, adaptation, translation, and outright copying of cinematic and other works, undertaken without permission from copyright holders, was an inexpensive, accepted, and even necessary strategy. It served to nourish the local economy and revitalize the culture and arts at affordable prices. The downside was that this situation favored a culture of translation over that of original creation. Now that Iranians have become producers of cinematic knowledge and their films have expanded beyond the confines of Western film festivals and art-house cinemas, the filmmakers can neither borrow film ideas with impunity from the outside world—as they did before—nor afford to disregard the damage that copyright violation of their own works abroad can cause them—without recourse, as long as Iran is not a signatory to the copyright conventions.

A case in point is Dariush Mehrjui's *Pari* (1995), whose screening at Lincoln Center in New York City—part of a major retrospective of his films—was cancelled in November 1998 after a protest by the writer J. D. Salinger. According to Salinger's representatives, in loosely adapting their client's work *Franny and Zooey* without permission, Mehrjui had breached international copyright laws.[42] Mehrjui is a gifted and savvy director who has managed a successful career under the autocratic regimes of both the shah and the Ayatollahs by employing literary adaptation to cope with a dearth of good ideas and good screenwriters in Iran. He has also worked with renowned and dissident local writers, such as Gholamhosain Sa`edi and Hushang Golshiri, to adapt their works for the screen. As a result, he is credited as either the writer or the cowriter of many of his films' screenplays. His literary adaptations brought him prestige, and his screenplay writing consolidated his position as an auteur filmmaker. Such adaptations and exchanges have served Mehrjui more than any other Iranian director, but if they are to continue to serve him and the Iranian cinema in general, the copyright issues must be solved at the national level.[43]

Today Iranians, both inside and outside Iran, are engaged in cultural productions of unprecedented quality and quantity (in literature, arts, music, and film). The free exchange of these ideas and products is hampered and the relevant industries are stymied not only by trade barriers and economic boycotts of the kind that the U.S. government has maintained against Iran, but also by the fear among Iranian authorities about the "cultural invasion" of the country by Western pop culture and their refusal to join the international copyright conventions.[44] It is time to seriously consider joining them. It appears that Iranian officials are taking note of the situation, as Ataollah Mohajerani, Minister of Culture and Islamic Guidance, recently advocated that Iran become a signatory to the copyright conventions to protect the rights of its artists at home and abroad.[45]

EXILIC AND DIASPORIC FILMMAKING AND EXCHANGE RELATIONS

Another novel dimension of the cinematic exchange between Iran and the West, which emerged only after the revolution, is the production and exhibition of films made by Iranians in their Western exile and diaspora. Immediately after their massive displacement in the late 1970s and early 1980s, Iranians began screening in rented commercial movie houses of Los Angeles (and a few other major American cities) over 130 fiction films made before the revolution. Most of them were B-grade movies, with comedies, melodramas, and tough-guy action genres predominant.[46] A few A-grade features and documentaries were also exhibited in universities and churches. A massive amount of television programs were also produced, chiefly in Los Angeles, and circulated or broadcast to the rest of the country and to Europe.[47]

Their film production effort took some time to take shape, but once it started it became a significant force, topping that of all other Middle Eastern filmmakers in exile. According to a study which I conducted in the late 1990s, Middle Eastern and North African filmmakers in Europe and North America form a surprisingly large and diverse group, numbering 321 filmmakers from sixteen sending countries who have made at least 920 films in twenty-seven receiving countries, mostly in Europe and North America. In terms of output, Iranian filmmakers topped the list with nearly a third of the 920 documentary, short subject, animated, and feature films tabulated. Although Iranian exile filmmakers are diverse politically and religiously, a majority of them are united in their opposition to the Islamist regime. While they work in different countries, making films in various languages, their films share certain features that mark them in specific ways. Theirs is part of an emerging global "accented cinema" that is centrally concerned with expressing the pains and pleasures of displacement and the problematic of multiple locations and identities.[48]

As expected, this accented cinema of displacement has evolved in several phases, in tandem with the evolution of Iranians' identity abroad—from total preoccupation with the homeland and its politics to concern with the problems of living here and now in exile. The older, highly politicized exiles, such as Sayyad and Allamehzadeh, are preoccupied with Iranian politics, and their works are made in the traditional feature and documentary forms. A new crop of male and female directors, such as Caveh Zahedi, Ramin Serry, Shirin Etessam, Shirin Bazleh, Shirin Neshat, Mehrnaz Saeed Vafa, and Mitra Tabrizian, are in dialogue with the host society and with the fact of displacement, and they experiment with narrative forms and filming style. Much of the exile output is small-scale, low-velocity, and amateurish, limited to ethnic or micro-audiences. However, the works of avant-garde filmmakers such as Neshat, Zahedi, and Tabrizian are well made and powerful, and enjoy the wider attention of the European and American art world and critical establishment. Other veteran filmmakers such as Amir Naderi, Sohrab Shahid Saless, Marva Nabili, and Rafigh Pooya, with varying degrees of success, have made more ambitious feature films that transcended the strict binary focus on Iranian and exilic issues. Together, all these films are contributing to a borderless Iranian national cinema, to the national cinemas of the countries in which the filmmakers reside, and to the emerging global cinema of diaspora and exile that is accented by our era's profound sense of displacement, fragmentation, and globalization.

The exchange relations between Iran and the West have become even more complicated thanks to two recent developments. One involves Iranian filmmakers locating part or all of their films abroad, such as Ebrahim Hatamikia's *From Karkheh to Rhine* (*Az Karkheh ta Rhine*, 1992), which was set partly in Germany; Davud Mirbaqeri's *The Snowman* (*Adam Barfi*, 1996) and Mohsen Makhmalbaf's *A Time to Love* (*Naubat-e Asheqi*, 1991), both of which were set entirely in Turkey; Makhmalbaf's *The Silence*, filmed in Tajikistan; and Puran Derakhshandeh's *Love Without Borders* (*Eshq Bedun-e Marz*, 1999), which is set in the United States. The reasons for relocating their stories abroad are many: among them, escaping Iranian moral and political censorship; the desire for fresh sites, sights, and insight; and the wish to expand their audience base to neighboring countries and beyond. Several of these films, such as *The Snowman* and *Love Without Borders*, proved to be very popular with audiences in Iran, earning very high box-office records.

The other significant development is the interaction of exile filmmakers with the Iranian cinema at home. With the passage of time and political change both at home and abroad, the early, antagonistic response of politicized exiles underwent a gradual, but major, shift. This has involved the return of several generations of filmmakers trained abroad to make films at home. Some New Wave filmmakers, such as Bahman Farmanara and Parviz Kimiavi— who each left Islamic Iran to work abroad for a number of years, the former in Canada and the U.S., the latter in France—returned to the Islamic Republic in the 1990s. Upon their return, however, they encountered difficulties, and it often took them several years to make their first post-return films. Kimiavi's *Iran is My Home* (*Iran Sara-ye Man Ast*, 1998) and Farmanara's *Smell of Camphor, Fragrance of Jasmine* (*Bu-ye Kafur, Atr-e Yas*, 1999) are Art Cinema films that proved to be very powerful and highly controversial (the first has yet to be released in Iran, while the second won the top directing award at the 2000 Fajr International Film Festival). A second generation of younger filmmakers, such as Masud Jafari Jozani, Shahram Assadi, Gholamreza Azadi, and Faryal Behzad, returned early in the postrevolutionary era to make films that also fall within the Art Cinema category. Now, a third generation of Iranians born or raised in Europe and the U.S. is returning to make documentary and feature films in Iran, including Rafi Pitz, Mahmud Behraznia, Babak Payami, Ramin Bahrami, Maryam Shahriar, Perzheng Vaziri, and Mohammad Akhaviani. The impact of these filmmakers is growing, as indicated by the 2000 Fajr festival roster, which for the first time included films from three such returnees. Some critics cynically ascribed the return of these filmmakers to economic reasons (it is cheaper to make films in Iran) or to political expediency (international film festivals are looking for films from Iran for their programming, and making films in Iran is the best way to get into these festivals).[49] These factors may be at work, but the impact of the reform movement in Iran (headed by Khatami) and the possible rapprochement between Western powers and Iran, particularly between the United States and Iran, are also important factors, as are the deeply personal reasons that must have motivated each filmmaker.

Not surprisingly, many of the third-generation exile films involve stories of return: return home, return to the past, or return to childhood. It is as though, to see Iran, it is necessary to view it retrospectively and nostalgically. Such a conceptualization of home is driven partly by the distance—real and metaphorical—from which these filmmakers view Iran. It is also motivated in part by their hybridized personal and national identity and by their liminal position within Iranian society and the culture industry, which sometimes encourage firmer attachment to roots, to atavistic times, and to authenticating experiences. It may also be driven by this new generation's indirect and imaginative contact with home, which is mediated by family memories, displacement, and the manner in which the postrevolutionary Art Cinema films have imagined and represented Iran (some of the third-generation filmmakers' first experience of Iran has been through these films).

CONCLUSION

The cinematic exchange relations between Iran and the West, which began a century ago on a limited scale, have undergone a gradual but steadily widening metamorphosis. Most recently, they have taken the form of multifaceted exchanges between Iranian cinema and foreign audiences, and between Iranian émigré and returnee filmmakers and Iranian cinema and society, which emphasizes a new fact about cinema in general and about Iranian cinema in particular: their globalization. With the Internet now becoming a growing venue for film distribution, and with recent legislation in Iran freeing the private consumption of all kinds of videotapes (including pornographic ones) and music (including Western pop music) and Internet access at home, Iranian films can become even more global without having to enter international film festivals, and Iranian audiences can become more cosmopolitan without having to leave their homes. Certain types of small-scale, marginal, or political films, made in Iran or by Iranian exiles, which could hitherto find no suitable screening place either in their home countries or in the international festivals, can now acquire worldwide exposure by being cybercast.

In a fragmented world, a series of borderless cinemas are emerging, of which the Iranian cinema—consisting of films made both inside and outside the country—is but one. By the same token, the definition of what is Iranian is now less dependent on residence within the territory called Iran; this is because acts of imagination and mediation—as constituted by cinema viewing and filmmaking—are also constitutive of national identity. It is also because national identity itself is similarly subjected to exchange relations with others.

NOTES

1. Hamid Naficy, *Iran Media Index* (Westport, CT: Greenwood Press, 1984), xii–xxi; and Hamid Naficy, "Mediating the Other: American Pop Culture Representation of Postrevolutionary Iran," in *The U.S. Media and the Middle East: Image and Perception,* ed. Yahya R. Kamalipour (Westport, CT: Greenwood Press, 1995), 73–90.

2. Hamid Naficy, "Self-Othering: A Postcolonial Discourse on Cinematic First Contact," in *The Pre-Occupation of Post-Colonial Studies,* ed. Fawzia Afzal-Khan and Kalpana Seshadri-Crooks (Durham: Duke University Press, 2000) 292–310.

3. Mozaffar al-Din Shah Qajar, *Safarnameh-ye mobarakeh-ye Mozaffar al-Din Shah beh farang,* transcribed by Mirza Mehdi Khan Kashani, 2nd ed. (Tehran: Ketab-e foruzan, 1361/1982), 160; and Jamal Omid, *Paydayesh va bahrehbardari, Tarikh-e sinema-ye Iran* (Tehran: Radyab, 1363/1984), 1:42.

4. Farrokh Gaffary, "Cinema i: History of Cinema in Persia," in *Encyclopaedia Iranica* (Costa Mesa, CA: Mazda, 1991), 5:567–72; and Farrokh Gaffary, *Le cinéma en Iran* (Tehran: Le Conseil de la Culture et des Arts, Centre d'étude et de la coordination culturelle, November 1973).

5. This film inspired Mohsen Makhmalbaf's *Once Upon a Time Cinema* (*Naser al-Din Shah, Aktor-e Sinema,* 1992).

6. Mohammad Ali Issari, *Cinema in Iran, 1900–1979* (Metuchen, NJ: Scarecrow, 1989), 172–73.

7. Hamid Naficy, "Cinema in Persia iii. Documentary Films," in *Encyclopaedia Iranica* (Costa Mesa, CA: Mazda, 1992), 5:579–85.

8. Hamid Naficy, "Cinema as a Political Instrument," in *Modern Iran: The Dialectics of Continuity and Change,* ed. Nikki Keddie and Michael Bonine (New York: State University of New York Press, 1981), 358.

9. Naficy, *Iran Media Index,* 4.

10. Among the feature films that were completed under this coproduction arrangement were Orson Welles's *F for Fake* (1976), Patrice Chereau's *La Chair de L'Orchidée* (1976), Junya Sato's *Gogol 13* (1976), Valerio Zurlini's *The Desert of Tartars* (1977), and Leslie Matinson's *Missile X* (1978).

11. "Persian Filmmakers Map Expansion into International Market; Eye Coproductions," *Variety,* 12 Nov. 1969; np.

12. For an extensive collection of reviews of Mehrjui's films and interviews with him, see Naser Zera'ati, ed., *Majmu'eh-ye maqalat dar mo'arefi va naqd-e asar-e Daryush Mehrju'i* (Tehran: Entesharat-e nahid, 1375/1996).

13. Hamid Naficy, "Islamizing Film Culture in Iran," in *Iran: Political Culture in the Islamic Republic,* ed. Samih K. Farsoun and Mehrdad Mashayekhi (London: Routledge, 1992), 183.

14. Naficy, "Islamizing Film Culture," 181.

15. Interestingly, this shift in the clerical leaders' opinion about cinema was presciently predicted by Ohanian in his film *Mr. Hajji, the Movie Actor,* in which the Hajji character changes from disliking cinema to embracing it for educational purposes.

16. *Toronto International Festival of Festivals Catalog* (4 Sept. 1992), 8. Judith Miller, "Movies of Iran Struggle for Acceptance," *The New York Times,* 19 July 1992; H9, H14.

17. The major concepts frequently promoted by Iranian authorities when speaking of "Islamic culture" can be classified under the following categories: nativism (return to traditional values and mores), populism (justice, defense of the disinherited [*mostaz`afin*]); monotheism (*tauhid*); anti-idolatry (anti-*taghut*); theocracy (*velayat-e faqih,* rule of the supreme jurisprudent); moralism and puritanism (*Amr-e beh ma`ruf va nahi az monkar*); self-sacrifice, martyrdom, and revolutionary patience; political and economic independence (*esteqlal*); and combating arrogant world imperialism (*estekbar-e jahani,* code words for the United States). The last two concepts were condensed in the oft-repeated slogan "neither East nor West." When Mohammad Khatami was elected President in 1997, new values were added: civil society, pluralism, tolerance of opposing views, and rule of law. These concepts were overdetermined in Iranian cinema, but they found their most natural expression in the Official Cinema films, particularly in those that dealt with the eight-year war with Iraq (1980–1988).

18. "Iran dahomin keshvar-e donya," *Mahnameh-ye Sinema'i-ye Film* 239 (Shahrivar 1378/Aug. 1999): 38.

19. For an analysis of censorship rules in cinema, see Naficy, "Islamizing Film Culture"; for the evolution of rules governing gender segregation, veiling, and ways of looking in cinema, see Hamid Naficy, "Veiled Voice and Vision in Iranian Cinema: The Evolution of Rakhshan Banietemad's Films," *Social Research* 67 (2000): 559–76.

20. Including in Jamsheed Akrami's feature-length documentary, *Friendly Persuasion: Iranian Cinema After the Revolution* (1999).

21. Quoted in "Jashn-e sinema avay-e mehrabani-ye mast . . . ," *Hamshahri* [internet version of Tehran's Persian-language daily] (September 15, 1999) [http://www.neda.net/hamshahri/780624/adabh.htm].

22. Parviz Sayyad, *Rah-e doshvar-e sinema-ye dar tab`id* (Los Angeles: Parsian, 1996).

23. Hamid Naficy, *An Accented Cinema: Exilic and Diasporic Filmmaking* (Princeton: Princeton University Press, 2001); and Hamid Naficy, *The Making of Exile Cultures: Iranian Television in Los Angeles* (Minneapolis: University of Minnesota Press, 1993).

24. Jalal Khosraushahi, ed., *Baztab-e sinema-ye novin-e Iran dar jahan* (Tehran: Entesharat-e ghazal, 1370/1991), 28–31.

25. "5000 Hozur va 330 Jayezeh-ye bainolmelali," *Mahnameh-ye Sinema'i-ye Film* 229 (Dai 1377/Dec. 1998): 11.

26. "Dar kuchehha-ye Kan," *Mahnameh-ye Sinema'i-ye Film* 92 (Tir 1376/June 1997): 84.

27. At different Cannes festivals, Kiarostami won the Rossellini Award for *And*

Life Goes on (Zendegi va Digar Hich, 1992) and the Golden Palm award for *Taste of Cherry (Ta`m-e Gilas,* 1997), and Jafar Panahi won the Best Film Award and the International Film Critics Award for *White Balloon (Badkonak-e Sepid,* 1995).

28. In the 2000 Cannes festival, Samira Makhmalbaf's *Blackboards (Takhteh Siyah)* shared the Jury Prize with *Songs from the Second Floor* by the Swedish director Roy Andersson, while the Golden Camera award for a first film was shared by Iranian filmmakers Hasan Yektapanah for *Jom`eh* and Bahman Ghobadi for *The Time for Drunken Horses (Zamani bara-ye asbha-ye mast).* Both directors had been Abbas Kiarostami's assistants on his previous films. *The Time for Drunken Horses* also won the International Film Critics Award at Cannes.

29. For example, Kiarostami edited *Where Is the Friend's House? (Khaneh-ye Dust Kojast?* 1986); Mohsen Makhmalbaf, *The Marriage of the Blessed (Arusi-ye Khuban,* 1988); and Baizai, *Maybe Some Other Time (Shayad Vaqti Digar,* 1988).

30. Based on the data that Zeitgeist Films provided the author.

31. *"Bachehha-ye Aseman yek* million dollar *forukht," Iran Daily,* 13 Sept. 1999, carried by *The Iranian* Web magazine: http://www.iranian.com/News/1999/September/hk.html. How much of these foreign earnings are channeled to the directors depends on individual contractual arrangements.

32. Mohammad Atebbai, "Bazaryabi-ye filmha-ye irani besyar movaffaq budeh ast," *Mahnameh-ye Sinema'i-ye Film* 230 (Dai 1377/Jan. 1999): 26.

33. Sina Alinejad, "Majidi Scores Double: At Movie Box Office with U.S. Reviewers," *Iran Times,* 28 April 2000, 2.

34. http://movies.yahoo.com/boxoffice/rank.html.

35. Mohsen Beigagha, "Economic Review of Iranian Cinema in Boom Year 1999," *Film International* 28 (Spring 2000): 15.

36. Alinejad, "Majidi Scores Double," 2, and Jonathan Curiel, "Iranian Director Majidi Finds His 'Paradise' Tale of Blind Boy a Huge Hit in Tehran," *San Francisco Chronicle* (4 April 2000); website: http://www.sfgate.com/cgi-bin/article.cg?file=/chronicle/archive/2000/04/DD88385.DTL.

37. Azadeh Farahmand, "Digesting the 'Cherry': Kiarostami in a Long Shot," paper presented at the annual Society for Cinema Studies conference, West Palm Beach, Florida, 15–18 April 1999, 5.

38. See Sayyad, *Rahha-ye doshvar-e sinema dar tab`id;* Reza Allamehzadeh, *Az dur bar atash: sokhani bar sinema va sansur* (Ontario, Canada: Afra Publishing, 1995); and Reza Allamehzadeh, *Sarab-e sinema-ye eslami-ye Iran* (Utrecht, Holland: Nashr-e navid/Take 7, 1991).

39. Todd McCarthy, "Cannes Taps 'Dancer,'" *Variety* (22 May 2000): 1, 45.

40. Ahmad Talebinezhad, "Hezar charkh-e sib," *Mahnameh-ye Sinema'i-ye Film* 229 (Dai 1377/Dec. 1998): 11–12.

41. During the film's screening, I could not identify any profanity in it.

42. Jesse McKinley, "Iranian Film Is Canceled after Protest by Salinger," *New York Times,* 21 Nov. 1998, A15, A22.

43. Mehrjui told the *New York Times* that, before making the film, he had written to Salinger to obtain permission to loosely adapt his work, but since he did not hear from the writer, "I just continued and made it" (McKinley, "Iranian Film Is Cancelled," A22).

44. In the mid-1990s, Islamist hard-liners began an extensive campaign against

what they claimed was an organized, multifaceted "cultural invasion" of the country by "Western imperialism," a campaign that led to the removal of many leading "liberal" figures, including the then Minister of Culture, Mohammad Khatami. This debate resurfaced again under a different guise during the presidency of Khatami, leading in 2000 to the closing of some eighteen "reformist" newspapers and the jailing of many editors.

45. "Behtar ast beh qanun-e jahani-ye kopirait beh paivandim," *Mahnameh-ye Sinema'i-ye Film* 259 (Farvardin 1379/March 2000): 25.

46. Hamid Naficy, "Popular Culture of Iranian Exiles in Los Angeles," in *Irangeles: Iranians in Los Angeles,* ed. Ron Kelley and Jonathan Friedlander (Berkeley: University of California Press, 1993), 325–64.

47. For a full list of these films, see ibid., 231–32.

48. Naficy, *The Making of Exile Cultures.*

49. Naficy, *An Accented Cinema.*

50. "Nasl-e avval, nasl-e chaharom . . . Iran bara-ye hameh-ye Iranian," *Mahnameh-ye Sinema'i-ye Film* 250 (Farvardin 1379/March 2000): 49.

Part IV

Political-Cultural Relations
with the Muslim World

12 / The Failed Pan-Islamic Program of the Islamic Republic: Views of the Liberal Reformers of the Religious "Semi-Opposition"

WILFRIED BUCHTA

Since its creation in 1979, the Islamic Republic of Iran has pursued an official policy aimed at bridging the gap between Shi`ism and Sunnism. To date, this ecumenical policy has been rather unsuccessful. This article examines the reasons for the failure of Iran's pan-Islamic efforts. Focusing on Iran's internal conditions, it discusses the difficulty of removing anti-Sunni elements from Iranian Shi`i dogma and popular belief, and points to a closed epistemology and an exclusionary historiography as major obstacles to a rapprochement between the two main branches of Islam. It also presents criticisms directed at the halfhearted and misguided nature of Iran's pan-Islamic project by several of Iran's leading intellectuals and religious scholars, among them Abdol Karim Soroush.

The Conference of the Organization of Islamic Countries (OIC), held in Tehran on December 8–10, 1997, was a total success for the host country: it earned the Islamic Republic de facto reinstatement as an official member of this organization of fifty-four Islamic countries.[1] This was a first concrete step toward overcoming the mistrust that Iran's Arab neighbors had harbored against the Islamic Republic since 1979 because of the perceived threat of its revolutionary ideology. A dramatic manifestation of this change of heart was the sensational participation of Saudi Crown Prince Abd Allah. Iran and Saudi Arabia had been bitter ideological and political enemies since 1979, and Ayatollah Khomeini had repeatedly labeled the Saudi regime the citadel of "American Islam." The old enmity seemed forgotten when the Iranian triumvirate of Supreme Leader Ali Khamenei, President Mohammad Khatami, and Deputy Head of the Council of Experts Ali Akbar Hashemi Rafsanjani put on a rare show of unity in preparing a warm welcome for Abdullah. This symbolized Iran's intent to pursue a policy of détente, guided by motives of national interest and pragmatism, and to give realpolitik priority over revolutionary ideology in order to turn Iran into the leading Gulf power. The first step toward a thaw in relations with Saudi Arabia, which had severed ties with Iran for four years after the bloody Hajj incident of 1987, had been taken in the early 1990s by President Rafsanjani (in office 1989–97). Yet real dynamism in the détente process awaited the accession to power of President Khatami in 1997. Khatami's call for internal democratic reform and his challenge to the West to engage in a "dialogue of civilizations" laid the groundwork for confidence building among Arabs concerning the seriousness of Tehran's intentions.[2] What, then, had become of the pan-Islamic project that had so emphatically informed Iran's foreign policy toward the Arab world from 1979 until the early 1990s?

The present essay, divided into two parts, seeks to answer that question. The first part provides an outline of the basic tools, content, and idiom of Iran's pan-Islamic policy and offers a brief overview of the most important domestic obstacles blocking the realization of this project. The second part outlines the criticisms leveled against this policy by some leading liberal dissidents from the religious "semi-opposition" within Iran. Among those, Abdol Karim Soroush is currently the most important and influential thinker, and he therefore receives the most attention.

The word "semi-opposition" requires some clarification. Following Hooshang Ahmadi, I see this as a series of individuals, groups, and intellectual currents critical of the current regime and operating in the gray area between the regime and civil society.[3] These individuals and groups criticize the regime using religious arguments and aim at a nonviolent transformation of the system within the parameters of the constitution. The leaders of this "semi-opposition" are mostly religious intellectuals and Shi`i clerics. Their strong involvement in the opposition to the shah inside and outside of Iran enabled them to attain high positions in the new state at the onset of the revolution, but later on their "liberal" tendencies pushed them to the margins of the system. They share a rejection of armed resistance to the regime, and it is precisely this position of nonviolence that has made them seem harmless to the majority of the ruling elite and has secured their lives. Some factions within the regime nonetheless spare no effort to minimize the effectiveness of these groups by restricting their access to the public via the media and public appearances.[4]

IRAN'S PAN-ISLAMIC PROJECT

The Islamic Republic of Iran (IRI) has been propagating Islamic unity and a rapprochement between Sunnism and Shi`ism ever since its creation in

1979.[5] In the next two years the regime took a series of measures designed to give credibility to its desire for an improvement of relations between the two Islamic branches, both inside and outside of Iran. These include:

1. A ban, proclaimed in 1979, on the official cursing of the first three caliphs that had been in place since the Safavids.[6]
2. A similar ban, issued in the same year, on the publication of those canonical Shi`i writings that include such vilification, most notably the sections on the hadith of the Imam in the *Bihar al-anwar* of the Safavid religious scholar Baqer Majlesi.
3. The issuance of a fatwa by Khomeini in October of 1979, allowing Iranian pilgrims to pray behind a Sunni imam in Mecca and Medina.[7]
4. The introduction of the Hafteh-ye vahdat (week of unity) in 1982, following a statement by Ayatollah Hosain Ali Montazeri.[8] On the occasion of the Birthday of the Prophet, the Iranian government organizes a yearly conference around the theme of Islamic unity (*vahdat-e eslami*), with Sunni and Shi`i participants from Iran and abroad.

Islamic unity is propagated in many ways, including in official speeches and publications that are directed abroad, as well as by official propaganda outlets such as the Sazman-e tablighat-e eslami (Organization of Islamic Propaganda). Two types of argument are advanced to buttress the need for Islamic unity.

1. All Muslims face the same enemy, that is, the militarily, economically, and culturally expansive West, which threatens the political independence and cultural and religious identity of the Islamic world.
2. All Muslims share a host of basic religious convictions, such as the belief in one God, one Prophet, the Day of Judgment, the Quran, and daily prayer. To concentrate on these basic elements of unity and brotherhood is to help overcome nonessential differences between Muslims.[9]

Conflict between Muslims, this reasoning holds, comes mostly because of foreign conspiracies and intervention by outside enemies or their agents.[10] The fundamental religious and political controversy between Sunna and Shi`a concerning the concepts of *imama* (imamate) and *khilafa* (caliphate) remains rather mute in this argument. This also holds for all derivative points of theological or dogmatic controversy, especially those involving *fiqh* (jurisprudence) and *usul al-fiqh* (principles of jurisprudence). Examples are the questions of whether *ijma`* (consensus) is obligatory or must be rejected, of *mut`a* (temporary marriage), and of *taqiya* (dissimulation), and the issue of whether the sayings (hadith) of the Imams rank on the same level as those of the Prophet.[11]

This propaganda only hints at a vague form of unity and points in its general direction, but says nothing about either its form or its content. Nor has it thus far had any discernible effect on the majority of Muslims within or outside of Iran.[12] External factors such as the antagonism between the IRI and countries like Iraq, Egypt, and Saudi Arabia, pushed to nationalist and religious extremes by the Iran-Iraq war of 1980–88, contributed to the failure of an envisioned political unity, but that discussion would require another article.

What characterized the pan-Islamic project launched by Tehran until 1990 was above all its lack of connection to the Islamic ecumenical movement that came out of Cairo in the 1940s to 1960s, the so-called Dar al-taqrib. The publishing enterprise of that name, founded in 1947 by the Shi`i cleric Mohammad Taqi Qommi, enjoyed the support of those among the Sunni establishment at al-Azhar who favored ecumenical relations with Shi`ism. In the 1950s, the Nasser regime was among those who supported the endeavor. The movement's greatest success was the fatwa issued in 1959 by the rector of al-Azhar, Mahmud Shaltut, which granted Shi`ism equal status with Sunnism as a fifth school.[13]

Beginning in 1960, the Dar al-taqrib movement felt the effects of the political rivalry between the Arab socialist Nasser regime and the pro-Western Pahlavi monarchy. This led to a disruption of the ecumenical dialogue between the Azhar scholars and their Shi`i counterparts in Iraq and Iran.[14] In the 1970s, the activities of the *Dar al-taqrib* movement in Cairo fizzled. In 1990, Iran's supreme leader Khamenei tried to revive the *taqrib* movement, this time under Iranian leadership. In the same year he founded an organization named Majma` al-taqrib bain al-madhahib al-islamiya. With this organization, financially supported by the supreme leader's office, Tehran mostly seems to pursue political objectives, though it projects an outward concern with a rapprochement between Sunna and Shi`a on issues of jurisprudence. Yet so far no breakthrough has been achieved in the uneasy relations between the two.[15]

Despite the success of the Islamic Revolution in Iran, several obstacles from the onset stood in the way of a realization of Islamic unity as propagated by Khamenei. One crucial one, and a source of the ambivalence and inconsistency Iran exhibits toward unity, is the cultural and religious imprint Shi`i history has left on Iran. Iran's national culture and history have been profoundly marked by the Shi`i Safavids who, following their conquest of the country in 1501, proclaimed Shi`ism its official religion and forced the population to profess it. Ever since, Shi`ism has been the national religion of Iran, the only Shi`i state in the world.[16] The Islamic Republic has not altered Iran's emphatic Shi`i identity, expressed in the proclamation of Twelver Shi`ism as the religion of the state and its president in the new constitution (article 12). This incorporation elicited much harsh criticism and bitter enmity, even among those in the Arab world who initially were favorably inclined toward the Islamic Republic. Thus, the Jordanian *Hizb al-tahrir* chided Khomeini in late 1979 for declaring Twelver Shi`ism the state religion, calling it an error of nationalism and unacceptable, since it endangered the unity of the *umma*.[17] Eight years later, the theoretician of the Syrian Muslim Brothers, Sayyid Hawwa, bitter and disillusioned, distanced himself from the IRI under Khomeini that he had initially endorsed.[18] At the height of the Iran-Iraq War, impressed by Baghdad's propaganda, Hawwa portrayed Shi`ism as an erroneous creed hostile to Arabs, and accused Khomeini of seeking control over an Islamic world remade in the image of Shi`ism.[19]

Another stumbling block for the government's pan-Islamism is the decentralized structure of Iran's higher clergy. This structure makes it impossible to make the ideas and beliefs of Islamic unity acceptable to all clerics, especially since many among the orthodox traditionalists still harbor a strong aversion to Sunni Islam. Underlying this problem is the hidden ethos of Shi`ism. This ethos is inspired by what Hamid Enayat calls "historical Shi`ism," a creed characterized by a complex system of historically grown collective views. Such views in part reflect religious dogmas, in part arise from individual interpretations and a clerical consensus that has grown over time but does not necessarily count among the principles and sources of the faith.[20] Many elements of this "historical Shi`ism" manifest themselves in popular and quasi-sacred practices and institutions that have become part and parcel of both popular beliefs and the theological convictions of the ulama. These include a distinctive *shahada* during the call to prayer, the cursing (*sabb wa la`n*) of the companions of the Prophet, and various forms of self-castigation during the *Ashura* passion plays of Moharram. The high-ranking ulama lead the masses of simple believers in religious and social questions, but are also dependent on them, as the power and influence of each *alim* depends on the number of believers who recognize and emulate him and pay him a tax known as the fifth (*khoms*).

From 1979 to 1981, many liberal and "leftist" individuals and groups left the leadership of the IRI. Examples are Mehdi Bazargan, Ebrahim Yazdi, Sadeq Qotbzadeh, and Abol Hasan Bani Sadr. Their positions quickly fell to a series of orthodox-traditionalist ulama. Many of these ulama, who initially had reservations about the Revolution and the doctrine of *velayat-e faqih,* later on moved into the top echelons of state and government, tempted by power. The participation of these traditionalists, who enjoy a considerable power base among the populace, strengthened the newly acceded radical wing of the Shi`i clergy around Ayatollah Khomeini. This group worked to absorb and control militant, revolutionary forces, to build a stable government, and to create the necessary basis for order and security, especially the security of ownership; in short, to consolidate and routinize the Revolution.[21] Given the opaque power structure of the IRI, we can only speculate about the influence on state and society of those orthodox clerics who oppose the idea of Islamic unity. There can be no doubt, however, that they have slowed down the realization of the officially sanctioned pan-Islamic project.[22]

Proponents of Islamic unity are to be found in the ranks of the liberals among the religious "semi-opposition." Below, the critical perspectives of four prominent Iranian reformers, Hojjatoleslam Yusefi Ashkevari, Hojjatoleslam Ne`matollah Salehi Najafabadi, the politician Ebrahim Yazdi, and the thinker Abdolkarim Soroush, will be discussed. All maintain a position of critical distance vis-à-vis the current regime and its entourage. They engage with the arguments of the opponents of unity in the ranks of the traditionalist ulama, who are unable to voice their reservations about a policy that enjoys official support, but only to refute them. Their views as presented here were mostly expressed in interviews conducted by the author. It is important to add that such interviews often reveal things not found in published writings (though some of these ideas have also been published).

The traditionalist ulama are divided among various currents and schools. What distinguishes them, among other things, is whether and to what degree they tacitly reject the official line about unity. Among the nongovernmental groups known both for their outspoken opposition to a rapprochement with Sunnis and for their quietist and apolitical stance, are, first, the Anjoman-e hojjati, which prior to the Revolution earned a reputation as fierce opponents of the Baha'is, and, second, a circle of arch-traditionalists around Ayatollah Morteza Askari.[23] It may be assumed that quite a few traditionalist ulama who were coopted by the Revolution and who publicly espoused the official line about unity secretly sympathize with the views of these two groups.[24]

Ne`matollah Salehi Najafabadi is a Shi`i *alim* who lives and works in Qom. Mostly known for his historical studies, he has for decades been critically engaged with sociopolitical themes.[25] He raised a storm of indignation with his book, published in 1968 and today in its fifteenth printing, *Shahid-e javid* (*The Eternal Martyr*), which examines the events surrounding the battle of Karbala and the death of the third Imam Husain. To date, thirteen books have been published in response, among them works by prominent ulama such as Grand Ayatollah Mohammad Golpayegani (d. 1993) and Ayatollah Mottahari (d. 1979). For this book, Najafabadi checked all relevant Shiʻi traditions, found many of them false or only partly authentic, and hence rejected them. He also used many Sunni hadith. The book's main thesis is that Husain pursued power just like his opponents, wanted to become caliph, and was unaware of his impending death (Husain's prior knowledge of his death through martyrdom is one of the central tenets of the Shiʻi faith).[26]

After 1979, Najafabadi repeatedly cast doubt on those Shiʻi traditions that, to him, seemed incompatible with a rational understanding of Islam. In his book *Tauteʻeh-ye Shah bar zedd-e Emam Khomaini* (*The Shah's Conspiracy against Imam Khomeini*, 1984), for instance, he refutes the anti-Sunni views of Shaikh Morteza Ansari (1799–1864), the first to gain unequivocal recognition as *marjaʻ-e taqlid* in Shiʻism. Ansari had written, in his *al-Makasib*, a work that today is still used in theological seminaries as a standard text, that the excoriation of Sunnis belongs to the basics of Shiʻi jurisprudence.[27]

Najafabadi, relying on a rationalist interpretation of hadith by the first and the fifth Shiʻi imams, Ali and Muhammad al-Baqir, and on the Quran itself, in his refutation of this fatwa, rejects the view reflected in it as time- and environment-specific. Contemporary ulama, he argues, ought to exercise *ijtihad* with more courage and freedom, and evaluate even the Traditions attributed to noted Shiʻi authorities more critically in regard to their compatibility with the exigencies of the modern world. He challenges them never to shy away from revisiting specific questions just because they could go against the majority opinion of the ulama.[28]

Najafabadi uses the same theme in his essay "Vahdat-e eslami" (1985), which was banned by the religious authorities of Qom shortly after its publication. In this work he posits that to strive for a unity solely built on empty political slogans is an exercise in futility. According to him, little is done in today's Iran to create a friendly and hospitable climate between Shiʻis and Sunnis. As a major obstacle, he notes the conviction among many Shiʻi ulama that Sunni *fiqh* is less valid than Shiʻi *fiqh*. In their view, a Sunni who follows Sunni *fiqh* would find less grace with God than a Shiʻi, even if the Sunni fulfilled all of his religious obligations.[29] Shaikh Shaltut, Najafabadi says, took the first courageous step toward unity on the part of the Sunnis. It is now up to the Shiʻis to reciprocate, for example by allowing a Shiʻi *faqih* to follow Sunni *fiqh* in specific cases when he considers doing so more appropriate.[30]

In a personal interview, Najafabadi explicitly stated that the spiritual and cultural climate in Qom after the Revolution was still marked by fanatical viewpoints and dogmatism. With his book *Shahid-e javid* he had intended to show that, though Husain was an extraordinary human being, he was not a supernatural being with miraculous capabilities, including a knowledge of the future, something that even the Prophets of Islam, Muhammad, Abraham, Lot, and Noah, lacked. Knowledge of the future he sees as false and extremist (*ghuluww*), to be rejected because it goes against the logic of the Quran and Islam itself. Rejecting such beliefs, he noted, could contribute to the building of unity between Sunnis and Shi`is.[31]

Such views are reportedly rather widespread, even in Qom, among a small circle of progressive *mollah*s who praised him for his book. Nonetheless, he knows no one who would have the courage to issue a fatwa to that effect. The risk is too great, since Najafabadi assumes that fanatical and ignorant *mollah*s would react by inciting the masses of uneducated simple believers against him and thus jeopardize his life. Even Ayatollah Montazeri, who, according to Najafabadi, is earnestly concerned with rapprochement, would not dare to take such a bold step in the current climate.[32] Najafabadi sees the current measures taken by Tehran to improve the atmosphere between Sunnis and Shi`is as positive, but also thinks that too little has been done to promote a climate in which unity can occur. Many Shi`i ulama, he contends, continue to consider their Sunni brothers unclean (*najes*), refusing to accept them as equal Muslims who might find acceptance and forgiveness from God on an equal footing. The government, Najafabadi maintains, does not do enough to change this perspective. Short of a step like the one taken by Shaltut in Egypt, unity cannot and will not progress.[33]

Ebrahim Yazdi (b. 1931), a U.S. graduate in pharmacology and molecular biology, served as interim prime minister and first minister of foreign affairs of the provisional government from February to November of 1979. He belongs to the second generation of leaders of Nehzat-e azadi-ye Iran, a liberal-Islamic movement that was founded in 1961 by Mehdi Bazargan, the grand old man of Islamic modernism in Iran.[34] Nehzat-e azadi-ye Iran, which already under the shah operated in the opposition, draws from the technocratic elite, parts of the bazaar, and the traditional middle class, and represents an oppositional movement loyal to the constitution of the IRI. Under Mehdi Bazargan, who was Khomeini's first prime minister, its membership comprised most of the ministers of the transitional government, mainly moderate and believing technocrats. Since it has been out of government, the movement has frequently leveled sharp criticism of the excesses of the Revolution, invoking Islam.

During his time in the United States (1961–77), Yazdi was one of the leaders of the Muslim Student Association (MSA) of the U.S. and Canada. He recounts how, in his capacity as secretary of religious affairs, he often had to intervene in disputes between the Sunnis and the Shi`is of the MSA, and in the process became familiar with their variegated theological and dogmatic differences. Yazdi calls himself a Muslim revivalist who thinks in modern terms and thus often rejects the views of the traditionalists. To him, Islam is a universal religion that nevertheless permits an ineradicable cultural and religious pluralism. He thinks attempts to homogenize all doctrine and rites are unrealistic, arguing that pursuing such unity can even be harmful. All that is attainable, Yazdi insists, is a unity of political action, which should start with dialogue and toleration while aiming for clearly defined goals.[35] He thinks the prerevolutionary intercultural dialogue associated with the ecumenical Dar al-taqrib in Cairo and with the names of Shaltut and Ayatollah Borujerdi (1875–1962) lacked a solid basis, as it was limited to only a few ulama. The Iranian revolution with its pan-Islamic overtones, on the other hand, aroused an interest among the Muslim masses to learn more about Shi`ism. Through it a historical opportunity was created to revive the dialogue, to pursue reconciliation, and to propagate mutual understanding and toleration. This opportunity has, however, been squandered, Yazdi claims, in part because of propaganda campaigns mounted by Sunni regimes that felt threatened by the Islamic Revolution. But the Iranians are also partly to blame for a failed rapprochement following the gradual takeover of the Revolution by Shi`i traditionalists, who began to emphasize its Shi`i character at the expense of its pan-Islamic tendencies.[36] He illustrates this with the examples of the issue of Shi`ism as state religion and of the concept of *velayat-e faqih,* two basic elements of the Iranian constitution, and a discussion of his own role in the elaboration of its first draft:

> In the first draft of the Constitution of the IRI we deliberately did not specify that the president had to be a Twelver Shi`i and male. We ignored these points. It was our underlying intention to teach the Islamic world not to be so stubborn and partisan. Of course, we knew that the likelihood of a Sunni or a woman being elected president in a country like Iran, with its overwhelmingly Shi`i majority, would be very small. . . . Yet such an event would have reflected our political philosophy and our universal worldview. Unfortunately, some of the clerics disagreed with us. They insisted on the insertion of this clause and pushed it through. Another issue is *velayat-e faqih.* As others have rightly said, *velayat-e faqih* does not fit in the other (Sunni) schools and is a novelty even in Shi`ism.[37]

Other pan-Islamic projects have failed because of traditionalist resistance as well, Yazdi claims. An example is the building of a Sunni mosque in Tehran.

In 1979, the provisional government made plans for this with the mayor, and an area of 5,000 square meters was set aside for it in the northern suburb of Yusofabad. Yet when the Bazargan government fell, the plans were immediately shelved.[38]

Yazdi sees the outlook of the ulama as one of the main obstacles to a political and religious rapprochement. Their views are informed by canonical works that contain numerous statements against the first three caliphs that are unacceptable to Sunnis. The influence of traditionalist ulama on Iran's domestic and foreign policy since 1979 has helped to make meaningful cooperation with the Sunni world ever more difficult. Yazdi cites the example of the IRI condemning the uprising of the Syrian Muslim Brothers in Hama in early 1982.[39] As he sees it, political cooperation with the Muslim Brothers might have been possible, especially given what he calls their modernist outlook. Iran's minister of foreign affairs, Ali Akbar Velayati, however, made a mistake with grave consequences when in 1982 he characterized the Muslim Brothers as agents and stooges of the CIA, thereby adopting the jargon of Syria's atheist Ba`ath regime. This, Yazdi insists, did a great deal of damage to the pan-Islamic claims of the IRI.

> Pan-Islamic movements should bear universal characteristics and be nonsectarian, or they will be without success. Unfortunately, this negative trend has gained ground. After a while the Iranian government ended up only supporting Shi`i groups in the various Islamic countries. This has not helped us in either India, Afghanistan, Kuwait, Bahrain, or anywhere else.[40]

After the death of Mehdi Bazargan in January 1995, Yazdi assumed the leadership of the Nehzat-e azadi-ye Iran, whose candidates have thus far not been allowed to participate in any presidential or parliamentary elections on account of the movement's rejection of *velayat-e faqih*. Marginalized for years, the movement has revived since 1997. The official ban on its activities is still in place, but the movement is now benefiting from the more liberal climate of free expression created by Khatami. Apparently, it has also regained a level of support among Iranian youth and students, which support, beginning in the 1970s, it had lost almost completely to radical leftist or leftist-Islamic groups.[41]

Born in Ashkevar, a small town in the northern province of Gilan, Hojjatoleslam Hasan Yusof Ashkevari received a classical theological education in Qom. During his studies, he became acquainted with the social revolutionary theories of Ali Shari`ati and Ayatollah Mahmud Taleqani. He had a seat in the first Parliament after the Revolution (1980–84), but retreated from politics after radical Islamists blocked the candidacy of those who represented groups critical of the regime. Since then he has the collaborated with a number of scholarly institutions inside and outside of Iran, such as the Da'erat al-ma`aref-e eslami and the Da'erat al-ma`aref-e tashayyo`, the latter being politically close to the leftist Islamists. In addition, he regularly writes for the bimonthly magazine *Iran-e Farda,* published by Ezzatollah Shabi, one of the "semi-opposition." In his articles, Ashkevari criticizes the dominant interpretation of Islam and seeks to demonstrate the fundamental compatibility between Islam and democracy.[42]

To Ashkevari, at the core of the controversy between Sunna and Shi`a is the principle of the imamate, which originally was a political concept employed by an oppositional minority but which over time has acquired a much larger theological, dogmatic, and esoteric significance. An attack on the principle of the imamate, Ashkevari insists, would be tantamount to an assault on many related elements in the Shi`i faith that would also be called into question. According to him, it is time for a critical reassessment of the ways in which both Sunnis and Shi`is approach history. Both sides should give up their belief that they own the exclusive truth and, if necessary, change their historical viewpoint. Their model, Ashkevari suggests, could be the time of the Prophet, when factionalism had not yet emerged. Without a willingness to reassesses one's own view of history and possibly admit error, no unity can emerge between Sunna and Shi`a.[43]

Ashkevari sees three positions among the clerics and intellectuals of the Islamic Republic on the question of Islamic unity. The first is that of the traditionalists, who strongly reject unity. One of their protagonists is Ayatollah Askari, who is seen as an historian by the Shi`i clerics but whose books, Ashkevari insists, are harmful to unity. The second is that of the leaders of state, who pay lip service to unity but in effect see it only as political unity directed against an outside enemy. Such a notion of unity does not reach very deep. Also, Ashkevari notes, the method toward its realization is unworkable because it is based on the claim of Iran's Supreme Leader to be the commander of the world's Muslims (*vali-ye amr-e moslemin-e jahan*). There is no chance that non-Iranian Muslims would ever accept this claim. Hence, the IRI is putting obstacles in the way of unity by thus arousing a great deal of suspicion among Sunnis outside of Iran.[44] The third position is represented by the religious intellectuals. These include, Ashkevari says, people like Ebrahim Yazdi, Mehdi Bazargan, and Abdol Karim Soroush. They aim to lead Muslims to a critical evaluation of their conception of history in order to bring about a unity of Muslims freed from the burden of history and sectarianism.

To promote unity, Muslims would have to work toward a new understanding of the tradition concerning whether the Prophet designated Ali as his successor, which caused the conflict over *velayat*.[45] To Ashkevari, it should be easy for Muslims today to achieve unity, because the Shi'i idea of a political imamate is in practice a moot one (*montafi shod*), since the last Imam has disappeared, remains in hiding, and the moment of his return falls outside the ken of humans. This situation raises the question of what currently would be the practical difference between Sunnis and Shi'is. Ashkevari sees no practical distinction between the concept of *velayat-e faqih* and that of the Caliphate. In the absence of an Imam, the issue of who holds greater legitimacy, the caliph, elected by the *umma*, as the Sunnis hold, or the Imam, designated by the Prophet, as the Shi'is maintain, is merely theoretical. Should Muslims heed the suggestion of Ayatollah Hosain Ali Montazeri to have the *vali-ye faqih* elected by the people, the Shi'is would be doing what the Sunnis have been demanding of them for fourteen centuries, and the difference would grow less.[46]

Ashkevari believes that elections by Muslims as stipulated by Montazeri would be a common denominator on which Sunni and Shi'i thinkers could agree. Ashkevari characterizes this as the principle of *mashrutiyat*. He believes that this, and not secondary questions of jurisprudence concerning theology and dogma, was a central principle for some of the most influential Sunni thinkers of the twentieth century, such as Sayyid Qutb (d. 1965) and Abu'l A'la Mawdudi (d. 1979). Ashkevari says that it is similarly important for Shi'is to accept that the power of the *vali-ye faqih* derives from the people. He believes that a government that adheres to the principles of *mashrutiyat* as stipulated by Montazeri would be acceptable to Sunnis as well. When both Sunnis and Shi'is employ similar concepts, such as civil government (*hokumat-e madani*) and democracy, they will be able to draw much closer than they are now. The question of the source of political power would then, he claims, inspire unity rather than intra-Muslim discord. Differences on theology and dogma between Sunnis and Shi'is have to be taken as natural. People could live with them, however, for such differences exist within the branches of Islam as well.[47]

Ashkevari is a self-proclaimed follower of the theses of the Egyptian al-Azhar judge Ali Abd al-Raziq (d. 1966), expressed in the latter's 1925 book, *al-Islam wa usul al-hukm* (*Islam and the Principles of Government*), for which he was ostracized by Egypt's religious establishment.[48] Like al-Raziq, Ashkevari believes that the caliphate lost its legitimacy after the era of the four rightly-guided caliphs (632–61) and cannot be considered an institution created by God or the Prophet. Ashkevari uses this absence of legitimacy to put the caliphate on the same level as *velayat-e faqih,* since the latter, too, lacks legitimacy in being unable to claim to be representative of the Hidden Imam of Shi`a Islam.[49]

The pan-Islamic program of the government, Ashkevari contends, is doomed to fail because it is based on the claim to leadership of the *velayat-e faqih:*

> *Velayat-e faqih* is a Shi`i concept of rule. The Sunnis outside of Iran, many of whom doubt that Shi`is are Muslims at all, will therefore never accept this principle. The suspicion with which Sunnis regard the pan-Islamic project of Iran's current government is being fueled by that very same government, which made Shi`ism the religion of state and reserved all leading governmental positions for Shi`is, all in clear and incontrovertible contradiction to the message of the Islamic Revolution. If the government does not work toward Islamic unity within Iran, how could it do so beyond the country's borders?

Without mentioning Iran's Sunni minority by name, Ashkevari in the last part of this quote hints at a group whose position has become worse since the 1979 revolution. Disappointed with Khomeini's broken promise that Sunnis and Shi`is would be treated equally before the law, Sunnis even formed small militant groups in the 1980s.[50]

Ashkevari's criticism of Iran's system has grown in volume and insistence since the accession to power of President Khatami. In April 2000 he participated in a Berlin conference on democratic change, organized by the Heinrich Böll Foundation. Following this, the Iranian justice system accused Ashkevari, and a number of other Iranian proponents of civil society participating in the conference, of so-called "support for tendencies inimical to the system."[51]

SOROUSH'S OBSERVATIONS ON ISLAMIC UNITY

Abdol Karim Soroush is currently the best known and most controversial of Iran's thinkers. Born in Tehran in 1945, he grew up in a traditional religious family. In the 1950s, he went to the Alavi High School in Tehran and between 1965 and 1973 studied Pharmacy at Tehran University.[52] Early on, his interests focused on Islamic philosophy and theology. In 1964, Soroush met Ayatollah Motahhari and asked to be accepted by him as his student. Montazeri, however, referred him to his own best student and Soroush studied for nine years with the latter, mastering the classical canon of Shi`i theology such as *usul al-fiqh, tafsir* (Quranic exegesis), and philosophy. In 1973,

Soroush went to England, where he studied chemistry at the University of London; at the same time he studied philosophy and epistemology in the Departments of History and Philosophy of Science. Graduating in chemistry after five-and-a-half years, Soroush returned to Iran shortly after the Revolution. There he started working as a teacher at Tehran University and researcher at the Anjoman-e hekmat va falsafeh (Society for Theosophy and Philosophy). Since 1978, Soroush has dealt with a wide range of topics, articulated in the form of speeches, lectures, sermons in mosques, and talks abroad, as well as numerous articles and books. These topics range from mysticism and the philosophy of religion to ethics, epistemology, and the philosophy of science. Between 1980 and 1984, Soroush also participated in Iran's cultural revolution. At the behest of Khomeini, he was appointed to the High Council of the Cultural Revolution (Shura-ye aliyeh-ye enqelab-e farhangi), whose tasks included the reorganization of the universities that had been closed between 1980 and 1983 and the adaptation of their curricula to the requirements of the Islamic Revolution. In 1984, Soroush resigned from the Council out of dissatisfaction with its work conditions and devoted his time solely to research and lecturing.[53]

Soroush's theories reflect the influence of classical Muslim theologians such as Muhammad al-Ghazali (1058–1111) and Islamic mystics such as Jalal al-Din Rumi (Maulana, 1207–73), as well as various Western philosophers including Immanuel Kant and, above all, Karl Popper. One of his main philosophical themes, worked out in numerous essays and books, centers on the construction of a modern Islamic worldview as an alternative to the value system of the West. He seeks to come to some kind of compromise with regard to central issues like human rights and democracy.

Among many devout intellectuals, government technocrats, and, above all, students, Soroush has enjoyed great respect since the 1980s, and he has apparently lost none of it since the state ceased to protect him in the last few years. The traditionalist clerics, on the other hand, are among his bitterest enemies. He aroused their ire primarily with a theory offered in his 1990 book, *Qabz va bast-e te'orik-e shari`at* (*Theoretical Observations on the Contraction and Expansion of Religion*). The core of this theory is a plea for a strict distinction between the part of religion that is consistent and unalterable, and our knowledge of religion. By the latter Soroush means mostly the traditional theological knowledge of Islamic scholars (*fuqaha*). Their wisdom, Soroush argues, is the product of different historical periods, situated in specific and changeable epistemological frameworks, and thus inconsistent and fallible. It is the fruit of history and can thus lay no claim to sacred status or to validity going beyond time and place, and it should be exposed to criticism, just like all other disciplines that are susceptible to change. In order to achieve a renewal of religious knowledge, the *fuqaha* should enter into a dialogue with modern scientific disciplines. Otherwise, they will not be able to offer satisfactory answers to the many challenges posed by modernity.[54]

Since 1991, the attacks from influential right-wing governmental circles on Soroush have increased in number and intensity, accusing him of spreading subversive ideas. As a result, Soroush lost the reputation as "philosophical darling of the Revolution" that he had held in the 1980s, and, gradually, all opportunities to spread his ideas via the airwaves or the state-controlled print media. When his opponents deprived him of his position as a university lecturer in 1996, the bimonthly journal *Kiyan,* run by friends of his, became the sole outlet for the dissemination of his ideas.

Soroush pleads for a distinction within pan-Islamism (as it is variously defined in today's Iran), between two dimensions: an inner and an outer one. The inner one concerns the unification of all Muslims of the *umma* vis-à-vis external enemies, and should aim, if possible, for a global extension of the *umma.* This inner dimension is interpreted by a majority of the Shi`i ulama as meaning that they are superior to the Sunnis. Soroush argues that in their hearts they never accepted the ideas of Jamal al-Din al-Afghani (1839–97) or those of Ali Shari`ati (d. 1977), with regard to the equality of all Muslims and their equal claim to the truth. Deep down, they still see it as their duty to convert Sunnis to Shi`ism in order to create an *umma* united under the Shi`i banner. Anyone who, for the sake of reconciliation, shows the slightest willingness to accommodate positions taken by Sunnis—for instance, on issues such as ijma`[55]—meets with bitter resistance from the traditionalist clerics, whose objections mostly involve the question of *velayat.*[56]

Conversely, Soroush sees Sunnis as more active and productive than Shi`is regarding reconciliation. Illustrative is the reissuing of what he calls the revolutionary and courageous fatwa of Shaikh Shaltut, to which the Shi`is have not responded with anything similar. Were a Shi`i *alim* to issue a fatwa declaring it legitimate to follow the fatwa of the Hanafi or Shafi`i school, a revolutionary step would be taken and a great softening would take place. Given a widespread conviction among the Shi`i ulama that the Sunnis are fundamentally in error, that God himself means ill for them and has condemned them to the fires of hell, this is out of the question. None of them believes that he should concede anything to the Sunnis or adopt any of their positions. Soroush realizes, though, that the majority of the Sunni ulama and the masses hold similar views toward the Shi`is.[57]

Based on this analysis, Soroush believes that even the highest echelons of Shi`i authority do not believe in a real reconciliation. Even Khomeini himself, despite his revolutionary personality, always remained an orthodox Shi`i, thinking in terms of traditional *fiqh* and *kalam* in religious matters.

> Ayatollah Khomeini was an orthodox Shi`i who insisted that the clause proclaiming Shi'ism as Iran's state religion be anchored in the constitution. He was the one to be emphatic and uncompromising about this. . . . He may have pursued reconciliation for political considerations, but he did not base the unity of Shi`a and Sunna on a firm intellectual foundation. Nor did he ever believe in it in his heart of hearts, as I see it.[58]

Soroush discusses arguments for unity that are used by the Islamic Republic and its representatives—that is, unity directed against a common external foe and inner unity inspired by religious common ground. He regards these arguments as partially valid, yet sees them as insufficient to realize unity. Unity against an external foe is defensive and can at best only be temporary. It collapses as soon as the external enemy disappears or is defeated. Without unity grounded in the hearts of Muslims, they are sure to revert to centuries-old hatreds.[59] As for religious common ground, Soroush says that Muslims have not been able in the last fourteen centuries to use their common religious principles as a platform for a stable inner unity. Hopes that they will now give up their conflicts to embrace unity are therefore unrealistic.[60] To Soroush, the oft-mentioned religious principles are more sources of strife than of unity, since each denomination uses different commentaries on the same Quranic verses or different interpretations concerning the Prophet. No basis for Muslim unity can exist without the introduction of a new epistemology and intellectual initiatives to give these a framework.[61]

In discussing obstacles to unity, Soroush lays much of the blame on Iran's domestic religious climate. His arguments here can be summarized as follows. The scope for Iran's pan-Islamic project is limited, since the government, instead of opening up new frontiers, has only followed the beaten path. What practical efforts have been made have all been challenged and put at risk by various groups. The Sunni world knows its Wahhabis, a literalist sect which brands all those who follow a line other than theirs apostates, and which should be condemned by all Muslims. The Iranian counterparts of the Wahhabis are certain arch-traditionalist ulama who enjoy a considerable backing in their society. Many strict believers, members of the Anjoman-e hojjati or similar groups, such as Ayatollah Askari, regard Sunnis as their mortal enemies, reject any concession toward Sunnis, and even cast doubt on the Shi`i character of Iran's current government. Some groups, disregarding the government's ban on such practices, apparently hold onto the cursing of the first three caliphs, if only secretly. Convinced of Shiʿism's monopoly on truth, they believe that the first Sunni caliphs were out to distort Islam. They see them as hypocrites (*monafeqin*), as enemies of Islam who were only Muslim in appearance. In their view, Umar led the Muslims on an erroneous path through falsifying history and hence must be seen as the one who caused the unbelief that has spread around the world.[62] Their current efforts thus focus on correcting Sunni falsification of the history of Islam, writing this history according to their own theology and their own worldview.[63]

Asked about the reasons for the failure of the idea of unity as promoted by Iran, Soroush says that the government's calls for unity, though sincere, are based on a one-sided and incomplete concept of unity. The government misjudges the comprehensive character of unity, which must include not just politics and jurisprudence but also a theological dimension that cannot be separated from the other dimensions. Islamic unity is either wholly accepted or wholly rejected. Regarding the Majmaʿ al-taqrib as supported by Khamenei, Soroush states that it would be a serious mistake if this organization mainly focused on *fiqh* at the expense of other aspects of unity. For *fiqh* is the least important aspect in the teachings and world view of Islam. The most pressing differences between Sunnis and Shiʿis concern questions that have little or nothing to do with *fiqh* but rather involve theology (*kalam*). Among the jurists of the various subdivisions within either Shiʿism or Sunnism, the differences in jurisprudence are sometimes greater than those between Sunnis and Shiʿis. These differences are surmountable and Muslims have become accustomed to them over the centuries. The crucial distinctions lie not in *fiqh* but in the different representations of the Imamate and of Islamic history. The Iranian government, Soroush argues, ignores these latter two aspects, convinced that it would be more judicious not to broach such subjects.[64]

Soroush sees erroneous epistemological categories employed by the ulama as another major obstacle to unity. God has created people with different temperaments, forms of conscience, and abilities to understand reality, and as a result differences arise in questions of faith and the interpretation of sacred texts. Willed by God, these differences are natural and legitimate and not the work of enemies out to sow discord among Muslims. That God did not expect to unite all people in one community the Prophet knew as well, and, endowed as he was with insight into human nature and God's plan, he too did not expect such unity. If Muslims, and above all their religious guides, the ulama, would recognize the inevitability and naturalness of religious conflict, then their approach to these schisms would change as well.[65]

Many of today's Shiʿi ulama, Soroush continues, are blind to the profound insights into human nature and the god-willed conflicts notably found in the poems and parables of the Iranian mystic Jalal al-Din Rumi (1207–73). Reflecting on them, he says:

> All those who try to unite all people of the world under the banner of one faith will fan the flames of discord so long as they have not gained this important insight. . . . All those who believe that they alone possess the pure truth, and that what others believe is null and void, pour oil on the fire of battle. We should reach the insight that in this world each individual human being is part of the truth and that the truth belongs to all people, and not just to the adherents of a specific persuasion.[66]

Soroush believes it is not the task of the ulama to ban evil and error from the world, to improve the world from the bottom up, and to alter human nature. It is, on the other hand, the task of the ulama to turn the eyes of the religious masses away from a struggle over futilities and instead to direct them to a higher plane in order to offer a spiritual and contemplative orientation. A great many Shi`i ulama, Soroush claims, are populists who adopt the masses' beliefs out of a lack of a fundamental inclination toward contemplation. Instead of resisting the passions of popular belief and steering the blind emotions of the masses in harmonious directions, they fall victim to these popular beliefs themselves.[67]

To Soroush, historiography permeated by theology, as it is among Shi`is and Sunnis alike, is the final, formidable obstacle to unity. Theological premises determine, consciously or not, historiographical writing. In the case of Shi`ism this means, for instance, that the belief in Ali's infallibility must lead to the conviction that his opponents were unjust, hypocrites, or enemies of Islam. Conversely, one would gain a completely different view of history if one assumed, with the Sunnis, that Ali was but a fallible, errant religious authority.

The identity of believers on both sides, Soroush notes, is a historical identity rooted in precisely those variants of Islamic history that are transmitted over time and narrated to the faithful from a specific vantage point— variants they are familiar with and understand. The decisive issue is the question of historical identity. At bottom, a mutual recognition is steadily hampered by divergent readings of a history saturated with theology. According to Soroush this leads to the notion that

> our Prophet is different from the Prophet of the Sunnis, the reason being that our historical profile of the Prophet is fundamentally different from that held by the Sunnis. I would say that our image of the Imam and even of the Quran is different from that current among Sunnis. There are many Shi`i Traditions about the Imams that our ulama regard as

significant commentary on specific Quranic verses. By contrast, these Traditions only have a secondary meaning among the Sunnis.[68]

The only exit from this dilemma, Soroush insists, is a rewriting of Islamic history through cooperation with experienced historians from a variety of Islamic currents, adding that this idea is likely to remain an ideal that will never be realized. Without serious steps in this direction, however, a reconciliation between Sunnis and Shi`is is impossible.[69]

The theoretical foundation of such a rewriting, Soroush submits while invoking Hegel, ought to make a strict distinction between essence and contingency in religious matters. Essential elements are the defining characteristics of a religion, that is, the traits without which it loses its inner meaning. In Islam those are *nubuwwa* (prophecy), *tauhid* (Oneness), and *ma`ad* (return). Contingent, by contrast, is everything that is derived from time and circumstance and that lies outside the shaping force of the Prophet, that is, all things that touch on human limitation and fallibility. These nonessential elements, most of which came about after the Prophet's death, might have taken totally different forms than they have. An example is Ali, who could have altered the course of Islamic history by taking up arms at the election of Abu Bakr as caliph.

If we accept the principles of *nubuwwa, tauhid,* and *ma`ad,* Soroush says, there are no differences between Sunna and Shi`a other than concerning the Imamate. To him the Imamate is a contingent matter that arose after the death of the Prophet. Even those who do not believe in the Imams are fully Muslim. Many problems with the Sunnis have been caused by the content of Imami *hadith.* The problem, Soroush insists, is that many representatives of both branches consider as essential multiple dogmas of faith that owe their existence to the accidental and capricious course of history or personal error or misunderstanding. So long as there is no fundamental mutual understanding about the necessity of separating contingency from essence among the ulama of both sides, there is no hope for a substantive unity of Muslims.[70]

CONCLUSION

Since 1979, despite official words in Iran favoring Sunni-Shi`i unity, there has been little progress toward such unity abroad or at home on the religious level, although better political relations with Sunni countries, including Saudi Arabia, may be reflected in a lessening of religious hostilities. One reason for the lack of progress toward religious unity has been the continued traditionalism of most religious leaders, a traditionalism that, as "semi-oppositional" thinkers point out, continues to insist on a view of Shi`ism that makes no concessions to Sunni beliefs or sensibilities. The often parallel experience of Western Protestantism and Catholicism suggests that ecumenism is a long, hard process, and may only come about when both religious leaders and the mass of believers cease to put so much stress on former core beliefs and practices that are totally unacceptable to the other group. In the modern West, this has often been a function of secularizing trends and an attendant loss of political and social power for individual denominations, which then saw themselves, for instance, forced to band together and form coalitions and merge separate parties into a large "Christian Democratic" party. In the Islamic world, a similar process is not observable (though recent findings point to an alarmingly low rate of religious observance among Iranians, with 75 percent of the general populace and 86 percent of high school and university students saying they did not pray).[71] The outlook for some form of ecumenical progress need not be totally bleak, however. Inasmuch as history shows that justifications for better religious relations have always been a function of cordial *political* relations between Iran and its Sunni neighbors, such progress would naturally require a relaxed political climate. Iran's relations with Sunni countries such as Saudi Arabia and Egypt—crucial interlocutors in the interfaith dialogue—have already improved in the 1990s. This was recently illustrated by the positive reaction of the rector of Cairo's al-Azhar University, Muhammad Sayyid Tantawi, who warmly accepted the invitation extended by Tehran's Majma` al-taqrib society to Egyptian ulama to participate in an Islamic Unity Conference in Tehran.[72] They might improve yet further if a less conservative brand of leaders came to power in Iran. A different political leadership might make sincere overtures toward the Sunni world and even persuade the arch-conservative ulama to relent on some minor issues, for a start. Total pessimism in this regard is only warranted if one believes that both Sunnis and Shi`is are inherently incapable of making any concessions. The history of the Christian church has given us some examples of ecumenical progress that do not necessarily presuppose a wholesale abandonment of all contradictory doctrines and practices and that let each faith retain its own core beliefs while acknowledging the existence and worthiness of the other. Over time, the doctrinal differences between Sunnism and Shi`ism may seem less important to most believers and ulama than they do today.

NOTES

Translated by Rudi Matthee. Thanks are due to Rudi Matthee for editing the paper down from the longer German version and for making numerous helpful editorial suggestions.

1. See Ruhollah K. Ramazani, "The Emerging Arab-Iranian Rapprochement," *Middle East Policy* 6, no. 1 (1998): 45–62.

2. For the progress in Iranian-Arab relations since December 1997, see Wilfried Buchta, *Who Rules Iran? The Structure of Power in the Islamic Republic* (Washington: Washington Institute for Near East Policy, 2000), 130–34.

3. Hooshang Ahmadi, "Emerging Civil Society in Iran," *SAIS Review* 26 (Summer–Fall 1996): 87–104.

4. For an overview of the most important members of the religious "semi-opposition," see Buchta, *Who Rules Iran?*, 78–101.

5. For Iran's pan-Islamic project between 1979 and 1989, see David Menashri, "Khomeini's Vision: Nationalism or World Order?," in *The Iranian Revolution and the Muslim World,* ed. David Menashri (Boulder, CO: Westview, 1990), 40–58.

6. Hojjatoleslam Sayyed Mohammad Khatami, the former Minister of Culture and Religious Guidance (1982–92) and currently president, told me in an interview that, following the revolution, Khomeini himself had expressed his rejection of any denigration of Sunnis before a small circle of students. According to Khatami, the attendants had interpreted this as an order to be strictly followed. Interview with Mohammad Khatami, Tehran, National Library, 27 July 1993.

7. The ban on praying behind a non-Twelver Shi`i person goes back to preeminent Shi`i scholars such as Abu Ja`far Tusi (d. 1067). See Etan Kohlberg, "Non-Imami Muslims in Imami Fiqh," *Jerusalem Studies in Arabic and Islam* 6 (1985): 99–105. For the Persian text of the fatwa, see Wilfried Buchta, *Die iranische Schia und die islamische Einheit 1979–1996* (Hamburg: Deutsches Orient-Institut), 74–80.

8. For the text of this statement, see Mostafa Ezadi, *Faqih-e Ali-qadr* (Tehran: Entesharat-e sorush, 1366/1987), 123–25.

9. For such arguments, see *al-Wahda al-islamiya. Darura wa hadaf. Min khutab Ayatullah Khamina'i qa'id al-thaura fi usbu` al-wahda al-islamiya li am 1410/1989,* ed. Islamic Propagation Organization (Tehran, 1989), esp. 21–31.

10. For this, see Masih Mohajeri, *The Background of the Islamic Unity* (Tehran, 1988).

11. A sound analysis of all fundamental theological and dogmatic issues between Sunna and Shi`a can be found in Werner Ende, "Sunniten und Schiiten im 20. Jahrhundert," *Saeculum* 36 (1985): 187–200, esp. 189–93.

12. Despite common enemies, there are many theological and dogmatic impediments to a political alliance between Sunni and Shi`i fundamentalists. See Emmanuel Sivan, "Sunni Radicalism in the Middle East and the Iranian Revolution," *International Journal of Middle East Studies* 21 (1989): 1–30.

13. For a detailed study of the *Dar al-taqrib* movement, see Rainer Brunner, *Annäherung und Distanz. Schia, Azhar und die islamische Ökumene im 20. Jahrhundert* (Berlin: Klaus Schwarz, 1996), 215–32.

14. For details, see Brunner, *Annäherung*, 238–43.

15. For this, see Wilfried Buchta, "Tehran's Ecumenical Society (*Majma` al-taqrib*): A Veritable Ecumenical Revival or a Trojan Horse of Iran?" in *The Twelver Shi`a in Modern Times: Religious Culture and Political History,* ed. Rainer Brunner and Werner Ende (Leiden: E. J. Brill, 2001), 333–53.

16. Said Amir Arjomand, *The Shadow of God and the Hidden Imam: Religion, Political Order, and Societal Change in Shi`ite Iran from the Beginning to 1890* (Chicago: University of Chicago Press, 1984), esp. 138 and 165.

17. Fritz Steppat, "Fundamentalistische Kritik an der Staatskonzeption der Islamis-chen Revolution im Iran," in *Studies zur Geschichte und Kultur des Vorderen Orients. Festschrift für Berthold Spuler zum 70. Geburtstag,* ed. Hans Roemer and Albrecht Noth (Leiden: E. J. Brill, 1981, 443–52.

18. See Sayyid Hawwa, *al-Khumainiya: Shudhudh fi al-aqa'id wa shudhudh fi al-mawaqif* (Cairo: Dirasat minhajiya hadifa, 1987).

19. Ibid., 44ff.

20. Hamid Enayat, *Modern Islamic Political Tought* (London: I. B. Tauris, 1982), 19ff.

21. Abbas Vali and Sami Zubaida, "Factionalism and Political Discourse in the Islamic Republic of Iran: The Case of the Hujjatiye Society," *Economy and Society* 124, no. 2 (1985): 139–73 (142).

22. See Buchta, *Die iranische Schia,* 159–64.

23. The orthodox-quietist *Anjoman-e khairiyeh-ye mahdaviyeh (Anjoman-e hoj-jati)* was led by Ayatollah Mahmud Halabi (1897–1999). Financed by conservative bazaar circles, it made a name for itself since the 1950s through its campaign against the Baha`i movement. Its rejection of the concept of *velayat-e faqih* earned it the rebuke of Kho-meini in 1983, and officially it dissolved at that time. It is clear, however, that the group survived. Because it is so averse to publicity and the taking of official positions, vir-tually no literature exists on the movement. See, however, Mehdy Naficy, *Klerus, Bazar, und die iranische Revolution* (Hamburg: Deutsches Orient-Institut, 1993), 139–46; and Vali and Zubaida, "Factionalism and Political Discourse."

24. For more details, see Buchta, *Die iranische Schia,* 132–47.

25. He thus criticized the concept of *velayat-e faqih* in the early 1980s, arguing that it should be brought up to date with modern notions of majority rule, social con-tract, and representation through rational arguments based on the Quran and Shi`a-hadith. See Ahmad Kazem Moussavi, "A New Interpretation of the Theory of Vilayat-i Faqih," *Middle Eastern Studies* 28 (1992): 101–07. For an important article on Najafabadi, see Evan Siegel, "The Politics of *Shahid-e Jāwid,*" in *The Twelver Shi`a in Modern Times,* ed. Brunner and Ende, 150–78.

26. For this controversy, see Enayat, *Modern Islamic Political Thought,* 190–94.

27. See Salehi Najafabadi, *Taute'eh-ye Shah bar zedd-e Emam Khomaini va rav-abet ba qatl-e Hojjatoleslam Shamsabadi. Janjal marbut beh shahid-e javid* (Tehran: Entesharat-e rasa, 2nd ed., 1363/1984), 192.

28. Ibid., 198.

29. Ibid., 174.

30. See Ne`mat Salehi Najafabadi, "Vahdat-e eslami," in *Majmu`eh-ye maqalat* (n.p., 1364/1985), 198.

31. Persian cassette interview with Hojjatoleslam Ne`matollah Salehi Najafabadi, Tehran, 12 August 1993.

32. Ibid.

33. Ibid.

34. See Houchang Chehabi, *Iranian Politics and Religious Modernism: The Liber-ation Movement of Iran under the Shah and Khomeini* (London: I. B. Tauris, 1990).

35. Persian cassette interview with the author, Tehran, 29 May 1993.

36. Ibid.

37. Ibid.

38. Interview with Ebrahim Yazdi, Tehran, 5 August 1993. Sayyid Hawwa simi-

larly describes the failure of Sunni mosques in Tehran as a reason for his disillusionment vis-à-vis the pan-Islamic tendency of Iran under Khomeini. See Hawwa, *al-Khumainiya*, 49.

39. For the political and religious background to the events in Hama, see the penetrating study of Hans-Günther Lobmeyer, *Opposition und Widerstand in Syrien* (Hamburg: Deutsches Orient-Institut, 1995), 259–336.

40. English cassette interview, Tehran, 29 May 1993.

41. For the current position of *Nahzat-e azadi-ye Iran*, see Buchta, *Who Rules Iran?*, 80–82.

42. See, for instance, Yusefi Ashkevari, "Eslam va demokrasi," *Iran-e Farda* 13 (1994): 26–30.

43. Persian cassette interview, 13 July 1993.

44. Ibid.

45. For the concept of *velayat*, see Mojan Moomen, *An Introduction to Shi`i Islam* (New Haven: Yale University Press, 1985), 15.

46. Persian cassette interview, 13 July 1993.

47. Ibid.

48. In his book, Al-Raziq held a plea for the separation between religion and state as sanctioned by Islam. For this thesis he was banned from al-Azhar. See Albert Hourani, *Arabic Thought in the Liberal Age, 1798–1939* (Cambridge: Cambridge University Press, 1962), 183–92; and Leonard Binder, *Islamic Liberalism: A Critique of Development Ideologies* (Chicago: The University of Chicago Press, 1988), 128–70.

49. Persian cassette interview, 13 July 1993.

50. For this, see Buchta, *Who Rules Iran?*, 103–11.

51. See *Frankfurter Algemeine Zeitung*, 25 April 2000, 7.

52. Biographical material provided by Soroush himself. English cassette interview, *Anjoman-e hekmat va falsafeh*, Tehran, 12 Sept. 1994.

53. Ibid.

54. See Abdol Karim Soroush, *Qabz va bast-e te'orik-e shari`at* (Tehran: Mo`asasseh-ye farhangi-ye sirat, 5th ed., 1373/1994), 493–523.

55. Sunnis and Shi`is use different criteria for ijma`. See Harald Löschner, *Die dogmatische Grundlagen des ši`itischen Rechts* (Cologne: Diez Verlag, 1971), 111–47.

56. The term *velayat* here stands for the belief in the leadership of the Hidden Imam. For strict Shi`is, anyone who renounces the Imam is considered an apostate, on the basis of a *hadith* going back to the fifth Imam, Muhammad al-Baqir. See Momen, *Introduction*, 157ff.

57. English cassette interview, 10 July 1993.

58. Ibid.

59. Cassette interview of a two-hour-long Persian speech of Soroush on the occasion of the Week of Unity, on 6 Aban 1376/29 Oct. 1988, held in Tehran. Cited hereafter as Speech of Soroush, Tehran, 29 Oct. 1988.

60. Ibid.

61. English cassette interview, 10 July 1993.

62. Ibid.

63. Though Askari ostensibly pursues objectivity so as not to fall victim to official censorship, his historical writings are marked by a latent anti-Sunni tendency. See, for example, Morteza Askari, *Naqsh-e a'emmeh dar ehya al-din* (n.p., 1991), 77–78.

64. English cassette interview, 12 Sept. 1994.

65. Speech of Soroush, Tehran, 29 Oct. 1988.

66. See Abdol Karim Soroush, "Sokhanrani dar bareh-ye vahdat-e eslami," *Saz-man-e tablighat-e eslami*, ed. Majmu'eh-ye sokhanraniha va maqalat-e dovvomin kofer-ans-e vahdat-e eslami (Tehran, 1367/1988), 73–95 (76).

67. Speech of Soroush on Islamic Unity, 29 Oct. 1988.

68. English cassette interview, 10 July 1993.

69. Ibid.

70. Ibid.

71. *Iran Times*, 21 July 2000.

72. See for this *al-Sharq al-Ausat*, 9 April, 2000, 16. For Iranian-Egyptian relations since 1979, see Asef Bayat and Bahman Baktiari's paper in this volume.

13 / Revolutionary Iran and Egypt:

Exporting Inspirations and Anxieties

ASEF BAYAT AND BAHMAN BAKTIARI

This chapter discusses the impact of revolutionary Iran on Egypt from the revolution of 1979 through the presidency of Muhammad Khatami. It explores some of the major intellectual, cultural, and political influences Iran has had on another ancient nation. It shows that the events of revolution and after have left imprints of both inspiration and anxiety. The revolution inspired many Egyptians of various social milieus—secular nationalists, Islamists, and ordinary people—in their desire to push for social and political change. Yet it generated a disproportionate anxiety amongst the political elites. We show that Iran's influence has been at its height when the nation embarked on social mobilization, democratic practice, and popular participation. In contrast, its political and intellectual impact was lowest when Iran was dominated by authoritarian rule, war, and repressive policies.

By virtue of their strategic location, size, historical tradition, and leadership qualities, Egypt and Iran have been major actors in the regional politics and culture of the Middle East in the later part of the twentieth century. Both countries were ruled for the most part by monarchies, and both monarchies were overthrown by revolutionary change, Egypt's in 1952 and Iran's in 1979. Being located at the crossroads of three continents, Egypt more than Iran since 1500 has been host to many foreign peoples and cultures, including Turks, Italians, Greeks, and Iranians. During the 1920s and 1930s, Iranian residents in Cairo formed a vibrant community of mostly merchants and intellectuals. The community had established associations, published many periodicals, and was highly active in trade. In the words of one historian, Cairo's major commercial center in the 1930s (today's Khan Khalili bazaar) "belonged entirely to the Iranian merchants."[1]

Iran-Egypt relations experienced a brief period of flourishing following the shah's marriage to Fauziya (Fuziyeh), King Faruq's sister, in 1939. The wedding itself caused an outpouring of panegyric on the warm relations between Egypt and Iran. In poetry especially written for the occasion, both countries were called cradles of civilization that had brought forth Ramses and Cyrus, respectively, and shining examples of an awakening East.[2] It also prompted al-Azhar University to introduce Persian into its language curriculum.[3] In the two decades that followed, relations were cordial, giving rise to the activities of the *Dar al-taqrib* movement. Founded in 1947 by the Iranian cleric Mohammad Taqi Qommi and led by Mahmud Shaltut, the rector of al-Azhar, this ecumenical movement aimed at a rapprochement between Sunnism and Shi`ism. Never evolving into a mass movement, it rather functioned as a forum for discussion and a publishing enterprise. Its achievements were few. It never managed to persuade al-Azhar to institute a chair of Shi`i jurisprudence, for example. Yet the 1959 fatwa of Shaltut, which recognized Twelver Shi`ism as a fifth school of Islam, must be seen as a landmark ruling and at least a symbolic measure of success. After the 1952 coup it initially enjoyed the support of Gamal Abdul Nasser, who saw it as a tool in his ambition to play a leading role throughout the Arab world.[4]

The Free Officers' coup in 1952, however, heralded a new era in Egypt-Iran relations. Under Nasser, the core of the Egyptian regime's ideology and the very basis of its legitimacy became Arab nationalism. This episode coincided with the anticolonial posture of the Iranian nationalist prime minister, Mohammad Mosaddeq, who had nationalized the British holdings in the Anglo-Iranian Oil Company. Inspired by Mosaddeq, Nasser nationalized the Suez Canal. A year later, in 1953, a CIA-backed coup removed Mosaddeq from power. From this time, Iran completely changed course, moving in exactly the opposite direction to that of Nasser's Egypt, courting the Western powers and joining military alliances with Britain and the United States.[5]

This was the beginning of a cold war between Iran and Egypt. The shah of Iran perceived Nasser as an "instrument of Soviet expansionism," and Nasser saw the shah's cooperation with Western powers and their allies, especially Israel, as detrimental to Arab interests.[6] By early 1960, Cairo's relationship with Tehran had reached a low point, with Egypt finally breaking off diplomatic relations with Iran in the summer of 1960, following Tehran's de facto recognition of the state of Israel.[7] However, a number of external events during the 1960s brought Iran and Egypt closer together. Egypt's unsuccessful military intervention in the Yemeni civil war of 1962, and Nasser's ambition to establish a foothold in southern Arabia, alienated the conservative sheikhdoms in the Persian Gulf, drawing them closer to Iran. The Iranian regime embarked on an assertive diplomacy and succeeded in isolating Egypt in the region.[8] But the devastating defeat in the June 1967 war with Israel convinced Nasser to reassess Egypt's ambitious policy in the Persian Gulf and to seek to reduce tensions with Iran. After Iran welcomed the "new Egyptian realism" in May 1970, Iran and Egypt restored diplomatic relations in August of the same year, a month before President Nasser's death.[9]

From the beginning, the shah and the new Egyptian president, Anwar al-Sadat, had a friendship that was to last until the shah's death in Cairo in 1980. Sadat had decided to steer Egypt away from the Soviet Union, and in the Persian Gulf adopted a less aggressive posture toward Arab causes and a more accommodating stance toward Saudi Arabia and Iran. Sadat visited Tehran in 1971, en route to Moscow. The October War of 1973 further cemented Tehran's relation with Cairo. The shah allowed Soviet planes delivering supplies to Egypt to fly over Iranian territory. The Pahlavi regime also provided loans and grants worth billions of dollars to Egypt for a giant project involving reconstruction of Port Said, widening of the Suez Canal, and a number of joint industrial and agricultural projects.[10] Sadat's decision to make peace with Israel also received strong support from the shah. Thus, Mohammad Reza Pahlavi became the second foreign leader, after U.S. President Jimmy Carter, to express his unequivocal support for the Camp David Accords. Vice-President Hosni Mubarak traveled to Tehran to brief the shah on the accords.[11]

It is against this historical background that the Iranian Revolution took place, causing a radical shift in diplomacy and influencing the course of political events and intellectual trends in Egypt. In the following sections, we discuss the dynamics of such influence in political and intellectual fields in Egypt. We show that the Iranian Revolution both inspired many Egyptians in their desire for change and caused much anxiety among political elites. We conclude by arguing that Iran's influence has been at its height when the nation undertook social mobilization, engaged in democratic practice, and showed popular participation. In contrast, its political and intellectual impact was at its lowest when Iran was dominated by authoritarian rule, war, and repressive policies.

THE IRANIAN REVOLUTION AND EGYPT

The Iranian Revolution undoubtedly caused shock waves in a region ruled by hereditary monarchs or lifetime presidents, from the Persian Gulf to Iraq, Greater Syria, and North Africa. At the time that Iran's revolutionaries were marching in the streets, Egypt was going through a historic shake-up. President Sadat was in the midst of his unpopular policy change of breaking with

Nasserist legacies. Sadat had suspended the strategic alliance with the Soviet Union and become a close ally of the West, especially the United States. Internally, he had launched his Open Door policy, repressed the Nasserists and the Communists, and encouraged the Islamists. At the time that Iranians were shouting slogans against the U.S. and Israel, Sadat signed the Camp David Accords with Israel. For the average Egyptian, this political contrast was tremendous.

When the ruling clergy took over the state power in Iran, the government-controlled press in Egypt ran articles questioning the legitimacy of Iran's Islamic claims. Editorials in *al-Ahram,* Egypt's leading newspaper, criticized Ayatollah Khomeini's concept of Islamic justice by referring to the summary executions of the former shah's officials, advising Khomeini to "return to the teachings of the Quran and implement the principles of true Islam in Iran."[12] By that time the shah had fled Iran to Cairo, and Sadat had received him warmly as a head of state. Thus, in April 1979, Iran broke diplomatic relations with Egypt. Recriminations between Iranian and Egyptian leaders reached a high point in late 1979. In an interview, Sadat stated that he was "sad for the Islamic nation, because Khomeini's fever is beginning to catch onto some Moslem leaders. But I will not hesitate to fight this disease if it tries to creep into some souls here."[13]

Khomeini used similar language. In a meeting with Muhammad Haikal, Ayatollah Khomeini said that "the Egyptian nation is one thing, and Mr. Sadat is something else. How sad I am to see that a person who says he is the leader of an Islamic country sits at the same table as two persons who are both enemies of Islam, the Israeli regime, the United States."[14]

When Sadat offered the shah and his family political asylum in March 1980, relations between Cairo and Tehran reached the breaking point.[15] The Iranian regime called for the overthrow of the "lesser Satan," in the words of Ayatollah Sadeq Khalkhali, the "hanging judge," considering it an act of Islamic revolutionary justice. The Egyptian government in turn called the Islamic Republic "a false purveyor of Islam and hatred." Ayatollah Khalkhali called for the execution of Sadat by Egyptian Islamic militants.[16] After a long battle with lymphatic cancer, the shah died in Cairo's Maadi Military hospital. In his last minutes, the shah told his doctor to avoid extraordinary measures, saying "I am fed up with living artificially; I don't want to die like Tito."[17] Even though he wanted a simple funeral, Sadat insisted on full military honors. He is buried in the al-Rifa`i Mosque, where his father Reza Shah was entombed for several years during World War II.

It was not surprising then that, in such circumstances, the Iranian Revolution appeared to many Egyptians, notably the intellectuals, as a genuine response of a Muslim nation to imperialist aggression in the region. Many members of the intelligentsia looked toward Iran in search of solutions to their own national problems: how to deal with Sadat, and how to tackle the Israeli occupation of Arab lands and American support for it. This sentiment prevailed in all currents within the intellectual class. As an Egyptian author recalled, there was a special enthusiasm in the al-Ahram Center for Strategic Studies, Egypt's most prestigious think-tank, for what had happened in Iran.[18]

Left-wingers impressed by the mass mobilization in Iran began to offer analyses, but also sought ways to emulate the model. The Workers Communist Party, for example, offered various observations regarding the events in Iran, in mostly structuralist Marxian language. Iranian mass mobilization became a model couched in ideological language. At the same time, however, the very complex nature of events in Iran confused most Marxists. On the one hand, they could not escape observing the magnitude of a popular revolution that had toppled a repressive regime backed by the West. On the other, it was a religious leadership that brought the revolution to victory. For such secular Egyptian observers, this remained a theoretical dilemma. The question was whether to support or oppose the revolution. Thus, a search for a realistic understanding of the Iranian phenomenon continued.

Given government and al-Azhar censorship of literature on the Iranian Revolution in Egypt, many enthusiasts looked to Beirut, where a liberal publication atmosphere had allowed the appearance of a number of original works by Iranians in Arabic. Such publications as Abol Hasan Bani Sadr's *Oil and Domination* (*Naft va solteh*), Mehdi Bazargan's *The Boundaries Between Religion and Politics* (*Marz miyan-e din va siyasat*), and a number of the Tudeh Party's works (published by the newspapers *al-Safir* and *al-Nahar*) were smuggled to Egypt, where they offered some original insights into the thoughts of some of the revolutionary leaders.[19] In addition, Egyptian observers added their own interpretations of the revolutionary events in Iran. Works such as al-Sayyidd Zahra's *al-Thaura al-iraniya. al-Wajh al-ijtima`iya* (*The Iranian Revolution: The Social Aspects*), Fathi Abd al-Aziz's *Khumaini: al-Badil al-islami* (*Khomeini: The Islamic Alternative*), Muhammad al-Sa`id Abd al-Mu'min's *Mas'ala al-thaura al-islamiya* (*The Question of the Islamic Revolution*), and Muslim Brotherhood member Muhammad Abd al-Rahman Anbar's *Nahwa thaura islamiya* (*Toward an Islamic Revolution*) found their places in Cairo's bookshops.[20]

The dramatic turn of events in Iran in the early 1980s, including executions ordered by the revolutionary courts, hard-line vigilante violence against leftist and liberal forces, repression of the Kurdish autonomy movement, and the banishment and arrest of many revolutionaries and respected clerical figures such as Ayatollah Kazem Shari`atmadari, turned the early enthusiasm and jubilance of Egyptian secular intellectuals into confusion and disappointment. The nationalist leftist periodical *Ruz al-Yusuf* commented that Egyptians had supported the Iranian Revolution because one of its objectives was to remove Iran from under American domination. But, the weekly argued, the Islamic rulers had now resorted to a kind of dictatorship that was worse than the shah's.[21] It seemed the revolutionary repression by the Islamic regime had confirmed the early pessimism of such outstanding intellectual figures as Louis Awad, who had described the events in Iran as "terroristic."[22]

THE IRANIAN REVOLUTION AND EGYPTIAN ISLAMISM

While secular intellectuals could find comfort in their preconceived ideas by explaining that a "religious revolution" would eventually turn into a disaster, for Islamists it was an entirely different story. The Islamic Revolution, of course, did not generate Egyptian Islamism. Islamism in Egypt has its own dynamics. However, the Iranian Revolution had a significant effect on its momentum, direction, and expansion.

As the Pahlavi regime began to crumble in 1978, most Islamic groups in Egypt criticized officials expressing support for, or at least sympathy with, the shah of Iran. Successive invitations extended to the deposed monarch to reside in Egypt exacerbated differences between the state and the Egyptian Islamic opposition. Defending his decision to invite the shah, Sadat said that Egypt had "acted in this respect in accordance with its values and principles. The shah stood by Egypt before, during and after the October war." The shah had ordered oil tankers bound for Europe to immediately divert to Egypt and unload their cargo.[23]

Some Islamic political actors challenged the official argument that the help provided now to the shah was an expression of gratitude for the substantial supply of oil and military and economic assistance he gave to Egypt in 1973 and thereafter. Instead, they referred to the oil the shah had provided for Israel at the time of the 1973 oil embargo, and the close military and intelligence relations he had established with Israel.[24] Thus, there is no doubt that the Iranian Revolution gained the sympathy of many political Islamic groups in Egypt. Pictures of Ayatollah Khomeini appeared in Cairo and in some provincial cities, and demonstrations were organized against the arrival of the deposed shah in Egypt.[25]

For most Islamists, then, the revolution realized a long-awaited dream, following years of defeat and humiliation by the West and Israel. Like secularists, they also thought for the first time in many decades that it was possible to defeat a tyrant as well as the West. And this had happened under the banner of Islam. "Iran fulfilled our dream; Iranians are ruling themselves," an enthusiastic Safinaz Kazim announced to a British TV journalist.[26] The message of revolutionary Islam entered universities, nongovernmental mosques, and popular sentiment. For many Egyptians, Iran represented a solution, an alternative model, and a successful one at that. It was an Islamic state with institutions, rulers, ideology, and popular support. One of the main Islamist leaders in Egypt recalls the impact the Iranian events had on him:

> As an Islamist, I was so much interested in the Iranian Revolution. Not just me, but most Islamists in the world. In 1980 I was at a conference in Kuala Lumpur, Malaysia. For the first time, I listened to a representative of Iranian youth. Of course, that was the time when millions of people were demonstrating in the streets in Iran. From this I became very interested in the Iranian Revolution. So I followed the media about the events, the departure of the shah, the return of Ayatollah Khomeini, et cetera. And, of course, the U.S. hostage issue, the war with Iraq, et cetera. All of these showed that Iran was one of the hottest spots in the world. I read a number of books about Iran, like Huwaidi's *Iran min al-dakhil*, or articles by Mr. Haikal and Salim al-Awa, and interviews from abroad. But then, of course, I read a lot about changes [in the 1990s] in Iran too, especially during Mr. Rafsanjani's government. Actually, I think the changes really began with Mr. Rafsanjani.[27]

Each branch of the heterogeneous Islamist movement in Egypt looked at Iranian Islamism through its own prism. Fahmi Huwaidi, a prominent Islamist journalist, enthusiastically followed the events. He traveled many times to Iran, where he met with Ayatollah Khomeini, and wrote a best-selling book on his findings, *Iran min al-dakhil* (*Iran From Within*).[28] In his articles and books he offered a sympathetic picture of the revolution. Indeed, once Iran entered into war with an Arab nation, Iraq, he was at pains to defend Iran in its struggle against Saddam Hussein. He went even further, arguing for historic and cultural proximity between the Arabs and Iranians, exemplified in the flow of culture, language, and food—elements that he claimed hostile politicians did not see.[29]

On the other hand, for Hasan Hanafi, a prominent philosopher at Cairo University, the Iranian Revolution offered a concrete alternative project for Islam—an alternative that he, as a leftist-Islamist of the Ali Shari`ati type, had envisaged. To him, the revolution represented the leftist face of Islam.[30] In his attempts to introduce the model to the Egyptian public, he published

Ayatollah Khomeini's classic text, *al-Hukama al-islamiya* (*Islamic Government*). He also, in cooperation with Muhammad Auda and Ibrahim Shita Dissuqi, founded the journal *al-Yasar al-Islami* (*The Islamic Left*), in which they discussed the Iranian experience as a new model, a philosophy, a political alternative, and a new interpretation of progressive Islam. Although this publication ceased after only its first issue, nonetheless it reflected the heightened hope and enthusiasm of the Islamic left at the time. Egyptian militant groups were encouraged by the success of popular confrontation against the authorities in Iran. The resoluteness of leaders such as Ayatollah Khomeini surely inspired armed struggle against what the Egyptian Islamists considered the internal *jahili* state (a term originally applied to pre-Islamic Arabia). An early declaration of support came from the Islamic Students' Association of Cairo University. They stated that the spirit behind the revolution was like that in early Islam, when religion and politics were inseparable.[31]

Like others, the Muslim Brothers expressed jubilance concerning the Islamic Revolution, seeing it as a manifestation of Islam's triumph in a political struggle. A member boasted of the global impact of the revolution, claiming that it would "turn political theories and contemporary political forces on their heads."[32] For many in the movement, the Iranian Revolution revitalized fond memories of earlier ties between the Muslim Brothers and Iran's Fedayan-e Islam organization. In fact, shortly after Abdul Nasser's accession to power in 1952, pro-Muslim Brotherhood students in Egypt invited Navvab Safavi, the founder of the Fedayan (executed by the shah's regime in the 1950s), to participate in a conference organized by them at Cairo University. They held him on their shoulders and introduced him as an Islamic leader.[33] The initiative of the likes of Navvab Safavi had now paid off in the Islamic Revolution. The duty of Muslims, according to statements issued by the Muslim Brothers, was to support it. Indeed, the United States tried to use the spiritual leader of the Muslim Brothers, Umar al-Tilmisani, to mediate for the release of the American hostages in 1980, although this mediation, like many others, failed to bear fruit.

Nevertheless, as the revolution evolved, the Muslim Brotherhood took an ambivalent position towards Iran. The Iranian Revolution, although Islamic, had posed a challenge for the Brotherhood. First, Iran had entered into war with Iraq, an Arab nation (even if Saddam Hussein had taken the lead in its outbreak). It also had allied itself with Syrian President Hafiz al-Asad and his Ba`ath regime, the great enemy of the Syrian Muslim Brothers. Though successful as a Muslim uprising, Iran's revolution was also clearly inspired by Shi`i Islam. "Shi`ism is a kind of extremism," a Muslim Brother paper commented, echoing a widespread sentiment in the Sunni world.[34] Moreover, this successful revolutionary experiment was at odds with the gradualist strategy of the Muslim Brothers. It represented a radical interpretation of Islam, thus encouraging more radical Islamist groups at the expense of the Muslim Brotherhood. Finally, while until the 1980s it was the Muslim Brotherhood whose pan-Islamist ideology inspired other groups in different Muslim countries, after the revolution Iran began to be a model for those Muslims who waged opposition to their own internal rulers and their Western allies. In short, Iran had become not a great ally, but a formidable rival.

For its part, not only did al-Azhar (the great Islamic university and official religious establishment) share many similar concerns, it went further, criticizing Iranian rulers for instigating Islamist sentiments abroad as part of revolutionary Shi`i activism, a concern entirely shared by the Egyptian regime. Official anxiety over the "danger" of a Shi`i conspiracy in the Egyptian media was expressed in the late 1980s and mid-1990s, when the state claimed to have uncovered groups of Shi`i activists in Egypt (see below).

Despite or perhaps partly because of such reservations on the part of the religious authorities in Egypt, Iran's revolutionary experience contributed tremendously to popular religiosity and Islamic mood, sentiments, and sensibilities in people's daily lives in Egypt. From the very start, Iran considered the emergence of Islamism in Egypt as part of the totality of Islamic revivalism led by Iran. This was clear from Iran's strong condemnation of the Egyptian regime for persecuting Egypt's Islamist activists.

THE PERIOD OF AMBIVALENCE

However, before long, the early expression of popular jubilance over the Iranian revolution turned into a mood of confusion. The news of repression from Iran, the hostility of Egyptian religious authorities towards the Islamist leaders in Iran, especially after the assassination of President Sadat by the Islamist Jihad group, and Iran's growing emphasis on Shi`ism created an ambivalent mood among average Egyptians. This ambivalence was exacerbated by cultural and religious misunderstandings between average Iranians and Egyptians. In the early days of the revolution, Egyptians had little idea about Iran. They invariably viewed Shi`ism of whatever variety as some kind of extremism (*tatarruf*). Indeed, many Egyptians still consider Shi`is as having deviated from true Islam by placing Imam Ali above the Prophet Muhammad. Some Egyptians even go as far as establishing an etymological link between the terms *Shi`i* and *shiyu`i* (communist). Conversely, Iran's insularity and sense of superiority toward Arabs made the regime's avowed effort to close the gap with Sunnism largely a theoretical option. What contributed to this gap at this juncture was the escalation of the Iran-Iraq war, in which Egypt supported Iraq, as an Arab and a Muslim nation, in an attempt to return to the old pan-Arab mode that had been virtually lost in the frenzy of the Camp David accords. The sympathy for Iran's revolutionary fervor started to subside.

For over a decade, from the early 1980s until the early 1990s, at the height of Egyptian Islamism, a mood of ambivalence and confusion emerged in Egypt. Iran began to fade from the public discourse. The Islamists, torn between Arab and Islamic solidarity, were unsure how to position themselves vis-à-vis the Iran-Iraq war and the increasingly friendly relations between Tehran and Damascus. Faced with an increasingly nationalist tone coming out of Iran and unable to ignore the revolutionary excesses, they chose to minimize their coverage of Iran, until they themselves were silenced by Sadat's 1981 crackdown on the Islamist press.[35] The Egyptian regime and the state-controlled media, in turn, never enamored of Iran's radical transformation, mostly continued to ignore Iran, except occasionally to highlight the oppressive nature of the regime. There was little for Egyptians to note about Iran except for some scattered reports about the Iran-Iraq war, the clash among the Islamic rulers, and accounts of political repression relayed by Iranian opposition groups in Europe. The country almost vanished from the Egyptian popular memory in this decade. Diplomacy ceased, trade ebbed, and cultural and intellectual exchanges almost disappeared.

What remained from Iran were the defunct Iran-Misr Bank, the almost deceased Bank Saderat of Iran, and a few other joint ventures, such as the Misr-Iran Shipping Company and a Suez textile plant. The old glory of a few carpet shops had faded under the dusty "Persian Carpets" signs. Indeed, there hardly remained any really Iranian merchandise. Streets named after Mosaddeq and Iran, and Pahlavi Square, in Cairo's Dokki district, did linger on. But they meant little to passers-by who were caught, perplexed, between the initial inspiration of an Islamic Revolution and subsequent images of "bloodbath," mass execution, and the brutality of the war with "Arab brothers." Only the Maidan Pahlavi was to assume political significance, later, in 2000, as a counterpoint to the Egyptian protest over Khalid Islambuli Street in Tehran, named after the assassin of Anwar Sadat. Even the corpse of the shah, buried in a lonely corner of the al-Rifa`i Mosque in Cairo, only added to the ambivalence in the Egyptian popular consciousness. In sum, this dim picture stood in stark contrast to the decade of the 1930s, when a vigorous Iranian community resided in Cairo, leaving its mark on social, commercial, and intellectual life.

Egypt's state-run media rarely conveyed an in-depth picture of Islamist

Iran. Real news, photos, and footage of Iranian leaders rarely appeared in print media or on TV screens. The transmission of mere words, then, left the actual picturing of events to the imagination of the average Egyptian. Few Iranians traveled to or, for that matter, lived in Egypt in these times.

Persian language and literature remained a major discipline in a dozen Egyptian universities, giving jobs to some tens of Egyptian professors. However, the dull, run-down, and silent hallways of Persian Studies programs spoke of bygone days. Many enthusiasts of Persian language could not find modern Persian texts to read, let alone follow events in Iran.

During the 1980s, there were some 150 mostly half-Iranian families, almost all coming from Western countries, working in international firms or UN agencies. They would gather together, organize gatherings, and reminisce, in the manner of exiled groups, about their fun times in the country that they saw being destroyed by the ravages of the Islamic Revolution and a seemingly endless war with Iraq. They would celebrate Nauruz, worry about their home country, and revive their national pride and identity by criticizing their host nation, Egypt, ranting and raving about its poverty, poor sanitation, and urban chaos. Chances for a meaningful relationship between this community and their Egyptian counterparts, then, remained feeble. Theirs was an expatriate Western life style. The main threads which linked such Iranians to their Egyptian upper-class counterparts were the stories of the failed marriage of the shah and Fuziyeh, and a common nostalgia for each other's old, pre-Islamic civilizations. The knowledge in the Iranian community of Egyptian culture did not go beyond some impressionistic observations. In turn, few Egyptians learned anything about Iran from this tiny community. In the experience of one of the authors, almost no Egyptian would guess, nor often believe, his (Asef Bayat's) Iranian origin. The image of an Iranian man was still one of a bearded, rough, and violent-looking *Pasdar* (Revolutionary Guard).

The more isolated Iran became internationally and the further it sank into the war with Saddam Hussein, the better Egypt's position in the region's political and economic scenes became. The war allowed Egypt to improve its position among the Arab countries in the Persian Gulf, which had suspended ties with Cairo following the Camp David Accords with Israel. In November 1987, the United Arab Emirates (U.A.E.) restored diplomatic relations with Egypt. Improved relations with other Arab countries followed, culminating in Egypt's readmission to the Arab League in May 1989. This was followed by the reestablishment of League headquarters in Cairo, and the leading role Mubarak played in gathering Arab support against Iraq's invasion of Kuwait in July 1990. The general belief that Iran was a major threat to Arab regimes in the Persian Gulf and beyond, and the fact that President Mubarak had distanced himself from Sadat's denunciations of other Arabs, made a rapprochement with the rest of the Arab world possible. By the time Syria renewed diplomatic relations with Egypt in May 1990, all Arab countries had reestablished diplomatic relations with Egypt.

In the economic domain, the U.A.E. increased trade with Egypt, from zero before Camp David was signed to over $30 million in 1986. Saudi Arabia's imports from Egypt rose from under $50 million in 1979 to over $80 million in 1985. Saudi exports to Egypt increased from about $40 million in 1979 to close to $250 million in 1984. Exports from Egypt to Kuwait showed a slight drop in 1978–1980, but by 1981 had already started increasing. There was a significant drop in imports from Kuwait to Egypt from 1978 to 1982, but between 1982 and 1985 they surged from about $10 million to about $90 million. In the meantime, Egypt replaced Iran as the main supplier of oil to Israel. From 1984 to 1987, Egypt supplied an average of 25 percent of Israel's oil import needs, reaching 43 percent in 1986.[36]

THE GRADUAL RETURN OF AN IMPROVED IMAGE

With the death of Ayatollah Khomeini, the end of the war with Iraq, and the beginning of postwar reconstruction under President Akbar Hashemi Rafsanjani (1989–1997), a new era began to unfold in Iran. In pursuit of reconstruction, the pragmatic president formed a technocratic cabinet, attempted to open up the economy, eased up foreign trade, pursued urban renewal, and went on to repair international relations.

The impact of such internal changes, on Egypt as much as on other countries, began to surface before long. The Iranian regime toned down its statements on the Egyptian government's crackdown on Islamist groups. In 1989, the Egyptian authorities claimed that they had arrested a group of forty-one persons considered to be the nucleus of a secret Shi`i movement alleged to have been formed when four Sunni militants converted to the Shi`i faith. They were charged with plotting to overthrow the Mubarak regime.[37] The fear of a Shi`i conspiracy exploded later, in October 1996, when the state security forces claimed to have discovered an organized Shi`i group displaying their literature and a portrait of Imam Ali. Shaikh Hasan Muhammad Shita, the preacher of a Giza mosque, was detained in this connection. The group of fifty-six Egyptians were allegedly seeking to propagate an Iranian-style revolution in Egypt.[38] Iranian authorities did not deny the fact that some members of the Egyptian Shi`i community had traveled to Iran, but commented that "from the viewpoint of the Egyptian rulers the exchange of ideas and meetings between different Muslim groups is against the law and considered as anti-state activities. The fact is that communications between Muslims is quite usual and natural and no person in his sound state of mind can accuse Muslims of subversive activities just because they pay a visit to another Muslim country or because they meet with Shi`i leaders."[39] While the Egyptian government intensified its crackdown on Islamists, Iran continued to make overtures to Egypt. Prior to Iranian foreign minister Ali Akbar Velayati's visit to Cairo in 1994 for the foreign ministers' meeting of the Islamic Conference, Iran communicated a message to Cairo stating that Tehran respected the authority of al-Azhar over Sunni Muslims and would refrain from criticizing Egypt peace policy towards Israel. It also stated that it would discourage Islamic radicals in Lebanon from backing Egyptian radical Islamist groups.[40] Especially significant was Iran's coordinated position with Egypt during the 1994 International Conference on Population and Development (ICPD), to which Iran sent a high-ranking Ayatollah, Ali Taskhiri, chief of the president's international affairs office and Head of the Islamic Propagation Organization. Taskhiri met a few times with Egyptian officials and visited al-Azhar.

The absence of revolutionary rhetoric from Tehran eventually changed the atmosphere and led to an increase in trade between the two countries. The defunct Iran-Egypt Bank resumed operation. Both countries began exploring avenues for cooperation in the fields of construction materials, industrial machinery, automotives, heavy industries, petrochemicals, and foodstuffs. In December 1994, Egypt and Iran reached an agreement to settle $149 million of Egyptian debt owed to Iran. The original debt was $283 million, but Iran agreed to reduce it in order "to create a favorable atmosphere for better economic and commercial relations." Egypt agreed to pay off the debt by constructing a number of sugar factories in Khuzestan province, in southern Iran.[41] Moreover, Iran and Egypt agreed to resume the activities of a joint Iran-Egypt textile company and an Iran-Egypt shipping line. Iran owns 49 percent of the latter company, which is situated in the Suez area and chaired by an influential Egyptian senator, Abd al-Hakim Hujjaj.[42] By the end of Rafsanjani's presidency, bilateral trade between Iran and Egypt was reported to be around $80 million.[43]

The impact of Rafsanjani's pragmatic approach could also be seen in Egyptian foreign policy in the Persian Gulf. Egypt, Syria, and the six members of the Gulf Cooperation Council (GCC) signed a security pact in Damascus in March 1991 calling for the creation of a pan-Arab peacekeeping force, with Egypt and Syria playing the leading roles. According to the pact, known as the Damascus Declaration, a peacekeeping force was envisioned for the Gulf to help protect the area from any possible aggression. The U.A.E. wanted Egypt to lead an Arab military intervention in the territorial dispute between the

U.A.E. and Iran. However, since Iran had promised not to encourage Islamic fundamentalist groups, Egypt reciprocated by not becoming militarily involved in the dispute between the U.A.E. and Iran. Usama al-Baz, top political advisor to President Mubarak, stated that "the situation there [in the Gulf] does not call at all for the adoption of any military steps. There is plenty of opportunity for political contacts and diplomacy."[44]

But domestic opposition to a full normalization of relations with Egypt was still strong in Iran. The daily *Resalat*, a conservative paper, argued that "given the fact that Egypt is still a lackey of Zionism, it is not clear why the future of relations between Tehran and Cairo, the two opposite poles of faith and blasphemy, resistance and compromise, have become a topic of discussion in political circles of the region."[45] In May 1993, a group of Tehran University students rallied at the university campus in a protest directed at the foreign ministry for normalizing ties with Egypt and Saudi Arabia. Nevertheless, Rafsanjani's government maintained the level of political dialogue and economic cooperation until his successor, Mohammad Khatami, took over in 1997. Since then, Iran has continued to distance itself from overt support for armed Muslim militants in Algeria, Egypt, and elsewhere.

ONCE AGAIN, IRAN AS A MODEL

The outcome of the presidential elections of 1997 in Iran, a resounding victory for a reformist cleric named Mohammad Khatami, was a watershed in Iran's return to the international scene, in particular in the Arab world. A moderate and not-well-known clergyman ousted the hard-line candidate, Ali Akbar Nateq-Nuri, who enjoyed the support of the conservative establishment. This heralded the onset of the "Khatami Era." In the course of three years, Khatami and his team have managed to popularize significant concepts that would shake the conservative power holders, emphasizing civil society, rule of law, tolerance, pluralism, and freedom of expression. Internationally, Khatami opted for rapidly improving relations with other nations based upon mutual respect and the "dialogue of civilizations."

These concepts spread in Iranian society, framing the ideological foundation of the "reform movement," which in turn pushed for policy and institutional changes in the country. To the dismay of conservatives, the reformist executive unleashed an unprecedented free press, civil-society organizations, and some cultural openness. The reformists captured a majority in the 1999 municipal elections and won over two hundred seats in the 290-seat parliament in the February 2000 elections. These electoral victories projected a new, intellectually vibrant, socially active, and democratic image of Iran abroad, especially in the Middle East. As "isms," such as pan-Arabism, Nasserism, Ba`athism, and fundamentalism have begun to vanish or lose luster, the phrase "Islamic reformation" has now been introduced. Perhaps of greatest importance is that the Iranian democratization is likely to have an impact on surrounding Islamic states, inspiring groups calling for political change in those countries to speak out more forcefully. Indeed, if successful, the Iranian democratization could have an impact on the region similar to that its revolution did some twenty years ago.

In regional diplomacy, Khatami's presidency coincided with the eighth meeting of the Organization of Islamic Countries (OIC) in Tehran in December 1997, the largest gathering of Islamic leaders in Tehran since the 1979 revolution. The timing was very providential for Iran. With a new, popularly elected president, Iran was uniquely situated to capitalize on the deep frustration felt by Arabs and Muslims at the intransigent policies of Israeli Prime Minister Benjamin Netanyahu, as well as Washington's failure to pursue a balanced strategy in Middle East peacemaking. The pro-American regimes of Egypt and Saudi Arabia, long hostile to revolutionary Iran, shunned invitations to attend a U.S.-backed regional economic conference that Israel attended in Qatar. Instead, both decided to go to Tehran along with other ostensible Arab allies of the United States.

Prior to the conference, Khatami's government embarked on an assertive campaign of diplomacy to prepare the groundwork for a successful conference. Iran Air resumed its flights between Iran and Saudi Arabia, while Iran attended a large trade fair in Jiddah, Saudi Arabia. Iraq subsequently opened its border to Iranian pilgrims, and, within days of Khatami's election, Cairo radio quoted Egyptian foreign minister Amr Musa as saying that Egypt was "looking to improve relations" with the Islamic Republic in light of the actions of Khatami, who had made a similar statement.[46] In short, the OIC changed the political language between the two countries. Accusations of treason and betrayal traded by Iranian officials and their Egyptian counterparts over the prior twenty years were now replaced with words of praise and an expression by both sides of a serious desire to mend ties. Egyptian dailies praised Iran's great efforts to ensure good preparations for the Islamic summit, stressing that Iran's success with this summit "helped it emerge from twenty years of isolation." They also hailed Iran for its new moderate course, which they saw contributing to the stability of the region.[47] For its part, the Iranian press also began to open a public debate on Egypt. For the first time since 1979, a daily asked, if the Islamic Republic could improve its relations with Saudi Arabia, what was keeping it from doing the same with Egypt?[48]

These events were followed by the first media delegations from Egypt and

Iran to visit Tehran and Cairo, respectively, in October and November 1999. In December 1999, Egyptian Minister of Information Muhammad Safwat al-Sharif traveled to Tehran to attend the Fifth Islamic Conference of Information Ministers (ICIM-5). In the meeting, President Khatami emphasized that the exchange of visits by Iranian and Egyptian officials, irrespective of differences of opinion and political stances, was beneficial to the region and the world of Islam.[49] As a further gesture of goodwill to the Egyptians, on January 4, 2000, a group of Iranian reformists formed an NGO to lobby for better relations with Egypt. The Iran-Egypt Friendship Society is headed by a prominent journalist, Ali Hekmat, and is supported by President Khatami. Although the Society was bitterly denounced by some hard-liners,[50] resulting in an attack on the headquarters of the Society, moves to normalize Iran-Egypt relations continued nonetheless.

These developments began to create a new image of Iran in the popular consciousness of Egyptians. Once again, a positive picture of Iran returned in the popular media. The era of confusion has given way to a time when Iranians are seen as "people who have found their way in this turbulent region." Iranian youth are praised as conscious agents, combatant and cultured.[51] Nothing better reflects this expression of admiration for Iranians than the ecstasy with which Egyptians cheered for Iran's team in its competition against the U.S. in the World Cup in 1998.[52]

The Iranian parliamentary elections of February 2000, resulting in a landslide victory for the reform candidates, were a turning point in Iran's new image. Iran became a new "model of democracy" in the Muslim Middle East. "After two decades as a source for inspiration for Islamic militants," the *Washington Post* reported, "Iran has become an example of political reform in the Middle East, prompting democratic activists and commentators in the generally less pluralistic Arab world to look east and wonder: What about us?"[53] This is true in a region where elections, if they take place at all, are usually little more than a pretext and rarely oust those in power. In contrast to Iran, the Arab world's political landscape has been at a standstill for decades, featuring monarchies with absolute rulers or republics with authoritarian presidents and pseudodemocracies. The Iranian experience is worrisome to these rulers because it provides an example of a society where change comes from the ballot box instead of through military coups.[54]

Governments in the region officially expressed satisfaction about the direction Iran was taking, in part because they see a decline in its extremism. Yet in reality they are worried that the consequences of the democratic change in Iran might undermine their own legitimacy. "Instead of Islamic revolution," the Egyptian newspaper *al-Wafd* warned, "this time Iran exports the idea of free elections."[55] An Egyptian writer, Wahid Abd al-Maguid, underscored the impact of the Khatami experiment by saying that "we in the Arab world have such a hunger for democracy that we are like a man starving to death who goes to the market. He eats anything in the belief it is good food, though it may not be."[56]

The timing of Iran's parliamentary elections was unfortunate for Egypt, where the compliant Majlis al-Sha`b (People's Assembly) had just extended the Emergency Law, then in effect for the last twenty years, for another three years. The law effectively restricts free expression and assembly, and renders detention without trial a routine procedure. The Assembly passed the law after one hour of debate. President Mubarak's congratulatory telegram to Khatami notwithstanding, he seemed to avoid this embarrassing situation by flying to Beirut to express support for the Lebanese people, including the Shi`i Hizbullah, in their struggle against the Israeli occupation of south Lebanon.

This happened against a background of unprecedented coverage of Iran, with extensive commentaries, photos, and footage in most Egyptian papers and on national television. For weeks, Iran's parliamentary elections were the talk of the town among politicians, journalists, intellectuals, and many students in the college corridors. Liberals, nationalists, and Islamists alike applauded the outcome. Although there were some who dismissed the event as "not really democratic," since no one from "outside the system" was allowed to participate,[57] nonetheless many acknowledged that Iran was a "regional power" that "we cannot afford to ignore." Whatever happens in Iran will affect Egypt, an *al-Ahram* commentator noted.[58] Significantly, Iran once again became a reference point, a "model," and a "lesson." Reflecting on the Iranian reform movement's major concern, "political development" (as opposed to the usual "economic development"), Salama Ahmad Salama argued that Egypt should follow similar policies as Iran. "It is no longer possible to argue," he said, "that economic reform must take precedence over democratization, to claim that there are no political parties capable of competing at the polls, or to exaggerate domestic problems or terrorist threats as a pretext for avoiding political change. Iran today seems far more advanced than many Arab and Islamic countries," he concluded.[59]

"Iran's model," another observer advocated, "can be and should be emulated by all Arab and Islamic nations."[60] To many, this experience pointed not only to the fact that ordinary people can cause significant political change, but also that Islam can embrace democracy. *Al-Azhar* was particularly emphatic on this latter point, despite its suspicions about Iran's Shi`i influence and support for militant Islamism. This "fusion of religious values and democratic principles" represents what Khatami describes as "Iran's innovation." A commentary in *Saut al-Azhar*, reflecting on the significance of this innovation, compared it with Britain's experience of "combining democracy with Christianity," although no one, the commentator argued, calls that system a religious state or theocracy. The reverberations of Iran's experience, the paper further suggested, would go beyond Iran to influence other Muslim countries, from Turkey to Egypt to Indonesia.[61]

The reform movement in Iran has generated a more active and diverse exchange between Iran and Egypt. The number of Iranians visiting Egypt has increased considerably and the number of those living in the country rose to some five hundred families. Once again, programs in Iranian Studies and Persian Language and Literature have been revitalized, with currently some one hundred professors specialized in these fields. Many Egyptian businessmen, intellectuals, and officials have visited Iran, attended workshops and conferences, and returned with positive impressions, often expressing a sense of surprise. Interest in Iran, its democratic readings of Islam, new politics, and culture, has been reinvigorated. Egyptian Muslim women have expressed their eagerness to learn from the experience of Iran's "Islamic feminism."[62] Professional workshops and conferences have been held to discuss the changes in Iran. A number of books on and by President Muhammad Khatami and other personalities are in Cairo's bookshops.[63] Currently, the Egyptian Iran-Egypt Friendship Society is waiting for an official permit. According to an Iranian foreign ministry official in charge of policy for Arab countries, "Iran's relations with Egypt are improving rapidly."[64]

CONCLUSION

When the revolutionaries swept to power in Iran in 1979, Arab rulers in neighboring states feared the success of Tehran's brand of radical Islam as a dangerous example for the region. Twenty-one years later, a new democratic wind is blowing out of Iran, and many of Iran's neighbors are just as fearful. In this article, we have discussed the impact of revolutionary Iran on Egypt since the revolution of 1979 by exploring some of the major intellectual, cultural, and political influences Islamist Iran has had on this ancient nation. Our analysis supports the conclusions drawn by Rudi Matthee and Shahrough Akhavi that the Iranian revolution did not generate Egypt's Islamism.[65] The Islamist movement in Egypt had its own internal causes and followed its own dynamics. However, the revolutionary developments in Iran contributed to an increasing mood of religiosity in Egypt and legitimized the activism of the Islamists, in particular their anti-Western perspectives.

The doctrinal shift currently underway among Islamist movements in general, to which the new changes in Iran have contributed, is likely to influence Egyptian Islamism. Some evidence already points to disarray in the Egyptian Islamist movement. The crisis has in part to do with state repression, and is in part a matter of internal strategy. Some factions are undertaking new ways of thinking about the notion of Islamic politics and its strategic objectives. The Hizb al-Wasat may represent the organizational form of such a revisionist trend in Egyptian Islamism.

On the other hand, the experience of relatively free elections in Iran, where an opposition actually took power, has made the Egyptian opposition bolder in demanding "clean elections." It was these calls and concerns that led opposition groups to form a committee in April 2000 to work together with the government to ensure clean, free, and fair elections for the Majlis al-Sha'b in November 2000. Yet what promised at first to be the fairest election since 1952 turned sour in the final stage.[66] It has also forced the Egyptian regime to pay more lip service to democracy and the rule of law. A review of Iran's presence in Egyptian popular imagery makes one thing very clear. In the past twenty turbulent years of Iranian-Egyptian political and intellectual relations, Iran's influence has been at its height when it experienced an increase in popular mobilization, democracy, the rule of law, and popular participation (that is, at the time of the revolution in 1979 and, currently, during a period of increased democracy and an active reform movement). Iran's impact reached its nadir when the country went through authoritarian rule, war, and repressive policies.

NOTES

We thank Rudi Matthee for his assistance with the paper and especially for the German sources he suggested.

1. The periodicals included *Sorayya, Parvaresh, Hekmat,* and, most importantly, *Chehrenema.* On the Iranian community in Cairo see Mohammad Yadegari, "The Iranian Settlement in Egypt as Seen Through the Pages of the Community Paper *Chihrinima* (1904–1966)," *Middle Eastern Studies* 16 (1980): 98–114.

2. See "Sahwat al-Sharq" and "Kusra wa Ramsis," in *Misr wa Iran. Al-Kalamat wa al-qasa'id alati ulqiyat fi haflat al-adabiya al-kubra alati aqamaha al-ittihad . . . Ibtihajan bi al-musahara al-malakiya al-sa`ida,* ed. Ittihad udaba al-Iskandariya (Alexandria: Matba`a al-faruqiya, 1939), 23–29. Also see Adel Sabit and Majed Farag, *The Imperial Wedding: Royal Albums of Egypt* (Cairo: Max Group, 1993).

3. Rainer Brunner, *Annäherung und Distanz Schia, Azhar und die islamische Ökumene im 20. Jahrhundert* (Berlin: Klaus Schwarz, 1996), 87.

4. Ibid., 225–32. Even Shaltut's fatwa was not free from political overtones, com-

ing as it did after the coup in Iraq and a call for support from the beleaguered Shi`i ulama in that country. See ibid., 236.

5. R. K. Ramazani, *The Foreign Policy of Iran: A Developing Nation in World Affairs, 1500–1941* (Charlottesville: University Press of Virginia, 1975), 102; Shahram Chubin and S. Zabih, *The Foreign Relations of Iran: A Developing State in a Zone of Great-Power Conflict* (Berkeley: University of California Press, 1974), 156.

6. Chubin and Zabih, *The Foreign Relations of Iran,* 157.

7. As Brunner, *Annäherung und Distanz,* 238, notes, Iran had had unofficial relations with Israel since the early 1950s.

8. *Tehran Journal,* 9 March 1965.

9. For a good analysis of Egypt under Nasser, see Raymond William Baker, *Egypt's Uncertain Revolution Under Nasser and Sadat* (Cambridge, MA: Harvard University Press, 1978).

10. R. K. Ramazani, *Revolutionary Iran: Challenge and Response in the Middle East* (Baltimore: Johns Hopkins University Press, 1986), 163.

11. *Al Ahram,* 24 Oct. 1978.

12. Ibid., 11 May 1979.

13. Associated Press (AP), 25 Dec. 1979.

14. Tehran Radio, 19 Dec. 1979, translated and rebroadcast by the BBC *Summary of World Broadcasts,* 21 Dec. 1979.

15. AP, 24 March 1980.

16. *The New York Times,* 25 March 1980. The fact that Sadat offered the United States use of Egyptian military facilities, if it wanted to make another attempt to rescue the American hostages in Tehran, provoked more harsh statements from Iran.

17. *Newsweek,* 11 Aug. 1980.

18. Interview with Nabil Abd al-Fattah, a prominent Egyptian writer to whom we are indebted for offering his insights on the Egyptian intellectual scene during the Iranian Revolution of 1979. Interview with Asef Bayat, Cairo, 24 April 2000.

19. Abol Hasan Bani Sadr, *Naft va solteh* (Beirut: Dar al-kalima li al-nashr, 1980); and Mehdi Bazargan, *Marz miyan-e din va siyasat* (Tehran: n.p., n.d.).

20. al-Sayyid Zahra, *al-Thaura al-iraniya. al-Wajh al-ijtima`iya* (Cairo: al-Ahram Strategic Studies Center, 1980); Fathi Abd al-Aziz, *Khumaini: al-Badil al-islami* (Cairo: Dar al-i`tisam, 1979); Muhammad al-Sa`id Abd al-Mu'min, *Mas'ala al-thaura al-islamiya* (Cairo: n.p., 1981); Muhammad Abd al-Rahman Anbar, *Nahwa thaura islamiya* (Cairo: Matba`a abirin, 1979).

21. Cited in Shahrough Akhavi, "The Impact of the Iranian Revolution on Egypt," in *The Iranian Revolution: Its Global Impact,* ed. John Esposito (Miami: Florida International University Press, 1990), 149.

22. Interview with Nabil Abd al-Fattah of the al-Ahram Center for Strategic Studies, Cairo, 24 April 2000.

23. Cairo Home Service, 27 Feb. 1979, BBC *Summary of World Broadcasts: The Middle East and Africa,* 1 March 1979.

24. Maridi Nahhas, "State Systems and Revolutionary Challenges: Nasir, Khomeini, and the Middle East," *International Journal of Middle East Studies* 17 (1985): 521.

25. See Salih al-Wirdani, *al-Haraka al-islamiya fi Misr; ru'ya waqi`iya li al-hiqbat al-saba`inat* (Cairo: al-Bidaya Publishing House, 1986), 197–202; and Henry Munson, Jr., *Islam and Revolution in the Middle East* (New Haven: Yale University Press, 1988), 135.

26. Cited in the British documentary, "The Sword of Islam," Channel 4, 1996.

27. Asef Bayat's interview with Abu al-Ala`a Madi, the leader of Hizb al-Wasat, Cairo, March 2000.

28. For an analysis of Huwaidi's views on Iran, see Wilfried Buchta, *Die iranische Schia und die islamische Einheit 1979–1996* (Hamburg: Deutsches Orient-Institut, 1997), 234–42. See also Rudi Matthee, review of *Iran min al-dakhil, Iranian Studies* 22 (1989): 12–14.

29. Fahmi Huwaidi, *al-Arab wa Iran. Wahm al-sira wa hamm al-wifaq* (Cairo: Dar al-shuruq, 1991).

30. Hasan Hanafi, "The Relevance of the Islamic Alternative in Egypt," *Arab Studies Quarterly* 4 (1982): 54–74.

31. Cited in Akhavi, "Impact of the Iranian Revolution," 141.

32. Muhammad Abd al-Rahman Anbar, quoted in ibid., 145.

33. Tariq al-Bishri, *al-Haraka al-siyasiya fi Misr 1945–1952*, 2nd ed. (Cairo: Dar al-shuruq, 1991); Abd Allah Imam, *Abd al-Nasir wa al-Ikhwan al-Muslimun* (Cairo: al-Mawaqif al-arabi, 1983), 60, 174.

34. In *al-Liwa al-Islami*, 27 Aug. 1987, cited in Johannes Jansen, "Echoes of the Iranian Revolution in the Writings of Egyptian Muslims," in *The Iranian Revolution and the Muslim World*, ed. David Menashri (Boulder, CO: Westview, 1990), 214.

35. For this, see Rudi Matthee, "The Egyptian Opposition on the Iranian Revolution," in *Shi`ism and Social Protest*, ed. Juan R. I. Cole and Nikki R. Keddie (New Haven: Yale University Press, 1986), 264–65.

36. Paul Sullivan, "Contrary Views of Economic Diplomacy in the Arab World: Egypt," *Arab Studies Quarterly* 21 (1991): 14, 29, 65.

37. Akhavi, "Impact of the Iranian Revolution," 143.

38. *Al-Ahram Weekly*, 24–30 Oct. 1996.

39. Voice of the Islamic Republic of Iran external service, Tehran, BBC *Summary of World Broadcasts*, 23 Oct. 1996.

40. *The Independent*, 23 July 1990.

41. *Iran News*, 5 Dec. 1994.

42. "Iran, Egypt, two cradles of human civilization approach each other," *Iran Commerce* 5, no. 2 (Summer 1998): 32–37.

43. Ibid. By this time, Iran had overtaken Saudi Arabia as the biggest user of Egypt's Suez-Mediterranean (Sumed) pipeline to significantly boost its oil sales to the European market. Islamic Republic News Agency (IRNA), 8 May 1996.

44. AP, 22 Sept. 1992.

45. *Resalat*, 22 July 1992.

46. IRNA, 29 May 1997.

47. Middle East News Agency, Cairo, BBC *Summary of World Broadcasts*, 10 Dec. 1997.

48. *Neshat*, 6 June 1999.

49. IRNA, 1 Dec. 1999.

50. See the editorial in *Jomhuri-ye Eslami*, 5 Jan. 2000.

51. These phrases are from a Cairo taxi driver during Asef Bayat's discussion with him in May 2000.

52. For the first time in twenty-one years, Egypt's national soccer team traveled to Tehran in early June 2000, and won a match against Iran. Later, an official of the Egyptian team said that "we hope this friendly match can strengthen the relations

between the two Muslim countries and act like the Ping-Pong diplomacy that finally ended the hostility between China and the U.S.," *Gulf News,* 11 June 2000.

53. Howard Schneider, "Democracy in Iran Prompts Arab Introspection," *The Washington Post,* 11 March 2000.

54. Farid al-Khazin, a political scientist at the American University of Beirut, Lebanon, predicts that Arab leaders who may have been toying with the idea of holding free elections will decide not to, in view of the outcome of Iran's elections. Quoted by Associated Press, 8 April 2000.

55. *Al-Wafd,* 4 March 2000.

56. Salama Ahmad Salama, *al-Ahram Weekly,* 2–8 March 2000.

57. See the commentary by Abduh Mubashir in *al-Ahram,* 5 March 2000.

58. Salah al-Din Hafiz, "Nahnu wa Iran. Hal tataghayyara qawa`id al-la`ba?" *al-Ahram,* 8 March 2000.

59. Salama Ahmad Salama in *al-Ahram Weekly,* 2–8 March 2000.

60. Muhammad Ali Shita, "Dars min Iran," *al-Wafd,* 5 April 2000.

61. *Saut al-Azhar,* 25 Feb. 2000.

62. The Egyptian Muslim feminist Heba Ra`uf, for instance, on a number of occasions expressed a strong interest in learning about Iran's Muslim feminist movement.

63. Muhammad Khatami, *al-Din wa al-turath wa al-hadara wa al-tanmiya wa al-hurriya* (Cairo: Dar nahdat Misr, 1999).

64. IRNA, 13 May 2000.

65. Matthee, "The Egyptian Opposition"; Akhavi, "The Impact of the Iranian Revolution."

66. Many polling stations in several governorates were sealed off by police forces to prevent the supporters of NDP rivals from voting. At the industrial suburb of Shubra al-Khaima, in the north of Greater Cairo, one person was killed and thirty people were wounded in clashes with police who prevented them from voting. At Ma`adi-Bassatin, south of Cairo, security forces prevented voters from casting ballots for the Brotherhood's candidate, Abd al-Fattah Rizq, who ran against Muhammad al-Murshidi, an NDP sympathizer. Many of Rizq's supporters were arrested. Nevertheless, in spite of numerous violations, 17 (out of 442) pro-Brotherhood candidates managed to get elected, making them the largest opposition bloc in the Assembly. See *al-Ahram Weekly,* 16–22 Nov. 2000; 13–20 Dec. 2000.

14 / The Iranian Revolution and Changes in Islamism in Pakistan, India, and Afghanistan

VALI NASR

The Iranian revolution of 1979 had a profound impact on the role of Islam in politics and society in South Asia and Afghanistan. The nature and scope of this impact changed over time. Initially, the revolution influenced mainstream Islamist thinking and activism. In time, the influence of the revolution on Islamism declined, but its impact on Shi`a activism became more pronounced. As the revolution came to be seen as a Shi`a phenomenon, it helped fan the flames of sectarian conflict and violence, thus polarizing Islamism and Muslim society in India and Pakistan. This development was accelerated first by regional rivalries between Iran, Iraq, and Saudi Arabia, and later by the Afghan war and the advent of the Taliban.

The Iranian Revolution of 1979 was a watershed event in the relation between Islam and politics. In the years immediately following the fall of the Pahlavi regime in Iran, the prospect of similar revolutionary change animated politics across the Muslim world. The revolution intensified Islamic activism as it invigorated Islamist challenges to the authority of secular states, and inspired new ways of thinking about legitimacy, authority, and the conduct of politics.[1] Although Islamism (also called political Islam, Islamic fundamentalism or Islamic revivalism), an interpretation of Islam that emphasizes a narrow reading of Islamic law and predicates salvation on gaining control of political power, was a force in South Asian politics long before the Iranian Revolution, still, the events of 1979 in Iran had a profound impact on the relation between religion and politics in that region.

The Iranian Revolution was at first a model for antistate activism. It encouraged a social revolution, rooted among radical youth and the disenfranchised, organized around an Islamic ideology. Where there existed Shi`a minorities, the revolution also served as a model for mobilizing the minority against the majority. Sunni opposition to the state was thus complemented with the minority Shi`a's drive for power. The interaction of these mobilizational drives produced new political dynamics that today stand as the revolution's legacy. Nowhere is this more evident than in South Asia.

Since the turn of the century, Islamism in South Asia (Bangladesh, India, and Pakistan) has produced broad-based social movements that have helped change the map of the region and define the structure of political authority there, as well as providing ideological perspectives that have been influential beyond the boundaries of South Asia.[2] The Iranian Revolution both strengthened existing Islamist tendencies and redirected their energies toward goals articulated in the Iranian Revolution that had not hitherto featured prominently in South Asian Islamist discourse. The revolution thus transformed Islamist discourse in South Asia, producing new patterns of religiopolitical activism, and new relations of power between state and society. Although the revolution's influence extended as far as Bangladesh, it was most evident and profound in Pakistan, producing trends that extended to India and Afghanistan as well. As such, Pakistan, along with areas within the arc that extends from Afghanistan into India, serve as case studies of the varied and at times unexpected impact of the revolution.

The impact of the Iranian Revolution on South Asian Islamism occurred in two phases and with differing, interrelated, outcomes. There are two fundamental reasons for this varied impact. First, Pakistan and Afghanistan were then already in the throes of an ascendant Islamist drive for power when the Iranian Revolution took place. Second, South Asian Muslim societies were comprised of both Shi`is and Sunnis, whose reaction to the revolution was different, and increasingly so over time. This was especially true in Pakistan, but was also important in India. The nature of the Iranian Revolution's impact in turn depended on how it was perceived by South Asian Muslims. I will argue that initially the revolution was viewed as an "Islamic" event, but later came to be seen as primarily a Shi`i one. Initially, the Iranian Revolution spurred a radicalization of Islamist activism, but, as it became predominantly associated with Shi`ism, the revolution catalyzed the rise of sectarianism in the region.[3] How the image of the Iranian Revolution changed, and the manner in which that change interacted with the realities of South Asian society and politics, will be elucidated below.

THE INITIAL IMPACT OF THE REVOLUTION:
RADICALIZING SOUTH ASIAN ISLAMISM

In 1979, Islamist forces in South Asia shared many of the objectives of the Iranian Revolution, but had evolved differently and played a different role in politics. The works of key thinkers, including lay intellectual activists such as Mawlana Mawdudi and the ulama of Jami`at-i Ulama-i Hind (Society of Indian Ulama), in India, and the Jami`at-i Ulama-i Islam (Society of Ulama of Islam) and Jami`at-i Ulama-i Pakistan (Society of Pakistani Ulama) in Pakistan, advocated a gradualist approach to change, anchoring the Islamization of society and politics in the education of the masses rather than in cataclysmic change.[4] In the works of Mawdudi, the most articulate and influential advocate of this approach, this process would eventually Islamize society and politics by winning over the hearts and minds of its leaders and power brokers and, through them, the lower echelons of society.[5] For Mawdudi, therefore, Islamic revolution was a piecemeal and peaceful process.[6] All activism in the political arena was justified as defensive and required to ensure the success of gradual Islamization.[7]

In Pakistan, the vicissitudes of political change, in practice, pushed Islamists to follow a different course of action. During the 1973–77 period, the growing opposition to the government of Prime Minister Zulfiqar Ali Bhutto was spearheaded by Islamist forces, most notably Mawdudi's Jama`at-i Islami.[8] The campaign to overthrow Bhutto nudged Islamist forces in the direction of agitation, belying their commitment to gradual change through education. The Iranian Revolution occurred while Islamism in Pakistan was absorbed in an internal debate over its future direction and mode of operation. The pertinent issues came into sharper focus with the Iranian Revolution and, later, the Afghan war—where the role of militancy reinforced support in Pakistan for moving in the direction of the Iranian Revolution.

This was most apparent in the Jama`at, the party most associated with Islamic activism in South Asia since 1947, which had been at the forefront of the anti-Bhutto campaign. The revolution came to fruition in the year Mawdudi died. Hence, the debate precipitated by the Iranian experience did not benefit from his input, and was, therefore, based on varying interpretations of his teachings. The Iranian Revolution not only led to debate on the meaning of the term "Islamic revolution," but also, by virtue of its success in Iran, put South Asian Islamists' prior praxis into question.[9] Similarly, the Afghan war proved the efficacy of radical action—"the only tangible victory for Islam" in the words of the Jama`at's then-current leader—which was more than Islamist forces could boast for their peaceful approach to revolution.[10]

Some in the Jama`at believed that Mawdudi's ideas should be reinterpreted to support revolutionary activism.[11] The examples of Iran and Afghanistan, for this group, pointed to the mobilizational potential of a true revolutionary stance. However, such a transformation would have required that Islamist forces dissociate themselves from mainstream politics and reject Pakistan's political order, which they had participated in for the past four decades. In India, Islamists had never accepted the Indian state as legitimate, but neither had they laid any claims to it. The changes afoot pushed them in that direction. However, laying claim to the state in India was not realistic, and, as a result, the Iranian model did not hold sway for very long—although it continued to encourage Islamist thinking.

In Pakistan, not only was such a *volte face* difficult, but for many Islamists the damage such a move could cause would not have been compensated by any tangible gains. In India, similarly, such a move could have precipitated social tension and a political backlash. The Iranian and Afghan models, therefore, did not completely transform South Asian Islamism, but their example continued to animate Islamist debates, especially since, thus far, local Islamist forces had failed to use the political process to their advantage. In Pakistan this point remains salient, as it is unlikely that Islamists can succeed in an electoral process controlled by the traditional elite of landlords and their patronage systems. That many of the younger Islamists in Pakistan have fought in Afghanistan—or attended *madrasas* (seminaries) that trained Afghan fighters and advocated jihad—has added to their eagerness to follow the same strategy in Pakistan. As the political process in Pakistan has stymied the progress of Islamism, it has pushed Islamists to consider a more agitational and violent posture toward the state. To date, although not yet keen to reorient themselves along revolutionary lines, South Asian Islamist forces remain open to this in the future—and some elements among them have taken steps in that direction.

Notable in this regard are youth belonging to the Deobandi and Ahl-i Hadith movements, who favor declaring the Pakistan state to be un-Islamic and waging jihad against it.[12] This approach amounts to adopting the Egyptian jihad groups' model, and would open the door to armed conflict with the state. This position has come under fire from mainstream parties like the Jama`at, the Jami`at-i Ulama-i Pakistan (JUP), and some in the Jami`at-i Ulama-i Islam (JUI) as well as from prominent Islamist thinkers such as Javid Ahmad al-Ghamidi.[13] These critiques of an escalation of violence argue that the Pakistan state cannot easily be declared un-Islamic, and add that the use of violence against Muslims—and against a professed Islamic state—is forbidden. Such criticism is aired by mainstream Islamists who often continue to have a stake in the state and benefit from its patronage. They have resisted the radicalizing impact of the Iranian Revolution.

Although the Deobandi and Ahl-i Hadith position has not found many advocates in Pakistan, its open airing is significant. More moderate and guarded versions of it are found in the pronouncements of the JUI's Fazlur

Rahman and in Sipah-i Sahaba Pakistan (Army of the Prophet's Companions, SSP) rhetoric, as well as in Qazi Husain Ahmad's warnings to Nawaz Sharif between 1997 and 1999. They all warned the government that if it followed pro-Western policies or faltered in its promotion of Islamization, it could face open conflict with Islamism. These relatively cautious statements suggest that, while Islamists may not be ready to declare the state un-Islamic now, they may do so in the future.

The initial impact of the Iranian Revolution on South Asian Islamism was to radicalize it. The revolution—along with the Afghan war and the struggle in Kashmir—compelled South Asian Islamists to reevaluate their understanding of "Islamic revolution" and the degree of activism that it required. The revolution made South Asian Islamists more "jihadist" and prone to agitation and antistate posturing, as it questioned Islamization through piecemeal change and education. Activists like Syed As'ad Gilani of the Jama'at-i Islami advocated a confrontational posture toward the state. Similar views were also advocated by the Jama'at's student organization and some others such as Israr Ahmad.

In this phase, the Iranian Revolution's impact on South Asia was similar to its radicalizing impact on other Muslim societies and Islamic movements. This impact was, however, short-lived, as perception of the revolution and of its moral and religious authority changed. Although the revolution's militancy continued to serve as a point of reference in Islamist debates—increasingly, through the course of the Afghan war—concern with the revolution's implications for the sectarian balance of power came to dominate the scene.

THE REVOLUTION AND THE RISE
OF SECTARIAN MILITANCY IN SOUTH ASIA

The more enduring impact of the Iranian Revolution in South Asia was in radicalizing Shi'i and Sunni identities. Shi'i-Sunni conflict is not new in South Asian politics. It has been a facet of social and political struggles for power since the rise of Shi'is to power in Awadh.[14] Still, after the Iranian Revolution the Shi'i-Sunni division emerged in Pakistan's politics as a stronger force, with a distinctly new aim, and with a more decisive impact on politics. It also developed into an ideology with a more systematic view of sectarianism and its place in politics.

The Iranian Revolution was at the outset perceived by Twelver Shi'is as a Shi'i affair, and by Sunnis as an Islamic event. It mobilized Shi'i consciousness first. In time, Sunnis reacted to the Shi'i mobilization by viewing the revolution as more Iranian and Shi'i than Islamic.[15] It was then that Sunni identity was mobilized in reaction to the revolution and its impact on South Asia. In essence, in the long run, local Shi`is were more decisive in the impact of the Iranian Revolution on Sunnis than was the rhetoric of the revolutionary elite in Tehran.

Initially, Sunnis saw the Iranian Revolution as the triumph of an Islamic movement, inspired by the example of the Prophet of Islam and the teachings of the Quran to combat secularism and to establish an Islamic order. Sunnis focused more on the implications of the collapse of the secular state in Iran and paid less attention to the specifically Shi`i aspects of the revolution. Local Shi`is, on the other hand, made more of the Shi`i particularities of the revolution. This led to tensions between Shi`is and Sunnis over the future course of Islamic activism in Pakistan, so that Sunnis became increasingly aware of the Shi`i elements of the revolution. That awareness led some Sunni activists to formulate positions designed to limit Iran's influence in Pakistan and to counter the Shi`i mobilization that followed the revolution. Sectarian mobilization occurred in both India and Pakistan; since then, developments in each country have been important in the other. Still, sectarianism has been first and foremost a Pakistani phenomenon.

Shi`is constitute 15–25 percent of Pakistan's population.[16] Unlike Arab Shi`i minority communities, Pakistan's Shi`is have not been underprivileged. Many of the Muslim League's early leaders and patrons, such as Muhammad Ali Jinnah (the country's founder and first leader), M. A. Ispahani, and Raja Mahmudabad, were Shi`is.[17] A number of Pakistan's top leaders during its first decade of existence were Shi`is, including Governor General and later President Iskandar Mirza, and prime ministers M. A. Bugra, H. S. Suhrawardi, and I. I. Chundigar. General Yahya Khan, Chief Martial Law Administrator between 1969 and 1971, and prime ministers Zulfiqar Ali Bhutto (1971–77) and Benazir Bhutto (1988–90 and 1993–96)—although the latter now claims to be a Sunni—can be added to this list. In addition, Shi`is have featured prominently among the feudal elite (the Bukhari, Hayat, Husain, Imam, and Qizilbash families in Punjab, or the Bhuttos in Sind), the top ranks of the military (including the general in charge of law and order in Islamabad during the Shi`i march on that city in 1980), the bureaucracy, the judiciary, and the industrial and entrepreneurial elite (such as the Ali, Gokal, Habib, Ispahani, and Raza families). The Shi`i community has, since before the partition of India, been very closely associated with the Pakistan independence movement and state.[18]

Hence, Shi`is have not displayed the oppositional positions that characterized relations between Shi`i minorities and the state in the Arab world.[19] To the contrary, Shi`is have at times been viewed by Sunnis as a privileged

Pakistani Shi`a leader, Lahore, 1986.*  *Pakistani Shi`a woman, Lahore, 1986.
Photo by Nikki Keddie. *Photo by Nikki Keddie.*

minority (although the percentage of urban and rural poor is higher in the Shi`i than in the Sunni community). The sociopolitical status of Shi`is in Pakistan became increasingly a point of contention as Pakistan's politics became anchored in Islamic concerns from late 1971 onwards.[20] In an Islamically conscious polity, whose definitions of orthodoxy and Islamicity were drawn from puritanical Sunnism, Shi`i status was increasingly open to challenge. In fact, by the late 1970s some Shi`is feared that Pakistan was moving in the direction of declaring Shi`is a non-Muslim minority—as it had done with the Ahmediya, a small branch of Sunni Islam, in 1974—thus excluding Shi`is from the mainstream and positions of power.[21]

Similar tendencies were also evident in India, where the growing influence of Islamism throughout the 1970s had created tensions between Shi`is and Sunnis and precipitated conflict in Lucknow and Hyderabad, where the two communities had a history of confrontation. In India, too, by the end of the 1970s there existed an effort to exclude Shi`ism from the mainstream of Muslim life and piety.[22]

The initial impact of the Iranian Revolution in both India and Pakistan was felt against this backdrop. The Iranian Revolution empowered South Asian Shi`is initially at the symbolic level, but, ultimately, more tangibly, in society and politics. As a matter of symbolism, a Shi`i religious leader had carried out in Iran the most spectacular Islamist victory to date against a secular state. Thus, Ayatollah Khomeini had fulfilled the promise of Islamism—largely a Sunni phenomenon up to that point—and, proving to be its most intractable and vigilant defender, Khomeini quickly dominated Islamism as he defined its goals and identified its enemies. For a time, he was widely popular in South Asia, and was viewed as the undisputed leader of Islamism. This catapulted Shi`is to the forefront of the Islamist struggle for power and gave them confidence in asserting their claims before the dominant Sunni order. That after the revolution Iran became the vanguard force in Islamist politics gave Shi`is a sense of pride: a community that was once worried about being declared "non-Muslim" now had claim to the leadership of Islamism. Hence, South Asian Shi`is were quick to claim the Iranian Revolution as a Shi`i event, and in so doing they undermined the more universalist claims of the revolution in Tehran as an Islamic rather than a purely Shi`i phenomenon.

More tangibly, the Iranian revolution provided South Asian Shi`is with a strong source of support in the face of Sunni challenges to their sociopolitical standing. It is an open secret in Pakistan that Ayatollah Khomeini warned General Muhammad Zia ul-Haq—then military ruler of Pakistan—in no uncertain terms regarding threats to the position of Shi`is in Pakistan. At one point in 1980, Khomeini told a Pakistani reporter during an interview that "if Zia continued to harass the Shi`is, he [i.e., Khomeini] would do unto him [i.e., Zia] what he had done to the Shah."[23] The Shi`i community believes that, had it not been for Ayatollah Khomeini's intercession, the Zia regime would have effectively marginalized them.[24]

The consequence of Iran's direct support for South Asian Shi`is and the feeling of empowerment that the revolution brought to that community changed the political attitudes and mode of operation of Shi`is. Palpable changes in Shi`i posture toward the Sunni community and the state, and in the interests and politics of the Shi`i community, set the stage for the more lasting impact of the revolution.

The Iranian Revolution introduced new forms of sociopolitical organization, leadership, and activism to South Asian Shi`ism. The revolutionary elite in Tehran was eager to export revolution, and, given the prevalence of Islamism in Pakistan's politics, viewed that country as a primary target. Iran initially approached the established (Sunni) Islamist parties of Pakistan, most notably the Jama`at.

The Jama`at was impressed with the Iranian Revolution, but, as mentioned, had not endorsed its model of Islamist activism. Moreover, it soon became apparent that Iran was interested in more than sharing its revolutionary experiences; through exporting the revolution, it intended to dominate the Islamist scene in Pakistan and beyond. Pakistani Islamists, the Jama`at in particular, viewed the Islamic Revolution as a positive step for Iranians and, perhaps, as a good omen for its own efforts in Pakistan. However, this did not mean that it would accede to Iran's desire to dominate Islamism across the Muslim world, which was what Khomeini believed Iran should do. The Jama`at, moreover, resisted Iran's attempts to influence Pakistani domestic political issues, and sided with the Zia regime when Iran demanded certain privileges for Pakistan's Shi`is.[25] Similarly, in India, Sunni organizations and leaders, from Imam Bukhari of Delhi to the influential Nadwatu'l-Ulama in Lucknow, rejected Iranian meddling in Indian Muslim affairs, and, especially, Iran's attempts to protect Indian Shi`is. Maulana Abu'l-Hasan Ali Nadwi, the widely popular and influential rector of the Nadwatu'l-Ulama, took the lead in resisting Iranian hegemony.

Rebuffed in its efforts to control South Asian Islamism, Iran invested more directly in the Shi`i communities of South Asia, which were more open to following Iran's model and acceding to its domination. Soon after the revolution, zealous emissaries of the Islamic Republic—such as the first commander of the Revolutionary Guards, Mohsen Zamani (Abu Sharif), who had been trained by AMAL in Lebanon and soon after the revolution became Iran's ambassador to Pakistan—began to organize Shi`i youth into militant organizations. This led to the emergence in 1979 and subsequent growth of the Imamia Student Organization (ISO, a Twelver Shi`i organization first formed in 1972) and the Tahrik-i Nifaz-i Fiqh-i Ja`fariya (TNFJ, Movement for Preservation of Ja`fari Law), in 1979 renamed Tahrik-e Ja`fariya Pakistan (TJP, Shi`a Movement of Pakistan), in Pakistan, and the emergence among the Shi`is of radical self-styled activists, such as Aqa Murtaza Puya, and charismatic "Khomeini-like" leaders, notably Allama Arif Husaini (d. 1988), in Pakistan, and Kalb-i (Qalb) Sadiq, in India.[26] Husaini's and Sadiq's prominence also signaled the growing clericalization of South Asian Shi`ism.

The new organizations were inspired by the Iranian Revolution, but had roots in the threat the Shi`a felt from the Zia regime and its Islamization policies, which favored Sunni Islam. The name of the main Shi`i organization, the TNFJ, bears testament to its defensive nature. The TNFJ was formed in April 1979 with the specific aim of protecting Shi`i interests in the emerging Islamic order.[27] It was to be a pressure group responding to General Zia's Islamization policies. Its architect was Mufti Ja`far Husain, a senior Shi`a *alim*, who had been appointed by General Zia to the Council of Islamic Ideology to safeguard Shi`i interests.[28] Mufti Ja`far was a moderate and was interested

in organizing Shi`is primarily to safeguard their communal interests. Still, the
TNFJ soon set for itself the goal of formulating an Islamic constitution for
Pakistan, based on Shi`i principles as expounded by Ayatollah Khomeini. This,
the organization believed, would unite the Shi`i community, protect Shi`i
rights, and actively involve them in national politics.[29] In addition, many in
the rank and file of the TNFJ gravitated toward the Iranian model, and were
encouraged to do so by revolutionary activists who were dispatched from
Tehran. Also in 1979, Shi`i students organized the form of the ISO, to stake
their claim on campuses and provide organizational muscle for the Shi`i com-
munity, a process that bears resemblance to the rise of AMAL in Lebanon in
the 1970s.[30] The ISO was closely associated with Iran and quickly became the
most militant force on Pakistan's campuses in the early 1980s. The ISO provided the TNFJ with its future workers and leaders.

It was soon clear that Mufti Ja`far's tempered approach to activism would
pass from the scene as the ISO and the TNFJ rank and file grew closer to Iran
and its model of revolutionary activism. The TNFJ gradually adopted a more
aggressive and confrontational style. The inevitable transition to a more radical organization came with the death of Mufti Ja`far in 1983. In 1984 the orga-
nization split into traditionalist and radical camps. The division reflected
tensions within the organization as to whether it should follow Mufti Ja`far's
moderate approach or adopt a more revolutionary style. The latter approach
won the day after Allama Arif Husaini emerged as the TNFJ's leader in 1984.
His charismatic revolutionary posturing consecrated the TNFJ's transformation into a militant body advocating radical sociopolitical activism with the
goal of bringing about an Islamic revolution—modeled after that of Iran and
following Khomeini's authority—in place of General Zia's Islamization initiative.[31] This aim went beyond protecting Shi`i interests in the existing order.
It gave organized activism in Pakistan a new meaning, and also defined the
nature of anti-Shi`i policies of the state and its allies among Sunni Islamist
groupings. Most notable in this regard was the confrontational style of the
TNFJ under Husaini, which set the tone for both Shi`i politics and the Sunni
opposition to it. It would not be until 1992—after Arif Husaini was assassinated, in 1988, and it had subsequently become clear that the TNFJ would neither be able to lead a revolution in Pakistan nor effectively represent Shi`is
in the democratic process—that the party tempered its stance.

The prospects for a TNFJ-led revolution appeared increasingly dim by the
end of the 1980s, and Shi`i landlords, politicians, and secular parties like the
Pakistan Peoples Party, which had originally been overshadowed by the TNFJ/
TJP, began to claim the bulk of the Shi`i vote. Under the leadership of Husaini's
successor, Maulana Sajjid Ali Naqvi, the TNFJ changed course in the early

1990s. In 1993 it changed its name to TJP to suggest its desire for inclusion in the political process—downplayed its connection with Iran, and once again advocated protection of Shi`i interests in lieu of Islamic revolution, which it now defined as part of a broader collaborative process with other Islamist forces in Pakistan. This change produced factionalism in the organization (especially after 1995) and gave rise to radical splinter groups such as Sipah-i Muhammad (Army of Muhammad), which emerged in 1991 to continue to promote the revolutionary model among Shi`is and to follow Iran's lead.[32] In this regard, there are interesting parallels between the TNFJ/TJP's history and those of AMAL and Hizbullah in Lebanon.[33]

Although the TNFJ/TJP has remained the main Shi`i political organization, it has lost some ground to other forces. SM, discussed below, is one, as is the Shura'-i Wahdat-i Islami (Council of Islamic Unity).[34] Created in 1988, the Shura' serves as an umbrella organization and claims to represent all Shi`i political forces and perspectives. The avowed mission of the Shura' is in effect to usurp the TNFJ/TJP's role. Although not as prominent as the TNFJ/TJP, its very rise was symbolic of the decline in that organization's authority. The challenge to the TNFJ/TJP had to do with disaffection with its leader, Allama Naqvi, who was resented for violating the consultative process within the organization's machinery in favor of centralized control. He was also accused of lax moral behavior after he entered into what was viewed as a scandalous marriage. The disgruntlement made it difficult for Naqvi to justify the TNFJ/TJP's increasing moderation at a time of escalation of Sunni sectarian violence, especially in September–October 1999, when, as a prelude to the military coup, forty-five Shi`i ulama and community leaders were assassinated across Pakistan, compelling the TJP to openly encourage a military takeover to end the bloodshed.

The TJP has proved incapable of containing dissent within its ranks or preventing the emergence of new organizations outside of its control. After the military coup of October 1999, the TJP's supreme council voted to remove Sajjid Naqvi, replacing him with Shahid Husain Naqvi as Acting President.[35] The party also dissolved all its organizational units to pave the way for revamping the party structure. With these moves, the TJP evolved beyond being the extension of a charismatic leader, which it had been under Arif Husaini and in the decade after his death. The moves also showed the gravity with which Shi`is view the sociopolitical crises facing them in Pakistan. The new leadership and party structure, it is hoped, will chart a new path for Shi`i political activism.

SM is today perhaps the most notable Shi`i organization, after the TJP. It was formed in 1991 by two ISO activists who believed that both the TNFJ and

ISO were too moderate in the face of the growing challenge of Sunni sectarian militancy: the young ulama Ghulam Raza Naqvi and Murid Abbas Yazdani, both of whom had received their seminary education in Qom.[36] Soon after its formation the SM became the most heavily armed Shi`i organization, and its penchant for violence placed it beyond the pale in the eyes of both the TNFJ/TJP and the ISO.[37] The SM quickly became active in sectarian violence, taking responsibility for bombings and assassinations. It also became embroiled in criminal activities, which it used to finance its campaign of violence against Sunni sectarian forces.[38] Its activists came from rural backgrounds, were attached to small, rural seminaries, and received military training in Afghanistan.[39] The SM is headquartered in the small Shi`i hamlet of Thokar Niaz Baig (outside of Lahore) and has created a broad network of militant activists across Pakistan.[40] Although it is an independent organization, it has maintained some ties with the TNFJ/TJP. It criticizes the larger organization for its failure to protect Shi`is, but avoids an open breach. The TJP, for its part, maintains its distance from the SM while avoiding an open and explicit condemnation of its activities.

In 1995, factionalism erupted in the SM over the organization's response to the initiative of the Milli Yikjahati Council (Council of National Reconciliation) that was formed by mainstream Islamist parties to end sectarian violence. After much internal bickering, the SM leader, Yazdani, joined the council, but was soon after assassinated in Islamabad in September on the orders of his lieutenant, Ghulam Raza Naqvi.[41] Although the two factions of the SM ultimately united, the organization was greatly weakened by concerted Sunni sectarian attacks against its members, infiltration by the police, who viewed the SM as a stumbling block to ending sectarian violence, and an end to Iranian support owing to pressure from Pakistan.[42] These pressures have fissured the organization considerably, reducing its ability to pursue a concerted campaign. As a result, although the SM remains a force in Shi`i politics—and the principal Shi`i force in the drama of sectarian violence—its powers have greatly diminished during the course of the past few years.

The new organizational activism among Shi`is after 1979 also institutionalized a new pattern of communal leadership. This leadership modeled itself after the Iranian revolutionary elite, and sought to replicate the role of the Iranian ulama in Pakistan's Shi`i community. In so doing, it sought to replace the landed elite and mainstream politicians as the spokesmen of the community, as had Imam Musa Sadr in Lebanon.[43] The rise of "Khomeini-like" revolutionary leaders, however, presented problems. First, traditional community leaders—the landed elite and mainstream politicians—commanded significant resources at their disposal to limit the reach of the TNFJ and ISO.

In particular, the Shi`i landed elite proved successful in keeping the new Shi`i activism out of rural areas. Second, the Iranian model faced obvious limitations in a society where Shi`is are no more than 15–25 percent of the population. The ultimate impact of an ulama-based and Shi`i-sectarian charismatic revolutionary leadership on Pakistan as a whole would be quite different from its impact on Iran.

Finally, there existed a strong source of resistance to the dominance of the Iranian model in the person of Ayatollah Abol Qasem Khu'i (d. 1992), a senior Shi`i cleric who lived in Iraq and was openly critical of the Iranian Revolution and its interpretation of the role of religion in politics, especially the *velayat-e faqih*.[44] Khu'i did not stop the radicalization of Shi`is but did limit Khomeini's impact. Khu`i enjoyed strong support across South Asia through the network of his students who served as ulama and community leaders. Many TNFJ leaders, including Arif Husaini, were his students—and that accounted for their authority. Khomeini was never able to replace Khu'i completely. In 1989–90, this author found many Pakistanis and Indians referring to Khu`i with the same lofty titles that Tehran reserved for Khomeini. Every time Iran pushed for an elevation of Khomeini's status, South Asian Shi`is would accord the same status to Khu'i as well—although Khu'i did not command the resources available to Khomeini in Iran. Khu'i was routinely referred to as *na'eb-e Imam* and continued to receive the lion's share of *zakat* and *khoms* funds, and many Shi`is insisted that, whereas in political matters they followed Khomeini, in religious matters they followed Khu'i. Khu'i thus limited the extent of Khomeini's control over Pakistani Shi`is and the degree to which they committed to revolution.

In addition, South Asian Shi`is have shown resistance to Iran's attempts to institutionalize the revolution as a foundational event of Shi`a history on a par with Imam Husain's battle at Karbala—rather than a mere reenactment of it—and to arrogate to Khomeini the status reserved for the infallible Shi`i Imams.[45] The Iranian Revolution continues to be seen in South Asia as a political event devoid of the mythology that Iran seeks to ascribe to it.

There were, however, circumstances in Pakistan that favored the institutionalization of Khomeini's authority. In the Northern Territories of Pakistan— the area close to the boundaries of India, Pakistan, and China and the disputed borders of Kashmir—Shi`is constitute a sizable portion of the population, and along with Isma`ilis constitute a majority.[46] In parts of this region, like the Hunza Valley, Shi`is and Isma`ilis predominate and live in close proximity. The Isma`ilis view their spiritual and communal leader, the Aga Khan, as a living Imam who commands unwavering obedience.[47] His authority exceeds what has been enjoyed by Shi`i ulama and approximates that of the infallible Shi`i Imams. In Hunza Valley, the Aga Khan model led local Shi`is to accept more readily Khomeini's claim to unchallenged and absolute authority. In a way, Khomeini was accepted as an "Imam" by Shi`is there, as he was seen as a Shi`i Aga Khan. This, however, saddled Khomeini's authority with unforseen demands and responsibilities. The Aga Khan's authority among Isma`ilis is not primarily political, nor is it tied to revolutionary struggle. It is, rather, sustained by generous investment by the Aga Khan Foundation in the advancement of the community.[48] Local Shi`is expected similar patronage from Iran, and in time began to compare their "Aga Khan" with the Isma`ili one. In the end, disagreement over the functions and duties of the living Imam limited Iran's control over Shi`is of the Northern Territories.

A new mode of Shi`i organizational activism and religiopolitical leadership surfaced in Pakistan after the Iranian Revolution, which has greatly influenced its internal politics as well as the Shi`is' role in Pakistan's politics. More important, these changes have produced reactions from Sunnis, thus setting in motion more fundamental changes in Islamism and sectarian relations in South Asia.

THE ESCALATION OF SECTARIAN CONFLICT

Changes in Shi`i politics exacerbated sectarian conflict between Shi`is and Sunnis. The scope of this conflict expanded over time to produce a distinct form of identity politics, one that extended beyond Islamist ideology and politics. It was argued above that by empowering, mobilizing, and organizing Shi`is, the Iranian Revolution bolstered communal and sectarian feelings among them. However, the revolution also entrenched similar feelings among Sunnis and contributed to the rise of a militant sectarianism which has, since the late 1980s, become the scourge of South Asian Muslim politics.

The Iranian Revolution and greater Shi`i activism in South Asia coincided with the ascendance of Islamism in the subcontinent. In Pakistan, Islamist ascendancy was encapsulated in the state's Islamization drive. The Zia regime went further than any other government in Pakistan to put in reforms that would anchor law, economy, and public policy in teachings of the shari`a. The Islamization initiative was, however, at odds with the Islamist demands of Pakistan's Shi`is. Zia's Islamization was largely Sunni, and viewed Shi`i activism as a threat.[49] Islamization established religious courts, inheritance laws, tax laws, punitive laws for transgressions against Islamic teachings, as well as for theft, adultery and the like, and enforced public observance of religion—all based on a strict interpretation of the Hanafi school of Sunni law.[50] This meant that in matters of religion Shi`is had to follow a view of

Islamic law very different from the Shi`i one. Moreover, Shi`is were expected to submit to a Sunni state in matters of religion, notably in paying religious taxes. As the secular state in Pakistan became an Islamic one, the sectarian and communal balance of power that had governed Shi`i participation in society and politics was disturbed, with reaction from Shi`is. The Islamization initiative in essence transformed Pakistan's Shi`is from a privileged minority into a disadvantaged one. The result was that Pakistan's Shi`is began to organize against the Sunni state.

The scope of Shi`i unhappiness became apparent when Shi`is refused to submit to Zia's *zakat* law, which mandated a government deduction of 2.5 percent from private savings accounts. Following large-scale and violent demonstrations in Islamabad by some 25,000 Shi`i demonstrators from across Pakistan on July 5, 1980, which shut down the capital, Islamabad received exemption from it.[51] Shi`i demonstrators defied martial law ordinances to rally against the *zakat* law, and their reliance on support from Tehran to organize the protests and assert their demands was disliked by the military. Hence, the exemption from the *zakat* law was followed by introduction of a provision to the constitution which made condemnation of the first three caliphs of Islam—reviled in popular Shi`i ceremonies—a legal offense. It has been argued that the martial law administrator of Punjab, General Ghulam Gilani, deliberately turned a blind eye to growing Sunni militancy, and the rise of armed bands centered in *madrasas*, after 1980, as a means of addressing the "problem" of Shi`i resurgence.[52] The result was anti-Shi`i militancy and violence, which reared its head first in Karachi in April 1983, when Sunni militants attacked two Shi`i Imambaras (places of worship associated with martyred Shi`i Imams), precipitating serious clashes.[53]

The state's capitulation to certain Shi`i demands was seen by advocates of Islamization as constricting the Islamic state and diluting the impact of Islamization. State-led Islamization was in effect being reduced to "Sunni" Islamization, which undermined its universalist claims. Many among Sunni Islamist activists argued that Pakistan's Shi`is were in no position to carp about "Sunnification" of Pakistan, since Iran had made Shi`i law into state law with no exemptions afforded to its Sunni minority.

The formation of the TNFJ and ISO in 1979 was seen as a sign of hardening of Shi`i identity, which led Sunni Islamizers to conclude that, owing to the Iranian Revolution, they would not be able to win over Shi`is and integrate them into their promised Islamic social order. In addition, sectarianism by Shi`i activists created antagonisms towards Shi`is at the local and popular level as well.

Some non-Shi`i Pakistanis who wished to distribute their estates according to Shi`i law (which favors women more) or avoid paying *zakat* to the government declared themselves Shi`is. Many Shi`i families who had been close to Sunnism gravitated back to their faith for the same reasons. The apparent rise in the number of Shi`is—and the faith's new position as a haven from state-led Islamization—was disheartening to General Zia and his Islamist allies. Sunni activists sought to undermine the exemptions given to Shi`is by claiming that the Ahmediya were abusing them by declaring themselves to be Shi`i and adopting Shi`i names. The Ahmediya allegation was useful in that it blurred the boundary between Shi`is and the much despised Ahmediya, and could lead to relegating Shi`ism to the same status as the Ahmediya.

Anti-Shi`i tendencies began to surface among Sunni Islamist groups. The Zia regime looked to militant Sunni organizations to counter the rising tide of Shi`i militancy. One of the first of such organizations was the Anjuman-i Sipah-i Sahaba (Society of Companions of the Prophet), which later became the Sipah-i Sahaba Pakistan (SSP).

Saudi Arabia and Iraq were also concerned about Shi`i activism in Pakistan and what they saw as Iran's growing influence there. These two countries were involved at the time in a bitter campaign to contain Iran's revolutionary zeal and limit its power in the region. In this campaign, Saudi Arabia looked to South Asian self-styled Islamist thinkers, such as Muhammad Salahu'ddin or Israr Ahmad in Pakistan,[54] and, more important, Deobandi ulama in India and the Ahl-i Hadith ulama in Pakistan. The Ahl-i Hadith is a puritanical school of Sunni Islam which, much like Wahhabism, has been strongly opposed to Shi`ism. Saudi assistance helped to establish new Ahl-i Hadith *madrasa*s in Pakistan, and to provide an inroad into the Afghan war for the Ahl-i Hadith through them. Proliferation of *madrasa*s and the greater power and prominence that came with it became tied to involvement with the Saudi Arabian sectarian project.

With Saudi encouragement, self-styled Islamist thinkers and the Ahl-i Hadith mounted a strong anti-Shi`i campaign through publication of books, pamphlets, and magazines, sermons in mosques (notably, Israr Ahmad's popular Friday sermons in Lahore), and activism centered in *madrasa*s.[55] Thinkers like Israr Ahmad and Allama Ihsan Ilahi Zahir, the chief of Jam`iat-i Ulama-i Ahl-i Hadith (Society of Ahl-i Hadith Ulama), formulated the first anti-Khomeini critiques from within Islamist/Islamic circles. More important, they began to produce a new style and language in criticizing Shi`ism, one that depicted that branch of Islam as outside the pale of the religion, and began to successfully transform doctrinal and theological disputes into communal ones.[56] This line of attack became increasingly focused on Shi`is as a people and not Shi`ism as an interpretation of Islam. Zahir's book, *Shi`is and*

Shi`ism, published in Lahore in 1980 and subsequently translated into Arabic and English and distributed across the Muslim world by Saudi Arabia, became the most celebrated effort in this genre. Zahir's views continue to appear in Ahl-i Hadith publications.[57]

It became customary for sectarian leaders to name their sons after Mu`awiya (d. 680) and Yazid (d. 683)—the first two Umayyad caliphs, whom Shi`is hold responsible for the martyrdom of their early leaders, Ali ibn Abi Talib and Husain ibn Ali—who had not theretofore enjoyed respect among Sunnis.[58] Eulogizing the two Umayyad caliphs soon became an important part of the new language of anti-Shi`ism, implying that, having opposed and killed the two Shi`i leaders—the first of whom was the fourth caliph and the son-in-law of the Prophet, and the second the Prophet's beloved grandson, facts difficult to gloss over for Sunnis, who are dedicated to exact emulation of the Prophet's life—they ought be venerated by Sunnis as defenders of the faith against infidels.[59] A popular SSP slogan in its campaign during Shi`i Muharram commemorations was *"Shi`a kafir Yazid kai munkir?"* ("Shi`is are the infidels. When was Yazid a denier [of the truth of Islam]?")[60]

The titles of some of the new genre of anti-Shi`i books that dominated the scene from this point on attest to the change in attitudes: *Shi`a hazrat ki Qur'an se baghavat* (Revolt of Shi`is against the Quran),[61] *Din main ghulluw* (Extremism within religion),[62] or *Shi`a hazrat ki Islam se baghavat* (Shi`is revolt against Islam).[63] In 1994, the SSP increased tensions when one of its leaders, A`zam Tariq, openly assailed Shi`i Imams.[64] This is a new chapter in Sunni polemics against Shi`ism, one that is controversial, as many Sunnis hold the family of the Prophet (*ahl al-bait*) in high esteem. The SSP would later introduce in the National Assembly the "Namus-i Sahaba" ("Honor of the Companions of the Prophet") bill which sought to add the name of the four rightly-guided Caliphs (632–661) to the list of those covered by the Blasphemy Law. The intention was to greatly limit the scope of popular Shi`i commemorations, during which aspersions are cast on the first three caliphs for usurping Ali's right to the caliphate. This was seen as a move to lay the grounds for declaring Shi`is a non-Muslim minority.

The Ahl-i Hadith's anti-Shi`i campaign eventually precipitated a confrontation with the militant Shi`i organizations, which soon turned violent. Shi`i activists sought to silence the Ahl-i Hadith ulama through a number of bomb blasts, most notably one on March 23, 1985, that killed Zahir, who had become the most vocal anti-Shi`i and anti-Khomeini among Ahl-i Hadith ulama. It became evident that the Ahl-i Hadith did not possess the organizational capacity or social base to confront the sizable Shi`i community and its formidable organizations. Although Ahl-i Hadith ulama, such as Sajjad

Above and opposite: Ceremonies for the ten days commemorating Imam Husain's death, Lahore, 1986. Photos by Nikki Keddie.

Mir, Ahl-i Hadith students, and organizations like Da'iat wa'l-Irshad (Call and Guidance [to Islam]) and its militant offshoot, Lashkar-i Tayyiba (Army of the Pure), continue to play a prominent role in articulating Sunni sectarianism, the Ahl-i Hadith were soon overshadowed by Deobandi organizations that surfaced to carry on with the anti-Shi'i campaign.

In 1984 the Indian Deobandi *alim*, Muhammad Manzur Nu'mani of Lucknow, wrote *Irani Inqilab: Imam Khumaini awr Shi'ayyat (Iranian Revolution: Imam Khomeini and Shi'ism).*[65] The book, which was prefaced by the rector of Nadwatu'l-Ulama of Lucknow, Sayyid Abu'l-Hasan Ali Nadwi, accepted the claims of the Iranian Revolution to represent the true Shi'i faith as well as the claims of Ayatollah Khomeini to be the undisputed leader of all Shi'is, only to point to the revolution's excesses as proof that Shi'ism was outside the pale of Islam. Owing to the high rank of its Deobandi and Nadwi authors, the book quickly made a stir. It was translated into English, Arabic, and Turkish, and was soon published in Pakistan in both Urdu and English. The book made Deobandis central to the ongoing sectarian confrontation in Pakistan.

Nu'mani's views were shaped in the context of Shi'i-Sunni conflict in Lucknow,[66] and his arguments drew on the tradition of anti-Shi'ism in the Deobandi school of thought. Deobandis had always maintained a belligerent attitude toward Shi'ism.[67] In Pakistan, politics within the Deobandi community were pushing it in the direction of anti-Shi'i sectarianism.[68] The growing importance of anti-Shi'ism to Deobandi politics opened the door for the rise of militant sectarian organizations among Deobandis.

In 1983, *maulanas* Salimu'llah and Isfandiyar of the Deobandi Sawad-i A'zam-i Ahl-i Sunnat (Majority of Sunnis) organization launched anti-Shi'i movements in Karachi with the financial backing of Iraq.[69] These efforts would, however, pale before those of the SSP, which was formed in Jhang in Pakistan's Punjab by Maulana Haqnawaz Jhangvi (d.1990), a local Deobandi *alim* of low rank.[70]

The SSP proved far more capable and willing to engage the militant Shi'i organizations. It built on the Ahl-i Hadith rhetoric, demanding that Shi'is be declared *kafirs* (infidels). The senior SSP leader, A'zam Tariq, for instance, declared, "If Islam is to be established in Pakistan, then Shi'is must be declared infidels."[71] More important, the SSP incited violent riots in Jhang and, later, in Multan and Kabirwala in southern Punjab, Peshawar (NWFP), and Karachi (Sind). One of its splinter groups, the Lashkar-i Jhangvi, retaliated for assassinations carried out by Shi'is with assassinations of its own, the most important of which was that of the Iranian cultural attaché in Lahore in 1990.[72]

The SSP has sought to involve Iran directly in the sectarian conflict. When

Maulana Jhangvi was assassinated in 1989, the SSP chose to retaliate by killing Iran's cultural attaché in Lahore instead of attacking a Pakistani Shi`i target. Again, in 1997, when a bomb blast killed and injured several SSP leaders and members in a courthouse in Lahore, the party's response was to set Iranian cultural centers in Lahore and Multan on fire. The SSP's actions have been directed at portraying Pakistan's Shi`is as agents of a foreign country, mobilizing Pakistan's Sunnis against Iran, and complicating relations between Islamabad and Tehran, all of which serve Iraqi and Saudi policies in the region. The anti-Iranian aim of Sunni sectarianism became clearer in September 1997, when five Iranian military personnel were assassinated in Rawalpindi.[73]

With the rise of the Taliban—who, like the SSP, are Deobandis and hail from the same *madrasa* structure and networks, and even the same training camps in NWFP and southern Afghanistan[74]—the scope of the SSP's strategic and political ties with Persian Gulf regional politics has expanded, and its penchant for violent action increased. The impact of the Taliban on Shi`i organizations and sectarian conflict in Pakistan became clearer with its victory over the Shi`i Hizb-i Wahdat (Party of Unity) in Afghanistan's Hazara region in August 1998. The Taliban massacred thousands of Shi`is in Mazar-e Sharif and, later, in Bamiyan. Thousands more Hazara Shi`is escaped to Quetta in Pakistan's Baluchistan province.[75] Not only did the predicament of Afghan Shi`is animate Pakistani Shi`is—who saw in the Afghan case a vindication of their worst fears of Sunni militancy—but many were prompted to reaction by the Hizb-i Wahdat. The Hizb, which is based in the Hazara region of Afghanistan, had maintained close ties with Pakistan's Shi`i organizations and helped train many of their activists, especially in the SM.

In addition, the Taliban victory in Hazara precipitated a serious conflict between Iran and Afghanistan that brought the two to the brink of the war. The tensions escalated sectarian violence in Pakistan and convinced the Shi`i community that its "Sunni problem" was part of a broader regional conflict. In October 1999, when sectarian violence claimed the lives of a number of TJP leaders and forty-five Shi`is altogether in the first ten days of October 1999, former Prime Minister Nawaz Sharif and his brother Shahbaz Sharif, Chief Minister of Punjab at the time, both accused the Taliban of promoting terrorism in Pakistan.[76] These developments led the TJP to call on the Pakistan military to intervene,[77] and brought Iran and Pakistan's Shi`is closer—especially as Pakistan's support for the Taliban may translate into a more concerted Pakistani state support for Sunni militancy, with the aim of limiting regional Shi`i resistance to the Taliban assumption of control over Afghanistan.

CONCLUSION

The Iranian Revolution has left a profound mark on Pakistan's politics, impacted the nature of Islamist activism in the Pakistan-Afghanistan corridor, and also influenced Islamist thought and practice in India. As was the case elsewhere in the Muslim world, the most immediate impact of the revolution was to underscore the importance of Islam to sociopolitical change, make Islamism central to oppositional politics, and provide impetus for Islamist activism. However, in the region under consideration here, the Iranian Revolution impacted religion, society, and politics in another regard as well. Here, Iran's drive to establish regional hegemony, combined with growing Sunni resistance to its Shi`i characteristics, exacerbated sectarian conflict. This conflict has fed on regional struggles for power between Iran and its Arab neighbors, and competition for resources and influence between Sunnis and Shi`is in South Asia. The result has been a new form of Islamist politics, one that draws on Islamism in tandem with identity politics. Its force has greatly impacted sociopolitical relations in the region. The more lasting impact of the Iranian Revolution in the region has not been promotion of Islamist activism, but deep division between Shi`is and Sunnis, a sectarian discourse of power, and deepening of social cleavages in the region.

NOTES

I would like to thank Nikki Keddie, Rudi Matthee, Muhammad Qasim Zaman, Mariam Abou Zahab, and S. Faysal Imam for their comments on earlier drafts of this paper, and the John D. and Catherine T. MacArthur Foundation for the Research and Writing Grant that made its writing possible.

1. R. K. Ramazani, *Revolutionary Iran: Challenge and Response in the Middle East* (Baltimore: Johns Hopkins University Press, 1988); John L. Esposito, ed., *The Iranian Revolution: Its Global Impact* (Miami: Florida International University Press, 1990); David Menashri, ed., *The Iranian Revolution and the Muslim World* (Boulder, CO: Westview Press, 1990); and Juan R. I. Cole and Nikki Keddie, eds., *Shi`ism and Social Protest* (New Haven: Yale University Press, 1986).

2. On this influence see S. V. R. Nasr, "Communalism and Fundamentalism: A Re-Examination of the Origins of Islamic Fundamentalism," *Contention* 4, no. 2 (Winter 1995): 121–39. See Freeland Abbott, *Islam and Pakistan* (Ithaca, NY: Cornell University Press, 1968); Leonard Binder, *Religion and Politics in Pakistan* (Berkeley: University of California Press, 1961); Seyyed Vali Reza Nasr, *Vanguard of the Islamic Revolution: The Jama`at-i Islami of Pakistan* (Berkeley: University of California Press, 1994); Farzana Shaikh, *Community and Consensus in Islam: Muslim Representation in Colonial India, 1860–1947* (Cambridge: Cambridge University Press, 1989); and David Gilmartin, "Religious Leadership and the Pakistan Movement in Punjab," *Modern Asian Studies* 13 (1979): 485–517.

3. Sectarianism here refers to organized, militant, religiopolitical activism, which aims to safeguard and promote the sociopolitical interests of a particular Muslim sectarian community (Shi`i or Sunni).

4. Yohanan Friedmann, "Jam`iyatul `Ulama-i Hind," Charles H. Kennedy, "Jam`iyatul `Ulama-i Islam," and Seyyed Vali Reza Nasr, "Jam`iyatul `Ulama-i Pakistan," in *Encyclopedia of the Modern Islamic World,* ed. John L. Esposito (New York: Oxford University Press, 1995), 2:365–67. On Mawdudi's ideas see Seyyed Vali Reza Nasr, *Mawdudi and the Making of Islamic Revivalism* (New York: Oxford University Press, 1996).

5. Sayyid Abul A`la Mawdudi, *A Short History of the Revivalist Movement in Islam,* Al-Ash`ari, trans., reprint (Lahore: Islamic Publications, 1963); idem, *The Process of Islamic Revolution,* 8th ed. (Lahore: Islamic Publications, 1980); and Ishtiaq Ahmed, *The Concept of an Islamic State: An Analysis of the Ideological Controversy in Pakistan* (New York: St. Martin's Press, 1987).

6. Hamid Enayat, *Modern Islamic Political Thought* (Austin: University of Texas Press, 1982), 103.

7. On the reflection of this approach in Pakistan's politics see Leonard Binder, *Religion and Politics in Pakistan* (Berkeley: University of California Press, 1961); Mumtaz Ahmad, "Islamic Fundamentalism in South Asia: The Jamaat-i-Islami and the Tablighi Jamaat," in *Fundamentalism Observed,* ed. Martin E. Marty and R. Scott Appelby (Chicago: University of Chicago Press, 1991), 457–530; and Nasr, *Vanguard.*

8. See Syed Mujawar Hussain Shah, *Religion and Politics in Pakistan (1972–88)* (Islamabad: Quaid-i-Azam University, 1996); Mumtaz Ahmad, "Islam and the State: the Case of Pakistan," in *Religious Challenge to the State,* ed. Matthew Moen and L. Gustafson (Philadelphia: Temple University Press, 1992), 230–40; and Nasr, *Vanguard,* 170–87.

9. Khurram Murad recollects that during his trip to Paris to meet with Ayatollah Khomeini, members of Khomeini's entourage, with the help of an American professor translating, severely criticized the Jama`at's irenic approach to revolution, arguing that the Jama`at should forthwith engage in open revolutionary activism against the Pakistan state; interview with Khurram Murad, Lahore.

10. Interview with Qazi Husain Ahmad, Lahore. Qazi Husain repeated this observation in several rallies as a justification for the Jama`at's support for the jihad in Kashmir since 1989.

11. Interview with ranking Jama`at leader Sayyid As`ad Gilani, Lahore.

12. For a survey of these parties and their positions see Amelie Blom, "Les partis islamistes: A la recherche d'un second souffle," in *Le Pakistan, carrefour de tensions régionales,* ed. Christophe Jaffrelot (Paris: Editions Complexe, 1999), 99–116. On the Ahl-i Hadith see Barbara Metcalf, *Islamic Revival in British India: Deoband, 1860–1900* (Princeton: Princeton University Press, 1982), 268–80.

13. Ghamidi has written prolifically on the subject in his journal *Renaissance.*

14. Juan R. I. Cole, *Roots of North Indian Shi`ism in Iran and Iraq: Religion and State in Awadh, 1722–1859* (Berkeley: University of California Press, 1988).

15. Samina Ahmad, "Pakistan at Fifty: A Tenuous Democracy," *Current History* 96, no. 614 (Dec. 1997): 423.

16. On Pakistan's Shi`is see Vernon James Schubel, *Religious Performance in Contemporary Islam: Shi`i Devotional Rituals in South Asia* (Columbia, SC: University of South Carolina Press, 1993), 1–34.

17. Ispahani was a prominent financier and advisor to Jinnah who became Pakistan's first ambassador the United States. Raja Mahmudabad owned the largest estate in the United Provinces in northern India. He was the League's most generous benefactor.

18. On Shi`i politics in Pakistan before the Iranian Revolution see Saleem Qureshi, "The Politics of the Shia Minority in Pakistan: Context and Developments," in *Religious and Ethnic Minority Politics in South Asia*, ed. D. Vajpeyi and Y. Malik (Delhi: Manohar, 1989), 109–38; and Munir D. Ahmad, "The Shi`is of Pakistan," in *Shi`ism: Resistance and Revolution*, ed. Martin Kramer (Boulder: Westview Press, 1987), 275–87.

19. See the various essays in Cole and Keddie, *Shi`ism and Social Protest.*

20. Some of these themes are explored in Nikki Keddie, "The Shi`a of Pakistan: Reflections and Problems for Further Research," Working Paper 23 (Los Angeles: The G. E. von Grunebaum Center for Near Eastern Studies, University of California, Los Angeles, 1993).

21. Interview with Dr. Karar Husain, senior Shi`i leader in Karachi.

22. On Shi`i-Sunni conflict in Lucknow see Cole, *Roots of North Indian Shi`ism;* Theodore P. Wright, "The Politics of Muslim Sectarian Conflict in India," *Journal of South Asian and Middle Eastern Studies* 3 (1980): 67–73; and Imtiaz Ahmad, "The Shia-Sunni Dispute in Lucknow, 1905–1980," in *Islamic Society and Culture: Essays in Honour of Professor Aziz Ahmad*, ed. Milton Israel and N. K. Wagle (New Delhi: Manohar, 1983), 335–50. For other dimensions of Shi`i-Sunni relations in India see David Pinault, "Shi`ism in South Asia," *The Muslim World* 87 (1997): 235–57.

23. Interview with Khalid Mahmud, editor of the daily *Nation* of Lahore.

24. Interview with Karar Husain.

25. On relations between Iran and Pakistan at the time see Mushahid Hussain, "Pakistan-Iran Relations in the Changing World Scenario: Challenges and Response," in *Pakistan Foreign Policy Debate: The Years Ahead*, ed. Tariq Jan (Islamabad: Institute of Policy Studies, 1993), 211–22.

26. On these organizations see Afak Haidar, "The Politicization of the Shias and the Development of the Tehrik-e-Nifaz-e-Fiqh-e-Jafaria in Pakistan," in *Pakistan 1992*, ed. Charles H. Kennedy (Boulder Co.: Westview Press, 1993), 75–93; Maleeha Lodhi, "Pakistan's Shia Movement: An Interview with Aref Hussaini," *Third World Quarterly* 10 (1988), 806–17; and Muhammad Qasim Zaman, "Sectarianism in Pakistan: The Radicalization of Shi`i and Sunni Identities," *Modern Asian Studies* 32 (1998): 687–716. On Indian Shi`is see John Norman Hollister, *Islam and Shia's Faith in India* (New Delhi: Taj, reprint 1989); Saiyid Athar Abbas Rizvi, *A Socio-Intellectual History of the Isna `Ashari Shi`is in India*, 2 vols. (Canberra: Ma`rifat Publishers, 1986); and David Pinault, *The Shiites* (New York: St. Martin's Press, 1992).

27. Haydar, "The Politicization of Shias," 79.

28. Ibid, 78.

29. Ahmed, "The Shi`is of Pakistan," 282.

30. Fouad Ajami, *The Vanished Imam: Musa al-Sadr and the Shia of Lebanon* (Ithaca: Cornell University Press, 1986); Helena Cobban, "The Growth of Shi`i Power in Lebanon and Its Implications for the Future," in *Shi`ism and Social Protest*, ed. Cole and Keddie, 137–55; and Augustus Richard Norton, "Shi`ism and Social Protest in Lebanon," in ibid., 156–78.

31. Zaman, "Sectarianism," 695–99.

32. *Herald* (Karachi) (Sept. 1998), 48a, 697–99.

33. Augustus Richard Norton, *Amal and the Shi`a: Struggle for the Soul of Lebanon* (Austin: University of Texas Press, 1987); Hala Jaber, *Hezbollah: Born with a Vengeance* (New York: Columbia University Press, 1997); and Martin Kramer, "The Oracle of Hizbullah: Sayyid Muhammad Husayn Fadlallah," in *Spokesmen for the Despised,* ed. R. Scott Appelby (Chicago: University of Chicago Press, 1997), 83–181.

34. *Herald* (Sept. 1998), 48a.

35. *Dawn* (6 Nov. 1999).

36. *Herald* (Dec. 1996), 57.

37. *Herald* (June 1994), 37.

38. *Herald* (June 1994), 37.

39. Zaman, "Sectarianism," 698.

40. *Herald* (June 1996), 57.

41. *Herald* (Dec. 1996), 55.

42. *Herald* (Dec. 1998), 29.

43. Ajami, *The Vanished Imam.*

44. Joyce N. Wiley, "Kho'ī, Abol-Qāsem," in *The Oxford Encyclopedia of the Modern Islamic World,* ed. Esposito, 2: 423.

45. On these policies of the Islamic Republic of Iran see Haggay Ram, *Myth and Mobilization in Revolutionary Iran: The Use of the Friday Congregational Sermon* (Washington, DC: The American University Press, 1994).

46. On Shi`i politics in this region see Tor H. Aase, "The Theological Construction of Conflict: Gilgit, Northern Pakistan," in *Muslim Diversity: Local Islam in Global Contexts,* ed. Leif Manger (London: Curzon, 1999), 58–79.

47. Azim A. Nanji, "Aga Khan," in *The Oxford Encyclopedia of the Modern Islamic World,* ed. Esposito, 1: 44–45.

48. S. S. Khan and M. H. Khan, *Rural Change in the Third World: Pakistan and the Aga Khan Rural Support Program* (New York: Greenwood Press, 1992).

49. On the confrontation between Shi`i and Sunni Islamism see Roy, *The Failure of Political Islam,* 123–24; and Chibli Mallat, "Religious Militancy in Contemporary Iraq: Muhammad Baqer as-Sadr and the Sunni-Shi`i Paradigm," *Third World Quarterly* 10 (1988): 699–729.

50. On Zia's Islamization see Syed Mujawar Hussain Shah, *Religion and Politics in Pakistan (1972–88)* (Islamabad: Quaid-i-Azam University, 1996); Afzal Iqbal, *Islamisation of Pakistan* (Lahore: Vanguard, 1986); Anita Weiss, ed., *Islamic Reassertion in Pakistan: The Application of Islamic Laws in a Modern State* (Syracuse: Syracuse University Press, 1986); Kemal A. Faruki, "Pakistan: Islamic Government and Society," in *Islam in Asia: Religion, Politics, and Society,* ed. John Esposito (New York: Oxford University Press, 1987), 53–78; Charles Kennedy, "Islamization in Pakistan: Implementation of Hudood Ordinances," *Asian Survey* 28 (1988): 307–16; and idem, "Legal Reforms in Pakistan: 1979–89," *Pacific Affairs* 63 (1990): 62–77.

51. Syed M. Zaidi, "Shi`a Activism in Islam: An Overview," unpublished manuscript, 36.

52. *Herald* (August 1992), 67.

53. On April 12, 1983, the Sunni activists attacked Markazi Imambarah in

Liaqatabad, producing clashes that led to the arrest of 135 people by the police. On April 15 there was another attack on an Imambarah in Golimar; cited in Zaidi, "Shi'a Activism in Islam," 36.

54. See, for instance, Israr Ahmad, *Sanihah-i Karbala* (*The Karbala Tragedy*) (Lahore: Maktabah-i Markazi Anjuman Khuddamu'l-Qur'an, 1983).

55. The government has begun to view stopping the dissemination of this literature as central to ending sectarian strife; *Nawa'-i Waqt* (Lahore), 29 August 1997.

56. See, for instance, Maulana Abdu'l-Ghaffar Hasan, *Din main ghulluw* (*Extremism within Religion*) (Karachi: Ribatu'l-ulum'u'l-islamiya, 1983).

57. Ahmad, "Revivalism," 17.

58. For instance, both Israr Ahmad and Maulana Haqnawaz Jhangvi named their sons Mu'awiya and Yazid, and Israr Ahmad insisted on celebrating his daughter's wedding on Ashura (tenth of Muharram), the Shi'i day of mourning for Husain ibn Ali.

59. See, for instance, Maulana Muhammad Tayyib, *Shahid Karbala awr Yazid* (*Martyr of Karbala and Yazid*) (Lahore: Idarah-i islamiyat, 1976).

60. *Herald* (August 1992), 66.

61. Azhar Nadim, *Shi'a hazrat ki Qur'an se baghavat* (*Revolt of Shi'is against the Quran*) (Lahore: Tahrik-i nifaz fiqh-i hanafiya, n.d.).

62. Hasan, *Din*.

63. Azhar Nadim, *Shi'a hazrat ki Islam se baghavat* (*Shi'is' Revolt against Islam*) (Jhang: Anjuman-i sipah-i sahaba Pakistan, n.d.).

64. *Herald* (May 1994), 46.

65. Muhammad Manzur Nu'mani, *Irani inqilab: Imam Khumaini awr Shi'ayyat* (*Iranian Revolution: Imam Khomeini and Shi'ism*) (Lahore: Imran Academy, n.d.).

66. On Shi'a-Sunni conflict in Lucknow see Wright, "The Politics of Muslim Sectarian Conflict in India"; and Imtiaz Ahmad, "The Shia-Sunni Dispute in Lucknow, 1905–1980."

67. Metcalf, *Islamic Revival*, 40–42.

68. Ibid., 15.

69. Ahmed Rashid, "Pakistan: Trouble Ahead, Trouble Behind," *Current History* 95, no. 600 (1996): 161; *Aghaz* (Karachi), 26 March 1983; *Herald* (Sept. 1998), 29.

70. See a biographical sketch of Jhangvi in *Herald* (March 1990), 39–40.

71. *Herald* (March 1995), 36b.

72. *Herald* (Jan. 1991), 69–70.

73. *Dawn* (Karachi), 20 Sept. 1997.

74. For the role of the Taliban in this regard see Kamal Matinuddin, *The Taliban Phenomenon: Afghanistan, 1994–1997* (Karachi: Oxford University Press, 1999), 12–16.

75. *The Washington Post*, 28 Nov. 1998.

76. *Dawn*, 10 and 11 Oct. 1999.

77. *Dawn*, 9 Oct. 1999.

Part V

The Politics of Iran's International Relations

15 / Iran's Foreign Policy:

A Revolution in Transition

GARY SICK

The Iranian Revolution of 1979 demolished the entire architecture of Iran's foreign relations and left Iran isolated and menacing to its neighbors. The excessive costs of such a policy became evident by the mid-1980s, when Iran began to cultivate better relations with Europe, its neighbors in the Persian Gulf, and even the United States. Although Iran created a new policy environment in the region, it was Saddam Hussein of Iraq who transformed the political and strategic landscape of the Gulf, chastened the Iranian Revolution, and set it on a new, more nationalistic and pragmatic path. The Iranian Revolution was like no other in modern times. Its attention to the popular will through the medium of elections created a new image that challenged U.S. sanctions and struggled to provide a model of a democratizing state in an Islamic context. The ferocious counterattack on the forces of democracy and openness by revolutionary ideologues and vested interests, however, demonstrated just how perilous and uncertain such an experiment would be.

T he foreign policy of any country is a function of its domestic politics. That truism was never more applicable than in the case of the Islamic Republic of Iran. The Iranian Revolution of 1979 demolished at a stroke the entire architecture of Iran's foreign relations, sweeping away an edifice of relationships that had been carefully constructed over more than a generation and replacing them with wild and unpredictable actions that threw its region into turmoil and inspired fear and undisguised hostility from its neighbors.

The extreme rhetoric of the revolutionaries was compounded by an organizational void. As the new leadership struggled to define itself, small groups of militants seized the opportunity to pursue their own vision of a global Islamic politics. As in any revolution, there were ancient grudges to be settled, and these enmities rippled out from Iranian territory, like Islam itself, acknowledging no borders and contemptuous of "Western" notions of temporal sovereignty. The earliest targets of attention by the revolutionaries were their brethren among the disadvantaged Shi`i populations of Iraq, Bahrain, Saudi Arabia, and Lebanon, but their zeal and revolutionary triumphalism were boundless.

This is the common experience of revolutions, which initially try to redefine the world in their own image, only to discover by bitter experience that the world does not so easily yield to their ministrations. Twenty years later, the radicals who confidently set forth to introduce Islamic rule to their neighbors would scarcely recognize the foreign policy practices of the Islamic Republic. When a senior Iranian official can remark casually that, in his view, "The revolution was not a renaissance. It was more a riot,"[1] without himself prompting a riot, it is clear that something important has happened.

IRAN'S LEARNING CURVE

In the exuberant atmosphere following the overthrow of the shah, Iranian leaders displayed no interest in diplomatic niceties, much less support for any legacies of the shah's rule. Revolutionary leaders almost casually let it be known that they did not consider themselves bound by any of the shah's agreements. Instead, spokesmen for the Islamic Republic pointedly noted that in traditional Islam there were no borders dividing the faithful. Those remarks, when coupled with fiery rhetoric calling for export of the revolution to all of the Islamic world, gave Iraq and other neighbors of Iran justifiable grounds for concern. The basic principle was written into Iran's constitution.[2]

Even the crucial 1975 border agreement with Iraq, which favored Iran, was allowed to languish in a kind of diplomatic limbo until a full month after Iraq launched its invasion in 1980. The war, however, had a sobering effect. By mid-1983, Iran's repeated failures to breach Iraqi defenses, combined with the growing effectiveness of Iraqi air strikes, compelled Iran to undertake a thorough reappraisal of its diplomatic and military policies. In October 1984, Khomeini summoned Iran's diplomatic representatives from abroad and instructed them to take a new approach.

> We should act as it was done in early Islam when the Prophet . . . sent ambassadors to all parts of the world to establish proper relations. We cannot sit idly by saying we have nothing to do with governments. This is contrary to intellect and religious law. We should have relations with all governments with the exception of a few with which we have no relations at present.[3]

Iranian Prime Minister Mir Hosain Musavi expanded on these comments, offering assurances to the nations of the region who had feared the export of Iran's revolution. "We do not want to export armed revolution to any country. That is a big lie. Our aim is to promote the Islamic Revolution through persuasion and by means of truth and courage. These are Islamic values."[4] These words of reassurance, repeated regularly by all senior Iranian leaders, appeared to be more than rhetoric, as Iranian subversion gradually subsided.

After the death of Ayatollah Khomeini in 1989, the new government of Ali Akbar Hashemi Rafsanjani initiated a major effort to repair relations with Europe, Iran's neighbors in the Persian Gulf and surrounding area, and even with the United States. Rafsanjani, who was a businessman as well as a cleric, made reconstruction of Iran's shattered economy his top priority, and he understood that this would require foreign investment and cooperation.

His plans, however, were repeatedly disrupted. The fatwa against Salman Rushdie that was issued by Ayatollah Khomeini before his death caused a major crisis with the British government and other members of the European Union, greatly complicating Rafsanjani's efforts to repair relations. In August 1991, just before Rafsanjani was scheduled to make the first Iranian state visit to France since the revolution, former prime minister Shahpour Bakhtiar was stabbed to death at his home while under the protection of French security services, and the visit was canceled. In Germany, the leader of a Kurdish opposition group was assassinated in 1992, eventually leading to the formal indictment of Iranian Minister of Information [Intelligence] Ali Fallahian. This was compounded in October 1993 when the Norwegian translator of Rushdie's novel, *The Satanic Verses,* was shot outside his home, eventually leading Norway to withdraw its ambassador.

These and other incidents gave the impression that there were several centers of power in Iran that were working at cross-purposes. Specifically, it appeared that the hard-liners in the Iranian intelligence services were pursuing an independent vendetta against enemies of the revolution and that they were not entirely displeased to embarrass the more moderate president and the foreign ministry. The killings in Europe stopped in about 1993, suggesting that Rafsanjani was finally able to exert some control. But the aftermath of those events continued to poison relations with Europe and other countries for years after.

A NEW BEGINNING

In March 1997, Rafsanjani met with Crown Prince Abdullah of Saudi Arabia during an Islamic summit in Islamabad. This was the beginning of a diplomatic rapprochement between these two major powers in the Persian Gulf region. This was particularly auspicious for three reasons. First, Ayatollah Khomeini had denounced the Saudi royal family in scathing terms in his will, so this opening represented a move away from the revolutionary orthodoxy of the past. Second, Saudi Arabia was the leading power in the Gulf Cooperation Council, which meant that a restoration of businesslike relations would speed the process of reconciliation with the other five members of the GCC, healing rifts that had been created by Arab support for Iraq during the Iran-Iraq war. Finally, since Saudi Arabia was a close political and military ally of the United States, the improved relations provided Iran with some independent maneuvering room at a time when the United States was maintaining severe economic sanctions against Iran.

The full effect of these policies was not felt, however, until the presidential election in May 1997 of Seyyed Mohammed Khatami, a reformist who campaigned on a platform of civil society, rule of law, and expanded personal liberty. In that election, 90 percent of the eligible voters went to the polls, and Khatami received 70 percent of the vote. His surprise landslide election was decided almost entirely on the basis of domestic issues. From the beginning, however, the new president indicated that his electoral themes could and would be extended to Iran's foreign policy. Contrary to expectations, some of the most striking early accomplishments of the Khatami government were in the realm of foreign policy. The former Minister of information, Fallahian, was removed. The previous foreign minister, Ali Akbar Velayati, who had been in office for nearly the entire postrevolutionary period and who symbolized the confrontational policies of the past, was replaced by a respected diplomat who had represented Iran for nearly nine years at the UN.

Before the end of Khatami's first year, Iran had mended its fences with many of its Arab neighbors in the Persian Gulf, invigorated its role in the United Nations, hosted a very successful Islamic summit, and restored relations with the European community, Turkey, and Bahrain. Most striking was the continued rapprochement with Saudi Arabia. Saudi Crown Prince Abdullah attended the Tehran summit of the Organization of Islamic Countries (OIC), met twice with President Khatami, and openly praised the new president.

During Khatami's first few years he consistently broke new ground. He visited Italy, France, Germany, China, Syria, Saudi Arabia, and Qatar. He restored full diplomatic relations with Great Britain, Norway, and Bahrain. He attended the United Nations and launched an international movement for "dialogue among civilizations." And he dramatically changed the international image of Iran. Khomeini had once remarked that "There is no joy

in Islam." The smiling visage of President Khatami, his emphasis on tolerance and rule of law, and the unmistakable love of much of the Iranian populace for him personally went very far to remove the dour and forbidding
visage of the Iranian Revolution and to inspire a degree of respect and even
trust among Iran's neighbors that would have been unimaginable only a decade
earlier.

THE ROLE OF SADDAM HUSSEIN

The Iranian Revolution terminated Iran's close relationship with the United
States and demolished the U.S. "twin pillar" policy of relying on regional states
to protect its interests. Although this transformed the foreign policy environment in the Persian Gulf, actual changes in the political and strategic landscape were due almost entirely to the actions of President Saddam Hussein
of Iraq, who reacted forcefully to the new circumstances and fundamentally
altered the regional balance of power. Iraq's invasion of Iran in September
1980, its invasion of Kuwait in August 1990, and its decade-long sparring with
the United Nations Security Council created an entirely new set of facts on
the ground. In effect, the Iranian Revolution was the trigger for a rampage
of more than two decades by Saddam Hussein's government that rewrote the
strategic situation in the Gulf, perhaps permanently. It is worth reviewing
the interaction between Iran and Iraq, these two traditional rivals whose
mutual depredations, like those of a pair of hateful Siamese twins, set off a
sequence of events whose end is still unknown.

In 1975, the shah of Iran and Saddam Hussein concluded an agreement
concerning their mutual border, and, particularly, the boundary line of the
Shatt al-Arab River. This major concession by Saddam Hussein, which
moved the boundary from the eastern bank of the river to the *thalweg*, the
center of the navigable channel, was undertaken while under pressure from
a Kurdish rebellion in northern Iraq supported by Israel and the United States
via Iran. Five years later, after the Iranian Revolution, the departure of the
shah, the near-collapse of the Iranian military, and a series of hostile acts by
Iran and its agents in Iraq, including some border skirmishes, Saddam Hussein publicly renounced the 1975 agreement as null and void. On the night of
September 21, 1980, Iraq launched a massive air and ground attack against
Iran. This military campaign was intended to restore total Iraqi control of the
Shatt al-Arab waterway, to conquer Iran's predominantly Arab province of
Khuzestan, which had long appeared as a lost province on Iraqi maps, and to
restore Arab control over the islands of Abu Musa and the Tunbs. But its
broader aims were probably intended to bring down the revolutionary Islamic
government in Tehran, to rescue the Gulf Arab states from the menace of rev-

olutionary Shi`i subversion, and to win recognition for Saddam Hussein's Iraq as the savior of the Arabs and the dominant power in the Persian Gulf.

The Iraqi invasion, modeled at least in part on Israel's Six-Day War against Egypt, encountered unexpected levels of Iranian resistance and dragged on for eight full years. It mobilized Arab support for Iraq, but it also persuaded the Gulf Arab states to begin to take their security into their own hands. Under the leadership of Saudi Arabia, the six smaller states banded themselves together as the Gulf Cooperation Council in May 1981, thus completing the third point of the strategic triangle with Iran and Iraq. Although the GCC was slow to develop a common defense policy, it evolved as a convenient—and often influential—forum for the political and diplomatic articulation of mutual interests.

The war also provided the one unequivocal example of Iranian revolutionary expansionism. In 1982, after Iranian forces had pushed Iraqi troops back to approximately the original border, there was a pause in the fighting. Iran had the option of either promoting a diplomatic settlement or else continuing the war and attempting to drive into Iraqi territory. At the time, Iran enjoyed what appeared to be a decisive advantage on the battlefield, and after intense internal debates Iran announced that its forces would march to Jerusalem via Baghdad. This was a catastrophic decision. Iraqi forces stiffened in the defense of their own territory, and Iran's "human wave" tactics proved incapable of overcoming Iraq's lines of defense and superior weaponry. The eventual cease-fire that was negotiated in 1988, which Ayatollah Khomeini likened to drinking poison, was probably not very different from the settlement that Iran could have obtained on its own terms in 1982. The decision to continue the war became a major point of contention for Iran's reform movement nearly twenty years later, when journalists began to raise questions about who was responsible for the enormous economic, political, and military costs it had produced.[5]

The war also brought the United States into the Persian Gulf far more directly than ever before. The key turning point came in March 1987, when the United States accepted a Kuwaiti request to reflag some Kuwaiti tankers and to provide military escort for some of their shipping that had begun to come under attack by Iran. This decision had three main effects: first, it linked U.S. military deployments explicitly to Kuwait and other Arab states of the Gulf, as opposed to the previous "over the horizon" policy; second, the United States began to construct a military support infrastructure in the region that would eventually become permanent; and third, the United States was soon drawn directly into the fighting between Iran and Iraq, including the sinking of an Iranian mine layer and retaliatory attacks on Iranian oil platforms and naval vessels. In July 1988, a U.S. naval ship shot down an Iranian civilian aircraft after mistaking it for a fighter plane, killing 290 people. In all but name, the United States became a party to the conflict and for the first time established a major, continuous, military presence in the region.

The U.S. "tilt" towards Iraq continued after the cease-fire in August 1988 and was maintained until Iraq's invasion of Kuwait in 1990. Unlike the invasion of Iran, which was largely ignored by the international community, the attack on Kuwait prompted an immediate and dramatic response. The UN Security Council immediately demanded an unconditional withdrawal of the invading forces and imposed on Iraq the most severe sanctions in the history of the international community. When Iraq failed to comply, the United States took the lead in organizing a massive military buildup that eventually defeated the Iraqi forces and ejected them from Kuwait. In the process, the United States developed, in close cooperation with the regional Arab states, a military infrastructure that was gradually formalized by a series of defense cooperation agreements, a high level of routine U.S. military deployments, and several huge depots of pre-positioned materiel.

THE NEW STRATEGIC LANDSCAPE

Thus, over a period of less than twenty years, the strategic landscape of the region had been almost totally redrawn. The Iran-Iraq-GCC triangle was expanded to a quadrangle, with the United States as a direct participant in regional affairs. With the signing of the Camp David Accords in September 1978, which removed the likelihood of a new Arab-Israel war, and with the simultaneous explosion of the Iranian Revolution, the center of gravity of Middle East strategy and politics shifted from the eastern Mediterranean to the Persian Gulf.

The Carter Doctrine of 1980 unequivocally asserted U.S. interests in the Gulf and expressed U.S. intentions to act—by military force if necessary—to prevent any attempt "by an outside force to gain control of the Persian Gulf."[6] This largely symbolic statement was given some teeth by the U.S. military buildup during the Reagan administration. Nevertheless, the U.S. presence remained relatively discreet and episodic until the mid-1980s. In fact, the roughly 40,000 U.S. military personnel deployed in the Persian Gulf during World War II to protect the supply lines to the Soviet Union represented the largest U.S. presence in the region until the buildup for Desert Storm in 1990 and early 1991.

Desert Storm also coincided roughly with the collapse of the Soviet Union and the end of the Cold War. For decades, U.S. strategy in the Persian Gulf had been based on two principles: access to the oil supplies of the region and opposition to control of those resources by the Soviet Union. By the 1990s, the threat from the Soviet Union had dissipated and was replaced, without fanfare, by Saddam Hussein's Iraq. Although Iran was officially given equal billing under the rubric of the U.S. "dual containment" policy, in reality Iran cooperated silently with the campaign to eject Iraq from Kuwait, confiscated Iraqi planes that were flown in to Iran without warning at the start of the war, and refused to make common cause with its recent enemy, despite Saddam's unilateral offer to restore the 1975 border agreement and to give Iran "everything you wanted."[7]

By 2000, the routine U.S. presence in the Gulf had become substantial. According to the Department of Defense, at any given time the United States had in the region some 17,000–25,000 personnel, about 30 naval vessels, and some 175 aircraft.[8] The reasons for this considerable level of permanent military presence were all related to Iraq.

A CHASTENED REVOLUTION

Iraq's effect on the Iranian Revolution was no less remarkable. In the early 1980s, Iran evinced boundless optimism and unlimited goals. By the end of its war with Iraq, the optimism had faded and the universalist Islamic goals had been replaced by a gritty nationalism. Even the composition of the Iranian government was changed. Immediately after the revolution, the primary qualification for any job was a past record of revolutionary action, preferably augmented by some religious training. Professional background and actual job experience were regarded as secondary or irrelevant. After eight years of conflict, a new generation of technocrats had begun to emerge, responding to the demands of the economy, military organization, and administration. The system was still very far from a meritocracy, but young seminarians who had taken to the streets for Khomeini could no longer count on automatic job preference.

After eight years of combat and austerity, there was a vast appetite for consumer goods and other benefits. The new generation of Iranians, many with little or no memory of the revolution or life under the shah, were now coming on the job market with only limited prospects. There was a shortage of housing, schools were overwhelmed by the tidal wave of youth produced by the pro-natal policies of the early revolutionary years, social services were limited, and the burst of consumer spending that accompanied the end of the war created a bubble of foreign debt that would take a generation to erase. Mismanagement of the economy and omnipresent corruption blighted the reputation of the revolutionary regime, dimming even its genuine accomplishments, such as the extension of roads, telephones, and electricity to the villages. The promises of the revolution to serve the "dispossessed" seemed little more than idle talk. Khomeini was once said to remark that the revolution was not about the price of melons. Suddenly, it seemed to be about little else.

IRAN AND ITS NEIGHBORS

After the dissolution of the Soviet Union and the creation of a series of new states in Central Asia and the Caucasus, Iran was left in the peculiar position of having land and direct sea borders with fifteen different states. It had fought an eight-year war with its neighbor to the west, suffering more than 600,000 casualties, including the most extensive use of chemical weapons since World War I.[9] Its eastern neighbor, Afghanistan, had been invaded by the Soviet Union and then collapsed in a civil war. From these various conflicts, Iran had inherited some two million refugees within its own borders, together with hundreds of square miles of minefields.

Another neighbor, Pakistan, itself a nuclear power, supported forces in Afghanistan that were hostile to Iran. Iraq harbored a terrorist organization that conducted cross-border operations into Iran. Northern Iraq was in an unstable balance of power between rival Kurdish factions, punctuated by periodic forays by both Turkish and Iraqi forces, while the Shi`i region of southern Iraq was the site of a prolonged, low-level rebellion. The United Arab Emirates and its Arab allies in the GCC pressed Iran to resolve the dispute over the islands of Abu Musa and the two Tunbs that had been occupied by Iran in 1971.

The new states of the former Soviet Union along Iran's northern border were all in the early stages of nation building, and the former Communist officials who dominated their governments were instinctively suspicious of Islamic movements. Many of these states were engaged in ethnic and territorial strife of their own, as they sorted out the residue of the Soviet empire.

Iran also had a superpower on its doorstep. The ships and planes of the United States operated in the confined waters of the Persian Gulf and conducted frequent exercises with the Arab states of the region. The United States also conducted periodic military reprisal raids against Iraq, and U.S. and British aircraft patrolled daily over northern and southern Iraq, just across the Iranian border.

Given this perilous situation, the Islamic Republic of Iran opted for a strategy of accommodation. In the period beginning after the Iran-Iraq war, and accelerating during Khatami's presidency, Iran muted its Islamic message when dealing with the new states on its northern border and deliberately tried to avoid a secular-Islamist rivalry with Turkey. Iran refused to take sides in regional disputes and offered its good offices on such thorny issues as Nagorno-Karabagh and Chechnya. Instead, it focused primarily on commercial and regional cooperation, taking a lead role in creation of the Economic Cooperation Organization (ECO) and offering technical assistance and even aid on engineering and other projects. While preserving its position in the complex dispute over division of resources in the Caspian, Iran refused to be provoked into an escalation of words, or worse. It vigorously argued in favor of a pipeline route from the Caspian to northern Iran and in opposition to the U.S. plan of a Baku-Ceyhan (Turkey) connection, with some modest success. Iran appeared to be more concerned with stability and good relations than with any short-term political or economic gains which might be achieved by a more aggressive stance.

With regard to Iraq, Iran maintained cool but businesslike relations while keeping its powder dry. Talks proceeded slowly on repatriation of POWs and on such mundane issues as pilgrim visits to the Shi`i shrines in Najaf and Karbala. Iran refused, however, to return some 125 aircraft that Iraq had flown to Iran without warning at the beginning of the war over Kuwait, insisting on reparations of up to one trillion dollars from Iraq in compensation for damages sustained as a result of the Iraqi invasion.

Both sides used surrogates to carry out hit-and-run operations against the opposition forces housed on either side of the border: the Mojahedin-e Khalq Organization (MKO), operating against Iran from a complex of bases and installations in Iraq, and the Supreme Assembly of the Islamic Revolution in Iraq (SAIRI), which had its headquarters in Tehran and conducted operations in southern Iraq. However, despite occasional exchanges of mortar fire and missiles, both sides resisted the temptation to push the confrontation to a climax. Iran gave lip service to the international sanctions against Iraq, but often looked the other way at the lucrative smuggling of Iraqi oil through Iranian waters. Neither side provided a level of support that would permit its surrogates to launch a major cross-border offensive.

At the same time, Iran pursued a determined program of missile development, indigenous production of weaponry and combat equipment, and regular military exercises along its border with Iraq. This demonstration of readiness and self-reliance was clearly intended to deter Iraq from any consideration of further military activities against Iran. Iraq, in turn, viewed the warming relations between Tehran and the regional Arab states as a betrayal of the Arab cause and as part of a greater plot by the United States to isolate the Iraqi government, but its blandishments had little effect.

An important element of Iran's deterrent policies was the burgeoning relationship with Russia. Following the collapse of the Soviet Union, Iran chose to cooperate with Russia in pursuit of stability along its northern border, to purchase modern military equipment that was unavailable from the West, to acquire nuclear technology for the power plant that Russia was building for Iran at Bushehr, and to develop some measure of diplomatic support for its positions, particularly in its running confrontation with the United States. The United States imposed some limited sanctions on Russian institutes, and the question of Iran became a perennial staple of U.S.-Russian relations. It was evident, however, that the Iranian-Russian connection was primarily a marriage of convenience and a matter of mutual commercial benefit. Neither side demonstrated desire for any long-term commitment; each seemed suspicious of the other and was willing to take opposing positions (on Caspian demarcation, pipeline strategy, and relations with particular Caspian states, for example) when it suited its immediate interests.

With regard to the GCC states, after about 1990 Iran made a concerted effort to develop a relationship of trust. In 1987, more than four hundred people had died when Saudi security forces confronted Iranian pilgrims during the annual Hajj. The pilgrims were performing a symbolic demonstration against the United States and Israel, contrary to Saudi rules against political demonstrations during the Hajj. This incident led to a three-year break in diplomatic relations between Saudi Arabia and Iran and marked the low point of relations between Iran and the Arab states of the Gulf. In later years, Iran took measures to prevent a recurrence of this tragedy by ordering its pilgrims to carry out their demonstrations on a small scale and within the confines of the Iranian encampment.

Iran also sent a string of goodwill emissaries to the Arab states and actively sought to change its earlier image of hostility and radicalism. Memories of Arab support for Iraq during the Iran-Iraq war were not forgotten on either side, but reconciliation was made easier by mutual acknowledgment of Iraq as the primary military threat in the region, following its invasion of Kuwait in 1990. After the election of Mohammed Khatami in Iran, high-level visits between Iran and the Arab regional states became commonplace, and Iran began to call for military confidence-building measures and for a regional security pact.

The terrorist bombing of the U.S. military barracks at Dhahran, Saudi Arabia, in 1996 killed nineteen American servicemen and raised concerns that Iran was behind the attack. Those charges were never proved, however, and the rapprochement between Saudi Arabia and Iran continued after a pause. Similarly, charges of Iranian complicity in Shi`i riots in Bahrain during the

early 1990s were eventually set aside, and the two countries restored full diplomatic relations in January 1998, after a thirty-month lapse.

By far the most persistent of the issues separating Iran and the Arabs of
the Gulf was the dispute over Iran's 1971 occupation of the islands of Abu
Musa and the two tiny Tunb islands. Both Iran and the United Arab Emirates were passionate in their claims of sovereignty, and scholars in both countries conducted elaborate historical research to support national claims.[10]
At the same time, new technology greatly reduced the strategic importance
of the islands, while commercial sharing of the undersea resources of the
islands was unaffected by political differences. Thus, the dispute became one
of competing symbolic claims and national pride, which, ironically, may have
rendered it even more difficult to resolve.[11] Although Iran offered talks, neither side showed the least interest in relinquishing its claims or seeking a compromise, suggesting that the islands issue would persist as a long-term irritant
in relations. It did not, however, prevent a gradual warming of relations
between the GCC states and Iran, including commercial relations with the
U.A.E. In fact, during the height of this controversy, Iran became the num-
ber-one trade partner of the U.A.E. in the Islamic world.[12]

One of the most significant areas of Iran's new policy of accommodation
was its participation in the Organization of Petroleum Exporting Countries
(OPEC). In a series of difficult decisions during the late 1990s and early 2000,
Iran generally set aside its earlier ideological objections and participated with
Saudi Arabia and others to increase oil-production quotas in 1998, and then
to reduce them in 1999 when oil prices collapsed in the face of the Asian financial crisis. After the recovery of oil prices above $30 per barrel, Iran argued
strenuously against a new increase in production levels. At the Vienna OPEC
meeting in March 2000, Iran formally disassociated itself from the consensus,
preserving its classic position as a price hawk and protesting U.S. pressure tactics, which was important in terms of its domestic politics. Once the decision
had been taken, however, Iran quietly increased its own production in accordance with other producers.[13] The very muted reaction of Saudi Arabia to Iran's
rhetorical protest suggested that this bit of posturing had been prearranged.
Throughout, Iran's production and exports remained well within the OPEC
guidelines, and the relationship with Saudi Arabia was carefully nurtured.

RELATIONS WITH THE UNITED STATES

The very close political, economic, and strategic relations between the United
States and Iran collapsed under the weight of the revolution and the hostage
crisis. Those events, and particularly the 444 days of the hostage-taking, cre-

ated an American image of Iran as a fanatic nation committed to undermining fundamental U.S. interests. That image was not improved in 1985–86, when the Reagan administration attempted a disastrously conceived opening to Iran that exploded in scandal and nearly brought down the government.

In the years after Iraq's invasion of Kuwait, the Clinton administration in effect declared a plague on both Iran and Iraq with the "dual containment" policy, which spelled out broad guidelines for containing and isolating both countries.[14] In the case of Iran, the objective was to persuade the Islamic Republic to change its policies in a number of areas: terrorism, subversion, violent opposition to the Arab-Israel peace process, and the pursuit of weapons of mass destruction. To that end, and despite the opposition of its allies, the United States instituted an array of unilateral measures intended to isolate and punish Iran, including a secondary boycott against foreign companies investing in the Iranian oil and gas sector.

The U.S. position began to change after the election of Mohammad Khatami as president of Iran. In January 1998, President Khatami spoke to the American people via an interview with CNN, in which he addressed the key issues of major concern to the United States.[15]

On terrorism: "Any form of killing of innocent men and women who are not involved in confrontations is terrorism. It must be condemned, and we, in our turn, condemn every form of it in the world."

On the peace process: "We have declared our opposition to the Middle East peace process, because we believe it will not succeed. At the same time, we have clearly said that we don't intend to impose our views on others or to stand in their way."

On weapons of mass destruction: "We are not a nuclear power and do not intend to become one."

In addition, Khatami went as far as any Iranian political figure could go in expressing regret about the 1979–81 hostage crisis, and he pledged that such "unconventional methods" would not and could not be employed in today's Iran.

In response, Secretary of State Madeleine Albright in June 1998 spelled out a new U.S. policy calling for the establishment of "a road map leading to normal relations."[16] Over the following two years, the United States made a series of small but significant gestures to Iran. U.S. officials softened their language and no longer referred to Iran as a "rogue" or "outlaw" state; removed Iran from the narcotics list; designated the Mojahedin-e Khalq (and its multiple front organizations) as a terrorist organization; cooperated with Iran on the "6+2" talks on Afghanistan at the UN; waived sanctions against foreign oil companies that invested in Iran; lifted restrictions on the sale of agricultural and medical goods to Iran; authorized the sale of spare parts needed to ensure the safety of civilian passenger aircraft previously sold to Iran; and eased visa regulations for academic exchanges and for travel by Iranian UN diplomats in the United States.

Following the February 2000 elections for the sixth Majles in Iran, which resulted in an overwhelming popular vote for candidates supporting Khatami's reform movement, Secretary Albright again addressed the issue of Iran.[17] She acknowledged the U.S. role in the countercoup that overthrew Prime Minister Mohammad Mosaddeq in 1953 and commented that "the United States must bear its fair share of responsibility for the problems that have arisen in U.S.-Iranian relations."[18] She further acknowledged that "aspects of U.S. policy towards Iraq during its conflict with Iran appear now to have been regrettably shortsighted." While reiterating U.S. grievances toward Iran, she welcomed the prospect of "regional discussions aimed at reducing tensions and building trust." She announced the lifting of U.S. sanctions on the purchase of Iranian carpets and food products such as caviar and pistachios, promised to remove impediments to the travel and operation of exchange programs and nongovernmental organizations, and vowed to increase efforts to conclude a global settlement of all outstanding legal claims (often incorrectly referred to as Iran's "frozen assets"). Reiterating U.S. willingness to enter into direct official discussions without preconditions, she added, "surely the time has come for America and Iran to enter a new season in which mutual trust may grow and a quality of warmth supplant the long cold winter of our mutual discontent."

This was the most far-reaching expression of U.S. interest in a rapprochement with Iran in the twenty-one years since the revolution. It came, however, at a moment of intense political conflict in Iran. Conservative forces were striking back at the reformists, closing many newspapers, throwing key journalists into jail, and attempting to assassinate Sa'id Hajjarian, a member of the Tehran Municipal Council and one of the architects of the reform movement.

Iran's supreme leader, Ayatollah Mohammad Ali Khamenei, was reportedly offended by a phrase in Albright's speech referring to the fact that many of Iran's institutions remained in the hands of "unelected" officials. He made a scathing attack on the U.S. position in a speech in Mashhad on March 25,[19] and Iran's official response to the Albright speech was muted and tended to fall back on the formulas of the past.

Remarkably, however, less than two weeks later an important reformist organization published an alternative analysis of the Albright speech. Without reference to the Khamenei address, the Organization of the Mojahedin of the Islamic Revolution of Iran (OMIR), which was closely associated with Behzad Nabavi, a key supporter of President Khatami in the sixth Majles, praised the candor of Albright's speech and concluded that it was "a kind of victory and an achievement for . . . Khatami's government." In a clear reference to the U.S. call for direct talks, the OMIR declaration asked Iranian policy makers "to carry out a logical, calculated and wise analysis of the changes that have come about in American stances and policies. Instead of relying upon a wave of blind emotions, they must act on the basis of national interests."[20]

Thus, although the Albright speech and the Iranian response could not be seen as a breakthrough, it was evidence of substantially changed attitudes in Washington and in some important circles in Tehran. Unlike the "dual containment" policy of the previous six years, after 1998 the United States deliberately began to make an explicit distinction between Iran, where it sought dialogue and eventual normalization of relations, and Iraq, where regime change was the objective.

A REVOLUTION LIKE NO OTHER

Iran is the exception to the history of modern revolutions. With the French Revolution as the intellectual model, we have come to anticipate certain stages through which any revolutionary society is likely to pass. We anticipate the rise of a radical clique that appropriates the revolution in the name of its own ideological persuasion, leading to a dictatorship, highly centralized authority, and one-party rule by the victors in the ideological combat. We have come to expect massive suppression of dissent and the enforcement of a strict ideological canon, leading almost inevitably to the use of mass terror and purges.

Iran had encounters with all of these symptoms, but it avoided the extremes of the French, Russian, or Chinese revolutions. The difference appeared to lie in a fundamental respect for the popular voice that was quite remarkable under such extreme economic and political circumstances.

The Iranian constitution is an ambiguous document. It leaves unanswered the central question of whether sovereignty and legitimacy arise from the people or from God. Iran is an Islamic Republic, and it is not clear whether the emphasis should be placed on "Islamic" or "Republic." At various times the pendulum has swung in different directions. Even in the earliest days, however, Iran insisted on elections. None of these elections rose to the level of international standards of "free and fair." Candidates were prescreened by a body of revolutionary overseers and severe limits were placed on the terms of public expression and debate. The Islamic nature of the revolution was not to be questioned, nor would criticism of the supreme leader be tolerated. The media were not equally available to all candidates, and radio and television remained in the hands of the conservative ruling elite, which was not hesitant to use them for its own ideological purposes.

Nevertheless, voting itself was generally unfettered and there appeared to be no effort to rig the vote, even when it was not what the conservative elite wanted or expected. Over time, and especially in the decade after Khomeini's death, candidates and the electorate demonstrated a willingness to challenge official orthodoxy and go their own way. The first major evidence of this was the 1993 presidential election, in which Ali Akbar Rafsanjani was running for his second term. He had won by 94 percent in his first election, when he was seen as a pragmatic reformer who would bring order and good management to the country. Partly due to the vagaries of the oil market and other developments that were not entirely under his control, the government's record in his first term was less than compelling, and the voters responded accordingly. In the election for his second term, 42 percent of the voters stayed home—a huge percentage in a country where voting was routinely described as a religious duty—and of those who voted, he received only 63 percent.

The watershed, however, was the presidential election of 1997. Mohammad Khatami, a virtual unknown, was paired against the well-known speaker of the Majles, Ali Akbar Nateq-Nuri. Khatami ran a Western-style campaign, whistle-stopping throughout the country with his unique message of civil society and rule of law. The youth population immediately embraced his message, and they went to work for him in a huge burst of enthusiasm and grassroots campaigning. Only weeks before the election, most observers in Iran and elsewhere confidently expected Nateq-Nuri to win, but the popular shift was irresistible.

This performance was repeated in the municipal council elections of February 1999 and especially the Majles elections of February 2000, which saw three of every four incumbents go down to defeat, while those associated with the newly organizing reform movement won almost everywhere. In each case, the conservative establishment fought a rear-guard action, disqualifying some elected candidates after the fact, closing reformist newspapers and hauling their publishers and journalists into court on trivial charges, and, most ominously, conducting a series of murders of intellectuals and writers. However, there was no systematic attempt to nullify the elections, and the hard-line tactics only reinforced the negative image of the antireform forces and eroded their legitimacy.

The Khatami forces gradually extended their control to an increasingly wide range of governmental institutions in a kind of envelopment strategy, slowly but surely excluding the ultraconservatives from one area after another, all without serious violence or involvement of the military. There was no precedent for such a development in any other major revolutionary society, and there was no real precedent for electoral rejection of an entrenched political elite anywhere in the Middle East, with the exception of Israel.

In some respects, former president Rafsanjani was both the emblem and eventual victim of this process. A cleric close to Khomeini, one of the organizers of the revolt against the shah, a coalition-builder and strategist behind the scenes, the consummate insider with perhaps the most distinguished résumé of all the revolutionaries of his generation, an early proponent of reform, and the sponsor of the first really successful party of largely nonclerical technocrats, Rafsanjani appeared to be the millennium man. In the 2000 elections, however, he was viciously attacked by the new breed of reform journalists, who asked why he had apparently done nothing to curb the past excesses of the intelligence ministry, why he had apparently supported the continuation of the war with Iraq in 1982, and how he could account for his considerable personal wealth.

Although Rafsanjani and his family genuinely—and with some considerable justification—saw themselves as the progenitors of the reform movement, their pained reaction to these highly personal attacks associated them with the conservative faction, and Rafsanjani came in at the very end of the list of thirty Majles candidates in Tehran.[21] The fact that he symbolized the past, which he would have expected to work in his favor, was the reason for his decline.

The new politics of Iran was less respectful, more aggressive and unintimidated in its efforts to get answers to some of the unanswered questions of the past. Rafsanjani was caught up in this maelstrom and was totally at a loss over how to handle it. It was clear, however, that a corner had been turned and the politics of the revolution were unlikely to return to their earlier status.

CONCLUSION: THE NEW IMAGE OF IRAN

At the start of the new millennium, Iran was one of the most interesting and politically innovative countries in the Middle East. Its freshly minted image of moderation and regional cooperation was still regarded with skepticism by some of its neighbors and by many in the United States who had watched the fanaticism of the earliest days of the revolution and who were unlikely soon to forget the sight. Moreover, doubts persisted about the ability of the reform movement to withstand the relentless counterattack by diehard conservatives who were willing to exploit—even abuse—their access to the courts and other institutions to preserve their own vision of the revolution.

This fierce struggle for the soul of the revolution was kept in check only by the determination of the reformists to operate peacefully within the constitution and by the equal determination of Iran's top leadership, especially the supreme leader and the president, to compromise at critical moments to prevent an outburst of violence. Could the popular demand for change by a youthful and restless electorate be accommodated within the context of a revolutionary Islamic state without collapsing into anarchy and violence? The answer could not be predicted, but the very effort to construct a new politics within an existing constitutional model was a unique experiment for the region.

Europe, Japan, and China, which had placed their bets early on the possibility of a working relationship with Iran, and which staunchly opposed U.S. unilateral sanctions, moved quickly to take advantage of emerging commercial opportunities while U.S. companies were still forbidden to compete. By early 2000, major European companies, particularly in the energy sector but also in other commercial areas, were setting up offices in Tehran. The Japanese, who had acceded for nearly a decade to U.S. demands to withhold development loans, once again began to signal that they would proceed with such loans despite U.S. objections. Even the World Bank disregarded U.S. pressure and approved loans for two long-standing Iranian development projects in May 2000, citing the promising direction of Iran's political reforms.

This new commercial dynamic was directly related to changes in U.S. policy. The partial lifting of U.S. sanctions on the purchase of Iranian non-energy products, and the absence of any U.S. reaction to a spate of European, Canadian, and Australian energy deals, seemed to indicate that the United States was no longer willing—or perhaps able—to resist international commercial pressures for an opening to Iran. It was also understood that the most onerous U.S. third-party sanctions (the Iran-Libya Sanctions Act of 1996) would expire in August 2001 and were unlikely to be renewed by any administration in Washington. The U.S. government certainly was not anxious to engage in another showdown with its allies in a quixotic effort to deprive Iran of revenues that might be used for military or other purposes. In fact, Iran's military budget had been pared back in favor of social programs, and its hard-currency expenditures on defense were smaller than those of any other country in the Gulf.

Close observers of Iran understood the power of the reform movement and the near-impossibility of putting the genie back in the bottle, but they were also aware of the tenuous balance between the forces of change and the resistance by an earlier revolutionary generation that saw its most cherished slogans being challenged or set aside. It was well understood that if the reformists failed to fulfill their early promises, they could share the fate of their predecessors, who also started with high hopes and wide public support.

This drama would not only play itself out domestically, it would be watched with rapt attention by Iran's neighbors. It was one of the great ironies of the Iranian revolution that its most significant "export" to its neighbors in the Middle East might prove to be a model of a democratizing system within an Islamic context. Some of those in the neighborhood might regard that as a threat at least as great as the export of radical Islamism. The ferocious counterattack by revolutionary ideologues and vested interests, however, demonstrated just how perilous and uncertain such an experiment would be.

NOTES

1. Hosein Valeh, political adviser to President Khatami, interview cited in Susan Sachs, "As Ballots Are Counted, Iran's Moderates Fear Backlash," *The New York Times*, 22 Feb. 2000, 1.

2. The Preamble of the Constitution of the Islamic Republic declares that "in the development of international relations, the Constitution will strive with other Islamic and popular movements to prepare the way for the formation of a single world community . . . and to assure the continuation of the struggle for the liberation of all deprived and oppressed peoples in the world."

3. Foreign Broadcast Information Service, 30 Oct. 1984.

4. Ibid.

5. Rightly or wrongly, this was one of the charges that reformist journalists attributed to Rafsanjani in the February 2000 Majles election, which contributed to his very poor showing as described later in this paper.

6. See Jimmy Carter, *Keeping Faith: Memoirs of a President* (New York: Bantam Books, 1982), 483.

7. Saddam Hussein, letter to President Rafsanjani of Iran, 15 August 1990. This letter, which revoked in a single stroke all of the war aims that Iraq had pursued during the eight years of conflict with Iran, was intended to secure Iraq's eastern border as its forces redeployed to Kuwait; or, as Saddam put it, "so as not to keep any of Iraq's potentials disrupted outside the field of the great battle." Foreign Broadcast Information Service, 16 August 1990.

8. Testimony of Alina L. Romanowski, Deputy Assistant Secretary of Defense for Near Eastern and South Asian Affairs, before the House Committee on International Relations, 23 March 2000, Federal News Service.

9. According to Hadi Qalamnevis, Director General of the Statistics and Information Department at the Islamic Revolution Martyrs Foundation, 204,795 Iranians lost their lives in the Iran-Iraq war, including 188,015 military and 16,780 civilians. Islamic Republic News Agency, 23 Sept. 2000, and *Iran Times*, 10 Nov. 2000, 4. Earlier estimates by Mohsen Rafiqdust, the former head of the Iranian Revolutionary Guard Force, had stated that 400,000 were wounded during the war. Robert Fisk, *The*

Independent, 25 June 1995. According to Iranian health officials, about 60,000 Iranians were exposed to Iraqi chemical weapon attacks during the war. Agence France Press, 13 March 2000. Over 15,000 war veterans suffering from chemical weapons syndrome reportedly died in the twelve years after the end of the Iran-Iraq war, according to Abbas Khani, the head of the Legal Office for War Veterans. Islamic Republic News Agency, 13 Nov. 2000.

10. For an excellent synopsis of the issue see Richard Schofield, "Border Disputes: Past, Present, and Future," in *The Persian Gulf at the Millennium: Essays in Politics, Economy, Security, and Religion*, ed. Gary G. Sick and Lawrence G. Potter (New York: St. Martin's Press, 1997), 142–56.

11. This issue was debated at length in the Gulf/2000 conference on "Confidence-Building Measures in the Gulf," in Salalah, Oman, 9–12 Nov. 1999. This conference brought together about forty Arabs and Iranians, with a few Westerners, to address mutual security issues.

12. The Islamic Republic News Agency, 13 Oct. 1998, reported that the value of U.A.E. exports to Iran in 1996 stood at $1.080 billion and its imports at $330 million. Saudi Arabia and Indonesia followed Iran in the list of major trade partners to the U.A.E. in 1996. Much of this trade involved re-export of consumer goods to Iran via Dubai, often circumventing U.S. sanctions against direct sales to Iran.

13. See, for example, James Gavin, "Odd Man Out," *Middle East Economic Digest*, 7 April 2000, 5. For a report on Iran's adherence in practice, see Reuters wire service report, "Reuters Survey, OPEC Adds One Mbpd Oil Output in April," 8 May 2000.

14. Martin Indyk, "The Clinton Administration's Approach to the Middle East," Keynote Address to the Soref Symposium on "Challenges to US Interests in the Middle East: Obstacles and Opportunities," Proceedings of the Washington Institute for Near East Policy, 18–19 May 1993, 1–8.

15. Cable News Network, 7 Jan. 1998, "Transcript of interview with Iranian President Mohammad Khatami."

16. Secretary of State Madeleine K. Albright, "Remarks at 1998 Asia Society Dinner," 17 June 1998, as released by the Office of the Spokesman, U.S. Department of State, 18 June 1998.

17. Secretary of State Madeleine K. Albright, speech to the American-Iranian Council, Omni Shoreham Hotel, Washington, DC, 17 March 2000.

18. *The New York Times* subsequently published key CIA documents on the coup in its issue of 16 April 2000.

19. See "Khamene'i Address in Mashhad," Voice of the Islamic Republic of Iran Radio 1, 25 March 2000, as translated by the Foreign Broadcast Information Service.

20. Declaration of the Organization of the Mojahedin of the Islamic Revolution of Iran, 4 April 2000, published in *Asr-e Ma* 156, 6 April 2000, 1, 6, 8. Translated by the Foreign Broadcast Information Service.

21. After charges of irregularities and a lengthy recount of many voting boxes, including invalidation of 720,000 votes in the Tehran constituency by the Guardian Council, Rafsanjani was eventually identified as number 20 on the Tehran list. He aligned himself squarely with the conservative faction and emerged as the key strategist in efforts to unseat the reformers.

The Contributors

BAHMAN BAKTIARI is director of the International Affairs Program and associate professor of political science at the University of Maine. His Ph.D. is from the Woodrow Wilson Department of Government and Foreign Affairs at the University of Virginia. He is the author of *Parliamentary Politics in Revolutionary Iran: Institutionalization of Factional Politics*. In 1999–2000 he was a visiting professor of political science at the American University in Cairo.

THOMAS BARFIELD is professor and chairman of anthropology at Boston University. His Ph.D. is from Harvard. He has conducted ethnographic research with nomads in Afghanistan and western China as well as historical work on steppe empires of Central Asia. He is the author of *The Central Asian Arabs of Afghanistan: Pastoral Nomadism in Transition*; *The Perilous Frontier: Nomadic Empires and China*; *The Nomadic Alternative* (coauthored with Alfred Szabo); and *Afghanistan: An Atlas of Indigenous Domestic Architecture*. He was recently a senior Fulbright scholar in Samarkand, Uzbekistan.

ASEF BAYAT is professor of sociology and Middle Eastern studies at the American University in Cairo. He is the author of *Workers and Revolution in Iran*; *Work, Politics, and Power*; and *Street Politics: Poor People's Movements in Iran*. He is currently writing a new book on Islamisms and social movement theory.

WILFRIED BUCHTA received his doctorate in Islamic studies from the Friedrich-Wilhelms University in Bonn and specializes in the modern history of Iran and Iraq. He has written two books on Iran, *Die iranische Schia und die islamische Einheit, 1979–1996* (The Iranian Shi`a and Islamic unity 1979–1996) and *Who Rules Iran? The Structure of Power in the Islamic Republic*. From 1998 to 2001 he served as the representative of the Konrad Adenauer Foundation in Rabat, Morocco. He currently works for the International Crisis Group in Amman, Jordan.

JUAN R. I. COLE is professor of Middle Eastern and South Asian history at the University of Michigan. His Ph.D. is from UCLA. He is the author of *Roots of North Indian Shi`ism in Iran and Iraq: Religion and State in Awadh, 1722–1859; Colonialism and Revolution in the Middle East: Social and Cultural Origins of Egypt's `Urabi Movement;* and *Modernity and the Millennium: The Genesis of the Baha'i Faith in the Nineteenth-Century Middle East.* He edited *Comparing Muslim Societies* and coedited, with Nikki Keddie, *Shi`ism and Social Protest.* He is the editor of the *International Journal of Middle East Studies.*

AHMAD KARIMI-HAKKAK received his Ph.D. from Rutgers University. He is professor of Persian language and literature and Iranian culture and civilization at the University of Washington. He wrote *Recasting Persian Poetry: Scenarios of Poetic Modernity in Iran.* He has also translated several volumes of Persian poetry into English and has written extensively on literary translation and translation theory as applied to Persian literature. He is currently working on modern Iranian redefinitions of the Persian classics, Rumi among them.

FIROOZEH KASHANI-SABET is assistant professor of history at the University of Pennsylvania. Her Ph.D. is from Yale. Her book *Frontier Fictions: Shaping the Iranian Nation, 1804–1946* looks at the significance of land in Iranian nationalism. She is currently at work on the subject of hygiene and humanism in the modern Middle East.

NIKKI R. KEDDIE is professor emerita of history, UCLA. Her Ph.D. is from the University of California, Berkeley. She has published eight single-author books, most recently *Qajar Iran and the Rise of Reza Khan,* and edited or coedited twelve collections, including *Women in Middle Eastern History* (coedited with Beth Baron). She is a 2002 recipient of the Award for Distinguished Scholarship from the American Historical Association. Her recent and current work is on women and on worldwide secularism and fundamentalism. She is proud of the students who worked with her at UCLA, among them six whose essays are included in this volume.

RUDI MATTHEE is associate professor of history at the University of Delaware. His Ph.D. is from UCLA. He has written extensively on Safavid and Qajar Iran. He is the author of *The Politics of Trade in Safavid Iran: Silk for Silver, 1600–1730* and is coeditor, with Beth Baron, of *Iran and Beyond: Essays in Middle Eastern History in Honor of Nikki R. Keddie.* He is currently working on a book about drugs and stimulants in early modern Iran. In 2002–2003 he is a fellow at the Institute for Advanced Study, Princeton, New Jersey.

GOLNAR MEHRAN is associate professor of education at Al-Zahra University in Tehran and is also a UNICEF education consultant. Her Ph.D. is from UCLA. Her publications are mainly on ideology and education, political socialization of schoolchildren, adult literacy, female schooling in postrevolutionary Iran, and girls' education in the Middle East. Her latest published work is "Lifelong Learning: New Opportunities for Women in a Muslim Country (Iran)," in *Comparative Education*, no. 35.

HAMID NAFICY is Nina J. Cullinan chair in art and art history and professor of film and media studies at Rice University. He has written extensively on Iranian cinema, theories of exile and diaspora, and cultures and media in exile. His Ph.D. is from UCLA. His books include *An Accented Cinema: Diasporic and Exilic Filmmaking*; *Home, Exile, Homeland: Film, Media, and the Politics of Place*; *The Making of Exile Cultures: Iranian Television in Los Angeles*; and *Iran Media Index*. He is also coeditor of *Otherness and the Media: The Ethnography of the Imagined and the Imaged*. His forthcoming book is *Iranian Cinema: A Social History*.

VALI NASR is associate professor of political science at the University of San Diego. He received his Ph.D. from M.I.T. He is the author of *The Vanguard of the Islamic Revolution: The Jama`at-i Islami of Pakistan*; *Mawdudi and the making of Islamic Revivalism*; and the forthcoming *The Islamic Leviathan: Islam and the Making of State Power*.

MONICA M. RINGER is Mellon Fellow at Williams College and a research fellow at Georgetown University's Center for Muslim-Christian Understanding. She received her Ph.D. degree from UCLA. She has been a visiting assistant professor of Islamic traditions at Oberlin College and of Middle Eastern history at the University of Massachusetts, Amherst. She is the author of *Education, Religion, and the Discourse of Cultural Reform in Qajar Iran*.

JASAMIN ROSTAM-KOLAYI teaches in the Department of History at California State University, Long Beach. She received her Ph.D. from the UCLA. Her dissertation is titled "The Women's Press, Modern Education, and the State in Early Twentieth-Century Iran, 1900–1930s."

GARY SICK is acting director of the Middle East Institute at Columbia University and executive director of Gulf/2000, an international research project on political, economic and security developments in the Persian Gulf. He was the principal White House aide for Iran during the Iranian Revolution and hostage crisis and is the author of *All Fall Down: America's Tragic Encounter With Iran* and of many other publications.

ABOLALA SOUDAVAR is an independent scholar based in Houston, Texas. He is the author of *The Art of the Persian Courts* and of many articles on Persian art history in both Persian and English.

NAYEREH TOHIDI is associate professor in the Women's Studies Department at California State University, Northridge, and a research fellow at the UCLA Center for Near Eastern Studies. She received her Ph.D. from the University of Illinois, Urbana-Champaign. She has been the recipient of a post-doctoral grant from Stanford University, a Fulbright lectureship, and a Woodrow Wilson Center scholarship. She has consulted with several United Nations bodies on women and development in the Middle East and the post-Soviet Caucasus. Her publications include *Feminism, Democracy, and Islamism in Iran* (in Persian); *Women in Muslim Societies: Diversity within Unity* (coedited with Herbert Bodman); and *Globalization, Gender, and Religion: Politics of Women's Rights in Catholic and Muslim Contexts* (coedited with Jane Bayes).

Index

Abbas I, Shah, 23, 72–74, 75, 106, 123, 124, 126, 130, 131, 132
Abbas II, Shah, 107, 132
Abbas Mirza, 115, 147, 150, 151, 152, 158
Abbasids, 3, 243
Abd Allah Qajar, 167
Abd al-Aziz, 100
Abd al-Aziz, Fathi, 309
Abd al-Maguid, Wahid, 321
Abd al-Mu'min, Muhammad Sa'id, 309
Abd al-Rahman Anbar, Muhammad, 309
Abd al-Raziq, Ali, 292
Abd al-Samad, 108, 109
Abdullah, Crown Prince, 281, 357, 358
Abol Fath Mirza, 135
Abraham, Prophet, 245, 288
Abu Bakr, 89, 299
Abu Musa, 359, 363, 366
Abu Sa'id, 108
Adil Shah, Yusuf, 25
Adil Shahi dynasty, 25
A'eneh-ye sekandari, 166
Al-Afghani, Jamal al-Din, 295
Afghanistan and Afghans, 5, 15, 21, 74, 75, 85, 130, 131, 149, 210, 219, 220, 225, 290, 328, 329, 338, 347, 363, 367
Africa and Africans, 174, 188, 246
Afshar, Mirza Mostafa, 150–52, 159
Afshar tribe, 72
Afsharid dynasty, 115
Aga Khan, 339, 340
Aga Khan Foundation, 340
Agha Khan family, 30
Agha Mohammad Khan Qajar, 134–35, 138

Ahl-i Hadith Movement, 330, 342, 343, 346
Ahmad, Israr, 231, 342
Ahmad, Qazi Husain, 331
Ahmad Shah Qajar, 175
Ahmadi, Hooshang, 282
Ahmadi-Khorasani, Nushin, 222
Ahmadnagar, 25
Ahmediya, 333, 342
Al-Ahram, 308, 321
Al-Ahram Center for Strategic Studies, 309
Akbar, Sultan, 16, 17, 20, 25, 109, 110
Akhaemenid dynasty, 66, 169
Akhavi, Shahrough, 322
Akhaviani, Mohammad, 273
Akhbar-e Iran (Iran News), 257
Akhundzadeh, Mirza Fath Ali, 165, 166, 168
Akkasbashi, Mirza Ebrahim Khan, 255
Alam, Muzaffar, 16–18
Alam-e Nesvan, 183, 191–98
Alborz College, 185, 189
Albright, Madeleine, 367, 368, 369
Alexander the Great, 130
Algeria, 209, 213, 318
Ali, Mir Sayyed, 108
Ali family, 332
Ali ibn Abi Talib, Imam, 23–24, 89, 105, 111, 115, 245, 246, 287, 292, 298, 299, 313, 343
Ali Nadwi, Maulana Abu'l Hasan, 335
Ali Naqvi, Maulana Sajjid, 336
Allamehzadeh, Reza, 261, 272
Alliance Française, 184
Alliance Israélite Universelle, 184

Alqas, 94
AMAL (Afwaj al Muqawama al Lub-
naniya), 335, 336, 337
Amanpour, Christiane, 227
Amasia, Treaty of, 103, 115
American College of Tehran, 185, 186,
187, 189
American Protestant Mission (Schools)
185–91
Amin al-Dauleh, 153
Amin al-Soltan Atabak, 154, 155, 156
Amir Kabir, 236
Amir Khusrau, 17, 21
Amnesty International, 213
Anatolia, 5, 63, 64, 65, 66, 70, 71, 74, 75,
89, 91, 103
Ancient Iran, 258
Andhra Pradesh, 26
Anglo-Iranian Oil Company, 306
Anglo-Persian Treaty of 1919, 169
Anglo-Russian Treaty of 1907, 167–68
Anjoman-e hekmat va falsafeh, 294
Anjoman-e hojjati, 286, 296
Anjuman-i Sipah-i Sabaha. *See* Sipah-i
Sabaha Pakistan (SSP)
Ansari, Shaikh Morteza, 287
Apple, The (*Sib*), 266, 268
Aqa Mirak, 101, 103, 104, 108
Aq-qoyunlu dynasty, 61, 70–71, 92, 93,
94, 100, 108
Arab League, 315
Arab world and Arabs, 5, 6, 7, 63, 64,
66, 67, 71, 74, 76, 128, 129, 165, 166,
236, 243, 247, 281–82, 285, 306, 315,
318, 320, 321, 332, 364, 365
A`rabi, Fereshteh, 209
Arabia, 24, 63, 65, 125
Arabic language and literature, 5, 22, 32,
110, 187, 218
Aram, Ahmad, 172
Arberry, A. J., 37
Ardabil, 71, 89, 106, 132
Aref, Muhammad, 111
Arefi Shirazi, Fathollah, 94
Aria, Fatemeh Mo`tamed, 263
Armenians, 123, 140, 171, 184, 185, 190,
192

Aryans and Aryan beliefs, 8, 165, 166,
174, 176, 177, 247
Arzu, 21
Al-Asad, Hafiz, 312
Ascent of Man, 258
Ashkevari, Hojjatoleslam Hasan Yusefi,
222, 286, 290–93
Ashtiyani, Abbas Eqbal, 174
Ashura, 285
Asia and Asians, 155, 188, 194, 223, 246
Askari, Ayatollah Morteza, 286, 291, 296
Aslani, Mohammad Reza, 261
Asr-e jadid, 150–51
Assadi, Shahram, 273
Assyrians, 185
Astarabad, 131, 134
Astarabadi, 21, 131
Astrakhan, 132, 133
Ataturk, Mustafa Kemal, 175–76, 256
Attebai, Mohammad, 270
Auda, Muhammad, 312
Aurangzib, 26, 107
Australia, 223, 263, 372
Al-Awa, Salim, 311
Awad, Louis, 310
Awadh, 20, 27, 28–30, 331
Ayyubid dynasty, 24
Az Karkheh ta Rhine. See *From Karkheh
to Rhine*
Azadi, Gholamreza, 273
Azerbaijan, 65, 70, 73, 76, 137, 177
Azerbaijan, Republic of, 210, 211, 212
Azeris, 190, 211, 212
Al-Azhar, 284, 292, 300, 305, 313, 317
Al-Azhar, 321
Aziz-Allah Khan, Mirza, 197

Babur, 16, 90, 95, 98, 106, 107
Bachehha-ye Aseman. See *Children
of Heaven*
Badi` al-Zaman, Mirza, 95, 98
Baghchehban, 237
Baghdad, 32, 70, 74, 103, 360
Baha'is, 171, 286
Bahar, Mohammad Taqi (Malek
al-Sho`ara), 166, 171, 175
Bahmani dynasty, 25, 26

Bahrain, 128, 290, 356, 358, 365
Bahram Mirza, 93
Bahrami, Ramin, 273
Baizai, Bahram, 259, 261, 264, 265, 268
Bakhtiar, Shahpour, 357
Bakhtiyari, 61, 73, 76, 190
Baku, 137, 210, 212, 364
Balkhi, Mahmud, 19
Baluchistan and Baluchis, 27, 61, 74, 83, 85, 347
Bamdad, Badr al-Moluk, 197
Bandar Abbas, 24, 124, 125, 126, 127
Bangladesh, 15, 225, 226, 328
Banie`temad, Rakhshan, 223, 264, 265
Bani Sadr, Abol Hasan, 285, 309
Bank Melli, 258
Bank Saderat, 314
Baqer Khan, 236
Barks, Coleman, 7, 36, 48, 50–51, 53–58
Basra, 124, 128
Ba`th Regime, Iraq, 243
Ba`th Regime, Syria, 290, 312
Bayezid I, 91, 103
Bayezid II, Sultan, 90–92, 95, 103
Al-Baz, Usama, 318
Bazargan, Mehdi, 285, 288, 290, 291, 309
Bazleh, Shirin, 272
Bedouins, 63, 64, 65
Behbahani, Aqa Ahmad, 19, 135
Behbahani clan, 20
Behraznia, Mahmud, 273
Behzad, 93
Behzad, Faryal, 273
Beijing, 212, 213, 216, 218, 220
Beirut, 309, 321
Bekovich-Cherkaskii, Alexander, 134
Bengal, 16, 20, 26, 27, 28, 30
Berlin, 224, 293
Bhagavad Gita, 22, 32
Bible, 37, 187
Bidel, 21
Bihar al-anwar, 283
Bijapur, 20, 24, 25
Binesh, Taqi, 177
Biruni, Abu Raihan, 22, 236
Blackboards (*Takhteh Siyah*), 266, 268
Bly, Robert, 37, 58

Bombay, 23, 30, 126, 129
Booth, Marilyn, 193
Borujerdi, Ayatollah, 289
Boyce, Annie Stocking, 187–90
Brahmins and Brahmanism, 22, 245
Braj Bhasha language, 22
Bruyn, Cornelis de, 132, 137
Budaq Qazvini, 105
Buddhists and Buddhism, 194, 217, 245
Bukhara, 17, 41, 42, 46, 82, 99, 100
Bukhari family, 332
Burhan al-Mulk. *See* Nishapuri, Mir Muhammad Amin
Burton, Antoinette, 196
Bushehr, 128, 365
Buttho, Benazir, 332
Buttho, Zulfiqar Ali, 329, 332
Bu-ye Kafur, Atr-e Yas. See Smell of Camphor, Fragrance of Jasmine
Buyid dynasty, 24, 66
Byzantine culture, 5

Cahiers du Cinéma, 265
Cairo, 32, 284, 289, 300, 305, 307, 308, 309, 310, 314, 315, 317, 320, 322
Cairo University, 311, 312
Camp David Accords, 307, 308, 314, 315, 316, 361
Canada, 224, 263, 266, 270, 273, 288, 372
Cannes International Film Festival, 265, 268
Carter, President Jimmy, 307
Carter Doctrine, 361
Caspian Sea and littoral, 130, 131, 133, 134, 140, 174, 211, 364, 365
Catherine II (the Great), 137, 138
Caucasus, 65, 73, 130, 138, 163, 209, 210, 363
Central Asia, 4, 7, 17, 19, 21, 42, 62, 63, 65, 66, 67, 70, 75, 82, 83, 134, 149, 156, 163, 209, 210, 211, 266, 363
Chaghatay Turkish, 16, 17
Chak dynasty, 25
Chaldiran, 72, 91, 93
Changiz Khan, 94, 95
Chehabi, Houchang, 171
Chehel Sotun, 107

Chehel tuti, 197
Chekalevskii, P., 137
Chicherin, Ivan Ivanovich, 132
Children of Heaven (Bachehha-ye Aseman), 266, 267, 269
China and the Chinese, 63, 67, 155, 192, 194, 195, 339, 358, 372
Chishti order, 27
Christianity and Christians, 6, 23, 123, 130, 158, 171, 183, 184, 185, 186, 187, 217, 245, 322
Chubak, Sadeq, 259
Chundigar, I. I., 332
Church Missionary Society, 183
CIA (U.S. Central Intelligence Agency), 290, 306
Civilisation, 258
Clinton, President Bill, 10; administration of, 367
CNN, 227, 367
Cohn, Bernard, 129
Cold War, 361
Color of Paradise, The (Rang-e Khoda), 264, 267, 269
Conference of the Organization of Islamic Countries (OIC), 281
Constitutional Revolution, 207, 236
Cossacks, 133, 140
Council of Guardians, 217
Cow, The (Gav), 258, 259
Crossroads of Civilization, 258
Crusaders, 24
Curie, Marie, 192

Dabestan-e mazaheb, 23
Da`iat wa'l Irshad, 346
Dailamites, 91
Da'irat al-ma`aref-e eslami, 291
Da'irat al-ma`aref-e tashayyo`, 291
Damascus, 70, 155, 317
Dar al-taqrib movement and publishing house 284, 289, 306
Dara Shikuh, 22
Dariush, 240
Darugheh, 95
Darya`i, Zinat, 225
Daryush, Hajir, 259

Daulatabadi, Mahmud, 259
Daulatshah, Mirza Mohammad Ali, 111, 115
Deccan, 27
Dehkhoda, Ali Akbar, 175
Delhi, 17, 21, 28, 29, 32, 75
Deobandi Movement, 330, 342, 346, 347
Derakhshandeh, Puran, 273
Desert Storm, 361
Dialogue of civilizations, 10, 318
Din main ghulluw, 343
Do Zan. See Two Women
Dokhtar-e Lor. See Lor Girl, The
Donne, John, 21
Dorrani, Ahmad Shah, 75
Dorrani dynasty, 27
Dorrani Pushtuns, 74
Dryden, John, 38, 39, 41, 42
Dutch, 124, 131

East India Company, Dutch, 124, 126, 127, 128
East India Company, English, 28, 122, 124, 125–29, 135
Ebadi, Shirin, 224
Ebrahim Mirza, 105
Ebtekar, Ma`sumeh, 220
Economic Cooperation Organization, 364
Egypt and the Egyptians, 8, 24, 149, 192, 193, 194, 195, 226, 263, 284, 288, 300, 305–23, 360
Elton, John, 128
Emam al-Hokama, Agha, 190
Enayat, Hamid, 285
England and the English , 8, 21, 28, 29, 30, 32, 39, 77, 121–22, 125–29, 130, 135–40, 150, 152, 153, 157, 175, 176, 177, 183, 194, 196, 221, 243, 294, 306, 322, 358
Erzurum, Treaty of, 111, 115
Esfahani, Mirza Abu Taleb (Khan), 135, 150
Esfahani, Mirza Nathan, 19
Eshq Bedun-e Marz, 273
E`tesami, Parvin, 171, 191, 237
E`tesami, Yusof, 191

E`tesham al-Din, Mirza, 150
Ettehadieh Nizam-Mafi, Mansoureh, 30
Ettesam, Shirin, 272
Europe and Europeans, 147, 148, 149,
    150, 152, 153, 154, 155, 156, 157, 159, 165,
    166, 167, 188, 192, 193, 194, 195, 196,
    223, 248, 264, 266, 268, 269, 270, 272,
    273, 310, 314, 357, 372

Facets Multimedia, 266
Fahmideh, Hosain, 241
Fajr International Film Festival, 273
Fallahian, Ali, 357, 358
Farabi Cinema Foundation, 262, 264,
    266
Farhang-e shahaneh, 92–93, 99
Farhangestan, 175
Farman Farma, Abdol Hosain Mirza,
    190–91
Farman Farmaian, Sattareh, 190, 191
Farmanara, Bahman, 259, 273
Farrokh Beg, 112
Fars, 77, 92, 126, 137
Faruq, King, 306
Farzaneh, 216
Fath Ali Shah, 150, 152
Fatima, 207, 209, 213, 214, 215, 220, 221,
    245
Fatimids, 24
Fauziya, 305, 315
Fayyazi, Faizi, 19
Fedayan-e Islam, 312
Fendereski, Mir, 22–23
Ferdausi, 236
Film International, 270
Fiske, Fidelia, 187
Fitzgerald, Edward, 39, 58
Forster, George, 134–35
Forughi, Abol Hasan, 176
Forughi, Mohammad Ali, 256
Fotuhat-e kompani, 135
France and the French, 16, 153, 157, 164,
    165, 176, 183, 184, 186, 187, 214, 221, 267,
    273, 358
Franco-Prussian War, 176
Franks, 123, 124, 125
Franny and Zooey, 271

Fraser, James, 137
Friendship, 126
*From Karkheh to Rhine (Az Karkheh ta
    Rhine)*, 273
Frost, David, 258
Fuziyeh. *See* Fauziya

Gadamer, Hans-Georg, 49
Gaffary, Farrokh, 259
Gav. See Cow, The
Georgia and Georgians, 16, 130, 132, 138
Geramizadegan, Ashraf, 222
Germany and Germans, 77, 176, 263,
    273, 357, 358
Al-Ghamidi, Javid Ahmad, 330
Ghazal, 41–48
Al-Ghazali, Muhammad, 32, 294
Ghazan Khan, 67–68
Ghaznavid dynasty, 61
Ghelza'i Pushtuns, 74, 75
Ghiyas al-Din, 21
Ghojdovan, 95, 98
Gholams, 73
Gilan, 92, 130, 131, 132, 133, 134, 140, 290
Gilani, General Ghulam, 341
Gilani, Syed As`ad, 331
Gobineau, Compte Joseph Arthur de,
    164, 165, 174
Gog and Magog, 130
Gokal family, 332
Golconda (Hyderabad), 20, 24, 25, 26,
    126
Golestan, 68
Golestan, Treaty of, 138
Golmakani, Houchang, 270
Golpayegani, Ayatollah Mohammad,
    287
Golshiri, Hushang, 259, 271
Golsorkhi, Morteza, 197
Gombroon. *See* Bandar Abbas
Greeks, 5, 32, 172, 305
Griboyedov, 151
Gujarati, Abd al-Latif, 19
Gulf Cooperation Council (GCC), 317,
    358, 360, 363
Gulf of Oman, 174
Gulf States, 209, 360, 365, 366

Habib family, 332
Habl al-Matin, 168
Ha'eri, Abdol Hadi, 122, 128, 136, 139
Haeri, Shahla, 210
Hafez, 4, 7, 37, 39, 42, 43, 44, 46, 48, 53,
   57, 58
Hafteh-ye vahdat, 283
Haider Mirza, 106
Haikal, Muhammad, 308, 311
Hajjarian, Sa'id, 368
Hajji Agha, Aktor-e Sinema, 256
Hajji Mohammad Khan, 140
Hakim Mirza, Muhammad, 110, 112
Halide Hanom, 192
Hamadan, 25, 183, 184, 186
Hamzeh Mirza, 106
Hamzeh-nameh, 109
Hanafi, Hasan, 311
Hanway, Jonas, 134, 137, 140
Haritash, Khosrau, 259
Harun al-Rashid, 32
Hasan, Imam, 111, 245
Hasan al-Askari, Imam, 24
Hashemi, Fa'ezeh, 219, 222
Hashemi, Fatemeh, 219
Hashemi, Fereshteh, 209
Hatamikia, Ebrahim, 273
Hawwa, Sayyid, 285
Hayat family, 332
Hazin Lahijani, Mohammad Ali, 21, 125,
   130, 136, 140
Hedayat, Mehdi Qoli Khan (Mokhber
   al-Saltaneh), 155, 156, 159, 160
Hefz-e sehheh-ye zanan va dokhtaran,
   197
Heidegger, Martin, 49
Heinrich Böll Foundation, 293
Hejab, 209–12, 214, 239
Hekmat, Ali, 320
Hekmat, Ali Asghar, 175
Hellenistic culture, 5
Herat, 19, 70, 74, 93, 94, 95, 99, 100, 110,
   166
High Council of the Cultural Revolu-
   tion, 294
Hindavi language, 16
Hindi language, 15, 29, 31

Hindus and Hinduism, 15, 18, 19, 22,
   23, 26, 28, 194, 217
Hizb al-tahrir, 285
Hizb al-Wasat, 323
Hizb-i Wahdat, 347
Hizbullah, 321, 337
Hoquq-e Zanan, 222
Hormuz, 74, 126, 139
Hosain Baiqara, Soltan, 94
Hosain Beg, 126
Hosain Mirza, Mozaffar, 95
Hosain-e Kord, 197
Hughli, 20, 24
Hujjaji, Abd al-Hakim, 317
Al-Hukuma al-islamiya, 312
Human Rights Watch, 224
Humayun, 20, 21, 32, 106–7
Hungary, 101, 263
Hunza Valley, 339, 340
Husain, Imam, 26, 27, 236, 245, 246,
   286, 339, 343
Husain family, 332
Husain, Mufti Ja'far, 335, 336
Husaini, Allama Arif, 335, 336, 337, 339
Huwaidi, Fahmi, 311
Hyderabad, 26, 27, 30, 333. *See also*
   Golconda

Ibn Hayyan, Jabir, 246
Ibn Khaldun, 7, 63, 64, 71
Ibn Sina, 236
Ijtihad, 287
Il-Khan dynasty, 61, 66, 70
Illuminationism, 32
Imam Bukhari movement, 335
Imam family, 332
Imam Jom'eh, 221
Imam Qoli Khan, 126
Imamia Student Organization (ISO),
   335, 336, 338, 341
India and Indians, 7, 15–32, 66, 83, 126,
   128, 129, 135, 136, 149, 150, 192, 194,
   195, 218, 245, 256, 290, 328, 330, 332,
   333, 335, 339, 342. *See also* Mughal
   dynasty; South Asia
Indo-European languages and peoples,
   8, 17, 164, 165, 166, 247

Indo-Persian literature, 21
International Conference on Population and Development, 317
International Congress on Woman and Islamic World Revolution, 214
International Women's Day, 206, 225
Iqbal, Muhammad, 31
Iran, Islamic Revolution and Republic, 3, 5, 6, 8, 9, 10 , 31, 171, 178, 206, 211–27, 232–50, 261, 268, 273, 281–300, 307, 310, 312, 327–48, 355–73
Iran Bethel College 185–91, 192, 196
Iran Is My Home (*Iran Sara-ye Man Aast*), 273
Iran min al-dakhil, 311
Iran Sara-ye Man Aast. See Iran Is My Home
Iran-e Farda, 291
Iran-Egypt Friendship Society, 320, 322
Irani, Ardeshir, 256
Irani Inqilab: Imam Khumaini awr Shi`ayyat, 346
Iranian Journal of International Affairs, 210
Iranian Women's Studies Foundation, 224
Iran-Iraq War, 206, 241, 243, 247, 284, 285, 311, 314, 315, 316, 356, 358, 359, 360
Iran-Libya Sanctions Act, 372
Iran-Misr Bank, 314, 317
Iranshahr, 163
Iraq, 24, 29, 62, 85, 209, 243, 284, 311, 312, 315, 339, 356, 358, 361, 363, 364, 367, 368, 369
Irons, William, 65
Isfahan, 15, 32, 65, 76, 107, 130, 131, 132, 133, 172, 183, 184, 190
Isfandiyar, Maulana, 346
Iskandar Mirza, President, 332
Al-Islam wa usul al-hukm, 292
Islamabad, 332, 338, 341, 357
Islamic Conference of Information Ministers, 320
Islamic Institute of Women, 216–17
Islamic Party of Azerbaijan, 211
Islamic Propaganda Organization, 317

Islamists and Islamism, 313, 314, 317, 327–48, 373
Isma`il, Imam, 24
Isma`il, Shah, 25, 71, 72, 89, 90–95, 98, 101, 107, 110, 240
Isma`il II, Shah, 72, 103, 105–6
Isma`ilis, 16, 24, 30, 339, 340
Ispahani, M. A., 332
Ispahani family, 332
Israel, 306, 308, 310, 315, 316, 317, 319, 360, 365, 367
Issari, Mohammad Ali, 258
Istanbul, 32, 106, 111, 155
Ivan IV, Tsar, 130

Jafari Jozani, Masud, 273
Jahangir, 20, 22
Jahanshah Qara-qoyunlu, 99
Jalali, Moluk Khanom, 190, 192
Jalali Sohravardi order. *See* Sohravardi order
Jalili, Abolfazl, 265
Jami, 23, 32
Jami`at-i Ulama-i Hind, 329
Jami`at-i Ulama-i Islam (JUI), 329
Jami`at-i Ulama-i Pakistan (JUP) 329, 330
Jam`iyat-e taraqqi khahan-e Iran, 168
Janissaries, 73, 91, 92, 101
Japan and the Japanese, 155, 156, 157, 192, 194, 195, 221, 372
Jaubert, Amédée, 138
Jebadar, Ali Qoli Baig, 107
Jens-e Dovvom?, 222
Jhangvi, Maulana Haqnawaz, 346, 347
Jihad Group, 313
Jones, Sir William, 7, 37, 38, 39, 41, 42, 43, 44, 46, 47, 48
Jordan, Mary Park, 186
Jordan, Samuel, 186, 189–90
Joseph, Prophet, 100
Journal of Foreign Policy, 218
Judaism and Jews, 6, 158, 171, 183, 184, 185, 190, 192, 194, 245

Kadivar, Hojjatoleslam Mohsen, 221
Kadivar, Jamileh, 221, 222

Kalantar, 137
Kamran Mirza, 107
Kant, Immanuel, 294
Kanun-e banovan, 171
Kanun-e Sinemagaran-e Pishro, 259
Kar, Mehrangiz, 207, 224
Karachi, 341, 346
Karbala, 246, 286, 339, 364
Karim Khan Zand, 76, 128, 129, 134, 135, 136, 137, 139, 240
Kashmir, 25, 26, 75, 339
Kashmiri, Khwaja Abd al-Karim, 19
Kavakchi, Marveh, 211
Kaveh, 169
Kayasth caste, 18
Kazim, Safinaz, 311
Kazim ibn al-Ja`far, 24
Keats, John, 46
Keddie, Nikki, 162, 165
Kermani, Mirza Aqa Khan, 166, 168
Kermanshah, 76, 184
Khadija, 245
Khadim al-Haramain al-Sharifain, 92
Khafi, 21
Khalifeh Soltan, 126
Khalkhali, Ayatollah Sadeq, 308
Khamenei, Ayatollah Ali, 216, 221, 281, 284, 368
Khamenei, Hojjatoleslam Hadi, 211
Khamseh confederacy, 61, 76, 77
Khatami, Mohammad, 9, 10, 213, 217, 219, 220, 233, 249–50, 267, 274, 281, 282, 290, 293, 318, 319, 320, 321, 322, 358, 365, 367, 368, 369, 370
Khatami, Mohammad-Reza, 211
Khatri caste, 18
Khayyam, Omar, 3, 39, 58
Khomeini, Ruhollah Ayatollah, 6, 178, 206, 209, 214, 215, 219, 221, 237, 240, 261, 281, 283, 285, 286, 288, 294, 295–96, 308, 310, 311, 312, 316, 334, 335, 336, 339, 340, 342, 346, 356, 357, 358, 360, 362, 370, 371
Khorasan, 19, 65, 66, 67, 73, 74, 76, 90, 94, 95, 99
Khorasani, Nushin Ahmadi, 207, 224, 226–27

Khosrau Parviz, 240
Khristoforov, K., 133
Khu'i, Ayatollah Abol Qasem, 339
Khumaini: al-Badil al-islami, 309
Khuzestan, 74, 317, 359
Khwarazm Shah dynasty, 61
Kiarostami, Abbas, 259, 261, 263, 265, 266, 267, 268
Kimiai, Masud, 258, 259, 261
Kimiavi, Parviz, 273
Kuchukov, Vasilei, 133
Kurds, 61, 62, 63, 76, 85, 190, 309, 357, 363
Kuwait, 290, 315, 316, 359, 360, 361, 362, 364

Lahiji, Shahla, 207, 224
Lahore, 17, 32, 338, 342, 343, 346, 347
Lashkar-i Jhangvi, 346
Lashkar-i Tayyiba, 346
Latin America and Latin Americans, 246, 266
Lazarist Catholic Mission, 184, 187
League of Muslim Women, 219
Lebanon, 214, 223, 317, 321, 335, 336, 337, 338, 356
Lezgis (Lezgees), 137
Lobanov-Rostovskii mission, 132
Lor Girl, The (Dokhtar-e Lor), 256
Lot, Prophet, 288
Louis XIV, 147
Love Without Borders, 273
Lucknow, 29, 135, 333, 335, 346
Lutis, 92, 101

Ma`ad, 299
Ma`adi Military Hospital, 308
Madrasa, 17
Mahayana Buddhism, 22
Mahmudabad, Raja, 332
Mahnameh-ye Sinema'i-ye Film, 270
Maidan Pahlavi, 314
Majidi, Majid, 263, 265, 266–67, 269
Majles, 167, 211, 215, 219, 221, 222, 368, 369, 370, 371
Majlesi, Mohmmad Baqer, 283
Majlis al-Sha`b, 321, 323

Majma` al-taqrib bain al-madhahib
 al-islamiya, 284, 297, 300
Majma` al-tavarikh, 131
Al-Makasib, 287
Makhmalbaf, Mohsen, 264, 265, 267,
 268, 269, 273
Makhmalbaf, Samira, 265, 268
Maknun, Soraya, 210
Makran, 74, 126
Maktubat-e Kamal al-Dauleh, 165
Malaysia, 217, 310
Malkom Khan, Mirza, 158, 163
Mamluk dynasty, 91–92
Manicheanism, 6
Maratha dynasty, 27
Marthiyah, 29
Marv, 74, 82, 95
Marvell, Andrew, 43, 48
Marz miyan-e din va siyasat, 309
Mas'ala al-thaura al-islamiya, 309
Mashhad, 76, 95, 212, 368
Matthee, Rudi, 322
Al-Maula, Sa`ud, 223
Mawdudi, Abu'l A`la, Mawlana, 292,
 329
Mazandaran, 130, 133, 134
Mazar-e Sharif, 220, 347
Mecca, 23, 91, 95, 155, 212, 283
Medina, 91, 283
Mehrjui, Dariush, 258, 259, 261, 264,
 265, 271
Mesopotamia, 65, 74, 89, 173
Milani, Tahmineh, 223, 265
Millet, Kate, 225
Milli Yikjahati Council, 338
Milton, John, 43, 48
Mir Ali, 100
Mir Mosavver, 108
Mir Sayyed Ali, 108, 109
Miramax Films, 266, 267, 269
Mirbaqeri, Davud, 273
Mirza Hosain Khan, 153
Mirza Kuchek Khan-e Jangali, 236
Mirza Mohammad, 137
Mirza Shafi`, 138
Misr-Iran Shipping Company, 314
Mo`ayyad al-Molk, 153

Mohajerani, Ataollah, 221, 263, 271
Mohammad, Soltan, 93
Mohammad Hosain, Mir, 135
Mohammad Khodabandeh, Shah, 72,
 106
Mohammad Reza, Pahlavi, 84, 169, 172,
 177, 240, 246, 248, 258, 288, 306, 307,
 310, 314, 315, 355, 359, 362, 371
Mohammad Shah, 152, 185, 186
Mohebbi, Shahid, 267
Mojahedin-e Khalq, 364, 367
Mokhber al-Saltaneh. *See* Hedayat,
 Mehdi Qoli Khan
*Moment of Innocence, A (Nun va
 Goldun)*, 269
Momtahen al-Dauleh, 153
Mongolia, 64, 65
Mongols, 7, 17, 61, 66, 67, 69, 70, 95, 236,
 243, 247
Monshi, Eskandar, 126
Montazeri, Ayatollah Hosain Ali, 283,
 288, 292, 293
Mosaddeq, Mohammad, 3, 177, 178, 236,
 256, 306, 314, 368
Moscow, 130, 131, 132, 307
Moses, 245
Mostafavi, Zahra, 209, 210, 219
Mostashar al-Dauleh, 163
Mottahari, Ayatollah, 287
Mozaffar al-Din Shah, 152, 153, 154, 155,
 157, 158–59, 186, 255
Mubarak, Hosni, 307, 315, 316, 318, 321
Mufti Ja`far. *See* Husain, Mufti Ja`far
Mughal dynasty, 16–27, 28, 29, 31, 32, 72,
 74, 75, 83, 90, 107, 108, 109
Muhammad, Prophet, 23, 30, 89, 235,
 240, 241, 245, 249, 283, 284, 291, 292,
 295, 298, 299, 313, 343
Muhammad II, Sultan, 90
Muhammad al-Baqir, Imam, 287
Muhammad al-Mahdi, Imam, 24
Muhammad Shita, Shaikh Ali Hasan,
 316
Mukhlis, Anand Ram, 18, 19
Mulla Sadr, 338
Mulla Sadra, 23, 32
Multan, 346, 347

Murad II, Sultan, 25
Murad III, 105, 106
Murad Bakhsh, 107
Murids, 27, 71
Musa, Amr, 319
Musa al-Kazem, Imam, 90
Musavi, Mir Hosain, 357
Mush va gorbeh, 197
Muslim Brothers (Egyptian), 307, 312,
    313
Muslim Brothers (Syrian), 285, 290, 312
Muslim Student Association, 288
Muslims, 183, 185, 186, 188, 190, 192, 194,
    217, 235, 236, 244–45, 248, 249, 283,
    284, 292, 295, 317
Mut`a, 209, 284

Nabavi, Behzad, 369
Nabili, Marva, 261, 272
Nader Shah, 20, 21, 28, 75, 128, 134, 137
Naderi, Amir, 259, 261, 272
Nadwatu'l-Ulama, 335
Nadwi, Sayyid Abu'l Hasan Ali, 346
Nafisi, Sa`id, 172–73
Naft va solteh, 309
Nagorno-Karabagh, 364
Al-Nahar, 309
Nahwa thaura islamiya, 309
Najafabadi, Hojjatoleslam Ne`matollah
    Salehi, 286, 287, 288
Najm-e Sani, 98
Napoleon, 129, 138
Naqhshabandi order, 27
Naqvi, Allama, 337
Naqvi, Ghulam Raza, 338
Naqvi, Shahid Husain, 337
Naser al-Din Shah, 152, 153, 154, 157, 159,
    186
Naser al-Din Shah, Aktor-e Sinema.
    See *Once Upon a Time Cinema*
Nasser, Gamal Abdul, 284, 306, 307,
    312
Nateq-Nuri, Ali Akbar, 318, 370
National Committee for Dialogue
    between Muslims and Christians, 223
National Iranian Radio and Television
    (NIRT), 257, 258, 259

Naubat-e Asheqi. See *Time to Love, A*
Nava'i, Shahin, 223
Neda, 209
Nehzat-e azadi-ye Iran, 288, 290
Nek Rai, 19
Ne`mat-Allahi order, 23, 26
Neoplatonism, 32
Neshat, Shirin, 272
Nestorians, 171
Netanyahu, Benjamin, 319
New York Film Festival, 261
Nezam al-Molk, 68
Nezam-e jadid, 147, 150
Niebuhr, Carsten, 135, 136
Nishapuri, Mir Muhammad Amin
    (Burhan al-Mulk), 28
Nishapuri dynasty, 28
Nizam of Haydarabad, 27
Nizam Shah, Burhan, 25
Nizam Shahi dynasty, 25
Noah, 245, 288
Noqtavis, 19
North Africa, 63, 65, 149, 307
North America, 223, 266, 269, 270, 272
Nubuwwa, 299
Nu`mani, Muhammad Manzur, 346
Nun va Goldun. See *Moment of Inno-
    cence, A*
Nur Jahan, 20, 32
Nurbakhshi order, 25
Nuri, Shaikh Fazlollah, 261

Obaidollah Khan, 98–101, 102, 103
October War, 307, 310
Office of Women's Affairs (OWA) 217,
    218, 219
Ogurtjoy people, 134
Ohanian, Avanes, 255, 256
Olearius, Adam, 123
Oman and Omani Arabs, 126, 127
*Once Upon a Time Cinema (Naser
    al-Din Shah, Aktor-e Sinema),* 269
Organization of Islamic Countries
    (OIC), 319, 358
Organization of the Mojahedin of the
    Islamic Revolution of Iran (OMIR),
    368–69

Organization of Petroleum Exporting Countries (OPEC), 366
Ormavi, Loqman, 94
Orumiyeh, 183, 184, 185, 187
Ottoman Empire and dynasty, 7, 16, 24, 70, 72, 73, 74, 75, 90–91, 94, 95, 101, 103, 105, 106, 108, 109, 110, 111, 115, 123, 125, 128, 132, 133, 147, 149, 192, 194
Oudh. *See* Awadh
Oxus River, 89, 95

Pahlavi dynasty and regime, 3, 5, 8, 83, 168–78, 243, 247, 248, 256, 257, 261, 263, 267, 310, 327
Pakistan, 9, 15, 27, 28, 31, 62, 209, 210, 213, 214, 217, 219, 328–48, 363
Pakistan Peoples Party, 336
Panahi, Jafar, 264, 265
Panipati, Nizam al-Din, 22, 23
Pari, 271
Pari Khan Khanom, 103
Paris, 111, 153, 154, 157, 184, 255
Parsis, 19, 23
Parthian dynasty, 6
Patna, 21, 23
Payam-e Hajar, 216, 217, 222
Payami, Babak, 273
Persian Gulf, 65, 74, 77, 89, 124, 125–29, 306, 307, 315, 317, 347, 357, 358, 359, 361, 363, 372
Persian language and literature, 5, 7, 15, 16–22, 29, 30, 31, 32, 36, 58, 92, 94, 110, 163, 168, 175, 234, 236, 315, 322
Peshawar, 27, 346
Peter the Great, 129, 130, 131, 132, 133, 137, 138, 140, 151
Philippines, 214
Pirzadeh, Hajji, 153–54, 159
Pish-ahangi, 171
Pishdadian dynasty, 95
Pitz, Rafi, 273
Point IV Program, 257
Poland, 263
Pooya, Rafigh, 272
Pope, Alexander, 39, 43
Popper, Karl, 294
Portugal and Portuguese, 74, 126, 131, 139

Potiphar, 45
Poya, Maryam, 213
Presbyterians, 186
Punjab, 16, 26, 27, 28, 75, 332, 341, 346, 347
Pushtuns, 62, 63
Puya, Aqa Murtaza, 335

Qabz va bast-e te'orik-e shari`at, 294
Qadiri order, 27
Qaisar, 258
Qajar, Ahmad Faruqi, 265
Qajar dynasty, 5, 8, 26, 30, 31, 61, 72, 75–77, 82, 83, 111, 115, 121, 122, 129, 134, 135, 136, 137, 138, 139–40, 163, 165, 169, 170, 175, 183, 185, 243, 256, 259, 261
Qandahar, 74, 75, 107
Qansu al-ghuri, 91
Qara-qoyunlu dynasty, 70
Qashqa'i, 61, 76, 77
Qasr-e Shirin (Zohab), Treaty of, 74
Qatar, 319, 358
Qavvali, 28
Qavvam family, 77
Qazvin, 15, 73, 131, 132
Qazvini, Asad Beg, 19
Qeshm, 128, 131, 225
Qizilbash, 16, 28, 61, 71, 89, 90, 91, 92, 95, 98, 99, 101, 106, 131
Qizilbash family, 332
Qom, 220, 286, 287, 288, 290, 338
Qommi, Mohammad Taqi, 284, 306
Qommi, Qazi Ahmad, 94, 103
Qotbzadeh, Sadeq, 285
Quest for Identity, The, 207
Quran, 100, 101, 111, 183, 197, 214, 234, 238, 283, 287, 298
Qutb, Sayyid, 292
Qutb-Shahi dynasty, 25–26
Qutbu'din, Sultan-Quli, 25

Rafsanjani, Ali Akbar Hashemi, 217, 219, 281, 282, 311, 316, 317, 318, 357, 370, 371
Rahman, Fazlur, 330–31
Rahnavard, Zahra, 209, 218–19
Rahnema, 167
Rahshan, Mehrtaj, 190

Ram, Haggay, 247
Ram Mohan Roy, 30
Rama, 22
Ramazani, Mohsen, 267
Rang-e Khoda. See *Color of Paradise, The*
Rawalpindi, 347
Raza family, 332
Razi, 236
Reagan, Ronald, presidency of, 361, 367
Regulating Act, 129
Renan, Ernest, 162, 164–65, 174, 178
Resalat, 318
Rex Theater, 260
Reza Shah (Khan), 8, 83–84, 169–77, 183, 190, 197, 198, 256, 308
Rhodes, 101
Al-Rifa`i Mosque, 308, 314
Riza, Imam, 245
Romans, 172
Romanticism, 39
Rostam al-Hokama, 135–36
Rothschild, Baron Edmond de, 111
Rushdie, Salman, 357
Rumi, Jalal al-Din, 3, 7, 23, 32, 36, 37, 48, 50, 51, 54–58, 294, 298
Rumlu tribe, 70, 72
Russia and the Russians, 8, 82, 121–22, 123, 128, 129–35, 137–38, 140, 151, 153, 155, 156, 157, 163, 165, 169, 196, 211, 243, 248, 365
Ruz al-Yusuf, 310

Sa`d Abad Pact, 176
Sadat, Anwar, 307, 308, 310, 313, 316
Saddam Hussein, 243, 311, 312, 315, 359, 362
Sadeq, Isa, 175
Sadeq Khan, 135, 136, 148
Sa`di, 4, 68, 236
Sadiq, Kalb-i (Qalb), 335
Sa`edi, Gholamhosain, 258–59, 271
Saeed Vafa, Mehrnaz, 272
Safavi, Navvab, 312
Safavids, 5, 6, 7, 8, 16, 17, 18, 19, 20, 24, 25, 26, 32, 61, 62, 70, 71–75, 83, 84,

89–115, 122–28, 130–34, 135, 136, 139, 140, 147, 163, 175, 183, 283, 284
Saffarid dynasty, 66
Safi I, Shah, 132
Al-Safir, 309
Sahhafbashi, Ebrahim Khan, 159, 255
Sa`idzadeh, Hojjatoleslam Mohsen, 219–20
Sajjad Mir, 343–46
Salahu'ddin, Muhammad, 342
Salama, Salama Ahmad, 321
Salimu'llah, Maulana, 346
Salinger, J. D., 271
Salnameh-ye Zanan, 207
Samanid dynasty, 66
Samarqand, 17, 41, 42, 46, 94, 98
Samarqandi, Abd al-Razzaq, 19
Sam Mirza, 93, 94, 100
Sanskrit, 17, 21, 22, 31
Sassanian dynasty, 66, 176, 236, 243
Satanic Verses, The, 357
Sattar Khan, 236
Saudi Arabia, 209, 210, 223, 226, 281, 282, 284, 300, 307, 316, 318, 319, 342, 343, 356, 357, 358, 365, 366
Saut al-Azhar, 322
Savad Kuh, 175
Sawad-i A`zam-i Ahl-i Sunnat, 346
Sayyad, Parviz, 259, 261, 264, 272
Sazman-e parvaresh-e afkar, 173
Sazman-e tablighat-e eslami, 283
Seh maktub, 166
Selim I, Sultan, 91, 92, 101
Selim II, Sultan, 103, 110
Selim III, Sultan, 111
Selim-nameh, 94, 105
Seljuqs, 5, 24, 61, 67, 70, 71
Sepenta, Abdol Hosain, 256
Serry, Rahim, 272
Shabi, Ezatollah, 291
Shafaq, Reza-Zadeh, 193–94
Shah Jahan, 26
Shahid Saless, Sohrab, 259, 261, 272
Shahid-e javid, 286, 287
Shahnameh, 93, 94, 105, 110, 111
Shahnameh-ye Selim Khan, 94
Shahsevan, 61, 76

Shaikh-oghlu, 95

Shakespeare, William, 43, 46, 48

Shaltut, Mahmud, 284, 287, 289, 295, 306

Shams Pahlavi, 171

Shari`ati, Ali, 290, 295, 311

Shari`atmadari, Ayatollah Kazem, 310

Sharif, Nawaz, 331, 347

Al-Sharif, Safwat, 320

Sharif, Shahbaz, 347

Shatt al-Arab, 359

Shekarlu, Mahsa, 226

Shelley, Percy Bysshe, 46

Sherkat, Shahla, 219, 221

Shi`a hazrat ki Islam se baghavat, 343

Shi`a hazrat ki Qur'an se baghavat, 343

Shibani, Mohammad Khan, 94–95, 96, 98

Shi`is and Shi`ism, 342–43

Shi`ism, 3, 5, 6, 9, 16, 19, 23, 24, 25, 26, 27, 28, 29, 30, 32, 71, 82, 89, 98, 163, 236, 240, 282–300, 306, 312–13, 327–48

Shiraz, 17, 24, 41, 42, 53, 65, 76, 77, 108–9, 135, 183, 184, 221

Shirazi, Mirza Saleh, 146, 147, 148, 150–52, 159

Shirdel, Kamran, 259, 261

Shirvani, Aflatun, 94

Shirvani, Ali b. Amir Beg, 94

Shissler, A. H., 165

Shita Dissuqi, Ibrahim, 312

Shore, John, 135

Shura'-i Wahdat-i Islami, 337

Shushtari, Abd al-Latif, 135

Siavoshi, Sussan, 248

Sib. See Apple, The

Sikhs, 27

Silence, The (Sokut), 267, 273

Sind, 27, 28, 75, 174, 332, 346

Sipah-i Muhammad (SM), 337, 338, 347

Sipah-i Sabaha Pakistan (SSP), 331, 342, 343, 346, 347

Siyasat-nameh, 68

Skipp, George, 135, 136

Smell of Camphor, Fragrance of Jasmine (Bu-ye Kafur, Atr-e Yas), 273

Sohravardi order, 27

Sokut. See Silence, The

Solaiman, Shah, 124, 133

Solaiman-nameh, 94

Soltan Hosain, Shah, 75, 127, 130, 131, 133

Soltanom, Princess, 107

Sony Classic Pictures, 267, 269

Soroush, Abdol Karim, 9, 282, 286, 291, 293–99

South Asia, 4, 5, 6, 8, 15–32, 327–48

Soviet Union, 176, 214, 215, 216, 248, 307, 308, 361, 362, 363, 365

Spenser, Edmund, 43

St. Vincent de Paul, Sisters of, 184

Stark, Freya, 149

Sten'ka Razin, 133

Subrahmanyam, Sanjay, 20, 31

Suez Canal, 306, 307

Sufism and Sufis, 16, 19, 20, 23, 25, 27, 28, 30, 32, 71

Suhrawardi, H. S., 332

Suleiman, Sultan, 94, 101, 103, 104

Sunnism, 6, 9, 16, 25, 26, 71, 82, 89, 90, 98, 282–300, 306, 327, 331

Supreme Assembly of the Islamic Revolution in Iraq, 364

Surat, 24, 126, 127, 128

Symposium on Women and Development, 217

Syracuse University, 257

Syria, 24, 70, 213, 226, 307, 312, 314, 316, 317, 358

Tabarra`iyan, 89

Tabataba'i, Gholam Hosain Khan, 135

Tabriz, 73, 91, 92, 93, 94, 106, 137, 183, 184, 186

Tabrizian, Mitra, 272

Tahmasb I, Shah, 72, 73, 90, 93, 94, 98–101, 103, 105–8, 110–11, 115, 130

Tahmasb II, Shah, 130

Tahmasb Mirza, 131

Taimurtash, Iran, 190

Taj-e haidari, 107

Tajik literature, 21

Tajikistan, 210, 273

Tajlu Khanom, 92

Takhteh Siyah. See Blackboards

Takhti, 237
Takkalu, 72
Taleqani, Azam Ala'i, 217
Taleqani, Ayatollah Sayyed Mahmud, 217, 290
Talesh, 130
Talesh, Shehab al-Din, 19
Taliban, 219–20, 347
Talpur nawabs, 27
Ta`m-e Gilas. See Taste of Cherry
Tamerlane. *See* Timur Lang
Tantawi, Muhammad Sayyid, 300
Taqizadeh, Sayyed Hasan, 169
Taqvai, Naser, 259, 261
Tarbiyat, Hajar, 173
Tarikh-e alam-ara-ye abbasi, 130
Tarikh-i Ja`fariya (TJ), 335
Tarikh-i Nifaz-i Fiqh-i Ja`fariya (TNFJ), 335, 336, 337, 338, 339, 341, 347
Tariq, A`zam, 343, 346
Tashkiri, Ayatollah Ali, 317
Taste of Cherry (Ta`m-e Gilas), 266
Tauhid, 299
Taute`eh-ye Shah bar zedd-e Emam Khomaini, 287
Tayyab, Manuchehr, 261
Tazeh-gu'i, 21
Tedesco, Juan Carlos, 233, 242
Tehran, 15, 76, 138, 183, 184, 185, 186, 187, 210, 211, 213, 219, 222, 225, 255, 267, 270, 281, 289, 293, 294, 300, 307, 314, 319, 320, 336, 359, 364, 368, 371, 372
Tehran University, 318
Telegu language, 22
Terek River, 132
Thokar Niaz Baig, 338
Tiflis, 138
Tikhanov, 132
Al-Tilmisani, Umar, 312
Time to Love, A (Naubat-e Asheqi), 273
Timur Lang, 16, 42, 70, 91
Timurids, 17, 61, 75, 92, 93, 94, 95, 98, 100, 107, 108
Tito, 308
Tiufiakin, Vasilei Vasil'evich, 131
Tofangchis, 73

Toghril, 67
Tolu`-e Fajr, 265
Topkapi Palace, 111
Torbat-e Haidariyeh, 19
Torkmanchai, Treaty of, 163
Toronto International Film Festival, 261
Trabzon (Trebizond), 91
Transcaucasia, 165
Transoxania, 95
Tudeh Party, 309
Tunbs, 359, 363, 366
Turan, 173
Turkestan, 74
Turkey, 62, 82, 83, 85, 175, 192, 195, 209, 210, 211, 214, 256, 263, 273, 322, 358, 363, 364
Turkish language, 17, 110, 218
Turkmen, 25, 61, 70, 71, 72, 73, 74, 77, 82, 90, 91
Turko-Mongols, 4, 5, 7, 17, 24, 62, 63, 64, 65, 66, 67, 69, 71–72, 77, 98
Turks, 6, 7, 41, 63, 64, 68, 71, 72, 77, 91, 166, 175, 194, 236, 247, 305
Twelve Imams, 24, 25
Two Women (Do Zan), 267
Tytler, Alexander, 38

Ulama, 24, 29, 153, 158, 159, 237, 285, 286, 287, 289, 297, 329, 338, 339, 342
Umayyads, 243, 343
United Arab Emirates, 210, 315, 316, 317, 318, 363, 366
United Nations, 216, 217, 315, 358, 359, 361, 367, 368
United States and Americans, 3, 155, 157, 177–78, 183, 184, 185–91, 192, 193, 194, 195, 196, 214, 222–23, 226–27, 243, 248, 254, 256, 257, 259, 264, 266, 267, 271, 273, 274, 288, 307, 308, 320, 357, 358, 359, 360, 361, 362, 363, 364, 366, 367, 368, 369, 371, 372
United States Information Service (USIS), 257
Upanishads, 22, 32
Urdu language and literature, 15, 21, 23, 29, 31, 218
Ustajlu tribe, 72

Uthman, 89, 111
Uzbeks, 16, 17, 72, 73, 74, 82, 90, 94–95, 98–101, 108, 109, 133
Uzun Hasan, 71, 92

Vaziri, Perzheng, 273
Velayat-e faqih, 286, 289, 290, 292, 295, 339
Velayati, Ali Akbar, 290, 317, 358
Venice International Film Festival, 259
Victoria, Queen, 192
Vienna, 101, 217, 366
Virgil, 38
VOC. *See* East India Company, Dutch
Volynskii, Artemii Petrovich, 132, 133, 134
Voznictsyn, Feodor, 133

Al-Wafd, 320
Wahhabism, 342
Wittgenstein, Ludwig, 49
Women's Social-Cultural Council, 218
Women's Society of the Islamic Republic of Iran (WSIRI), 209, 213, 214, 215, 219
World Bank, 372
World Conference of Islamic Countries, 219
World Conference on Human Rights, 217
World Conference on Women, 212–18
World Organization of Muslim Women, 219
World War I, 77, 169, 194, 363
World War II, 177, 256, 308, 361

Yahya Khan, 332
Al-Yasar al-Islami, 312

Yazd, 19, 183
Yazdani, Murid Abbas, 338
Yazdi, Ebrahim, 285, 286, 288–90, 291
Yazid, 343
Yemen, 306
Yoga Vasistha, 22, 23
Yomut Turkmen, 74
Yusof Khan, 132
Yusofabad, 290

Zagros mountains, 76
Zahedi, Caveh, 272
Zahir, Allama Ihsan Ilahi, 342, 343
Zahra, al-Sayyid, 309
Al-Zahra University, 210, 219
Zainab, 245
Zamani, Mohsen (Abu Sharif), 335
Zan, 222, 223
Zanan, 216, 219, 221, 222
Zand dynasty, 20, 26, 76
Zan-e Ruz, 214, 221, 222
Zeitgeist Films, 266
Zell al-Soltan, Mas'ud Mirza, 155, 157–58
Zia ul-Haq, 334, 335, 340, 341, 342
Zinat, 225
Zionism, 216, 318
Zobdat al-tavarikh, 131
Zohab, Treaty of. *See* Qasr-e Shirin, Treaty of
Zoka al-Molk, Mirza Hosain Khan, 176
Zolaikha, 45
Zoroastrianism and Zoroastrians, 5, 6, 16, 19, 23, 171, 185, 190, 192, 194, 236, 245
Zu'lqadir, 72

LaVergne, TN USA
22 June 2010
187075LV00001B/54/P